Building Construction

BOOKS BY HUNTINGTON, W. C.:

Building Construction. Third Edition
Earth Pressures and Retaining Walls

Building Construction
materials and types of construction

THIRD EDITION

WHITNEY CLARK HUNTINGTON, *Honorary Member of American Society of Civil Engineers, Professor of Civil Engineering Emeritus and Retired Head of Department, University of Illinois*

JOHN WILEY & SONS, INC., New York · London · Sydney

FIFTH PRINTING, JUNE, 1967

Library of Congress Catalog Card Number: 63–17478

Printed in the United States of America

Preface

This book deals with the materials and types of construction used for the various parts of buildings and not with the structural design except in its qualitative aspects. It is written for sophomore and junior students in civil engineering and architecture; structural engineers, whose experience has been with other types of structures and who wish to become familiar with the construction of buildings; electrical and mechanical engineers, whose work requires a knowledge of the structural make-up of buildings; and for those young men associated with architectural and construction organizations who have not yet gained, through experience, a detailed knowledge of building materials and types of construction. Particular attention has been paid to the terminology used in building construction. Definitions and illustrations of the many special terms used in this field are included.

The book has been thoroughly revised and largely rewritten in order to include the developments that have taken place during the past two decades. Some of the more significant of these are the revisions of building code requirements and standards, the manufacture and uses of plastics, foundation construction for deep basements, reinforced brick masonry, the progress in glued laminated timber construction, the increased use of welding and high-strength bolts in steel construction, types of shell roofs, the addition of an entire chapter on precast and prestressed concrete construction including the common forms of structures as well as lift-slab and tilt-up construction, new flooring and roofing materials, new types of windows and doors, and modern curtain wall construction. The material concerning rigid frame, arch and dome roofs constructed of timber, steel and concrete has been expanded, and cable-supported roofs have been included.

A list of numbered references is included at the end of each chapter. These lists include references which have been helpful in preparing the text. Each of these is referred to by a number in parentheses at an appropriate place in the text. All references and quotations have been made with permission of the publishers except those from building codes, standard specifications, and government publications. Some publications not referred to by the author are included with the thought that they may be helpful to the reader.

I wish to acknowledge the services rendered by Milo S. Ketchum and W. S. Kinne, Jr., each of whom prepared an article for this edition, my associates Ralph B. Peck, Chester P. Seiss, Edwin H. Gaylord, and Seichi Konzo who reviewed parts of the manuscript, and Clarence L. Eckel and Elmer F. Heater for assistance in the preparation of the drawings. Acknowledgment is also made to the technical periodicals, and especially to the *Engineering News-Record* and to the many technical societies and manufacturers' associations whose publications provided much valuable material. Special mention is made in the text where such material is referred to. Finally I wish to acknowledge my indebtedness to Dorothy Pringle who expertly performed the extensive typing required for this edition.

WHITNEY C. HUNTINGTON

Urbana, Illinois
June, 1963

Contents

1 Introduction

1. BUILDING CODES

Introduction. Building codes include types of construction; quality of materials; floor, roof, and wind loads; allowable stresses; health and safety; mechanical and electrical equipment; and other requirements related to buildings.

The codes issued by various agencies are quite similar in their basic requirements. There are, however, significant differences, and therefore the code adopted by a given municipality must be satisfied by buildings constructed within its limits. The requirements of various codes are included in this treatise for illustrative purposes, but for a specific building the governing code should be consulted.

Authority for Building Codes. According to reference 2,

The building code derives its justification from the police power. This is the inherent power of government to protect the people against harmful acts of individuals insofar as matters of safety, health, morals or the like are concerned. It is the power forming the basis for State acts and municipal ordinances dealing with these matters and is of indefinite extent, although certain limitations concerning its use are to be found in the Federal and State constitutions and in court decisions. Fundamentally, under our system of government, the police power resides in the State and may be transmitted to local authorities through enabling acts authorizing the adoption of building requirements or may be conferred upon municipalities when a charter is granted.

If a code requirement is unnecessary to accomplish the protection referred to in the preceding quotation, it will not be supported by the courts.

Agencies Issuing Building Codes. All cities and many towns have building codes. Towns that do not have building codes often adopt, by reference, all or parts of certain established codes.

Many states have established building codes which may or may not control all building construction within the state unless they are specifically adopted by municipalities, as stated in the preceding paragraph. An example of such codes is the State Building Construction Code adopted by the State of New York. As stated in that code: "The municipalities of the state have the option to accept or not to accept the applicability" of this code.

Several regional agencies have formulated building codes. These have been prepared to assist municipalities in preparing codes, or a municipality may adopt such a code, by reference, if such action is authorized by the statutes of the state in which the municipality is located. Among such codes are the following:

- *"Modern Standard Building Code,"* Midwest Conference of Building Officials, 205 W. Wacker Drive, Chicago 6, Illinois.
- *"Uniform Building Code,"* International Conference of Building Officials, 610 South Broadway, Los Angeles 14, California. The Pacific Coast Building Officials Conference is a subsidiary.
- *"State Building Code,"* State of New York, Division of Housing, 270 Broadway, New York 7, New York.
- *"Basic Building Code,"* Building Officials Conference of America, Inc., 51 East 42nd Street, New York 17, New York.
- *"Southern Standard Building Code,"* Southern Building Code Congress, Brown-Marx Building, Birmingham 3, Alabama.
- *"National Building Code,"* the National Board of Fire Underwriters, 85 John Street, New York 38, New York. This code has assisted many municipalities in framing their codes, and many have adopted the entire code or parts of it, by reference.

Other Agencies. Many agencies have contributed to the control and the advancement of knowledge related to building construction.

The American Society for Testing and Materials, 1916 Race St., Philadelphia 3, Pennsylvania, has adopted standard specifications for nearly all materials entering into the construction of buildings. These specifications have been incorporated in most building codes.

Other standards and recommendations concerning specific materials have been issued by numerous organizations, some of which have been adopted in building codes. Only a few of these organizations are included in the following list, for illustrative purposes.

- American Concrete Institute, 18263 West McNichols Road, Detroit 19, Michigan.
- American Institute of Steel Construction, 101 Park Avenue, New York 17, New York.

- American Standards Association, 70 East 45th St., New York 17, New York.
- American Welding Society, 33 West 39th St., New York 18, New York.
- Metal Lath Manufacturers Association, Engineers Building, Cleveland 14, Ohio.
- National Lumber Manufacturers Association, 1319 Eighteenth St., N.W., Washington 6, D. C.
- National Board of Fire Underwriters, 85 John St., New York 38, New York.
- Structural Clay Products Institute, 1520 Eighteenth St., N.W., Washington 6, D. C.

Various agencies of the United States government, especially the Bureau of Standards, Washington, D. C., and the Forest Products Laboratory, Madison, Wisconsin.

Extensive lists of material and construction standards and their issuing agencies are included in reference 3. Much information can be obtained, often at little or no cost, by writing these agencies. Publications by agencies of the federal government are obtained by writing the U. S. Government Printing Office, Washington, D. C.

Fire-Resistance Ratings. Building codes commonly classify buildings according to type of construction and according to use or occupancy. The most important factor in the classification according to type of construction is the resistance to fire exposure. In classifying buildings in this manner, it is therefore necessary to have some measure of the performance of the various structural parts of a building under fire-exposure conditions. To do this it is necessary that the fire-resistive properties of materials and members be measured and specified according to a common standard expressed in terms which are applicable to a wide variety of materials, situations, and conditions of exposure.

The *Standard Fire Test* accomplishes these objectives. This test has been established by the American Society for Testing Materials designated as ASTM E119. It consists of exposing samples of the material or the building member to a fire of specified intensity and, in some cases, to a fire hose stream when the sample is in a heated condition. Performance is defined as the period of resistance to standard exposure elapsing before the first critical point in behavior is observed, and it is expressed in hours. For example, a material is given a 2-hour rating if it withstands the test for a period of 2 hours.

Most of the common building materials and assemblies of materials have been tested and rated and the results published. For this reason, it is not often necessary to make fire tests in connection with the design of individual buildings. An extensive report on such ratings is given in reference 4.

Building Content and Fire Severity. Burnout tests conducted in fire-resistive buildings indicate that the fire severity due to the combustion of such materials as wood, paper, cotton, wool, silk, straw, grain, sugar, and similar organic materials may be considered to be as shown in Table 1-1. The values in this table enable fire severity to be visualized (11).

Fire Limits, Zones, or Districts. The New York State Code includes the following definition: *"Fire limits.* Boundary line establishing an area in which there exists, or is likely to exist, a fire hazard requiring special fire protection."

Two classes of fire limits are included in this code. "Fire limits A comprising the areas containing highly congested business, commercial and, or industrial occupancies, wherein the fire hazard is severe; and or, Fire limits B comprising the areas containing residential, business and, or commercial occupancies or in which such uses are developing, wherein the fire hazard is moderate.

"All of those areas not included in fire limits A or B are designated herein as outside the fire limits."

The areas within fire limits are often called *fire zones* or *fire districts*.

Building Classification

Building code requirements are based primarily on building occupancy or use, type of construction, and location.

Table 1-1

Relation of Amount of Combustibles and Fire Severity

w	hr	w	hr	w	hr	w	hr	w	hr
5	$\frac{1}{2}$	10	1	20	2	40	$4\frac{1}{2}$	60	$7\frac{1}{2}$
$7\frac{1}{2}$	$\frac{3}{4}$	15	$1\frac{1}{2}$	30	3	50	6		

Key: w is average weight in lb. per square foot of floor area
    hr is fire severity in hours.

Classification According to Occupancy. The classification of buildings according to occupancy, as included in the National Building Code, is as follows.

assembly occupancy means the occupancy or use of a building or structure or any portion thereof by a gathering of persons for civic, political, travel, religious, social, or recreational purposes.

business occupancy means the occupancy or use of a building or structure or any portion thereof for the transaction of business, or the rendering or receiving of professional services.

educational occupancy means the occupancy or use of a building or structure or any portion thereof by persons assembled for the purpose of learning or of receiving educational instruction.

high hazard occupancy means the occupancy or use of a building or structure or any portion thereof that involves highly combustible, highly flammable, or explosive material, or which has inherent characteristics that constitute a special fire hazard.

industrial occupancy means the occupancy or use of a building or structure or any portion thereof for assembling, fabricating, finishing, manufacturing, packaging, or processing operations.

institutional occupancy means the occupancy or use of a building or structure or any portion thereof by persons harbored or detained to receive medical, charitable, or other care or treatment, or by persons involuntarily detained.

residential occupancy means the occupancy or use of a building or structure or any portion thereof by persons for whom sleeping accommodations are provided but who are not harbored or detained to receive medical, charitable, or other care or treatment, or are not involuntarily detained.

storage occupancy means the occupancy or use of a building or structure or any portion thereof for the storage of goods, wares, merchandise, raw materials, agricultural or manufactured products, including parking garages, or the sheltering of livestock and other animals, except when classed as a high hazard.

Classification According to Type of Construction. Buildings are classified in building codes according to types of construction based on the fire resistance of their structural members or assemblies. Codes vary in the details of such classifications, but the objectives sought are similar. The *New York State Building Construction Code* will serve as an example.

According to this code, if the temperature required to ignite and support combustion of a material, or combination of materials, is below 1382°F., the material is designated as *combustible,* and if a higher temperature is required it is designated as *noncombustible.*

The principal combustible materials used in buildings are wood, organic fiber boards, and plastics. The principal noncombustible materials are steel and aluminum, concrete, and masonry materials such as brick, stone, and structural clay tile, as well as plaster and glass.

According to the New York State Code, buildings are classified into five types as follows.

Type 1. Fire-Resistive Construction. That type of construction in which the walls, partitions, columns, floors, and roof are noncombustible with sufficient fire resistance to withstand the effects of a fire and prevent its spread from story to story.

Type 2. Noncombustible Construction. That type of construction in which walls, partitions, columns, floors, and roof are noncombustible and have less fire resistance than required for *fire-resistive construction.*

Type 3. Heavy Timber Construction. That type of construction in which the exterior walls are of masonry or other noncombustible materials having an equivalent structural stability under fire conditions and a fire resistance rating of not less than 2 hours; in which interior structural members including columns, beams and girders are timber, in heavy solid or laminated masses, but with no sharp corners or projections or concealed or inaccessible spaces; in which floors and roofs are of heavy plank or laminated wood construction, or any other material providing equivalent fire-resistance and structural properties. Noncombustible structural members may be used in lieu of heavy timber, provided the fire resistance rating of such members is not less than ¾ hour.

Type 4. Ordinary Construction. That type of construction in which the exterior walls are of masonry or other noncombustible materials having equivalent structural stability under fire conditions and a fire resistance rating of not less than 2 hours, the interior structural members being wholly or partly of wood of smaller dimensions than those required for *Heavy Timber Construction.*

Type 5. Wood Frame Construction. That type of construction in which walls, partitions, floors, and roof are wholly or partly of wood or other combustible material.

Each of the five types of construction which have been described, except Type 3, is divided into two subtypes which vary according to the degree of fire resistance required. The requirements for subtypes *a* are more severe than those for subtypes *b*.

The fire-resistance ratings required for the various types and subtypes are shown in Table 1-2.

From Table 1-2, it will be noted that the highest required fire rating is 4 hours. This rating is required in the higher type of *Fire-Resistive Construction* for exterior bearing walls, for party walls, and for interior firewalls, bearing walls, and partitions. It is also required for columns, beams, girders, and trusses supporting more than one floor. These are the most important structural elements in a building. It is also required for the party walls and fire walls of *Heavy Timber Construction.*

Table 1-2

Minimum Fire-Resistance Requirements of Structural Elements
(By types of construction; fire-resistance ratings in hours)

Structural Element	Type 1 (fire-resistive)		Type 2 (non-combustible)		Type 3 (heavy timber)	Type 4 (ordinary)		Type 5 (wood frame)	
	1a	1b	2a	2b		4a	4b	5a	5b
Exterior									
Bearing walls	4	3	2	nc	2	2	2	¾	c
Nonbearing walls	2	2	2	nc	2	2	2	¾	c
Panel and curtain walls	¾	¾	¾	nc					
Party walls	4	3	2	2	4	2	2	2	2
Interior									
Fire walls	4	3	2	2	4	2	2	2	2
Bearing walls or partitions	4	3	2	nc	2	¾	c	¾	c
Partitions enclosing stairways, hoistways, shafts, other vertical openings; and hallways									
on outside exposure	2	2	2	2	2	2	2	¾	¾
on inside exposure	1	1	¾	¾	¾	¾	¾	¾	¾
Nonbearing walls and partitions separating spaces	1	1	¾	¾	¾	¾	¾	¾	¾
Columns, beams, girders and trusses (other than roof trusses)									
supporting more than 1 floor	4	3	2	nc	c	¾	c	¾	c
supporting 1 floor	3	2	¾	nc	c	¾	c	¾	c
Floor construction including beams	3	2	1	nc	c	¾	c	¾	c
Roof construction including purlins, beams, and roof trusses	2	1	¾	nc	c	¾	c	¾	c

Key: nc = noncombustible, c = combustible.
The code includes special requirements and exceptions which are not included in this table.

The lowest fire rating required is ¾ hour. It is required for panel and curtain walls in *Fire-Resistive Construction* and in the higher type of *Noncombustible Construction,* and interior partitions and nonbearing walls for all types of construction except *Fire-Resistive.* It is also required for bearing walls and nonbearing walls for the higher type of *Wood Frame Construction* and for various other members in *Ordinary and Wood Frame Construction.* *Noncombustible Construction* without a fire rating is required for various members in the lower type of *Noncombustible Construction.* *Combustible Construction* is permitted in some parts of *Heavy Timber Construction* and in several parts of *Ordinary and Wood Frame Construction.*

The highest type of construction, designated as *Fire-Resistive* in Table 1-2, is often designated as *fireproof.* However, it is not feasible to construct a building which is really fireproof, and therefore that term is being replaced in building codes by the term *fire-resistive.* The term *mill construction,* which often is used instead of *Heavy Timber Construction,* had its origin in New England where construction using heavy timber was developed many years ago to decrease the fire hazard in textile mills. This type of construction is also called *slow-burning construction* for obvious reasons. These terms are occasionally used in building codes. The types of construction known as *Heavy Timber Construction, Ordinary Construction,* and *Frame Construction* are used in nearly all codes. A classification not given here but often found in codes includes buildings with unprotected steel structural members. It is considered to have a fire resistance lower than *Ordinary Construction* because the strength of steel decreases at high temperatures. Such a classification is designated as *unprotected metal, metal frame, light incombustible frame.*

Classification According to Fire Hazard. All codes recognize the differences in fire hazard as determined by the kind of occupancy within each general occupancy class. For example, the New York State Building Construction Code includes the following classifications according to fire hazard.

low hazard. Business buildings.
moderate hazard. Mercantile buildings. Industrial and storage buildings in which the combustible contents might cause fires of moderate intensity as defined in the code.
high hazard. Industrial and storage buildings in which the combustible contents might cause fires to be unusually intense, as defined in the code, or where explosives, combustible gases, or flammable liquids are manufactured or stored.

Height and Area. The height and fire area of a single story are defined in each code. For example, the following definitions in the New York State Code are typical.

Building Height. Vertical distance measured from the curb or grade level to a flat or mansard roof, or the average height of a pitched, gabled, hip or gambrel roof, excluding bulkheads, penthouses and similar constructions enclosing equipment or stairs, providing that they are less than 12 feet in height and do not occupy more than 30 per cent of the area of the roof on which they are located.
Fire Area. The floor area of a story of a building within exterior walls, party walls, fire walls, or any combination thereof.

The permissible height and fire area of a building are determined by its occupancy, construction, and fire hazard classifications, the fire protection equipment installed in the building such as sprinkler systems, and the accessibility for fire protection equipment.

The permissible heights and fire areas included in the New York State Code for Low-Hazard buildings are illustrated in Table 1-3. This code also includes tables for other classes of occupancy and moderate and high hazards. Other codes have similar requirements stated in various ways.

Table 1-3

Permissible Height and Fire Areas
Low-Hazard Business, Industrial, and Storage Buildings

		Basic Fire Area in 1000 sq. ft.							
Maximum Height		Type 1 Fire Res.		Type 2 Noncomb.		Type 3 Heavy Timb.	Type 4 Ordinary		Type 5 Wood Frame	
st.	ft.	1a	1b	2a	2b		4a	4b	5a	5b
1	un	un	un	un	18	21	18	12	9	6
2	40	un	un	21	15	18	15	9	6	3
3	55	un	un	18	np	15	12	6	np	np
4	70	un	un	15	np	12	9	np	np	np
5	85	un	un	12	np	np	np	np	np	np
6	100	un	un	np	np	np	np	np	np	np
Over 6	Over 100	un	un	np	np	np	np	np	np	np

Key: st = stories, un = unlimited, np = not permitted.

The fire areas in this table are based on a frontage on one street or legal open space at least 50 ft. wide. If a fire area faces or abuts such streets or spaces on two sides, it may be 50 per cent larger than the area shown in the table; on three sides, 75 per cent larger; and on four sides, 100 per cent larger, provided that such open areas are served by fire hydrants and are unobstructed and accessible at all times for fire-fighting equipment. Specified increases in height and fire area are permitted if approved automatic sprinklers are installed.

Restrictions Based on Fire Districts. Most building codes prohibit *Wood Frame Construction* within fire districts with specified exceptions such as small private garages, greenhouses, and sheds. If buildings with such construction are located outside the fire limits, there are fire restrictions concerning the distance from property lines, and the fire area and the height, as illustrated in Table 1-3 for Type 5, and there are restrictions on kinds of roofing materials.

Other types of construction are permitted within the fire limits subject to certain requirements about the fire ratings of their various parts (illustrated in Table 1-2), the fire areas and heights (illustrated in Table 1-3), and other regulations mentioned in the preceding paragraph.

Other Regulations. Codes include requirements such as those for exits, stairways, elevator shafts, corridors, roofs, protection of openings in exterior walls, interior finish, flooring materials, doors and doorways, and building contents.

Many references are made elsewhere in this treatise to code requirements for various parts of buildings. The code requirements for the loads carried by buildings are considered in Art. 2. Codes include allowable working stresses for the many materials included in a building. They are of great importance in structural design but do not fall within the scope of this book. The allowable bearing pressures for foundations, illustrated by Table 18-1, are included in codes.

Codes also include requirements for ventilation, sanitary features such as plumbing and wastes disposal, electric wiring, and mechanical equipment, which do not fall within the scope of this treatise.

2. LOADS CARRIED BY BUILDINGS

Definitions. The loads to which buildings are subjected may be divided into four classes: dead loads, live loads, lateral loads, and other loads.

dead loads include weights of all parts of the building such as walls, structural frame, permanent partitions, floors, roofs, stairways, and fixed equipment.

live loads include the weights of the occupants, furniture, movable equipment, stored material, and snow that may accumulate on the roof.

lateral loads include distributed horizontal loads which act above the ground level and are assumed to have effects equivalent to those produced by wind pressures. For some regions they include lateral loads which are assumed to have effects corresponding to those produced by earthquake shocks. Also included are horizontal loads on foundation walls caused by earth pressure and water pressure.

Dead Loads. The magnitudes of dead loads to be used in design are determined by the weights of the building materials, the assemblies of materials, and the fixed equipment which are used in the construction of buildings.

Live Loads. The magnitudes of the live loads on floors are determined by the types of occupancy of the various units into which a building is divided. There is a marked uniformity in building code requirements for the minimum live loads for which the floors of buildings are to be designed. These loads refer to normal conditions. Any special conditions to which a floor may be subjected must be considered. The floor loads recommended by the American Standards Association are given in Table 2-1 (8). It will be noted that the floor load for offices included in this table is 80 lb. per sq. ft. Many codes require only 50 lb. per sq. ft. for this occupancy. An additional load of 20 lb. per sq. ft. is often included for masonry partitions not included in the initial plans, if there is a possibility that such partitions may be installed at a later date. Many codes provide for a load of 2000 lb. concentrated on any 2½-ft. sq. area if such a load on this otherwise unloaded area produces stresses greater than the required uniform load. Other special provisions for live loads are included in various codes.

Codes include requirements for minimum live *roof loads*. The simplest requirement is a load of 20 lb. per sq. ft. of horizontal projection in addition to the wind load regardless of the slope of the roof. In most parts of the United States, provision must be made for a *snow load*. It may cause a greater load than the required minimum. Of course, the possible snow load varies widely throughout the country. According to the New York State Code, the required snow load on a flat roof varies from 20 to 60 lb. per sq. ft. according to the building's location on a snow map included in the code.

Another factor in the snow load is the slope of the roof. In the New York State Code, no load is required for slopes of 60 degrees or more with the horizontal. The required load varies for roof slopes between

Table 2-1

Minimum Uniformly Distributed Live Loads
American Standards Association, 1955 (8)

Assembly halls, fixed seats	60	Residential. Dwellings	
Movable seats	100	First floor	40
Corridors, first floor	100	Second floor	30
Other floors, same as occu-		Habitable attics	30
pancy served except as		Uninhabitable attics	20
indicated		Residential. Hotels	
Dance halls	100	Guest rooms	40
Dining rooms and restaurants	100	Public rooms	100
Garages, passenger cars	100	Public corridors	100
Gymnasium floors and balconies	100	Private corridors	40
Hospitals, operating rooms	60	Schools. Classrooms	40
Private rooms and wards	40	Corridors	100
Libraries, Reading rooms	60	Stairs, fire escapes, exitways	100
Stackrooms	150	Stores. Retail	
Manufacturing	125	First floor	100
Office buildings, offices	80	Upper floors	75
Lobbies	100	Stores. Wholesale	125
Residential. Multifamily		Warehouse, light storage	125
Private apartments	40	Heavy storage	250
Public rooms	100		
Corridors	60		

Key: Pounds per square foot of floor area.

0 and 60 degrees in a specified manner which is somewhat higher than would be given by a linear variation.

If a roof is also to be used as a floor, it must be designed for the live load it is to carry but for not less than the minimum live load required for floors, the magnitude depending upon the type of use of the roof.

Reductions in Live Floor Loads. The probability that the required live floor load will not cover the entire floor area contributing to the load on the supporting members is recognized by all codes. For example, the New York State Code permits the following reductions.

Uniformly distributed live loads on beams or girders supporting other than storage areas and motor vehicle parking areas, when such structural member supports 150 square feet or more of roof area or floor area per floor, may be reduced as follows:

When the dead load is not more than 25 lb. per sq. ft., the reduction shall not be more than 20 per cent;

When the dead load exceeds 25 lb. per sq. ft. and the live load does not exceed 100 lb. per sq. ft. the reduction shall be not more than the least of the following three criteria: 60 per cent or 0.08 per cent per sq. ft. times square feet of area supported; or 100 per cent times (dead load in lb. per sq. ft. plus live load in lb. per sq. ft.) divided by (4.33 times live load in lb. per sq. ft.).

For columns, girders supporting columns, bearing walls, and foundation walls supporting 150 square feet or more of roof area or floor area per floor other than storage areas and motor vehicle parking areas, the uniformly distributed live loads on these members shall not be less than the following percentages of total live loads on the following levels [Table 2-2].

Table 2-2

Percentage of Each Live Floor Load To Be Included

Roof	80	5th floor below roof	65
Floor immediately below roof	80	6th floor below roof	60
2nd floor below roof	80	7th floor below roof	55
3rd floor below roof	75	8th floor below roof	50
4th floor below roof	70	All other floors	50

According to the Modern Standard Code: "For determining the total live loads carried by columns, the following reductions [in Table 2-3] shall be permitted, the reduction being based on the assumed live loads applied to the entire tributary floor area.

It will be noticed that these requirements are on different bases. In the first, the percentage of the total live load on *each* floor and the roof

Table 2-3

Percentage Reductions in Total Live Floor Loads

Tributary Area	A	B	C	Tributary Area	A	B	C
Roof	0	0	0	4 floors and roof	15	30	30
1 floor	0	0	0	5 floors and roof	20	30	40
2 floors and roof	5	10	10	6 floors and roof	20	30	45
3 floors and roof	10	20	20	7 or more floors and roof	20	30	50

Key: A = Warehouse and Storage, B = Manufacturing, Stores, and Garage, C = All Other.

contributing to the column load is given. In the second, the percentage of reductions of the total live floor and roof load on *all* the areas contributing to a *specific* column is given. For a specific column, and the same live floor and roof loads, the first requirement would result in larger column loads than the second.

Wind Pressures. The wind pressures, or wind loads, on buildings vary with the geographical location and, for a given location, with the height above the ground surface. Winds are assumed to act in any horizontal direction in spite of the direction of prevailing winds. There are positive pressures on the windward side of a building and negative pressures, or partial vacuums, on the leeward side. Design pressures are based on the total resultant pressure, which is equal to the sum of these pressures.

Extensive studies of wind pressures by the National Bureau of Standards, are reported in reference 7 at the end of this chapter, and they form the basis for the Building Code Requirements of the American Standards Association as given in reference 8. The comments in this article are based on these references.

The recommended design pressures are computed from measured velocities of gust winds, and the rectangular shape of exposed building surfaces and many other factors that affect wind pressures are taken into consideration.

The minimum allowable resultant wind pressures for various parts of this country at a height 30 ft. above the ground surface are shown on the map in Fig. 2-1.

The design wind pressures for various height zones above the ground surface and various minimum wind pressures for the height of 30 ft. above this surface are given in Table 2-4. For example, if the pressure at the height of 30 ft. as given on the map in Fig. 2-1 is 30 lb. per sq. ft., the design wind pressure at a height of 100 ft. is 45 lb. per sq. ft. as shown in the table.

As stated in reference 7,

The wind pressures and suctions in the immediate path of tornadoes are considered to be so great that construction strong enough to withstand them is not economically feasible. Therefore, in recommending design wind pressures, building codes do not take into consideration the violent forces that can be expected within the narrow path of a tornado.

Experience has shown, however, that buildings designed for wind pressures even less than those recommended have not collapsed but have survived without irreparable structural damage and relatively few, if any, casualties.

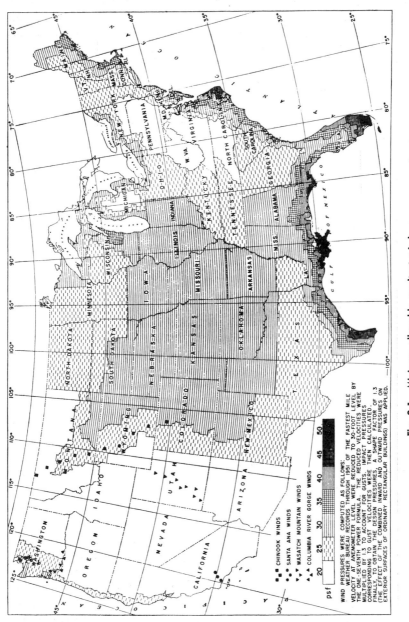

Fig. 2-1. Minimum allowable resultant wind pressures.

Table 2-4

Design Wind Pressures for Various Height Zones

Height Zone above Ground Level, ft.	Wind Pressure Map Areas, lb. per sq. ft.						
	20	25	30	35	40	45	50
	Design Wind Pressures, lb. per sq. ft.						
Less than 30	15	20	25	25	30	35	40
30 to 49	20	25	30	35	40	45	50
50 to 99	25	30	40	45	50	55	60
100 to 499	30	40	45	55	60	70	75
500 to 1199	35	45	55	60	70	80	90
1200 and over	40	50	60	70	80	90	100

Wind pressures tend to overturn buildings as a whole and parts of buildings above any elevation. To avoid this, codes require that the resistance of the dead load of a building to overturning above any elevation be one and a half times the overturning effect of wind, both factors being measured by their moments about the leeward edges. For the condition which includes the effects of wind loads in the computed stresses in the resisting members, codes permit the allowable stresses to be increased one-third. However, the allowable stresses must not be exceeded for the condition that does not include wind load.

Building codes include factors for adjusting horizontal wind loads to sloping roofs and for the uplift pressures on roofs caused by wind loads.

Earth and Water Pressures. A portion of a foundation wall may be below the ground surface (Fig. 2-2a). For this condition, the lateral earth pressures may be assumed to equal one-half of the corresponding water pressures.

If there is a uniform vertical pressure of p_v lb. per sq. ft. on the ground surface, the unit lateral pressure p_s acting on the height h may be assumed to equal one-third of p_v.

If the groundwater level is above the bottom of the wall (b), the additional pressures caused by the water may be assumed to equal four-fifths of the water pressures which would act on the submerged portion of the wall if no soil were present.

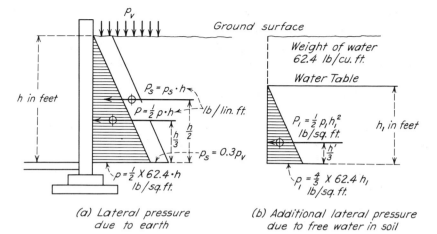

Fig. 2-2. (a) Lateral pressure due to earth. (b) Additional lateral pressure due to free water in soil.

The reduction of one-fifth in the water pressure is assumed to offset the reduction in earth pressure on the submerged portion of the wall owing to the buoyant effect of the water on the submerged soil.

Foundation walls retaining expansive clay soils may be subjected to very large earth pressures because of their increase in volume as their moisture content increases, even if they are entirely above the groundwater level. If these are thin walls supporting low buildings, they may fail under the action of such pressures. It may not be feasible to construct a wall thick enough to resist these pressures. Under these conditions, a wall should be backfilled with a nonexpansive soil for a considerable distance from the wall.

Earth pressures against free-standing walls require special consideration, as explained in reference 9.

If the groundwater level is above the bottom of a basement floor and the groundwater is in contact with this surface, the floor must be designed to resist an *uplift pressure* equal to the water pressure to which it is subjected. This is equal, in pounds per square foot, to 62.4 times the vertical distance, in feet, between the ground water level and the bottom of the floor.

Earthquake Shocks. The disastrous effects that earthquakes have had on buildings in many parts of the world are well known. A relatively small portion of this country has not experienced at least minor earthquakes during the period for which records are available. The most severe earthquake damage has occurred in California, and the possibilities of further damage are recognized in codes covering that area.

Examples of code requirements to resist earthquake shocks are included in the following:

The *National Building Code* of the National Board of Fire Underwriters.

The *Uniform Building Code* of the International Conference of Building Officials, of which the Pacific Coast Building Officials Conference is a subsidiary.

The *Minimum Design Loads in Buildings and Other Structures* of the American Standards Association.

The addresses of these agencies are given on page 3.

The effects of earthquakes on many buildings are too complex to be covered adequately by codes. Structural engineers well versed in earthquake-resistant design should be consulted on the design of major buildings to be constructed in regions subject to severe earthquake shocks (10).

3. BUILDING COST ESTIMATES

Types of Estimates. Two general types of estimates may be prepared for the cost of a building. The first is a preliminary estimate, which may be required to determine approximate cost before detailed plans and specifications are prepared. Such an estimate may be used to inform the prospective builder, who knows the approximate amount of money he will have available for the project, of the approximate floor area that can be provided with that amount. Or he may know what floor area he requires and wish to know approximately what it will cost.

Such estimates are usually necessary before the architect is asked to incur the expense of preparing the complete plans and specifications.

The second type of estimate is prepared by the contracting organization to determine the amount of the *bid* or *proposal* on which he would enter into an agreement or contract with the owner to complete the building. This is called a *lump sum contract*. Under this form of agreement, bids are received from several contracting organizations.

Both the owner and the contractor may prefer a *cost plus* contract, one by which the contractor agrees to construct a building for the amount it costs him plus a percentage of this cost, or plus a fixed fee. Sometimes the contractor agrees to a *guaranteed maximum* cost to the owner. When a cost plus contract is used, the owner usually selects the contracting organization with which he wishes to enter into an agreement, and there is no competitive bidding. The owner usually requires, however, that he be provided with at least an approximate cost estimate.

Gross Floor Area Estimates. A standard for computing the *gross floor* area, or architectural area as it is sometimes called, adopted by the American Institute of Architects is as follows: "The *architectural area* of a building is the sum of the areas of the several floors of the building, including basements, mezzanine and intermediate floored tiers and penthouses of headroom height measured from the exterior faces of exterior walls or from center line of walls separating buildings. Covered walkways, open roofed-over areas which are paved, porches and similar spaces shall have their architectural areas multiplied by an area factor of 0.5. The architectural area does not include such features as pipe trenches, exterior terraces or steps, chimneys, roof overhangs, etc." The areas of pilasters and buttresses should also be excluded.

A preliminary cost estimate is made by multiplying the gross floor area in square feet by an appropriate total cost per square foot. This cost is selected on the basis of costs of similar buildings. Such costs may be based on the architect's experience, a contractor's suggestions, or published values.

Costs vary from year to year and have increased significantly in past and recent years as indicated by the *Engineering News-Record* Building Cost Index (Fig. 3-1). In this index the cost for the year 1913, just before World War I, is considered to be 100. In 1960 this index was 550, or five and one-half times the 1913 value. By using this index, given monthly in that publication, available square-foot costs for buildings already constructed can be brought up to date. Cost for buildings erected in a city other than that in which the contractor is to build can be adjusted to the locality by other cost indexes included regularly, for many cities, in issues of the *Engineering News-Record.*

Cubage Estimates. A procedure similar to the one explained in the preceding paragraph is based on the cost per cubic foot, or *cubage,* of a building. A standard for computing the cubage or architectural volume adopted by the American Institute of Architects is as follows: "The *architectural volume* of a building is the product of the total areas defined above (architectural areas) and the height from the average depth of footings to finish floor, floor to floor, to the average height of the surface of the finished roof above, for the various parts of a building." In other words, it is the total volume of the building included between the horizontal surfaces at the average footing depth and roof height.

The bases of the selected cubage costs and the adjustments for date of construction correspond to those given in the preceding paragraph.

Other Approximate Methods. Other even cruder methods are sometimes used in the early stages of a project. Some of these are based on the cost per unit of capacity, such as the cost of a school per pupil or classroom, a hospital per bed, or a hotel per room.

Detailed Estimates. Final estimates on which a contractor's bid is based require complete plans, or working drawings, and specifications. They involve a *quantity survey* or *takeoff*, that is, a survey of the quantities of various materials and equipment items required in the building. The number of hours and kinds of labor involved in placing these items must be estimated, and finally the material and labor costs must be estimated to determine the *direct costs*.

To the direct costs must be added the *indirect costs* for construction equipment, supervision, purchasing, transportation, financing, administration, insurance, cleaning the building for occupation, site development, and numerous other items not included in the direct costs of the building. Finally, the anticipated profit must be added.

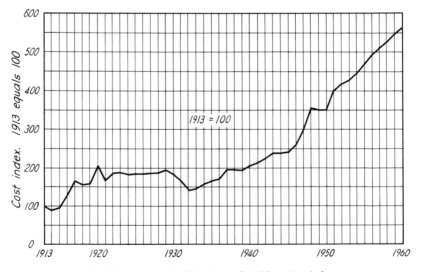

Fig. 3-1. *Engineering News-Record* Building Cost Index.

Table 3-1

Approximate Contract Costs per Square Foot of Gross Floor Area

Type	Cost	Type	Cost
Residences	$15	Schools	$22
Apartments	15	Hotels	28
Warehouses	14	Hospitals	30
Retail stores	20	Office Buildings	30

In addition to these costs, allowance must be made for the fees of the architects, engineers, and special consultants.

Approximate Costs. The costs of buildings of the same type of construction and occupancy vary with the date of construction and the location, as has been explained. Other factors such as the labor supply, weather conditions, and economic conditions affect building costs. Table 3-1 includes recent values for contract prices to give the reader some idea of the magnitude of building costs.

The qualities of materials used in building construction are controlled by standard specifications, most of which have been prepared and recommended by the American Society for Testing Materials. Usually, these have been adopted by the various agencies which have prepared codes and by architects and engineers who are preparing specifications.

The *allowable* or *working stresses* used in the design of the various structural elements which enter into the construction of a building depend upon the properties of the materials of which they are made, the condition under which the elements are used, and many other factors. These stresses are specified in the codes.

References

1. *Building Codes, Their Scope and Aims,* National Board of Fire Underwriters, 85 John Street, New York 38, New York.
2. *Preparation and Revision of Building Codes,* Building Materials and Structures Report 116, National Bureau of Standards, 1949.
3. *Selected Bibliography on Building Construction and Maintenance,* Building Materials and Structures Report 140, National Bureau of Standards, Second Edition, 1956.
4. *Fire Resistance Ratings,* National Board of Fire Underwriters, 85 John Street, New York 38, New York. Copies of this publication will be sent on request.
5. B. L. Wood, *Fire Protection through Modern Building Code,* American Iron and Steel Institute, 1945.

6. *Fire-Resistance Classifications of Building Constructions,* Building Materials and Structures Report 92, National Bureau of Standards, 1942.
7. *Wind Pressures in Various Areas of the United States,* Building Materials and Structures Report 152, National Bureau of Standards, 1959.
8. *American Standard Building Code Requirements for Minimum Design Loads in Buildings and Other Structures,* A58.1, American Standards Association, 1955.
9. Whitney C. Huntington, *Earth Pressures and Retaining Walls,* John Wiley and Sons, 1957.
10. *Recommendations, Earthquake Resistant Design of Buildings, Structures, and Tank Towers,* Pacific Fire Rating Bureau, 1950.
11. *Building Materials List,* Underwriters Laboratories, Inc., sponsored by National Board of Fire Underwriters, issued periodically.

2 Building materials

4. GENERAL DISCUSSION

Introduction. Before giving more detailed consideration to the various materials used in building construction, it seems desirable to summarize the basic properties of a few of them. These are assembled in Table 4-1. Materials included under one name often vary widely in properties, and in such cases the range in values is given. In others, average values are included. For example, the properties of concrete vary over a wide range according to the proportions of cement, aggregate, and water. There are also extreme variations in the properties of plastics, for reasons too complex to consider at this point. The modulus of elasticity of a material is the measure of its stiffness.

The objective of Table 4-1 is to make broad comparisons possible, not to give specific values for use.

The materials considered in this chapter are those that are used in many parts of a building. Other materials whose use is limited to one part of a building are considered in the appropriate chapters.

Masonry materials such as brick, stone, hollow clay tile, concrete block and tile, and cast stone are considered in Chapter 4 on masonry construction. Flooring materials such as clay tile, magnesite composition, asphalt tile, and linoleum are considered in Chapter 10. Roofing materials are considered in Chapter 11, and glass in Chapter 14.

To help the reader understand the methods of manufacture of building materials, some of the fundamental principles of chemistry will be explained in this article.

The Elements, Compounds, and Mixtures. All substances are made up of elements. An *element* may be defined as a substance which cannot be separated by any known mechanical or chemical means into substances different from itself. There are about 100 known elements. If two or more substances are mixed together and can be separated

Table 4-1

Basic Properties of Common Building Materials

Name of Material	Weight, lb./cu. ft.	Ultimate Strength, 1000 lb./sq. in.	Mod. of Elasticity, Million lb./sq. in.	Melting Point, °F.
Steel				
Cold-drawn wire	490	200–300t	30t	
Alloys	490	80–115t	30t	2200–2800
Structural	490	60–72t	30t	2750
Wrought iron	485	48t	27t	2800
Cast iron, gray	450	80c	11t	2000
Aluminum	170	12t	17t	1200
Alloys	170	13–83t	10t	850–1250
Copper	550	25t		2000
Alloys	510–530			1300–1900
Lead	710	3t		620
Tin	450	2t		460
Zinc	445	8t		790
Brick, hard	130	3–12c		
Stone	120–175	5–30c	3.3–8.4c	
Concrete	145	2–5c	2–5c	
Lightweight	33–104	0.3–4.0c	0.2–2.7c	
Woods, soft	23–44	2.6–4.4c	0.8–1.6c	(Softening point)
Plastics	62–125	1.5–13t	0.1–2.0t	150–450
Laminates		10–37t	0.9–2.5t	

Key: c indicates compressive properties and t tensile properties.

by mechanical means, a *mechanical mixture* is formed; but if they combine in definite proportions to form a homogeneous mass whose components cannot be separated mechanically, a *chemical compound* is formed. *Alloys* and *solutions* are formed by mixing substances together to form other substances which are homogeneous and cannot be separated into their components mechanically, but these substances need not be in definite proportions and therefore are not chemical compounds.

Atoms and Molecules. According to the atomic theory, an *atom* is the smallest particle of an element which can exist either alone or in combination with similar particles of the same or of a different element. It is now possible, however, to divide atoms by nonchemical methods, but the products have chemical properties different from those of the atom. The atoms of one element have the power of attracting atoms of other elements to form *compounds*. The combination of atoms forms *molecules* which are the smallest particles of a compound that can exist. Given elements always combine in definite proportions when they form the same substance. For instance, when hydrogen and oxygen combine to form water, they always unite in the proportions of 2 atoms of hydrogen to 1 atom of oxygen. The weight of an atom of oxygen is 16 times as great as the weight of an atom of hydrogen; therefore, by weight, 2 units of hydrogen combine with 16 units of oxygen to form 18 units of water. The same elements may sometimes combine in different proportions to form different substances. For instance, 1 atom of carbon will combine with 1 atom of oxygen to form 1 molecule of carbon monoxide, and 1 atom of carbon will combine with 2 atoms of oxygen to form 1 molecule of carbon dioxide.

Chemical Symbols, Formulas, and Equations. For convenience, each element is designated by a *symbol*. The elements that compose practically all building materials and the symbols for these elements are

Aluminum	Al	Nickel	Ni
Calcium	Ca	Nitrogen	N
Carbon	C	Oxygen	O
Chlorine	Cl	Phosphorus	P
Copper	Cu	Potassium	K
Hydrogen	H	Silicon	Si
Iron	Fe	Sulfur	S
Lead	Pb	Tin	Sn
Magnesium	Mg	Zinc	Zn
Manganese	Mn		

Compounds are designated by *formulas* formed by combining the symbols of the component elements. The number of atoms of each element in the molecule of the compound is indicated by a subscript figure. For instance, the formula for water is H_2O. This indicates that water is formed by a combination of hydrogen and oxygen in the proportions of 2 atoms of hydrogen to 1 atom of oxygen.

The changes that occur when elements or compounds combine are indicated by chemical *equations*. For instance, the equation for the chemical change when the elements hydrogen and oxygen combine to form the compound water is

$$2H + O = H_2O$$

A more complicated change occurs when the compound quicklime (CaO) absorbs the compound carbon dioxide (CO_2) from the air while setting to form the compound calcium carbonate. This is indicated by the equation

$$CaO + CO_2 = CaCO_3$$

One of the changes that takes place in a blast furnace in the manufacture of pig iron is the reaction of three molecules of carbon monoxide (CO) with one molecule of iron oxide (Fe_2O_3) to form three molecules of carbon dioxide (CO_2) and two molecules of iron (Fe):

$$3CO + Fe_2O_3 = 3CO_2 + 2Fe$$

In all equations the number of atoms of each element on one side must equal the number of atoms of that element on the other side; in other words, the equations must balance.

Many other details might be explained, but enough have been given so that a general idea of the use of equations can be formed.

Acids, Bases, and Salts. Most compounds may be classed as acids, bases, or salts. *Acids* are compounds, containing hydrogen, which will react with the metallic oxides known as *bases*, to form neutral compounds called *salts*.

Some of the common acids are hydrochloric (HCl), sulfuric (H_2SO_4), and nitric (HNO_3). Quicklime (CaO), magnesia (MgO), and potash (K_2O) are examples of bases. Ordinary salt is sodium chloride (NaCl) and is formed by adding hydrochloric acid to the base soda:

$$Na_2O + 2HCl = H_2O + 2NaCl$$

Common Compounds. The chemical names and the chemical formulas for some of the more common compounds used in building construction are given in Table 4-2.

All these compounds are called *inorganic*. Carbon is included in many of them. It is also the basic element in many other compounds, all of which are classified as *organic*. Common examples of organic compounds or materials are the plastics, considered later in this chapter, rubber, wood, coal, oil, and vegetable fiber.

Table 4-2

Formulas for Chemical Compounds

Substance	Chemical Name	Formula
Alumina	Aluminum oxide	Al_2O_3
Carbonate of lime	Calcium carbonate	$CaCO_3$
Quicklime	Calcium oxide	CaO
Slaked lime	Calcium hydroxide	$Ca(OH)_2$
Sulfate of lime	Calcium sulfate	$CaSO_4$
Magnetite	Magnetite	Fe_3O_4
Hematite	Ferric oxide	Fe_2O_3
Litharge	Lead monoxide	PbO
Red lead	Red lead oxide	Pb_3O_4
White lead	Basic lead carbonate	$2PbCO_3 \cdot Pb(OH)_2$
Magnesia	Magnesium oxide	MgO
Magnesium carbonate	Magnesium carbonate	$MgCO_3$
Manganese dioxide	Manganese dioxide	MnO_2
Silica	Silicon dioxide	SiO_2
Sulfur dioxide	Sulfur dioxide	SO_2
Salt	Sodium chloride	$NaCl$
Zinc white	Zinc oxide	ZnO
Zinc sulfate	Zinc sulfate	$ZnSO_4 \cdot 7H_2O$
Muriatic acid	Hydrochloric acid	HCl
Nitric acid	Nitric acid	HNO_3
Sulfuric acid	Sulfuric acid	H_2SO_4
Vinegar	Acetic acid	$HC_2H_3O_2$
Carbonic acid gas	Carbon dioxide	CO_2
Water	Water	H_2O

5. PIG IRON, CAST IRON, AND WROUGHT IRON

Pig Iron

Definition, Composition, and Uses. *Pig iron* may be defined as the product obtained by the reduction of iron ores in the blast furnace. It contains 91 to 94 per cent iron, 3.75 to 4.50 per cent carbon, 0.25 to 3.50 per cent silicon, 0.03 to 1.00 per cent phosphorus, and less than 0.10 per cent sulfur. A vertical section through a blast furnace is shown in Fig. 5-1.

Pig iron may be used directly in making castings, but its most impor-

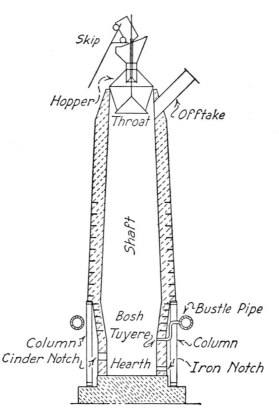

Fig. 5-1. Blast furnace.

tant use is in the manufacture of cast iron, wrought iron, and steel where it may be used in a molten state direct from the blast furnace or in the form of *pigs*, which are castings made from the pig iron as it is drawn from the furnace.

Raw Materials. The raw materials used in the manufacture of pig iron are the iron ores which furnish the iron; the fuel which furnishes the heat and the *reducing agent* to reduce the carbon content; the *flux* which provides a fusible *slag* that carries off ash of the fuel and some of the impurities of the ore; and the air which supplies the oxygen for the combustion of the fuel.

The principal iron ores of commercial importance may be divided into four classes: iron oxides, iron carbonates, iron silicates, and iron sulfides. Only the oxides are of importance in this country. The oxides of iron used in the manufacture of pig iron are

Hematite, Fe_2O_3, containing about 70 per cent iron when pure;

Limonite, Fe_2O_3, n.H_2O, which is hydrated hematite containing about 60 per cent iron when pure;

Magnetite, Fe_3O_4, containing about 72 per cent iron when pure.

Impurities in the ore, such as sand and clay, are called the *gangue*.

The fuel has two functions in the manufacture of pig iron: to furnish the necessary heat and to supply the reducing agent to combine with the oxygen of the ore. The fuel used is coke because of its porosity and resistance to crushing.

The functions of a *flux* are to make the impurities in the ore and fuel, such as silica and alumina, more easily fusible and to provide a fusible slag in which these and other impurities may be carried off. The flux used in the blast furnace is usually limestone, which, when pure, is calcium carbonate and has the chemical formula $CaCO_3$, although a considerable amount of magnesium carbonate ($MgCO_3$) is usually present.

The Blast Furnace. The blast furnace is a structure 100 ft. or more in height, approximately cylindrical in shape, built of fire brick, enclosed more or less completely in a steel shell. The furnace is divided into three main parts: the *hearth*, or *crucible*, the *bosh*, and the *stack*, *as* shown by the diagram in Fig. 5-1.

The hearth is provided with an *iron notch* and a *cinder notch* through which the iron and slag are periodically removed. Just below the bosh a ring of 10 to 16 *tuyeres* penetrates the lining. The air necessary for the process is blown through these tuyeres, which are all connected to the *bustle pipe* encircling the furnace. This pipe is in turn connected to the hot-blast stoves, which heat the air, and finally to the blowing engines which provide the air at a pressure of from 15 to 30 lb. per sq. in.

At the top of the furnace is a device that permits the raw material to be charged into the furnace but prevents the escape of the gases. These gases are heated to a very high temperature and contain a large amount of carbon monoxide (CO), which is combustible. Formerly these gases were permitted to burn as they left the furnace, but now they are used in the hot-blast stoves, under steam boilers, and in internal-combustion engines. This practice results in a considerable saving in fuel.

Operation. A blast furnace is operated continuously by charging the *burden,* which consists of ore, fuel, and flux in proper proportions, in the top of the furnace and drawing off the slag and iron at the bottom, the slag being tapped at intervals of about 2 hours and the iron at intervals of about 5 hours. The iron may be used in the molten state in the manufacture of wrought iron or steel or may be cast into bars called *pigs* for subsequent use.

Chemical Changes. Air contains about one part of oxygen to four parts of nitrogen and other inert gases. The air enters the blast furnace through the tuyeres at a temperature of about 1000°F. and a pressure of from 15 to 30 lb. per sq. in. It immediately comes into contact with hot coke, and the oxygen of the air combines with the carbon of the coke forming carbon dioxide (CO_2):

$$C + O_2 = CO_2 \tag{1}$$

Because of the excess of carbon, the carbon dioxide is reduced to carbon monoxide (CO):

$$CO_2 + C = 2CO \tag{2}$$

The ore as it moves down through the furnace encounters this carbon monoxide, which is a powerful reducing agent, and the following reactions result, the first occurring near the top of the furnace at a temperature of approximately 600°F., and the last, in the lower part of the stack at a temperature of about 1400°F.:

$$2Fe_2O_3 + 8CO = 4Fe + 7CO_2 + C \tag{3}$$

$$3Fe_2O_3 + CO = 2Fe_3O_4 + CO_2 \tag{4}$$

$$Fe_3O_4 + CO = 3FeO + CO_2 \tag{5}$$

$$FeO + CO = Fe + CO_2 \tag{6}$$

Reactions 1 and 3 produce most of the heat required by the other reactions and heat to dry the raw materials, to decompose the limestone, to flux the impurities, and to melt the iron and slag. The temperatures in the furnace increase from about 400°F. at the top to about 3000°F. in the crucible.

Other changes occur, but they are too confusing to consider here. However, it may be well to mention that the heated coke acts as a reducing agent in much the same manner as the carbon monoxide already considered.

The limestone in the charge breaks up into calcium oxide and carbon dioxide at about 1600°F:

$$CaCO_3 = CaO + CO_2 \tag{7}$$

The CO_2 is reduced to CO when it encounters the hot coke. At about this same temperature the iron, which is in a spongy form, absorbs carbon from the coke. This lowers its melting point and it becomes fluid.

At the top of the bosh, the lime (CaO) combines with some of the gangue, a little unreduced iron oxide, and manganese oxide from the ore and forms slag which, with the molten iron, runs down through the coke to the hearth. There the slag and the molten iron separate into two layers because of the difference in their densities; the slag, being the lighter, remain on top.

In the hearth, part of the oxides of manganese (Mn_3O_4), silicon (SiO_2), and phosphorus (P_2O_5) are reduced by the carbon of the coke, which extends through to the bottom of the furnace, and join the iron. The remainder of the oxides are not acted upon by the carbon, and are found in the slag. All the phosphorus present in the charge is found in the iron, but the amount of silicon and manganese in the pig iron depend upon furnace conditions. Sulfur is introduced into the blast furnace mainly as an impurity in the coke in the form of iron sulfide. Some of this reacts with the lime to form calcium sulfide and joins the slag, but the remainder is found in the iron, for iron sulfide is soluble in iron. Conditions that tend to decrease the amount of sulfur present in the iron also tend to increase the amount of silicon.

Cast Iron and Malleable Cast Iron

Production. Cast iron is manufactured by remelting pig iron in a *cupalo*, which is similar to a blase furnace but much smaller, and pouring it into molds to form castings of the desired shape when the metal solidifies in cooling. Scrap iron, consisting chiefly of discarded castings, is used with the pig iron because it is less expensive than pig iron. No chemical changes of importance take place during the process of remelting. Cast iron contains from 2.5 to 4.0 per cent carbon.

Molds and Patterns. The process of making castings is called *iron founding.* The molds are made of sand; the impressions in the sand are usually made by *wood patterns.* In *loam molding* no pattern is used, the impression being formed in the sand by hand or machine.

Patterns must be slightly larger than the objects to be cast, to allow for the shrinkage of the metal in cooling. Vertical surfaces must be slightly tapered to facilitate the withdrawal of the pattern from the mold. This taper is called *draft*.

Gray and White Cast Iron. When molten cast iron solidifies, the carbon which is present remains combined with the iron as *carbide of iron* (Fe_3C) or may separate from the iron as *graphite*. White cast iron contains carbon chiefly in the combined state. It has a white metallic fracture and is very hard and brittle. Gray cast iron contains carbon chiefly in the form of graphite mechanically mixed with the iron, but some carbon is present in the combined state. It has a gray, crystalline fracture and is not as hard and brittle as white cast iron. The graphite in cast iron is in the form of flakes, which reduce its strength materially. Slow cooling and the presence of silicon tend to increase the amount of graphite in cast iron, whereas rapid cooling and the presence of manganese and sulfur tend to hold the carbon in the combined state. Cast iron increases in strength as the amount of combined carbon is increased up to about 1.2 per cent. Further increases cause a loss of strength. The hardness and brittleness increase as the amount of combined carbon is increased. In general, cast iron has a high compressive strength and a low tensile strength.

Chilled Castings. Chilled castings are produced by using molds with certain surfaces made of iron. The iron that comes in contact with these surfaces is therefore cooled suddenly and the carbon in the iron remains in a combined state (Fe_3C) for a certain depth, forming white cast iron which is very hard. The remainder of the iron cools naturally and forms gray cast iron which is not as hard but is less brittle. Surfaces of cast iron which are subject to wear are often chilled to increase their life.

Malleable Cast Iron. Castings made of white cast iron may be made malleable and ductile by subjecting them to an annealing process which converts the combined carbon into free carbon in a very finely divided state. The annealing may be accomplished by packing the castings in some inert material such as sand or clay and heating to a red heat which is maintained for several days, after which the castings are slowly cooled.

Better results may be secured by packing the castings in an oxidizing material such as iron oxide. The oxide draws the carbon from the castings to a depth of $\frac{1}{16}$ in. or more, forming a skin of soft iron on the castings in addition to converting the combined carbon in the body of the castings into free carbon.

White cast iron is used so that all the free carbon will be in the form of very minute particles evenly distributed throughout the castings and not in the form of large flakes which have such a weakening effect on gray cast iron.

Malleable castings are used for small articles such as builders' hardware. Malleable iron washers are extensively used in timber construction.

Wrought Iron

Manufacture. Formerly, wrought iron was produced by melting pig iron in a reverberatory puddling furnace, the hearth of which was lined with iron oxide. At present the Aston-Byers process is used. Instead of using a puddling furnace, the pig iron is refined in a Bessemer converter, described in Art. 6 and illustrated in Fig. 6-1a. The molten metal is then poured into a ladle containing a previously prepared molten slag of an appropriate composition. The temperature of the slag is lower than that of the molten iron and, because the iron is cooled suddenly, innumerable small explosions occur. These explosions divide the iron into small globules which are coated with slag. These form a *puddle ball* which is squeezed and rolled to form a solid mass of wrought iron.

Properties and Uses. Wrought iron is composed of very pure iron mechanically mixed with a small amount of slag. The rolling process has elongated the particles of iron and slag which existed in the puddle ball so that a fibrous structure is produced. The properties of wrought iron correspond to those of pure iron, which is tough, ductile, easily welded, and comparativley low in tensile and compressive strength. It is superior to ordinary steel in resisting corrosion. In building construction, wrought iron is used for pipe and for ornamental iron work.

6. STEEL

Comparison of Steel with Other Ferrous Products. The various methods and processes for manufacturing steel have as their primary object the reduction of the amount of carbon present in pig iron, but the amounts of phosphorus, sulfur, manganese, and silicon are also controlled.

Steel differs in physical properties from pig iron, and it differs from cast iron by being ductile rather than brittle and by being malleable. It differs from malleable cast iron by being malleable without treatment after being cast. Low-carbon steel differs from wrought iron chiefly by the process of manufacture and structure, rather than by any great difference in other physical properties.

Steel differs in chemical composition from pig iron, cast iron, and malleable cast iron chiefly by having a much lower percentage of carbon, but also by the smaller amounts of manganese, silicon, and phosphorus present. Low-carbon steel and wrought iron differ very little in chemical composition, but in wrought iron the iron itself contains a smaller percentage of impurities because a part of the impurities are in the slag which is mechanically mixed with iron.

Effect of Composition on Properties. The element that has the most pronounced effect on the physical properties of steel is carbon. The amount of carbon present in steel may vary from almost 0 to about 1½ per cent. Increasing the amount of carbon increases the strength, hardness, and brittleness of steel but decreases its ductility. Steel may be classified according to carbon content approximately as follows.

	Carbon Content, Per Cent
Low-carbon steel................	0.06 to 0.30
Medium-carbon steel............	0.30 to 0.50
High-carbon steel..............	0.50 to 0.80

There is no distinct line of demarcation between the various grades, so these limits are subject to considerable variation.

Silicon, in the amounts usually found in steel, has little effect on its properties, but when present in amounts as high as 0.3 or 0.4 per cent it increases the strength without a sacrifice in ductility.

Sulfur has little effect on the strength or ductility of steel, but it makes steel brittle and likely to crack when worked at red heat. This property is called *red shortness*. The maximum amount of sulfur permitted by specifications for structural steel is about 0.05 per cent.

Phosphorus causes steel to be brittle at ordinary temperatures, or *cold short*, and is therefore very objectionable. The maximum amount of phosphorus permitted by specifications for structural steel is about 0.06 per cent.

Manganese in amounts ordinarily present is beneficial to steel, but its action is too complex to consider here.

Effect of Mechanical Working. Hammering, pressing, and rolling steel while it is hot tend to eliminate flaws. If the working is continued while the metal is cooled past a certain critical temperature, the steel will be fine grained, owing to the breaking up of the crystals and to not permitting them to form again.

The cold-working of steel increases the strength and elastic limit but decreases the ductility.

Effect of Heat Treatment. Heating, annealing, and sudden cooling have very marked effects on the strength, ductility, and grain size of steel, but this subject is too complex for consideration here.

Processes of Manufacture. The principal processes used in manufacturing steel are the Bessemer and open-hearth processes, which produce steel by purifying pig iron. The open-hearth process has replaced the Bessemer for structural use.

Bessemer Process

The acid and the basic Bessemer processes are used in the manufacture of steel. The acid process will be considered first.

Plant. In the acid Bessemer process for making steel, molten pig iron is charged into a vessel called a *converter,* constructed as shown diagrammatically in Fig. 6-1a. This converter consists of a steel shell with a lining composed chiefly of silica, and it has tuyeres in the bottom through which air may be forced. The converter is mounted on a horizontal axis on which it can be rotated. The capacity of a converter is about 20 tons of pig iron.

Operation. While being charged with molten pig iron, the converter is tipped, as shown in Fig. 6-1b. The blast is turned on and the converter is rotated to a vertical position (Fig. 6-1a). The pressure of the blast varies from 10 to 25 lb. per sq. in. The blow is continued for about 10 minutes, during which time a flame issues from the mouth of the converter. This flame is caused by the burning of the gases given off during the process. The operator judges from the appearance of the flame when the process is complete and pours the steel into a *ladle* by tipping the converter. From the ladle the steel is poured into *ingot molds* to form *ingots.*

Removal of Impurities. The oxygen in the air blast combines with the silicon, manganese, and carbon in the pig iron, forming the oxides SiO_2, MnO, and CO. The oxides of silicon and manganese form a *slag*

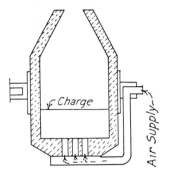

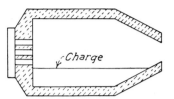

(b) *Bessemer Converter*
(In position for receiving charge)

(a) *Bessemer Converter*

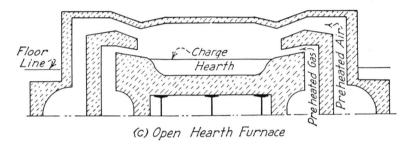

(c) *Open Hearth Furnace*

Fig. 6-1. Bessemer converter and open-hearth furnace.

which separates from the iron, and the carbon monoxide, being a gas, passes out through the open end of the converter where it combines with oxygen from the air to form carbon dioxide (CO_2). The phosphorus and sulfur present in the pig iron are not removed by this process, and the pig iron used must not contain large enough amounts of these materials to be objectionable in the steel. Since all the phosphorus which is present in the ore charged into the blast furnace joins the pig iron, it is evident that the only ores that can be used for acid Bessemer steel are ores that do not contain enough phosphorus to injure the steel. Such ores are not plentiful in this country. They are therefore expensive and place a limit on the use of the acid Bessemer process.

Sources of Heat. The melting point of the purified iron is higher than that of the pig iron, so if no heat were generated in the process the iron would not remain in a molten state. The heat required for the process is furnished primarily by the oxidation of the silicon, but the oxidation of the carbon and the manganese furnish some heat.

Recarburizing. During the process, all the carbon is removed from the pig iron and some iron oxide is formed. The amount of carbon desired in the steel is introduced by adding a *recarburizer* to the molten metal while it is still in the converter, or after it has been poured out into the ladle. The recarburizer has other functions to perform: the deoxidation of the steel, the introduction of elements such as manganese to improve the quality of the steel, and the removal of the small amount of carbon monoxide gas that tends to remain in the steel and cause blow holes. The material used as a recarburizer is a special pig iron that is high in manganese and carbon.

The Basic Process. The process just described is called the acid process because the slag formed is acid in character and requires a converter lining, also acid in character, to prevent chemical action between the lining and the slag. Phosphorus can be removed by the basic process in which lime is charged into the converter to produce a slag basic in character. The phoshorus is the chief source of heat in the basic process, and ores, in order to be suitable for this process, must be high in phosphorus. The basic process is not used in the United States largely because of the lack of suitable ores.

Advantages and Disadvantages. The chief advantages of the Bessemer process are its rapidity, the simplicity of the plant, and the saving in fuel. The disadvantages are the lack of suitable ores and the variability of the product, for the process depends largely on the skill of the operator in judging the time required for the reactions by the appearance of flame issuing from the mouth of the converter. Bessemer steel is no longer used for structural purposes in this country.

Open-Hearth Process

Plant. The open-hearth process for manufacturing steel is carried out in an open-hearth furnace (Fig. 6-1c). There are two open-hearth processes, the acid and the basic. The basic process will be considered first.

The Basic Process. The furnace consists essentially of a hearth in the central portion and two openings, called *ports*, at each end. The hearth is lined with calcined magnesite, with anhydrous tar as a binder. Under the action of heat the tar burns to coke and becomes hard and firm. The capacity of the furnaces in use varies from 100 to 200 tons in 12 hours.

Operation. In charging the furnace, pig iron, steel scrap, iron ore, and limestone are placed on the hearth through doors on one side of the furnace. The furnace is heated by introducing preheated gas through one port at one end of the furnace and preheated air through the other port at the same end. The gas and air ignite at the ports. The exhaust gases are drawn through both ports at the other end by natural draft. These gases pass through regenerators filled with checker brick and heat the brick to a high temperature. In about 20 minutes, valves are turned so that the direction of flow of the gases is reversed. The gas and air are preheated by passing through the regenerators that were heated by the exhaust gases. Regenerators are provided at each end of the furnace, so that one set is always being heated by the exhaust gases while the other is heating the incoming gas and air. The direction of flow is changed at intervals of 15 or 20 minutes. The regenerators make it possible to heat the furnace to a temperature high enough to melt the charge in 4 or 5 hours. The process requires 6 to 12 hours to remove the impurities. Then the furnace is tapped through a tap hole, and the molten steel is run into ladles.

Removal of Impurities. The oxygen in the iron ore of the charge is the oxidizing agent that combines with the silicon, manganese, and phosphorus present in the charge, forming the corresponding oxides which, with the lime of the charge, form the *slag*. The carbon present in the materials charged into the furnace is oxidized by the oxygen of the iron ore, forming carbon dioxide gas, which leaves the furnace with the other exhaust gases. The elimination of sulfur is uncertain.

Sources of Heat. Some heat is supplied by the oxidation of the impurities, but most of the heat is obtained from the combustion of the fuel, which may be gas, fuel oil, or powered coal.

Recarburizing. The process is always continued until the amount of carbon present is less than the amount desired in the finished steel. The additional carbon is supplied by adding ferromanganese with coal, charcoal, or coke to the metal in the ladle.

The Acid Process. The process just described is the basic process because the slag formed is basic in character and requires a basic lining for the hearth in order to prevent any chemical action between the slag and the lining. Phosphorus can be removed by the basic process but not by the acid process; and since all the ores in this country contain phosphorus in objectionable amounts, the acid process is of very little use.

The acid process differs from the basic in the following respects: the lining of the hearth is acid in character instead of basic, the charge must be low in phosphorus, and the recarburizing may be done in the furnace instead of in the ladle as it is in the basic process.

Advantages and Disadvantages. The chief advantage of the open-hearth process over the Bessemer process is the possibility of better control owing to the slowness of the process. The chief disadvantages are the time required and the additional fuel necessary, the heat in the Bessemer process being supplied entirely by the oxidation of the impurities in the charge. Open-hearth steel is generally specified for structural purposes.

Properties and Uses. As has been stated, the strength, ductility, and other properties of steel are affected by its composition, the mechanical treatment it receives when it is hot and cold during processing, and many other factors. In general, it may be classed as a relatively high-strength and low-cost metal. Its most significant defect is its lack of resistance to corrosion.

Steel is the most important metal used in building construction. Its uses are so numerous and so well known that it seems unnecessary to mention them here, but many of them are considered in detail in subsequent articles.

Alloy Steels

Various alloying elements are introduced into steel to change the properties in some desired manner, such as to increase the strength. Included in these elements are silicon, manganese, copper, nickel, chromium, tungsten, molybdenum, and vanadium. They may be introduced singly, or two or more may be used. Such steels are called *alloy steels*.

A common steel used for curtain walls, decorative purposes, sinks and counter tops, and other building purposes is *stainless steel*, which resists corrosion, takes a high polish, and is attractive in appearance. Some types of it are made by adding from 10 to 30 per cent of chromium to steel. In others, from 5 to 15 per cent of nickel also is included.

The melting points of various steels vary from 2600 to 2800°F. Their weight is 490 lb. per cu. ft. Small amounts of copper, ranging from 0.15 to 0.30 per cent, introduced in steel increase its resistance to atmospheric corrosion without having a significant effect on its other properties. *Copper-bearing steel* is extensively used for sheet-metal products.

7. NONFERROUS METALS AND ALLOYS

Concentrating. The first step in the production of most nonferrous metals from their ores consists of increasing the proportion of metal present by removing much of the waste material. This process is called *concentrating*. It includes various mechanical treatments, such as crushing, grinding, and screening, which do not involve heat and cause no chemical changes.

Copper

Ores. Copper is found in the native or pure state and in a great variety of ores, of which the sufides are the most common.

Extraction. The stages in the extraction of copper from concentrated sulfide ores are as follows.

1. *Roasting* the sulfide ore by heating it in an oxidizing atmosphere where a part of the iron sulfide ore is converted into the oxide by the burning out of the sulfide. The temperature is not high enough to melt the ore. The roasted ore contains chiefly copper sulfide, iron oxide, and siliceous gangue, although some copper oxide may be present.

2. *Smelting* in a blast furnace with coke as a fuel or in a reverberatory furnace. Copper sulfide and iron sulfide settle to the bottom forming a *matte,* and the slag, containing the *gangue* or earthy materials and iron oxide, forms on top where it may be drawn off.

3. *Converting* the molten *matte*, containing the sulfides of copper and iron, in a converter similar to that used in the manufacture of Bessemer steel. Air is blown through the molten matte and provides oxygen, which combines with the iron sulfide to form a slag of iron oxide on top of the remaining copper sulfide. By continuing the process, the sulfur is burned out of the sulfides, forming sulfur dioxide which passes off as a gas and leaving an impure form of copper known as *blister copper.*

4. *Refining* the blister copper either in a reverberatory furnace or electrolytically. In *furnace* or *fire refining* the blister copper is melted

in a reverberatory furnace; the slag which is formed is skimmed off; and air is blown over the molten bath and oxidizes the impurities which either pass off as gas or form slag on top of the molten metal. Some of the copper is oxidized and must be reduced by adding charcoal and stirring with a green wood pole. Steam formed by the water in the green pole agitates the bath and the carbon from the charcoal combines with the oxygen of the copper oxide, forming carbon monoxide which passes off as a gas, thus leaving fairly pure copper which is cast into ingots.

In the *electrolytic process* anodes of blister copper or fire-refined copper and cathodes of pure copper are placed in a copper sulfate bath. An electric current is passed through the bath and causes pure copper to be transferred from the blister copper anode to the pure copper cathode. The impurities, which often include the precious metals, are not soluble in copper sulfate, and being of higher specific gravity they fall to the bottom of the bath and are removed.

Fire-refined copper is not as pure as that obtained by the electrolytic process. The former is used for wires, tubes, and plates, and for making brasses and bronzes. The latter is used primarily for electrical purposes which require the purer form.

Properties and Uses. The most important properties of copper are its electrical conductivity and its resistance to corrosion. Its strength and ductility are greatly affected by the mechanical and heat treatment it receives. If heated to a red heat and cooled slowly it is brittle, but if cooled quickly it is malleable and ductile. It may be cast and welded and may be rolled or drawn when hot or cold. Cold working increases its strength but decreases its ductility. When exposed to moist air, as when used for a roofing material, a thin coating of the green basic carbonate is formed. This protects the copper so that no further treatment is required.

Copper is used primarily for electrical purposes, but it is also used extensively as a constituent of brasses and bronzes and for sheet-metal roofing and shingles, gutters, rain conductors, flashing, and pipe for plumbing. Copper wire is formed by drawing through dies. If it is cold-drawn, it produces what is called *hard-drawn wire* which is springy.

Zinc

The ores of zinc are the sulfide (ZnS), the carbonate $(ZnCO_3)$, the silicates $(Zn_2\ SiO_4\ H_2O)$ and $(Zn_2\ SiO_4)$, and franklinite, which is composed of the oxides of zinc, manganese, and iron. The most common source of zinc is the sulfide zinc blende.

Extraction. The stages in the extraction of zinc from its ores are as follows.

1. *Roasting* the ore to drive off the sulfur from sulfides and the carbon dioxide from the carbonates to form zinc oxide.

2. *Mixing* the oxide with a nearly equal amount of finely ground anthracite coal and placing it in fire-clay retorts.

3. *Heating* retorts to a white heat so that the coal will form carbon monoxide which will combine with the oxygen of the zinc oxide to form carbon dioxide and zinc vapor.

4. *Condensing* the zinc vapor at a temperature above the melting point of zinc to form molten zinc, which is poured into molds and allowed to cool forming *zinc spelter,* the form commonly used. If the temperature at which the condensation is carried on is too low, *zinc dust* is formed. This cannot be melted to form a solid mass and has a limited use in the powdered form.

Properties and Uses. Zinc has a fairly high resistance to corrosion. For this reason it is used as a roofing material in the form of sheet zinc. Exposure to the weather causes dull-gray zinc carbonate to form on the surface and protect the remainder of the metal.

If zinc is cooled suddenly from the molten state it is malleable, but if cooled slowly it is hard and brittle. Commercial zinc is quite brittle, but if heated to about 250°F. it becomes malleable and ductile. It may then be drawn into wire or rolled into sheets which are ductile and malleable when cool. Molten zinc shrinks very little in solidifying and casts well.

Zinc is extensively used as a protective coating for steel in the *galvanizing* and *sherardizing* processes. It is also used as one of the constituents in brass, nickel silver, and other alloys and in making electric batteries.

Lead

Ores. The only important ore of lead is *galena,* the sulfide (PbS) mixed with gangue.

Extraction. There are two stages in the extraction of lead from its ores.

1. *Roasting* by charging crushed ore into a reverberatory furnace where it is heated at a low temperature in an oxidizing atmosphere.

Part of the sulfur in the sulfide is oxidized forming lead oxide and sulfur dioxide gas, and some lead sulfate is formed:

$$PbS + 3O = PbO + SO_2$$

$$PbS + 4O = PbSO_4$$

2. *Smelting* the lead oxide, the lead sulfate, and the remaining lead sulfide in a blast furnace with limestone, coke, and some other materials to form lead and sulfur dioxide:

$$PbS + 2PbO = 3Pb + SO_2$$

$$PbS + PbSO_4 = 2Pb + 2SO_2$$

The molten lead thus formed is drawn off and cast into ingots. This lead must usually be purified before it is ready for the market.

Properties and Uses. The important physical properties of lead are its resistance to corrosion, its plasticity, and its malleability.

Lead sheets are used to a considerable extent for water-tight pans under the floors of shower baths and in similar positions. They are used to a limited extent for roofing, particularly for curved or irregular surfaces to which lead can be easily fitted by stretching and working. Lead has a high coefficient of expansion and is difficult to hold in place, particularly on pitched roofs.

A roofing known as *hard lead* is composed of lead and antimony. It is stronger and has a lower coefficient of expansion than ordinary lead and can be used on any slope.

Lead pipes are used in plumbing but not as much as they were in former years. The pipe is formed by forcing the metal through dies by means of hydraulic presses. The term *plumber* is derived from the Latin word *plumbum* meaning lead.

Solder is an alloy of lead and tin.

Aluminum

Ores. Aluminum occurs abundantly in nature in combination with oxygen, sodium, fluorine, and silicon. The chief source of aluminum is *bauxite*, which is hydrated oxide of aluminum and iron with some silicon. The most extensive occurrence of aluminum is as the oxide *alumina* (Al_2O_3), which is the principal constituent of clay. No process has yet been devised to obtain aluminum from clay in commercial quantities.

Extraction. The stages in the extraction of aluminum from bauxite are:

1. *Roasting* bauxite to drive off the water.

2. *Grinding* roasted bauxite and heating under pressure with a solution of sodium hydrate forming sodium aluminate.

3. *Precipitating* aluminum hydroxide by heating sodium aluminate solution with aluminum hydroxide or with carbon dioxide.

4. *Separating* aluminum hydroxide with filtering and dehydrating by heating to form alumina (Al_2O_3).

5. *Extracting* aluminum from alumina by the electrolytic decomposition of alumina in a molten bath of cryolite which is the fluoride of alumina and sodium.

In the last-named process the containing vessel is lined with carbon in the form of graphite or coke which forms the cathode. Carbon rods suspended in the bath form the anode to which the oxygen goes. The cryolite is melted by the heat generated by the passage of the electric current across a gap which exists between the anodes and the cathodes. When the cryolite bath becomes molten, alumina is thrown on the bath and as it melts it is broken up into molten aluminum, which settles on the cathode, and oxygen, which goes to the anode with which it combines, forming carbon monoxide which escapes as a gas. The molten aluminum is tapped off as it accumulates. The heat for the process is supplied by the electric current.

Properties and Uses. Aluminum has a low electrical resistance which makes it valuable for transmission lines and other electrical uses. It is a good heat conductor and is noncorrosive. Because of its lightness it has many special uses; its weight is only about one-third that of iron, but it is usually alloyed with other metals which increase its strength. It is very malleable, quite ductile, noncorrosive, and strong in proportion to its weight. It may be drawn into wire, rolled into structural shapes and very thin sheets, extruded through dies, cast, and shaped in other ways.

Tin

Ores. The principal source of tin is the black oxide (SnO_2), known as *cassiterite* or *tinstone*. Tin is the only important metal not found in the United States.

Extraction. The stages in the extraction of tin from its concentrated ores are as follows.

1. *Roasting* in a reverberatory furnace to oxidize the sulfur and arsenic which exist as impurities. These oxides pass off as gases.

2. *Smelting* in reverberatory or blast furnaces. The oxygen of the tin oxide combines with carbon to form carbon dioxide, the carbon being mixed directly with the ore in the furnace, or the oxygen combines with carbon monoxide derived from the partial combustion of coal used as a source of heat. The molten tin accumulates and is drawn off. This crude or raw tin contains copper, iron, arsenic, sulfur, and other impurities.

3. *Refining* by liquidation and boiling. The ingots of crude tin are placed in a reverberatory furnace, and as the temperature is gradually increased the tin melts and is removed, leaving the unfused impurities. The molten tin thus obtained is still further purified by boiling while bundles of green twigs are held submerged in the molten tin. The steam given off by the green twigs develops violent boiling which causes the impurities to become oxidized by coming in contact with the air. These oxides form a scum on the surface. This scum is removed and the tin is cast into ingots. Some of the impurities are heavier than the tin and do not pass into the scum but settle toward the bottom. For this reason the tin that comes from the top of the vessel is purer than the tin that comes from the bottom. The former is called *refined tin* and the latter *common tin*. The common tin is often liquefied and boiled again.

Properties and Uses. Tin is extremely malleable and may be rolled into very thin sheets called *tinfoil*. It is very resistant to corrosion. Its principal use is in coating sheet iron or steel for use as a roof covering. *Tin plate* used for roofing does not have a coating of pure tin but of an alloy of 25 per cent tin and 75 per cent lead. This is known as *terne plate* and is much less expensive than *bright tin plate*, which is coated with pure tin.

Tin is used in making bronzes and other alloys.

Alloys

The Brasses. The *brasses* are alloys of copper and zinc. The most useful brass alloys range in composition from 60 per cent copper and 40 per cent zinc to 90 per cent copper and 10 per cent zinc. Standard brass contains two parts of copper to one part of zinc and is the most commonly used of all the brasses. Those carrying a large amount of copper are copper red in color, and those with a small amount of copper are a silvery white.

Brass may be shaped by casting, hammering, stamping, rolling into sheets, or drawing into wire or tubes.

Muntz metal contains 60 per cent copper and 40 per cent zinc.

The addition of even small amounts of tin to brass greatly increases its resistance to corrosion.

The Bronzes. The *bronzes* are alloys of copper and tin ranging in composition from 95 per cent copper and 5 per cent tin to 75 per cent copper and 25 per cent tin. The chief effect of tin on copper is to increase its hardness.

Gun metal contains 90 per cent copper and 10 per cent tin. It is the strongest of the bronzes. *Bell metal* contains 80 per cent copper and 20 per cent tin. It is hard and is used for making bells. *Speculum metal* contains two parts copper and one part tin. It is a hard white metal which will take a polish and is used for making mirrors.

Phosphor bronze is a copper-tin alloy to which a small amount of phosphorus has been added as a deoxidizer to eliminate copper oxide. This results in a very marked improvement in the strength and quality of the bronze. It is highly resistant to corrosion.

Manganese bronze is really a brass, for it contains a large amount of zinc and little or no tin. The manganese acts as a deoxidizer and does not appear in the resultant alloy since it has been oxidized and removed in the flux. The addition of manganese greatly improves the strength of the alloy. Manganese bronze is an excellent material for castings and is very resistant to corrosion.

Monel Metal. An important alloy of nickel and copper is *Monel metal,* which is about two-thirds nickel, somewhat less than one-third copper, and has small amounts of iron, manganese, carbon, and silicon. It is resistant to corrosion, takes an attractive finish, and is easily worked. Monel metal is used for counter tops, sinks, and other purposes in buildings.

8. PLASTICS

Definition. Many materials used in building construction are plastic, that is, they will continue to deform under a constant load, for varying conditions of temperature and stress intensity, and with duration of stress. The large and ever-increasing group of materials known as plastics, however, includes certain common characteristics. A plastic may be defined as follows.

A *plastic* is a material that contains as an essential ingredient an organic substance of high molecular weight which, although solid in the finished state, is soft enough at some stage of its manufacture to be formed into various shapes, usually through the application, either singly or together, of heat and pressure.

Essential Ingredients. All *organic substances* contain carbon. The ones that are involved in the manufacture of plastics are complex substances called *resins.* These may be natural resins, but they are usually synthetic resins built up by chemical processes from such materials as coal, petroleum, natural gas, water, salt, and air. The chemical elements whose atoms form the molecules of plastic resins are principally carbon, hydrogen, oxygen, and nitrogen.

Many kinds of resins are used, with other materials, in the manufacture of plastics to produce products with a great variety of physical and chemical properties. The other materials included in plastics are called plasticizers, fillers, and colorants. These are considered in a subsequent paragraph.

Formation of Large Molecules. The large size of the molecules in a plastic resin is an important factor in determining its properties and those of the plastic of which it is the essential ingredient. In forming synthetic resins, long chain-like molecules are built up by linking small molecules together by processes involving various combinations of heat, pressure, or chemical action. In some plastics, the long molecular chains become attached to each other by cross links, when heated, forming net-like structures.

Broad Classification of Plastics. All plastics include tangled masses of long resin molecules. They are divided into two classes according to their behavior when heated and cooled during manufacture.

Thermoplastics are softened by heat during the manufacturing process and regain their original properties as they solidify during cooling to form the finished products. No chemical changes occur and the process can be repeated.

The resin molecules of thermoplastics are chain-like with few if any cross links between molecules. They form a tangled mass, but they can slide over each other when the plastic is stressed. If the stress is not too large, they will slowly recover their original relative positions when the stress is removed, and the deformation caused by the stress will disappear.

Thermosetting plastics change chemically when heated during manufacture, solidify while still hot, and assume the form of the finished products. The process cannot be repeated.

Cross links form between the chain-like molecules of the resin and bind them together into a net-like structure which is retained on cooling. The cross links restrict the relative movement of the molecules when the plastic is stressed so it tends to become rigid. Plasticity decreases as the number of cross links increases.

Other Ingredients. As has been stated, the essential ingredient of all plastics is some type of resin. However, nonresinous ingredients are included in plastics to achieve certain desired properties, facilitate processing, or reduce the cost. These are classified as plasticizers, fillers, and colorants.

Plasticizers are materials which may be included in plastics to make them more plastic or flexible at ordinary temperatures and during the manufacturing process. They are usually organic compounds. Their primary, but not exclusive, use is in thermoplastics. Plasticizers are usually liquids which have high boiling points and act as solvents for the resins.

Fillers are materials included in plastics to provide or improve certain properties and lower their cost. They may be powders or fibrous materials. Powdered quartz or slate may be added for hardness; mica, clay, and asbestos fiber for heat resistance; wood flour for bulk and malleability; and glass and cotton fiber for tensile strength and flexibility. By the addition of appropriate fillers, plastics with widely varying properties can be made from the same kind of resin. A considerable portion of the volume of a plastic may be due to the filler. Fillers are extensively used in thermosetting plastics.

Colorants are responsible for one desirable feature of plastics. This is the great variety of colors in which they are available. These are obtained by the addition of coloring materials which include organic dyes and pigments, and inorganic pigments which are usually metallic oxides.

Solvents. Plastics are used in liquid form as one of the ingredients of some surface-coating materials. Among such materials are various kinds of paint, varnish, enamel, and lacquers. Most of the resins suitable for use in such products are hard and brittle. To convert them to liquids, as required in the manufacture and application of these products, appropriate organic solvents are used. The resin hardens as the solvent evaporates after a coating is applied. Solvents are also used to liquify the granular or powdered compounds as required in some manufacturing processes.

Shaping or Processing Plastics. Plastic products can be manufactured in a great variety of forms or shapes by selecting the appropriate kinds of resin and other materials and using suitable equipment and processing procedures. The compounds to be converted into manufactured products are supplied in granular or powdered forms, both commonly called *molding powder,* or in liquid form. The molding powders are heated to form viscous liquids during processing.

The temperatures required to make plastics sufficiently fluid for processing are relatively low compared with those required for most metals. Plastics cannot withstand high temperatures.

In the *molding processes,* the liquid is forced by pressure into molds, to produce the desired shape. There it solidifies either by cooling, as with thermoplastics, or by the cross linking of the molecules of thermosetting plastics.

In the usual *extrusion process,* a viscous liquid thermoplastic is forced through an orifice or die shaped to yield a product of the desired cross section. After passing through the die, the extruded plastic is deposited on a moving belt or other device. The extruded material may be cooled in various ways. The processes are usually continuous. Simple dies can be shaped to form solid rods and sheets. Special devices are used to form tubes and to coat wires with plastic. Instead of using long shallow dies or orifices for extruding films or sheets, such forms are more commonly produced by splitting large extruded tubes longitudinally and spreading them out to flatten.

In the *calendering process,* molding powder warmed to a dough-like consistency is fed between the first pair of a series of heated horizontal rolls and emerges from the last pair of heated rolls as a flat plastic film or sheet whose thickness is determined by the gap between the rolls. It is then cooled by a chill roll and may be stored for further processing on a takeoff roll. This process is extensively used for producing thermoplastic film or sheeting.

In the *casting process,* liquid plastics are poured into molds where they harden slowly. The plastic may be supplied in liquid form or in granular or powdered form which may be liquified by heat or adding solvents. Both thermoplastics or thermosetting plastics are used. The former will solidify at room or relatively low temperatures, but the latter require heating. No pressure is involved for either.

Laminates are usually formed by impregnating sheets of cloth, paper, asbestos, or woven glass fibers with liquid thermosetting resins; stacking them in layers; and curing by heat and pressure to form solid sheets. If low pressures are used, they are called *low-pressure laminates* or, more commonly, *reinforced laminates.* The latter designation is used especially if the impregnated sheets are woven glass fabric. Reinforced laminates differ from molded plastics in which the fibrous materials are not in layers but are included to increase their flexural strength. If high pressures are used, the products are called *high-pressure laminates.*

Plastic foams may be made by introducing air or some other gas into liquid thermosetting resin and solidifying by heating and curing. The foam may be formed mechanically by whipping air into the liquid resin, by dissolving a gas in the resin under pressure and then lowering the pressure to permit the gas to expand, or by producing gas in the liquid resin by chemical action of materials introduced into the resin. Such foams may be rigid or flexible. They are effective as heat insulation and are very lightweight.

In *sandwich constructions,* two thin, dense, strong, and hard facing layers of plastic, metal, or wood are bonded with adhesives to a core of lightweight material to form a panel. For the panel to function effectively, the core and adhesive must be strong enough to resist the shearing and compressive stresses due to normal loads and impacts. Plastics used for cores are either foamed or honeycombed, the former having superior heat-insulating properties.

Common Properties. The physical and chemical properties of plastics vary over wide ranges depending upon the type of resin, the kinds and proportions of fillers and plasticizers, the presence of reinforcing fabrics, and the temperatures, pressures, types of equipment, and other factors involved in the manufacturing processes. The following comments refer to many plastics used in building construction.

They are formable into a great variety of shapes, and available in a wide range of colors.

Most plastics have strengths comparable with those of wood or concrete, but those of some laminates and reinforced plastics are very high.

Stiffness is relatively low.

They have relatively light weight as compared with most building materials except wood and lightweight concrete.

They have a high coefficient of expansion, a low thermal conductivity, and the range of temperature resistance, from low to high, is relatively limited.

They will burn but not support combustion.

They are noncorrosive for conditions encountered in buildings.

Deformation due to creep tends to disappear when load is removed.

When considering many other properties, distinction should be made between thermoplastics and thermosetting plastics.

Thermosetting plastics are superior to thermoplastics in resistance to heat.

Table 8-1

Properties, Forms, and Uses of Plastics

Chemical Type	Properties	Forms	Uses
		THERMOPLASTICS	
Acrylics	Transparent, hard, weather-resistant, shatter-resistant, easily scratched	Cast sheets	Window and skylight glazing
Polyethylene	Flexible, tough, translucent, low cost, easily scratched	Film and sheet	Vapor barriers, temporary glazing and building enclosing, protection of materials stored outdoors
		Open mesh	Window screen
Polystyrene	Hard, clear, brittle, water- and chemical-resistant, low cost	Tile and sheet	Wall covering and tile
Vinyls	Tough, wear- and stain-resistant	Tile and sheet	Floor and wall tile, and sheet covering
		Coated glass fiber	Window screen
Polyamides (Nylon)	Tough, hard, wear-resistant, expensive	Cast	Rollers and bearings
		THERMOSETTING PLASTICS	
Alkyds	Weather-resistant, tough, good adhesive properties	Liquid and solid	Surface coatings such as paints, enamels, etc., molded products
Melamines	Hard, durable, abrasion-resistant, chemical- and heat-resistant	Sheets	Decorative laminates, high-pressure laminates, counter tops
Polyesters	Weather- and chemical-resistant, stiff, hard	Corrugated and flat translucent laminates, woven glass reinforced	Window glazing and skylights

Thermoplastics are usually tough but may be soft, flexible, and tough, or hard, rigid, and brittle depending upon composition.

Thermosetting plastics are usually rigid.

Thermosetting plastics are elastic for the stresses to which they are usually subjected.

All plastics are subject to creep under load, but this tendency is much greater for thermoplastics than for thermosetting plastics.

Thermoplastics are soluble in some solvents, but thermosetting plastics are mostly insoluble.

Some thermoplastics have excellent light-transmitting qualities.

Names of Plastics. A plastic may be designated by the chemical type of resin used as its essential ingredient or by a trade name given by the manufacturer. For a comprehensive list of trade names, their chemical types, and manufacturers, see reference 3.

Specific Properties, Forms, and Uses. The pertinent properties, forms, and uses of various plastics employed in building construction are summarized in Table 8-1.

Epoxy Resins or Epoxies

Introduction. Epoxy resins, often called epoxies, are thermosetting plastics introduced into building construction in about 1954. That epoxies have remarkable properties is known to architects and engineers. They have not yet made full use of them, largely because they are cautious in the use of materials whose value has not been demonstrated by experience and few workmen are skilled in their use. As time goes on and experience demonstrates the wide field of usefulness of epoxies in building constructions, they seem destined to assume an important role in this field.

The following comments are based on material presented by the American Railway Engineering Association in reference 15 and by the *Engineering News-Record* in reference 16.

Definitions. The term *epoxy* refers to a three-member ring structure containing two hydrogen atoms and one oxygen atom. Materials containing an average of more than one epoxy group per molecule are considered as *epoxy resins* 15.

Epoxy resins alone are chemically stable and may be stored indefinitely, but they are useless. By adding a *curing agent* or *hardener* to the resin in its liquid state, infusible and insoluble solids are formed. The length of time that an epoxy mixture is usable after the curing agent is added is called the *pot life*.

Substances added to epoxy resins during the manufacturing process to alter the properties of the cured resins are called *modifiers*.

Manufacture. The basic resins, together with the modifiers, are cooked under pressure by the manufacturer.

For resins used in construction, the cooking is terminated when the resins are honey-colored liquids having viscosities about the same as those of a 20-to-30-weight motor oil.

The characteristics of the manufactured product depend upon the ingredients, the temperature, the pressure, the cooking time during manufacture, and other factors. Each manufacturer produces a variety of resins suitable for various uses.

Modifiers. The basic resins without modification are useless. The modifiers added during the manufacturing process to provide the desired properties are classified as flexibilizers, fillers, pigments and dyes, and diluents.

Flexibilizers or *plasticizers* are always required to increase the flexibility. Ordinarily they are mixed with the curing agent by the manufacturer. Among the materials used are a synthetic rubber in liquid form and various coal tar products.

Fillers are added to provide certain desired properties or to reduce the cost. They extend the pot life, lower shrinkage while curing, and reduce the coefficient of expansion. Materials used as fillers are coal tar products, which react chemically with epoxy resins, and inert materials such as clay, asbestos or glass fibers, powdered metals, aluminum oxide, silica, mica, powdered glass, fine sand, or marble dust, which merely occupy space. Inert minerals are the most commonly used fillers for epoxies used in construction. Powdered metals and aluminum oxide are used in coatings and paints.

Pigments and Dyes. The color of many epoxy formulations is satisfactory for most uses but may be modified as desired by using appropriate pigments or dyes.

Diluents are added to improve workability, permit the application of thinner coats, reduce viscosity, or increase penetration. There are few applications except in paints and other coatings.

Curing Agent or Hardener. The curing agent or hardener may be reactive and become a part of the molecules in which case it imparts to the molecules some of its own characteristics. It may also act as a catalyst to facilitate the reaction but not become a part of the molecules.

The pot life may be controlled to a few minutes or a few hours depending upon the ingredients and the temperature created by the chemical changes which take place or by heat applied externally, both of which are affected by the size of the batch. On construction work only the former is used, but factory production may utilize the latter for some products. The curing agent completes the chemical changes which were interrupted when the manufacturing process was terminated.

Properties. Epoxies cannot be classed together as materials with specified properties.

"An epoxy can be as brittle as glass or as resilient as rubber. It can be a high molecular weight solid of great density, or a low molecular weight liquid of such low viscosity that it will leak out of containers capable of holding water. And it can be anywhere between these two extremes" (16).

The properties of cured resins may be varied within wide limits with the proper choice of curing agents, modifiers, and diluents.

Some of the more significant properties that can be achieved are the following (15).

(a) The liquid resin is convenient to use in many different types of applications.

(b) The curing time may be controlled by selecting the curing agent from the variety of those available.

(c) The properties of cured resins may be varied within wide limits with the appropriate choice of modifiers and curing agents.

(d) The overall strength properties such as tensile, compressive, and flexural strength are excellent. In general, their strength is greater than that of most of the materials they are used on.

(e) The shrinkage during curing is small.

(f) Hardness, toughness, and resistance to abrasion are outstanding.

(g) The resistance to corrosion, salts, acids, petroleum products, solvents, and other chemicals of many kinds is exceptionally good.

(h) Adhesion to the surfaces of most materials is excellent. Their ability to bond similar or dissimilar materials is exceeded by no other organic compounds.

(i) The color is satisfactory for most purposes. Epoxies can be formulated to be almost any color.

(j) Modification of resins to improve one property usually results in a sacrifice in one or more of the other properties.

Application. Cured epoxy compounds may be applied by brush, spraying equipment, trowel, squeegee, or other means appropriate for the characteristics of the material being applied and the type of operation.

The curing agent is added to the modified resin immediately before application. The operations must be completed during the pot life of the mixture.

Before applying, the materials must be properly mixed. Careful preparation of the surfaces to be joined, repaired, or protected is required. Any dust, loose material, oil, or grease must be removed from any surfaces involved and rust, surface coatings, and mill scale must be removed from steel.

Epoxies should not be applied when the air temperatures are below 60 or above 95 degrees unless special precautions are taken to protect them from the effects of lower or higher temperatures. Workmen experienced with the use of epoxies are required.

As stated in reference (15),

Prolonged or frequent skin contact of materials used in epoxy resin systems may cause dermatitis for some individuals. The reactive diluents used in epoxy resins are found to be sources of skin irritation. . . . Most persons can work with these materials for some time without taking any precautions to avoid skin irritation. A few persons under these conditions may suddenly break out with skin irritations which will disappear when transferred to other types of work.

Among the precautions suggested in the references, the following are included.

1. Care in preventing skin contact.

2. Regular washing of hands, arms and face with warm soapy water. Solvents should not be used.

3. Use of plastic or rubber gloves and protective clothing which have not been contaminated by prior use.

4. Complete protection of the body by clothing including a hat when spraying epoxies. Exposed body surfaces should be coated with protective cream, and a respirator should be used.

Uses. As has been stated, epoxy compounds have many remarkable properties and seem destined to assume an important role in building construction. The current uses mentioned in this paragraph are only suggestive of future possibilities.

In general, they are used as bonding materials to join most similar and dissimilar materials, as bonding agents for aggregates, as watertight crack and joint sealers, and as protective coatings including paints. They are expensive, but where their special characteristics are important they can be extremely economical. An epoxy compound must be specially suitable for the purpose for which it is to be used. Some of the uses which have been made or suggested are given in the following paragraphs.

Terazzo floor surfaces are installed with epoxies as the matrix rather than portland cement. The required thickness is only ½ in. instead of the usual thicknesses of 1 or 2 in., with the resultant saving in dead load.

Concrete overlays can be bonded to eroded or worn concrete surfaces.

Precast concrete piles, which have proved to be too short to achieve the required bearing capacity when driven, can be spliced to obtain the required strength in a few minutes, and driving can then be continued to attain the required bearing capacity.

Corners which have broken off of concrete slabs and pieces which have been broken off of concrete members can be replaced by coating the broken edges with epoxies or by replacing the broken parts with new concrete sealed with epoxies to the remaining parts.

Bonding the components in composite steel and concrete construction.

"Cold-welding" structural steel components instead of welding, bolting, or riveting under certain conditions.

Repair of cracked or checked timber members.

Adhesive for laminated timber and other timber parts, and for bonding precast or cast-in-place concrete slabs to timber or steel girders.

Waterproofing concrete surfaces by brush or spray coatings.

Corrosion-resistant coatings for steel.

The full use of epoxies will provide many entirely new methods of construction.

9. WOOD

Definitions. The terms wood, lumber, and timber are often used synonymously, but in the building industry the terms have distinct meanings. *Wood* is the hard fibrous substance that forms the major part of the stem and branches of trees. *Lumber* is wood that is the product of the saw or planing mill, not manufactured further than sawing, resawing, and passing lengthwise through a standard planing machine, crosscutting to length, and working (8). *Timber* is lumber 5 in. or larger in least dimension (8).

The term *millwork* is applied to the wood building materials manufactured in planing mills and millwork plants and includes such products as doors, window frames, shutters, porch work, interior trim, stairways, mantels, panel work, and moldings, but not flooring, ceiling, and siding.

Classification of Trees. Timber for construction purposes is furnished by two classes of trees: the *needle-leaved conifers* such as the pine, fir, and spruce, and the *broad-leaved trees* such as the maple, oak, and poplar. The woods furnished by the conifers are commonly classed as *softwoods* and those furnished by the broad-leaved trees as *hardwoods*, although poplar is as soft as pine and some of the softwoods are as hard as the harder hardwoods.

Manner of Growth. The conifers and broad-leaved trees grow by adding a layer of wood to all parts of the tree each year. This layer shows in the cross section as a new ring surrounding the old wood and under the bark. The rings thus formed are known as *annual rings*.

Structure. The cross section of a tree consists of the annual rings surrounding the *pith* at the center of the section and surrounded by the *bark*. The pith varies in diameter from $\frac{1}{20}$ in. in some kinds of wood to nearly $\frac{1}{4}$ in. in others.

The annual rings near the outside of the section form the *sapwood* and are lighter in color than those near the center which form the *heartwood*. The sapwood is active and assists in the life processes of the tree by storing up starch and conducting sap. The heartwood is dead, its only function being to contribute to the strength of the tree.

Each annual ring is made up of an inner portion which is relatively soft and light-colored and an outer portion which is harder and darker in color. The inner portion is formed early in the growing season and is known as *spring wood*, whereas the outer portion is formed later and is known as *summer wood*. In some woods there is a distinct line of demarcation between the spring wood and summer wood, but in others the spring wood merges gradually into the summer wood.

Wood is composed primarily of long thin cells or fibers closed at the ends with their length parallel to the length of the tree. In addition to these cells there are other groups of cells running radially and forming the *medullary* or *pith rays*. In the conifers the sap is conducted through the cells by passing through the walls, but in the hardwoods the sap passes through cells with open ends set one above another to form continuous tubes called *pores* or *vessels*. In some of the conifers, such as pine and spruce, there are intercellular passages called *resin ducts* which store and conduct resin. They occur horizontally, in the medullary rays, as well as vertically. The functions of the medullary rays are to store food and to provide for the passage of sap between the bark and the sapwood.

Though similar in many respects, the conifers and broad-leaved trees are very different in the structure of their wood. The structure of the wood of the conifers is simple and regular with a uniform type of cell or fiber. The wood of the broad-leaved trees is quite complex in structure with many different types of cells or fibers and a very irregular arrangement.

Chemical Composition. Dry wood, by weight, is one-half carbon and one-half oxygen and hydrogen with about 1 per cent of nitrogen and 1 per cent of earthy materials. When wood is burned, the constituents that were derived from the air return to the air, and those that were derived from the soil return to the soil in the form of ashes. There is little variation in the chemical composition of the various kinds of wood. However, there are great differences in the structures, and these are largely responsible for the differing physical properties. The chemical elements that have been mentioned form the cellulose and lignin of which wood is composed.

Softwood Lumber Classification. According to the American Lumber Standards for Softwood Lumber (8), softwood lumber is classified according to use, size, and extent of manufacture as follows.

A. USE CLASSIFICATION
   1. *Yard lumber.* Lumber of those grades, sizes, and patterns which is generally intended for ordinary construction and general building purposes.
   2. *Structural lumber.* Lumber that is 2 or more inches in thickness and width for use where working stresses are required.
   3. *Factory and shop lumber.* Lumber that is produced or selected primarily for remanufacturing purposes.
B. SIZE CLASSIFICATION. (nominal, rough green sizes)
   1. *Boards.* Lumber less than 2 inches thick and 1 or more inches wide. Boards less than 6 inches wide may be classified as *strips*.
   2. *Dimension.* Lumber from 2 inches to, but not including, 5 inches thick, and 2 or more inches wide. Dimension may be classified as framing, joists, planks, rafters, studs, small timbers, etc.
   3. *Timbers.* Lumber 5 or more inches in least dimension. Timber may be classified as beams, stringers, posts, caps, sills, girders, purlins, etc.
C. MANUFACTURING CLASSIFICATION. (Extent of manufacture)
   1. *Rough lumber.* Lumber that has not been dressed (surfaced) but has been sawed, edged, and trimmed at least to the extent of showing saw marks in the wood on the four longitudinal surfaces of each piece for its overall length.
   2. *Dressed (surfaced) lumber.* Lumber that has been surfaced by a planing machine (for purposes of attaining smoothness of surface and uniformity of size) on one side (S1S), two sides (S2S), one edge (S1E), two edges (S2E), or a combination of sides and edges (S1S1E, S1S2E, S2S1E, or S4S).
   3. *Worked lumber.* Lumber which in addition to being dressed has been matched, shiplapped, or patterned.
       (a) *Matched lumber.* Lumber that has been worked with a tongue on one edge of each piece and a groove on the opposite edge, to provide a close tongue-and-groove joint by fitting two pieces together; when *end-matched* the tongue and groove are worked on the ends also.

(*b*) *Shiplapped lumber.* Lumber that has been worked or rabbeted on both edges of each piece to provide a close lapped joint by fitting two pieces together.

(*c*) *Patterned lumber.* Lumber that is shaped to a pattern or a molded form, in addition to being dressed, matched, or shiplapped, or any combination of these workings.

Grading. The designation of the quality of a manufactured piece of wood is called the *grade.* Lumber may be stamped by a mark which designates its grade and the mill where it was produced. Such lumber is said to be *grade-marked.* The reasons for grading are given in Circular 64 of the U. S. Department of Agriculture entitled "How Lumber is Graded," by H. S. Betts, as follows:

The boards cut in a sawmill from logs of various kinds vary widely in quality. Some boards are very knotty, others have a few knots, and still others are clear. Some contain checks or splits and others have bark on the edges or are somewhat decayed in places. The clear boards are more valuable for most purposes than those with knots, so it becomes necessary to separate the lumber as it comes from the mill into classes or grades. The lumber in these grades varies in quality from practically clear boards in the highest grade to lumber in the lowest grade containing so many knots, checks, and other defects that it is unfit for anything except perhaps temporary construction or for cutting up to obtain small, clear pieces, the defective parts being discarded.

The use to which lumber is to be put determines the number, size, and position of the defects it may contain and still be satisfactory. In siding, for example, a reasonable number of knots on the edges which are covered when the siding is in place may evidently be allowed. In flooring some knots and other defects on the under side are allowable, since they will not show when the flooring is in use. Sheathing and subflooring may have a considerable number of defects, since both kinds of lumber are entirely covered by finishing material. Covered lumber, such as sheathing, should, of course, be free from decay, even if it does not show, as the decay is quite likely to spread rapidly. Door panels are an example of very high grade lumber that should be clear on both sides.

The location of defects in a piece of lumber determines the length and width of clear pieces that can be cut from it and the waste that will occur when the cuttings are made. Furniture requires comparatively short, wide pieces of clear lumber, while rails for porches and stairs require long, narrow, clear lengths. Lumber from which a large proportion of furniture stock should be cut might yield very little rail stock.

The condition of defects may also influence the grade of a piece of lumber. Tight knots in certain grades of siding or ceiling may be allowed, whereas loose knots likely to drop out would be objectionable.

The American Lumber Standards for softwood lumber serve as a basis for the grading rules that each regional softwood lumber manufacturers' association adopts and applies to its own species of lumber. The various associations' grading rules are those by which softwood lumber is graded. Corresponding grading rules have been adopted by various hardwood manufacturers' associations, but each set of grading rules applies to specific products such as maple flooring, oak flooring, dimension stock, trim, etc.

A grade is representative of the quality of lumber included in the grade and is not to be made up completely of pieces that meet only the minimum requirements for that grade.

Standards for Grading Softwood Lumber. The comments on grading given next are included in the American Lumber Standards for Softwood Lumber (8).

A. GENERAL

1. To the extent to which differences in the characteristics of species, in the quality of logs, in the conditions of manufacture, and in the uses to which the product is put will permit, in practical application, the basic provisions for grading of lumber shall be uniform.

2. The grading of lumber cannot be considered an exact science because it is based on visual inspection of each piece and on the judgment of the grader. Grading rules, however, shall be sufficiently explicit to establish 5 per cent below grade as a reasonable variation between graders.

3. If any grading rules indicate that a grade qualifies under two use classifications, the grade provisions shall satisfy the requirements for both classifications.

B. YARD LUMBER

1. The grading of yard lumber is based on the uses for which the particular grade is designed, and is applied to each kind with reference to its size and length when graded, without consideration to further manufacture.

2. On the basis of quality, the basic grade classifications of American standard yard lumber are as follows.

   (a) *Select.* Lumber of good appearance and finishing qualities. (The commonly used designations, grades A to D, have been substituted for the general designations i and ii in each of the two select grades given in the Standards).

      (1) Suitable for natural finishes.

         Grade A. Practically clear.

         Grade B. Of high quality, generally clear.

      (2) Suitable for paint finishes.

         Grade C. Adapted to high-quality paint finishes.

         Grade D. Intermediate between higher finishing grades and common grades and partaking somewhat of the nature of both.

   (b) *Common.* Lumber suitable for general construction and utility purposes. (The commonly used designations, No. 1 to No. 5, have been substituted for general designations i, ii, etc. used in the Standards).

      (1) For standard construction use.

         No. 1. Suitable for better types of construction purposes.

         No. 2. Well adapted for standard construction.

         No. 3. Designed for low-cost temporary construction.

(2) For less exacting construction purposes.

No. 4. Low quality.

No. 5. Lowest recognized grade but must be usable.

C. STRUCTURAL LUMBER

As stated in the use classification, structural lumber is lumber that is 2 in. or more in thickness and width for use where working stresses are required.

Structural lumber is graded according to the allowable stresses that can be used in computing its safe load-carrying capacity. The *stress-grades* are established in accordance with the National Design Specification for Stress-Grade Lumber and Its Fastenings recommended by the National Lumber Manufacturers Association. This specification is based on the strength and variability of the wood and the effects of various factors such as species of wood, density, moisture content, knots, cross grain, checks, and splits on the strength of a member.

For each stress-grade in each species of wood, the specification includes tabulated information concerning the specific set of rules under which it is graded and the allowable unit working stresses and stiffness factors.

D. FACTORY AND SHOP LUMBER

Factory and shop softwood lumber is graded with reference to its use for doors and sash, on the basis of characteristics affecting its use for general cut-up purposes, or on the basis of the size of cutting. Since the builder is concerned with the manufactured product itself and not with the grading of the lumber from which the product is made, no consideration will be given to the grading of this class of lumber.

Hardwood Lumber Grading. The standard rules for the grading of hardwood lumber are those of the National Hardwood Manufacturers Association. The basis of this grading is the amount of clear usable lumber in a piece. The standard grades are firsts, seconds, selects, No. 1 common, No. 2 common, No. 3A common and No. 3B common. The extremes in quality may be illustrated by the difference between firsts and No. 2 common. The former must have a minimum width of 6 in., and $91\frac{2}{3}$ per cent of the surface measure of a piece must be able to be cut into clear face material. The latter must be cut into clear face material. The number of pieces into which a piece can be cut to give the required percentage of clear material depends upon the grade and upon the size of the piece. For example, a piece with 14 sq. ft. of surface measure can be cut into only 2 pieces with a minimum size of 4 in. by 5 ft., or 3 in. by 7 ft. if the piece is to be classed as firsts; but a piece of No. 2 common of this size can be cut into 7 pieces with a minimum size of 3 in. by 2 ft. There are other requirements which are not mentioned here.

Special grading rules are used for hardwood flooring, interior trim, and dimension stock.

For a summary of hardwood grading see reference 7.

Plain- and Quarter-Sawed Lumber. Boards sawed from the logs with their face tangent to the annual rings are called *plain-sawed, slash-grained,* or *flat-sawed,* whereas those sawed in a perpendicular direction are called *quarter-sawed* or *edge-grain.*

Boards in which the annual rings or grain is neither tangent nor perpendicular to the sides are classed as quarter-sawed if the grain makes an angle greater than 45° with the side of the board. If this angle is less than 45°, the boards are classed as plain-sawed. Quarter-sawed lumber shrinks and warps less than plain-sawed lumber and wears better. The exposed grains of wood that is quarter-sawed are different from those of wood that is plain-sawed. In some cases more attractive effects are secured in quarter-sawed boards, but in others the plain-sawed boards have the advantage. Quarter-sawed lumber is less plentiful than plain-sawed lumber and is more expensive.

Units of Measure. The principal unit of measure for lumber is the *board foot,* which is the quantity of lumber contained in, or derived from, by drying, planing, or working, or by any combination of these means, a piece of rough green lumber 1 in. thick, 12 in. wide, and 1 ft. long, or its equivalent in thicker, wider, narrower, or longer lumber (8). Lumber less than 1 in. thick is considered as 1 in. thick.

This method of measurement is called board measure and is abbreviated b.m. The common unit is 1000 board feet, designated as M. For example, if a lot of lumber contains 25,000 board feet it is designated as 25 M.b.m.

Moldings are measured by the lineal foot, and shingles by the number of pieces of a specified size.

Size Standards. Because of shrinkage and the waste due to sawing and dressing, softwood yard lumber designated as 1 in. thick is required to be $2\frac{5}{32}$ in. thick after surfacing, and 2-in. material is required to be $1\frac{5}{8}$ in. thick. Corresponding allowances varying from $\frac{3}{8}$ in. to $\frac{3}{4}$ in. are made in the widths; the amount in each case depends upon the width of the material, a smaller allowance being made for a piece whose nominal width is 4 in. than for one whose nominal width is 12 in. Rough lumber is larger than surfaced lumber by the amount necessary for surfacing. Lumber usually is designated by its rough, green, or nominal size, not its actual size. The manufacturers in some regions do not follow this practice. An effort is being made to formulate a practice on which all can agree.

Hardwood lumber is cut oversize so that it will be full size when dry. When it is sufaced on one side the thickness is $\frac{1}{8}$ in. less than the rough size, and when surfaced on two sides it is $\frac{3}{16}$ in. less than the rough size.

The standard lengths for softwood lumber vary by 2-ft. increments from 4 ft. up, the most common lengths being 12, 14, and 16 ft. A few odd lengths as 9, 11, 15, and 17 ft. are considered standard for specified sizes. The standard lengths of hardwood lumber vary by increments of 1 ft. from 4 to 16 ft., but not over 15 per cent of the odd lengths is permitted by grading rules.

Seasoning. The *seasoning* of timber is simply the natural drying out from exposure to the air. This drying-out process may be hastened by subjecting the timber to high temperatures in a kiln. This is called *kiln drying.* The principal effects of seasoning and kiln drying on timber are reduction in weight; decrease in the amount of shrinking, checking, and warping after the timber is placed; increase in resistance to decay; and increase in strength.

Defects. In applying grading rules, it is necessary to standardize the definitions for the defects which affect the grade of lumber. Some of the definitions included in the American Lumber Standards for Softwood Lumber (8) are as follows.

bark pocket. Patch of bark partially or wholly enclosed in wood.

check. Lengthwise grain separation usually occurring through the growth rings as a result of seasoning.

cross break. Separation of wood across the width.

cup. See *warp.*

decay. Disintegration of wood substance due to action of wood-destroying fungi. Also known as *dote* or *rot.*

gum pocket. An opening between growth rings which usually contains or has contained resin or bark, or both.

gum seam. Check or shake filled with gum.

gum streak. Well-defined accumulation of gum in a more or less regular streak.

hit-and-miss. Series of surfaced areas with skips not over $\frac{1}{16}$ in. deep between them. See *skip.*

honeycomb (decay). Honeycomb is indicated by large pits in the wood.

knot. Branch or limb embedded in the tree and cut through in the process of lumber manufacture; classified according to size, quality, and occurrence.

machine burn. Darkening or charring due to overheating by machine knives.

pitch. Accumulation of resin in wood cells in a more or less irregular patch.

pitch pocket. An opening between growth rings which usually contains or has contained resin or bark, or both.

pitch seam. Shake or check filled with pitch.

pitch streak. Well-defined accumulation of pitch in a more or less regular streak.

pith. Small soft core in structural center of a log.

pith fleck. Narrow streak resembling pith on the surface of a piece, usually brownish, up to several inches in length, resulting from burrowing of larvae in growing tissue of a tree.

raised grain. Roughened condition of the surface of dressed lumber in which the hard summerwood is raised above the softer springwood but not torn loose from it.

shake. A lengthwise separation between or through the growth rings; may be further classified as a ring shake or pith shake.

skip. Area of a piece that failed to surface.

split. Lengthwise separation of the wood extending from one surface through the piece to the opposite surface or to an adjoining surface.

stain. Discoloration on or in lumber other than its natural color.

torn grain. Part of wood torn out in dressing.

wane. Bark or lack of wood from any cause on the edge or corner of a piece.

warp. Any variation from a true or plane surface; includes bow, crook, cup, or any combination thereof.

Decay. The decay of timber is caused by low forms of plant life called *fungi,* which feed on the cell walls and destroy them. In order to develop, these fungi require warmth, air, and moisture. At low temperatures the fungi are dormant but are not destroyed. They are killed, however, by very high temperatures. Timber that remains under water will last indefinitely because the air that fungi require is excluded. Pieces of timber have lasted for thousands of years under water. If moisture is not present, wood will not decay. Even in *dry rot* moisture is present. It may be caused by sealing the surface of a timber with paint or embedding the timber in masonry in such a way that the moisture present in the timber cannot escape and is therefore available for the development of fungi.

Insect Damage. Various boring insects attack timber and may cause considerable damage. Among these are *bark beetles,* which may damage wood by tunneling under the bark when the bark is left; *ambrosia beetles, roundhead borers,* which get into freshly cut timber; *powderpost beetles,* which attack freshly cut and seasoned hardwood by burrowing holes about $\frac{1}{16}$ in. in diameter through the wood; and *termites* or *white ants,* which are the most destructive of all and will be given further consideration. Most of the insect damage in wood construction is caused by termites, which are light-colored, resemble ants in appearance, and like ants live in colonies and thus are commonly called white ants.

Two types of termites, the subterranean and the drywood, are found in this country. The *subterranean termites* live in the soil but leave the soil in order to attack trees and wood structures. To live, termites of this type must have access to moisture from the ground. Therefore they build shelter tubes from the ground to the spots where they are working. They bore holes along the grain on the interior of the wood members, leaving only the shell. A piece may appear to be in good condition but actually be on the verge of failure. The most effective means of control is to prevent the passage of the termites from the soil to the wood. This may be done by using concrete foundations reinforced so that they will not open where cracks form, or by using cement mortar in brick and stone masonry, taking care to fill all the joints solidly so that termites cannot work their way through the joints. *Termite shields* of sheet copper or other noncorrosive metal should be placed between the top of the foundation walls and the wood plates or sills that are placed on them (Fig. 9-1). These should extend 2 in. over the edges of the wall and be bent down at an angle of 45°. This projection prevents the termites from building their shelter tubes from the foundation walls to the wood plates or sills. Extreme care should be used to remove all scraps of lumber from the building site. Wood treated with preservative by a process that penetrates to the interior will resist termites but, since termites attack timber from the interior, surface coatings and sprays are ineffective. Subterranean termites are prevalent in nearly all parts of this country.

Drywood termites attack wood directly and do not maintain contact with the ground. They are confined to the extreme southern parts of this country and are not such a serious menace as the subterranean

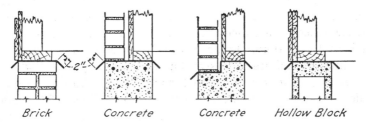

Brick   **Concrete**   **Concrete**   **Hollow Block**

Fig. 9-1.   Termite shields.

termites. All structures in this country constructed wholly or partially of wood, except those of temporary character, should be protected against subterranean termites.

Marine Borers. Wood located in salt water, such as timber piles for marine structures, may be attacked by marine wood borers such as the *teredo* or *shipworm* and the *limnoria* or *wood louse.* Various methods of protecting wood against these borers have been devised, including impregnating with creosote, but since marine structures are not considered in this treatise, no further attention will be given to the subject.

Wood Preservation. Proper seasoning of timber is the simplest way to prevent decay but, when timber is used where moisture is present, seasoning naturally loses its effectiveness. Under these conditions the best method for checking decay is to introduce substances into the timber that will poison the fungi. The substances commonly used for this purpose are zinc chloride and creosote. Zinc chloride is made by dissolving zinc in hydrochloric acid. Creosote is obtained from the distillation of coal tar. Zinc chloride is soluble in water and is suitable for use only where it will not be leached out by the action of water and when the method of application is such as to secure considerable penetration of the zinc chloride into the timber. Creosote does not suffer from these handicaps.

Creosote may be applied with a brush or spray, but this method is not very effective for the coating is thin and it is difficult to fill all the cracks. The advantage of this method is the low cost. Another simple method consists of dipping the timber in a tank of hot creosote. This method is more effective than brushing or spraying, but only a slight penetration of the creosote into the wood is secured.

In the *open-tank process* the timber to be treated is first placed in a tank of hot creosote and then in a tank of cooler creosote. While the timber is in the first tank, the air contained in the timber expands and some air is forced out. When the timber is placed in the second tank the air contracts and draws the creosote into the wood, thus securing a deeper penetration than is obtained by dipping in hot creosote alone.

Various processes are used to secure a deeper penetration of the preservative into the timber by pressure. These processes require extensive equipment and are expensive, but their use is justified where the most effective treatment is required, as in piling. These processes use cylinders as large as 8 ft. in diameter and 150 ft. long. The material to be treated is loaded on cars and run into a cylinder, the ends of which are then closed by tight doors. In one process, the first step is to exhaust some air from the cylinder in order to draw the air and

Table 9-1

Broad Classification of Wood According to Characteristics and Properties

(Prepared Chiefly from Data in Selection of Lumber, U. S. Department of Agriculture, Farmers' Bulletin 1756)

Kinds of Wood	Hardness	Weight, dry	Freedom from shrinkage	Freedom from warping	Ease of working	Paint holding	Nail holding	Decay resistance, heartwood	Proportion of heartwood	Amount of figure	Bending strength	Stiffness	Strength as a post	Toughness	Number of knots	Size of knots	Number of pitch defects	Size of pitch defects	Number of other defects	Size of other defects	Exterior trim	Interior trim, natural finish	Interior trim, paint finish	Framing	Wall sheathing	Sub-floors	Roof boards	Siding	Lath	Shingles	Sash	Doors	Millwork, general	Flooring (only vertical grain for B)	Plywood	Veneer
Beech	A	A	C	C	C		A	C	B	B	A	A	B	A	B	B	None	None	A	A		B	B	b		b							A			
Birch	A	B	C	B	C		A	C	C	B	A	A	B	A	C	B	None	None	B	B		A	A	b	A	b		A	B	A			A			H
Cedar, northern white	C	B	A	A	A	A	C	A	A	C	C	C	C	C	A	B	None	None	B	B	A				A			A	B	A						
southern white	C	B	A	A	A	A	C	A	A	C	C	C	C	C	C	B	None	None	B	C	A				A			A	B	A						
western red	C	C	A	A	A	A		A	A	B	C	C	C	C			None	None	C	C	A				A			A	B	A	H					H
eastern red	A	A	A	A	B			A	B	B	B	C	A	B	A	C	None	None	C	C	A			—												
Cherry	B	B	B	A	C			C	B	B	A	A	B	B	C	B	None	None	B	B		A	A	b	A	b	A	A	B		A	H	W	H		W
Chestnut	B	B	B	B	B		B	C	C	A	C	C	C	B	C	B	None	None	B	A	B		B	b	B	A	B	B	B		A	W		B	B	
Cypress, southern	B	B	B	B	B	A	B	A	C	A	B	A	B	B	C	C	B–B	B–B	B	B	B	A	B	A	B	A	A	C	B		B		W	B	W	
Douglas fir	A	A	B	A	C	C	B	B	B	A	A	A	A	B	B	C	None	None	B	A	B	A	B	A	B	B	A	A	B		W	W	W	A	W	
Fir, white	C	C	B	B	B	B	A	C	C	B	B	B	B	B	B	C	None	None	A	B	B	B	B	b	B	b	A	A	B				W			
Gum, red	B	B	C	C	B		B	B	B	B	A	A	B	A	C	A	None	None	C	C	B	A	A	c	A	B	B	B	A		A	H	W	B		W
Hemlock, eastern	B	B	B	B	B		B	C	C	A	C	C	B	B	B	B	None	None	A	A	B		B	b	B	B	B	C	B		B	W				
western	A	A	C	A	C	A	B	B	C	A	B	A	B	B	B	C	C–C	C–C	C	B	B	B	A	b	A	A	A	A	B		A	W	W	A		
Larch, western	A	A	B	B	C	C	A	B	C	B	A	A	A	C	A	C	A–C	A–C	C	B	B	B	B	A	B	A	A	A	A		A	W	W	A		
Maple, hard	A	A	C	A	C	B	A	C	B	B	A	A	B	B	B	C	None	None	B	B		B	B	b	B	b		A	A	H	A		W	W		W
Oak, red	A	A	C	C	C		A	C	B	B	A	A	B	A	C	A	None	None	A	A	A	A	A	b	A	b	B	B	A		A	H	W	A		W
white	A	A	C	C	C		B	A	A	C	A	A	B	A	C	B	None	None	B	B	B	A	B	b	B	b	A	C	B		B	W	W	B		W
Pine, ponderosa	C	B	A	B	A	C	B	C	B	C	A	A	B	C	B	C	B–B	B–B	B	B	B		B	b	A	B	B	A	B		A	H	W			
southern yellow	C	C	B	A	C	A	A	A	C	C	B	B	A	B	B	C	A–C	A–C	A	A	A		A	A	B	B	A	A	A		A	W	W	B		
northern white	C	A	A	B	A	A	B	B	B	C	C	C	C	B	C	C	C–C	C–C	C	B	A		A	b	A	b		C	B		A	H	W			
western white	C	B	B	A	A	A		A	B	C	C	C	C	C	C	C	C–C	C–C	C	B	A		A	b	A	b		A	B		A	W	W			
sugar	C	C	A	A	A	A		A	B	C	C	C	C	C	A	B	None	None	B	B			B	b	A	b		A	A		A	W	W			
Poplar, yellow	C	B	B	A	A		B	C	B	B	B	A	B	C	C	A	None	None	C	C	A	A	A	b	A	b		B	A		A	H	W	B		W
Redwood	B	B	B	A	B	A	B	A	A	B	B	A	A	B	A	A	None	None	C	B	A	B	B	b	A	B		A	B		A	W		B		
Spruce, eastern	C	B	B	B	B	B	B	C	C	B	B	B	B	B	B	B	None	None	B	B	B		A	B	B	B	B	B	A	H	B			W		
Sitka	C	B	B	B	B	B		C	C	B	B	B	B	A	C	C	C–B	C–B	B	B	B	B	A	B	A	B		B	A		A		W	A		
Walnut	A	A	B	A	B			A	A	A	B	B	B	A	C	B	None	None	C	C	A	A	A	a	A	B		B			A	H		A		W

A. Includes woods that are relatively high in the specific property or characteristic listed or which combine in a high degree the usual requirements for use.
B. Includes woods that are intermediate in the specific property or characteristic listed or which combine in a good degree the usual requirements for use.
C. Includes woods that are relatively low in the specific property or characteristic listed or which combine in a fair degree the usual requirements for use.
a, b, and c have the same meanings as A, B, and C except that the woods are not used extensively because of their adaptability to more exacting uses or because they are difficult to work.
W. Data obtained from "Wood Handbook" (7).
H. Data obtained from "Wood Construction" by Dudley F. Holtman.

Note: For the Cedar rows, "Lining cedar closets (H)" is noted spanning the interior trim columns.

moisture from the timber. Creosote is then introduced into the tank and forced into the cells of the wood by pressure. The treatment is completed by drawing off the creosote and removing the timber after the excess creosote has been permitted to drip off. This process leaves the cells, to the depth to which the creosote has penetrated, full of creosote. It is known as the *full-cell process.*

In another process the creosote is first forced into the timber by pressure and then the creosote, which is in the cells, is removed by creating a vacuum. Only the creosote in the cell walls remains. This is known as the *empty-cell process* and is therefore less expensive than the full-cell process.

When zinc chloride is used as a preservative the full-cell process is adopted.

Kinds of Wood, Their Properties, and Uses. The more common woods used in building construction, their properties and other characteristics, and their principal uses are summarized in Table 9-1.

10. CEMENTING MATERIALS AND MORTARS

Gypsum Plasters

Raw Material. The basic material in all gypsum plaster is the mineral gypsum which occurs in three forms; *gypsum rock, gypsum earth* or *gypsite,* and *gypsum sand. Alabaster* is a pure form of gypsum.

When pure, gypsum is composed of one molecule of sulfate of lime and two molecules of water as indicated by the chemical formula $CaSO_4 + 2H_2O$. Gypsum is rarely found in a pure state but contains clay, limestone, iron oxide, and other impurities. Pure gypsum is a soft, white mineral.

Classification. Gypsum plasters are divided into four classes:

1. Plaster of paris.
2. Cement, hard-wall, or patent plaster.
3. Hard-finish plaster.
4. Special plasters.

Changes in Manufacture and Setting. When gypsum is heated to temperatures between 212°F. and 400°F. it loses three-fourths the combined water as indicated by the equation

$$(CaSO_4 + 2H_2O) + Heat = (CaSO_4 + \tfrac{1}{2}H_2O) + 1\tfrac{1}{2}H_2O$$

The one and one-half molecules of water are driven off as steam. The remaining product is *calcineol gypsum*, or *plaster of paris* if pure gypsum is used in the process, and *cement plaster* or *hard-wall plaster* if certain impurities are present or are added, these impurities causing the product to set more slowly than the rapid-setting plaster of paris. For a discussion of the various kinds of cement plaster see Art. 81.

If gypsum is heated above 400°F. practically all the combined water is driven off as indicated by the formula

$$(CaSO_4 + 2H_2O) + Heat = (CaSO_4) + 2H_2O$$

forming *dead-burned, hard-burned,* or *anhydrous* plaster. If certain substances such as alum or borax have been added, *hard-finish plaster* is produced. *Keene's cement* is one variety of hard-finish plaster.

The setting of gypsum plasters is due to the recombination of the dehydrated lime sulfate $CaSO_4$, or the partially dehydrated lime sulfate $(CaSO_4 + \frac{1}{2}H_2O)$, with water to form the original hydrated sulfate $(CaSO_4 + 2H_2O)$. The necessary water is added when the plasters are used.

Methods of Manufacture. Plaster of paris and cement plaster are made by calcining or burning gypsum in large kettles or in rotary kilns. If kettles are used the gypsum is finely ground before burning, but in the rotary kilns the gypsum is crushed to a size of about 1 in., the final pulverizing being accomplished after burning.

The most common form of hard-finish plaster is Keene's cement. This material is formed by calcining lump gypsum, immersing it in a 10 per cent alum solution, recalcining, and finally pulverizing it to produce the finished product.

The time of set of cements or hard-wall plasters is regulated to suit the convenience of the workmen who are to use them. Ordinarily the setting must be delayed, and therefore a *retarder* consisting of such materials as glue, sawdust, or blood is added. The working qualities and sand-carrying capacity of cement or hard-wall plaster are improved by adding clay or hydrated lime by the manufacturers, and their cohesiveness is increased by the addition of cattle hair or wood fiber. For use in localities where good sand is not available, plaster mixed with the proper amount of sand for use in plastering may be obtained from some manufacturers.

Uses. Plaster of paris is used for ornamental castings, but because of the rapidity with which it sets it is not suitable for use in a wall plaster or for mortar.

Cement or hard-wall plaster is extensively used as a wall plaster for buildings, but it will not withstand weathering action and is therefore not suitable for exterior use. Blocks for use in fireproofing steel members and in constructing partitions, floors, and roofs of buildings are also made with cement plaster. It is also used in the manufacture of gypsum board, which consists of a core of plaster with a covering of cardboard, pressed into sheets ¼ in. to ⅝ in. thick. Floor and roof slabs of skeleton steel construction are sometimes constructed of cement plaster and an aggregate reinforced with steel in a manner similar to reinforced concrete. Hard-finish plasters are employed as wall plasters when a waterproof and unusually hard surface is desired. *Keene's cement* is the best known of these plasters. *Parian cement* is another form.

For a discussion of the use of gypsum plasters see Art. 82.

Special Plasters. Included in such plasters are those with vermiculite or pearlite aggregates. These aggregates weigh only about 10 lb. per cu. ft. and have excellent fire-resistive and heat insulation properties. *Vermiculite* consists of tiny flakes of mica that have been greatly expanded by heating to a very high temperature.

Pearlite is derived from siliceous volcanic rock that has exploded at a high temperature, causing a cellular structure produced by the expansion of occluded gases as the pressure was released during the explosion.

Quicklime

Definition. *Quicklime* is the product of the burning of limestone at a temperature sufficiently high to drive off the carbon dioxide.

Raw Materials. Pure quicklime is calcium oxide (CaO) and is obtained from pure limestone $(CaCO_3)$, but commercial quicklime contains varying amounts of magnesium oxide (MgO) resulting from the presence of magnesium carbonate $(MgCO_3)$ in the raw material. The chemical formula for the raw material used in lime manufacture is

$$xCaCO_3 + yMgCO_3$$

x and y being variables. Impurities such as silica, alumina, and iron are always present.

Classification and Grades. Quicklime is divided into four classes depending on the relative amounts of calcium oxide and magnesium oxide present: *high-calcium,* containing 90 per cent or more of calcium oxide; *calcium,* containing 75 to 90 per cent of calcium oxide; *mag-*

nesian, containing between 25 and 40 per cent of magnesium oxide; *high-magnesian* or *dolomitic,* containing a high percentage of magnesium oxide. Common practice recognizes the division of quicklime into only two classes, *calcium limes* and *magnesian limes.*

Quicklime is divided into two grades: *selected,* which is a well burned lime free from ashes, core, clinker, and other foreign material; and *run-of-kiln,* which is well-burned lime without selection.

Hydrated lime is furnished in two classes according to plasticity. *Masons' hydrated lime* has lower plasticity than finishing hydrated lime and is used for mortar and for the scratch and brown coats of plaster. *Finishing hydrated lime* has high plasticity and is used for the finish coat of plaster in addition to the uses made of masons' hydrated lime.

Manufacture. Quicklime is made by burning limestone in kilns at a temperature sufficient to drive off the carbon dioxide. If pure limestone is used the process may be shown by the following formula:

$$CaCO_3 + Heat = CaO + CO_2$$

Calcium oxide (CaO) is a white solid, and carbon dioxide (CO_2) is a gas. If magnesium carbonate is present a corresponding reaction occurs, leaving magnesium oxide and driving off carbon dioxide gas.

The fuel used in the process is coal or coke.

Slaking. In preparing lime mortar, quicklime is mixed with water forming calcium hydroxide, $Ca(OH)_2$. This is a fine white powder, but an excess of water is always used, forming a paste called lime paste or *lime putty.* The chemical change that occurs in slaking pure quicklime is shown by the formula

$$CaO + H_2O = Ca(OH)_2$$

A corresponding reaction occurs when magnesium oxide is present. The form of lime known as *hydrated lime* is simply the hydroxide formed by adding water to quicklime at the place of manufacture instead of on the job. While this change is occurring a considerable amount of heat is generated, and a marked increase in volume occurs.

The calcium limes slake more rapidly than the magnesium limes and give off a greater amount of heat. For quick-slaking limes, the lime should be added to the water, and when escaping steam appears the lime should be hoed and enough water added to stop the steaming. For medium-slaking and slow-slaking limes, add the water to the lime. Care must be taken to avoid cooling slow-slaking lime, and in cold weather it may be necessary to heat the water. There is little danger that too much water will be added to the quick-slaking calcium limes, but an excess of water may cause magnesium lime to be "drowned." If too little water is added to either calcium or magnesium limes they may be "burned." In either burning or drowning a part of the lime is spoiled, for it will not harden and the paste is not as viscous and plastic as it should be.

Slaked lime should be allowed to age for 2 weeks before it is used for plastering, but 24 hours may be sufficient if the lime is to be used for masons' mortar.

In making putty or paste from hydrated lime, the lime is sifted slowly into the water, the mixture being stirred constantly. The putty is allowed to age or soak at least 24 hours. The aging process increases the workability and sand-carrying capacity of the putty. Since hydrated lime has been slaked before shipping, the increase in volume while the putty is being made is small. A sack of hydrated lime weighing 50 lb. and containing 1 cu. ft. will make about 1.1 cu. ft. of lime putty.

Setting. In setting, the excess water is evaporated and the calcium hydroxide combines with carbon dioxide from the air to form calcium carbonate, as shown by the formula

$$Ca(OH)_2 + CO_2 = CaCO_3 + H_2O$$

A corresponding reaction occurs when magnesium hydroxide is present. The absorption of carbon dioxide occurs very slowly, and in heavy masonry walls the setting may never occur.

The term *air-slaked* is often applied to quicklime that has become slaked by absorbing moisture from the atmosphere; but the process does not stop when this change has occurred, for the hydroxide thus formed absorbs carbon dioxide to form calcium carbonate, which has lost its cementing properties.

Forms of Lime. The following definitions for various forms of manufactured lime have been adopted by the American Society for Testing Materials.

quicklime. A calcined material, the major part of which is calcium oxide or calcium oxide in natural association with a lesser amount of magnesium oxide, capable of slacking in water.

hydrated lime. A dry powder obtained by treating quicklime with water enough to satisfy its chemical affinity for water under the conditions of its hydration. It consists essentially of calcium hydroxide or a mixture of calcium hydroxide and magnesium oxide and magnesium hydroxide.

lump lime. Quicklime as it comes from the kilns.

pulverized lime. Quicklime that will pass a fine sieve of specified size, usually ¼ in.

Hydrated lime is furnished in 50-lb. paper bags and pulverized lime in 50-lb. paper and plastic bags, cartons, and 200-lb. steel drums. Lime is not available in lump form.

Portland Cement

Raw Materials. The materials necessary in the manufacture of port-land cement are lime, silica, and alumina. These materials are obtained by mixing an impure limestone, containing considerable clay, with pure limestone; by mixing limestone and clay or shale; or by mixing limestone and blast-furnace slag. They must be mixed in the proper proportions as determined by chemical analysis.

Manufacture. The steps in the manufacture are as follows:

1. Crushing the raw materials.
2. Drying the raw materials.
3. Grinding the raw materials.
4. Proportioning the raw materials.
5. Pulverizing the raw materials.
6. Burning to form clinkers.
7. Cooling the clinkers.
8. Adding the retarder to control the time of set.
9. Pulverizing the clinker to produce cement.
10. Seasoning of the cement.

The chemical changes that occur in the manufacture of portland cement are too complex to be considered here.

Several types of portland cement are used to accomplish special results. The two most commonly used are *high-early-strength cement* and *low-heat cement.* They are manufactured by the same process and from the same materials as standard portland cement, but they differ in the proportions of the ingredients used and vary in fineness of grinding. As the name implies, high early-strength cement attains strength more quickly in the early stages. Low-heat cement generates less heat in setting and acquires strength slowly. Both these special cements produce concrete which ultimately acquires about the same strength as that made with standard cement. *Air-entraining portland cements* contain very small quantities of certain air-entraining materials, which are incorporated by intergrinding them with the clinker during manufacture. They produce concrete which is more frost-resistant than other concretes. Concrete made with these cements contains minute, well-distributed, and completely separated bubbles, there being many millions of them in a cubic foot of concrete (9).

Setting and Hardening. When water is added to portland cement a paste is formed. This paste soon loses its plasticity and begins to harden owing to complicated chemical changes which are started when the water is added. The process of setting is divided into two stages by specifications, *initial set* and *final set*. The progress of the setting is measured by the penetration of weighted needles constructed according to standard specifications. Initial set should not take place in less than 45 minutes and final set should not require more than 10 hours. The hardening of portland cement continues for many months.

Uses. Portland cement is used as a cementing material in mortar and concrete.

Masonry Cement

There are two types of masonry cements included in the ASTM standards. They are as follows.

Type I. For use in masonry construction where high strength is not required.
Type II. For general use where mortars for masonry are required.
Where no type is specified, the requirements for Type II shall govern.

Comments on the composition and the use of masonry cements in mortars for clay masonry are included in Art. 26.

11. CONCRETE

Concrete is made by mixing portland cement and water with inert materials, such as sand, gravel, and crushed stone, which are called *aggregates*. The cement and water form a paste which, by chemical action, sets and hardens, binding the inert materials together to form a rocklike mass. In order to secure a durable concrete possessing the desired strength and other necessary characteristics, at a minimum cost, care must be exercised in selecting the materials, in determining the proportions of the various ingredients including water, in choosing the type of mixing equipment and controlling the mixing time, in transporting the concrete to the forms and placing it in the forms, and in curing the concrete for a period of several days after placing.

Materials. The portland cement used in concrete should conform to the specifications of the American Society for Testing Materials, although it must be recognized that all such cements are not alike in their behavior and properties. Special portland cements are often used to satisfy special conditions. If it is desirable to secure high strength quickly, as is often the case, *high early-strength cement* may be used; and if the amount of heat generated by the chemical reactions which take place in setting is objectionable, *low-heat cement* may be advantageous, particularly in massive structures from which heat escapes slowly. *White portland cement* is sometimes used to carry out desired architectural effects.

The water should be free from any injurious amounts of oils, acid, alkali, organic matter, or other deleterious substances, but water suitable for drinking purposes is usually satisfactory for making concrete. The surface water which is nearly always present in aggregates, even though they appear to be dry, must be allowed for in determining the amount of mixing water to be used. Also, if dry aggregate is used, corrections must be made for the amount of water that the aggregate will absorb. In any event, the quantity of water that is important is the net amount that actually enters the cement paste.

The inert material, called *aggregate,* is usually divided into two classes according to size. A common practice is to consider all aggregate that will pass a sieve with $1/4$-in. openings as *fine aggregate* and all that will be retained on a sieve of this size as *coarse aggregate,* but other size limits are in use. Aggregates graded in size so that the finer particles progressively fill up the voids in coarser particles have a smaller percentage of voids than aggregates consisting of particles that are uniform in size. For this reason, the graded aggregates are more economical because a smaller amount of cement paste is required to fill the voids. Specifications ordinarily contain clauses that insure the size grading of each aggregate.

Fine aggregate is usually sand, and coarse aggregate gravel or crushed stone, but when sand is not available fine aggregate can be made by crushing rock in rolls. Crushed, air-cooled, blast-furnace slag is sometimes used for fine or coarse aggregate. Various special aggregates are used to produce concrete with special characteristics. Among those used to produce *lightweight concrete* are cinders and coke breeze which, because of their sulfur content, tend to corrode steel reinforcing and embedded steel pipes; burned clays and shales, which expand and become vitrified during the burning process; vermiculite ore, which is micaceous aluminum, magnesium silicate, greatly expanded by sudden heating that causes the water between its minutely thin layers to vaporize to steam and form greatly expanded lightweight cellular granules; pearlite, which is a volcanic siliceous rock that has been crushed and heated to a high temperature, causing its combined water to vaporize and form innumerable tiny bubbles inside lightweight glassy particles; and natural lightweight stones such as lava, pumice, and tufa. Aggregates that will produce *nailable concrete* into which nails can be driven and maintain their grip include asbestos fiber, sawdust, and cinders.

Concrete is sometimes made by using natural mixtures of sand and gravel just as they come from a gravel pit, with no attention paid to grading and without washing. This is called *pit-run gravel*. It is not a satisfactory aggregate because of the uncertainty about the quality of the resultant concrete. Better and cheaper concrete can normally be secured by giving attention to the grading because of the saving in cement that can usually be accomplished.

Aggregates should consist of clean, strong, hard, and durable particles, which are not coated with dust, clay, silt, or other substances, and which will not change in volume in the concrete under the action of water or react chemically with the cement. Shale and some cherts are particularly objectionable because of their volume change or *unsoundness*. Flat, elongated, and angular particles, if present in large quantities, reduce the workability of concrete. Aggregates are screened to secure the desired gradings and washed to remove objectionable impurities that are in the finely divided state.

The maximum usable size of aggregate depends upon the character of the work. The size should not exceed one-fifth the width or thickness of the member in which it is being placed or three-fourths the clear space between reinforcing bars. A maximum size of 3 in., for use in any case, is often specified. Aggregates that are questionable should be tested because it may be impossible to make from them concrete of the desired quality, regardless of the proportions used. The tests that may be made include a sieve analysis and analyses for organic impurities, mortar strength, compressive strength of concrete cylinders, soundness, and resistance to freezing and thawing. The compressive strength of concrete is a good index of the quality of the aggregates used and of the durability, water tightness, and other desirable qualities of the concrete itself.

Proportioning. The proportioning of materials used to form concrete has been the subject of much study and research, and many methods for proportioning have been devised. A method that has been in vogue for many years and will doubtless continue in use for a long period because of its simplicity and in spite of its shortcomings calls for *arbitrary proportions* that do not take into consideration the characteristics of the materials. Moreover, it pays little attention to the amount of water used. For example, a 1:2:4 concrete consists of 1 part cement to 2 parts fine aggregate and 4 parts coarse aggregate, all measurements being by volume. This is not a satisfactory method to use on important work.

At the present time, emphasis is being placed on the *water-cement-ratio method* of proportioning. The strength of the cement paste that binds the aggregate particles together to form concrete is determined by the proportion of water used in making the paste. In order to obtain a workable plastic paste, much more water must be used than is actually necessary to satisfy the chemical changes that take place as the paste sets and hardens. However, increasing the proportion of water beyond that required to produce the plastic mixture dilutes the paste and reduces its strength and durability. The result is a reduction in the strength of the concrete made from that paste because the strength of the aggregates is usually greater than that of the paste and is therefore not a determining factor.

The ratio of the quantity of water to the quantity of cement is called the *water-cement ratio*. It is expressed in terms of United States gallons of water per sack of cement. Increasing the proportion of cement paste beyond that required to produce a workable mix does not increase the strength or durability of concrete. The proportion of cement paste required to produce a workable mix depends upon the grading of the aggregates. There is less total surface to be covered by the cement paste if the particles are coarse than if they are fine. It is therefore desirable to use the lowest proportion of fine aggregate that will fill the voids in the coarse aggregate. An excess of coarse aggregate causes the mixture to be harsh and difficult to place. To correct this situation, there is a tendency to increase the amount of water, thus reducing the strength and durability. The proper procedure is to increase the workability by better grading of the aggregates, but if this is not possible the proportion of cement paste must be increased. Rounded aggregates produce a concrete that is more workable for a given water-cement ratio than those that are angular in shape. In other words, for the same workability, concrete composed of rounded aggregates has a lower water-cement ratio and therefore a higher strength than concrete made from angular aggregates.

As has been stated, the strength and durability of concrete are determined primarily by the water-cement ratio, so that the proportioning of concrete, according to this method, consists essentially of selecting the water-cement ratio that will produce concrete of the desired strength and durability required by the conditions of exposure to which the concrete is to be subjected. The next step is to determine the amount and proportions of aggregate that can be added to a given amount of cement paste to produce a workable mix. The *consistency,* or state of fluidity, that gives concrete the required workability in any case depends upon the job conditions. Concrete that is to be placed in a large mass without reinforcing bars can be stiffer than concrete that is to be placed in small, reinforced members. Also, vibrating the concrete in the forms, by means of special equipment designed for that purpose, permits the use of stiffer mixtures.

The water-cement ratio that produces concrete of the required strength can be determined by tests made with the materials to be used. If such tests are not made, the table of water-cement ratios will serve as a guide.

Permissible Water-Cement Ratios

Minimum compressive strength, lb. per sq. in. at age of 28 days	2000	2500	3000	3500	4000
Gallons of water per sack of cement	8	$7\frac{1}{4}$	$6\frac{1}{2}$	$5\frac{3}{4}$	5

The consistency required in any case is commonly specified by means of the *slump test,* which is a convenient measure of the degrees of plasticity or workability. In making this test a sample of concrete is taken from the mixer and placed in an open-ended, sheet-metal mold shaped like the frustrum of a cone. It is 12 in. high with a top diameter of 4 in. and a bottom diameter of 8 in. and rests on a flat surface. The concrete is placed through the open top in three layers, rodded in a specified manner, and the top surface is struck off even with the top of the mold. The mold is immediately removed by lifting vertically. The distance which the top surface of the concrete drops is called the *slump.* A stiff mixture obviously will have a small slump and a fluid mixture a large slump.

Bulking. The volume of a given quantity of sand may be much greater when damp than when dry. This increase in volume due to increase in moisture content is called *bulking.* When the weight of the moisture reaches about 6 per cent the weight of the sand, the bulking may be as high as 20 to 30 per cent. Further additions tend to decrease the amount of bulking until the sand is completely inundated when there is practically no bulking. The bulking of fine material is more for a given percentage of moisture than that of coarse material. Coarse aggregate bulks very little. Methods of measuring sand should be such that bulking can be avoided.

Mixing. Concrete is usually mixed by power-driven machines which turn out the concrete in *batches*. These have capacities of from 2 cu. ft. to 8 cu. yd. or more. The strength and uniformity of concrete increase with the mixing time, but the improvement after the first minute or two, measured from the time when all the materials are in the mixer, is not usually considered enough to justify longer mixing times. The speed of rotation of the mixing drum, within reasonable limits, has little effect on the quality of the concrete. The minimum mixing time permitted is 1½ minutes. The rotation speed for the drum should be that for which the mixer is designed.

In many cities, concrete can be purchased from *central mixing plants* which deliver mixed concrete to the job in dump trucks. Where there is likely to be considerable delay in the placing of concrete from central mixing plants, the concrete may be placed in an *agitator* where it can be kept in a workable condition for an hour or more. No water should be added in the agitator. The ingredients for concrete, except the water, may be mixed in a *central batching plant* and dumped into *transit mixers* mounted on trucks where the water is added and the mixing completed while the concrete is on its way to the job.

Transporting. Concrete is transported from the mixer to its place in the forms by wheelbarrows, two-wheeled buggies, power buggies, bottom-dump buckets, dump cars, dump trucks, and chutes, or it may be pumped through hoses and steel pipes. Concrete placed by pumping is called "Pumpcrete." The mode of transport is selected after considering the quantity to be placed, the layout of the job, the equipment available, and other factors. The method employed and the procedure must prevent the separation of the materials, called *segregation,* and insure that concrete of good quality is deposited in the forms. The use of long chutes has fallen off during recent years because segregation of the materials is likely to occur in the chutes, but short chutes do not have this failing.

Wheelbarrows and buggies may be transported vertically by elevators and concrete often is deposited from bottom-dump buckets placed in position by cranes.

Placing. Before concrete is placed, the forms should be carefully cleaned out and, except in freezing weather, the forms should be thoroughly sprinkled unless oiled forms are used. The concrete should be so placed that no segregation occurs. Dropping concrete is objectionable because of segregation and because air is trapped in the concrete. The concrete next to the forms should be spaded and tamped to prevent honeycombing and to improve the appearance of the exposed surface, but these operations should not be carried too far or segregation will result.

Concrete is said to be *honeycombed* when it contains areas where the coarse aggregate is not surrounded with fine aggregate and mortar. When excess water is used, fine inert particles from the cement and aggregate, called *laitance,* accumulate in the water on the top surface of concrete. As this water evaporates, this fine inert material is deposited and, if it is not removed, forms a plane of weakness. Because of the excess water, or *water gain,* the concrete below the thin layer of laitance is usually porous and lacks durability. The formation of laitance should be prevented by avoiding excess water rather than trying to remove the laitance after it has formed.

The quality of concrete can be improved by means of *vibration,* which assists in its consolidation. Some types of *vibrators* are attached to the forms, others are placed on the surface of the freshly deposited concrete such as slabs and pavements, and still others are inserted in the concrete. They may be driven by electricity or compressed air. If vibrators are used, the concrete can be stiffer with a smaller slump and therefore can have a lower water-cement ratio and still be placed satisfactorily. Thus stronger and more durable concrete is formed from the same materials. If strength is the controlling factor, leaner mixes can be used when the concrete is vibrated and the same strength secured. Vibration also facilitates the flow of concrete around closely spaced reinforcement and into places that would be difficult to reach by ordinary methods.

Partially hardened concrete should never be used even though its plasticity is restored by *retempering,* which means adding water and remixing.

The placing of concrete under water should be avoided if possible. However, if concrete must be placed in this manner, a procedure must be adopted that will not require the concrete to fall through the water, because this would wash out the cement. Two devices for depositing concrete under water are in use, that is, the bottom-dump or drop-bottom bucket and the tremie. The *drop-bottom bucket* is so arranged that the bottom opens when it touches the surface on which the concrete is to be deposited or previously has been deposited. The *tremie* is a steel pipe long enough to reach through the water to the points where the concrete is to be deposited. In starting operations, the bottom is plugged to exclude water and to retain the concrete with which it is filled. It is then lowered into position with the lower end at the point where the first concrete is to be deposited. The plug is then forced out and concrete flows out the bottom of the pipe to its place in the forms, without passing through the water. Concrete is supplied at the top of the pipe at a rate sufficient to keep the pipe always filled. The rate of flow of concrete in the pipe is controlled by changing the length of embedment of the lower end of the pipe in the deposited concrete. The upper end of the pipe may be funnel-shaped, or a hopper may be provided to facilitate placing concrete in the tremie. Care must be exercised to keep the tremie from losing its charge and filling with water because this will usually necessitate starting again with the plugged tremie. If a richer concrete is used, however, some engineers permit the operation to continue while the water is being forced from the tremie by the concrete, the additional cement being used to take the place of that washed out of the concrete by the water in the tremie. After the concrete is placed, it is not spaded or puddled as is concrete in air.

Curing. The chemical reactions that take place as cement hardens continue for a very long period if conditions remain favorable. This results in a gradual increase in the strength of the concrete and an improvement in other properties. In order for these reactions to continue, moisture must be present and the temperature must be favorable. An excess of water is always present when the concrete is placed. If the evaporation of this water is prevented or reduced, the water necessary to continue the chemical operations will probably be present. Evaporation is reduced by covering the surface with wet burlap, by sprinkling, by coating the surface with a waterproof paint or spraying with various liquids, by covering slabs with sand or earth which is kept moist, and in other ways. This protection against evaporation should be continued for 7 days or longer.

Concrete must be protected from freezing at least during the first 7 days after it is placed. The heat generated by the chemical reactions of the concrete is an important factor in maintaining desirable temperatures. The mixing water may be heated and, if more heat is required, the aggregates may also be heated, especially to remove the frost and ice. Specifications often require that concrete be maintained above 50°F. for the first 7 days after placing, but the materials should not be heated enough to raise the placing temperature of the concrete above 70°F. After concrete has been placed it can be protected by enclosing it in some manner and maintaining heat in the enclosed space. Covering a temporary frame work with canvas *tarpaulins* is a common method. The heat may be supplied by steam which is allowed to escape into the enclosed space to provide moisture for curing. *Salamanders,* which are commonly oil-burning stoves, are also used to provide heat. The freezing point of concrete can be lowered by the use of salt or other chemicals, but this practice is objectionable.

Concrete should never be placed on frozen ground because settlement may occur when the ground thaws. All ice and frost should be removed from forms before concrete is placed in them.

Pneumatically Applied Concrete. Concrete or cement mortar can often be advantageously placed by a pneumatic procedure to coat concrete or masonry surfaces, to fill small spaces without using forms, or to patch or repair defects in concrete surfaces. In this procedure, a dry mixture of cement and sand is forced through a hose by compressed air. At a nozzle on the end of the hose, which is held in the hand, water is supplied to the mixture in a water chamber. Directing the nozzle deposits the mortar in the desired place. Because the apparatus resembles a gun, the product is often called *gunite* and, because it is "shot" into place, it is also called *shotcrete.*

If properly proportioned mixtures are skillfully applied, the finished product will be strong, dense, and highly impermeable to water penetration.

Dry Packed Mortar. It often is necessary to place cement mortar, which will be strong and have minimum shrinkage, in small relatively inaccessible spaces. Examples of such spaces are the construction clearances provided between the bottoms of column bases and the tops of footings; open spaces provided at construction joints so that overlapping bars which project from the ends of adjacent members can be welded to establish continuity; and other small spaces provided for any purpose. Bolt holes in concrete and surface defects due to improper placing must also be filled or patched.

The mortar used to fill such spaces usually consists of a relatively rich mixture of sand and cement with a minimum moisture content and a putty-like consistency which will not develop surface moisture when pressed or shrink when setting. It is commonly placed by hand tamping with suitable devices and protected against premature drying. It is often referred to as *dry pack,* although some moisture is present.

12. ROCK AND STONE

General Discussion. The term *rock* is used by the geologist to include both the solid and unconsolidated material forming the earth's crust, the former being designated as *bed rock* and the latter as *mantle rock*. In its engineering usage, the term *rock* includes only the solid or bed rock, the unconsolidated material being called *soil* or *earth*. In agriculture, the term *soil* applies only to the few inches of surface or *top soil* that supports vegetation, the underlying material being known as *subsoil*.

The terms *rock* and *stone* are often used synonymously, but there is actually some distinction between them. Both of these terms apply to the same material but, in general, if geologic formations are being considered the term *rock* is used, whereas smaller or quarried pieces of rock are called *stone*. However, these distinctions between rock and stone are not always made.

Rock formations are of interest to the structural engineer and architect because they are used to support the foundations of many structures, and stone is of interest because of its use in stone masonry, as concrete aggregate, in the manufacture of many materials, and in numerous other ways.

Rocks are divided into three classes according to the method of formation. These classes are igneous, sedimentary, and metamorphic. Rocks are also divided into classes according to their chemical composition. The most important of these classes are argillaceous, siliceous, and calcareous. *Argillaceous rocks* are composed primarily of alumina (Al_2O_3), the chief component of clay. *Siliceous rocks* are composed primarily of silicon dioxide (SiO_2), the principal ingredient of quartz sand. *Calcareous rocks* are composed primarily of calcium carbonate or lime ($CaCO_3$).

The earth's crust is made up almost entirely of eight chemical elements. These are estimated to be present in the amounts shown in Table 12-1.

From this table, it can be seen that oxygen comprises nearly one-half the earth's crust and silicon over one-quarter. These elements exist in combination with many other elements to form the minerals mentioned in the next paragraph.

Nearly all rocks are made up of one or more *minerals,* which are definite chemical compounds usually with crystalline structures, but some consist of natural glass or volcanic dust. The most common

Table 12-1

Chemical Elements in Earth's Crust (14)

Oxygen	49.20%	Calcium	3.39%
Silicon	25.67	Sodium	2.63
Aluminum	7.50	Potassium	2.40
Iron	4.71	Magnesium	1.93
	Total	97.43%	

rock-making minerals are *quartz,* or silicon dioxide; the *feldspars,* or potassium, sodium, or calcium aluminum silicates; the *micas,* which are complex hydrous silicates of aluminum with other elements such as potassium, magnesium, and iron; *hornblende,* which is primarily calcium magnesium silicate; *kaolinite,* or hydrous aluminum silicate; *calcite,* or calcium carbonate; and *dolomite,* or magnesium carbonate.

Igneous Rocks. Igneous rocks are formed from the solidification of molten rock. If this solidification occurs below the earth's surface, the rock is called *plutonic* or *intrusive,* but if it occurs on the surface, *volcanic* or *extrusive rock* is formed. If the molten rock is erupted violently into the air, *pyroclastic rocks* are formed. The term *lava* is also applied to solidified extrusive rock. The molten rock from which igneous rocks are formed consists of a hot solution composed principally of feldspar, quartz, mica, and gases such as water vapor and carbon dioxide. The solidification of igneous rocks is due to a decrease in both temperature and pressure. Their texture is influenced greatly by the rate of cooling and by the volatile substances present. It may be coarse-grained if the cooling is very slow and fine-grained if the cooling is somewhat more rapid. If the cooling is very rapid, a *glass* is formed. The volatile substances facilitate crystallization. Extrusive sheets have a *vesicular* or porous structure owing to the gases trapped in the mass as it solidifies.

The more common igneous rocks are granite, felsite, basalt, and obsidian. *Granite* is usually a strong, durable, nonporous, and practically insoluble rock which is a desirable foundation and building material. *Felsite* is a light-colored, fine-grained, volcanic rock which usually occurs as dykes or lava sheets. It is usually less porous than basalt. *Basalt* is a dark-colored rock which occurs chiefly in lava sheets or dykes. It is likely to be porous, cavernous, and may be badly fractured. Basalt is practically insoluble, the caverns being due to its method of formation and not to the solvent action of water, as is true of limestones. *Obsidian* is a volcanic glass formed by rapid cooling of molten rock. *Pyroclastic rocks* include *volcanic ash,* which is composed of fine, glassy particles deposited at considerable distance from the volcano by which they were formed; *lapilli,* which are formed from the gravel-like particles deposited closer to the volcano; and *breccias* and *tuffs,* which are formed by consolidation of the coarser particles falling near the volcano. The volcanic material corresponding in fineness to sand is known as *puzzolana. Trap* or *trap rock* is a commercial term applied to certain fine-grained, dense, durable igneous rocks, such as basalt, which are very difficult to quarry and work and so are not suitable for building stone.

Sedimentary Rocks. Sedimentary rocks are formed from the disintegration products derived from igneous rocks or from other sedimentary rocks. This disintegration is brought about by the action of weathering agencies. The principal *weathering agencies* are *temperature changes,* which produce cracking because of unequal coefficients of expansion of the minerals that compose a rock and also because of unequal temperatures in different parts of a rock mass; *alternate freezing and thawing,* which, because of the increase in volume of water when it freezes in the pores of the rock, exerts a repeated disruptive action; *abrasion* resulting from the action of moving glacial ice, running water, and wind, with their effectiveness accelerated by the solid particles they carry; and *chemical action* of atmospheric gases and of rain water that has absorbed atmospheric gases or ground water carrying chemicals in solution.

These products of rock disintegration may remain in place or may be transported by running water, wind, or glacial ice and deposited as sediments. The deposits may remain unconsolidated, as soil, or may be solidified through pressure exerted by overlying material and through the action of cementing materials included in the deposits or supplied subsequently by infiltration. Other important factors in the formation of rocks are the sea organisms, which form their shells from calcium carbonate originally derived from rocks, transported by water, and carried in solution in sea water. These shells accumulate on the sea bottom as the organisms die, are ground by the movement caused by shifting currents, and become solidified by pressure and the cementing action of the calcium carbonate itself. The time required by this continuous cycle of rock disintegration, transportation, deposition, and solidification to form rock again is measured in thousands of years.

Characteristic of sedimentary rocks are the layers or *strata* into which they are divided. The process of deposition of a given deposit has rarely been uniform and continuous, but variations have occurred in the velocity of the water or the wind and, therefore, in the size and composition of the material carried in suspension or the composition of the material carried in solution. These variations have resulted in the division of deposits into layers which differ somewhat from each other. The dividing surfaces between these strata are called *bedding planes* or *beds*. Because of this division into strata, many sedimentary rocks are also called *stratified rocks*, but some limestones show so little stratification that they are called *freestones*, their structure being uniform in all directions. The *beds* between strata may be planes of weakness so far as shearing forces are concerned, particularly if they contain clay which, when it is wet, becomes very slippery. Since movement may take place easily along such surfaces, they are sometimes called *gliding planes*. Sedimentary rocks are formed chiefly of the minerals quartz, kaolinite, calcite, and dolomite. The more common sedimentary rocks are sandstone, conglomerate, limestone, and shale.

Sandstones are formed by the consolidation of beds of sand that have been deposited by water carrying sand in suspension. The consolidation is due to pressure exerted by overlying material and to a cementing material which may be clay, calcium carbonate, iron oxide, or silica. The character of the cementing material has a pronounced effect on the properties of sandstone, those in which silica is the cementing material being the strongest and most durable. The properties are also affected markedly by the degree of cementation, which may vary greatly. Pure sandstone is silicon dioxide. *Conglomerates* are similar to sandstones but consist of cemented gravel instead of cemented sand. *Pudding stone* is conglomerate in which the pebbles are well rounded, and in *breccia* they are angular. Sandstones that are pure silicon dioxide are white in color, the various shades of yellow, brown, and red being due to the presence of different iron oxides.

Limestones are sedimentary rocks formed chiefly from the accumulation of shells on ancient sea bottoms which may now be many miles inland. Some limestones show fossils, but others show no trace of their origin because of the fine grinding to which the shells were subjected after deposition. The cementing material is calcium carbonate. Pure limestone is calcium carbonate, but magnesia, silica, alumina, and iron oxide are present in varying amounts. *Travertine* is a limestone formed by the chemical precipitation of calcium carbonate from hot groundwater. A characteristic of this stone is the small irregularly shaped cavities it contains. *Oolitic limestone* is one that contains many very small rounded particles called *oolites*. These consist of concentric layers of calcium carbonate deposited around a nucleus. All limestones are slightly soluble in water. This is not a defect of any importance in connection with building stones or foundations. However, during past geologic periods, *solution channels* and *caverns* may have been formed in a limestone deposit. The most common color of limestone is gray, but it may also be buff or brown.

Shales are formed by the compacting or by the compacting and cementing of clays, muds, and silts and may grade into sandstones if a large amount of siliceous material is present or into limestone if they are formed from silts containing an abundance of calcareous material. They have a finely stratified structure and are quite impermeable. Those that have been formed by compaction without cementation slack and disintegrate when acted upon by water after partial or complete drying. These shales are also unsatisfactory for supporting heavily loaded foundations because they gradually flow under load. This phenomenon is known as *plastic flow*. Shales in which the grains have been cemented as well as compacted by pressure do not disintegrate as do the shales which have been compacted only, and they are not subject to plastic flow. For these reasons they are more satisfactory to support foundations. Shales do not possess the requisite durability for building stones.

Metamorphic Rocks. Metamorphic rocks are either igneous or sedimentary rocks whose physical or chemical characteristics have been altered by the action of pressure resulting from earth movements or from temperature changes caused by intrusions of molten rock or by vapors or liquids that have permeated the rocks. The changes are in mineral composition, texture, and structure, and include cementation by siliceous matter. The changes in mineral composition depend upon the chemical composition and, since all kinds of rocks may be subjected to metamorphic action, there is a wide range of variation in the mineral composition of metamorphic rocks. Such rocks are highly crystalline in structure regardless of their origin. They usually have a *foliated* or laminated structure similar to the stratified structure of sedimentary rocks, and if so they are known as *schists*. The common metamorphic rocks are *gneiss,* a laminated rock with a mineral composition similar to granite; *schist,* a laminated crystalline silicate rock that splits easily; *slate,* a fine-grained argillaceous rock that splits easily into slabs; *quartzite,* a hard durable crystalline quartz rock derived from sandstone; and *marble,* a crystalline rock that can be polished. Marble is derived from limestone and is therefore composed chiefly of calcium carbonate. There is no definite line of demarcation between many of the metamorphic rocks. For instance, schist may sometimes grade into gneiss and at other times into slate. In the building industries limestones that can be polished are commonly classed as marbles.

Rock Structure. The methods of formation of the various rocks have been considered. After rocks have been formed their structures may be greatly changed by movements of the earth's crust so that the formations become bent and fractured as shown in Fig. 12-1a. The bends that have been formed are called *folds,* and the fractures are called *joints* if there is no movement along the fracture or *faults* if the rocks on one side of the fracture have moved with reference to the rock on the other side, as shown in *b.* The rock adjacent to a fault may be broken into fragments, as shown in *c,* which may afterward become cemented together to form fault breccia, or it may become finally pulverized and then it is called *gouge.* Sedimentary rocks are usually deposited in horizontal layers or *strata,* as has been explained, but because of the folding previously referred to they are found at various slopes. The angle that a bed makes with the horizontal is called the *dip,* and the direction of the line of intersection

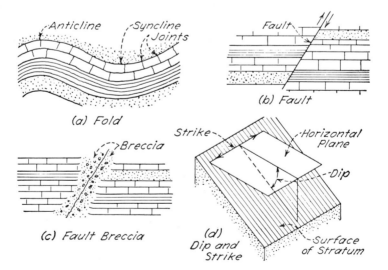

Fig. 12-1. Rock structure.

of the bed with a horizontal plane is called the *strike*, as shown in *d*.

Because limestone is soluble, there is always the possibility that a limestone formation will be *cavernous* or contain *solution channels*, owing to the action of groundwater. Such defects are particularly objectionable because they may cause failure of building foundations located immediately above such an opening. If defects of this type are discovered before a structure is built, they can usually be remedied by pressure grouting, by cleaning out the openings and filling with concrete, or by other means.

Occasionally large areas will be encountered whose rock formations have been broken up and the rock crushed to great depths even though there may be little evidence of such action on the surface. Such areas are called *shear zones*.

Physical Properties. The physical properties of stone that are most important in connection with the use of stone in its natural position to support foundations or in masonry structures are strength, durability, permeability, solubility, workability, fire resistance, color, and appearance. Some of these have been considered in the preceding paragraphs, to which the reader is referred.

Strength is an important property of rocks whether they serve to support foundations or are built into stone masonry. Sound bedrock is usually strong enough to support any load that can be carried to it by a concrete pier. Stone of such quality that it is durable when exposed to weathering in a masonry wall is also usually strong enough to support the loads it is called upon to carry. The loads placed on rock formations and stone masonry are principally compressive, but the flexural or bending strength is important in stone lintels over openings and in resisting stresses caused by unequal settlement and improper bedding of the individual stones. Stone is not used in a manner that will subject it to tensile stresses. The compressive strengths of rock or stone may vary from low values up to 50,000 lb. per sq. in. or more, so no specific values can be given. Stratified rocks have greater compressive strength normal to their bedding planes than parallel to them. Tests would be required if the strength of a given stone were in question. However, most rocks or stones that would be considered for foundations or construction purposes are amply strong for the loads they are to carry.

The *durability* of building stone is probably its most important property. Building stones are acted upon by most of the weathering agencies that act on rock formations. These have been described in preceding paragraphs. The rate of weathering depends upon the composition, texture, and structure of the stone. The durability of sandstone depends largely upon the kind of cementing material that holds the grains together, silica being the most durable and clay usually the least. Limestone and marble are slightly soluble in water containing carbon dioxide, but the rate at which these stones dissolve is usually so slow that this action is of no importance in building stones. However, this factor may receive consideration if a polished surface is to be maintained, as when marble is used. The possibility of solution channels and caverns in limestone that supports foundations must also be investigated.

The *porosity* of a building stone, which is the proportion of pore volume to the total volume, is often taken as an indication of its resistance to frost action. However, it is not the amount of pore space that is important but its continuity as measured by its *permeability*, its ability to permit water to pass through its pores. A stone may be very porous and still be quite impermeable, because of lack of continuity in the pores. For this reason it may not be seriously affected by alternate freezing and thawing. Moreover, an open, free-draining texture may be more resistant to frost action than a fine texture that holds water in the pores by capillary action.

The best method for determining the durability of a stone is by examining outcrops or the parts of a quarry where the stone has been exposed for a long period. Similarly, examination of the same rock in structures that have been in existence for many years is a good index of its weathering properties. Other properties that may indirectly give some indication of the durability of a stone are its weight and its compressive strength, high values for these properties usually, but not always, being favorable. Accelerated freezing and thawing tests carried on in the laboratory are also of value. Blocks of stone that have been quarried for a short time may contain a considerable amount of water called *quarry sap*. Such stones are frequently broken by freezing, but if they are allowed to season they will probably not break.

In some cases, the *fire resistance* of a stone may be an important consideration. No building stone will stand very high temperatures. This fact is particularly true when the heated stone is subjected to a stream of water, as frequently happens in burning buildings. Because of its low resistance to fire, the use of stone for interior piers, caps, and bond stones is sometimes prohibited by building codes, but this practice is probably too severe. Building stones may be arranged in order of their fire resistance as folows: fine-grained sandstone with silica binder; fine-grained granite or oolitic limestone; ordinary limestone; coarse-grained granite; marble. Limestone fails by calcination at a relatively low temperature.

Workability is another important property of building stones. Stones that are durable, strong, and attractive in appearance may not be suitable for building purposes because of the labor required to work them into the desired shapes. Some stones that would not be suitable for ashlar may be satisfactory for rubble or squared-stone masonry, which requires a relatively small amount of labor in shaping. Stones soft enough to work readily are frequently not durable. Ornamental work such as moldings and carvings requires a stone with an even grain which is free from seams and other defects. Stones easily worked in any direction and free from stratification are called *freestones*. Stones are more easily worked when they are *green* than after they have seasoned and the quarry sap has drained out and evaporated.

Abrasive resistance is important in steps, door sills, and floors.

The *color* of a stone may be a determining factor in its selection for a given building.

13. SOIL

Formation of Soils. As explained in the preceding article, the upper part of the earth's surface consists of solid rock called *bedrock*, which is either exposed or overlaid with water or unconsolidated material, called *mantle rock, soil,* or *earth* by the engineer, formed by the weathering of the solid rock. This unconsolidated material may rest on the rock from which it is derived and gradually grade into that rock, or it may be eroded and transported by water, wind, or glacial ice and deposited at some other place. Soil that remains in position over the rock from which it was formed is called *residual soil*. Soil that has been transported by water and deposited at another site is called *alluvial soil* or *alluvium*. The sizes of the particles in soil transported by water depend upon the velocity of the water from which they are deposited, the size of grains deposited decreasing as the velocity of the water decreases. Changes in velocity may take place gradually along a water course and result in fairly uniform deposits over a wide area, or they may take place quickly within a short distance and produce deposits with marked variations. Because of the method of formation, soil deposits are usually arranged in layers or are *stratified*. An important soil type formed by windblown material is known as *loess*. Because of the way it was transported, loess consists of fine particles.

Rock fragments and particles of all sizes that had fallen on glaciers, or had been picked up by them as they moved forward, were finally deposited as the glaciers melted and formed *moraines* of sometimes considerable size. These deposits may be in the form of ridges, called *terminal moraines,* crossing valleys and located where the forward movement of a glacier was just balanced, for a considerable period of time, by the rate of melting; they may be *lateral moraines,* which are ridges, paralleling the valley, formed by debris deposited along the sides of glaciers as they melted. Or the debris, if deposited to considerable depth over a wide area as a glacier receded by melting, would form *ground moraines.* Unless modified by subsequent action of water, the material deposited consists of material of all sizes mixed together in an unstratified mass called *till.* Fine particles, ground off bed rock as a glacier moved over it and deposited when the glacier melted, are known as *rock flour.*

Classification of Soils. As stated previously, soils have been formed by the disintegration of igneous rocks or sedimentary rocks, which were in turn formed by the solidification and cementation of unconsolidated materials originally derived from igneous rocks. Soils may also be formed from the disintegration of metamorphic rocks derived from igneous or sedimentary rocks, as has been explained.

The principal types of soils may be divided into two classes according to the sizes of the grains of which they are composed. The *coarse-grained soils* are gravels and sands, and the *fine-grained soils* are silts and clays.

Soil deposits usually consist of mixtures of various classes of soil and may also contain organic material such as *peat,* which consists primarily of partially decomposed vegetable fibers, and *muck,* which is often found with peat and consists primarily of fine clay or mud.

There are various systems for classifying soils according to their grain size. The system of classification of grain soils in the table is adapted from that of the U. S. Department of Agriculture.

Classification of Soils by Grain Size

Gravel, $\frac{1}{12}$ in. and over	Silt, 1/12,500 to $\frac{1}{5000}$ in.
Sand, $\frac{1}{500}$ to $\frac{1}{5000}$ in.	Clay, less than 1/12,500 in.

This classification should not be confused with that used in classifying concrete aggregates for which the grain size separation between fine and coarse aggregates, such as sand and gravel, is $\frac{1}{4}$ in.

The classification of soils according to grain size is convenient because grain size analyses are relatively simple to make, but it is unsatisfactory because grain size is only one factor, and not the most important, determining the behavior of soils as it affects engineering works. Sand may be ground to a fineness that would lead to its classification as clay according to grain size, but finely ground sand will not possess the properties usually associated with clay.

Most sands and gravels are composed primarily of grains of silicon dioxide or quartz. However, the grains may be composed of granite, basalt, and other rocks. The shapes of the grains vary from angular to rounded.

As the table shows, the grain size of clay is extremely small. The grains are composed primarily of hydrous aluminum silicate with various compounds such as quartz and iron oxide. The particle shape is flat or flake-like, similar to mica.

The grain size of silts is not a true indication of their behavior. Some silts, such as rock flour (described in the preceding article), resemble rounded sand grains in shape and behavior. They are usually composed of silicon dioxide. Other silts resemble clay in their composition, particle shape, and behavior. Some soils are intermediate between these two soils in composition and behavior and are called *silty clays*.

Structure of Soil. The *structure* of a soil deposit also bears an important relation to its properties. When sand grains are deposited in water they are carried by gravity into positions that result in relatively dense deposits, whereas the fine clay grains attach themselves to other clay grains without being carried by gravity to positions that would result in high density. These processes are illustrated in Fig. 13-1. A clay deposit consists of a sort of mesh or network of solid grains with the intervening spaces, called *voids* or *pores*, filled with

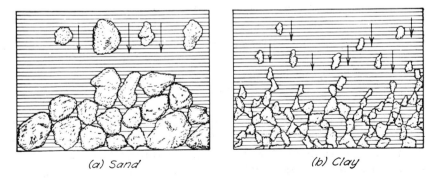

(a) Sand   *(b) Clay*

Fig. 13-1. Formation of sand and clay deposits.

water. Loads are transmitted through the deposit along the network which, as it yields, increases the pressure of the water in the pores, called the *pore pressure*. If the network is broken up by disturbance of any kind, the grains become wholly or partially surrounded with water and the soil mass loses a part of or all the rigidity, in which event it is said to be *disturbed* or *remolded*. Samples of clay obtained without changing its structure are called *undisturbed samples*.

Voids in Soil. The voids may be filled with air or other gas, with water, or partially with air or other gas and partially with water. The specific gravity of the grains is about the same regardless of their composition or size, generally falling between 2.5 and 2.8. Even though the specific gravity of the grains of most soils is fairly constant, the weight of a cubic foot of soil may be as low as 70 lb. or as high as 150 lb., because of differences in proportions of voids, depending upon the grading of the grain sizes; the moisture content, the extent to which it has been *consolidated* or compressed by overlying material or superimposed loads, or has been *compacted* by rolling, tamping, or vibrating.

In a volume of equal spheres, the space occupied by the voids may vary from a minimum of one-fourth (26 per cent) to a maximum of one-half (48 per cent) of the total volume, depending upon the arrangement of the spheres but not on the size. If the spheres are of mixed sizes, the percentage of voids is of course reduced, the smaller spheres progressively filling in the voids between the larger spheres. The ratio, expressed as a percentage, of the volume of voids in a soil to the total volume is called the *percentage of voids,* while the ratio of the volume of voids to the volume of the solid particles is called the *void ratio*. The percentages of voids, and therefore the void ratios, of sands are relatively small, whereas those of clays are large.

Percentages of Voids and Void Ratios

	Percentage of Voids	Void Ratios
Sands	30 to 45	0.43 to 0.82
Clays	35 to 95	0.54 to 19.00

From this table it is seen that in sand the volume occupied by the voids is less than the volume occupied by the solids, but in extreme cases the volume of the voids in clay may be many times the volume of the solids. The voids of sand will be filled chiefly with air if the sand is above the groundwater level and with water if below the groundwater level, but, except near the surface, the voids in most natural deposits of clays are filled with water regardless of the location of the groundwater level. Artificial clay fills may contain considerable *trapped air.* Sometimes gases other than air exist in the voids of clay. Occasionally these are inflammable and, with air, form explosive mixtures. Clay and silts in nature do not contain a measurable amount of air if they are below the zone of temporary desiccation.

Permeability. An important property of any soil is its *permeability,* its ability to permit water to pass through its voids or pores. Because of the large grains, the pore spaces between the grains of sand are large and offer relatively little resistance to the passage of water. In contrast to those of sand, the grains of clay are very small and the pore spaces, although usually much greater in total volume for a given volume of soil, are extremely small and offer great resistance to the passage of water. Sand, therefore, is very permeable and clay is very impermeable, while silts are intermediates in permeability. There may be great differences, however, in the permeability of different clays, and the presence of a small amount of clay may greatly affect the permeability of a sand. Some clays are 1000 times as permeable as others, and "the addition of 10 per cent of bentonite to a quartz sand may reduce the permeability of the sand about 10,000 times" (11). As will be explained later, the permeability of a soil has a marked effect on the rate at which it compresses or consolidates under foundation loads and also on the water tightness of the foundations.

Soil Water. Water may exist in soils in four states: capillary water, gravitational water, hygroscopic water, and adsorbed water. *Capillary water* is contained in the minute pores that are small enough to cause capillary action to take place. It is considered in the following paragraph. Water that flows through soil and can be drained or pumped out is called *gravitational water.* Water that surrounds the individual grains with a thin film which cannot be removed by air drying is called *hygroscopic* or *film water.* It can be removed by oven drying. *Adsorbed water* clings to the surface of the soil grains and cannot be removed by drying. The soil grains themselves do not absorb water but may contain *chemically combined* water, which is not considered here. The ratio of the weight of the water in a given quantity of soil to the dry weight of the soil, expressed in per cent, is the *moisture content.*

The water contained in the voids or pores of soil is often called *pore water,* and the pressure of this water is referred to as *pore pressure.* Pore pressure resists external pressures which tend to compress or consolidate the soil and, by partially holding the soil grains apart, reduces the frictional resistance between grains and therefore reduces the shearing strength. For this reason, tests of the shearing strength of a given soil that do not take into account the pore pressure are of no value. Since sand is very permeable, the pore pressure in sand equals the hydrostatic pressure caused by the head of water above the point at which the pressure is determined except when the water is flowing. Because clay is very impermeable, the pore pressure under a loaded area may be much higher than that in the surrounding soil. This inequality is gradually reduced as the water is forced from the pores of the soil under the loaded area and equilibrium is approached. This process may require hundreds of years.

The density or weight per cubic foot of clayey soil that is compacted in fills is dependent on the amount of moisture it contains. For a given size of tamper and for a given number of tamps on a given area of soil deposited in layers of a given thickness, there is a moisture content which will give the greatest density at the time of placement, as shown in Fig. 13-2. This is called the *optimum moisture content.*

Capillarity. When water and air are present in soil, a concave surface, called a *meniscus,* forms on the pore water where it comes in contact with the air. This is often called a film. The *surface tension* in these so-called films binds the grains together. This effect is illustrated

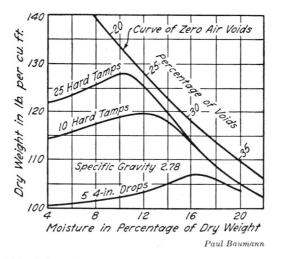

Paul Baumann

Fig. 13-2. Relation between moisture content and dry weight of soil.

by damp sand. The pores of soils also serve as capillary tubes which cause water to be present in soils above the groundwater level. The *capillary rise,* or the height above the water surface to which water is raised by capillary action, varies inversely with the diameter of the tube; in soils it varies with the diameter of the pores which is, in turn, a function of the grain size. The grain size of sand is so large that this soil possesses practically no capillarity; but the capillary rise in clays, with the small grain size, is very great. For this reason, the pores of clay are usually filled with water even though the groundwater level is many feet below, except in partially dry soil near the surface. The rate at which capillary water is transmitted depends upon the size of the pores; it is very slow in clay. Capillary water cannot be drained out of soil by any system of drainage.

Swelling and Shrinking. The volume of clay soils tends to change as the moisture content changes even though there is no change in the external load to which it is subjected. This *volume change* may be an increase in volume called *swelling* or a decrease called *shrinking.* The change in volume is brought about by stresses set up by capillary action in the pores of a soil; the pores may be considered as bundles or networks of irregularly shaped capillary tubes running in all directions through the soil. At each point where a pore is exposed to air, a concave curved surface called a *meniscus* forms on the water in the pore and over the end of the pore. As water evaporates across this surface from the soil to the air, the volume of the water in the pore decreases but the menisci remain at or near the ends of the pore. This action, in all the pores, results in a pulling together, compressing, or *shrinking* of the soil. If menisci come in contact with water, because of rains, flooding, or other causes, they are destroyed and *swelling* occurs. There is a limit to the amount of shrinkage that can take place. The moisture content below which no volume decrease occurs and above which the volume increases is called the *shrinkage limit.* The pore size of sands is so great that no volume change occurs because of this capillary effect; but in clays this phenomenon is very pronounced, as evidenced by the deep cracks that form in clay deposits as they dry out and disappear after rains.

The action that causes clay to shrink as it dries out can be compared with the changes that take place in an elastic tube (Fig. 13-3). These changes are greatly exaggerated in the figure for purposes of illustration. A tube of small diameter is shown in *a.* This tube is nearly filled with water (*b*). A curved surface called a *meniscus* is

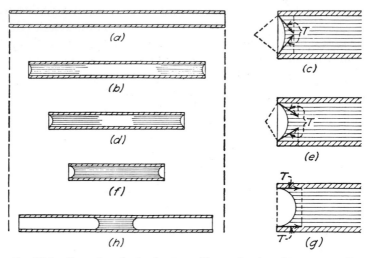

Fig. 13-3. Shortening of tube due to capillary action (greatly exaggerated).

formed at each end, shown enlarged in *c*. There is *surface tension* at each meniscus which exerts a pull *T* around the perimeter of the end of the tube. This is a constant force for each unit of length of the perimeter and exerts a compressive force *C* on the tube, causing the tube to shorten. As the volume of the water decreases (*d*) owing to evaporation of water across the meniscus, the radius of curvature of each meniscus decreases (*c*); and the angle that *T* makes with the walls of the tube decreases. Since the magnitude of *T* remains constant, *C* increases and the tube is shortened. This action continues (*f*) until the menisci become tangent to the walls of the tube, shown enlarged in *g*. The magnitude of *C* now equals *T*, its maximum value has been reached, and the tube has reached its minimum length. Further decrease in the volume of the water, owing to evaporation, causes the meniscus to recede into the tube (*h*). The tube increases in length because now only a portion of the length of the tube is compressed under the action of the meniscus. If all the water is evaporated or if the menisci are destroyed by flooding, the tube will return to its original length (*a*). Because of the complexity of the network of voids in soil, the action that takes place in soil is much more complicated, but the basic causes of shrinking and swelling are the same. Soil does not expand to its original dimensions, as the tube does, when all the water is evaporated. In soil, menisci form wherever there is air in the voids as well as at exposed surfaces.

Shearing Strength. The *shearing strength* of soils depends upon the friction between the soil grains, called *internal friction,* and upon *cohesion,* which is due partly to the molecular attraction of the grains of the soil for each other, called *true cohesion,* and partly to the binding of the soil mass together by the capillary action of the water in the pores of the soil, called *apparent cohesion.* Molecular attraction between two bodies varies directly as the product of the masses of the bodies and inversely as the squares of the distances between their centers of gravity. Because of the size of sand grains, the distance between their centers of gravity is so large that the molecular attraction is negligible in proportion to the number of grains; but the grain size of clay is so small, the grains so flat, and the number of grains in a given volume so large, that molecular attraction is a factor in the cohesive strength. In addition, because of the large size and the correspondingly large pores of sand grains, the capillary action in sand is slight, but in clay, with its small grains and pores, it is very important. Therefore, the shearing resistance of sand is due to internal friction and that of clay to both internal friction and cohesion. If clay is submerged and capillary action destroyed, apparent cohesion disappears. Submerging has little effect on internal friction in sand. There are many difficulties in determining the shearing resistance of clay, but they will not be discussed here.

Compressibility. The magnitude of the settlement of a foundation depends to a large extent on the *compressibility* of the soil on which it rests. For the unit pressures encountered in the soil under foundations, the unit stresses in the soil grains are relatively low considering the materials that make up the soil grains. The amount of compressive deformation in the grains themselves is negligible. The compressibility of a soil is therefore due to the decrease in the volume of the voids. For sands, with their bulky grains, there can be relatively little decrease in the voids unless the grains are rearranged by a sudden shock or by vibration. For clays, with their scale-like grains and large percentages of voids, the decrease in the volume of voids due to foundation pressures may be large. The compressibility of dense sand is therefore quite low, but for clays it is high, and in some clays, such as those encountered in Mexico City with void ratios as high as 14, it is very large. If the voids are filled with water, a part of this water must be squeezed out to permit the voids to decrease in volume, because the compressibility of water is negligible for the pressures encountered in foundations. Because of its permeability, sand offers little resistance to the passage of water, and the final degree of compression is reached almost as soon as the load is applied even though the pores may be filled with water. On the other hand, clay is quite impermeable, and the pores of natural deposits are normally filled with water so that compression takes place very slowly and continues over a long period of time. Air is forced out of the voids of sand almost instantaneously as pressure is applied and offers no resistance to compression. Air trapped with the water in the pores of clay, especially in artificial fills, may remain in place for a considerable period but compresses as soon as pressure is applied; therefore a certain amount of compression can occur instantaneously in clay if air is present in the voids. The process of squeezing water out of clay and thereby decreasing its volume is called *consolidation*. Consolidation can take place only when the stresses are large enough to break the bond between the soil particles.

Elasticity and Plasticity. When a body is stressed, its dimensions change. If, when the stresses are released, the body returns to its original form and dimensions, it is said to be elastic or to possess the property of *elasticity*. Sands are not elastic, but clays may have considerable *elasticity* when the stresses are small in comparison with rupture values.

The capacity of a soil to undergo changes in shape, or to flow when subjected to steady forces without a noticeable change in volume, is called *plasticity*. Sands are not plastic but clays are plastic when the stresses are high.

Solubility. Solubility is not a factor in soil that is to support the foundations of buildings. The most soluble material found in soil is gypsum; limestone is slowly soluble.

Contrasting Properties of Sand and Clay. Sand and clay represent the two extremes of the properties that are of interest to architects and engineers. This is shown by Table 13-1, which was prepared from a similar one by H. S. Gillette (13). It must be kept in mind that sands and especially clays vary widely in their compositions and properties but that they possess certain general characteristics, such as those mentioned, but to varying degrees.

Other Types of Soil. The discussions in this article have been confined to sands and clays for the sake of simplicity and to avoid con-

Table 13-1

Contrasting Properties of Sand and Clay

Property	Sand	Clay
Grain size	Large and bulky	Minute and scaly
Pore size	Large and wide	Small and narrow
Void ratio	Relatively small	Usually high
Internal friction	Large	Very small *
Cohesion	Small	Usually large
Capillary effects	Very small	Very large
Permeability	High	Low
Compressibility	Low	High
Shrinkage	Very low	High
Elasticity	Low	High for low stresses
Plasticity	None	High for high stresses

* Internal friction of clay is large when no pore water is present. Pore water is usually present and holds the grains apart causing the "apparent" internal friction to be low.

fusion. Other soils and other names applied to soils are considered briefly in the following list.

silt. Intermediate in properties to fine sand and clay.

gravel. Rounded particles more than 2 mm. or $\frac{1}{12}$ in. in diameter. It is composed chiefly of quartz but may contain granite, limestone, basalt, and other rocks. The lower limit of the size of gravel grains is sometimes taken as $\frac{1}{4}$ in.

pebbles. The smaller constituents of gravel with diameters up to 2 or 3 in.

boulders. The larger constituents of gravel, or very large, rounded blocks of rock many feet in diameter.

loam. Various mixtures of sand and clay usually containing organic matter.

marl. A mixture of quartz, clay, and calcium carbonate.

gumbo. Dark-colored, sticky clay.

adobe. Sandy, calcareous clay.

bentonite. Clay formed by the weathering of volcanic ash. It increases in volume very markedly when water is added and shrinks correspondingly when dried. Its void ratio is very high.

loess. Light-colored silt or silty clay transported and deposited by wind.

quicksand. Any finely divided sand subjected to the lifting action of water flowing upward through its mass so as to counteract the downward effect of the weight of the particles and thus cause it to behave as a liquid.

peat. A highly fibrous organic material with easily recognizable plant remains. It compresses to a large degree when subjected to pressure.

muck. Primarily decomposed black organic material with a considerable amount of finely divided mineral soil and a few fibrous remains.

rock flour. Finely divided rock particles, similar to silt, ground off the surface of bed rock by glacial action.

hardpan. A sedimentary formation consisting of mixtures varying from clay to gravel which are cemented together to form a material intermediate between soil and rock and difficult to excavate.

Uses of Soils. Soil is an important building material. In its natural position, it serves as the support for the foundations of most structures, only the foundations for some of the major structures being carried to rock unless rock is readily accessible.

Clay is used as the sole or an important material in the manufacture of brick, structural clay tile, terra-cotta, roofing tile, floor and wall tile, sewer pipe, farm tile drains, porcelain plumbing fixtures, and in many other ways in connection with buildings. The clay is selected for the particular purpose for which it is to be used and is transformed into the finished product primarily by the application of heat.

Clay is one of the principal ingredients of portland cement. When used for this purpose, it is mixed with the proper amount of limestone, pulverized, burned to a clinker, and pulverized again.

Sand is an essential ingredient in mortar used in laying brick, stone, and other masonry units, and in plaster and stucco. When used for these purposes, it is mixed with water and with some cementing material such as portland cement, lime, or gypsum plaster.

Probably the most important structural use of sand is as one of the four principal ingredients of concrete, the others being portland cement, gravel or crushed stone, and water.

Sand and gravel are used where a free-draining material is required, as under concrete floor and pavement slabs. Sand is used as a cushion under brick floors and pavements to secure an even bearing. Sand is one of the principal ingredients of window and structural glass.

References
1. Melvin Nord, *Engineering Materials,* John Wiley and Sons, 1952.
2. *Modern Plastics Encyclopedia,* Modern Plastics, Berskin Publications, 1960.
3. Herbert R. Simonds, *A Concise Guide to Plastics,* Reinhold Publishing Corporation, 1957.
4. Edward B. Cooper, "Plastics Used in Building Construction," *Plastics in Building,* Building Research Institute, 1955.
5. *Plastics as Building Materials,* Circular Series D.4.0, Small Homes Council, University of Illinois, 1956.

6. William Dudley Hunt, Jr., *The Contemporary Curtain Wall,* F. W. Dodge Corporation, 1958.

7. *Wood Handbook,* Agriculture Handbook 72, Forest Service Laboratory, U. S. Department of Agriculture, 1955.

8. *American Lumber Standards for Softwood Lumber,* U. S. Departme· t of Commerce, Simplified Practice Recommendation, R.6-53.

9. *Design and Control of Concrete Mixtures,* Portland Cement Association, 1952.

10. Charles Terzaghi, "Physical Differences Between Sand and Clay," *Engineering News-Record,* December 3, 1925, p. 912.

11. R. E. Grim, "The Clay Minerals in Soils and Their Significance," *Proceedings of Purdue Soil Mechanics Conference,* 1940.

12. R. R. Proctor, "Fundamental Principles of Soil Compaction," *Engineering News-Record,* Vol. III, 1933.

13. H. S. Guillette, *Elementary Soil Fundamentals,* University of Oklahoma Press, 1936.

14. Joseph M. Trefethen, *Geology for Engineers,* D. Van Nostrand Company, 1959.

15. Application of Synthetic Resins and Adhesives to Wood Bridges and Trestles, *American Railway Engineering Association* Bulletin 562, February 1961, p. 526.

16. Those Wonderful Epoxies, *Engineering News-Record,* July 12, 1962, p. 28.

3 Foundations

14. DEFINITIONS AND GENERAL DISCUSSION

Definitions.   The part of a building below the surface of the ground is called the *foundation* or *substructure,* and that above the ground the *superstructure.*   The soil or rock on which a building rests may also be called the foundation, and its surface the *foundation bed.*   In this book, the part of a building which bears directly on, and transmits the building load to, the supporting soil or rock is called the *foundation,* whereas the rock or soil is called the *foundation material.*   Walls below the surface of the ground and resting on the foundations are called *foundation walls.*

Various terms are used in building codes to describe the design of foundations.   Those used in this treatise may be defined as follows.

The *bearing pressure* is the intensity of pressure between the bottom of a foundation and the foundation bed.   The *allowable bearing pressure* is the maximum bearing pressure permitted to insure against excessive settlement or rupture of the foundation material.   If the foundation material is soil, allowable bearing pressures are called *allowable soil pressures.*   The *ultimate bearing capacity* is the maximum bearing pressure a foundation material can sustain without rupture.

Bearing power is a general term which refers to the ability of a foundation material to carry loads safely.

All these values are usually expressed in pounds or tons per square foot of bearing surface.

Variations in Foundation Materials.   As stated in Art. 13, the upper portion of the earth's surface consists of rock, called *bedrock,* overlaid with unconsolidated material called *soil,* which has been derived from rock.   Foundations may be supported on soil or they may be carried to bedrock.   Bedrock may be exposed on the surface or it may be several hundred feet deep.   Rock is not solid over large areas but is broken up into relatively small units by joints, bedding planes, faults, and other structural features. It may also contain caverns and solution channels. Bedding planes may be horizontal, as originally formed, or inclined. Marked variations in kind and properties of rock may occur within short distances or at different depths. Soils are also subject to wide variations in general type and in physical properties. A soil with high bearing power may be underlaid with one with low bearing power. Layers of peat, which deforms greatly under load, may cause excessive settlement if not discovered and provided for.

The formation, the composition, and the properties of rock and soil have been discussed in Arts. 12 and 13 and should be kept in mind in this chapter.

Groundwater. A large portion of the land surface of the earth is underlaid with *groundwater,* which occupies the pores and other open spaces in the soil and rock. This water flows in the same manner as surface water. Its surface is called the *groundwater table* or simply the *water table.* The groundwater table usually is not horizontal but follows, in a general way, the contour of the ground surface. The elevation of the groundwater table at a given point is called the *groundwater level.* Reference is often made to the *permanent groundwater level,* but it should be understood that there is no permanent groundwater level in most locations. The elevation of the water table varies with the amount of rainfall and with the amount of pumping for water supply or for other purposes and may be lowered very markedly by the construction of sewers, drains, subways, and other underground works.

The location of the groundwater table is of particular importance in selecting the type of foundation, in foundation design, and in planning construction procedures, even though it is below the lowest basement floor and is not a factor in the design of the basement walls.

Subsurface Exploration. Because of uncertaintities about underground conditions, adequate subsurface explorations should be made before the foundations of buildings are designed or possibly, in some cases, before a site is purchased. Methods for making such exploration are described briefly in Art. 15.

Types of Foundations. Building loads may be transmitted to the earth in the following ways.

1. By *spread foundations* bearing on soil over a sufficient area so that undue settlement or rupture does not occur. Foundations of this type may consist of individual *footings* under walls or columns, as

shown in Fig. 14-1a, or a single, heavy, reinforced concrete slab called a *mat* or *raft* may cover the entire area of the foundation and support all the building loads, as shown in *b*. Foundations of the latter type are often called *floating foundations,* although this term is commonly applied to all types of spread foundations.

2. By *pile foundations* in which the load is distributed into the soil by slender, vertical members of timber, concrete, or steel, called *piles,* or is transmitted directly to hardpan or rock by piles which pass through soil, with little or no bearing power, until their lower ends bear on the hardpan or rock. Foundations of this type may consist of individual footings called *pile footings,* under walls and columns, as shown in *c* to *e*, supported on groups of piles, or they may consist of a single member called a *mat* or *raft,* as in spread footings, with more or less uniformly spaced piles under the mat.

3. By *pier foundations* in which concrete piers are carried down through soil of inadequate bearing capacity until a satisfactory foundation bed is reached. This may be firm clay, in which case the pier is usually *belled out* at the base (*g*) to increase the bearing area; it may be hardpan, which usually requires that the piers be belled out (*g*); or it may be rock (*h*).

If the character of the soil is such that belling out is not possible or if the dimensions of the superstructure determine the dimensions of a pier, as may be true with bridge piers, piers may be made hollow (*f*). Such piers are rarely used for buildings.

The choice of foundation depends upon many factors, which are discussed in subsequent paragraphs.

Minimum Depths. The depth to which foundations must be carried depends upon the space requirements of the building, the depth of adjacent foundations, the loads that must be carried, the character of the foundation material, and climatic conditions. Except where bearing on rock, foundations that may be exposed to freezing temperatures must be carried below the *frost line* in order to prevent heaving due to frost action. A minimum depth of $1\frac{1}{2}$ ft. below the frost line is usually specified. The depth to the frost line, which is the maximum depth to which the ground freezes, varies with the locality. In the northern parts of this country, the frost line may be as low as 6 ft. below the surface, whereas in parts of the South the ground never freezes. In most cities, the depth to the frost line is fairly well indicated by the depth at which water mains must be placed to prevent freezing.

Subsurface explorations, described in Art. 15, should be carried a

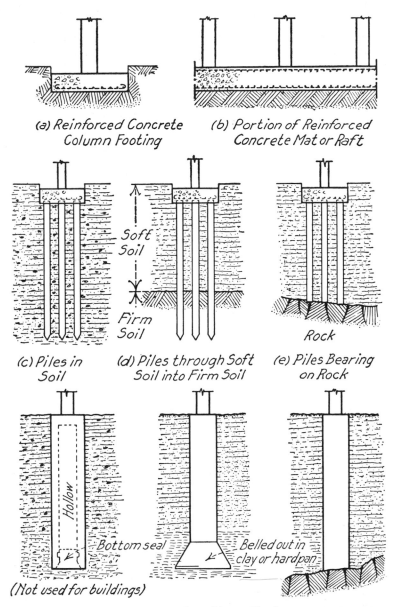

(a) Reinforced Concrete Column Footing

(b) Portion of Reinforced Concrete Mat or Raft

(c) Piles in Soil

(d) Piles through Soft Soil into Firm Soil

(e) Piles Bearing on Rock

(f) Piers in Soil (g) Piers on Firm Clay or Hardpan (h) Piers on Rock

Fig. 14-1. General types of foundations.

sufficient depth into soil to insure that there are no layers of low bearing power underlying the site to cause excessive settlement of spread or pile foundations, and that no cavities or weak areas exist under piers founded on rock. Layers of peat below the points of piles have caused excessive settlement of pile foundations.

Excavations Affecting Adjoining Property. In excavating for the basement and the foundations of a new building, it is often necessary to make some provision to prevent the adjoining land from suffering damage by the caving of the banks and to prevent injury to the buildings on adjoining land because of disturbing or undermining of the foundations. This may require that the foundations of such buildings be extended to greater depths.

Because the responsibility for the protection of adjacent property varies, a careful investigation of the local requirements should be made before preparing an estimate for a proposed building and before starting building operations.

15. SUBSURFACE EXPLORATION

General Discussion. Before a building site is purchased, or at least before the foundation plans are prepared, an investigation must be made to determine the character of the underlying material which will be called upon to support the building and the depth to the groundwater table. Even where groundwater does not affect the design of a building, it may have an important effect on the cost because of construction difficulties. With important structures on questionable soil, it is desirable to estimate the amount of settlement of foundations which may be expected, and the possibility of swelling of the soil should be investigated also. When settlement predictions are made, it is necessary to secure samples of the soil at various depths below the bottoms of the foundation. In taking such samples it is desirable, if possible, to keep them in their natural, undisturbed state. They are called *undisturbed samples*. Various devices have been developed to secure such samples.

Loading tests may be made to determine the bearing capacity of the soil, but before a decision to make such tests is made, the possibility of their being of any value should be considered. As is explained in Art. 18, such tests may be of little or no value because the bearing capacity of some soils does not vary in direct proportion with the area, and the soil a few feet below the elevation of the test area may be of a very different character from that contributing to the test results. In a loading test over a small area, usually 1 sq. ft., only the soil for a short distance below the loaded area carries sufficiently high stress to affect the results significantly, whereas the character of the soil for a considerable depth below an actual foundation contributes to the settlement of the foundations, as explained in Art. 18. The larger the foundation, the greater the depth that affects the results. This depth is usually about $1\frac{1}{2}$ times the width of the foundation.

Methods of Subsurface Exploration. Various methods are used in determining the character of the material underlying a building site. The usual methods may be listed as follows.

(*a*) Test pits.	(*e*) Churn drilling.
(*b*) Sounding rods.	(*f*) Diamond drilling.
(*c*) Soil augur boring.	(*g*) Shot drilling.
(*d*) Wash boring.	(*h*) Geophysical methods.

The methods listed from *a* to *e* are appropriate for soils, whereas *a* and *e* to *g* are used in rock. Since buildings are founded on soil or on bedrock, it is only necessary to drill into bedrock, and then only far enough to insure that the solid rock encountered is thick enough to carry the proposed load. Methods *d* and *e* are used to penetrate boulders encountered in soil. Method *a* can be used in rock, but the information necessary for examining rock for building foundations can be secured more cheaply by other methods. Geophysical methods, listed under *h*, make use of variations in the properties of various rock and soil formations to transmit sound or electricity in predicting the subsurface conditions. They are not used in the investigation of building sites and so will not be considered further. Each of these methods, except the geophysical methods, will be explained briefly. A concluding paragraph is devoted to obtaining soil samples.

TEST PITS. The most satisfactory method for securing reliable information about subsurface conditions in soil is by means of *test pits*, for this method permits the examination of the soil in its natural, undisturbed state. However, this method is relatively expensive. The pits must be large enough for a man to work in. They are shored to prevent caving, and in loose soil they must be lined by horizontal or vertical members, properly supported.

SOUNDING ROD. The *sounding rod* consists of a steel rod or pipe about ¾ in. in diameter, arranged in lengths of about 5 ft., joined by standard couplings, and provided with a point at the lower end. It is driven by hand into soil with a maul or drop weight, lubricated with water if necessary, and turned with a pipe wrench to reduce the tendency to stick. Some idea of the nature of the soil is obtained from the number of blows required to drive the rod. Driving should continue until the rod "refuses" to penetrate further. This may mean that rock has been struck, particularly if the rod "brings up" with a sharp ring. The effect is the same if a large boulder is encountered, and therefore other probings should be made nearby to see whether rock is encountered at about the same elevation, or whether the progress of the rod may have been stopped by a boulder. After driving has been completed, the rod is pulled up by means of a lever and chain or by some other device. This method, of course, yields no samples of the soil penetrated, but experienced operators may be able to judge the soil at various depths by the way the rod drives. At any rate, the results are of little value except for determining the depth to rock if it is within reach of the rod.

SOIL AUGER BORING. Holes may be bored into soil with *soil augers* rotated by hand or power. The augers are of various types, depending upon the material to be penetrated and upon the kind of power used. They vary in diameter from $1\frac{1}{2}$ to 12 in., one type being similar to the wood auger. They are mounted on sections of pipe, and new sections are added as the boring progresses. If the material being penetrated is damp sand or if it contains considerable clay, the hole may not cave but if caving occurs, the auger is operated inside a metal casing which may go down easily as the boring progresses or may have to be driven. If the soil being penetrated will adhere to the auger, some idea of its nature can be obtained from examining this soil. Below the groundwater level, in sand or silt, it may be necessary to use a bailer to remove the soil, and sometimes this device has to be used above the groundwater level by adding water to the hole and mixing it with the soil to be removed. If boulders are encountered, they are drilled with a churn drill or shot with explosive charges.

WASH BORING. One method for boring test holes into unconsolidated materials is *wash boring*. This method is also used for penetrating boulders and rock. A bit is mounted on the lower end of a pipe, called a *drill rod,* through which water is forced. The drill rod is worked up and down or churned in the hole and rotated slowly. The bit strikes the soil or rock at the bottom of the hole and gradually penetrates it. The bits used are of various types, depending upon the material to be penetrated, but in every instance they are provided with holes that permit the water to pass from the drill rod through the bit and against the sides of the hole. The width of the bit is greater than the diameter of the drill rod, to provide clearance. The cuttings are washed to the surface by the water's rising in the annular space between the rod and the sides of the hole. This operation gives the process its name. In soil, the drill is removed and a casing is installed before a depth is reached at which caving occurs. The casing is driven down at intervals as the drilling progresses. The nature of the soil penetrated is often judged by examining the borings or cuttings brought to the surface by the wash water, but such information is very unreliable. Experienced operators may be able to form some estimate of the character of the soil being penetrated by the "feel" of the equipment. A more satisfactory method consists of removing the bit and the drill rod from the hole and replacing the bit with an open-ended pipe or special forms of samplers. The apparatus is again placed in the hole and the pipe is driven into the soil at the bottom of the hole. The pipe or sampler is brought to the surface and the sample is removed and examined. It is called a *dry sample* to distinguish it from the samples brought up in the wash water, but it is not dry. Such a sampling procedure is, of course, not adaptable to rock. This boring method is used for penetrating sand, gravel, clay, boulders, and solid rock.

CHURN DRILLING. The *churn-drilling* or *dry churn-drilling* method is similar to the wash-boring method, just described, with the exception of the means of removing the cuttings. In removing the cuttings, only enough water is used to fill the bottom portion of the hole. The cuttings become mixed with this water as the churning proceeds, and at intervals the drill stem is withdrawn, the cuttings and water being removed by means of a sand pump or bailer lowered into the hole. The samples are usually obtained from the bailer and are very unreliable indicators of the material penetrated. The method is used in soil, boulders, and rock. If reliable soil samples are required, they may be obtained in the same way as "dry samples" in the wash-boring method; or core samples of rock may be secured at intervals with diamond drills, shot drills or saw-toothed drills, as described in the following paragraphs, the churn-drill equipment being removed while the cores are being obtained.

DIAMOND DRILLING. The *diamond drill*, which is only suitable for drilling in rock, consists of a hollow steel cylinder with black diamonds set on the outside and on the inside edges of the bottom to form a bit. The diamonds are set to provide a small amount of clearance so that the hole bored will be slightly larger than the outside diameter of the drill cylinder and so that the outside diameter of the core will be slightly smaller than the inside diameter of the cylinder. The drill is rotated by some kind of power and cuts into the rock by abrasive action. Water is forced down the drill rod to the bottom of the hole and rises in the annular space between the drill rod and the sides of the hole. This water removes the cuttings and keeps the bit cool.

The bit is not attached directly to the drill rod, but a cylinder called a *core barrel* is placed between the two to provide space for a length of core up to 10 ft. or so. The portion of core in the core barrel is removed at intervals by withdrawing the drilling apparatus. The *core lifter* automatically grips the core so that it is removed in the barrel. The core provides a more or less continuous record of the material penetrated. Gaps usually exist in the record because the recovery of cores is not often complete. This method is expensive but rapid. The size of core is commonly $1\frac{1}{8}$ in. and the size of hole is 2 in. Large holes can be drilled, but the cost increases rapidly with the diameter of the hole. The diamond drill can drill in any direction.

SHOT DRILLING. The *shot drill* is used to secure cores from rock. It consists of a cylindrical bit rotated by a drill rod, to which it is attached, and it cuts a circular groove in the rock. The cutting action is provided by chilled steel shot which are fed into the hole from above and find their way under the rotary bit. The cuttings are washed from the cutting surface by water which is pumped through the drill rod and bit to the bottom of the hole which rises in the annular space between the drill rod and the sides of the hole. A core barrel is provided between the bit and the core rod, as in the diamond drill.

The drill rod is considerably smaller in diameter than the core barrel and the bit so that the velocity of flow of the water which rises upward in the annular space between the drilling apparatus and the sides of the hole is much less above the top of the core barrel than below it. For this reason, the cuttings accumulate in a space provided on top of the core barrel and are removed when each section of core is withdrawn.

When cavities or open seams are encountered, progress stops because the shot disappears into the open spaces and do not remain in contact with the lower edge of the bit. At such times, the open spaces are filled with cement grout. After this sets, drilling is resumed, the bit cutting through the grout. The size of hole is usually 4 or 5 in.

Soil Sampling. As has been stated, the information obtained about the soil penetrated by some exploration methods is usually inadequate for foundation design. To obtain information about the properties of the soil at various depths, the bits attached to the drill rods are replaced at intervals by various types of samplers forced or driven into the bottom of the hole. The objective of the sampling operation is to obtain a sample with a minimum disturbance of the soil, called an *undisturbed sample.*

The simplest type of sampler, which is suitable only for cohesive soils such as clay, is a thin-walled seamless steel tube not less than 2 in. in diameter and from 2 to 3 ft. long; the tube is filled with soil by forcing it into the bottom of the hole. In the testing laboratory, the tube and its contents are cut into lengths of about 6 in. The soil is forced from these short lengths of tube to obtain specimens for testing.

Other devices consist of open-ended cylinders, called *sampling spoons,* especially designed for either sand or clay. They are forced into the ground and become filled with soil which, when extracted, provides test specimens. In performing a *standard penetration test,* the number of blows of a 90-lb. weight falling a vertical distance of 30 in. required to force a sampler with a 2-in. outside diameter 1 ft. into the ground is recorded. From this *penetration resistance,* the relative density of sand deposits and the stiffness of clay deposits can be judged. Such information is useful in selecting allowable soil pressures for foundation design.

16. TYPES OF SPREAD FOUNDATIONS

Definition and General Discussion. *Spread footings* include all the types designed to spread the building loads over a sufficient area of soil to secure adequate bearing capacity.

They may be divided into the following classes according to the manner in which they receive the loads:

wall footing. Supports a wall by extending along the entire length of the wall (Fig. 16-1a, c, and e).

isolated or *independent footing.* Supports a single column, pier, or other concentrated load (Fig. 16-1b, d, f, and g). One that supports a column is called a *column footing.*

cantilever footing. Supports two column loads and consists of two footings connected by a beam, often called a *strap.* A footing of this kind is sometimes called a *connected footing* or a *strap footing* (Fig. 16-2e and f).

combined footing. Supports two column loads or sometimes three column loads not in a row (Fig. 16-2a, b, and c).

continuous footing. Supports a row of three or more columns (Fig. 16-2). A *two-way continuous foundation* consists of continuous footings placed at right angles to each other (Fig. 16-3).

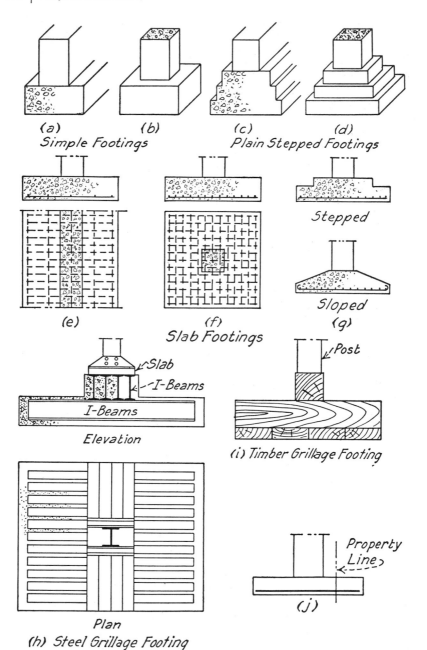

(a)   (b)
Simple Footings

(c)   (d)
Plain Stepped Footings

Stepped

Sloped

(e)   (f)   (g)
Slab Footings

Slab
I-Beams
I-Beams
Elevation

Post
(i) Timber Grillage Footing

Property Line
(j)

Plan
(h) Steel Grillage Footing

Fig. 16-1.   Spread footings.

raft or *mat foundation.* Extends under the entire building area and supports all the wall and column loads from the building (Fig. 16-3*b*, *c*, and *d*). It is often called a *floating foundation,* but this term is usually applied to any spread foundation.

Footings are divided into the following groups according to their structural characteristics.

simple footing. Projects only a few inches beyond the edges of a wall or column (Fig. 16-1*a* and *b*). Such footings are used only for light loads, and the stresses in the material are low.

stepped footing. Provides for a wider distribution of the load over the soil. It is made of brick and stone masonry and plain concrete, and at one time it was used extensively (Fig. 16-1*c* and *d*). It has now been largely replaced, however, by reinforced concrete slab footings.

slab footing. Consists of a reinforced concrete slab supporting a wall (Fig. 16-1*e*); a single column (Fig. 16-1*f* and *g*); two columns (Fig. 16-2*a* and *c*); several columns (Fig. 16-2*g* and *h*); and all columns of a building (Fig. 16-3*b*).

grillage footing. The structural elements are tiers of parallel steel I-beams or timber beams (Figs. 16-1*h* and *i*, and 16-2*b* and *e*).

WALL FOOTINGS. Wall footings may be simple footings constructed of plain concrete if the loads are light and do not require projections of more than about 6 in. beyond the edges of the wall. The depth of such footings is usually required to be equal to at least twice the projection. It is usually desirable to provide light, longitudinal reinforcement in simple concrete wall footings in order to distribute shrinkage and temperature cracks so that they will not be objectionable, and to bridge over soft spots in the soil. Similar dimension requirements prevail for wall footings constructed of hard-burned brick and flat stones, but these materials are rarely used. Greater footing widths can be provided by stepped footings; usually the depth of each step must equal at least twice the width. Stepped footings are rarely used.

The most common wall footing is the reinforced concrete slab footing of constant depth, but occasionally the top surface of the footing is stepped or sloped to save concrete. However, the increased labor cost may offset this saving. If footings with steps are used, there is a tendency to pour each step separately and allow the concrete to set at least partially between operations. This practice should not be permitted, because in design it is assumed that the whole footing will act as a unit. The main reinforcement in a spread footing for a wall is perpendicular to the wall and near the bottom of the slab to keep the projections from cracking off near the wall lines. The reinforcing bars tend to slip in the concrete because of high bond stresses. This condition makes it necessary to obtain a large surface area on the reinforcing bars by using small, closely spaced bars rather than large bars spaced farther apart. Longitudinal reinforcement is provided for the reasons given under simple footings. Spread footings are more desirable than unreinforced stepped footings because the latter occupy more space in a basement, or if they are kept below the basement floor a greater amount of excavation and material is required. The weight of stepped footings is greater and therefore adds to the load on the soil. The saving in reinforcing steel by the use of stepped footings is partially or wholly offset by the increased cost of the concrete and form work.

COLUMN FOOTINGS. Column footings are the most common type of isolated or independent footings. For light loads they may be of the simple type, but most column footings are slab footings with two-way reinforcing (Fig. 16-1f) with constant depth. As in wall footings, small, closely spaced bars should be used to provide greater bond strength. The comments about stepped and sloping top surfaces made under wall footings apply to column footings also. Grillage footings may be constructed of tiers of timber beams (i). The upper beam or beams, whose end view shows in the figures, is placed under the column base and distributes the load to a tier of tranverse beams. In the timber grillage footing, a layer of heavy planks is placed under the lower tier of beams to distribute the load to the soil. In the steel grillage footing (h), the beams are held in position by spacers placed between them, a layer of concrete 6 or 8 in. thick is placed under the lower beams, and the entire footing is filled solidly with concrete and encased in concrete with a minimum thickness of 4 in. Timber grillage footings are permitted only for temporary buildings and for frame buildings when the footings are below the "permanent" groundwater level. Steel grillage footings have been largely replaced by reinforced concrete slab footings.

COMBINED FOOTINGS. Footings of this type are most frequently used to support wall columns which are close to the property line. If such a column were centered on an isolated footing (j), the footing might project over the property line. If it were placed near the edge of such a footing, the foundation pressures would not be symmetrically distributed and the footing would tend to settle unevenly. This condition can be overcome by combining the wall column footing and the nearest interior footing into a single footing (Figs. 16-2a, b, and c). Combined footings are so proportioned that the centroid of the area which bears on the soil is on the line of action of the resultant of the

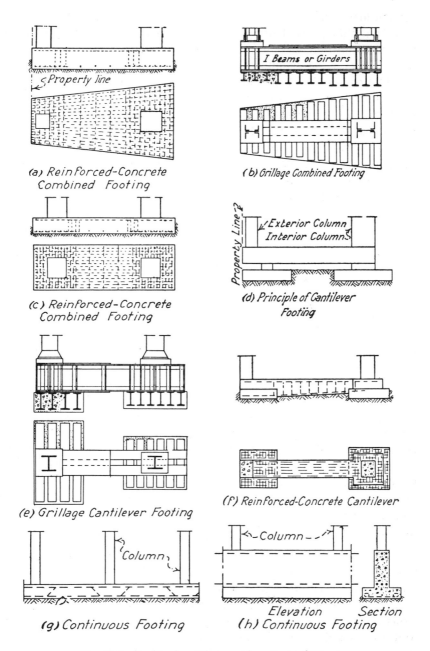

(a) Reinforced-Concrete Combined Footing

(b) Grillage Combined Footing

(c) Reinforced-Concrete Combined Footing

(d) Principle of Cantilever Footing

(e) Grillage Cantilever Footing

(f) Reinforced-Concrete Cantilever

(g) Continuous Footing

(h) Continuous Footing

Fig. 16-2. Combined, cantilever, and continuous footings.

column loads, in order to avoid any tendency to rotate. The result is usually a trapezoidal footing. It is ordinarily assumed that this arrangement also produces uniform pressure distribution under the footing. However, as explained in Art. 17, this result is not achieved. The footings for a wall column and two adjacent interior columns may be combined, and many other arrangements are made, particularly at the corners of buildings. Combined footings are usually constructed of reinforced concrete (Fig. 16-2a, but grillage footings (b), have been extensively used in the past. A combined footing may be rectangular in plan (c). If the interior column load is greater than the wall column load, a footing of this form can be so proportioned that the centroid will be on the line of action of the column loads, by adjusting the inward projection of the footing. The building codes of some cities permit foundations adjacent to streets and alleys to project over property lines, to simplify the foundation construction.

CANTILEVER FOOTINGS. Footings of this type are designed to serve the same function as combined footings by permitting a wall column load to be placed near the edge of a footing. The principle of the cantilever footing is illustrated in d. The load of the wall column is considered supported near the end of a beam which has one support over the center of the wall footing and the other support at the adjacent interior column. Since the beam projects beyond its support on the wall footing, it is said to "cantilever" beyond the support. Cantilever footings are usually made of reinforced concrete (f), but steel grillage footings of this kind (e) have been used extensively in the past. The cantilever principle is not evident in actual footings, because in both types an actual fulcrum is not used and in the reinforced concrete footing the beam is merged into the slabs. However, it is evident that the beam prevents uneven settlement of the wall footing, because of the eccentric load, by holding it in a horizontal position. The beam connecting the footings is called a *strap beam*, and footings of this type are often called *connected footings*.

CONTINUOUS FOOTINGS. Continuous footings usually consist of reinforced concrete slabs extending continuously under three or more columns (g). They tend to reduce the differential settlement between columns. This action is more effective if the foundation wall is constructed as a reinforced concrete girder (h). If the footing and the wall are poured separately, as is usually done, the lower reinforcing should be placed at the bottom of the wall, but if they are poured in one operation, this steel is more effective when placed near the bottom of the footing. Transverse reinforcing must be provided near the bottom of the slab (h). Corresponding steel is required in the footing illustrated in Fig. 16-2g. Continuous foundations of the type shown in h may be used to support bearing walls as well as columns. This type of construction is desirable because it reduces differential settlement due to variations in the soil and reduces the amount of cracking in the walls bearing on the foundation wall as well as in the foundation wall itself. If there are windows in the upper portion of the foundation walls, the upper band of reinforcement should be placed just below the windows with light reinforcement over the openings. Poured-concrete foundation walls reinforced in this manner are appropriate even for small structures such as residences. The additional cost is small, and the results may be worth many times this cost. Two-way continuous footings may be constructed (Fig. 16-3a), to reduce differential settlement more effectively than can the one-way continuous footing. Foundations tied together in this manner are desirable from the point of view of earthquake resistance.

RAFT OR MAT FOUNDATIONS. These usually consist of reinforced concrete slabs from 4 to 8 ft. in thickness (b) covering the entire foundation area. These slabs or mats are reinforced with layers of closely spaced reinforcing bars running at right angles to each other and about 6 in. below the top surface of the mat and other layers about 6 in. above the bottom. It is preferable to pour the entire slab in one operation in order to avoid construction joints. Another form of raft or mat consists of inverted T-beams of reinforced concrete (c), with the slab covering the entire foundation area. The beams run in both directions and intersect under the columns. These are poured at the same time as the slab, forming a *monolithic* structure which will act as a unit. Before the basement floor is placed, the space between these beams may be filled with cinders or other materials as shown in the figure. If the slab is placed at the top of the beams and monolithic with the mat (d), the mat may serve as the basement floor and save excavation and filling. This construction is suitable for a soil that will stand without caving so that the space occupied by the beams can be excavated and the whole mat poured without the use of forms. Raft or mat foundations are used when the bearing capacity of the soil is so low that spread footings cannot be used and where piles cannot be used advantageously or are not necessary. Foundations of this type are commonly called *floating foundations*.

RIGID FOUNDATIONS. During recent years there has been a tendency to use the term floating foundations in a more restricted sense to apply to foundations where the earth is excavated to a depth that will make the

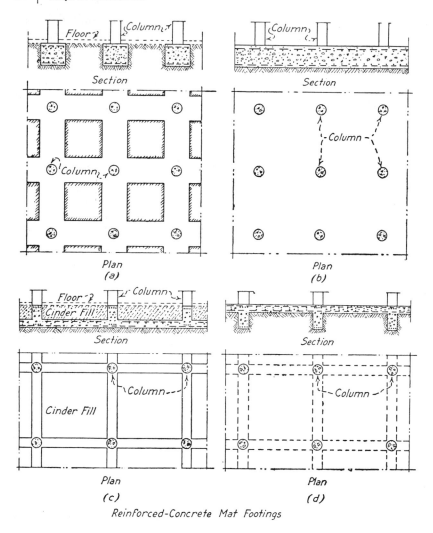

Reinforced-Concrete Mat Footings

Fig. 16-3. Raft or mat foundations.

weight of the earth removed about equal to the building load, just as the weight of a body floating on a liquid is equal to the weight of the liquid displaced. In such a case, the total vertical pressure on the soil under the building is about the same after the building is completed as it was before the excavation was started and the settlement is reduced to a minimum. All settlement may not be eliminated because there may be an elastic rebound in the soil when the earth load

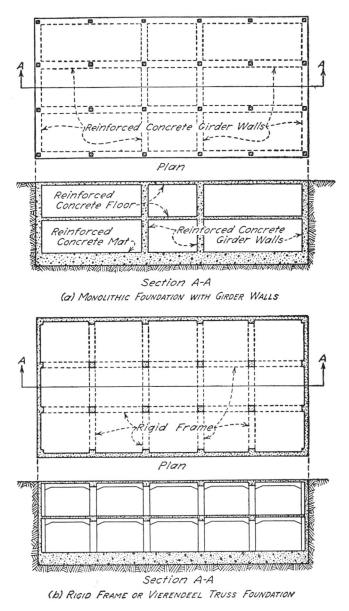

Section A-A
(a) Monolithic Foundation with Girder Walls

Section A-A
(b) Rigid Frame or Vierendeel Truss Foundation

Fig. 16-4. Rigid foundations.

is removed and a corresponding deformation when the building load is added. If a foundation is not rigid and is well below the ground surface, the central portion of the building will probably settle more than the outer portion.

In order to reduce this differential or uneven settlement to a minimum, foundations must be so constructed that they are very rigid. There are two ways of accomplishing this. One way is to make use of rigid, reinforced concrete outside and crosswalls in the basement of the building, to form a box-like structure (Fig. 16-4a). The other is to design the basement floor and the first or second floor as chords and the columns as posts of rigid frames (b). Frames of this type are called *Vierendeel girders* or trusses. They are not really trusses, as defined in Art. 34, because they are not made up of triangular frames. Because the diagonal members are omitted, the members and their intersections must be designed to carry bending stresses. These rigid girders may also be carried through two or more stories if necessary to secure the required rigidity. This is conveniently done if there is a subbasement, as there often is, or if one is provided to remove the weight of this soil in order to offset the building load. Reinforced concrete trusses with diagonals have been used instead of Vierendeel girders. Reinforced concrete interior walls restrict the use of basement space. Openings in these walls reduce the rigidity of the walls and introduce problems in design. Reinforced concrete trusses with diagonals also restrict the use of the space, but Vierendeel girders do not.

17. SOIL PRESSURES UNDER SPREAD FOUNDATIONS

General Discussion. The design of spread foundations and settlement computations are based on the distribution of pressures at the surfaces of contact between the foundation and the soil, often called the *foundation bed,* and in the underlying soil. These pressures have been measured by various investigators, and methods for computing them have been developed. The measured pressures are subject to the uncertainties existing in most *pressure cells* that have yet been developed for measuring soil pressures, but reasonably satisfactory data are available to correlate experiment and theory. The computed pressures are determined by analytical methods which assume that soils have certain properties which they possess only to a fair degree. The most widely used method, developed in 1885 by Boussinesq, is for a homogeneous, isotropic, elastic solid with the load applied at the surface and normal to it. Various proposals have been made for modifying Boussinesq's solution so that it will more nearly apply to soils, but none has received general recognition. The pressures which are of interest in foundation computations are the unit vertical pressures on horizontal surfaces at various depths below the surface. The calculation of these pressures, using Boussinesq's method directly, is quite laborious, but a procedure developed by Newmark (2) has greatly simplified the computations. Boussinesq's solution is applied to the pressures produced in the soil by superimposed loads. These pressures are of interest in settlement computations.

Contact Pressures. The distribution of the normal pressure on the surface of contact between the bottom of a footing and the soil is worth noting. The analytical solution based on the idealized properties that have been mentioned and with the footing assumed to be perfectly rigid gives the stress distribution in Fig. 17-1a with infinite, unit, normal pressures at the edges. Actually no material could be perfectly elastic for infinite stresses, and therefore the pressures under the edges will have some large finite value. The distributions for rigid plates on clay and sand have been determined experimentally, with the results shown in Fig. 17-1b. The contact pressures for clay were found to have a distribution similar to that given by the analytical solution. As the depths of the footing below the surface increased, the proportionate difference between the edge pressures and the center pressure decreased. It also seems probable that the pressure distribution in clay will gradually change and become more uniform as the clay consolidates under pressure (3). The contact pressures for sand were found to be a maximum at the center and zero at the edges, where the footing was on the surface. This fact would be expected because the sand grains under the edge of the footing have no lateral support and so can carry no vertical stress. With clay, cohesion provides this lateral support. When the footing is below the surface, edge pressures are developed because the sand grains under the edge now have lateral support which is proportional to the depth below the surface. Lateral support increases, however, as the center of the footing is approached, and the pressures increase accordingly. The usual practice in the design of footings is to assume a uniform pressure distribution (Fig. 17-1c). The effect of other distributions should at least be considered, especially in combined and continuous footings and in raft foundations. The effect of the elastic deflection of the foundation itself on the distribution of foundation pressures should be considered in some instances.

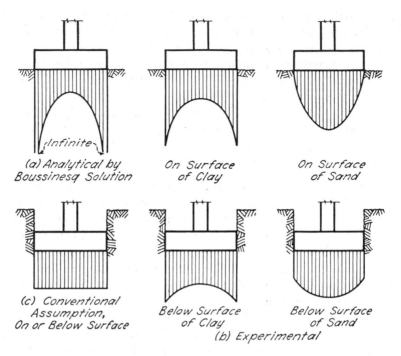

Fig. 17-1. Contact pressures.

The effect of the distribution of contact pressures on the unit vertical pressures under a footing does not extend deep enough to be of any importance in settlement computations.

Pressure Bulbs. The *unit vertical pressures* under a square footing, as computed by Boussinesq's solution, are shown in Fig. 17-2*a*, and experimental values for a circular plate on sand, determined by Kogler and Scheidig (4), are shown in Fig. 17-2*b*. In each of these figures the values given are for unit vertical pressures at points in a vertical plane parallel to the paper and through the center of the loaded surface. The magnitudes of the pressures at various points are indicated by lines, sometimes called *isobars*, drawn through points of equal vertical pressure. These figures are called *pressure bulbs* because of their form. The dimensions of computed pressure bulbs are directly proportional to the width of the loaded area. It is assumed that this proportionality applies to pressure bulbs in actual soils, but the variations in the soil do have some effect on the dimensions of the bulb. The dis-

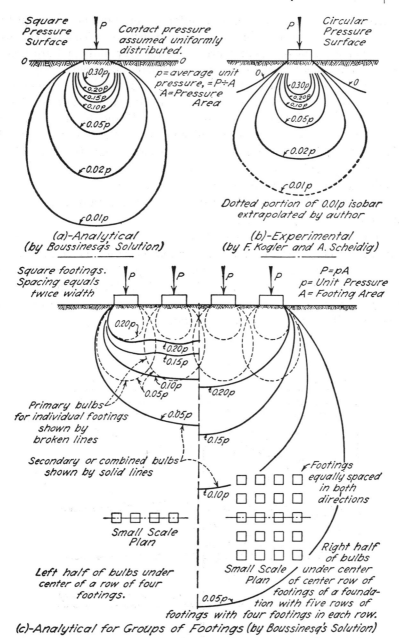

Square Pressure Surface

Contact pressure assumed uniformly distributed.

Circular Pressure Surface

0

0.30p
0.20p
0.15p
0.10p

0.05p

0.02p

0.01p

p = average unit pressure, = P÷A
A = Pressure Area

0.30p
0.20p
0.10p

0.05p

0.02p

0.01p

Dotted portion of 0.01p isobar extrapolated by author

(a)-Analytical
(by Boussinesq's Solution)

(b)-Experimental
(by F. Kögler and A. Scheidig)

Square footings. Spacing equals twice width

P = pA
p = Unit Pressure
A = Footing Area

0.20p

0.20p
0.15p

0.10p
0.05p

0.20p

0.05p

0.15p

Primary bulbs for individual footings shown by broken lines

Secondary or combined bulbs shown by solid lines

0.10p

Footings equally spaced in both directions

Small Scale Plan

Left half of bulbs under center of a row of four footings.

Small Scale Plan

Right half of bulbs under center of center row of footings of a foundation with five rows of footings with four footings in each row.

0.05p

(c)-Analytical for Groups of Footings (by Boussinesq's Solution)

Fig. 17-2. Bulbs of pressure for spread footings.

tribution of the contact pressures is different for clay and sand, but the effect of this difference extends only a short distance below the surface. The upper portions of the pressure bulbs for clay and sand are therefore different, but otherwise they are considered identical.

The isobar for zero stress is at the surface for Boussinesq's solution, (Fig. 17-2a), but for the experimental bulb it extends downward and outward from the edge of the footing (b). It should be noted that the isobar does not close. It cannot pass under the footing, as do all other isobars, because nothing would be supporting the load along the surface of which this line is a trace.

Buildings are usually supported on several footings. The pressure bulbs for the individual footings gradually merge into a single bulb for the entire foundation (c).

The pressure bulb for a square mat supporting all the columns of a building is identical to that for a square footing (Figs. 17-2a and 17-3).

Most of the settlement of a footing, a group of footings, or a mat is due to the unit vertical pressures included within the bulb for pressures of $0.2p$. Pressures outside of this bulb can be neglected. For convenience, this will be referred to as the *significant bulb* of *pressure*.

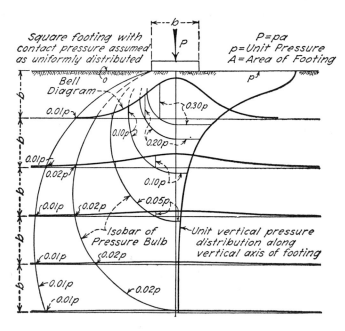

Fig. 17-3. Relation between bell diagrams and bulb of pressure.

Bell Diagrams. The distribution of unit vertical pressures along horizontal planes at various depths under a footing is illustrated by the diagram in Fig. 17-3. These are called *bell diagrams* because they are bell-shaped. The "stress volume" included under each of these diagrams is equal to the load. The pressure bulb corresponding to the bell diagrams is shown in the figure. The ordinate of the bell diagram at each point where an isobar crosses the corresponding horizontal line is equal in magnitude to the pressure represented by the isobar. The distribution of unit vertical pressures along a vertical line through the center of a footing is shown in Fig. 17-3. The abscissas in this figure are equal to the corresponding midordinates of the bell diagram. A pressure bulb corresponds to a contour map, and a bell diagram to a profile.

18. PROPORTIONING THE BEARING AREAS OF SPREAD FOOTINGS

Basic Requirements. The bearing areas of spread footings must be so proportioned that the following requirements are satisfied.

1. There must be an adequate factor of safety against failure by rupture of the underlying soil; the underlying soil ruptures when the shearing stresses in the soil, produced by the footing loads, exceed the shearing strength of the soil. The factor of safety commonly required for stresses produced by dead and live loads only is 3, and if stresses produced by wind loads or earthquake shocks are included, the factor is reduced to 2. The latter loads are not considered to act simultaneously. This phenomenon is considered in greater detail later in this article.

2. The settlement of any footing from the compression of the underlying soil must not be more than existing conditions permit.

3. The relative, or differential, settlement between any adjacent footings must not be excessive. The amount of differential settlement permitted depends on the consequences of such settlement, as considered in Art. 19. In the absence of more specific information, differential settlement is often limited to ¾ in.

Code Values for Allowable Soil Pressures. The most common procedure for selecting values for the allowable pressures on various soils is to consult the building code of the municipality in which a building is to be constructed or values recommended by various other agencies. This information is sometimes supplemented by bearing capacity tests carried on in accordance with specified procedures, described later. In any case, more or less elaborate subsurface investigations, as described in Art. 15, should be made. The extent of these investigations depends upon the importance of the building and general knowledge of difficulties that might be encountered at the site.

The maximum allowable bearing pressures recommended by the American Standards Association are given in Table 18-1. These values are supposed to insure against excessive settlement due to the compression of the soil and deformation due to shearing stresses and to provide an adequate factor of safety against the rupture of the supporting soil because of excessive shearing stresses.

Uncertainties in the selection of appropriate values for the allowable soil pressures from such tables are due partially to the indefinite de-

Table 18-1

Allowable Bearing Pressures
(in tons per square foot)

American Standards Association (5)		
Class	Material	Pressure
1. Massive crystalline bedrock such as granite, diroite, and trap rock in sound condition		100
2. Foliated rocks such as schist and slate, in sound condition		40
3. Sedimentary rocks such as hard shales, siltstones, sandstones, limestones; also thoroughly cemented conglomestes, in sound condition		15
4. Soft or broken bedrock of any kind except shale		10
5. Exceptionally compacted or partially cemented gravels, sands, and hardpan		10
6. Gravel, sand-gravel mixtures, compact		6
7. Gravel, loose; coarse sand, compact		4
8. Coarse sand, loose; sand-gravel mixtures, loose; fine sand, compact		3
9. Fine sand, loose		2
10. Stiff clay and soft shales		4
11. Medium stiff clay		2.5
12. Medium soft clay and soft broken shales		1.5
13. Except in cases where, in the opinion of the building official, the bearing capacity is adequate for light frame structures, fill material, organic material, and silt shall be treated as being without any presumptive bearing capacity. The bearing value may be fixed by the building official on the basis of tests or other satisfactory evidence		

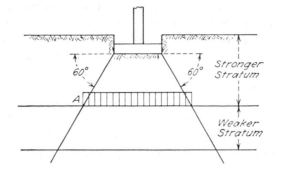

Fig. 18-1. Assumed distribution of vertical pressures under a footing.

scriptions of the soils. They are subject to wide differences in inter-pretation. This is true especially for clays.

Factors that are not recognized in code values or in the conventional procedure for proportioning the bearing areas may have significant effects, under some conditions, on the behavior of foundations. Some of these are summarized in Art. 19.

The allowable soil pressure for an underlying stratum, as determined by settlement, is in some instances less than that of the soil on which a foundation rests. This discrepancy is provided for by the requirement that the unit pressure due to the footing load computed on the top surface A–A of the weaker stratum (Fig. 18-1), shall not exceed the allowable soil pressure for the material in that stratum. The load here is considered uniformly distributed over the area intercepted on the top surface of the weaker stratum by planes sloping from the edges of the foundation at an angle of 60° with the horizontal, as shown in the figure. This is an arbitrary assumption and does not follow the form of the bell diagram in Fig. 17-3. However, the procedure is considered sufficiently accurate for its intended purpose and is simple in its application.

In estimating settlement, the allowable pressures on underlying soil are considered as pressures that the building can add to the pressures already there. This is equivalent to neglecting the weight of the soil in determining the pressures on underlying soil, for comparison with allowable values.

Bearing Capacity Tests. Tests are often made to help select the allowable pressure. The tests are conducted in a pit with a bottom several feet below the ground surface, under conditions that correspond with those in the soil on which the foundations are to be placed. Loads are applied in some manner to a test area at least one foot square on the bottom of the pit. There should be no other loads on the bottom of the pit.

According to one procedure a load equal to the proposed allowable soil pressure is applied to the test area, and settlement readings are taken at least every 24 hours. The test is continued until there is no increase in settlement during a 24-hour period. The load is then increased 50 per cent, and the settlements under the increased load are observed.

The proposed allowable soil pressure is considered satisfactory if it causes a settlement of not more than ¾ in. and if the additional settlement due to the increase in load is not more than 60 per cent of the settlement due to the proposed soil pressure. The settlement due to the proposed soil pressure is sometimes limited to ½ in. The test is repeated, as required, until an appropriate value can be selected.

A test area of 4 sq. ft. is sometimes required, especially for foundation materials with the lower allowable soil pressures. Tests for several test areas may also be required as a guide for selecting the allowable soil pressures when there are major differences in the sizes of the footings to be used.

Procedures for interpreting loading-test data are arbitrary and not entirely satisfactory. Test loads are usually applied in pits which have bottoms at the elevation of the bottoms of the proposed footings. The results are affected by the relation between the test area and the area of the bottom of the pit. If the test area occupies a large portion of the area of the pit bottom, the loaded soil receives considerable support from the soil surrounding the pit, but if only a small portion of the bottom is loaded, this support may be unimportant. Experienced judgment, guided by examination and tests of the underlying soil, must be used in the interpretation of such test results.

This type of test may have no value in determining allowable soil pressure. The soil pressures under a footing that account for most of the settlement are those included within the bulb for pressures equal to $0.2p$ (Figs. 17-2a and 17-3), which is located above a depth equal to about one and one-half times the width of the footing. This may be called the *significant bulb of pressure*. As may be seen in Fig. 18-2a, this bulb for a load test extends only a short distance below the loaded surface, but for an actual footing (b), it extends much deeper. If the latter should pass through an underlying soft stratum, much of

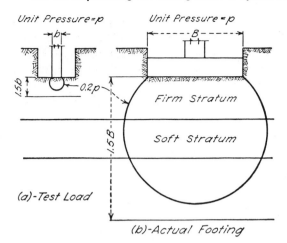

Fig. 18-2. Comparison of pressure bulbs for test load and for actual footing.

the settlement of the footing might be due to the compression of this stratum. The amount of settlement due to the compression of soil under a given unit pressure varies directly with the dimensions of the loaded area, in the same manner as that by which the bulb of pressure increases.

Ultimate Bearing Capacity. The bearing capacity of a building foundation may be determined by the permissible settlement or by actual rupture of the soil. When a load is placed on soil, shearing stresses set up in the soil cause the grains to move in relation to each other. This fact is demonstrated by the photograph in Fig. 18-3, a time exposure taken as a rod was forced into sand contained in a box with the exposed side made of plate glass. A flat side of the rod was placed next to the glass. The path of movement of each grain of sand in contact with the glass, during the period when the camera shutter was open, is recorded on the photograph (6). A similar phenomenon has been observed in clay (7). The vertical movement of the rod in Fig. 18-3 is greater relatively than would be permitted for a footing, but the photograph illustrates the tendency for the soil under a footing to be displaced laterally and upward. The soil grains in the region near the rod move outward and upward along curved paths, and heaving occurs at the surface on each side of the rod. Outside a fairly definite boundary, the soil is not displaced. In the disturbed region the shearing stresses along the curved paths caused by the load exceed the shearing resistance of the soil, but in the undisturbed region the shear-

Fig. 18-3. Displacement of sand by surface load.

ing resistance exceeds the shearing stresses. The displacements that occur are illustrated by the diagram in Fig. 18-4. Analytical solutions have been devised for computing the maximum load that a soil with a known shearing strength will carry.

Failure of Earth Slopes. Earth slopes of cohesive soil may fail by rupture with no load except that of the weight of the earth itself, as evidenced by landslides. Buildings placed on or close to a sloping earth surface may contribute to such failures and may be damaged or destroyed by them. For some buildings, the failure is very slow and is foretold by excessive cracking in the building, if only a part of the building is affected, or by gradual settlement. In other buildings, the failure may be sudden, owing to weakening of the soil by rain, to the increased weight of the soil because of rain water absorbed, and to the force exerted by water seeping through the soil. In some regions, the effect of earthquake shocks must be considered.

The usual manner of failure of earth slopes is shown in Fig. 18-5a. A portion of the earth embankment designated as *ABCD* tends to slide on the curved surface *BC* and pile up in the position shown by irregular lines. If a part or all of a building occupies the portion of the horizontal surface affected, the building will be damaged or will collapse entirely. Experience has shown that earth slopes, except clean

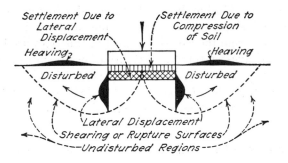

Fig. 18-4. Causes of settlement of footing.

sand or gravel, fail on roughly curved surfaces. In computations of the stability of earth slopes, it is usually assumed that failure will occur on a smooth curve that may be considered an arc of a circle, called a *slip circle*. The portion of the slope that tends to slide is considered as tending to rotate about O, the center of the circular arc. The resistance to failure is offered by the shearing strength of the earth along the arc. If the moment $W \cdot a$ (in Fig. 18-5a) of the forces tending to cause failure is greater than $T \cdot r$, the moment of the resisting forces, failure will result. If $W \cdot a$ is less than $T \cdot r$, the slope is stable, the factor of safety being measured by $T \cdot r \div W \cdot a$. The arc BC, on which failure is most likely to occur, must be located by trial, since it is the arc that will give the least factor of safety in the computations. If a building is located on top of the slope (Fig. 18-5b), the weight W' with the moment arm b must be included in the computations. Where forces other than these exist, they are of course taken into account. A slope that is stable before a building is built may fail because of

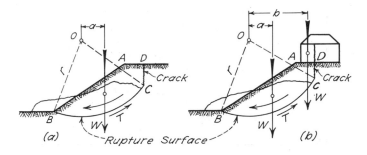

Fig. 18-5. Failure of earth slopes.

the load added by the building. Buildings should not be located on or close to clay slopes unless serious consideration is given to the danger of failure from the causes outlined in this paragraph. Analytical methods for investigating the stability of earth slopes are available.

Instead of passing through a building (Fig. 18-5b), the top of the rupture surface may be at a considerable distance behind the building. Then the entire building moves with the sliding block of soil and may be destroyed.

Bearing Capacity of Rock. Rock gradually grades into soil, and therefore no definite value can be given for its bearing capacity. Allowable values for the bearing capacity of rock are given in Table 18-1. It is often said that sound bedrock will carry any load that can be transmitted to it by a concrete pier, for the allowable unit compressive stress in the concrete of the pier would be less than the allowable bearing stress in the rock. A given material is stronger in bearing when the load is applied to a small portion of its surface than it is in a prism such as a pier. Failure in bearing could occur only by shear, in a manner similar to the failure of soil that carries a surface load (Fig. 18-4). As stated in Art. 13, some shales yield by plastic flow when subjected to bearing pressures. For this reason, shales should always be carefully investigated before they are subjected to heavy bearing pressures.

When rock that is being considered for foundation support is of doubtful quality, compression tests should be made to help determine a safe bearing value. Allowable bearing pressures given in Table 18-1 are in general terms.

Other factors that must be taken into account in examining rock for proposed foundations are the direction of stratification illustrated in Fig. 18-6; structural defects, such as excessive fractures; caverns and solution channels in limestone; possibly weak underlying strata.

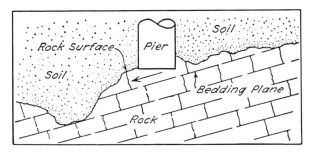

Fig. 18-6. Tendency to slide along bedding plane.

If a fault crosses the building site, the possibility of movement along the fault and the consequences of such movement should be considered.

As has been stated, a test hole yielding a core should be drilled to a depth of 10 ft. or so in the bottom of a rock excavation on which a pier is to be placed. The hole and the core will reveal any objectionable structural defects or unsatisfactory underlying material that may be present.

19. SETTLEMENT OF SPREAD FOUNDATIONS

General Discussion. All foundations, except those supported on sound rock, settle. When the supporting soil is dense, coarse sand or gravel, the amount of settlement is relatively small, unless the loads are excessive, and occurs as soon as the load is applied. In contrast to sand and gravel, if the supporting soil is clay the settlement may be large and will continue over a period of many years. In extreme cases, the settlement of structures founded on clay is measured in feet.

Settlement may not be objectionable if the entire foundation of a building settles uniformly, if the amount of settlement is not excessive, and if it can be predicted within reasonably close limits before construction starts. Such settlement causes no structural damage to the building. However, *differential settlement,* or different amounts of settlement in adjacent parts of a foundation, introduces stresses that may seriously weaken a building, throw various parts of the building out of plum, cause unsightly cracks in walls, partitions, floors, and ceilings, cause floors to be out of level and uneven, cause roofs to leak, interfere with the operation of doors, and throw mechanical equipment out of adjustment.

It is usually assumed in the design of spread foundations that, if the supporting soil is fairly uniform over the building site, settlement will be uniform when the unit pressures exerted by the foundations, where they come in contact with the soil, are the same for all parts of the foundation. In computing these pressures, only the weight of the building and the portion of the contents that remains in place for long periods are considered to cause settlement. In addition, the maximum unit pressure in any part of the foundation for any possible condition of loading is usually limited to some rather arbitrarily adopted allowable soil pressure. That this practice is unsatisfactory, particularly for cohesive soils such as clays, has become increasingly evident.

Experience with actual foundations and experimental and theoretical investigations show that, within certain limits at least, the settlement for a given unit pressure on a given soil increases as the lineal dimension of that area increases. This practice has also been unsatisfactory because of the inadequate and faulty methods used for determining the allowable bearing pressures for soils.

Causes of Settlement. The possible causes of settlement of foundations supported by soil are as follows.

1. Compression of the soil grains themselves.
2. Lateral displacement of the supporting soil.
3. Reduction in the volume of the voids of the supporting soil and, therefore, in the volume of this soil.
4. Actual rupture of the soil.

The first of these possible causes is negligible because the unit stresses in the soil grains, for the loads placed on foundations, are too small to be of any consequence.

For the loads usually placed on building foundations, the lateral displacement of the soil is so small that it need not be considered unless the lateral support of the soil is reduced by adjoining excavations or unless shallow foundations bear on soft clay.

The principal and usually the only important cause of settlement of building foundations is the third, that is, the reduction in the volume of the voids in the supporting soil.

The property of soil which is a measure of this action is called its *compressibility* and is considered in Art. 13.

As explained in Art. 16, the most effective method for reducing the settlement of foundations supported on a deep bed of soft clay is to excavate the basement of the building to a depth sufficient to make the weight of the soil removed equal to the weight of the building and its permanent contents. In this way, any increase in the soil pressure from the building load is avoided.

Settlement Predictions. Settlement predictions for structures founded on clay are based on the consolidation phenomenon mentioned in Art. 13. They are made by computing the unit vertical pressures, caused by the building load, at various depths below the bottom of the foundation and by making consolidation tests on representative samples, at various depths, of the soil that is to support the building. The procedures followed in computing the unit vertical pressures are considered in Art. 17. The consolidation test is made in a specially designed apparatus in which the soil sample is compressed and the time rate at which the sample deforms under a given unit pressure is observed, provision being made for water to escape at the top and bottom surfaces of the sample. Mathematical relationships have been developed which enable the settlements to be estimated from the unit foundation pressures and the consolidation characteristics of the samples, due consideration being given to the location of porous strata. These samples should be in the same condition in the test apparatus as in the ground, or should be *undisturbed samples*. Settlement predictions require specialized knowledge and experience in that field and are not usually made by structural engineers and architects.

Lowering of Water Level. The position of the water level may have important effects on the settlement of foundations bearing on soil. The water level is often lowered after a building has been completed. Many years may elapse before this occurs. It may occur because of the installation of sewer or drainage systems, or the construction of subways, depressed highways, or other underground works.

If foundations are located on sand or gravel with an underlying stratum of clay and the water level is in these permeable materials, the pressures on the underlying clay stratum may be increased by lowering the water level, because of the reduction of the buoyant effect of water or the effective weight of submerged sand or gravel.

If the foundations are located on clay, lowering the groundwater level will promote the consolidation of the clay, as explained in Art. 13. Also, the clay soil may be compressed further by the increased capillary tension in the soil as explained in Art. 13 and illustrated in Fig. 13-3.

Effects on Adjoining Buildings. Foundations of existing buildings supported on water-bearing sand or silt may be undermined by adjoining excavations, because of pumping operations to control the water, and soft clay soils may squeeze into excavations for piers and walls. This condition is evidenced by the excess of the excavated material over the volume of the excavation. Excess of excavation, or *lost ground*, may result in a corresponding settlement of adjoining foundations.

Even though a building is constructed only to the limits of its own site, it causes vertical as well as lateral pressures in the soil of the adjoining sites. Because of the increase in the vertical soil pressures under the foundations of an existing building by the construction of a new building on an adjoining site, the existing building may settle.

A building may be damaged from upheaval of the soil resulting from the reduction of soil pressures when an adjoining building is removed, but soils that will produce this effect are rare.

Shrinkage and Swelling. As explained in Art. 13, clay soils shrink and swell as the moisture content changes with changing seasons or more markedly during long periods of drought or rainy weather. These effects are most pronounced in the upper few feet of soil and therefore involve buildings on shallow foundations. Some clays are more susceptible to this action than others, those with high percentages of bentonite being especially objectionable. Shrinking and swelling tend to be more pronounced on exterior footings than on interior footings because of the greater protection given to the latter by the building. Extensive damage may occur for the first time many years after a building is constructed.

In some buildings the exterior footings have settled considerably more than the interior footings because of shrinkage, and in others the exterior footings have risen considerably above the interior footings because of soil expansion.

The possibility of such actions should be considered when building in regions where they have taken place or where expansive clays are known to exist.

The only means of avoiding such difficulties appears to be by carrying the foundations to depths where they will not be affected.

Summary. Comments about settlement may be summarized as follows.

1. For footings bearing on a given soil and causing equal soil pressures on the bearing area, the following relationships prevail for uniform deposits of sand, gravel, and clay foundation materials.

(*a*) The settlements are approximately proportional to the widths of wall footings and to the linear dimensions of isolated footings which have the same ratios between their lateral dimensions.

(*b*) The settlements of wall footings are greater than those of isolated footings.

2. The settlement of footings founded on sand or gravel occurs during a short period of time and then ceases, but for those founded on dense clays the settlement may continue for many years.

3. For uniform deposits of sand or clay, most of the settlement of a footing acting independently is due to the vertical soil pressures included in a depth equal to one and one-half times the width of the footing, as indicated by the pressure bulb for $0.20p$ in Figs. 17-2a and 17-3, which may be called the *significant bulb of pressure.*

4. In uniform deposits of sand or clay, most of the settlement of one row of isolated footings is due to the significant bulb of pressure shown on the left side of Fig. 17-2c. The bulb of pressure for several rows of isolated footings is shown on the right side of Fig. 17-2c.

5. If the underlying deposits of soil are more compressible than the soil on which a footing is founded, they may contribute significantly to the settlement of the footing or of a foundation consisting of several isolated footings, especially if they lie within the significant bulbs of pressure.

6. The settlement of shallow footings founded on some clays may be increased significantly by lowering the moisture content during periods of drought, or such footings may heave during periods of heavy rainfall.

7. Foundations on sand or gravel that is not dense may settle owing to decreases in the void space caused by excessive vibrations within a building or by operations adjacent to the building. Foundations on clay are not affected in this manner.

8. Foundations on clay or underlain with clay deposits may settle if the groundwater level is lowered.

20. TYPES OF PILES AND PILE FOUNDATIONS

Types of Pile Foundations. Pile foundations are similar to spread foundations in some respects. In spread foundations, the loads are transmitted directly to the soil by the foundation, but in pile foundations the loads are transmitted first to the piles which, in turn, transmit them to the soil or rock. The upper end of a pile is called the *head* or *butt,* and the lower end the *point* or *tip.* The types of pile foundations are much the same as those for spread foundations, as far as the part bearing on the piles is concerned. An *isolated* or *independent pile footing* is illustrated in Fig. 20-1*a*. The member into which the upper ends of the group of piles are embedded is called the *pile cap.* A *cantilever pile footing* is illustrated in Fig. 20-1*c*, and a *raft or mat* in Fig. 20-1*d. Combined* and *continuous pile footings* corresponding to these spread footings are used extensively. Several types of piles are used, the most common being wood piles, precast concrete piles, cast-in-place concrete piles, structural steel piles, and steel pipe piles. Each of these types is discussed briefly in the following paragraphs.

WOOD OR TIMBER PILES. In the United States, wood piles are usually tree trunks with the branches and bark trimmed off. They are driven with the small end down, except under special conditions. This end may be cut off square, it may be pointed, or it may be provided with a metal point called a *shoe.* When driving is not difficult, unpointed

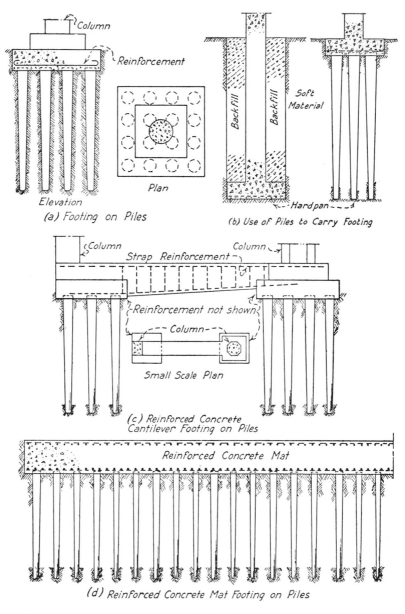

Fig. 20-1. Pile foundations.

piles are used, especially if the points rest on a hard stratum, as in the *end-bearing* or *point-bearing piles*. Driving through firm clay may be made easier by cutting blunt points on the piles. If the material penetrated contains boulders or other obstructions, metal points may be desirable.

Wood piles that are permanently below the groundwater level will last indefinitely, but consideration should be given to the possibility of the lowering of this level, as mentioned in Art. 14. Wood piles above the groundwater level may be weakened or destroyed by decay or in other ways as described in Art. 9. They may be made more resistant to decay by preservative treatments. The preservative usually used on piles is creosote. So far, experience with treated wood piles for building foundations has not extended over a period long enough to insure their permanence.

Almost any kind of sound timber that will stand driving, and that has adequate strength for the loads to be carried, can be used for piles that are to be below the "permanent" groundwater level. The most commonly used woods, however, are the cedars and cypress, which are very decay resistant; Douglas fir, from which very long piles of excellent quality can be obtained; southern pine; white and red oak; and spruce. Douglas fir, southern pine, and red oak respond better to treatment processes than the other woods. In general, heartwood is more resistant to decay than sapwood, but better results are secured with sapwood than with heartwood in the treatment processes.

The required dimensions for wood piles are determined by the load to be carried and the nature of the use. The diameter is rarely less than 6 in. at the tip and 12 in. at the butt, and the taper should be uniform. Wood piles should be free from short or reversed bends, and a straight line extending from the center of the butt to the center of the tip should lie wholly within the pile. Limbs and knots should be trimmed flush with the surface of the pile. In the better classes of work, piles should be peeled smooth.

PRECAST CONCRETE PILES. Piles constructed of reinforced concrete are used extensively. Sizes have varied from as small as 6 in. to as large as 30 in., and lengths have exceeded 100 ft. Piles are usually square or octagonal in cross section; but they may be round, usually of uniform section except at the point or sometimes tapered. The piles must be designed for the stresses caused by handling and driving, as well as for those produced by the loads to which they are subjected in service. In general, the bearing capacity of a pile is determined by

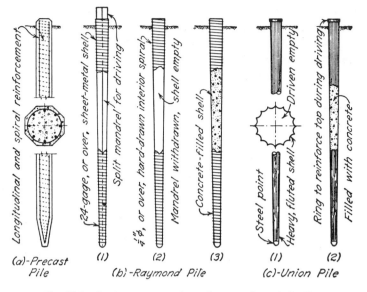

Fig. 20-2. Precast concrete pile and cast-in-place shell piles.

the resistance offered by the soil to the load which tends to move the pile through the soil, rather than by the strength of the pile itself. The reinforcement consists of longitudinal bars with hoops or spirals (Fig. 20-2a). If the reinforcing is provided only because of the stresses due to handling and driving, the thickness of the concrete outside the reinforcing need not exceed 1 in.; but if the reinforcing is required by the service loads, it should be protected by at least 1½ in. of concrete; and, if exposure conditions are extreme, the protection should be 3 in. The top and point of the pile should be provided with additional lateral reinforcement to withstand the driving stresses. For piles driven in plastic clay soils, the point preferably should be blunt or even flat; for those driven in sand or gravel or for those that must penetrate hard strata, a long tapering point should be used. Where conditions are extremely severe, a metal point or shoe may be desirable. If piles are to be jetted into position, as described later, a pipe may be cast into the pile along its axis, the end of the pipe being contracted to form a nozzle.

Piles of this type are occasionally prestressed in the same manner as columns, described in Art. 59. The principal advantage of prestressing such piles is the avoidance of cracks that could permit corrosion of the reinforcement by groundwater.

CAST-IN-PLACE CONCRETE PILES. Concrete piles that are cast in place, or *in situ,* in the ground are of two general types, the shell or cased piles and the shell-less or uncased piles.

A *shell pile* is formed by driving a sheet-steel shell or casing, closed at the point, into the ground and filling it with concrete. In the *Raymond pile,* shown in Fig. 20-2*b*, the tapered shell is made of relatively thin sheet steel. Straight-sided shells are also available. This pile is formed by (1) placing a steel *mandrel* or core inside the shell and driving the mandrel and shell into the ground; (2) removing the mandrel and inspecting the interior of the shell; and (3) filling the shell with concrete. For piles up to 40 ft. in length, the shell is in 8-ft. sections which lap over each other; and for longer piles up to lengths exceeding 100 ft., the shell consists of sections screwed together at the joints. The *Union* or *Monotube pile* (Fig. 20-2*c*), is formed by (1) driving a heavy, fluted, sheet-steel, tapered shell into the ground and inspecting the interior; and (2) filling with concrete. For piles up to 40 ft. long, the shell is in one piece, and for longer piles, up to 100 ft. or more, sections are welded together at the factory or in the field. The *MacArthur cased pile* is formed by (1) driving into the ground a heavy steel casing with an inserted core; (2) removing the core and inspecting the casing; (3) inserting a corrugated steel shell; (4) filling the shell with concrete; and (5) placing the core on top of the concrete and withdrawing the casing leaving the concrete-filled shell in the ground.

A *shell-less pile* is formed by (1) driving into the ground a shell with an inserted core; (2) withdrawing the core; and (3) filling the shell with concrete and withdrawing the shell. This type is illustrated by the *Simplex pile* in Fig. 20-3*a* and by the *Pedestal pile* in Fig. 20-3*b*. The concrete in the Simplex pile is forced against the soil, as the casing is removed, by the fluid pressure of the concrete and by impact during placing. Greater pressure may be exerted, if desired, by tamping the concrete.

The *Pedestal pile* (Fig. 20-3*b*) is formed by (1) driving a casing and core into the ground; (2) removing the core and placing concrete in bottom of casing; (3) replacing the core and pulling the casing up 1½ to 3 ft. while exerting pressure on concrete with the core; (4) ramming concrete to form pedestal; and (5) removing the core, filling casing with concrete, replacing the core to exert pressure on concrete, and pulling casing to form the finished pile.

COMPOSITE PILES. Wood piles and cast-in-place concrete piles are combined to form *composite piles* (Fig. 20-3*c*), to take advantage of the

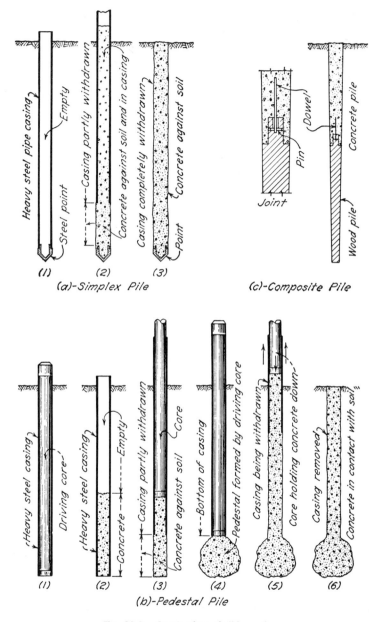

Fig. 20-3. Cast-in-place shell-less piles.

lower cost of wood piles for the portion below the groundwater level and the durability of concrete piles for the upper portion. If the Raymond pile is to be used, a wood pile is first driven nearly its full length into the ground. The shell and mandrel are then placed on the top of the wood pile and driven. The mandrel is removed and the shell filled with concrete, forming a concrete pile on top of a wood pile. The joint must be designed to stand driving and to exclude water and soil, and also designed so that the two sections will not separate because of heaving soil when adjacent piles are driven. If the MacArthur cased pile is used, the wood pile is driven inside the casing and the concrete pile is then formed in the usual manner.

PIPE PILES. Piles of this type consist of heavy steel pipe filled with concrete (Fig. 20-4a). Pipes are driven with open ends or, for the smaller sizes, with the bottom end closed. The usual types of pile

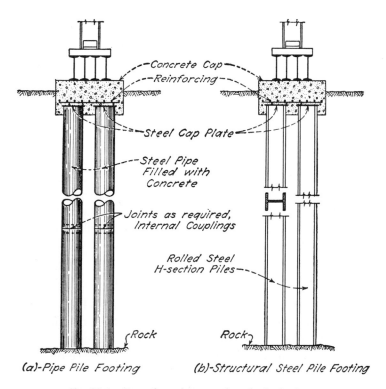

Fig. 20-4. Pipe pile and structural steel pile footings.

hammers are used, or hydraulic jacks are used when there is a load to jack against, as in underpinning.

The resistance to penetration is reduced by cleaning out open-end piles as the driving progresses. This is particularly true for piles driven through sand, because the sand plugs the end of a pile and the resistance offered is the same as though the end were closed. Cleaning out is usually done with compressed air. It is accomplished by pushing a pipe 2½ in. or more in diameter down into the soil in the pipe and forcing air through it at a pressure approaching 100 lb. per sq. in. This air pressure blows the soil out of the pipe. Water may be mixed with the soil to facilitate its removal. Pipe piles are also cleaned with small orange-peel buckets and earth augers. Clay cores which enter open-end pipe piles have been removed by withdrawing the pipe and core, forcing the core out with a plunger, and redriving the pipe. The pipes may be placed in sections with joints which will hold the sections in position, will insure good bearing between the ends of the sections, and will not project on the outside of the pipe. Concrete is placed by dumping it at the top of the pile, but the bottom portion of long piles should be placed with drop-bottom buckets to avoid segregation. Water should be removed from the pipe before the concrete is placed, but if this is not possible the bottom can be sealed with concrete placed with a drop-bottom bucket. After this seal has set, the water can be pumped out and the remainder of the concrete placed in the dry. After the concrete is set, a steel plate may be grouted over the upper end of the pile to secure good bearing on the steel and the concrete. In determining the bearing capacity of pipe piles, both the steel and concrete are considered as carrying stress, due allowance being made for the different moduli of elasticity or stiffnesses of the two materials. The pipes are commonly ⅜ in. thick, but thinner and thicker pipes are used. The diameters vary from 10 in. upward. In strength calculations, a deduction of ¹⁄₁₆ in. is sometimes made in the thickness to allow for corrosion. Available information indicates this is not necessary for piles driven in undisturbed soil (25).

STRUCTURAL-STEEL PILES. Rolled-steel H-sections (Fig. 20-4b), have been increasingly used for bearing piles. This type of pile is particularly advantageous for use in driving to bearing on sound rock through ground where driving is difficult because of the presence of boulders or thin strata of hardpan or rock which are underlaid with weaker strata and therefore do not have adequate bearing capacity. Because of their small sectional area, piles of this type displace only a small volume of soil and are not effective in increasing the bearing power of loose sands by compaction. They are not economical for use as ordinary friction piles because they are relatively expensive. Moreover, the full surface area is not available for frictional resistance because soil becomes wedged between the flanges and causes the pile to act as a square pile. Available information indicates that corrosion is not a serious factor in piles of this type and that protection against corrosion is required only for such piles driven in disturbed soils.

Comparison of Types. Untreated wood piles should be used only where they will be below the permanent groundwater level. Their life can be prolonged for many years, however, by impregnating them with creosote under pressure. As has been stated, buildings founded on creosoted timber piles have not been in existence long enough to insure their permanence above the groundwater level. Concrete and steel piles do not have this limitation. A considerable reduction in excavation, masonry, and load to be carried may sometimes be accomplished by the use of concrete piles because of the requirement that wood piles be below the permanent groundwater level.

Precast concrete piles are usually more suitable than cast-in-place piles for use where the piles project above the ground surface, although the shell type can be reinforced longitudinally and can give satisfactory service under these conditions. Precast piles must be reinforced to withstand the flexural stresses which occur during handling and the stresses due to driving; but the stresses are usually compressive, after the piles are in the ground, and do not require reinforcing. Tensile stresses may be induced in piles, however, by the heaving of the soil brought about by the driving of adjacent piles. This may cause the rupture of shell-less cast-in-place piles. The rebound of the soil and the driving of adjacent piles may reduce the section or otherwise may injure shell-less cast-in-place piles before the concrete has set. The driving of adjacent piles may collapse the shells of shell-type cast-in-place piles before the concrete is placed or may injure the piles themselves immediately after the concrete is placed. To avoid injury to cast-in-place piles by the driving operations for adjacent piles, it is usually required that all the shells or removable casings for a group of piles be driven before the concrete is placed in any of them, or at least that any pile not be poured that is to be within 5 ft. of a pile to be driven. The shell-type cast-in-place pile excludes water and earth from contact with the fresh concrete of the pile. The required lengths of precast piles must be determined before they are ordered. They must be cut off in the field and the excess length wasted if they cannot be driven to the ordered depth. Withdrawing the casing in forming shell-less cast-in-place piles, or encased piles in which the shell is inserted in the casing before withdrawal, releases the stresses set up on the soil during driving and makes any dynamic pile-driving formula inapplicable.

Pipe piles and structural steel piles are usually carried to rock, or at least to hardpan, to develop their carrying capacity, and they are usually used to carry heavy loads. Structural steel piles can penetrate hard strata and gravel. The corrosion of the steel of pipe piles or of structural steel piles is not an important consideration, except under unusual conditions.

The allowable load on individual piles varies from 15 tons to 150 tons, depending upon the type of pile, the supporting material, and other factors. The minimum value is for a wood-friction pile and the maximum value for a large steel-pipe pile bearing on rock. Of course, larger loads can be carried by steel-encased concrete cylinders, constructed in the same way as pipe piles; but cylinders with 24-in. or larger diameters are sometimes classed as *piers*.

Almost any type of pile can be secured or constructed in lengths exceeding 100 ft. Pipe piles have been used in lengths as great as 140 ft. Structural steel H-section piles 194 ft. long were used on the Potomac River Bridge at Ludlow Ferry, Maryland.

Further comparisons are made in the following article.

Pile Driving. Piles of various types and dimensions may be driven by means of a pile driver operating in conjunction with a drop hammer, various types of power hammer, or a water jet.

When a drop hammer is used, the pile is lifted into vertical position by the pile driver. A heavy weight called a *drop hammer* is then dropped on the head of the pile, driving it into the ground, the weight being guided in its fall by the *leads* of the pile driver. The hammer is raised by a steam engine, a gasoline engine, or an electric motor, and the process is repeated until the desired penetration has been secured. This type of hammer is almost obsolete.

The *steam hammer* is extensively used instead of the drop hammer. It rests on the head of the pile all the time while driving, its driving power being derived from the reciprocating parts of the hammer itself which strike blows in such rapid succession that the pile is kept in almost continuous motion. Steam hammers are single acting and double acting. A *single-acting steam hammer* consists of a heavy ram which is raised 2 to 4 ft. by steam admitted under pressure to a cylinder located above the ram, and which falls by gravity when the steam is exhausted. The steam pressure acts against the underside of a piston in the cylinder, and the piston is connected to the ram by a piston rod. The ram is guided in its fall, and the various parts are held together by a frame (Fig. 20-5a). The hammer is placed in position on top of the pile by using a pile driver or by suspending it from the boom of a derrick or from a gin pole. A *double-acting steam hammer* is similar to a single-acting hammer. The ram is raised 4 to 20 in. by steam admitted under pressure to the cylinder on the lower side of the piston, but instead of falling by gravity alone, as in the single-acting hammer, the ram is forced down by steam under pressure admitted to the cylinder on the upper side of the piston at the same time that the steam on the lower side is exhausted. The principle of the double-acting hammer is shown in Fig. 20-5b.

Special devices are used for protecting the heads of concrete piles during driving and for fitting over the heads of sheet piles. Steam hammers may be operated with compressed air as *pneumatic hammers.* Some types may be arranged to operate under water. Steam hammers may be inverted for use in pulling sheet piles and sheeting. Power hammers drive piles more rapidly than drop hammers and injure them less. Hydraulic pressure and diesel hammers are also used.

The *water jet* is extensively used in driving piles. It consists of a pipe placed at the side of a pile through which water is forced, washing the material away from the point of the pile. The pile drops into the space formed by the water jet. Some water from the jet rises

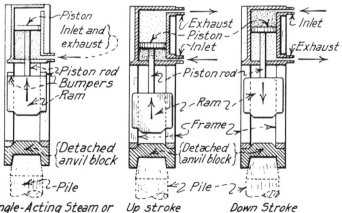

(a) Single-Acting Steam or   Up stroke   Down Stroke
Air Hammer on Up Stroke (b) Double-Acting Steam or Air Hammer

Fig. 20-5. Steam or air hammers.

to the surface along the sides of the pile and acts as a lubricant in decreasing the friction of the surrounding earth, thus assisting materially in driving. A load may be placed on the pile to assist in forcing it down, or else light blows may be struck with a pile hammer. In addition to the jet that delivers water to the point of the pile, jets may be used to deliver water along the side of the pile to assist in decreasing the frictional resistance. After the driving by the jet is completed, the earth settles around the pile and develops frictional resistance to correspond with that developed in driving without the jet. The final penetration is usually given with a pile hammer after the jet has been turned off.

The pipe used in jetting is about 2½ in. in diameter, with the lower end decreasing in diameter to 1½ in. to form a nozzle. The upper end of the pipe is connected to a force pump by means of a hose. Concrete piles often have the jet pipe cast in place along the axis of the pile. Piles driven with a water jet are not injured in driving, and therefore this method is particularly suitable for precast concrete piles. The water jet may be used in many classes of material, but it operates most successfully in sand. Many building codes do not permit the use of the water jet except by special permission.

The pipe for pipe piles used in underpinning is often forced into position by *hydraulic jacks* that act against the building. This operation requires less space than a pile driver and causes less disturbance.

21. BEARING CAPACITY AND SETTLEMENT OF PILE FOUNDATIONS

General Discussion. For convenience, it is usually stated that piles are used to support foundations. It must be kept in mind, however, that piles are intermediate members which transmit foundation loads to the underlying soil of rock. Piles used in this manner are called *bearing piles* to distinguish them from *sheet piles* and other kinds of piles, such as *fender piles* and *guide piles*. Sheet piles are driven close together to form a continuous barrier or sheet which will retain earth or to form a reasonably watertight diaphragm. Fender piles and guide piles have special uses, as indicated by their names.

In Art. 14 and in Fig. 14-1, the use of bearing piles in connection with foundations was mentioned and illustrated. Types of piles and pile foundations are considered in Art. 20. The soil into which the piles are driven may be fairly uniform throughout the length of the piles as far as bearing capacity is concerned (Fig. 14-1c), in which case the load is transmitted from the pile to the surrounding soil; the piles may penetrate through soft soil with little or no bearing power into firmer soil, to which the load is transmitted by the piles (d); or the piles may penetrate through soft soil to hardpan or rock, to which the load is transmitted by the ends of the piles (e). The entire load on a pile foundation is considered to be transmitted through the piles with no load transmitted directly to the soil by the pile cap.

Design Requirements.   Pile foundations must satisfy the following requirements.

1. The pile caps or mats must be structurally adequate to transmit the building loads to the piles.

2. Each pile must have adequate strength to carry its load and adequate bearing capacity to transmit its load to the supporting foundation material.

3. The foundation must be so proportioned that the settlement of the building as a whole with reference to its surroundings is not excessive.

4. The differential settlements between adjacent footings must not exceed permissible values. The consequences of such settlements are the same as they are for spread foundations as explained in Art. 19.

5. The shearing stresses in the supporting soil must not exceed values that would provide an adequate factor of safety against rupture of the soil. A factor of safety of 3 is considered adequate for dead load plus full live load, and 2 is adequate when loads due to wind or earthquake shock are included, the design being based on the most critical condition.

6. To insure stability, a minimum of two rows of piles should be used to support a continuous or wall pile footing and a minimum of three piles to support an isolated or column footing.

Causes of Settlement.   The causes of settlement of pile foundations supported by soil may be listed as follows.

1. An individual pile may settle by moving through the soil that surrounds it (Fig. 21-1a). An individual pile normally settles because of the compression of the surrounding soil to which it transmits stress, as indicated by the bulb of pressure in b. However, piles are not used individually.

2. A group cluster of piles supporting a footing, together with the enclosed soil, may settle by yielding as a unit and moving downward in relation to the soil that surrounds it (c).

3. A pile footing and the soil that surrounds it will always settle because of the compression of the soil to which the foundation load is transmitted by the piles, as shown by the bulb of pressure in Fig. 21-1d.

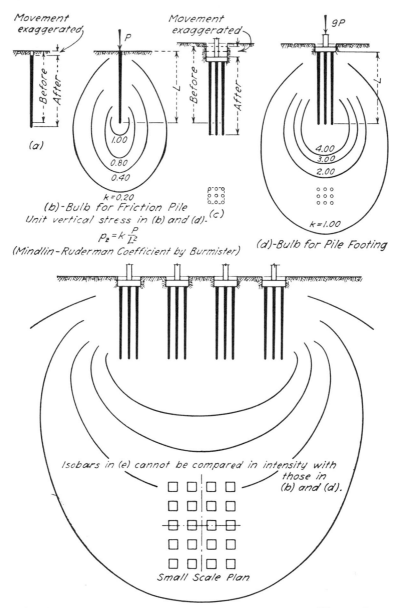

Movement exaggerated

P

Movement exaggerated

9P

Before — *After*

L

Before — *After*

L

L

(a)

1.00

0.80

0.40

k=0.20

(b)-Bulb for Friction Pile

Unit vertical stress in (b) and (d)- (c)

$$p_z = k \frac{P}{L^2}$$

(Mindlin-Ruderman Coefficient by Burmister)

4.00

3.00

2.00

k=1.00

(d)-Bulb for Pile Footing

Isobars in (e) cannot be compared in intensity with those in (b) and (d).

Small Scale Plan

(e)-General Form of Bulb of Pressure for Groups of Pile Footings

Fig. 21-1. Bulbs of pressure and settlement of piles and pile footings.

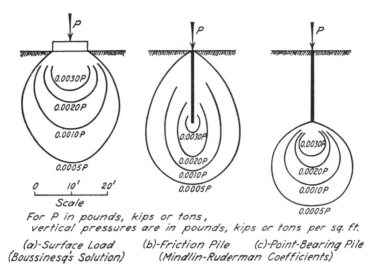

For P in pounds, kips or tons,
vertical pressures are in pounds, kips or tons per sq. ft.

(a)-Surface Load   (b)-Friction Pile   (c)-Point-Bearing Pile
(Boussinesq's Solution)   (Mindlin-Ruderman Coefficients)

Fig. 21-2. Comparison of bulbs of pressure.

4. An entire pile foundation, consisting of several pile footings, will settle because of the compression of the soil underlying the structure as a whole. This condition is normal for building foundations consisting of a number of isolated footings; but unexpected settlements of large magnitude may be caused by layers of soil, such as peat, with low bearing capacity, whose presence was unknown because of inadequate subsurface exploration. To avoid this difficulty, the soil should be investigated for a considerable distance below the tips of the piles. The settlement of a foundation is due to the compression of the soil, and results from the stresses transmitted to it by the piles, as indicated by the bulb of pressure in Fig. 21-1e.

Other causes of settlement are the lateral movement of the soil under a foundation because of excessive loads, removal of lateral support or undermining, compacting of loose sands by vibrations, and the injury of piles during driving.

Pile Action. Unless resting on hardpan or rock, a pile may be supported by *skin friction* along its length and *point resistance* at its lower end, both exerted by the soil that surrounds the pile. A pile supported primarily by skin friction is called a *friction pile* or a *floating pile* and one supported primarily by point resistance, a *point-bearing* or *end-bearing pile*. The distribution of the load between skin friction and point resistance depends upon the type of soil penetrated and is discussed in a subsequent paragraph. Below the point of the pile the load is, of course, carried entirely by the underlying soil. A pile, therefore, increases the bearing capacity of an area by distributing the load over a wider area and deeper into the soil. The pressure distributions due to a plate or footing on the ground surface, a friction pile, and a pile that transmits its load primarily by point resistance are illustrated in Fig. 21-2.

The form of pressure bulb for a loaded area is fairly well established. The form of pressure blub for a pile, however, can be shown only diagrammatically because adequate information is not yet available.

Piles driven in deposits of loose sand compact the sand and thereby increase its bearing capacity. When piles are driven for this purpose only, they are called *compaction piles*. When this has been accomplished to the degree desired, the piles have served their purpose.

Pile Clusters or Groups. Piles are not used singly but are arranged in groups or clusters centered under the loads to be carried, these loads being distributed to the individual piles by rigid *pile caps,* which are usually of reinforced concrete and are similar to spread footings. A footing bearing on piles is called a *pile footing.*

It is sometimes assumed that the bearing capacity of a group of piles is equal to the bearing capacity of one pile multiplied by the number of piles. This is true when the piles rest on rock or if the piles are spaced so far apart that the overlapping of the pressure bulbs is of no consequence. Piles that depend primarily on point resistance can be spaced more closely than friction piles, the controlling factors in this form being the compressive strength of the piles and the bearing capacity of the layer into which they are driven or on which they bear.

There is no satisfactory criterion for the spacing of friction piles. It is sometimes considered that the perimeter of the group of such piles should equal at least the sum of the perimeters of the individual piles. This conclusion is based on the assumption that the shearing resistance per unit of surface area is the same for the piles as for the prism of earth included within the perimeter of the pile group (Fig. 21-1c). The center-to-center spacing of piles is usually required to be not less than $2\frac{1}{2}$ or 3 times the diameter of round piles or the diagonal of rectangular piles, but the minimum of 2 ft. 6 in. is often used.

The distribution of vertical pressures on a horizontal plane at the points of the piles is somewhat as shown in Fig. 21-3. In this figure it is assumed that the piles act independently and that the total vertical

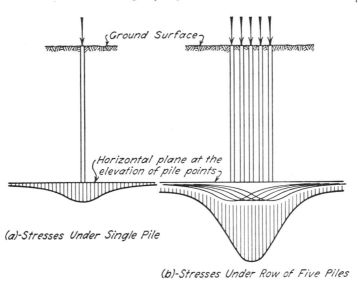

(a)-Stresses Under Single Pile

(b)-Stresses Under Row of Five Piles

Fig. 21-3. Vertical pressure distribution at elevation of pile points.

pressure at any point on the horizontal plane is equal to the sum of the vertical pressures at that point produced by the individual piles. On this basis, the settlements of the center piles would obviously be greater than those of the outside piles. Clusters of piles, however, are always capped with a rigid cap that would cause all the piles to settle nearly the same amount. This fact would tend to increase the pressure under the outer piles and decrease it under the center pile, but the pressure under each center pile would still be greater than it would be under a single pile. Mat footings founded on piles as shown in Fig. 20-1d tend to settle more at the center than at the ends, because of this effect.

A simple procedure that is often used assumes that the load from a group of piles is distributed outward and downward, at an angle of 60° with the horizontal, from the perimeter of the group of piles, at the elevation where the piles enter a stratum that has satisfactory bearing capacity. The soil pressures are considered uniformly distributed on the portions of horizontal planes included within the 60° limiting planes. This procedure is illustrated in Fig. 21-4. Each pile is assumed to carry by point resistance a load equal to the allowable unit soil pressure at the point of the pile multiplied by the area of the

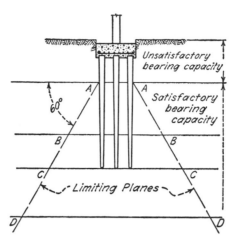

Fig. 21-4. Assumed distribution of vertical pressures under pile footing.

point. The remainder of the load is assumed to be carried by skin friction and to be transmitted to the surrounding soil at a uniform rate along the length of the pile between the elevations A–A and C–C. On this basis, the unit soil pressure at elevation B–B is equal to the load carried by skin friction divided by the horizontal area between the 60° planes minus the area of the piles. The unit soil pressure at elevation C–C, or just below the points of the piles, or the elevation D–D at some distance below C–C, is equal to the total foundation load divided by the horizontal area at C–C or at D–D. The actual soil pressures at the depths where the soil type changes are computed in this manner and compared with the allowable soil pressures, given by the code being followed, for these soils. These allowable soil pressures must not be exceeded. Only the pressures due to the foundation load are included. Overlap of planes of adjacent footings must be considered.

Effect of Width of Foundation. Half bulbs of pressure for a spread footing and a friction pile footing are compared in Fig. 21-5a. It is seen that the piles lower the bulb of pressure significantly and thereby increase the bearing capacity. Half bulbs of pressure for a mat or raft foundation supported on the ground surface and on friction piles are shown in Fig. 21-5b. It is seen that the piles have little effect on the bulb of pressure, except near the ground surface, and therefore are not effective in reducing the settlement or increasing the bearing capacity of the mat footing (9).

Effects of Type of Soil. When a pile is driven into soil it occupies space. That space can be made available only by compressing the surrounding soil or by displacing the volume of soil equal to the space occupied by the pile. In the latter case, the only way the soil can move to compensate for the volume displaced by the pile is upward so that the surface of the soil surrounding the pile rises or *heaves*. In some soils, the space occupied by the pile may result partially from compression and partially from heaving.

The bearing capacity of loose sand or other compressible fill may be improved by compacting it by means of piles. The spacing of piles required to produce the necessary bearing power by compaction is determined by trial. Advantage is taken of the compacting effect of piles in loose sand or in other compressible soil when *sand piles* are used. To place sand piles, a hole is formed in the sand by driving and withdrawing a pile or by some other method. The hole thus formed is gradually filled with sand which is thoroughly tamped during the operation. The tamping of the sand enlarges the hole in which it is

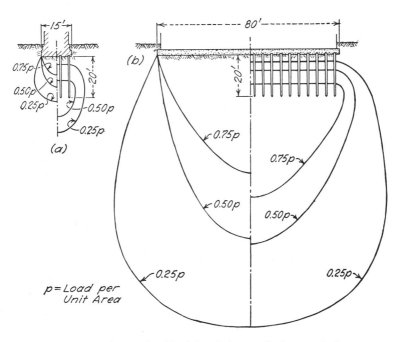

Fig. 21-5. Relation of width of foundation to effectiveness of piles.

placed and thereby compacts the surrounding sand. Sand piles are rarely, if ever, used in the United States.

It may be difficult or impossible to drive piles into dense sand or gravel without the aid of a water jet acting at the point to decrease the point resistance and, in some instances, along the length of the pile to decrease the frictional resistance. The jet washes the sand grains away from the point of the pile and up along its surface to the top of the ground. If a jet is used, the final penetration of the pile should be secured by driving with the hammer only. Jets are not as effective in clay soils. If the usual heaving of such soils must be reduced because of its effect on adjacent piles, or for other reasons, holes may be bored, or cored out with driven open-end pipe, to receive the piles which are driven into final positions. The depth of the holes is less than the length of the piles.

The point resistance of a pile driven into clay does not contribute significantly to its bearing capacity, but it is an important factor in the bearing capacity of piles driven into dense sand.

When piles are driven through a layer of partially consolidated soil and into firm soil, the load on the piles may be gradually increased as the layer consolidates and settles. The increase is caused by the frictional drag on the piles as the settlement progresses and may result in increased settlement of the foundation or even failure of the piles.

The bearing capacity of a pile may increase or decrease after the driving is completed. If the pile is driven into coarse sand that can drain freely, there is little change after a period of rest. In fine sand and silt, which are less permeable than the coarse sands, and in clay, the displacement of soil by the pile will build up pressure in the water in the voids of the soil surrounding the pile. This pressure resists the penetration and increases the point resistance. Since the soil is slowly permeable, however, water pressure will gradually be dissipated, and the point resistance will decrease accordingly. Piles driven into clay displace the corresponding volume of clay, causing heaving, and compressing the clay very little, but a small amount of water is squeezed out of the clay adjacent to the pile point and rises around the pile. This lubricates the surface of the pile and reduces its frictional resistance. The vibration of the pile during driving makes the hole slightly larger than the pile and forms a space around the pile into which the water can flow. After driving, the clay surrounding the pile gradually reabsorbs the water and "sets" around the pile, thereby increasing the skin friction. Since most of the bearing capacity of piles driven in clay is due to skin friction, the increase in skin friction, after a period of rest, increases the bearing capacity (10).

Except in clean sands and gravels, the adhesion between the soil and a pile is usually greater than the shearing strength of the soil itself, so that the resistance along the sides of a pile is usually the shearing strength of the soil immediately surrounding the pile. This shearing resistance depends upon the internal friction and the cohesive strength of the soil. Because of the compacting effect of the pile during driving, the shearing strength of the soil close to the pile may be greater than that of the soil at some distance from the pile. The shearing area, of course, increases as the distance from the pile increases.

When clusters of piles are being driven in clay soils, the driving of one pile may cause adjacent piles already in place to move upward and become unseated. If this occurs, all the piles so affected must be seated by partial redriving.

Bearing Capacity of Individual Piles. The bearing capacity of individual piles is estimated by means of pile formulas or measured by applying loads to *test piles*. The formulas used may be static or dynamic. These formulas refer to the resistance offered by a pile to loads that tend to cause it to move or slip in relation to the soil immediately surrounding it, and not to the bearing power of the surrounding soil. Settlement of the pile may be due to movement of the pile with reference to the soil, or to the movement of the pile and the surrounding soil as a unit, because of the compression of the soil under the action of the pressures induced in it by the load transmitted from the pile to the soil.

Static formulas estimate the bearing capacity by computing the shearing resistance along the surface of the pile and the bearing resistance of the point. The shearing resistance and the point resistance are obtained experimentally. Because of the extreme variation in soils of the same general class, it is difficult to determine suitable values for the pertinent properties to use in estimating shearing and bearing resistance.

Dynamic formulas are used to compute the bearing capacity of a pile from its behavior during driving. The factors used in all formulas are the energy used in driving and the average penetration produced by the last few blows. Other factors that may be included are the weight of the pile, its cross-sectional area, its length, and the modulus of elasticity of the material of which it is composed. These factors are used to compute the energy lost during the impact of the hammer on the pile and is, therefore, not available to produce penetration.

The formula most commonly used in this country is the *Engineering-News* formula, which is as follows:

$$P = \frac{2Wh}{s + c}$$

where P is the allowable load on the pile; W is the weight of a drop hammer, or the weight of the moving parts of a single-acting steam or air hammer; h is the distance through which a drop hammer falls, or the stroke of a steam or air hammer, expressed in feet; s is the penetration of the last blow or, ordinarily, the average penetration for the last few blows, expressed in inches; and c is a constant equal to 1.0 for a drop hammer and 0.1 for a steam or air hammer. The values for P and W are expressed in the same units, either in pounds or tons. The product Wh is the energy exerted by the hammer in striking one blow. The ram of the single-acting hammer is raised by pressure but drops under the action of gravity only, as explained in Art. 20. When the double-acting hammer is used, the ram is forced down by steam or air pressure so that the product of the pressure and the area of the piston represents the force driving the ram. This force is added to the weight of the ram and the weight of other moving parts in determining the total force that acts through the distance h in striking the pile. The *Engineering-News* formula has the advantage of simplicity.

The frictional resistance and the point resistance of a pile in permeable materials, such as sand, gravel, and permeable fills, are nearly the same during driving as under static load. When a pile is driven into such materials, a theoretically sound, dynamic formula can be expected to give good results. The frictional and point resistances that prevail during driving, however, differ greatly from resistances that act when a pile is at rest, if a pile is driven in relatively impermeable materials such as fine-grained silts and soft clays. As explained in the previous section, skin friction in soils of this type is reduced during driving by water squeezed out of the soil, which lubricates the surface between the pile and the soil; and point resistance is increased by the pressure built up in the pore water as the point displaces the soil. After a period of rest, the water along the pile surface is absorbed by the soil and frictional resistance is restored, but the point resistance decreases because the excess water pressure at the point is dissipated as water gradually moves from the region in which the pressure is built up by driving.

Dynamic pile-driving formulas are applied to cast-in-place concrete piles. The formula may be logical when applied to shell piles where the shell is rigid enough to maintain the compression in the soil surrounding the pile. With shell-less piles, the conditions are changed so radically by removing the casing that such a formula is not a good indicator of bearing capacity.

The most satisfactory method of determining the bearing capacity of individual piles supported in soil is by actually loading piles and observing their behavior during driving and under static load. Such piles are called *test piles*. Enough test piles should be used to make certain that the variations in the soil conditions in different parts of the site are determined. A common requirement is that the allowable load on a pile shall not be greater than one-half the maximum load which causes no settlement for 24 hours, and the total settlement shall not exceed 0.01 in. for each ton of test load. Another requirement is that the design load shall not be greater than 50 per cent of the load which causes a permanent settlement of $\frac{1}{4}$ in. in 48 hours. Other modifications of this requirement are in use. To be of value, the test loads should not be applied immediately after the pile is driven, but sufficient time should elapse to enable the soil to adjust itself to static conditions and thereby avoid the temporary effects of driving on the frictional and point resistance, as explained in the previous section. The bearing capacity of a pile may increase after a period of rest if driven in some soils, may decrease if driven in others, and may not change at all. In driving a test pile, the penetration per blow, or the average penetration for several blows, at the conclusion of driving should be observed. When the penetration per blow of the other piles, driven in the same material, is equal to or less than the final penetration per blow of the test pile, those piles can be assumed to have a bearing capacity at least equal to that of the test pile. In using the test pile as an index of the bearing capacities of other piles, the piles themselves, the kind of soil, the hammer, and the procedure used in driving the piles must be the same as those associated with the test pile. This comparison of the final penetrations of piles with that of the test pile is not usually followed, but it is a desirable one.

The procedure just described is satisfactory for determining the bearing capacity of individual piles as controlled by permissible settlement but, as has been explained, the bearing capacity of a group of friction piles is not usually equal to the bearing capacity of one pile multiplied by the number of piles, because of the overlapping of their bulbs of pressure. Occasionally, groups of three or four piles may be loaded with test loads, but the cost of applying the necessary loads to pile groups is so large that groups of piles are not often tested. Any adjustment of the design load for the number of piles in a group is based on judgment, although some building codes include formulas for this purpose.

Settlement Prediction. The procedure used in predicting settlement of pile foundations supported by clay is similar to that for spread foundations outlined briefly in Art. 19. The vertical pressures in the soil supporting the foundation are computed on the basis of Boussinesq's method. Representative undistributed samples of the soil are subjected to consolidation tests, which give data about the amount that they are compressed when subjected to given pressures. By mathematical procedures, the total effect of the compression of all the soil under a building in producing settlement is predicted from the vertical pressures and from the behavior of the samples. The presence of the piles complicates the situation in the region covered by the depth to the tips of the piles. Below that elevation the conditions are identical with those under a spread foundation. It is necessary only to include the soil to a depth of about twice the width of the entire foundation, because at greater depths the soil pressures are so low that they have very little effect on the settlement, provided, of course, that there are no layers of peat or other soft soil at greater depths.

Formulas for the bearing capacity of piles can only give information about the loads that individual piles will carry without being moved through the soil that surrounds them. They give no data concerning settlement. A loading test gives data concerning the amount of settlement of an individual pile under a given load produced by any movement of the pile with reference to the soil and to any compression of the soil surrounding the pile during the relatively short period covered by the test. Since clay compresses very slowly, the total settlement of test piles driven in clay is not obtained from the tests. Furthermore, because of the overlapping of the bulbs of pressure of the individual piles and of groups of piles to form the composite bulb of pressure for the entire foundation, as indicated in Fig. 21-1, the settlement of an individual test pile, due to the compression of the soil, is not an index of the settlement of that pile when it is under a foundation. The settlement of each pile is contributed to by the loads on adjacent piles because of the overlapping bulbs of pressure. As indicated by the depths of the significant bulbs of pressure, deep-lying strata that would have no effect on the settlement of individual piles or on individual pile footings contribute to the settlement of the foundation as a whole. This condition may be particularly significant if there are deep-lying layers of soil which yield excessively.

The lack of effectiveness of friction piles in reducing the settlement of raft foundations is illustrated in Fig. 21-5. The same situation may prevail in buildings supported on several isolated, friction-pile footings. There are cases in which the settlement has greatly exceeded the settlement of an individual pile carrying the same load during a loading test. The common assumption that settlement will be uniform if all piles are loaded equally is not correct.

The settlement of buildings founded on sand or gravel is usually not large, and friction piles are not often used for these buildings except when the sand is not in a dense state and vibrations from machinery, etc., may cause the sand, and the building it supports, to settle. Any settlement will take place within a relatively short period. Present methods for computing settlements are based on the theory of consolidation and apply only to soils such as clay, in which settlement is due to the squeezing of water out of the soil.

22. PIERS

Introduction

General Comments. Buildings are frequently supported on concrete piers carried to the depth required to reach a material such as dense sand or gravel, firm clay, hardpan, or bedrock, which will have the necessary bearing capacity (Fig. 14-1g and h). Such buildings are usually of steel or reinforced-concrete construction, in which the foundations are called upon to support columns and not bearing walls. The column load is distributed over the pier by grillage beams or by rolled or cast-steel slabs frequently 6 in. and more in thickness. The top 2 or 3 ft. of such piers is usually reinforced with steel spirals or hoops. If the height does not exceed twelve times the diameter or if the diameter is 6 ft. or over, reinforcement is not required, but special reinforcement is sometimes used to reduce the size. Piers higher than twelve diameters, with diameters of less than 6 ft., should be reinforced with vertical steel spaced uniformly around the pier about 3 in. from the surface.

If a pier is to rest on bedrock which is at least as strong as the concrete, the uniform section shown in Fig. 14-1h is used. If the supporting material is clay or hardpan, the bearing area must be greater than the required area of the pier; therefore the pier is belled out (Fig. 14-1g), in soils such as firm clay or hardpan, which will stand without support while the bell is being excavated. The side slopes of the enlarged section usually make an angle of about 60° with the horizontal. The sides are again made vertical for a distance of about 6 in. at the bottom. The bell should be designed as a spread footing, with reinforcing near the bottom to carry tensile stresses if they exceed allowable values for plain concrete footings, but this is not necessary unless the slopes are flatter than 60°.

Various methods are used in excavating for piers. In all these methods some device, such as sheeting, sheet piles, or caissons, is used to hold back the earth and to keep out water. In one method, mudladen water in the excavation prevents caving of clay until some form of casing is provided. The sheeting or sheet piles may be removed as the concrete is placed in the well, but ordinarily they are left in place. Caissons are always left in place and become a part of the piers. At one time brick and stone were used in the construction of the piers, but now concrete is used exclusively. Timber and steel used during the process of excavating and left in place will not rot or rust excessively if they are below the groundwater level.

The eccentric effect of wall columns adjacent to the property line is taken care of by reinforced concrete or steel cantilever girders extending from the wall piers to the nearest interior columns (Fig. 22-1).

The methods used for excavating wells for concrete piers may be divided into two general classes, with several subdivisions under each class as follows.

Open-well method Caisson methods
   Simple excavation   Open caisson
   Vertical sheeting   Pneumatic caisson
   Vertical lagging
   Horizontal sheeting
   Sheet piling
   Steel cylinders
   Drilling

In the open-well methods, the excavation is carried on under atmospheric conditions, the earth and groundwater being held back in various ways. Caissons are used only where groundwater is present in large amounts. The earth is held back by the caisson, but the excavation is carried on through the water or the water is held back by a plug of earth in the bottom of the caisson, so that open-air methods can be used, or the water is held back by compressed air while the excavation is carried on by men working in the compressed air.

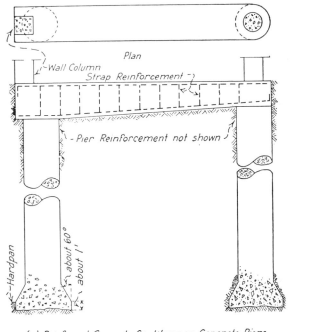

(a) Reinforced Concrete Cantilever on Concrete Piers

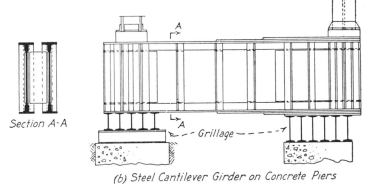

(b) Steel Cantilever Girder on Concrete Piers

Fig. 22-1. Cantilevers on concrete piers.

Definitions. The construction used in open-well methods can be classified as cofferdams if groundwater is present. A *cofferdam* may be defined as a structure built to exclude water from a given area so that work can proceed in that area under atmospheric conditions, or *in the dry*. Some leakage usually occurs, but it is controlled by pumping if the cofferdam is successful. It may be temporary or part of a permanent structure. Sometimes it is difficult to distinguish between a cofferdam and a caisson. In general, if the structure is self-contained and does not depend upon the surrounding soil for support, it is a *caisson,* but if it requires such support, as in the case of sheeting and sheet piling, it is a cofferdam.

It is the well-established practice in some localities to call all foundation piers caissons, regardless of the real meaning of the term caisson. Foundation piers are sometimes called *subpiers* to distinguish them from piers located above ground.

When excavating, it is usually necessary to support an exposed vertical face of earth to prevent its caving into the excavation. To do so, a diaphragm, ordinarily made of wood planks, is braced against the exposed face. Various terms are used to designate the members that compose this diaphragm, or the diaphragm itself, all of which have the same or similar meanings. The most common term is *sheeting,* also called *sheathing.* It usually consists of vertical members, but they may be horizontal. Vertical sheeting often is called *lagging,* but this term generally implies that the members are parts of a curved diaphragm, such as the staves of a barrel or drum. Occasionally lagging members are called *poling boards.* Horizontal sheeting members are often called *breast boards* because they are placed against the face or breast of an excavation as the work progresses. They also are called *cribbing* if they form a rectangle.

The diaphragm supporting the earth is often constructed of vertical members called *sheet piles,* which may be of wood, steel, or occasionally of reinforced concrete. Sheet piling is distinguished from vertical sheeting because it is driven into the ground in advance of the bottom of the excavation, whereas sheeting is driven or placed as the excavation progresses.

Wide-flange steel beams are often driven vertically into the ground a few feet apart and along the edge of a proposed excavation. These are called *soldier beams* because they stand erect rather than in the usual position of beams. As the excavation progresses, horizontal sheeting, or breast boards, is supported on the flanges of the beams to retain the earth.

Vertical sheeting, sheet piles, and soldier beams are supported by horizontal members, called *wales* or *waling,* placed at intervals along their height, which are in turn supported by one end of *struts* or *braces,* the means of support for the other end depending on the conditions which prevail. Inclined struts or braces supporting wales are also called *rakes* or *rakers* and *spur bracing.*

The meanings of these terms will be made more clear as the discussion proceeds.

Type of Soil. The method adopted in any excavation depends upon the nature of the soil, the depth of the excavation, the type of foundation under adjacent buildings, and many other factors. The simplest material, for excavation is firm clay. This soil is usually sufficiently watertight for the excavation in clay to be carried far below the groundwater level by open-air methods of excavation, any leakage of water that develops being taken care of by pumps. Water-bearing seams of sand and gravel introduce complications that may make it necessary to use a different procedure than would normally have been followed, but it may be possible to seal off these seams. Firm clay is a simple material to excavate for another reason, that is, it will stand unsupported without caving while excavation is being carried on for several feet of depth and will give ample time to provide support. Some wells excavated in clay for caissons over 100 ft. deep have stood unsupported for several hours.

Hardpan causes no difficulty in excavation if it is reasonably watertight, and it will usually stand unsupported until the concrete for the pier is poured.

Saturated sand offers little resistance to the penetration of caissons, but special methods must be used to keep soil that surrounds an excavation from flowing into the excavation. Excavated soil in excess of the volume occupied by the pier may have come from under adjacent foundations and have caused them to settle. This is called *lost ground*. Every effort is made in constructing foundations for buildings to avoid lost ground. This may not be serious if the piers are located in areas that are not built up or do not include adjacent water mains, sewers, or subways.

Boulders are often present on rock strata that are to be used to support piers. By some methods boulders are difficult to remove, and they may interfere with the advancing of the caisson and the establishing of the necessary seal between a caisson and the rock.

Usually piers founded on rock rest on the rock surface or are carried only a short distance into the rock to secure sound bearing. Very little excavation, therefore, is required in rock except for deep basements.

Two or more of these methods are frequently combined in a single well where different types of soil are encountered as the excavation progresses.

The various methods used in excavating for piers will now be described.

Open Wells

Simple Excavation. Wells or pits may often be excavated in stiff clay with no support whatever to prevent caving and with no provision for keeping out water. The excavation is carried on with pick and shovel in the usual manner or with air spades, described later, and the excavated material is removed in buckets hoisted by hand or power.

Vertical Sheeting. In excavating wells or pits for concrete piers the earth sides may be held in place by members called sheeting. Sheeting may be of wood planks placed vertically and supported by wood frames consisting of longitudinal members called *wales* or *rangers* and of transverse members called *braces* or *struts* (Fig. 22-2a). The sheeting is driven down and braced as the excavation proceeds. It is not practicable to drive sheeting that is more than 10 to 16 ft. long; so for excavations deeper than this it is necessary to drive a second set of sheeting a few inches inside the first, and so on, until the required depth is reached, as shown in Fig. 22-2b. This method is not used to any extent at the present time for excavating deep wells, principally because of the decreasing area of the section as the depth increases.

The decreasing section provided by the method described in the last paragraph may be avoided by sloping the sheeting outward sufficiently to permit the driving of the next set without decreasing the section. This method is illustrated in Fig. 22-2c. The outward inclination of the sheeting creates an objectionable condition at the corners which makes this method unsatisfactory in material such as loose sand, for it is difficult to keep this material from running through at the corners.

Chicago Method. In material such as clay, which will stand well, vertical sheeting, also called *poling boards and lagging,* may be placed in short lengths of 4 or 5 ft. as the excavation proceeds (Fig. 22-2d), instead of driving the sheeting, as described in the previous paragraphs. Wells excavated in this manner are usually circular. In starting a well, the first 4 or 5 ft. of depth is excavated and a set of sheeting is placed, the boards being held in place by metal rings placed inside, forcing them against the earth, which must be accurately excavated if good results are to be secured and lost ground is to be avoided. After the first set is in place, another 4- or 5-ft. section is excavated, another set of sheeting is placed, and this process is repeated until the desired depth is reached. If difficult material is encountered, the sections may be as short as 18 in. or 2 ft. The earth is excavated by pick and shovel, or the pneumatic spade may be used. The pneumatic spade operates on the same principle as the air drill, but the drill is replaced

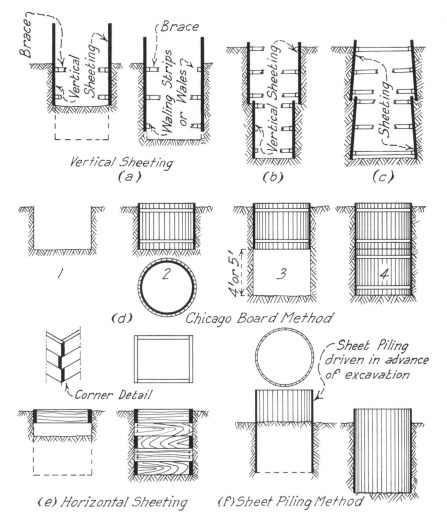

Fig. 22-2. Horizontal and vertical sheeting and sheet piling for open wells.

with a spade. As the handle of the spade is pushed, the spade is driven into the earth by compressed air. The earth is hoisted to the surface in buckets by hand or power. A tripod supporting a sheave wheel is placed over the well for convenience in hoisting.

The sheeting is 2-in. or 3-in. tongue-and-groove lumber with edges beveled to fit the curve, and the rings vary in size from 3 in. by ¾ in. to 4 in. by 1 in. The rings are divided into semicircles with flanges at the ends so that they may be bolted together in pairs to form the complete circle. In the wells for the Cleveland Union Terminal Building, some of the clay squeezed into the excavation threatened to collapse the lining. This was prevented by inserting, where necessary, heavy wooden drums divided into two segments which were forced against the lining by jack screws. These drums were removed as the wells were filled with concrete (Fig. 22-13).

When using this method for excavations carried below the groundwater level some pumping will usually be necessary, for water will enter through seams in the otherwise impervious clay. It is necessary to supply fresh air to the men who are working in the wells. If pneumatic spades are being used the exhaust may be sufficient for this purpose, but occasionally poisonous and explosive gases are encountered, and it becomes necessary to supply a large amount of air by blowers which force the air through air lines extending to the bottom of the wells (Fig. 22-13).

This method is called the *Chicago method*, for it originated in Chicago. The sheeting placed by this method is often called a caisson, but it is really a cofferdam.

The deepest foundations that have yet been placed were constructed by this method. Sixteen piers for the Cleveland Union Terminal Building were carried to a depth of 262 ft. below the curb and nearly 200 ft. below the groundwater level. A combination of horizontal sheeting, steel-sheet piles, and sheeting was used, as shown in Fig. 22-13.

Horizontal Sheeting. Planks to retain earth may be placed horizontally (Figs. 22-2e and 22-13), the wells excavated in this manner being square or rectangular in section. The excavation here need only be carried a few inches below the last set of sheeting to provide room for the next set; thus the method is applicable to soils that would not stand if a considerable depth were exposed. The sheeting usually consists of 2-by-8-in. or 2-by-10-in. planks called *breast boards* or *curb planks,* placed on edge, but in difficult material the width may be 6 in. or even 4 in. The earth is excavated with pick and shovel or with pneumatic spades and is hoisted in buckets operated by hand or power.

Sheet Piling. Instead of supporting the earth with sheeting, as in the methods just described, sheet piling may be driven around the perimeter of a well in advance of the excavation (Fig. 22-2f). The enclosed earth is usually removed by pick and shovel or by pneumatic spades and is hoisted in buckets. If driving is easy, the sheet piling may be driven its entire length before the excavation is commenced, but in all cases the piles are kept well in advance of the excavation.

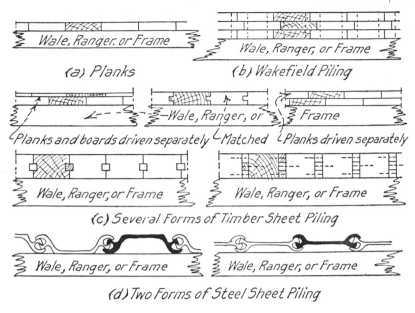

Fig. 22-3. Types of sheet piling.

The piles are braced by horizontal frames placed as soon as the progress of the excavation will permit.

Sheet piling may be made of wood or steel. The simplest form of wood-sheet piling consists of wood planks driven side by side, as shown in Fig. 22-3a. This type will hold back earth but will not keep out water. A common form of wood-sheet piling is the *Wakefield piling*, illustrated in Fig. 22-3b, consisting of three planks spiked together to form a tongue and groove. Other forms of wood-sheet piling are shown in Fig. 22-3c. With the exception of the simple planks, all the forms are intended to keep out water as well as to hold back earth. Two forms of interlocking steel piling are shown in Fig. 22-3d. If wood piling is used, the well should preferably be square or rectangular in section (Fig. 22-4a), but if steel piling is used, a circular section gives good results.

Wakefield piling will stand the impact of drop hammers, but steel-sheet piling is usually driven with steam or air hammers. Wood-sheet piling is sometimes driven with heavy wood mauls.

For wells over 20 or 25 ft. deep it may be desirable to employ two or more sections of piles, offset as shown in Fig. 22-4b. The second section is driven a few inches inside the first section, after the excavation has been completed to a point near the bottom of the first section,

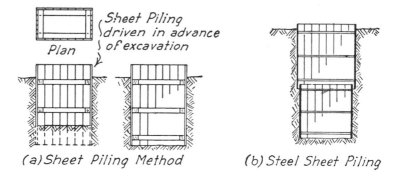

Fig. 22-4. Use of sheet piling.

and so on for other sections, allowing sufficient overlap to provide a water seal in each case.

This method has been used for wells up to 60 ft. in depth and, if some form of watertight steel piling is used, it is applicable for use in digging wells below the groundwater level if the amount of water that enters the excavation is not too great to be removed by pumping or not great enough to wash an excessive amount of the material surrounding the piling under the piling into the well. Frequently the piles are driven through porous water-bearing material until the ends of the piles are embedded in clay. The clay effectively seals the bottom of the excavation so that water cannot enter.

Telescoping Steel Cylinders. Telescoping steel cylinders from 5 to 8 ft. in length may be used in place of vertical sheeting or sheet piling. These cylinders differ in size by 2-in. increments. The largest cylinder is sunk first, as shown in 1, Fig. 22-5, by excavating below the cutting edge and driving the cylinder down. The excavation is carried on by hand methods. After the first cylinder is in position, the second is sunk in the same manner and others in succession until the desired depth is reached, as shown in 2. A bell, as shown in 2, is excavated at the bottom if the soil permits. After the excavation is completed, the space is filled with concrete, as shown in 3, the cylinders being withdrawn as the concrete is placed until the completed pier, as shown in 4, is formed. The waste of concrete caused by the decreasing section may be avoided by using a small cylinder as a concrete form for the entire depth, the space between the concrete and the outer lining being filled with sand. Telescoping cylinders can be used in water-bearing soils where the material will not hold its shape as required by the

Chicago method, the cylinders being driven well in advance of the excavating to keep the surrounding soil from flowing into the excavation. A bell cannot be formed unless the final excavation is in a suitable material such as clay. This is one form of the *Gow pile* and might be classed as an open caisson.

Drilling Methods

Introduction. Various types of equipment, truck, crawler, or otherwise, mounted for maneuverability, have been devised for drilling wells into which concrete foundation piers are poured. The material to be penetrated is loosened or broken up and removed by drills mounted on the lower ends of power-driven vertical shafts, called *Kelley bars,* held in vertical alignment by the machine, or drills may be suspended from power-operated cable hoists and guided as they fall by the cylindrical steel casings in which they operate.

There are three types of drill in common use; the auger and the bucket, which penetrate by rotation, and the hammer-grab, which penetrates by vertical impact. Other types of drill are or have been used, and still others will undoubtedly be developed in the future.

In some cases, wells may be excavated to their full depth without requiring protection against caving. In others, protection may be required for only a portion of the depth, and in still others protection may be required for the full depth. When required, protection against caving is provided by vertical lagging, or steel cylinder casings from $\frac{1}{4}$ in. to $\frac{3}{4}$ in. thick may be used as described later. If water-bearing

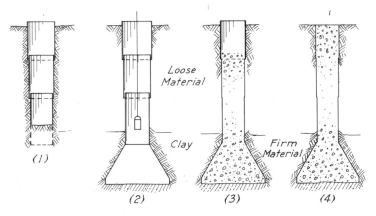

Fig. 22-5. Telescoping steel cylinders.

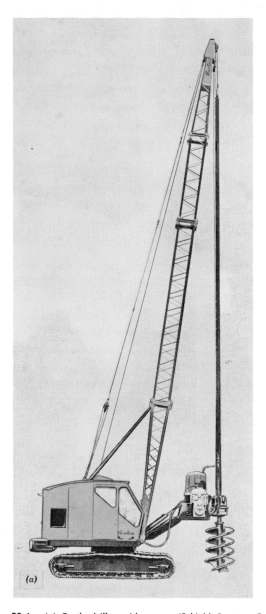

Fig. 22-6. (a) Earth driller with auger (Schield Bantam Co.).

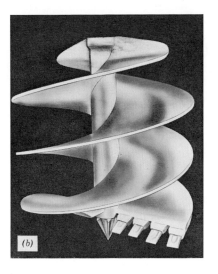

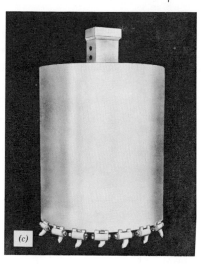

Fig. 22-6. Earth driller. (b) Auger drill. (c) Core barrel. (d) Bailing bucket.

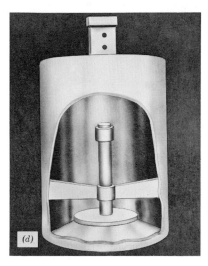

formations are encountered, water may be excluded from the well by steel cylinder casings, as will be explained. Lagging or steel casings may remain in place permanently or may be removed as the concreting progresses.

Auger Drill. An *auger drill* (Fig. 22-6b) is similar to a wood auger. It is mounted on the lower end of a power-driven solid or telescoping vertical shaft, or Kelley bar (Fig. 22-6a). When drilling operations start, the drill is placed in contact with the ground. As the shaft is rotated, the drill bores a hole in the ground as a wood auger drills a hole in wood. The auger has two cutting edges and from three to five helical turns or flights. When the drill has been rotated sufficiently to fill the helical turns with earth, the shaft and earth-laden auger are raised to the surface and spun around rapidly to throw the earth from the auger by centrifugal force. This operation forms a ridge of earth around the hole which must, of course, be disposed of. Reaming devices, which can be attached to the drill, are available for excavating holes larger in diameter than the drill or excavating bells at the bottom of piers (13, 20).

The auger drill is suitable for excavating clay, sand, gravel, some hardpans, and other material which will remain on the helical turns while the auger is being withdrawn.

Although used primarily for large buildings, small-diameter piers bored with earth augers through clay are sometimes used for small buildings such as residences. Pier foundations may be desirable when soil suitable for supporting the foundation is at a considerable distance below the ground surface, and especially when the soil is an expansive clay, as mentioned in Art. 19. The bottoms are often belled out. For wall-bearing buildings, the walls are supported on grade beams on top of the piers.

Bucket Drill. A *bucket drill* consists of a short steel cylinder or bucket mounted with its axis vertical on the lower end of a vertical shaft called a Kelley bar, as shown in Fig. 22-7. The bottom of the bucket is so constructed that, when the drill is rotated with its bottom in contact with the soil, it scoops up the soil, fills the bucket, and advances into the ground. One type of bucket is illustrated in Fig. 22-7. When the bucket is full, the shaft and bucket are raised and rotated horizontally to clear the hole. The bucket is then dumped through its movable bottom and is ready for another lowering and filling. Buckets with various diameters are used, depending on the diameter of the well and the equipment available. Wells with larger diameters than the buckets that drill them, and wells belled out at the bottom, can be drilled by attaching adjustable reamers or trimming arms to the bucket or shaft so that the trimmed earth falls into the bucket, as illustrated in Fig. 22-7 (13).

The bucket shown in Fig. 22-6c is called a *core barrel*. It is provided with replaceable teeth around its bottom edge. This type of bucket is suitable for excavating into solid or broken consolidated material of intermediate hardness.

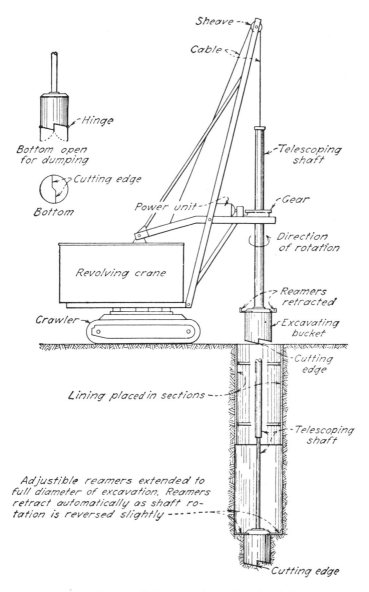

Sheave

Cable

Hinge

Bottom open
for dumping

Cutting edge

Bottom

Power unit

Telescoping
shaft

Gear

Direction
of rotation

Revolving crane

Crawler

Reamers
retracted

Excavating
bucket

Cutting
edge

Lining placed in sections

Telescoping
shaft

Adjustible reamers extended to
full diameter of excavation. Reamers
retract automatically as shaft rotation is reversed slightly

Cutting edge

Fig. 22-7. Well bored in clay with bucket drill.

The *bailing bucket* shown in Fig. 22-6d is designed to remove water or mud, which may contain small rocks. A valve in the bottom opens and admits the material while the bucket is being lowered, closes as it is being hoisted, and can be opened to discharge the contents. It is not rotated.

Protection Against Caving and Groundwater. The caving of soil being penetrated by auger and bucket drilling operations may be prevented by installing vertical wood lagging when necessary, as in the Chicago method illustrated in Fig. 22-7, or by inserting steel cylinder casings. These linings are placed in sections as the drilling progresses or after the excavation is completed, depending upon conditions. Steel casings are also employed where required to exclude groundwater encountered as the drilling progresses. When they are used, the bottom of the casing is kept far enough in advance of the excavation that a plug of earth which excludes the water is formed in the bottom portion of the casing. A steel casing may also be driven in advance of the excavation until it penetrates an impervious formation of soil or rock enough to form a water seal which excludes groundwater and enables the water to be pumped out. Penetration into the impervious formation may be obtained by impact on top of the casing or, when sealing in rock, by providing saw teeth on the bottom of the casing and rotating it as a drill while a vertical thrust is being exerted. The latter procedure is facilitated if the casing is somewhat smaller than the well. To avoid "lost ground," however, it is necessary to fill the annular space solidly between the casing and the well. Wood wedges have been used for this purpose below the permanent ground water level to avoid decay (13).

Lagging or steel casings may be left in place, or they may be removed for further use if financial reasons make it advisable. Some installations have the characteristics of cofferdams, and others have those of open caissons, which are described later.

Hammer-Grab. The *hammer-grab* or *Benoto drill*, shown in Fig. 22-8, is a device, several feet long and weighing $1\frac{1}{2}$ tons or more. It is a hammer similar in action to a drop hammer used in pile driving, but it has a grab on its lower end which is similar to an orange-peel or clam-shell bucket. The unit is operated by a power-driven cable hoist, by which it is alternately dropped and raised. The hammer-grab is operated in a steel cylinder casing which guides its fall. When the hammer-grab is dropped, the jaws of the grab are open. They penetrate or chop, by impact, into the material to be excavated. When the cable is hoisted, the jaws of the grab close and grab a load

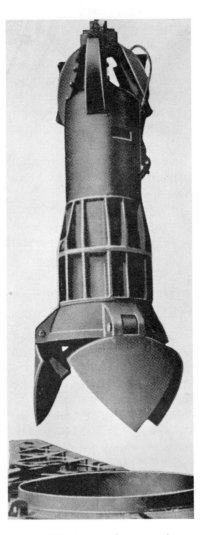

Fig. 22-8. Benoto hammer-grab.

of soil, and then hoist it to the surface and dump it. In addition to guiding the hammer-grab in its fall, the casing prevents the material being penetrated from caving and excludes groundwater. The length of the tube or casing is extended, as required, by adding sections. The sections are joined by a special interlocking device or butt welding.

When the material is difficult to penetrate, the jaws of the grab are locked open temporarily so that the material can be broken up by dropping the grab several times. The lower end of the casing has a toothed cutting edge. It may be kept slightly ahead of the grab; it may be kept 3 or 4 feet ahead to form an earth plug which excludes water from the casing if water-bearing soil is being penetrated; or, if hard dry material is being penetrated, the grab may be kept slightly ahead of the casing to facilitate the downward progress of the casing. After the well has been excavated to the required depth, its bottom is prepared to receive the pier, and concreting the pier starts. The casing is withdrawn progressively while the concrete is being placed. The casing is advanced and withdrawn by hydraulic rams, which exert longitudinal forces combined with partially reciprocating rotary motions.

The hammer-grab is suitable for excavating any type of material including solid rock. In a large-diameter well a "diving bell," or short vertical steel cylinder with an air lock on top, can be lowered into a well containing water to provide a working chamber where one or two men can work with pneumatic drills or place explosives for blasting. Such an arrangement can be used for the excavation of very hard ground or rock.

General Comments. The diameters and depths of piers placed by drilling depend upon the structural requirements, the depth to a formation capable of sustaining the loads and other geological conditions, the drilling equipment available, and other factors. There are no arbitrary limits on the diameters or depths of wells. When conditions are favorable, drilling is usually the most rapid method available of excavating for piers. In selecting a method for a specific project, relative costs and the time required are, of course, major factors for consideration. Wells for piers can be drilled in any type of material with appropriate equipment. A firm clay which does not require support against caving before the concrete for the pier is poured and which contains no water-bearing seams is the ideal soil for drilling, but ideal conditions are rarely found. Auger and bucket drills are only suitable for use in soil and some hardpans, but the hammer-grab drill can penetrate rock as well. Churn drills and special rotary drills are used in wells to excavate into rock formations and, if groundwater has been excluded, hand methods are also used.

Open-Caisson Method

Outline of Method. The open-caisson method consists of the following operations (Fig. 22-9).

1. *Constructing* the caisson, and preparing the site of the pier to receive it.

2. *Placing* the caisson over the site of the pier.

3. *Excavating* the soil on the interior of the caisson, and *advancing* the caisson so that its cutting edge is at or below the bottom of the excavation and continuing this process until the foundation stratum is reached.

4. *Sealing* the bottom of the caisson to exclude water and soil.

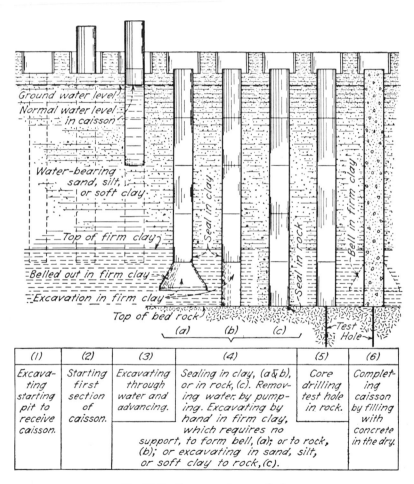

(1)	(2)	(3)	(4)	(5)	(6)
Excava-ting starting pit to receive caisson.	Starting first section of caisson.	Excavating through water and advancing.	Sealing in clay, (a & b), or in rock, (c). Removing water by pumping. Excavating by hand in firm clay, which requires no support, to form bell, (a); or to rock, (b); or excavating in sand, silt, or soft clay to rock, (c).	Core drilling test hole in rock.	Complet-ing caisson by filling with concrete in the dry.

Fig. 22-9. The open-caisson method.

5. *Preparing* the excavated space to receive concrete, and *examining* the foundation bed.

6. *Placing* the concrete to form the pier.

Construction. The caissons are usually cylindrical, from 2 ft. to 8 ft. or more in diameter, and are made of steel plates riveted or welded together or of reinforced concrete. The thickness of the steel plates depends upon the size of the caisson, upon the material to be penetrated, upon the method of advancing, and upon other factors. The thickness varies from $\frac{1}{4}$ in., or even less, to a maximum of about $\frac{3}{4}$ in. The cutting edges are often reinforced with steel bands placed on the inside. A steel caisson may be a single unit for the entire length, or its length may be increased by adding sections as the sinking progresses. The length of a reinforced concrete caisson is normally increased by pouring new sections, in lifts, as the sinking progresses.

A caisson is usually started in a sheeted *starting pit* above the groundwater level. To maintain the caisson in a vertical position it can be propped against the sides of the pit, but it is often necessary to erect towers for this purpose.

Excavating. The method used to excavate within a caisson depends upon the method used to advance it into the ground; therefore these two phases of the operation must be considered together. The various methods of performing each operation, however, will be listed separately. There are two methods for removing the soil from the interior of the caisson.

(*a*) Hand methods using the pick and shovel or the pneumatic spade to loosen the soil and to place it in buckets in which it is hoisted to the surface. Such methods are, of course, suitable for use above the groundwater level, and they are useful below the groundwater level only when the water which flows under the cutting edge and into the caisson can be controlled by pumping (Fig. 22-10*b*).

(*b*) Orange-peel and small clam-shell buckets which can be operated through water (Fig. 22-10*a*). These are often called *grab buckets* because they "grab" the soil and fill themselves.

Advancing. Methods of advancing the caisson into the soil are as follows.

(*a*) By the weight of the caisson itself. This is always a factor in

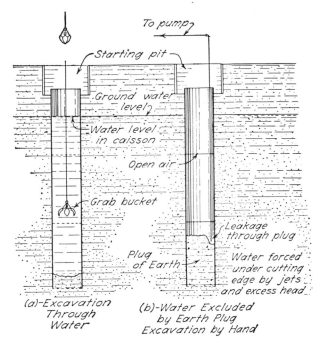

Fig. 22-10. Methods of excavating in open-caisson method.

advancing the caisson; and, in some soils, reinforced concrete caissons may have enough weight so that no other force need be applied.

(*b*) By loads applied to the top of the caisson. These may be large concrete blocks, steel rails, pig iron, etc.

(*c*) By driving the caisson with pile hammers. This procedure is applicable only to steel tubular caissons reinforced at the top and thick enough to stand driving. One hammer, acting on a beam across the top of the caisson, may be sufficient; or two hammers, acting simultaneously but not necessarily synchronized, may be required.

(*d*) By reducing the resistance to penetration with water jets around the cutting edge to loosen and displace the soil. Water jets supplement the weight of the caissons and are often used with loaded caissons or caissons driven with hammers.

(*e*) By reducing the resistance to penetration by drilling and blasting below the cutting edge to break up material that is difficult to penetrate, and by blasting near the cutting edge to jar the caisson loose momentarily and permit it to fall a short distance. These procedures are occasionally used to supplement other methods.

(*f*) By driving the caisson with hydraulic jacks. This is possible only when there is a load to jack against, as there usually is in underpinning.

The usual procedure consists of advancing the caisson by placing loads on its top and excavating by hand until the groundwater level is reached. Below this level, water will usually enter the caisson under the cutting edge at such a rate that it cannot be controlled satisfactorily by pumping unless large quantities of soil are carried into the caisson. Excavation is, therefore, continued by means of an orange-peel or clam-shell bucket. A serious objection to this procedure is the possibility of undermining adjacent footings by the *lost ground* brought into the caisson by the incoming water, even when excavating through water. If the soil being penetrated is fine sand this action is quite pronounced, but it may cause no difficulty in some clay soils. If the soil being penetrated is clay with seams of permeable water-bearing soil, it may be possible to use hand-excavation methods while the clay is being penetrated and to resort to grab buckets only while penetrating the permeable seams. Penetration may be facilitated by water jets if excavation is being made through water. In some soils, water jets may make the addition of loads to the top of the caisson unnecessary.

If the caisson is being driven with pile hammers or being forced down with hydraulic jacks, the cutting edge may be driven far enough in advance of the excavation so that the plug of soil in the bottom of the caisson, as shown in Fig. 22-10*b*, reduces the flow of water until it can be readily handled by pumping and is so slow that there is little ground lost. Under these circumstances the soil can be moved by hand methods.

Water Seal. If the pier is to be founded on firm clay or hardpan, the caisson is carried down far enough into the material to form a seal, as shown in Fig. 22-10*b*, 4, and any water present is pumped out. Bells for the enlarged pier bases are formed by excavating in the dry, using hand methods. If clay or hardpan lies immediately above rock which is to be used as a foundation bed, the seal is established (Fig. 22-9), 4, and excavation is carried on through these materials to rock, using the procedures just given, the clay walls being supported by sheeting or by whatever is necessary. Usually no support is required in hardpan, and often none is required for clay.

If the porous water-bearing soil continues until rock is reached, the caisson is carried to the rock and a seal must be established between the bottom of the caisson and the rock. Where the excavation has been carried on through a water-filled caisson, the rock is cleaned off as well as possible with a grab bucket or other devices, possibly with the aid of a diver who makes all possible preparation and examination of the foundation bed. A concrete seal is then placed in the bottom of the caisson, using a bottom-dump bucket. After this seal has set, the caisson is pumped out and is ready for concreting.

When the caisson has been driven or forced down with a hydraulic jack, an effort is made to drive the bottom of the caisson far enough into the rock to form a seal. If a plug of soil has been maintained in the bottom of the caisson to retard the flow of water enough to permit the use of hand excavation methods, this plug cannot be removed until the seal is established. Cement grout, pumped around the cutting edge, may be of assistance in this operation. An uneven or sloping rock surface adds greatly to the difficulty of making the seal.

If the various methods described for making a seal between the bottom of a caisson and the rock are unsuccessful, or if a seal placed through water is considered unsatisfactory because of the lack of opportunity for preparing and examining the foundation bed, the open caisson can finally be converted into a pneumatic caisson by placing a top on the caisson and attaching air locks. Any water is removed, and the work of preparing and investigating the foundation bed and of sealing the joint between the caisson and the rock is carried on under compressed air, as described under the pneumatic caisson method. It may be necessary to resort to this procedure before rock has been reached if boulders or other obstructions are encountered which cannot be passed in any simpler way. Layers of boulders are often found on top of bedrock.

Concreting. After the water seal has been established, the water is pumped out and the caisson is filled with concrete, using bottom-dump buckets, to complete the pier.

Concrete Piers with Structural-Steel Core. The capacity of concrete piers in steel-plate open caissons can be increased by inserting a structural-steel H-section (Fig. 22-11). Because of the introduction of the steel core, the bearing capacity at the surface of the rock stratum may be insufficient to carry the load transmitted by the pier. The required additional capacity is secured by drilling into the rock a hole whose diameter is equal to that of the outside of the shell. The H-section is carried several feet below the surface of the stratum. The shell and the hole in the rock are then filled with concrete, as shown in the

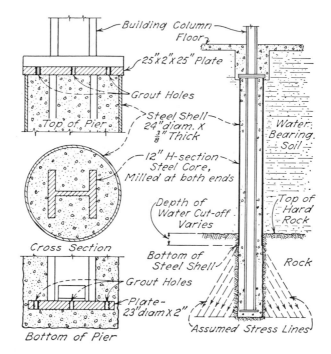

Fig. 22-11. Concrete pier with structural steel core.

figure. By this means, the pier load is distributed over a much greater area at the elevation of the bottom of the pier than it would be if the pier were supported on the surface of the rock. The assumed distribution of the stress in the rock is shown on the figure. It is determined by the allowable bond strength between the pier and the surrounding rock and by the assumed direction of the lines of stress.

In constructing this pier, the steel-caisson shell is driven to rock, the excavation being made through water. The hole in the rock is drilled deep enough to form a watertight seal after the caisson has been driven down into the rock. The caisson is then pumped out and the remainder of the rock excavation carried on in open air.

Pneumatic Caissons Method

Construction of Caisson. Pneumatic caissons are used for constructing building foundations that consist of piers carried through water-

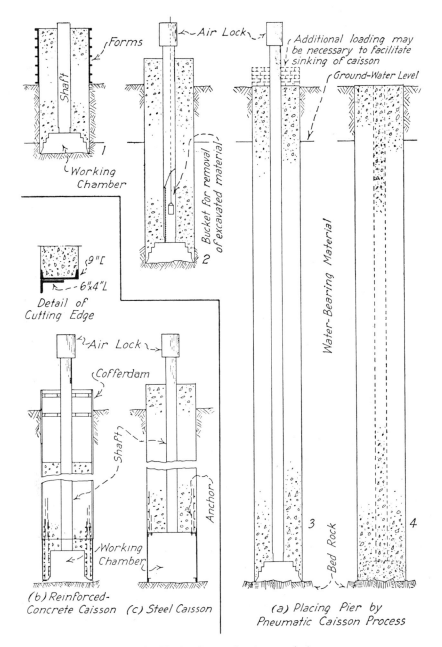

Forms

Shaft

1

Working
Chamber

Air Lock

Bucket for removal
of excavated material

2

9"⌐

6"x4"L

Detail of
Cutting Edge

Additional loading may
be necessary to facilitate
sinking of caisson

Ground-Water Level

Water-Bearing Material

Air Lock

Cofferdam

Shaft

Working
Chamber

Anchor

3

Bed Rock

4

(b) Reinforced-
Concrete Caisson   (c) Steel Caisson

(a) Placing Pier by
Pneumatic Caisson Process

Fig. 22-12.   Pneumatic-caisson method.

bearing material to bedrock. The essential parts of a pneumatic caisson are the *working chamber,* the *shaft,* and the *air locks,* as shown in Fig. 22-12*b*. The working chamber may be constructed of timber, steel, or reinforced concrete. The shaft is usually constructed of steel.

The pneumatic-caisson process is illustrated in Fig. 22-12*a*. The lower end of the caisson including the working chamber is first constructed and placed on the surface of the ground or in a hole excavated to receive it, as shown in 1.

Excavating and Advancing. Excavation is carried on in the working chamber, and the caisson sinks either because of its own weight or because a necessary load was placed on it. As soon as the ground-water level is passed by the cutting edge, water begins to rise in the working chamber; therefore the air locks are placed at the upper end of the shaft as shown in 2, and sufficient air pressure is applied to the working chamber to force out the water. Men can now work in the working chamber without the interference of water. As the caisson sinks, the pressure in the working chamber must be increased to balance the water presure.

The part of the caisson above the working chamber may be surrounded with a timber *cofferdam,* as shown in Fig. 22-12*b*, to hold back the earth and water as the caisson sinks. Concrete is placed in the cofferdam to form a part of the pier and to serve as a weight to assist in forcing the caisson down. Removable forms may be used instead of the cofferdams, as shown in *c*. The top of the concrete is always kept well above the top of the ground. Frequently, if required by the depth from the surface to rock, the entire pier is completed before the sinking starts.

The earth exposed in the working chamber is excavated by any convenient method, such as pick and shovel or air spade, and is hoisted to the surface in buckets through the air locks. If the material is quite fluid it may be disposed of by blowing it to the surface through a pipe, the air in the working chamber providing the necessary pressure. Spoil that is to be blown out is heaped over the end of a stiff hose placed on the bottom of the working chamber and connected to the pipe leading to the surface. A valve is provided so that this pipe may be closed when not in operation.

Water Seal and Concreting. When the cutting edge of the caisson has reached bedrock, as shown in 3 of Fig. 22-12*a*, the surface of the rock is prepared to support the pier. A layer of concrete thick enough to resist the hydrostatic pressure is placed in the bottom of the working chamber and allowed to set. This seals the caisson so that water cannot enter. The air pressure is released, the air locks and possibly the shaft are removed, and concrete is carefully placed under atmospheric pressure in the remaining portion of the working chamber and the shaft, as shown in 4. Care must be excerised to avoid air pockets and to overcome the effect of the shrinkage that occurs in the concrete while it is setting.

Advantages and Disadvantages. The advantages of the pneumatic process are as follows.

When properly operated, the only excavation required is that represented by the volume occupied by the pier, and therefore adjacent foundations are not undermined as they may be in the open-caisson process. An opportunity is afforded to examine and prepare the foundation bed properly to receive the pier. This is not possible in the usual form of the open-caisson process.

The disadvantages are as follows.

The depth below the groundwater level is limited to about 110 ft. because men cannot work safely in the air pressure required by greater depths. The length of shift, or working period, that men can endure without ill effects decreases as the required pressure increases. This condition and the relatively high wages paid result in high labor costs.

The cost is relatively high compared with that for other methods.

Combined Methods for Pier Construction

It is frequently not feasible to use one method for the construction of the entire depth of a well, and two or more methods may be combined.

If a stratum of water-bearing material, such as water-bearing gravel or sand, lies on top of a thick stratum of clay which is underlain with hardpan or rock, sheet piling may be driven through the top stratum of sand into the clay a sufficient distance to form a watertight seal. The rest of the depth may then be excavated by the Chicago method.

At the site of the Cleveland Union Terminal Building this condition existed, but the groundwater level was a few feet below the level at which the excavation for the well was started. The upper part of the well down to the groundwater level made use of horizontal sheeting, (Fig. 22-13). Below this, and extending to the surface of the clay, steel-sheet piles were used and the remaining distance was excavated by the Chicago method.

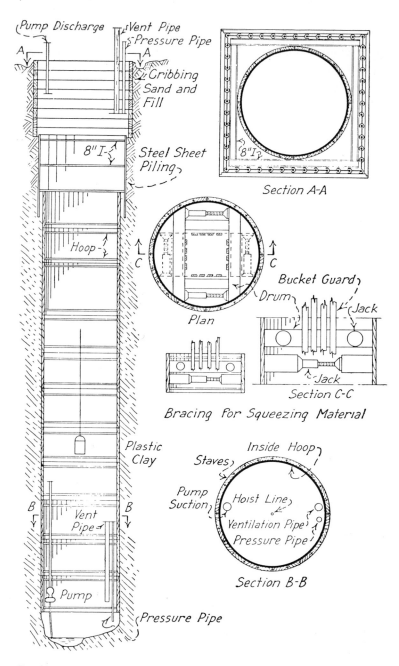

Fig. 22-13. Horizontal sheeting, steel-sheet piling, and lagging in a single well.

Another combination of methods, illustrated in Fig. 22-14a, has been developed to meet the situation in which a stratum of water-bearing gravel and boulders lies on top of the rock stratum where a pier is to rest, above which is a thick layer of clay. The Chicago method is used in the clay. Before the water-bearing gravel stratum is reached, the well is stepped out, as shown in the figure, to give sufficient room to drive steel-sheet piling through the gravel to rock. The bottom of the sheeted excavation is kept far enough above the top of the gravel stratum that the remaining clay acts as a seal to exclude water from the excavation. The sheet piling is driven into the bottom of the sheeted excavation and extends to rock. The piles are so driven that they form a seal between their lower ends and the rock; the enclosed earth gravel and boulders are cleaned out; the foundation

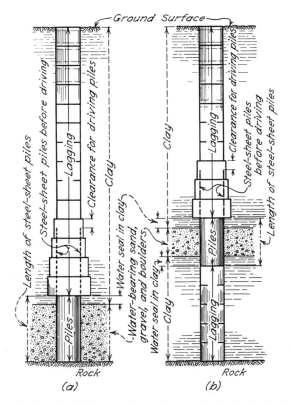

Fig. 22-14. Combined vertical wood lagging and steel-sheet piling.

bed is prepared to receive the pier; and the concrete pier is poured. If water-bearing strata are encountered between two layers of clay, they can be passed if sheet piling is used following this procedure (Fig. 22-14b), or they can be sealed off with steel cylinders with inside diameters large enough to clear the sheeting.

Because of their relatively low cost, open caissons may be used to penetrate a water-bearing stratum of sand, gravel, or silt; but they may be so arranged that locks can be placed on top of the dredging wells to convert them into pneumatic caissons. This procedure may be adopted as a precaution should material which the open caisson will not penetrate be encountered; or it may be considered desirable to secure the advantages of the pneumatic-caisson method in preparing the foundation bed and in filling the caisson with concrete.

23. DEEP BASEMENT WALLS

General Comments. The basements of tall buildings may extend several stories below the ground level and also below the groundwater level. The problems encountered in constructing basements and the methods employed for overcoming them are similar to some of those explained for pier foundations. Procedures for bracing basement walls to resist lateral pressures while the permanent building frame is being constructed, however, are quite complex. After the frame is in place, it resists these pressures.

The construction methods include the use of vertical and horizontal sheeting, sheet-pile cofferdams, and pneumatic-caisson cofferdams. Only in rare instances have open caissons been used for buildings because of the danger of undermining adjacent foundations and other underground works by excessive lost ground. They may be suitable, however, for use in areas which are not built up, or in some built-up areas if special precautions are taken to avoid settlement of adjacent buildings because of lost ground.

A combination of methods may be used. The upper portion of the excavation, above the groundwater level, may be protected by a single diaphragm of sheeting or sheet piling, and the lower portion by a double-wall steel-sheet piling cofferdam within which the basement wall is constructed, or a pneumatic-caisson cofferdam may be used for this portion.

The sheeting, sheet piling, or cofferdam surrounds the entire area to be excavated.

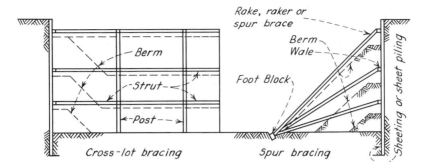

Fig. 23-1. Lateral bracing for sheeting or sheet piling.

Methods of Bracing. For relatively shallow excavations, vertical sheeting or sheet piling may be supported temporarily by sets of inclined timber braces or struts called *rakes* or *rakers*. The upper end of each brace bears against a wale and the lower end against a timber *foot block*, shown on the right-hand side of Fig. 23-1, all struts bearing against a single foot block. Such bracing is sometimes called *spur bracing*.

Before the bracing can be placed, the interior excavation is carried down to the elevation of the underside of the lower basement floor or to the level below which another method of construction is to be used. Portions of the earth to be excavated, called *berms*, are left in place, as shown by the dashed lines in the figure, until the wales and inclined struts can be placed successively to support the sheeting or sheet piling. The basement wall is then constructed inside the sheeting or sheet piling, the bracing being altered as required to serve as temporary bracing for the wall. The bracing must be wedged tightly in place to minimize movement. Strictly speaking, berms are horizontal surfaces that form breaks in earth slopes. The term, however, is often used as defined above.

The bracing method which has been described cannot be used for deep excavations. For this condition, bracing is carried across the entire area to be excavated to the opposite side of the excavation from which it receives its support, as shown on the left-hand side of Fig. 23-1. This is called *cross-lot bracing*. Normally, it would extend in both directions across the excavation. It may be temporary timber bracing, and if so it must be arranged to clear the members of the permanent structure. The excavation is carried on, as shown by the dashed lines in the figure, leaving temporary berms for lateral support while the bracing is being installed progressively downward. To reduce the cost, members of the permanent structure may be installed instead of temporary bracing. In both cases the supporting members must be stressed with wedges or jacks to minimize any lateral movement.

Soldier Beams and Breast Boards. A common method for basement excavation consists of vertical wide-flange *soldier beams* driven full length at intervals into the ground before excavating, with horizontal timber *breast boards* or sheeting inserted between them and supported on their flanges as the excavation proceeds. This method is illustrated in Fig. 23-2.

The soldier beams are spaced a few feet apart. The breast boards are timber planks, varying in thickness from 2 to 4 in. and long enough to provide end bearing on the flanges of the beams. They are placed as the excavation progresses and may be supported against the inner flanges (*a*) or against the outer flanges (*b*). Wedges are driven between the breast boards and the flanges to force them against the earth, which is trimmed to receive the boards.

The soldier beams are supported laterally by wales placed at intervals along their height, which are in turn supported by spur or cross-lot bracing (Fig. 23-1).

For the arrangement in *a*, the wall is cast between the soldier beams,

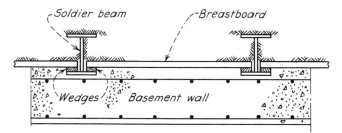

(a) Breastboards supported by inner flanges

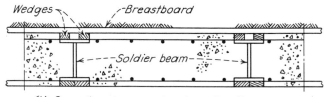

(b) Breastboards supported by outer flanges

Fig. 23-2. Soldier beam and breastboard construction.

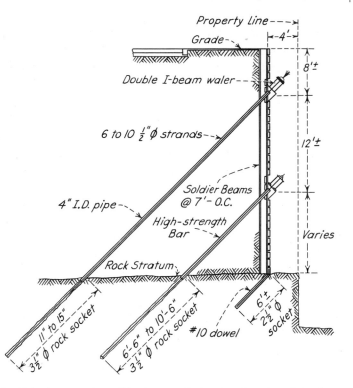

Fig. 23-3. Tiebacks supporting soldier beams. *Engineering News-Record*, April 18, 1961.

and for that shown in b, in front of the beams to which it is anchored. The wall is reinforced as required by the lateral pressures.

Instead of spur or cross-lot bracing, soldier beams may be supported by tiebacks with one end of each anchored in rock outside the area to be excavated and the other attached to a wale (Fig. 23-3). Rock in which to anchor the tiebacks must be available for this method to be used. After the soldier beams have been driven, and excavation and placing of breast boards to a depth just below the top line of wales have been completed, a pipe is driven at an angle of 45 degrees from the wale to the top of the rock formation. A socket is then drilled to the required depth in the rock formation by a drill operating through the pipe. The pipe and socket are cleaned out with an air or water jet. The lower end of the wire tendon is grouted in the socket with high-early-strength cement grout. The tendon is prestressed by jacks and anchored to the wale. This procedure is repeated for each tendon located at each soldier beam. The wales consist of double I-beams set at an angle to receive the tendons as shown in the figure. If necessary the lower ends of the soldier beams are anchored as shown. The many advantages of this procedure, when it can be used because of unobstructed working space, are apparent. It was originated by Spencer, White and Prentis, Inc. These comments are based on reference 16.

Double-Wall Steel-Sheet-Pile Cofferdam. As illustrated in Fig. 23-4a, it is assumed that a deep basement and foundation are to be constructed at a site which explorations have shown is underlain progressively downward with a layer of filled material, an unconsolidated permeable water-bearing formation, a relatively impervious rock formation with low bearing capacity, and finally, sound bedrock on which the foundation is to be supported. The basement extends into the impervious rock with low bearing capacity.

The fill is supported by a single row of steel-sheet piles or in some other manner, with spur bracing installed as the enclosed area is excavated, as shown in *a*. Two rows of interlocking steel-sheet piles are then driven through the permeable water-bearing formation until their bottoms form a water seal in the relatively impervious rock formation. Steel diaphragms are installed at intervals between the two rows of piles to form cells. The material is then excavated from the cells. As the excavation proceeds, wales and braces, consisting of I-beams, are installed to resist the lateral pressure of the earth and water. In this manner, a double-wall steel-sheet-pile cofferdam is constructed completely around the area to be excavated. Finally, a trench is excavated through the relatively impervious rock with low bearing capacity to bedrock. No lateral support is required in this formation.

All the preparations required for starting the construction of the outside wall, as shown in *b*, have now been completed. First, the trench is filled with concrete, using forms on the face to be exposed in the basement. Above this point the wall forms are constructed in sections in the cofferdam and concreted, the original wales and cross braces being removed progressively as required and replaced with wales and shorter braces bearing against the completed concrete and the exposed row of sheet piles. The horizontal construction joints between successive wall sections are keyed to preserve alignment and are provided with water stops.

While the construction of the outside walls is under way, the interior portion of the basement is excavated, leaving berms of unexcavated material to provide lateral support. These berms and the top of the

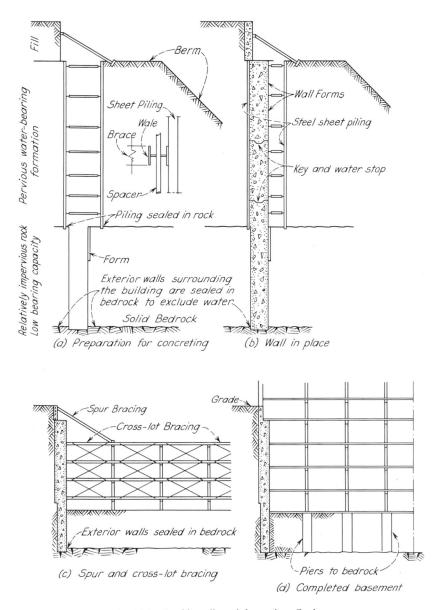

Fig. 23-4. Double-wall steel-sheet-pile cofferdam.

general excavation are lowered progressively to permit the installation of the cross-lot bracing, as illustrated in Figs. 23-1 and 23-4c, the spur bracing being carried by this bracing. The use of spur bracing can be avoided by extending the top of the outer row of sheeting to the ground surface, if conditions permit.

After the cross-lot bracing is in place, the piers supporting the interior columns can be constructed, and finally the basement floor, as shown in d, together with the necessary waterproofing and underdrainage, can be installed as described in Art. 24. The remainder of the building is then constructed (d).

This discussion is based on references 14, 15, and 18, to which the reader is referred for descriptions of actual projects in which these procedures were used.

Open-Caisson Cofferdams. Monolithic open-caisson cofferdams have been used in excavating for deep basements. One example is illustrated by the half section in Fig. 23-5. The caisson, which is cylindrical with an external diameter of 187 ft., was sunk with its cutting edge 91 ft. below the ground surface and sealed in compact clay. The diameter at the cutting edge is about 8 in. larger than that of the upper portion of the caisson. The resulting 4-in. annular space which surrounds the caisson was injected full of bentonite slurry, which acted as a lubricant to facilitate sinking and as waterproofing for the excavation. The portions of the structure shown by the heavy black areas were constructed progressively as the soil under the cutting edge was removed and the caisson sank. Further details are given in reference 19, on which these comments are based. The architect was Fritz Jenny.

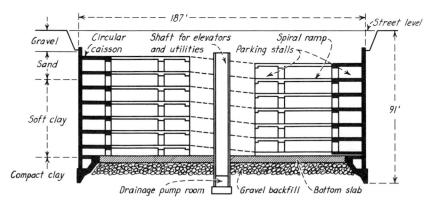

Fig. 23-5. Open-caisson cofferdam.

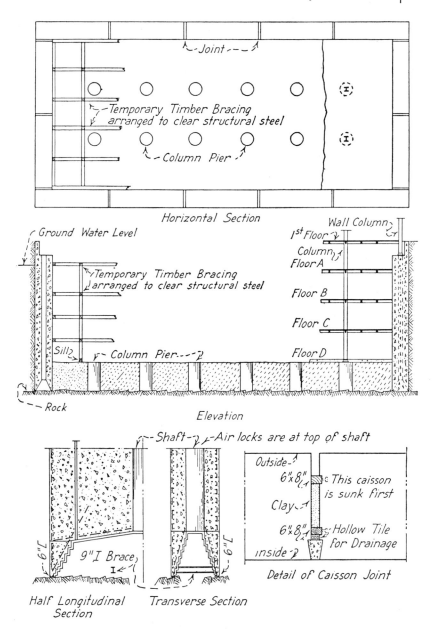

Horizontal Section

Elevation

Half Longitudinal
Section

Transverse Section

Detail of Caisson Joint

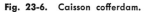

Fig. 23-6.   Caisson cofferdam.

Pneumatic-Caisson Cofferdams. The exterior walls of deep basements may be constructed by the pneumatic-caisson method and consist of a cofferdam of rectangular reinforced concrete caissons (Fig. 23-6). Each caisson is sunk to rock, sealed, air locks removed, and the working chamber and shafts filled with concrete. Excavation and bracing can then proceed. See p. 186.

Well-Point Method. The well-point method for excavation in water-bearing material consists of surrounding the area to be excavated by one or more rows of closely spaced well points placed along each side and lowering the water table in that area by pumping the water through the well points. The excavation within the area can then be carried on in the dry. A well point is a pipe provided with a point at its lower end and with a screen or filter along the lower 3 or 4 ft. of its length. Some types of well points are designed for driving with a maul, whereas others are designed for jetting into position. The well points are set about 3 ft. apart, the top of each point being connected to a header pipe connected to a pump. The water level may be lowered as much as 20 or 30 ft. Greater lowering may be accomplished by arranging well points in two or more vertical stages. This method is used chiefly in trench excavation and in unwatering the whole area occupied by a building, but is also applicable to excavation for piers. It may be necessary to provide sheeting to keep banks from caving, but the sheeting does not need to be watertight.

Grouting Soil and Rock Formations. Certain soils can be made more stable and more impervious, and structural defects in rock formations such as cracks, joints, fissures, and cavities which weaken them or cause them to be permeable can be filled, by injecting grout into them under pressure. The grouts used may be chemical solutions or mixtures of water and portland cement, portland cement and finely ground sand, or clay.

Various methods are used for chemical grouting. In general, each makes use of two solutions which react chemically when mixed and gel or solidify. They may be mixed in the formation by injecting one and then the other. This is called a *two-shot method.* In the *one-shot method,* the two chemicals are mixed immediately before or during injection and gel at a predetermined time after injection. Injections are made by specially designed pumps and connections which force solutions into the formation through a driven pipe, a cased drill hole, or an uncased drill hole, depending upon the character of the formation. Techniques are available for confining the grout to desired locations. After the grouting has been completed, the formations treated become more stable and relatively impermeable.

One chemical grouting method makes use of a mixture of sodium silicate and calcium chloride. Another utilizes a mixture of acrylamide and methylenebisacrylamide and is called AM-9 Chemical Grout (22). Others are in use, and still others doubtless will be developed. Chemical grouting may be effective in gravel and sand formations but not in silt or silty sand. It has been used successfully in some hardpans.

Portland cement, portland cement and fine sand, and clay grouting are extensively used to make rock foundations for dams more impermeable or more stable, but these methods are rarely, if ever, used in constructing foundations for buildings. The grouts formed by mixing these materials with water are pumped under pressure into holes drilled in rock foundations.

Injection procedures are expensive and involve uncertainties because of unknown subsurface conditions, and the results are sometimes disappointing. The operations are complex and require skilled and experienced operators.

24. DRAINAGE, DAMPPROOFING, AND WATERPROOFING OF BASEMENTS

Introduction. Basements whose floors are above the groundwater level must often be protected against dampness and infiltration of rainwater which penetrates permeable backfills but is under little if any pressure. Such protection is called *dampproofing*. Basements below the groundwater level must be protected to resist water infiltration and pressures caused by water under hydrostatic pressure. At any point on an exposed wall, the latter is equal to the unit weight of water multiplied by the vertical distance of the point below the groundwater surface or, in pound and foot units this pressure equals 62.4 y. This pressure may also exist on the underside of basement floors unless it is relieved in some manner.

Dampproofing. Water in the pores of a backfill may pass through cracks in a basement wall, through small but continuous passages in permeable concrete or masonry units, or through defective joints between these units. Moisture from wet or damp backfills may also penetrate walls by capillary action through continuous channels of capillary size, causing the interior surfaces of the walls to be damp and contributing by evaporation to the humidity of the inside air.

Dampproofing may be divided into various stages, some of which may not be required under favorable conditions, for example, walls not adversely affected by dampness, an arid climate, or impermeable

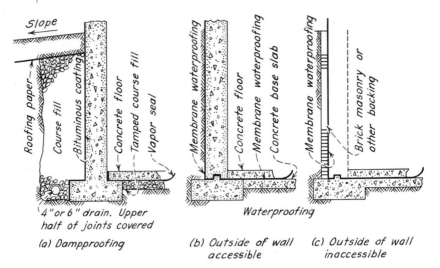

Fig. 24-1. Dampproofing and waterproofing basements.

backfill. These stages, some of which are illustrated in Fig. 24-1a are as follows.

1. Drainage of surface water away from the building by sloping the ground surface and conducting the rainwater from downspouts, which discharge on the ground surface, away from the building in paved channels.

2. Applying a dampproof coating to the exterior surfaces of the portions of exterior walls below the ground surface to increase their resistance to moisture penetration. This coating may consist of one of several materials which include:

(*a*) Bituminous materials applied in liquid form by brushing or spraying or in plastic form by troweling.

(*b*) One or two coats of portland cement mortar, which may include a water repellent, troweled on or pneumatically placed to give a smooth final surface finish.

The coating in *a* can be applied directly to smooth concrete surfaces, but if the surface is rough, or if the coating is to be applied to the surface of a masonry wall, a smooth mortar coating (*b*) should first be applied. The latter coating may be sufficient without the former.

The coatings described will seal a wall against the passage of moisture by capillary action from a damp or wet backfill, and of water filtering in through minor defects, but they are, of course, not effective in sealing cracks that develop after they are applied.

3. Providing granular fills under floors and installing vapor seals. Concrete floors laid directly on fine-grained soils tend to draw moisture from the soil into a basement by capillary action. Such a floor should always be laid on a tamped granular base from 4 to 6 in. thick, made of gravel, crushed rock, or sometimes cinders. As an additional precaution against moisture penetration, a layer of heavy roll roofing or a *4-mil polyethylene film* may be laid on the top surface of the granular base, care being used to avoid puncturing the vapor barrier when placing the concrete. Since free water is not present, or should not be, the edges of the sheeting need only be lapped but not sealed.

4. Installing a backfill drainage system to keep rainwater and wet soil away from basement walls. Included in this system are the *footing drains* which discharge into a storm sewer or, when feasible, into a *dry well*. A dry well is a pit excavated in permeable soil, or one having its bottom in such soil, and filled with gravel or crushed rock. It may also consist of a lined pit with a cover but no bottom, not filled.

The footing drains consist of 4- or 6-in. drain tile perforated or laid with open joints. The upper half of open joints is covered with strips of roll roofing to exclude soil. The drain tile are surrounded with gravel or crushed rock. A *blanket drain* of this material, at least 12 in. thick, is placed against the wall and extends upward to within a foot or so of the ground surface. The remainder of the backfill consists of ordinary soil tamped in place. The portion of the backfill above the top of the blanket drain is ordinary soil to support vegetation and to prevent the free access of surface water into the blanket drain. The latter objective may be accomplished more effectively by placing a strip of roll roofing over the top of the blanket drain and extending it into the ordinary soil. This accomplishes the further objective of preventing the ordinary soil from working into the drain.

There are other less important factors which deserve consideration. In residence construction, the basement may occupy only a portion of the area under the first floor, thereby leaving an exposed ground surface. Fine-grained soil may serve as a "wick" in drawing moisture into the basement from the underlying soil by capillary action. This action can be reduced or prevented by covering the exposed surface with a heavy polyethylene film held in place, especially at the joints, by earth. Crawl spaces should be treated in the same manner.

Dampproofing coatings are sometimes placed on the inside surface of exterior walls. Such coatings of either bituminous materials or cement mortar may eventually lose their bond with the wall and fail. If they are used, special care should be taken to insure good bonding.

Waterproofing. The portion of a basement below the groundwater level must be designed to exclude water and to resist the earth and any hydrostatic pressures to which it is subjected. The procedures followed in a given case to accomplish these objectives depend upon prevailing conditions.

An extensively used method for waterproofing basements consists of providing a continuous bituminous membrane around the portions of the outside walls that are below the groundwater level and on the underside of the basement floor (Fig. 24-1*b*). This membrane is built up of three to five or more layers or plies of bituminous saturated felt, or cotton fabric, or a combination of these materials. It is sealed together and held to the wall surface with coal-tar pitch mopped on hot, as it would be in constructing a built-up roofing surface as described in Art. 77, but without a gravel outer surface.

A surface to which a membrane is to be applied should be smooth and dry. A unit masonry surface will usually require a coat of smooth troweled portland cement plaster to provide a smooth surface. The surface is mopped with hot pitch before the first ply is applied, and the exposed outer surface is also mopped.

A wall membrane should be protected against indentation by the backfill and abrasion caused by its settlement by a coat of portland cement mortar, a layer of asphalt-impregnated fiber board, or preferably a single wythe of brick masonry.

Before placing a floor membrane, a tamped base of gravel or crushed rock 4 in. or more thick must be provided. A cement mortar or concrete leveling bed at least 1 in. thick is placed on this base to receive the membrane.

Finally, a concrete basement floor slab is placed. The membrane must be continuous under all columns, interior walls, and exterior walls, as shown in the figures. The membrane must also be continuous across the joint between the floor and exterior wall membranes.

The wall must be designed to resist the lateral earth and water pressures, and the floor to resist any hydrostatic uplift pressures that may develop.

Obviously, the basement cannot be excavated and the procedure just outlined carried out if the groundwater cannot be lowered below the basement floor level during the construction period. The only means of doing so is by pumping. Methods of constructing basements below the groundwater surface are considered in Art. 23.

If the exterior surface of the basement wall is accessible, the membrane and its protection are applied to this surface (Fig. 24-1*b*). If it is not accessible, because of an adjacent building or the construction procedure adopted to exclude water during basement excavation or to prevent caving of the embankment, the procedure is modified, as shown in Fig. 24-1*c*.

According to the modified procedure, the protective wythe of brick masonry is placed, rigidly supported against outward movement and plastered with a coat of portland cement mortar. The membrane is then applied to this surface. Finally, the wall is constructed with the protective layer serving as one side of the form if the wall is of concrete. If it is a masonry wall, any spaces between the outer surface of the wall and the masonry must be filled tightly with mortar or grout.

The quantity of water that must be pumped from a basement excavation depends upon the groundwater level and the permeability of the soil. If the basement walls penetrate into a clay stratum which acts as a water seal, the quantity may be relatively small. Under such conditions, it may prove desirable to replace the built-up membrane under the basement floor with a vapor seal, provide a tile drainage system in the granular base, discharge this system into a pit called a *sump,* and elevate the water collected by means of an automatic electric *sump pump* which discharges intermittently into a storm sewer. Under these conditions no uplift pressure is exerted on the underside of the basement floor.

Basements extending as many as six stories below the ground surface have been constructed. The pneumatic-caisson cofferdam surrounding the building, carried to rock, and sealed against water penetration as illustrated in Fig. 23-5 has been used extensively in New York City but its use has declined markedly because of the development of less costly methods. Multistory basement walls are also constructed in double-wall steel-sheet-pile cofferdams carried to rock and sealed to exclude water, as shown in Fig. 23-4. In such cases, the walls are constructed so as not to require membrane waterproofing. Drainage systems are also provided under the bottom basement floor, the water that accumulates is removed by sump pumps, and no uplift pressures develop.

Construction joints in walls not protected by membranes must be sealed with noncorrosive metal waterstops which permit movement without rupture.

References

1. Ralph B. Peck, Walter E. Hanson and Thomas H. Thornburn, *Foundation Engineering*, John Wiley and Sons, 1953.
2. N. M. Newmark, *Influence Charts for Computation of Stresses in Elastic Foundations*, Engineering Experiment Station, Series 338, University of Illinois, 1942.
3. A. Casagrande, "The Structure of Clay and Its Importance in Foundation Engineering," *Journal of Boston Society of Civil Engineers*, April, 1932.
4. F. Kogler and A. Scheidig, "Druckverteilung im Baugrunde" (Pressure Distribution in Building Soil), *Bautechnik*, 1927, Nos. 29 and 31; 1928, Nos. 15 and 17; 1929, Nos. 18 and 52.
5. *Building Code Requirements for Excavations and Foundations*, American Standards Association, A56.1-1952.
6. M. L. Enger, *Transactions American Society of Civil Engineers*, No. 85, 1921, p. 1581.
7. W. S. Housel, "A Penetration Method for Measuring Soil Resistance," *Proceedings of American Society for Testing Materials*, Vol. 35, 1935.
8. A. E. Cummings, *Lectures on Foundation Engineering*, Circular Series 60, University of Illinois, Engineering Experiment Station, 1949.
9. Karl Terzaghi and Ralph B. Peck, *Soil Mechanics in Engineering Practice*, John Wiley and Sons, 1948.
10. Charles Terzaghi, "Science of Foundations," *Transactions of the American Society of Civil Engineers*, Vol. 93, 1929.
11. H. A. Christine, "Boring Machine Digs Wells for Concrete Piers," *Engineering News-Record*, July 28, 1932.
12. Construction Methods. "Rotary Drills Speed Caisson Shaft Construction in Wet and Dry Soils," November, 1932.
13. "Big Augers Go Deep So Big Buildings Can Go High," *Engineering News-Record*, May 25, 1961, p. 32.
14. Robert C. Johnson, "Deep Foundations for Pittsburgh Skyscrapers," *Engineering News-Record*, December 7, 1950, p. 39.
15. Robert C. Johnson and Nicholas W. Koziakin, "Foundation Design and Methods Cut Skyscraper Cost," *Engineering News-Record*, July 24, 1958, p. 34.
16. "Tiebacks Remove Clutter in Excavation," *Engineering News-Record*, June 8, 1961, p. 34.
17. Edward E. White, "Deep Foundations in Soft Chicago Clay," *Engineering News-Record*, November, 1958, p. 36.
18. "Chemicals Seal Foundation for New York Building," *Civil Engineering*, October, 1957, p. 47.
19. "Caissons Dig Out a Seven-Story Basement," *Engineering News-Record*, July 6, 1961, p. 42.
20. Ralph B. Peck and Sidney Berman, "Recent Practice for Foundations of High Buildings in Chicago," *Symposium on the Design of High Buildings*, Golden Jubilee Congress, University of Hong Kong Press, 1961.
21. *Construction Methods*, August, 1957.
22. R. H. Carol, *Soils and Soil Engineering*, Prentice-Hall, 1960.
23. Chester W. Campbell, "Chemicals Seal Foundation of New York Building." *Civil Engineering*, October, 1957, p. 47.
24. "3 Uses of Chemical Grout Show Versatility," *Engineering News-Record*, May 31, 1962, p. 68.
25. "Pile Foundations," 4th Ed., American Iron and Steel Institute.

4 Masonry wall construction

25. DEFINITIONS AND GENERAL DISCUSSION

This article is concerned with definitions and comments which apply to all types of masonry construction used in buildings, but it does not consider the details of various types; Arts. 26 to 29 are devoted to these details. The specific code requirements for wall thickness, bonding of masonry units to form walls, anchoring of walls to other walls and other structural members, fire-resistance ratings, and other factors are assembled in Art. 30 to avoid repetition.

Walls constructed of masonry are used to enclose buildings to keep out the weather and make them usable and to subdivide the floor areas as required. They may carry their share of the weight of a building and other loads, they may carry only their own weight, or they may be carried by the structural frame of the building. They serve as barriers to the transmission of heat and sound and may be required to resist the spread of fire.

Definitions

Masonry may be defined as a built-up construction or combination of building units of such materials as clay, shale, concrete, glass, gypsum, or stone, set in mortar, or plain concrete (1). Masonry may consist wholly or in part of *hollow masonry units* or *solid masonry units* laid contiguously in mortar.

The various types of masonry units are illustrated and described in subsequent articles of this chapter.

Mortar may be defined as a plastic mixture of cementitious materials, fine aggregates, and water, used to bond masonry or other structural units. Mortar of pouring consistency is called *grout* (1).

Classes of Walls. Walls are divided into many classes according to their positions, functions, and types of construction.

apron wall or apron. Portion of spandrel wall between windowsill and floor level or between a sill and the head of the window below. See Fig. 25-1*a*.

bearing wall. One that supports any vertical load in addition to its own weight (1).

blank wall. See *dead wall.*

cavity wall. One built of masonry units or of plain concrete, or a combination of these materials, arranged to provide an air space within the well, with or without insulating material. The inner and outer parts or wythes of the wall are tied together with metal ties (1).

composite wall. See *faced wall.*

curtain wall. An exterior nonbearing wall built between columns or piers and not supported at each story. This definition is used the most often in building codes, but the term is also considered to be synonymous with panel wall.

dead wall. One without openings; also a *blank wall.*

division wall. One used to divide the floor area of a building into separate parts for fire protection, for different uses, for restricted occupancy, or for other purposes. More commonly called a *partition.*

dwarf wall. A wall or partition that does not extend to the ceiling.

enclosure wall. See *panel wall.*

faced wall. One in which the masonry facing and the backing are of different materials and are bonded to exert a common reaction under load (1); also called *composite wall.*

fire wall. One constructed to subdivide a building to restrict the spread of fire and extending continuously from the foundation through the roof. A *fire division wall* is similar in function to a fire wall but is not necessarily continuous from the foundation through the roof.

foundation wall. One built below the ground level, below the curb level, or below the floor level immediately above the ground level. See Fig. 25-1*b*.

grouted masonry wall. A wall made with clay brick or solid concrete brick units, in which the horizontal or bed joints are made in the usual manner and the vertical joints between wythes are filled by grout poured as the work progresses.

hollow wall. One of masonry arranged to provide an air space within the wall between the inner and outer parts or wythes of the wall (1). If the outer and inner wythes are bonded together with masonry units, it is called a *masonry-bonded hollow wall.* If they are bonded with metal ties, it is called a *cavity wall.*

inclosure wall. See *panel wall.*

knee wall. A low interior wall whose top abuts against a sloping ceiling. Commonly used in attics under sloping roofs.

nonbearing wall. A wall that supports no vertical load other than its own weight (1).

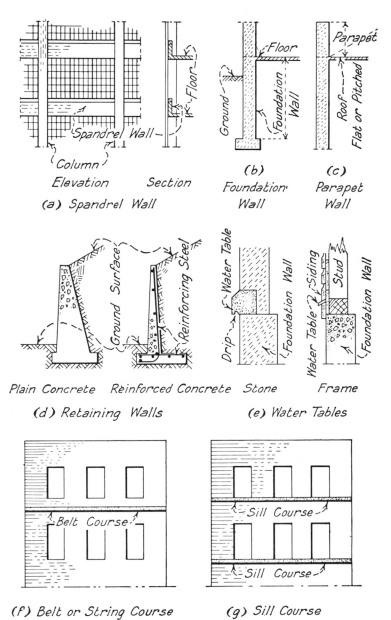

Spandrel Wall—

Column

Elevation   Section

(a) Spandrel Wall

(b)
Foundation
Wall

(c)
Parapet
Wall

Plain Concrete   Reinforced Concrete   Stone   Frame

(d) Retaining Walls   (e) Water Tables

Belt Course

Sill Course

Sill Course

(f) Belt or String Course   (g) Sill Course

Fig. 25-1. Walls and parts of walls.

panel wall. A nonbearing wall built between columns in skeleton construction and wholly supported at each story. This corresponds to the usual building code definition, but panel walls are usually called *curtain walls;* also called *enclosure walls.*

parapet wall. That part of any wall entirely above the roof (1). Also called a *parapet.* See Fig. 25-1c.

partition. An interior wall one story or less in height which subdivides the floor area of a building.

party wall. One on an interior lot line used or adapted for joint service between two buildings (1).

reinforced grouted brick masonry wall. Grouted brick masonry wall in which reinforcement is provided in the horizontal or bed joints and in the grouted vertical joints between wythes; also called *reinforced brick masonry wall.*

retaining wall. A free-standing wall whose chief function is to resist the lateral pressure of earth or other granular material. See Fig. 25-1d.

sandwich wall panels. Wall panels constructed of two thin slabs, usually of reinforced concrete, separated by a core of rigid heat-insulating material and connected with some form of metal ties.

solar screen. A perforated exterior wall used as a sunshade for the principal exterior wall.

tilt-up wall. One constructed in a horizontal position and tilted into its final vertical position by means of a crane or otherwise.

veneered wall. One having a facing of masonry or other material securely attached to the backing, but not so bonded as to exert a common reaction under load (1).

Parts of Masonry Walls

apex stone. The stone at the junction of the two inclined copings of a gable. Also called a *saddle stone.* See Fig. 25-2e.

arcade. A series of arches including the supporting piers or columns; also a covered passageway involving a series of arches.

arch. A curved construction over an opening made up of masonry units arranged to transmit the superimposed load laterally to the sides of the opening. See the next sections on parts and types of arches.

back. The inside surface of a wall.

bracking. The material included between the facing and the back; also called *back-up.*

back plaster. A coat of plaster applied to the inner surface of the facing of an exterior wall before the backing is placed, to improve the resistance of the wall to moisture penetration. Sometimes placed on the outer surface of the backing before the facing is placed.

base course. Usually a course of weather-resistant stone placed just above the ground level; also called a *plinth* and a *water table.*

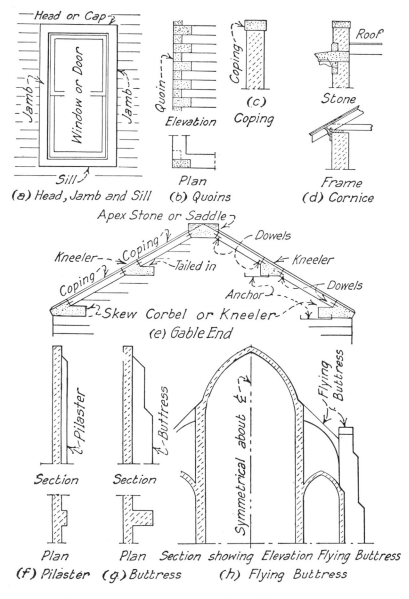

Fig. 25-2. Parts of a wall.

bed joint. See *joint.*

belt course. A horizontal band of masonry which runs across the face of a wall, flush with the wall surface or projecting, and is either plain or molded; also called a *string course.* See Fig. 25-1*f.*

bond. The interlocking of masonry units in the face of a wall by overlapping them in such a manner as to break the continuity of vertical joints. See Fig. 26-2.

bonder. A masonry unit which ties two or more wythes of the wall together; also called a *header* (1). See Figs. 26-4 and 27-5*c.*

build joint or build. See *joint.*

buttress. A vertical projection built into the face or back of a wall to increase its lateral rigidity or to support one end of a beam or girder. Similar to a *pilaster* but with a greater projection. See Fig. 25-2*f* and *g.*

cap. Upper member forming the top of a column, pier, chimney, etc.

collar joint. See *joint.*

coping. Exposed top course of a wall, such as a parapet wall, to protect the wall from the weather and provide a finish. See Fig. 25-2*c* and *e.*

corbel. A horizonal projection on the face of a wall, pier, or chimney formed by one or more courses, each projecting over the course below. May be a short bracket or a corbel course.

cornice. A horizontal projecting member at or near the top of an exterior wall, usually molded for decorative effect; also a molding at the junction of the side walls and ceiling of a room. See Fig. 25-2*d.*

counterflashing. See *flashing.*

course. A continuous horizontal layer of masonry units forming part of a wall.

dado. See *wainscot.*

drip. A groove along the bottom of the projecting portion of a sill, belt course, or coping which causes water to drip rather than follow along the face of a wall. See Figs. 25-1*e* and 27-1*b.*

engaged pier. A pier constructed as an integral part of a wall. Same as *wall pier, buttress,* or *pilaster.*

facade. The face of a building, usually the front or principal face.

face. The outer surface of a wall.

facing. The material forming the face of a wall.

flashing. Strips, usually, of sheet metal built into the joints of masonry walls and in other locations, such as at the junction of a roof and wall or chimney and in roof valleys. *Through-wall flashing* is flashing that extends through the entire thickness of a wall. See Fig. 25-7. *Counterflashing* is flashing built into a joint and extending downward over upturned flashing to keep water from penetrating between the wall surface and the flashing. See Fig. 25-7.

flying buttress. A masonry pier placed at some distance from a wall and connected to it by an inclined arch. Flying buttresses are more effective than buttresses in transmitting the thrusts of arched or vaulted roofs to the ground. They were developed for medieval Gothic cathedrals but are not used in modern buildings except those patterned after the older structures. See Fig. 25-2*h.*

footing. The part of a wall in contact with the ground, designed to spread the wall load over a sufficient area so that the allowable bearing capacity of the soil is not exceeded. See Fig. 16-1*a.* A *pile footing* is one supported on piles.

foundation. The masonry structure below the first floor on which a building is supported; also the structure at the bottom of a wall designed to transmit the wall load to the earth. This may be some form of footing or a more elaborate structure as described in Chapter 3.

furring. Construction that provides an air space between the interior finished face of a wall and the wall itself. See Fig. 25-5 and descriptive material that accompanies it.

gable. Triangular piece of wall closing the end under a gable roof. See Fig. 25-2*e.*

head. Member at the top of a window or door frame. See Fig. 25-2*a.*

header. See *bonder.*

head joint. See *joint.*

isolated pier. One that is free-standing or unattached to other masonry. See *pier.*

jamb. A side of a window or door opening or frame. See Fig. 25-2*e.*

joint. The mortar-filled space between adjacent masonry units. A *bed joint* is a horizontal joint between units on which the units are *bedded* during laying. A *collar joint* is a vertical joint between wythes. A *head joint* is a vertical joint between the ends of adjacent units; also called a *build.*

kneeler. A coping stone built securely into a gable wall to resist the sliding tendency of inclined coping. See Fig. 25-2*e.*

leaf. See *wythe.*

lintel. Horizontal member supporting the masonry above a wall opening.

lug sill. See *sill.*

parapet. The part of a wall above the roof; also called a *parapet wall.* See Fig. 25-1*c.*

pier. A prism of masonry serving as a column, or a relatively narrow portion of a wall included between window or door openings. See *engaged pier* and *isolated pier.*

pilaster. Same as a buttress, except it has a smaller projection beyond the face or back of the wall. Projection sometimes limited to half the width. Same as *engaged pier.* See Fig. 25-2*f.*

quoin. A masonry unit or group of units placed at an external corner of a wall. Usually a decorative unit emphasized by the fact that it projects somewhat beyond the faces of the walls, by difference in material, color, or surface finish, or by arrangement in a pattern. See Fig. 25-2*b*.

reveal. The part of the jamb of an opening which is exposed between a door or window frame and the face or back of a wall.

saddle stone. Same as *apex stone.*

sill. The member at the bottom of a window or door opening. A *slip sill* has the same width as the opening. The ends of a *lug sill* project into the masonry at each end of the sill. See Fig. 25-2*a*.

skew corbel. Same as a *kneeler.*

slip sill. See *sill.*

string course. Same as a *belt course.*

through-wall flashing. See *flashing.*

tie. See *wall tie.*

veneer. An exterior facing of masonry or other material attached to the masonry backing but not bonded to exert common reaction under load. See Fig. 27-5*d*.

wainscot. A facing applied to or built into the lower portion of an interior wall for protection or decorative effect. May be ceramic tile, facing tile, portland cement and plaster, marble, wood, or other materials. Sometimes distinguished only by the contrasting color of a painted surface. Also called a *dado,* although this term is sometimes restricted to a molding along the top of a wainscot.

wall pier. Same as an *engaged pier* or *pilaster.*

wall tie. A bent rod or metal strip inserted in a bed joint to tie the facing to the backing. Also called *anchor.* See Figs. 26-5*c* and 27-5.

wash. A sloping surface on the exposed top surface of a sill, belt course, or coping to shed water. See Fig. 27-1*b*.

water table. A projecting course of stone on the outside of a wall, near the ground, to deflect rainwater from passing over the wall surface below. See Fig. 25-1*e*.

wythe or *withe.* A continuous vertical section or layer of a wall one masonry unit in thickness and tied to its adjacent vertical layer or layers, in front or back, by bonders or headers, metal ties, or grout (1); also called a *leaf* or *tier.*

Parts of a Masonry Arch. The parts of a masonry arch are indicated in Fig. 25-3 and may be defined as follows.

arch ring. The curved ring of masonry forming the arch.

span. The width of the opening.

rise. The height of the curved portion of the opening.

soffit. The concave or lower surface of the arch ring.

back. The convex or upper surface of the arch ring.

faces. The exposed vertical planes or sides of the arch ring.

intrados. The line of intersection of the soffit and a vertical plane parallel to the faces.

extrados. The line of intersection of the back and a vertical plane parallel to the faces.

springing lines. The lines of intersection or tangency of the soffit and the vertical, or nearly vertical, sides of the opening.

crown. The highest part of the arch ring.

spandrel. The space between the back of the arch ring and a horizontal plane tangent to the back of the arch ring at the crown.

voussoirs. The blocks of masonry of which the arch ring is composed.

keystone. The voussoir at the crown.

springers. The voussoirs just above the springing lines.

haunches. The sides of the arch ring.

skewbacks. The upper surfaces of the springers.

abutments. The masses of masonry at the sides of the opening which resist the thrust of the arch. Masonry arches which are parts of a wall do not have well-defined abutments, for the wall itself serves in this capacity.

arcade. A series of arches which includes the supporting members between the arches such as piers, columns, etc.

Curve of Arch Ring. Many curves and combinations of curves are used in laying out arches. When strength and economy of material

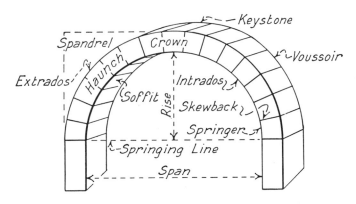

Fig. 25-3. Parts of an arch.

are important factors, as they are in arch bridges, the curve of the arch ring is determined by the span and rise of the arch and the characteristics of the loading. For the ordinary arches over openings in the walls of buildings, appearance is a more important factor in design than strength and economy of material. The most common cause of the failure of arches used in building construction is the spreading of the abutments or the masonry that serves as abutments. This spreading occurs when arched window or door openings are placed too near the wall corners or the abutments at the ends of the arcade are insufficient.

Types of Arches. The curve of the intrados is often a portion of the arc of a circle or a combination of the arcs of various circles with different radii and centers. Four types that have one center, as shown in Fig. 25-4a, are the *semicircular;* the *segmental,* which includes less than a semicircle; the *horseshoe,* which includes more than a semicircle; and the *stilted,* which consists of a semicircular-arch ring with straight vertical sections added on each side.

Two-centered arches are shown in *b.* The three types, blunt, equilateral, and lancet, differ only in the relation between the radius and the spacing of the centers. In the *blunt* or *drop arch* the centers are within the arch. In the *equilateral* or *Gothic arch* the radius of the intrados equals the span, and the centers are therefore on the springing lines. The centers for the *acute* or *lancet arch* are outside the arch.

There are two types of three-centered arch (*c*). In the first, one center is used for the arc of the central portion of the arch and two centers for the arcs at the ends of the arch ring. In the second, one center serves for the two arcs at the ends of the arch ring, and two centers are required for the central portion of the arch ring.

The four-centered or *Tudor arch* (*d*) is similar to the second type of three-centered arch, but the centers for the lower section of the arch ring do not coincide as in the three-centered arch. The vertical alignment of centers shown in the figure is not essential to this type.

The *flat arch* (*e*) may be supported by arch action, but it is usually carried on a concealed lintel.

The *two-cusped arch* is illustrated in *f.* Many forms of cusped arch have been used for decorative effect. Structurally they are very inefficient.

The *elliptic arch* is similar in shape to the three-centered arch shown in *c,* but the curve of the intrados is a semiellipse.

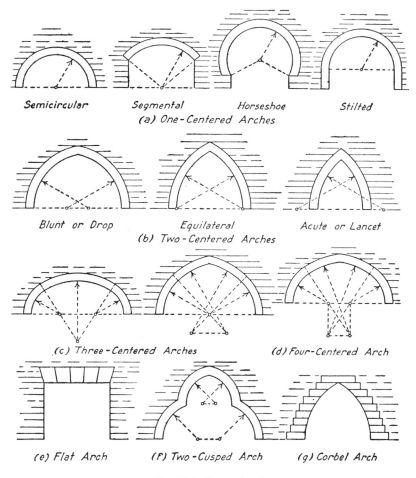

Semicircular   Segmental   Horseshoe   Stilted
(a) One-Centered Arches

Blunt or Drop   Equilateral   Acute or Lancet
(b) Two-Centered Arches

(c) Three-Centered Arches   *(d) Four-Centered Arch*

(e) Flat Arch   *(f) Two-Cusped Arch*   *(g) Corbel Arch*

Fig. 25-4. Types of arches.

The *parabolic arch* is similar in shape to the three-centered arch shown in *c*, but the curve of the intrados is a parabola with its axis vertical.

The *corbel arch* (*g*) is not really an arch but is called an arch because of its shape. There is no real arch action, each course being corbeled or cantilevered out over the course below until the two sides meet. This is the oldest form of arch and is not used in modern building construction. A *stepped arch* is one whose back is stepped to correspond with courses of masonry units in the wall above the opening.

Wall Furring, Moisture Penetration, and Flashing

Wall Furring. In general, *furring* consists of a light frame of wood or metal strips called *furring strips* applied to a surface to support plaster, stucco, or other surfacing material. It may be used to form an even surface over a rough or irregular wall or structural form; to form a hollow frame on which an imitation column, vault, or other decorative feature of plaster is placed; or to provide an air space between the rough inner surface of an outside wall and the finished surface of plaster or other finishing material. This is called *wall furring.*

Wall furring has three functions.

1. The air space intercepts any moisture that might pass through an outside wall, damage the wall finish and decorations, and cause unwholesome living conditions.

2. If humid air in a building comes in contact with a cold wall surface, there will be condensation on the surface, which will be just as objectionable as water passing through the wall. The air space acts as an insulator and prevents condensation.

3. The insulating properties of the air space reduce the heat transmission through a wall and thus save fuel in cold weather and keep a building cooler in hot weather.

There are two general methods for furring. One consists of lath and plaster placed on vertical furring strips fastened to the wall. The other consists of specially designed block of structural clay tile or gypsum applied to the wall. The blocks are coated with plaster after being placed. The use of metal lath on wood furring strips is illustrated in Fig. 25-5a, and metal lath on metal furring strips in b. Structural clay furring tile (c) are fastened to masonry walls by driving nails in the mortar joints and hooking the heads over the tile. Gypsum blocks (d) are applied in the same way.

The following comments on furring are quoted from the "Recommended Minimum Requirements for Small Dwelling Construction" by the Building Code Committee of the Department of Commerce, and are applicable to all classes of buildings.

1. In regions subject to low temperature, high winds, heavy rains, or extreme humidity of considerable duration, furring of solid masonry exterior walls is practically a necessity to avoid unwholesome living conditions caused by damp walls, and the danger of ruining wall decorations.

2. In arid localities, where low temperatures are infrequent, furring may be

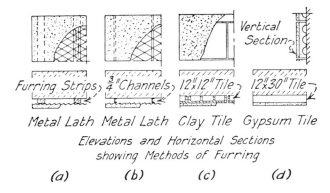

Elevations and Horizontal Sections
showing Methods of Furring

Fig. 25-5. Wall furring.

omitted without serious results, but should be used wherever economy in construction cost is a secondary consideration.

3. Waterproof paints or compounds applied to the interior of solid masonry walls help considerably to prevent moisture penetration, but have little effect on preventing condensation, and make it difficult to bond plaster to such treated walls.

4. Furring is somewhat less necessary on masonry exterior walls of hollow units, since the enclosed air cells help to check transmission of heat and moisture. However, mortar joints running through the wall are found to conduct moisture readily when poorly or incompletely made, and walls having such continuous joints require furring.

5. Furring a masonry wall lessens its heat conductivity, thus saving fuel, which saving, of course, continues throughout the life of the structure and may repay many times over the increased cost of furring.

6. Since hollow walls are good heat insulators, it has been found in many places that furring may be omitted and plaster applied directly to the interiors of the walls which are built with a continuous hollow space, or in which the mortar joints extend but part way through the wall.

7. In concrete house construction provision for insulation of exterior walls is recommended. A dead-air space within the wall itself or formed by furring and plastering has been found effective and this requirement seems to be favored by those recommending the use of concrete external walls.

In applying plaster to furring lath, it is important that the keys shall not project through so as to touch the wall, or be allowed to drop off and form a solid mass between the plaster and the wall. In either case moisture from the wall is liable to be transmitted through the plaster producing troublesome results, such as staining the wall, and ruining the lath—wood lath by dry rot and metal lath by corrosion. It is claimed that excellent results in furring 8-in. brick walls are obtained by attaching a layer of tarred paper to the back of the furring strips, or by using a lath of which such paper forms an integral part. Hollow tile or gypsum furring blocks are much used and are quite satisfactory. They have grooves in the back face which furnish air spaces between the wall and the plaster. There are also several forms of metal

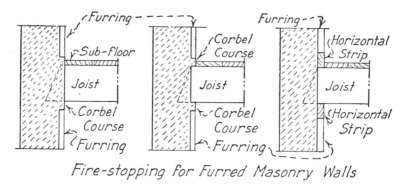

Fire-stopping for Furred Masonry Walls

Fig. 25-6. Firestopping for wall furring.

furring to which metal lath is attached and which serve the same purpose. Where walls are likely to be continuously damp, hollow tile furring will be more satisfactory than gypsum.

To prevent the passage of fire from floor to floor behind the furring, it may be necessary to corbel the masonry walls, as shown in Fig. 25-6. This is not necessary if fireproof floors, coming in close contact with the walls, are used. Wood strips are also used for this purpose, as shown in the figure, but are less effective than masonry.

Permeability. The following comments are quoted from Report BMS 82, "Water Permeability of Walls Built of Masonry Units," by Cyrus C. Fishburn (2).

1. Brick walls, in which labor and mortar were used sparingly, so that the interior of the vertical joints were left open and not filled with mortar, were highly permeable and leaked excessively.

2. Brick walls, in which the vertical joints were filled with mortar or grout and built of bricks having a low "suction" when laid, were highly resistant to water penetration.

3. There was little practical difference in the performance of walls in which the vertical joints were filled (a) by heavily buttering the bricks with mortar before placing them in the wall, (b) by slushing mortar into the joints from above, (c) by pouring in a grout, or (d) by shoving the bricks into a heap of mortar placed on the bed (pick-and-dip method).

4. Twelve-inch brick walls in which the head joints were lightly buttered at the exposed faces only, but which contained a mortar parging applied to the backs of both the first and second wythes, were highly resistant to water penetration. Eight-inch walls of this type were more permeable than similar 8-in. walls in which the vertical joints (head and collar joints) were completely filled.

5. There was no significant difference in the permeability of brick walls in which mortar for the bed joints was leveled or furrowed before placing the bricks, sufficient mortar having been used to cover the bed.

6. Brick walls, 8 in. thick, containing cored bricks and in which the vertical joints were completely filled, were highly resistant to water penetration and were slightly but significantly less permeable than similar walls built of solid bricks.

7. The least permeable brick walls were built of units having a low brick suction.

8. Low-absorptive bricks or those in which the "suction" was greatly reduced by prewetting, but which did not contain excessive amounts of absorbed water, were laid without difficulty in a mortar of high water retentivity. When such bricks were used with a mortar of low water retentivity, the construction of the walls was marked by excessive bleeding or by extrusion of the mortar from the joints. However, the walls so constructed were highly resistant to water penetration.

9. When the bricks had a high suction and were laid in a mortar having a low water retentivity, the walls were difficult to build and they were also more permeable than if a mortar having a high water retentivity was used.

10. Twelve-inch walls faced with brick and backed with hollow units were more permeable than similar all-brick walls. The kind of hollow unit used in the backing had no consistent or important effect on permeability, but the walls containing the end-bearing units appeared to be slightly less permeable than those containing side-bearing hollow units.

11. Walls of concrete units, without protective facings or coatings, were highly permeable.

The effects of exterior surface coatings of cement-water paints and other waterproofings on the permeability of highly permeable masonry wall specimens investigated by the Bureau of Standards were summarized in the abstract of Report BMS 95, as follows (3):

The cement-water paints were effective waterproofings and could be applied to the best advantage on the walls of concrete blocks with stiff, rather than soft, brushes. The admixture of fine sand to the paint for the first coat applied to coarse textured concrete block increased the effectiveness and durability of the paints. Thick paint films resulting from the application of excessive amounts of paint were effective when first applied but were much less durable than thinner coatings. The permeability of the paint films of average thickness was lower after weathering than before.

The colorless waterproofings were generally ineffective. Only one of the colorless waterproofings was satisfactory when first applied, but it was not durable and was much more permeable than the best cement-water paint treatments. The data confirm results previously obtained, which indicate that the only effective and durable method of waterproofing brick walls without changing their appearance was by repointing or grouting of the face joints.

The bituminous coatings applied to the inside faces of the walls was ineffective as waterproofing.

Considering the results of these investigations, no colorless water-proofing should be assumed to be satisfactory unless its performance has been demonstrated by reliable tests or performance.

Flashing and Calking. Flashing and calking, or caulking, are important factors in reducing rainwater penetration into masonry walls and in reducing the harmful effects of water that does penetrate. Water that penetrates the outer layer of face brick or stone may pass through the wall or flow downward through the joints and between the layers until it finds an outlet over a door, window, or other opening. This condition may be especially bad over bay windows or where an exterior wall becomes an interior wall because of an extension of the building in the lower stories. The reduction in the amount of water penetration by proper selection of materials and good workmanship has been mentioned previously. Flashing and calking are used as additional precautions at critical locations, such as under the copings on parapet walls and chimney tops, under window sills, and over and under projecting belt courses. The function of calking is always to exclude water, but flashing may have the additional function of conducting water outward so that its effects will be less harmful. This is particularly true over openings in a wall. Typical uses of flashing and calking are illustrated in Fig. 25-7.

The materials used for flashing are sheets of copper, lead, zinc, aluminum, galvanized iron, and terne plate; bituminous roofing papers; and copper-backed paper. The material selected should always be appropriate for the quality of the construction, keeping in mind that it is much more expensive to replace defective flashing than to install high-quality flashing initially.

Calking consists of filling joints or cracks in the exterior of a wall and around door and window frames with thick ribbons of plastic calking material resembling soft putty. Calking is applied by extruding from a calking gun through a nozzle about ¼ in. in diameter and moving the gun along to form the ribbon. A good calking compound will adhere to the surfaces with which it comes in contact and will harden slowly, shrink very little, and not stain. Calking compounds differ considerably in composition, but most of them consist of finely ground and fibrous materials mixed with a vehicle consisting of a drying or semidrying oil and some volatile thinner. The finely ground material is usually calcite, but quartz, dolomite, and other materials are used. The fibrous material is usually asbestos. The oils most commonly used are fish, soybean, linseed, and tung. The thinner is usually mineral spirits.

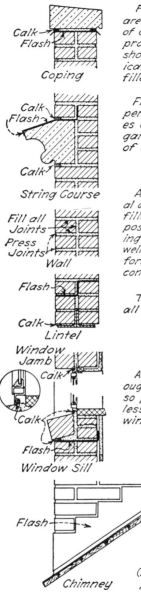

Few copings, except vitrified clay tile, are dampproof. Few joints between sections of coping can be made permanently damp-proof. Consequently, through flashing should be placed under coping. The vertical joints in the coping should be filled with plastic mortar or calking.

Flashing is placed over or under, depending on detail, all projecting courses of masonry, ornamental trim, etc., regardless of its character, unless it is of impervious terra cotta, well calked.

All joints in brickwork, internal, vertical and horizontal, should be completely filled with mortar. Failure to do this is possibly the most common cause of leaking walls. The face joints should be well tooled with considerable pressure to form a dense slick facing and thorough contact with the brick

Through flashing should be provided over all lintels.

All window and door frames should be thoroughly calked. Frequently such calking is so poorly done as to be practically worthless. Flashing should be placed over all window and door openings.

Flashing should be placed at the juncture of a chimney and roof, and also at gables and walls. Provision for adequate roof drainage should be made to prevent overflow or clogging in downspouts causing the water to spill over the face of the wall.

(Adapted from Tech. Bul. No. 8 of Brick Manufacturers Assn. of N.Y., by J. H. Hansen)

Fig. 25-7. Flashing and calking.

Efflorescence. *Efflorescence* is a white deposit which frequently appears on the surface of masonry walls. It is caused by soluble salts, such as calcium and magnesium sulfates, contained in the masonry unit or mortar being dissolved out by water's penetrating the unit or mortar and being deposited on the surface of the wall as the water evaporates.

For efflorescence to form, it is essential that both the water and the salts be present. Efflorescence may be minimized by selecting materials that contain a minimum amount of the materials causing efflorescence and by keeping water out of the wall. This may be accomplished, in part at least, by using water-repellent mortar and solidly filled joints; by capping walls with copings that have tight joints and are arranged to drip free of the wall or to drain toward the roof instead of toward the face of the wall; by effective flashing and calking; by providing drips for all sills, cornices, and projecting courses; by providing a waterproof layer on top of foundation walls; and by protecting the walls so that rain and water from melting snow cannot enter them during construction.

Efflorescence can be removed by washing the wall with a weak solution of muriatic acid and water. This treatment is not desirable for limestone, which is soluble in this solution, or for polished surfaces on other stones.

26. BRICK MASONRY WALLS

Brick for structural purposes may be made of clay or shale, portland cement and sand, or lime and sand.

Clay and shale brick exterior walls are used in all classes of building construction, from small dwelling houses to the finest public buildings. Concrete or cement brick and sand-lime brick are used to a limited extent.

Manufacture, Properties, and Classes of Brick

Manufacture. Clay and shale brick are made by three different processes, the soft-mud process, the stiff-mud process, and the dry process. In all these processes, the brick are molded to the desired shape, dried, and burned in kilns. The chief difference in the processes is in the method of molding.

In the *soft-mud process*, the clay is mixed with water and worked into a uniform plastic mass. Brick are shaped by pressing this material into molds by hand or machinery. To keep the brick from sticking to the molds, the molds may be wet with water or sanded. If the molds are wet, the method is known as *slop molding* and the brick are called *water-struck brick*. If the molds are sanded, the method is known as *sand molding* and the brick are called *sand-struck brick*.

In the *stiff-mud process*, just enough water is used with the clay to produce a mixture which may be forced through a die, forming a ribbon with a cross section equal to that of the flat side or bed of a brick or to that of the end. The brick are cut from this ribbon by tightly stretched wires, forming *wire-cut brick*. If the beds are cut by the wires the brick are called *side-cut*, but if the ends are cut they are called *end-cut*.

In the *dry-pressed process*, the clay of dry consistency is pressed into gang or multiple molds with plungers, exerting a heavy pressure. This process produces the most accurately formed brick.

Brick pressed in oversize molds, dried, and repressed to the correct size are called *repressed brick*. Such brick are accurately formed and strong. Stiff-mud brick are frequently repressed.

Clay and shale brick are extensively used in all parts of the country. By selecting clays and shales and introducing certain oxides, face brick of various colors are produced.

Concrete or cement brick are usually made by pressing a rather dry mixture of portland cement, sand, and water into gang molds. Because of the dry mixture used, the molds can be removed immediately without waiting for the cement to set. The brick are placed in an atmosphere of steam or are sprayed with water while the cement is setting. This class of brick should be called *concrete brick* rather than cement brick.

The ordinary concrete brick is a dead cement color which is not suitable for face brick. Different finishes are made on the exposed face by putting aggregates or colored cements on one side of the mold before pressing and backing this up with an ordinary mixture. Concrete brick are used in some parts of the country, particularly where suitable clay for brick making is scarce.

Sand-lime brick are made of a mixture of sand and hydrated lime, pressed into shape in molds and cured in an atmosphere of steam which causes chemical action to take place between the sand and lime, cementing the materials together.

Size, Shape, and Unit of Measure. The following dimensions are actual rather than nominal. The standard size for *American face brick* is

2¼ by 3¾ by 8 in. but brick made in the same size molds will differ in size because different clays vary in the amount of shrinkage in burning. *Roman brick,* which are used to a limited extent, are 1⅝ by 3¾ by 12 in., *Norman brick* 2¼ by 3¾ by 12 in., *English brick* 3 by 4½ by 9 in., and the *SCR brick* 2³⁄₁₆ by 5½ by 11½ in. Various sizes of brick are shown in Fig. 26-1a.

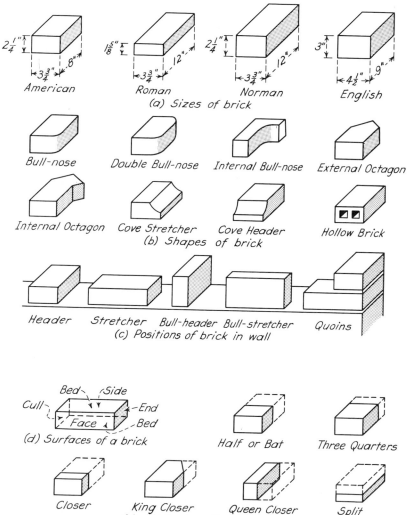

Fig. 26-1. Brick types and dimensions.

Special shapes are available for use in forming a finish around openings or for moldings. These special shapes are not usually used for ordinary brickwork, but are available in face brick and in the glazed and enameled clay brick described later. The most common forms are the *bull-nose* and *double bull-nose* (*b*), for use where a rounded corner is desired. Other shapes are the *internal bull-nose*, the *external octagon*, the *internal octagon*, the *cove header*, and the *cove stretcher*. *Hollow brick* are used as face brick or backing brick to reduce the weight of a wall and to gain the advantage of the air space in heat insulation and checking the passage of moisture through the wall.

The six surfaces of a brick are sometimes called the *face*, the *side*, the *end*, the *cull*, and the *beds* (*d*).

Brick may be cut into pieces of various shapes, the more common of which are shown in (*e*). They are known by the following names: *half* or *bat, three-quarter, closer, king closer, queen closer,* and *split.* They are used to fill in the spaces at the corners and other places where the full brick will not fit.

Brick may be solid, or it may contain vertical cylindrical *cores* which do not reduce the bearing area more than 25 per cent and do not come within $3/4$ in. of any face. They are advantageous because of weight reduction. One bearing face of a brick may have a rectangular recess or depressed panel, called a *frog*, whose depth does not exceed $3/8$ in., and no part of the recess may come within $3/4$ in. of any face. Deeper frogs may be used, however, if the net area through the frog is at least 75 per cent of the gross area.

Brick are always sold by the thousand.

Hardness of Clay Brick. The durability of a clay and shale brick depends largely upon the degree of burning it has received in the kilns. When removed from a kiln, brick are sorted according to their hardness, which depends upon the degree of burning. The brick that immediately surround the fire are usually overburned and are badly warped and discolored. These are known as *arch* or *clinker brick* and are suitable for use in foundations or similar places, for they are very durable but unattractive. The brick that have received the right amount of burning are known as *hard* or *well-burned brick* and are suitable for general use. The brick that are the most remote from the fire are underburned and are known as *soft brick*. These brick are weak and will not resist the action of the weather. They are suitable for use only as backing brick, where moisture is not encountered and where strength is not an important factor. The terms *salmon, pale,* and *light* are often applied to soft red brick.

Color of Clay Brick. *Common* or *building brick* used where appearance is not a factor are usually made of clay which burns red, but sometimes common brick are white or cream-colored. Very attractive walls are built of common brick by careful selection of the brick, the type of joint, and the bond.

Brick used on exposed faces of walls where appearance is a factor are known as *face brick*. By mixing clays and introducing certain oxides a great variety of colors may be secured. The most common colors are various shades of red, brown, and gray. Many effects are produced by the fire markings in burning.

Surface Finish of Clay Brick. The exposed face of brick may be smooth or roughened by *wire cutting* or by *combing*, as in *tapestry brick*.

Salt glazed brick are smooth-faced brick of special composition which will permit a glaze to be formed on the face exposed to the gases produced in the furnace by throwing salt into the fires of the kiln. This is called a *salt glaze* and does not require an additional burning. The common colors of salt glaze are gray, brown, and green. Salt-glazed brick are impervious, smooth, and easily cleaned. They are suitable for interior as well as exterior use, the whole wall surface being covered or only the wainscoting. Glazed and facing hollow clay tile are made for use with corresponding brick as described in Art. 28.

Ceramic glazed or *enameled brick* are made by spraying the surface of smooth unburned clay brick of special composition with a coating which gives an enameled surface when the brick are burned. The common colors are white, green, and brown. The surface may have a bright, medium, or dull finish. Enameled brick are impervious, smooth, and easily cleaned. They possess these qualities to a higher degree than salt-glazed brick and are more expensive. Enameled brick are suitable for interior and exterior use. They are particularly desirable for swimming pools, hotel kitchens, and other positions where wall tile might also be used.

Fire-flash or *fire-mark* brick are those which have acquired a surface marking by exposure to the fires of a kiln.

Face, Backing, and Common Brick. Brick are divided into *face brick* and *backing brick*, according to the part of the wall in which they are placed. Face brick are used in the exposed face of a wall, and backing brick are used in the back of the wall. Face brick are of higher quality, greater durability, and better appearance than backing brick. Backing brick may often come from the same kiln as the face brick, but they are of inferior quality from underburning or overburning.

Brick are also divided into *face brick* and *common* or *building brick*. In this classification, brick made especially for facing purposes by selecting the clays to produce the desired color or by special surface treatment are called face brick, whereas brick made from the natural clay without a special surface treatment are called common brick. Selected common brick are frequently used for face brick. They often have attractive fire marks.

Quality of Brick. The quality of brick is determined by its strength, durability, and appearance.

Specifications for building brick made from clay or shale have been prepared by the American Society for Testing and Materials. These specifications divide such brick into three grades, depending on exposure conditions for which they are suitable, as follows (4).

Grade SW. Brick intended for use where a high degree of resistance to frost action is desired and the exposure is such that the brick may be frozen when permeated with water.

As a typical example, brick used for foundation courses and retaining walls in portions of the United States subject to frost action should conform to this grade. Compliance with this grade is also recommended where a high and uniform degree of resistance to disintegration by weathering is desired.

Grade MW. Brick intended for use where exposed to temperatures below freezing but unlikely to be permeated with water, or where a moderate and somewhat non-uniform degree of resistance to frost action is permissible.

As a typical example, brick used in the face of a wall above ground should conform to this grade. Such exposure is not likely to result in permeation of brick by water if horizontal surfaces are protected.

Grade NW. Brick intended for use as back-up or interior masonry or, if exposed, for use where no frost action occurs, where the average annual precipitation is less than 20 in.

Specifications for facing brick provide for two grades as follows (5).

Grade SW. Brick intended for use where a high and uniform degree of resistance to frost action and disintegration by weathering is desired, and the exposure is such that the brick may be frozen when permeated with water.

Brick exposed in parapets and horizontal surfaces may become permeated. When suitably protected from above by flashings or overhanging eaves, ordinary exposure in the vertical face of an exterior wall is unlikely to result in permeation unless resulting from defective workmanship or faulty drainage.

Grade NW. Brick intended for use where a moderate and somewhat non-uniform degree of resistance to frost action is permissible or where they are unlikely to be permeated with water when exposed to temperatures below freezing.

In those sections of the United States where temperatures seldom fall below freezing, the degree of durability called for by grade SW of these specifications is unnecessary.

Three types of facing brick are recognized, the distinctions between types being on the basis of color range, variation in size, and mechanical perfection.

Brick Masonry

Brick masonry consists of brick built up to form walls or other structural elements. In order to secure an even bed for the brick, to hold brick in position, to make a tight wall, and to improve the appearance, mortar is used between the brick and forms the *joints*. The bricks are held together to act as a unit by arranging them so that they lap over each other and break the vertical joints. The various arrangements used are called *bonds*, and they affect the appearance of the masonry. Brick may be arranged to carry out designs or *patterns* that have no bonding effect.

Headers, Stretchers, etc. Brick may be placed in various positions in a wall. If they are laid flat with the end exposed they are called *headers*, and if laid flat with the long side exposed they are called *stretchers*. Half-brick which are used to give the appearance of headers but which do not project into the backing are called *false headers*. For sills, belt courses, etc., brick may be placed on edge with the end exposed and are called *bull headers*. Occasionally they are laid on edge with the flat side exposed forming *bull stretchers*. Belt courses and flat arches may be formed of brick set on end with the narrow side exposed. Such brick are called *soldiers*. *Quoins* are brick placed at corners with one end and one side exposed. These classes of brick are illustrated in Fig. 26-1c.

Bonds. The arrangement of brick in a wall to tie the parts together by lapping the brick in various ways is called the *bond*.

In *running* or *stretcher bond* the face brick are all stretchers, as shown in Fig. 26-2a, the face brick being tied to the backing by metal ties placed in the horizontal joints, by using clipped or secret bond as described later, or by splitting the face brick of every sixth course in half lengthwise so that a continuous row of headers may project halfway through the course and into the backing.

In *common* or *American bond* every sixth course of stretcher bond is usually made a header course (b), and gives a much stronger wall than that secured with metal ties.

English bond consists of alternate courses of headers and stretchers, the vertical joints in the header courses all coming over each other

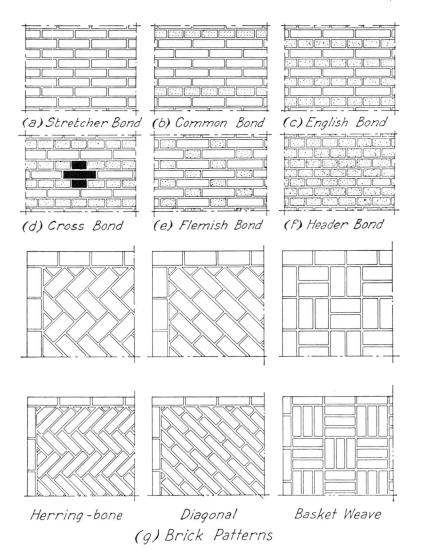

(a) Stretcher Bond (b) Common Bond (c) English Bond

(d) Cross Bond (e) Flemish Bond (f) Header Bond

Herring-bone Diagonal Basket Weave

(g) Brick Patterns

Fig. 26-2. Brick bonds and patterns.

and the vertical joints in the stretcher courses also being in line. The vertical joints in the stretcher courses bisect alternate brick in the header courses (*c*).

English cross bond, Dutch bond, or *cross bond* is similar to English bond, but the alternate courses of stretchers break joints (*d*). This wall is built up of interlocking crosses consisting of two headers and a stretcher, one of which is shown black in the figure to illustrate the cross.

In *Flemish bond* each course consists of alternate headers and stretchers, the alternate headers of each course being centered over the stretchers in the course below (*e*).

Header bond consists entirely of headers laid to break joints. An entire wall would not usually be laid in header bond, but certain areas of a wall may be laid in header bond for decorative effect (Fig. 26-2*f*). A large part of the headers may be false headers.

In *clipped* or *secret bond* face brick are laid in running bond, but the inside corners of the brick in every sixth row are clipped to permit a tie to be made with backing by headers laid diagonally. This bond offers very little resistance to the separation of the face and backing, so it is frequently desirable to use metal wall ties in addition to the clipped bond. These ties should be used on every brick of the course halfway between the diagonal header course. This construction gives a stronger wall than the use of wall ties only, but is not as satisfactory as the other bonds that have been described.

Face brick are sometimes laid with the vertical as well as the horizontal joints continuous. This arrangement is called *stack bond*, because the brick are arranged in stacks. The objective is to secure a decorative effect, but obviously there is no bond between adjacent brick. Horizontal reinforcement may be provided by including $\frac{1}{4}$-in. rods in the joints.

The bond requirements of the American Standard Building Code (1) are given in Art. 30, Sec. E.

Patterns. A great variety of patterns may be worked out by the use of headers and stretchers arranged in various ways. These may be emphasized by using headers differing slightly in color from the stretchers. Other patterns are secured by arranging face brick in diagonal and vertical positions. The most common patterns of these are the *herringbone*, the *diagonal*, and the *basket-weave patterns* shown in Fig. 26-2*g*.

Skintled Brickwork. *Skintled brickwork* consists of setting the face brick as in running bond but so that they are out of line with the face of the wall. The corners may project or be recessed from $\frac{1}{8}$ in. to $\frac{1}{4}$ in. or more. The mortar that squeezes out of the joint may be allowed to remain. This type of brickwork is likely to leak and collect dirt.

Joints. The mortar filled spaces between brick are called *joints*. The joints used in brick masonry may be as thin as $\frac{1}{8}$ in. for enameled or glazed brick walls where an easily cleaned surface is desired, or they may be as thick as ¾ in. to secure certain architectural effects, the most common thickness being from ⅜ to ½ in.

The joints in brickwork are usually made by the following operations, all of which are performed with a trowel.

1. Spreading enough mortar to form the horizontal joint for three or four brick.

2. Cutting off the mortar that projects over the edge to keep it from running down over the face of the wall.

3. Bedding the brick one at a time by tapping with the trowel until they are in position.

4. Cutting off the mortar that has been forced over the edge by the bedding process, and buttering the end of the brick to form the next vertical joint. This process forms a rough-cut joint.

5. Jointing or finishing the exposed surface of the joints. The various kinds of joints are shown in Fig. 26-3. This method does not fill the vertical joints.

In operation 1, a shallow longitudinal furrow is formed in the mortar with the trowel. It has been found that such a furrow is necessary to permit the brick to be placed accurately in position. If the furrow is not made too deep, the joint will be completely filled with mortar as required to make exterior walls watertight (1).

Push or *shove* joints are formed by placing a brick on a heavy bed of mortar and pushing or shoving it into position against a brick already placed in the same course, so that the vertical joint between the two is entirely filled with mortar. Walls constructed in this manner are stronger and more watertight than walls constructed in the usual way.

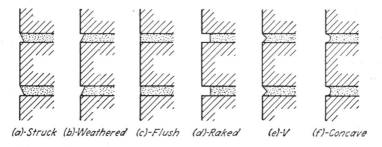

(a)-Struck (b)-Weathered (c)-Flush (d)-Raked (e)-V (f)-Concave

Fig. 26-3. Types of joints.

Buttered joints are formed by holding the brick bottom up and buttering mortar on the bottom around the four edges of the bed and on the vertical edge that will come in contact with the last brick laid. The brick is then placed and tapped with the handle of the trowel to set it accurately. Narrow joints in enameled or glazed brickwork are commonly formed in this way. At one time, face brick were set with buttered joints $\frac{1}{8}$ in. wide, but this practice has been practically discontinued. With buttered joints, the mortar is around the edges of the brick but not under the central part.

The exposed face of mortar joints may be finished in various ways. This finish is always formed at the time the brick are laid and not afterwards as in pointing stone work.

The *struck joint,* shown in Fig. 26-3*a*, is the most common type used when a finished joint is required. It is likely to produce leaky exterior walls.

The *weather joint* (*b*) is similar to the struck joint but slopes in such a way that it sheds water more effectively. The weather joint is more difficult to form than the struck joint and so is rarely used, but it is more watertight.

In the *flush joint* (*c*), the mortar is cut off flush with the face of the brick. This type of joint is common for unexposed interior surfaces and is also used for face brick.

The *plain* or *rough-cut joint* is similar to the flush joint but is not made as carefully. It is the cheapest and easiest joint to form and is used where appearance is not a factor.

The *raked joint* (*d*) is formed by raking out the mortar to the depth of about $\frac{1}{2}$ in.

The *stripped joint,* similar to the raked joint, is sometimes formed by placing wood strips in the joints as the brick are being laid. These strips insure a joint of uniform thickness. They may be removed as soon as the mortar has set slightly.

The *V joint* (*e*) is made with a special tool which is run along the joint before the mortar has set.

The *concave joint* (*f*) is also made with a special tool which is run along the joint before the mortar has set.

The best joint, from the point of view of water tightness and cost, is the concave joint. The struck joint, although easily made, is not watertight and is suitable for interior walls only. Raked and stripped joints are suitable only for interior masonry. They are relatively expensive and are not watertight. All joints in exterior walls, including the vertical joints and the interior joints, should be entirely filled with mortar to reduce moisture penetration. The outside face of the joints should be made smooth and dense by exerting considerable pressure on the tool with which they are formed.

The brickwork for all party walls, fire walls, and bearing walls that carry heavy loads should be laid solid with all joints filled with mortar.

Mortar. The mortar requirements for the joints in various kinds of masonry walls are considered in Art. 30, Sec. B., Pars. 2 and 3.

Mortars for clay masonry are considered by the Structural Clay Products Institute in reference 19, from which the following comments are quoted.

Air-entraining portland cement, because of air entrainment, has the definite detrimental effect of reducing bond between mortar and masonry units or reinforcement and should be used cautiously, if at all. If they are used for any reason, investigate bond strengths by laboratory tests before specifying such mortars.

Masonry cements are proprietary mixtures whose formulae are seldom disclosed by their manufacturers. Because ASTM specifications place no limitations on their compositions, the constituents of masonry cements vary widely among available brands. Most Type II masonry cements weigh about 70 lb. per bag, consisting of approximately equal parts of portland cement and ground inert limestone by weight. Additives are included to provide workability, water retentivity, and air entrainment. When one such bag is mixed with 3 cu. ft. of sand, the approximate resultant proportions by volume are one part portland cement, 2 parts ground inert limestone and 9 parts of sand. Essentially, such a mix has 1 part cementitious material and 11 parts of aggregate.

In masonry cements, commonly used additives include; salts of wood resins; tall oils and their derivatives; water-repellent fats; fatty acids and their salts, such as stearates and tallows; and wetting and air-entraining agents.

The Structural Clay Products Institute (SCPI) cannot recommend masonry cements *per se.* Their use should be based on performance records and laboratory tests.

Mortar of almost any color may be produced by mixing mineral mortar colors with the mortar. Mortar colors may be in the form of a paste or a powder. The usual colors are red, brown, chocolate, and black but many other colors are available or can be secured by mixing colors.

Bond Required. Every sixth course on both sides of a wall should be a header course, except where walls are faced with brick in Flemish bond and English bond, in which case the headers of every fourth course should be full brick bonded into the backing. The remaining headers may be half-brick called false headers. Where running bond is used, it should be bonded into the backing by using clipped bond combined with metal wall ties, as described in the paragraph on clipped bond, or by using split stretchers, as described in the paragraph on running bond.

In walls more than 12 in. thick, the inner joints of header courses should be covered with another header course which breaks joints with the course below.

Desirable methods of bonding brick walls of various thickness and types are shown in Fig. 26-4.

Face brick should be laid at the same time as the backing. The walls of each story should be built up the full thickness to the top of the beams or joists above.

For further consideration of bonding see Art. 30, Sec. E.

Anchorage at Wall Intersections. All walls should be securely anchored and bonded at points where they intersect. Where such walls are not built at the same time, the perpendicular joint should be regularly toothed with 8-in. maximum offsets, and the joint should be provided with anchors of not less than $1\frac{1}{2}$- by $\frac{1}{4}$-in. metal, with bent-up ends or cross pins to form anchorage; such anchors to be not less than 2 ft. long, extending 12 in. on each side of the joint, and spaced not more than 4 ft. apart in height. See Art. 30, Sec. E, Par. 1*b*.

Wetting Brick before Laying. Brick should usually be wet just before being laid, except in freezing weather, when they should be laid dry. The bricks are wet to keep them from soaking the water out of the mortar where it is necessary for proper setting, to secure a better bond between the brick and mortar, and to wash off the dust on the brick. See Art. 30, Sec. J, Pars. 2 and 3.

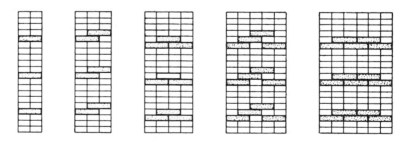

Methods of Bonding Brick Walls

Fig. 26-4. Methods of bonding brick walls.

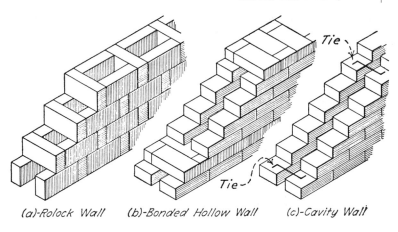

(a)-Rolock Wall   (b)-Bonded Hollow Wall   (c)-Cavity Wall

Fig. 26-5. Hollow walls of brick masonry.

Hollow Walls. Brick walls may be made hollow so that the open space will not permit rainwater to pass through completely. Water that penetrates the outer layer should be conducted out again by flashing. There are three kinds of hollow wall: the *rolock* or *rowlock wall*, consisting of bull stretchers and bull headers, as shown in Fig. 26-5a; the *masonry-bonded hollow wall* (b), in which the layer of face brick is separated from the backing by an air space of from 2 to 3 in., through which the headers pass to bond the face brick to the backing; and the *cavity wall* (c), which replaces the headers with metal ties.

The hollow wall with headers is not as effectively bonded as the solid wall with the same number of layers. The headers in the rolock and masonry-bonded hollow walls may collect water and cause moisture penetration.

In the cavity wall, the metal ties, if properly made, do not facilitate moisture penetration. They are effective in keeping the two layers or wythes from separating, but no part of a load applied to the inner layer can be transmitted to the outer layer by the ties. Secondary advantages of hollow walls are improved heat insulation, elimination of furring, and, as with the rolock wall, a saving in material. Hollow walls of brick are not widely used in this country, but the cavity wall is extensively used in England and on the Continent. They appear to have possibilities that deserve serious consideration because of their successful use abroad.

Permissible Wall Heights. For recommendations concerning permissible wall heights see Art. 30, Sec. D, Par. 4.

Stucco on Brick. Exterior walls of brick are frequently covered with stucco. In this case the surface brick should be rough hard-burned brick set in portland-cement mortar with joints not less than ⅜ in. thick, and with the mortar raked out for at least ½ in. from the face to give a better bond between the stucco and brick. The surface of the brick should be brushed free of all dust, dirt, and loose particles, and should be wetted to such a degree that water will not be rapidly absorbed from the stucco, but not to such a degree that water will remain standing on the surface when the stucco is applied.

The composition and placing of the stucco are discussed in Chapter 12.

Face Brick with Structural Clay Tile or Hollow Brick Backing. Face brick may be backed with structural clay tile or with concrete block, as discussed in Art. 28. The facing should either be bonded to the backing with a row of headers every 16 in. or be attached to the backing with metal wall ties bedded in the mortar joints. Such ties should be spaced not farther apart than 1 ft. vertically and 2 ft. horizontally. When metal ties are used, the face brick cannot be considered as a part of the backing in determining the required thickness of the wall, but if brick headers are used the face brick may be included.

Structural clay tile backing may be used to decrease the weight, when panel or curtain walls are supported by a steel or reinforced concrete frame, to increase the resistance to the passage of heat, or to reduce the cost when tile backing is cheaper than brick.

Hollow brick of standard brick size may be used to form the inside face of exterior walls, the air cells in the brick increasing the resistance of the wall to the passage of heat.

Brick Walls Faced with Stone. Brick may be used for backing walls that are faced with stone ashlar. The ashlar should not be less than 3¾ in. thick, and each stone should be reasonably uniform in thickness, but all stones need not be of the same thickness.

Each block of ashlar should be bonded into the backing or securely anchored to the backing with metallic anchors, as described in Art. 27.

Frame Walls Veneered with Brick. This type of wall is discussed in Art. 37.

Trimstone. Cut stone, as described in Art. 27, is frequently used as a trim around window and door openings and for belt courses, copings, and cornices of brick walls.

Cleaning. After the plasterer has completed his work, all surfaces of face brick should be thoroughly cleaned with a 5 to 10 per cent solution of muriatic acid in water. A stiff wire brush may be used to remove spots and stains. After cleaning, the surface should be carefully washed with water to remove all traces of acid.

Efflorescence. See Art. 25 under that paragraph heading.

Permeability. See Art. 25 under that paragraph heading.

Brick Arches. Brick arches are used over openings in brick walls and in many other parts of buildings. Various forms of arches are discussed in Art. 25.

Brick arches may be constructed of one or more rows of brick on edge with the end exposed (Fig. 26-6a), forming a rowlock arch; with one or more rows of brick on end with the narrow edge exposed (b); with the courses forming the arch ring bonded (c); or with bonding courses at intervals (d).

The brick may be adjusted to the curvature of the arch by making wedge-shaped mortar joints or by shaping the brick to fit the spaces they are to occupy and using joints of uniform thickness. Arches constructed of brick so shaped are called *gaged arches* (Fig. 26-6c, d, and g). This shaping is accomplished by laying the arch out on the floor and cutting and rubbing the brick to the proper shape before the work of placing is started. Arches of other types than the rowlock usually have to be gaged.

Two forms of flat or jack arches are shown in (e) and (f). The arch illustrated is often supported on a concealed lintel, but if so it is not a true arch.

Brick arches are often constructed over lintels in the backing of brick or stone walls (Fig. 26-6i). These arches are used to take the load from the lintels and are called *relieving* or *discharging arches*.

Reinforced Brick Masonry. Ordinary brick masonry has considerable compressive strength but very little tensile or flexural strength. By embedding steel reinforcing bars in some of the horizontal bed joints, horizontal tensile resistance may be provided. In addition, by placing vertical reinforcing bars in grout in the vertical joints between wythes, vertical tensile resistance may be increased. Such arrangements are illustrated in Figs. 26-7a, b, and c (6). By omitting the center course of brick at vertical intervals in the center wythe of a three-wythe wall, and placing grout-surrounded reinforcing bars in this space, as shown in Fig. 26-7d, larger bars can be introduced to provide greater tensile resistance. The head and bed joints in the outside wythes are made

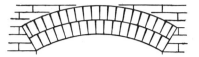

(a) Row-lock Arch

(b) Segmental Arch

(c) Bonded Arch

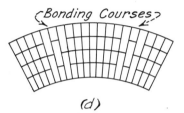

(d)

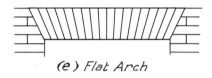

(e) Flat Arch

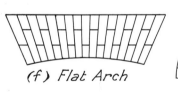

(f) Flat Arch

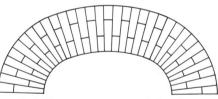

(g) Three Centered Arch

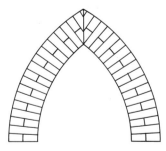

(h) Pointed Arch

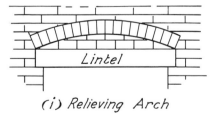

(i) Relieving Arch

Fig. 26-6. Brick arches.

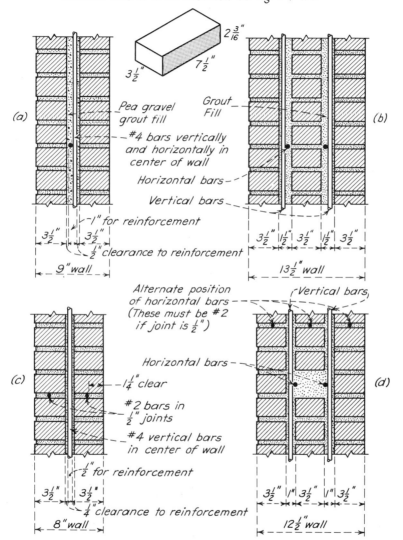

Fig. 26-7. Reinforced brick masonry walls. Structural Clay Products Institute (6).

in the usual manner, care being taken to keep the joints between wythes free from mortar. This type of construction is also called *grouted masonry*. See Art. 30, Sec. F.

The following statement appears in reference 7.

During recent years, a method of construction known as the "High Lift Grouting System" has been developed in the San Francisco Bay Area. This consists of placing vertical reinforcement, then building one wythe of brick masonry on each side of the reinforcement, with a space between of 2 in. or more to be filled with grout. The two wythes are tied together by metal ties providing construction similar to cavity wall. When the masonry is built to a maximum height of 12 ft., the cavity is filled with grout either by coal scuttle, concrete bucket, or by mechanical pumping equipment.

Reinforced brick masonry is used in areas subject to earthquake shocks and in blast-resistant construction because of its superior resistance to lateral forces. It is also desirable for parapet walls which are subject to extreme temperature ranges and which tend to crack because of tensile stresses resulting from longitudinal contraction.

Reinforced brick columns are constructed by casting square or rectangular reinforced concrete columns in vertical openings provided within brick masonry walls, piers or columns. The vertical reinforcement should have an area of not less than $\frac{1}{2}$ nor more than 4 per cent of the gross column area and should consist of not less than four $\frac{1}{2}$-in. bars. Lateral reinforcement of ties or spirals, as described in Art. 50, should be provided.

Many other forms of reinforced brick masonry have been developed (8) (11).

The following requirements are included in the *Building Code Requirements for Reinforced Masonry* approved by the American Standards Association as American Standard A41.2-1960, National Bureau of Standards Handbook 74, 1960.

All masonry units used in grouted masonry shall be laid plumb in full head and bed joints and all interior joints, cores, or spaces that are designed to receive grout shall be solidly filled. The grouted longitudinal joints shall not be less than $\frac{3}{4}$ in. wide. Mortar fins shall not protrude into spaces to be filled with grout. When the least clear dimension of the longitudinal vertical joint or core is less than 2 in., the maximum height of the grout pour shall be limited to 12 in. When the least clear dimension of the longitudinal vertical joint or core is 2 in. or more, the maximum height of the grout pour shall not exceed 48 times the least clear dimension of the longitudinal vertical joint or core for pea gravel grout nor more than 64 for mortar grout but not to exceed 12 ft. Grout shall be agitated or puddled during placement to insure complete filling of the grout space. When grouting is stopped for 1 hr. or longer the grout pour shall be stopped $1\frac{1}{2}$ in. below the top of a masonry unit. Masonry bonders (headers) shall not be used, but metal wall ties may be used to prevent spreading of the wythes and to maintain vertical alignment of the wall.

In reinforced grouted masonry, vertical reinforcement shall be accurately placed and held rigidly in position before the work is started. Horizontal reinforcement may be placed as the work progresses. . . . The thickness of grout or mortar between masonry units and reinforcement shall not be less than ¼ in. except ¼ in. bars may be laid in ½ in. horizontal mortar joints and No. 6 gage or smaller wires may be laid in ⅜ in. horizontal joints. Vertical joints containing both horizontal and vertical reinforcement shall be not less than ½ in. larger than of the diameters of the horizontal and vertical reinforcement contained therein.

Minimum Wall Thickness. See Art. 30, Sec. D.

Foundation Walls. See Art. 30, Sec. D.

Bonding and Anchoring. See Art. 30, Sec. E.

Fire Resistance Ratings. See Art. 30, Sec. L.

27. STONE MASONRY WALLS

Kinds of Building Stone and Their Uses. The composition, methods of formation, and properties of the various kinds of stone are considered in Art. 12. Stone masonry and cut-stone facings are extensively used in exterior and interior walls where appearance is an important factor; and *trimstone* in the form of belt courses, cornices, quoins, sills, jambs, and heads is widely used in exterior brick masonry walls. Stone is also used on the interior of buildings for wainscoting, mantels, hearths, floor tile, steps, and stairways and in many other ways. Concrete has largely replaced stone masonry for foundation walls, but stone masonry is still used where a suitable stone can be obtained locally at low cost.

Many stones that are satisfactory for interior use cannot be used outside because of climatic conditions; and some stones that are satisfactory for ordinary building purposes cannot be used for steps, door sills, and floors because of their low resistance to abrasion. Stones that are durable, strong, and attractive in appearance may not be suitable for building purposes because of the labor required to work them into the desired shapes. Some stones that are not used for high-class masonry which requires the stones to be accurately shaped and carefully finished are satisfactory for the cruder forms of masonry. Stones soft enough to work readily are frequently not durable. Ornamental work, such as moldings and carvings, requires a stone with even grain which is free from seams and other defects. Stones that are easily worked in any direction are called *freestones*. Delicate carvings require a stone of considerable strength to withstand injury. The architectural treatment of a building may demand stone of a certain color. Many other factors may enter into the selection of a stone for a specific purpose.

Granite quarries are located in several states, but most of the granite produced in this country is from quarries in eastern United States, from Maine to Georgia, and in Minnesota and Wisconsin. Vermont produces more granite than any other state. Granites are the hardest and most difficult to work of all building stones, but can be finished with a highly polished surface. They are available in a great variety of colors, including white, gray, pink, red, and green. Granite is used for masonry, steps, platforms, sills, trimstone, and as a thin facing or veneer over other masonry. It is also used in base courses and other locations requiring an extremely durable stone.

Marble deposits are rather widely distributed over this country. About 90 per cent of the marble produced comes from Tennessee, Vermont, and Georgia. Pure marble is white, but the other substances present produce a great variety of beautiful colors and color variations, characteristic of marble. The color patterns, together with the stone's ability to take a high polish, make marble a valuable medium for decorative uses. Marble is used as a veneer for monumental buildings. In general it is used for exterior and interior decorative purposes, including wainscoting, panels, mantels, hearths, floor tile, and stairs.

Limestones are found in all parts of this country. Indiana leads all states in the quantity produced. As Indiana limestone or Bedford limestone, limestone from this state is shipped to all parts of the country. This stone varies in color from buff to gray, it is durable and easily worked in saws, planes, lathes, and other machines, and can be carved effectively and cheaply. Because of the low cost of working Indiana limestone, it can compete with local stones in most parts of the country despite transportation costs. Limestone is used for masonry, veneer over other masonry, trimstone, steps, sills, coping, flagstones, floor tile, and is used in many other ways on the exterior and interior of buildings. *Travertine* is a form of limestone that is used to a limited extent for ornamental purposes and floor tile. It contains small irregular cavities. This stone is imported from Italy, but travertine quarries are gradually being developed in Colorado, California, and Montana.

Sandstones are found in nearly every state, but Ohio produces more than half the sandstone used in this country. It is sold chiefly in the Middle West. The stones from Ohio are blue, gray, and buff in color. They have good working qualities and are durable. Sandstones are used for the same purposes as limestones. *Bluestone* and *brownstone* are names applied to sandstones because of their color, although some stones that resemble bluestone in their physical properties are called bluestone even though they are not blue. Bluestone is very strong and durable and splits readily into thin slabs. It is used for sidewalks, steps, flagging, and sills.

Detailed information concerning building stones can be obtained from *The Stone Industries* by Oliver Bowles (9), which has been consulted in the preparation of this article.

Quarrying. Quarrying consists of separating rough blocks of stone from rock formations. In small quarries the work may be done entirely by hand tools with more or less assistance from explosives, but in larger quarries machines are used. Explosives are used to a limited extent because of the waste they cause. Their chief use is in removing the overburden to expose the solid stone.

The nature of the rock formation has an important bearing on the quarrying methods. The stratified sandstones and limestones have been deposited in layers as explained. The surfaces of contact of adjacent layers are called *beds*. In quarrying, advantage is taken of these beds, because they offer planes along which separation is easily accomplished. The beds may be so close together that the stone is only useful for *flagging*, or they may be so far apart or so indistinct that they are of little assistance in quarrying; but the stone may be of greater value in spite of this fact, for the size of the stones is then not limited by the beds.

The unstratified rocks such as granite do not lie in separate layers but have a massive structure, and surfaces of separation have to be made by artificial means. Such rocks may split more easily in one direction than in another.

Both stratified and unstratified rock formations may be divided by *seams* running in any direction. The presence of these seams may be an advantage in quarrying or a disadvantage because of the limit they place on the size and shape of the pieces removed. These seams may be very conspicuous and offer a distinct surface of separation; they may not be discovered until considerable work has been done on a stone; or they may even cause failure after a stone has been placed in a structure. *Streaks* may occur in stone without necessarily reducing its strength.

If a formation is badly broken up by beds and seams, the rock may be removed with crow bars, picks, and wedges; but *dimension stones* are difficult to secure under these conditions except in small sizes.

Building stone is removed from the quarry in rough blocks, which are later cut into pieces of the desired size. In separating the rough blocks from the rock formation, the rock may be broken along a line by drilling a row of closely spaced holes by hand or machine along that line and splitting the rock between the holes by means of *plug and feathers*. The plug is a steel wedge and the feathers are wedges rounded on one side to fit the outline of the hole and flat on the other to form a surface over which a wedge is driven, as shown in Fig. 27-1*a*. Plug and feathers are placed in each hole, and the plugs are gradually driven in with a hammer, driving each plug a little at a time and in succession. By continuing this operation, a force of sufficient intensity to split the rock is developed. In stratified stones the blocks are split along a plane parallel to the bed, which gives a natural surface of separation. In unstratified rocks, plug and feathers may be used along two planes at right angles to each other. Plug and feathers are also known as *wedge and shims*.

The splitting is sometimes accomplished by wooden plugs driven in the holes and soaked with water. The water causes the plugs to expand and exert forces that split the rock.

Channeling machines are widely used for quarrying. These ma-

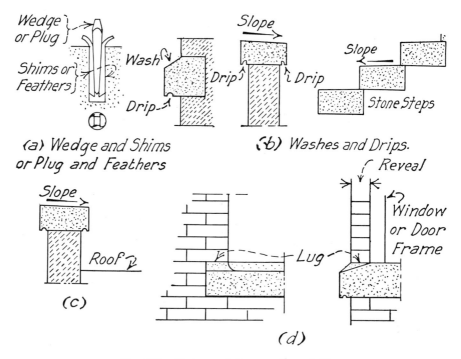

Fig. 27-1. Wedges and shims, washes and drips.

chines cut narrow channels along the face of the block to be cut out. The channels are cut vertically and may be as deep as 10 or 15 ft. The blocks are separated from the quarry ledge at a bedding plane, or they may be split along a horizontal plane by drilling holes and using wedges.

The plug-and-feathers method may be used on any kind of stone and is the method used in granite quarrying. The channeling method is not suitable for granite but is the method commonly used for quarrying limestone, marble, and sandstone. For the harder varieties of sandstone, however, the plug-and-feathers method is more suitable.

In many localities, stones found loose in the field are used for building purposes. These are called *fieldstones*. They may be used in the shape in which they are found, or they may be split or shaped with the hammer. *Cobblestones*, which may be defined as large pebbles, are used in the same way.

Milling. The converting of quarried blocks of stone into the finished product is called *milling*. It includes such operations as *sawing* the blocks into slabs of the desired thickness with *gang saws* or *circular saws*; *planing* them to improve the surface finish or cutting moldings on their surfaces; *turning* columns, balusters, etc., in *lathes*; *milling* recesses, patterns, and lettering on the faces of stones by means of a *milling machine*; *carving* the stone into various forms with hand tools, or with pneumatic tools operated by hand; and *finishing* the surface, as described in the next paragraph.

Cut stone or dressed stone is the product of the stone mill. Stones of large size or special shape, or any stone for which all dimensions are specified in advance, other than finished cut stone, are called *dimension stones*.

Surface Finish. There are various methods of finishing the exposed surface of building stone. The finish that is suitable for a given surface is governed by the kind of stone and the manner in which it is used and varies from the rough face formed in quarrying to the highly polished face often used on marbles and granites. The hand tools used in finishing are described in Vol. VI of the *Transactions of the American Society of Civil Engineers*.

A *quarry face* is a face which is on a stone when it comes from the quarry. It may be formed by the quarrying operations, or may be due to a natural seam and is then called a *seam face*. Quarries producing seam-face stone are traversed in all directions by natural seams forming relatively small blocks of stone of irregular shape and size. Seam faces are often highly colored by deposits from mineral-laden

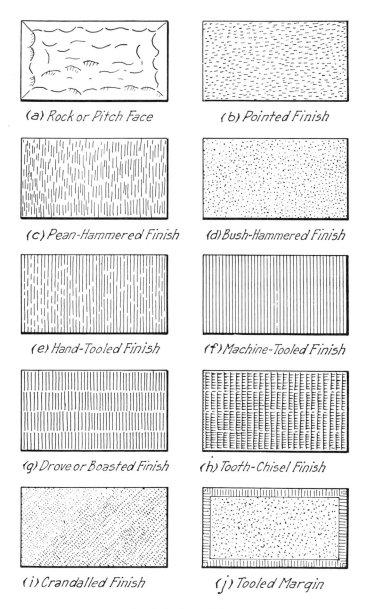

(a) *Rock or Pitch Face*

(b) *Pointed Finish*

(c) *Pean-Hammered Finish*

(d) *Bush-Hammered Finish*

(e) *Hand-Tooled Finish*

(f) *Machine-Tooled Finish*

(g) *Drove or Boasted Finish*

(h) *Tooth-Chisel Finish*

(i) *Crandalled Finish*

(j) *Tooled Margin*

Fig. 27-2. Stone finishes.

waters which have penetrated into the seams. A *split face* is formed by splitting a rock. Other types of surface finish, formed with various tools, are shown in Fig. 27-2.

A *sawed finish* is the surface produced by the saws in cutting a stone to size. The marks of the saws are visible.

A *smooth finish* is produced by planers without hand work other than the removal of objectionable tool marks.

Rubbed and *honed finishes* are produced by grinding or rubbing a sawed or pointed surface by hand or machine, small surfaces and moldings usually being finished by hand. The grade of rubbing is determined by the extent to which this process is carried. Coarse rubbed finish will show small scratches, but a honed finish gives a smooth dead surface practically free from scratches.

A *polished finish* is secured by polishing surfaces which have been previously honed. Granite and marble will take and hold a polish but most other stones will not.

The *margin* or *border* of a stone may have one type of finish and the remaining area another type. Figure 27-2*j* shows a tooled margin with the remainder of the surface bush-hammered. Stones finished in this manner are called *drafted stones.*

Sand blasting is used to cut lettering and designs into the surface of granite. In this operation, the polished surface is coated with a molten rubberlike compound called *dope,* which solidifies to form an elastic covering. The design to be executed is cut into this covering with a sharp tool exposing the stone surface which is to be cut. A blast of sand is then blown with compressed air through a nozzle and against the stone. The part that is covered with the elastic coating is unaffected, while the exposed stone is cut as deeply as desired. As stated by Bowles (9), "The delicate and exquisite detail attained would be impossible with hand tools, and the time required is reduced to a mere fraction of that which hand carving demands."

Selecting Surface Finish. The appropriate finish to be used depends upon the type of masonry, the kind of stone, its position and use in the building, the architectural effect desired, the atmospheric conditions, and the funds available.

All the types of finish just described may be used on granite and marble and, with the exception of polishing, they may be used on sandstone and limestone. Limestone that can be polished is usually classed as marble. The hammered finishes are suitable only for the harder sandstones and limestones, for on the softer stones the ridges will not stand up but will break off leaving a bruised face. These finishes are often called *hard-stone finishes*, for they are not suitable for soft stone. The tooled finishes are similar to the hammered finishes and are more suitable for soft stones.

In selecting a finish, the type that will give the desired results for the least cost would naturally be used. Very satisfactory results are often produced at low cost with quarry, seam, or split-face rubble masonry.

In general, rubble masonry will be quarry-face; squared-stone masonry will be quarry-face or pitched-face; and ashlar or cut-stone masonry will have a pointed or hammered face if it is granite and a sawed, smooth, or rubbed face if it is limestone or sandstone. Marble will usually be rubbed or honed for exterior use, and either honed or polished for interior use. A quarry face or pitch face may also be used for ashlar.

Because of the ease in cleaning, polished surfaces are often used for the base courses and other parts that may be splashed with mud by passing vehicles and for lower stories exposed to a smoky atmosphere. The fine finishes keep clean longer than the coarse finishes.

The sawed finish is the cheapest finish for limestone and sandstone, except the harder grades.

The finer finishes are more suitable for use on interior surfaces than the coarser finishes; but on the exterior the finer finishes will not show if used above the first story, so that the cheaper finishes are more suitable.

Washes and Drips. The exposed top surfaces of cornices, copings, belt courses, sills, steps, platforms, and other stones which should shed water are provided with sloping surfaces called *washes*. See Fig. 27-1*b*.

Projecting stones such as cornices, belt courses, and sills are provided with a groove or channel on the under surface of the projection and near the outer edge. This groove is called a *drip* for it causes water to drip from the lower edge of the projecting stone rather than follow along the surface of the wall. Drips should be at least ½ in. wide by ¼ in. deep, but larger drips are better if they can be provided. See Fig. 27-1*b*.

The stonework will usually be soiled or streaked where the washes pitch toward the face of the stonework. For this reason it is desirable that copings pitch toward the roof and that the water be drained off of projecting stones rather than be allowed to run over the face of the stone even though it drips from the lower edge. See Fig. 27-1*c*.

Where other work is built on stones provided with a wash, it will usually be necessary to cut *raised seats* and *lugs* on the stones to form level beds for the work which is built on them. See Fig. 27-1*d*.

Classification of Stone Masonry. In classifying stone masonry, it is necessary to take into account the degree of refinement used in shaping the stones, the way the face stones are arranged in the wall, and the surface finish of the stones.

There are no accepted standards for classification, but in general the crudest type of masonry, constructed of stones with little or no shaping, is called *rubble,* and the highest type, constructed of stones accurately shaped so as to make thin joints possible, is called *ashlar.* Between these two extremes, there are various degrees of refinement in shaping the stones and many ways of arranging them in the wall. The most common classification divides masonry into *rubble, squared-stone masonry,* and *ashlar,* according to the care used in shaping the stones, and into *range, broken range,* and *random,* according to the arrangement of the stones in the wall. The latter classification does not apply to rubble. Rubble is classed as *coursed* and *uncoursed.* Ashlar is also called *cut stone.* See Fig. 27-3.

There is no definite line of demarcation between ashlar and squared-stone masonry or between squared-stone masonry and rubble. When stratified stone is used, the horizontal joints of rubble may be as narrow and as uniform as those of squared-stone masonry, and the distinction between the two classes would lie in the vertical joints. If the work done on such stone consists only of knocking off loose rock or sharp corners, rubble would probably result; but, if the stone is shaped to give a uniform vertical joint, squared-stone masonry would be produced. If the end joints are not vertical but are uniform in thickness, the class of work would be the same as that on squared-stone masonry; but such masonry could not logically be placed in that class because of the shape of the stone.

Sometimes the joints are as thin as ashlar joints but the end joints are not vertical. Such masonry should probably be classed as ashlar. If the stones are irregular in shape without parallel surfaces and are shaped to fit the spaces they are to occupy, the joints may be neither vertical nor horizontal. Such masonry is classed as *polygonal masonry* because of the shape of the face of the stone. In this type of masonry the stones are sometimes accurately cut with joints as uniform and as thin as in ashlar. Often the stones are only roughly shaped, and the joints are not uniform in thickness. This type of masonry is often called *mosaic rubble* or *cobweb rubble.*

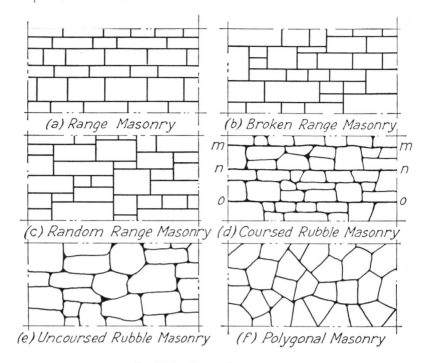

Fig. 27-3. Classes of stone masonry.

The *American Standard Building Code Requirements* includes the following definitions of types of masonry (1).

Ashlar Masonry. Masonry composed of rectangular units usually larger in size than brick and properly bonded, having sawed, dressed or squared beds, and mortar joints.

Ashlar Facing. Facing of a faced or veneered wall larger in size than brick, having sawed, dressed or squared beds, and mortar joints.

Rubble.

Coursed Rubble. Masonry composed of roughly shaped stones fitting approximately on level beds, well bonded, and brought at vertical intervals to continuous level beds or courses.

Random Rubble. Masonry composed of roughly shaped stones well bonded and brought at irregular intervals to discontinuous but approximately level beds or courses.

Rough or Ordinary Rubble. Masonry composed of nonshaped or field stones laid without regularity or coursing.

Arrangement of Courses. In *range masonry* the stones are laid in courses, each course being uniform in thickness throughout its length. All courses, however, need not be of the same thickness (Fig. 27-3a).

In *broken-range masonry* the stones are laid in courses but the courses are continuous for short distances only (*b*).

In *random masonry* no attempt is made to form courses (*c*).

The terms range, broken range, and random are usually applied only to ashlar and squared-stone masonry; but, where rubble masonry is constructed of stratified stones, the upper and lower surfaces may be parallel and random masonry results. In general, however, rubble masonry is divided into coursed and uncoursed rubble.

In *coursed rubble* the masonry is leveled at specified heights (*d*) or is laid in fairly regular courses marked *m–m, n–n, o–o* in the figure.

In *uncoursed rubble* the masonry is not leveled as in coursed rubble (*e*).

In *polygonal masonry* the stones are irregular in shape without parallel edges and are shaped to fit the spaces they are to occupy, the joints being more or less uniform in thickness (*f*). This type of masonry is also called *mosaic rubble* and *cobweb rubble*. It is undesirable structurally and architecturally.

Backing. In rubble masonry the face and backing are usually of rubble, the better stones being picked out for the face, but concrete backing may be used.

The backing for squared-stone masonry and ashlar masonry may be rubble masonry, brick, structural clay tile, or concrete block. Rubble masonry is not suitable for backing thin walls such as panel walls. If rough blocks are shipped to the building site and are there worked into shape, the stone that would otherwise be wasted is used in the rubble backing. Ashlar or squared-stone masonry is not used for backing.

Concrete is also used for backing, but it should not be placed against limestone facing or against brickwork in contact with such stone without providing a waterproof layer between the stone and the concrete. If such a layer is not provided, the stone may be discolored and stained. Certain stones may not require such a coating, but it should not be omitted without making a thorough investigation. Ashlar is often used as a veneer for concrete walls or other surfaces which are already in place.

The stones used in facing over brick- or structural clay-tile backing should preferably be of such a height that they will work in with the backing, the horizontal joints of the face and backing coming at the same level at the intervals desired for bonding, as described in the next section.

For illustrations of walls with stone facing and structural clay-tile backing see Fig. 28-3.

Setting. Placing stone in position in a structure is called *setting*. Stones are usually lifted with derricks, the stone being held with *grab hooks,* as shown in Fig. 27-4a, with *lewises* (b), or with *pin lewises* inserted in inclined holes (c). If lewises are used, *lewis holes* must be provided. The most common type of lewis is assembled in the hole, as shown in (b).

Stratified stone should be dressed so that it may be set in the building with the natural quarry bed horizontal. This is important in stratified stone because of its greater strength when it is placed in that direction and also because of its greater resistance to weathering. When the quarry bed is placed vertical, water enters the stone more freely and weathering progresses more rapidly than when the quarry bed is horizontal. If the quarry bed is placed vertical and parallel to the face, many stones scale off badly.

Little attention need be paid to the setting of Indiana limestone on its natural quarry bed. The great majority of such ashlar is sawed with the grain parallel to the face of the wall, and monolithic columns are produced with the grain running vertical. However, most limestones are somewhat weaker, when loaded, parallel to the bedding than when the loading is perpendicular to the bedding.

Door and window sills that have their ends built into the masonry should be bedded only at the ends, the space between being left entirely free from mortar except for the pointing mortar which is applied later.

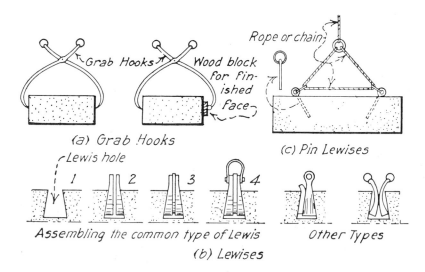

Fig. 27-4. Methods of lifting stone blocks.

If this practice is not followed, the sills will be quite certain to break when the ends become loaded as the work progresses. This type of sill is called a *lug sill*. Very often window sills are made slightly shorter than the opening and are independent of the rest of the masonry, except, of course, of the bed on which they rest. The bed is completely filled with mortar. Such sills are called *slip sills*. Exterior steps and sills are set with a slight pitch to the front so that they will drain.

The following comments on the setting of limestone are based on specifications prepared by the Indiana Limestone Institute. Many of these comments apply to other kinds of stone masonry.

Before setting, all stones should be cleaned on all sides by steam cleaning or washing, using fiber brushes and soap powder when necessary, and finally be drenched with clean water.

Except in freezing weather, all stone not thoroughly wet, should be sponged off or drenched with clean water just prior to setting to prevent the absorption of moisture from the setting mortar and thus insuring its proper hardening.

In general, every stone should be set on a full bed of mortar with all vertical joints flushed full of mortar and all anchor, dowel, lewis, and similar holes completely filled.

Lead buttons should be used where necessary to prevent crushing of mortar under heavy loads. Wood wedges should not be used for this purpose.

The joints between all sections of large diameter columns should be made of sheet lead cut back approximately 2 in. from the face and with center cut out to allow space for squeezing.

Heavy stones or projecting courses should not be set until the mortar in courses beneath has hardened to support them.

Projecting stones should be securely propped or anchored until the mortar in the wall above has set.

All cornices, copings, projecting belt courses and stones forming gutters should be set with the vertical joints unfilled. The exterior profiles of these joints should be calked with rope yarn or picked oakum and the joint filled full from above with mortar grout and raked out on top to a depth of ¾ in. After the grout has set, the calking is removed and the joint pointed.

In general, mortar should be raked out of joints to a depth of ¾ in. from the face of the stone for pointing. The face of the stone should be washed clean along all joints.

Avoid splashing exposed faces of stone with mortar. Droppings and splashings should be removed immediately with a clean sponge and water.

Face stone should not be set more than two courses in advance of the backing.

Limestone grade courses should not be set until the top of the foundation has been waterproofed or protected against the danger of staining due to capillarity.

Mortar including ordinary portland cement as an ingredient will stain limestone.

The mortar used in setting limestone facing, and preferably its backing, should be nonstaining.

The process of applying a waterproof coat of cement mortar to the back of the facing masonry or the face of the backing material is called *parging, pargeting,* or *back plastering.* To prevent staining of the facing by soluble salts carried in solution from the backing by rainwater which has penetrated into the wall, the parging may be applied. The use of nonstaining cement mortar, however, makes parging for this purpose unnecessary and is preferred if the backing masonry is free from soluble salts, but it increases the resistance of the wall to moisture penetration. The painting of the sides or backs of facing stones, called *back-painting,* with bituminous waterproofing for this purpose is considered objectionable.

Bondstones and Anchors. In stone masonry, longitudinal bond is secured by breaking joints as in brick masonry, although in broken-range and random masonry a vertical joint may sometimes be three stones in height.

Bond between the face and backing may be secured by headers or bondstones as in brick masonry, by bond courses, by metal anchors, or by bond courses or stones and metal anchors used together.

The bond or anchorage required between the face and backing depends upon whether the wall is a bearing wall or a nonbearing wall and upon whether the facing is to be considered in the required thickness of the wall.

Headers extending entirely through the wall are shown in Fig. 27-5a.

Bondstones arranged in courses projecting into the backing an amount equal to the thickness of the other facing stones are shown in *b,* with one bed of every stone in contact with a bondstone. The arrangement shown in *c* makes every other course a bond course. All the stones in a bond course are not usually bondstones; and in broken-range and random masonry the bondstones are distributed at random throughout the wall, with each stone providing the tie for a given surface area. *Noncorrosive metal anchors* are extensively used to tie the facing to the backing (*d*). Bond courses and anchors are usually used together. In *e* the anchors are supplemented by a bond course bearing on the spandrel beam of each story. The combination of bond courses and anchors is shown in *f.* Every stone not a bondstone may be anchored to the backing, as shown in *g.* The method of anchoring a cut-stone cornice is illustrated in *h.* Special anchors should be provided for cornice and belt-course stones that do not have sufficient bearing to balance on the wall. These anchors should be

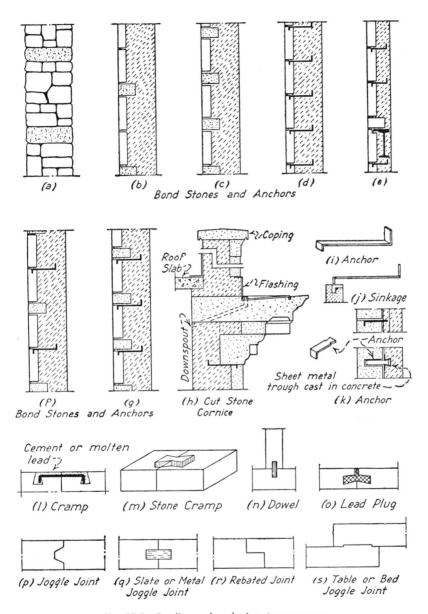

(a)

(b) (c) (d) (e)
Bond Stones and Anchors

(f) (g) Bond Stones and Anchors

(h) Cut Stone Cornice

Coping

Roof Slab

Flashing

Downspout

(i) Anchor

(j) Sinkage

Anchor

Sheet metal trough cast in concrete

(k) Anchor

Cement or molten lead

(l) Cramp   (m) Stone Cramp   (n) Dowel   (o) Lead Plug

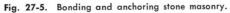

(p) Joggle Joint   (q) Slate or Metal Joggle Joint   (r) Rebated Joint   (s) Table or Bed Joggle Joint

Fig. 27-5. Bonding and anchoring stone masonry.

hooked into the stone at least 2 in. and should be spaced about 2 ft. apart, with at least two anchors to a stone.

Further discussion of the bond required between the facing and backing is given in the paragraph on faced and veneered walls.

The requirements of the American Standard Building Code (1) for bonding and anchoring are given in Art. 30, Sec. E.

Construction and Placing of Anchors. Anchors are usually placed in the horizontal joints and hooked into the tops of the stones, but at times it is desirable to place anchors in the vertical joints near the top and near the bottom of the stone and hooking into the side, especially when structural clay tile backing is used. A typical form of anchor is shown in *i.*

Anchors should not be placed in the mortar joint, but a *sinkage* or depression of ample width and of a depth slightly greater than the thickness of the anchor should be provided at the back of anchor holes (*j*). There are two reasons for providing sinkages. With the ¼-in. joints usually used in ashlar masonry there would be difficulty in placing the anchors in the joints, and the stones would tend to rest on the anchors rather than to secure uniform bearing on the mortar joint. This condition would tend to cause the stones to crack. The sinkages do not fit the anchor accurately but are usually larger than necessary and are crudely formed. Anchor holes should be kept about 2 in. from the outer surface of the stonework so that the anchor may be adequately protected. The anchors should be completely embedded in mortar.

Anchors should be made of noncorrosive metal or steel galvanized after cutting and shaping. Galvanizing is required to prevent rusting, which may stain the stonework, split the stone by expansion while rusting, or finally destroy the anchor. Coating anchors with paint will not take the place of galvanizing but may be done as an additional precaution.

A form of anchor which is convenient for use in anchoring a stone facing to a concrete wall is shown in Fig. 27-5*k*. Before the wall is poured, sheet-metal troughs are tacked to the side of the form for the outer face. They are placed vertically at the proper intervals. When the forms are removed, the trough is exposed in the face of the wall. It is beveled on the sides to receive an anchor with a dovetailed end. The anchors may be moved up and down to fit into the joints. This type of anchor is more convenient and much more effective than most types of anchors, which are cast in concrete walls and are bent out into the mortar joints of the facing.

Lewis Anchors, Cramps, Dowels, etc. Forms of anchors other than those just described are sometimes required. When it is necessary to suspend the soffits of openings from steelwork above, lewis anchors, similar to the ordinary lewis, are used. The lewis holes for the anchors should be from 3 to 4 in. deep.

Clamps or *cramps* are used to keep coping stones, stair rails, etc., from pulling apart. They are made of flat iron, varying from 1¼ by ¼ in. for light work to 1½ by ½ in. for heavier pieces. These are turned down 1½ or 2 in. at the ends and vary in length from 6 to 12 in. They may be set in sinkages in the tops of the stones, or they may be set under the stones with their ends turned upward into the stones. *Cramps* should be heavily galvanized after being bent to shape. On high-quality work they may be protected by pouring molten lead around them (Fig. 27-5*l*), the holes being larger at the bottom than at the top in order to hold the lead and anchor in place. Cramps or keys made of slate or other stone or of metal may occasionally be used in place of cramps (*m*). The lead plug shown in *o* serves the same purpose but is rarely used. In forming the lead plug, molten lead is poured in the vertical channel and fills the dovetailed holes, which are sloped so that the lead can easily fill the holes. Brass or bronze dowels made of solid rods or of pipe are ordinarily used to hold the ends of balusters, window mullions, and similar pieces in position (*n*). The ends of inclined copings may be doweled into the kneelers (Fig. 25-2*e*).

Joggled, Tabled, and Rebated Joints. Two types of joints which are rarely used are the *joggled joint* shown in Fig. 27-5*p* and the *table joint* or *bed joggle joint* shown in *s*, designed to prevent movement along a joint. These joints are very expensive to form. A slate or metal joggle joint (*q*) may be formed more cheaply. The joint is not usually continuous. A *rebated joint* is shown in *r*. This type of joint is sometimes used for coping stones placed on a slope.

Faced and Veneered Walls. Stone walls may be classed as faced walls and veneered walls according to the provision made for bonding the face to the backing. If the facing and backing are securely bonded together so that they will act as a unit, the entire thickness of the wall may be considered in strength calculations and in satisfying the requirements for minimum thickness. Such walls are called *faced walls*. If the facing is not attached and bonded to the backing to the extent that it forms an integral part of the wall, the wall is called a *veneered wall*, and only the backing may be considered in strength calculations and in satisfying the requirements for minimum thickness.

Joints and Pointing. The mortar layers between stones are called *joints.* Horizontal joints are *bed joints* or simply *beds,* and vertical joints are known as *head joints* or *builds.*

In rubble masonry the joints are neither uniform in thickness nor constant in direction; they simply fill the spaces between stones of irregular shape. Large spaces in the backing may have small pieces of stone called *spalls* embedded in the mortar.

In squared-stone masonry the joints are horizontal and vertical and are more or less uniform in thickness, the stones having been roughly dressed to shape. In general the joints in squared-stone masonry are ½ to 1 in. thick.

In ashlar or cut-stone masonry the stones are accurately dressed to shape so that the joints do not exceed ½ in. in thickness. A very common thickness of joint for the ashlar facing of buildings is ¼ in. Joints ⅛ in. in thickness are sometimes used for interior stonework but are not desirable for exterior work.

The mortar in the horizontal and vertical joints of ashlar masonry is kept back from the face in setting the stone or is raked out to a depth of about ¾ in. In this space a special mortar is placed to make a tighter and more attractive joint. This process is known as *pointing.* The various types of joints formed by pointing are shown in Fig. 27-6. Pointing is done after the mortar in the joint has set and usually after all the stone has been placed and the wall has received its full load.

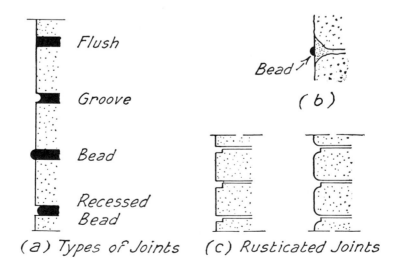

Fig. 27-6. Joints for stone masonry.

Squared-stone masonry may be pointed in the same manner as ashlar, or the joint may be finished at the time the stone is set.

The joints in rubble masonry are usually finished when the stones are set, and no pointing is done.

Often the joints of squared-stone masonry or rubble are made flush with the surface of the stones, and after the mortar has set a narrow bead of colored mortar is run on the wide joints to give the effect of narrow joints. See Fig. 27-6b. The wide joint is frequently made the same color as the stone and the narrow joint a contrasting color.

The joints are often emphasized by shaping the stones to form *rusticated* or *rebated* joints (*c*). This type of joint is frequently used in the stonework on the lower stories of buildings to give a massive appearance.

Mortar. See Art. 30, Sec. B.

Trimstone. Cut stone is frequently used as a trim around window and door openings and for belt courses, copings, and cornices in walls constructed of brick or rubble masonry. Stone used in this manner is called *trimstone*.

Cast Stone. The use of cast-concrete units, commonly known as *cast stone*, to replace cut stone has been growing in recent years. Cast stone consists of molded blocks of concrete with special surface treatment. They may be formed in any of the shapes obtained by cutting the natural stone and may have surface finishes which resemble the rubbed finish often used on limestone and other stones, or any of the tooled finishes. Special aggregates may be used next to the face or for the entire block so that when the cement surface film is removed by etching with acid or tooling the face will resemble granite, marble, and other natural stones, or the aggregate may be chosen simply to produce an attractive finish without attempting to imitate any natural stone.

One of the problems in connection with the manufacture of cast stone is the prevention of *crazing*. Crazing consists of small cracks of web-like nature which often form on the surface of cast stone.

Minimum Wall Thickness. See Art. 30, Sec. D.

Flashing and Calking. See Art. 25 under that paragraph heading.

Permeability. See Art. 25 under that paragraph heading. Stone masonry, however, is not mentioned specifically.

Efflorescence. See Art. 25 under that paragraph heading.

Protection against Freezing. See Art. 30, Sec. J, Par. 2.

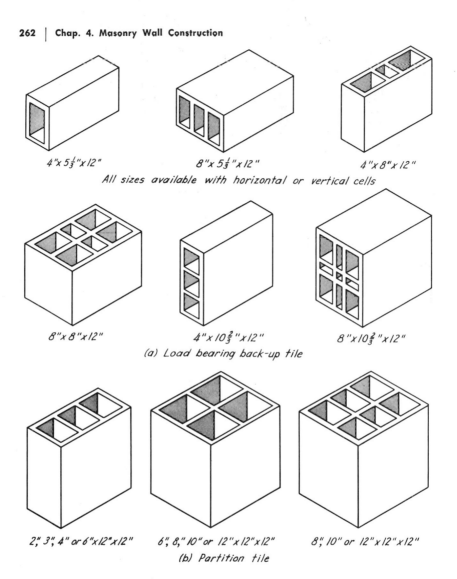

4"x 5⅓"x 12"   8"x 5⅓"x 12"   4"x 8"x 12"

All sizes available with horizontal or vertical cells

8"x 8"x 12"   4"x 10⅔"x 12"   8"x 10⅔"x 12"

(a) Load bearing back-up tile

2", 3", 4" or 6"x 12"x 12"   6", 8", 10" or 12"x 12"x 12"   8", 10" or 12"x 12"x 12"

(b) Partition tile

Fig. 28-1. (a) and (b) Structural clay load-bearing and partition tile.

28. HOLLOW-UNIT MASONRY WALLS

Classes of Hollow Units. Hollow units made of burned clay or shale, concrete, gypsum, and glass are extensively used in the construction of walls and partitions. The terms tile and block are used to represent a single unit or collectively for a number of such units, as in the case of brick. The term terra-cotta, meaning "burned earth," is sometimes applied to structural clay tile, but this term is preferably

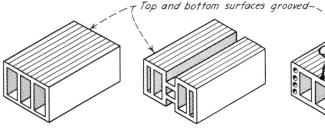
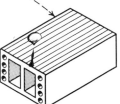

Top and bottom surfaces grooved

Solid-shell unit   *Double-shell unit*   *Cored-shell unit*
8 X 5⅓ X 12 in. side construction tile

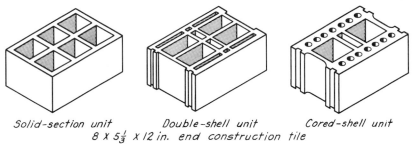

Solid-section unit   *Double-shell unit*   *Cored-shell unit*
8 X 5⅓ X 12 in. end construction tile

(c) Facing tile

Fig. 28-1. (c) Structural clay facing tile.

reserved for ornamental building units of burned clay which are usually classed as architectural terra-cotta. Hollow clay tile are usually called structural clay tile.

Structural Clay Tile

These units, illustrated in Fig. 28-1 (10), are manufactured by extruding or forcing a plastic clay through specially formed dies, cutting it to the desired dimensions, and burning it in kilns to various degrees of hardness, depending upon the grade being manufactured. The hollow spaces in the tile are called *cells*. The outer walls are called *shells*, and the inner partitions that divide the tile into cells are called *webs*. The shells are ¾ in. or more in thickness and the webs ½ in. or more. The nominal length is usually 12 in., although for some types of units it is 16 in. The actual lengths often are made ½, ⅜, or ¼ in. less than the nominal lengths to allow for the mortar joints and still to maintain the 4-in. *module*. The same is true for the other dimensions.

Many other types of units than those illustrated are manufactured.

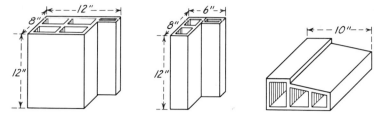

(a) Jamb and sill tile for end construction

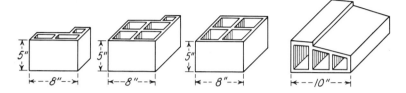

(b) Jamb, corner and sill tile for side construction

Fig. 28-2. Jamb, sill, and corner structural clay tile.

Special shapes (Fig. 28-2) are available for *corners* and *jambs* so that the ends of the cells will not be exposed if the cells are laid horizontally. *Sills* and *headers* are available to receive the ends of brick headers so that cutting will not be required.

Specifications for structural clay tile include requirements for absorption and, for load-bearing units, compressive strength.

Classes of Structural Clay Tile. Structural clay tile are divided into two classes (Fig. 28-1) according to the direction of the axes of the cells when the units are placed in masonry. In *side-construction tile*, the cells are placed horizontally, and in *end-construction tile*, vertically. The compressive strength, based on the gross area of a horizontal section included within the outer surfaces of a tile, is about 45 per cent higher for end-construction tile than for side-construction tile. Structural clay tile are divided into two classes according to loading conditions, *loadbearing* (Fig. 28-1a and c) and *nonloadbearing* (b). Nonloadbearing tile are usually called *partition tile* because of their use in nonbearing partitions.

Structural clay tile are divided into two classes according to the position they occupy in a multiple unit wall: *backing* or *back-up* tile used to back up various kinds of facing units such as brick and stone or to receive stucco; and *facing tile*, which has a finished surface on one or two sides whch are to be left exposed to view. Facing tile may have *solid shells, double shells,* or *cored shells* (*c*). They are available in thicknesses of 2, 4, 6, and 8 in., heights of 4, 5⅓, 6, and 8 in., and lengths of 8 and 12 in. for 4- and 5⅓-in. heights, 12 in. for 6-in. heights, and 12 and 16 in. for 8-in. heights.

Surface Texture and Color. The surface finish selected for structural clay tile depends upon the use to be made of the tile. The following finishes are available: natural or smooth, scored, combed or roughened by wire cutting or wire brushing, salt glaze, and ceramic glaze.

The natural or smooth finish may be used on exposed surfaces that are to be untreated or painted. The scored finish is provided to increase the bond of plaster or stucco finishes, although investigations have shown that the smooth finish provides an adequate plaster bond if it has no glaze. The roughened finishes are provided to achieve a desired texture, but they may be used to receive plaster. The salt and ceramic glazes are provided to achieve the desired appearance as well as low water absorption and easy cleaning.

Tile with *natural* or *smooth* and *roughened* finishes are produced in a wide variety of colors, depending upon the composition of the clay and the degree of burning. Such colors include cream, gray, buff, brown, and various shades of red, purple, and black comparable to the colors of face brick.

A *salt glaze* is produced on tile made of light-burning clays by introducing common salt and other chemicals into the fire box of the kilns near the end of the burning process. The vapors formed by the action of heat on the salt when they come in contact with surfaces of the tile react chemically and form a glaze. The usual colors of salt-glaze units are cream and buff.

Ceramic glazes or *enamels* are formed on surfaces of facing tile by spraying them with mineral glazing materials before burning. They are so constituted that they will fuse together during burning and form a glass-like coating on the surface of the tile. They may form single or multicolor shades. Some of the single-color shades are white, light gray, ivory, yellow, coral, tan, blue, and green. Multicolor glazes include mottles of white, gray, cream, and green with a trim shade of black.

Wall Construction. Structural clay tile backing units for exterior walls are used with facings of various other types of masonry units such as brick, stone, and structural clay tile facing units (Fig. 28-3). The backing units may be either end construction or side construction.

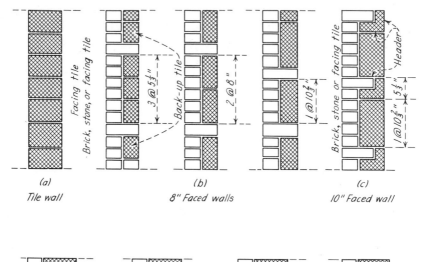

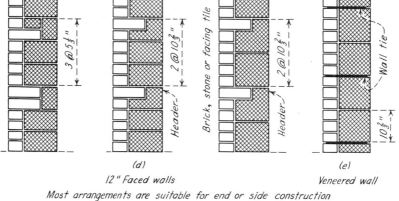

Fig. 28-3. Structural clay tile in wall construction. Adapted from Structural Clay Products Institute.

The figure illustrates the use of brick facing for 8-, 10-, and 12-in. walls, but similar arrangements are used with the other types of facing mentioned. In most of the illustrations, the facing is bonded to the backing by headers or bonders. In *e*, however, metal ties are used to anchor the facing to the backing.

The tile are normally laid with the vertical joints staggered as in the stretcher bond of brick masonry (Fig. 26-2*a*), but they are altered to provide for bonders as required.

The tile joints should provide full mortar coverage of the ends and edges of the face shells in both vertical and horizontal directions, as stated in Art. 30, Sec. E, Par. 2. For the type of mortar required, see Art. 30, Sec. B, Par. 3, and the paragraph on mortar in Art. 26.

Minimum Wall Thickness. See Art. 30, Sec. D.

Bonding and Anchoring. See Art. 30, Sec. E.

Fire-Resistance Ratings. See Art. 30, Sec. L.

Architectural Terra-Cotta

Architectural terra-cotta consists of hard-burned glazed or unglazed building units, which may be plain or ornamental, machine-extruded or hand-molded, and generally larger in size than brick or facing tile.

The units may be hollow or ribbed and may be made in a great variety of surface finishes, textures, and colors. Their function is decorative rather than structural.

Ceramic veneer is architectural terra-cotta characterized by large face dimensions and thin sections. The thinner sections may be held in place by adhesion to mortar placed between the terra-cotta and the backing, and the thicker sections by grout and wire anchors connected to the backing.

In selecting terra-cotta for outside use, care must be taken to obtain a product that will not spall or crack and one whose exposed surface will not craze or flake off under the weather conditions to which it will be subjected.

Concrete Block

Materials. Concrete block, three types of which are illustrated in Fig. 28-4, are made of portland cement concrete with *heavyweight*

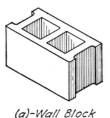 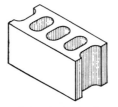

(a)-Wall Block   (b)-Wall Block   (c)-Partition Block

Fig. 28-4. Concrete block.

aggregates such as sand, gravel, crushed stone, and air-cooled slag; and *lightweight aggregates* such as coal cinders, expanded shale, clay or slag, and natural lightweight materials such as volcanic cinders and pumice.

Manufacture. The block are formed in machines with steel molds, the concrete being consolidated by vibrating and compacting. This treatment provides accurately formed block and permits dry mixtures to be used. Thus the molds can be removed immediately after compaction.

Small-scale operations may be carried on by small hand-operated single-mold machines with low production rates, but most of the production is by power-driven machines, with gang molds, each of which can produce several thousand units per day. The block are cured and dried as described in the following paragraph.

Curing and Drying. The curing and drying of concrete block after they have been formed in the manner described are of extreme importance because of the tendency of undercured block to shrink and cause unsightly cracks after they have been placed in a wall.

During the curing operation the block are kept moist so that setting and hardening can take place satisfactorily. During the drying operation the moisture content is reduced so that, at the time of laying, it will not be further reduced or increased by the air with which it is in contact for average air humidity conditions.

Curing and drying may be carried on in the open air with protection from the weather by enclosing stacked block and hastening the process by blowing heated air through them; by high-temperature steam curing in sealed kilns; or by high-pressure steam curing in a pressure vessel, called an *autoclave,* filled with saturated steam at a temperature of about 370°F.

The open-air procedure requires from 2 to 4 weeks, the heated-air process is more rapid, steam curing may be accomplished in 24 hours, and high-pressure steam curing in about 12 hours. While the units are stored, either at the plant or on the job site, they should be protected against absorbing moisture from rain or snow.

Sizes and Shapes. The most common sizes are shown in Fig. 28-4. The unit with the nominal dimensions of 8-in. width, 8-in. height, and 16-in. length has corresponding actual dimensions of $7\frac{5}{8}$ by $7\frac{5}{8}$ by $15\frac{5}{8}$ in. to allow for $\frac{3}{8}$-in. joists and thereby conform with the *modular coordination of design* which is based on the 4-in. module. The same dimensional relationship is maintained on all other units.

Other nominal widths are 3, 4, 8, 10, and 12 in., and other heights are $3\frac{1}{2}$ and 5 in. The usual length is $15\frac{5}{8}$ in., but half-lengths are also manufactured. Special shapes are available for single and double square and bullnose corners, jambs, and header block to receive the ends of headers. The area occupied by the cores may be as small as 25 per cent of the gross area, but it is usually from 40 to 50 per cent. Many other special shapes are manufactured to meet specific requirements and secure desired architectural effects. Pierced grille block are sometimes used for solar screens. Block may have solid faces with patterns to match pierced block.

The relative weights of block made from heavyweight and lightweight aggregates are illustrated by the weights of 8-by-8-by-16-in. blocks which vary from 40 to 50 lb. for the heavy and 25 to 35 lb. for the light.

Specifications for concrete block include requirements for moisture content, absorption, and compressive strength.

Surface Finish. The exposed surfaces are usually plain. The surface finish or texture may be fine, medium, or coarse depending upon the grading of the aggregates.

Concrete block with glazed exposed surfaces are available. The glazed surface, from $\frac{1}{8}$ to $\frac{3}{8}$ in. thick, is formed by a mixture of selected mineral aggregates, pigments, and a thermosetting plastic binder. The binder hardens at the temperatures prevailing in the high-pressure curing process which is used. Block of the usual sizes are manufactured in a variety of colors.

Wall Construction. Concrete block walls and partitions are normally one block thick laid with broken or staggered vertical joints. Concrete block are used as backing for exterior walls faced with brick or stone in the manner illustrated for structural clay tile backing (Fig. 28-3). Special units are available for corners, jambs, and other purposes as has been explained. Half-block may also be obtained.

Cavity walls are constructed of two wythes of blocks each at least 4 in. thick, separated by an air space of from 2 to 3 in. and tied together, as required, with noncorrosive metal ties.

The mortar in the bed joint usually covers only the shells, but if strength is an important factor the webs are also covered. The mortar covers only the shells in forming the head or vertical joints. The normal joint thickness is $\frac{3}{8}$ in. The V and concave joints illustrated for brick walls in Fig. 26-3e and f are preferred. They are made by running special tools along full or flush joints after the mortar has partially set, and exerting pressure. They are more watertight than other types of joints. In addition, to secure the maximum resistance to moisture penetration extreme care must be used to completely fill the joints. Even then, exposed exterior wall surfaces should be treated as described later.

Steel reinforcement of various types is often embedded in a part or all of the bed joints of concrete block masonry. Such reinforcement may consist of two $\frac{3}{16}$-in., or smaller, uncoated or galvanized, plain or corrugated longitudinal rods connected by welded perpendicular cross rods or, in truss-like form, by continuous cross rods bent back and forth at various angles and welded at their points of contact with the longitudinal rods. Galvanized woven-wire mesh is also available, similar in pattern to poultry wire, integral with two longitudinal wires along each edge.

Such reinforcement distributes the cracks due to block shrinkage or temperature change so that they are not visible, and does not permit such cracks to form at larger intervals where they may be seen. This action is similar to that of temperature and shrinkage reinforcement in reinforced concrete slabs. It is also effective in reducing cracking caused by differential settlement or deflection over openings in the wall and, by controlling cracking, increases resistance to water penetration. It is used to tie the wythes of cavity walls together as well as for walls one-unit thick. It is lapped or otherwise carried around corners and serves to anchor intersecting walls together.

Surface Treatments. In regions subject to driving rains, exterior, above-grade, concrete block walls are quite likely to leak because of water which penetrates the joints or the block. Such leakage can be prevented by the application of portland cement stucco or by coating with portland cement paint as described in the paragraph on permeability in Art. 25. Such paints are mixed with water and are available in a variety of colors.

The outside face of concrete block foundation walls should be waterproofed with two coats of portland cement mortar with a total thickness of at least $\frac{1}{2}$ in.

Interior wall surfaces require no treatment except for decorative purposes. Neither exterior nor interior wall surfaces of glazed block, of course, require surface treatment, but extreme care should be used in laying exterior block to secure watertight joints.

Wall Thickness. See Art. 30, Sec. D.

Bonding and Anchoring. See Art. 30, Sec. E.

Fire Resistance Ratings. See Art. 30, Sec. L.

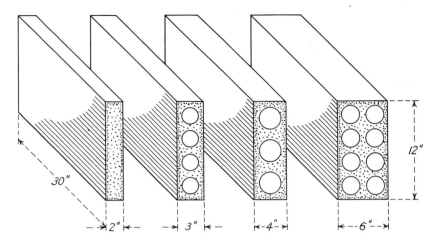

Fig. 28-5. Gypsum partition tile or block.

Gypsum Tile or Block

Gypsum tile or block are composed primarily of calcined gypsum to which water is added, resulting in the chemical reaction and setting as explained in Art. 10. They may or may not include aggregates. If combustible aggregates, such as wood fiber, are included, their weight must not exceed 15 per cent of the weight of the dry tile.

Some of the forms of gypsum tile are shown in Fig. 28-5. They are rectangular in shape and may be solid or cored. Special shapes are also available.

Gypsum tile are used for interior nonbearing partitions and as fire protection of structural steel members. They should not be used where walls are subject to continuous dampness. They are set only in gypsum mortar and do not form a suitable base for portland cement or lime plaster, but they provide an excellent base for gypsum plaster. See Art. 30, Sec. D, Par. 5c.

Glass Block

Glass block, as shown in Fig. 28-6, are hollow, colorless, translucent masonry units formed by fusing, at high temperature, two sections that have been cast separately. Their primary function is to transmit light through walls and thereby to replace windows. The process of manufacture seals the block and produces a partial vacuum in the in-

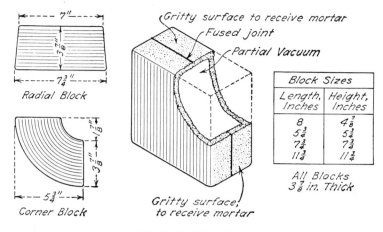

Fig. 28-6. Glass block.

terior. Various patterns are available for the exposed faces. The interior or exterior surfaces of each face may be smooth or may have horizontal or vertical ribs or other patterns. If the patterns are on the interior surfaces, the exposed surfaces are smooth. This smoothness permits easy cleaning.

Glass-block panels are used primarily to transmit light where window openings are not required for ventilation or where clear glass is not needed for visibility. They diffuse the light that passes through them. Suitable patterns can be provided on the interior surfaces to direct the light to the ceilings of rooms from which it is reflected downward on work surfaces which may be at some distance from the wall. They are more resistant to heat and sound transmission and condensation than is ordinary glass.

Special block are available which are more resistant to heat transmission and more effective in brightness control than regular block. These special properties are achieved by dividing the interior cavity with fibrous glass screens during manufacture, or in other ways. In some cases, the screen has a blue-green color and imparts this color to the block (20).

Glass block are used in exterior walls and interior partitions but cannot be used to carry any load other than their own weight. Glass block are not laid with the vertical joints broken or staggered as in other masonry, but the vertical joints as well as the horizontal are continuous.

See Art. 30, Sec. H.

29. PLAIN AND REINFORCED CONCRETE WALLS

Concrete without reinforcement or lightly reinforced, as described later, is classed as *plain concrete* or *masonry*. Other concrete with reinforcement is classed as *reinforced concrete.*

Uses. Concrete has largely replaced stone and brick for foundation walls, for it is usually cheaper than brick or stone masonry and more substantial and watertight than either. However, brick masonry will stand uneven settlement, without serious cracking, better than plain concrete. Bearing walls above ground may be constructed of concrete. Attractive buildings with concrete exterior walls are being constructed. In some, the exposed surfaces are left as they come from the forms, with very little touching up, but in others special surface treatments are used.

When the interior of the building is to be of reinforced concrete construction the usual practice is to use, except for low buildings, the skeleton type of building with wall columns and beams, and enclosure walls of concrete, brick, structural clay tile or some special type of curtain wall. This article will deal only with concrete walls, the other types having been considered in other articles.

Concrete is used to a limited extent in constructing bearing partitions and fire walls, but it is not usually suitable for nonbearing partitions because of its weight, the cost of forms, and the difficulty of installing it after the floors are in place. Concrete partitions cannot be poured much thinner than 4 in.; therefore other forms of construction, being hollow and in some cases thinner, have a distinct advantage in weight and are at least as satisfactory in other respects, including cost.

Concrete Foundations or Basement Walls. Foundation or exterior basement walls may be of several types. The simplest type is that shown in Fig. 29-1a, which supports the vertical load from walls above and withstands the lateral pressure of the earth. Ordinarily the earth pressure is not considered in this type of construction because its effect is small compared with that of the vertical loads, but for low buildings with deep basements the earth pressure may be an important factor in design. Walls of this type are frequently constructed without re-

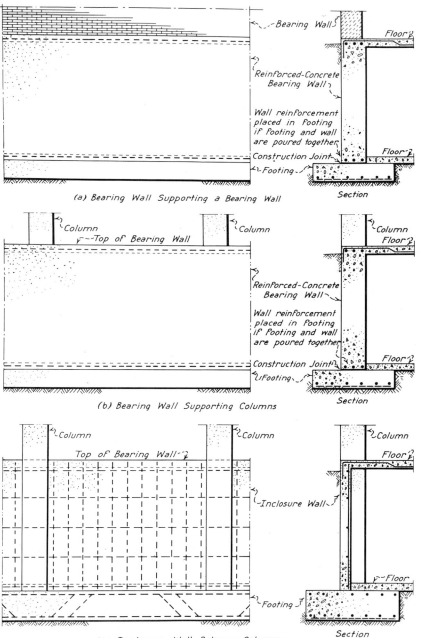

(a) Bearing Wall Supporting a Bearing Wall

Section

(b) Bearing Wall Supporting Columns

Section

(c) Inclosure Wall Between Columns

Section

Fig. 29-1. Reinforced concrete foundation walls.

inforcement except that in the footings, but longitudinal reinforcement is desirable to reduce the danger of objectionable cracking produced by temperature changes, shrinkage, and uneven settlement. This reinforcement is placed near the top of the wall and near the bottom, just above the footings. Longitudinal reinforcement placed in the footings is not fully effective in the beam action of the wall because of the construction joint between the footing and the wall. If special provision must be made for earth pressure, the wall may be made thicker than would otherwise be necessary, or steel reinforcement may be placed vertically near the inner surface of the wall so that the wall will act as a vertical slab supported at the bottom by the basement floor and at the top by the first floor construction.

The type shown in Fig. 29-1b is designed to carry the concentrated loads of columns instead of the uniform load of a wall. Since there is now a definite beam action, the wall must be designed as a continuous reinforced concrete beam. The effect of earth pressure and the provisions for such pressure are the same as in the walls of the first type.

Instead of resting the columns on a bearing wall, they may be carried down to a continuous footing (Fig. 29-1c). The walls are now required to carry only the lateral earth pressure and possibly a load contributed by the first floor. The lateral earth pressure may be provided for by reinforcing the wall as a vertical slab supported by the basement and first floors, as shown in the figure, or the main reinforcement may be placed horizontally, the necessary support being provided by the columns.

In Fig. 29-2a the columns are carried on independent footings, and the wall carries only the lateral earth pressure and possibly a load contributed by the first floor. The wall is designed as a vertical slab supported at the top by the first floor and at the bottom by the basement floor, the main reinforcement being placed vertically near the inner face. In b the wall is supported by the columns, and the main reinforcement is placed horizontally near the inner face. Windows or other openings in the wall will determine the most desirable method of support, or it may be economical to design the wall as a slab supported on four sides.

Deep basement walls of larger buildings are described in Art. 23.

Plain and Reinforced Concrete Walls. All walls constructed of concrete should contain some reinforcement to provide against cracks due to temperature changes, shrinkage, or unequal settlement. Building codes divide concrete walls into two classes, plain and reinforced.

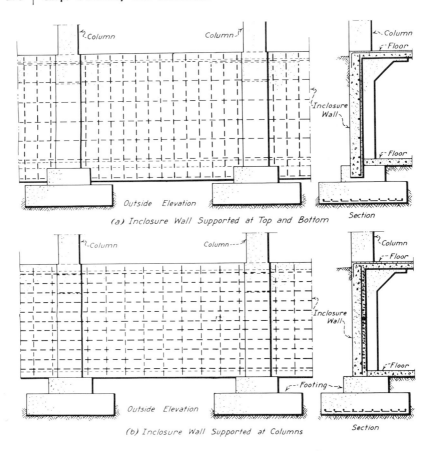

(a) Inclosure Wall Supported at Top and Bottom

(b) Inclosure Wall Supported at Columns

Fig. 29-2. Reinforced concrete foundation walls.

According to the Building Code of the American Concrete Institute (13), *reinforced concrete* walls are required to have horizontal reinforcement whose area equals at least 0.25 per cent of the area of the vertical cross section of a wall and vertical reinforcement with an area equal to at least 0.15 per cent of the area of the horizontal cross section. Walls with less reinforcement, or none, are classed as *plain concrete*.

Plain Concrete Walls above Ground. Bearing and nonbearing walls above ground may be constructed of plain concrete without steel reinforcement, but to avoid cracks caused by unequal settlement, shrinkage, and changes of temperature it is desirable to use some reinforcement, particularly at corners and around openings. Horizontal reinforcement is much more essential than vertical reinforcement. In exterior walls classed as plain concrete, it is frequently desirable to place a band consisting of one or two bars all around the building just above the window openings and another band just below these openings. It is also desirable to place a similar band of steel near the bottom of the wall.

Reinforced Concrete Walls above Ground. Reinforced concrete is extensively used for panel walls in skeleton construction and to a lesser degree for bearing and nonbearing walls. In skeleton construction the exterior walls rest on wall beams and are carried by the structural frame. They are called *panel walls* and are usually installed after the structural frame is completed.

Panel walls are required to carry only the wind pressure, and thus their thickness is usually determined by the minimum thickness which can be poured and which will be watertight and satisfy code requirements. The thickness should never be less than 4 in. and will rarely be over 12 in. Enclosure walls should be reinforced with wire fabric or small rods. A weathertight joint between the column and the wall is secured by a metal diaphragm or by other methods. A turned-up spandrel beam may serve as a panel wall.

The structural requirements for reinforced concrete bearing walls are given in the following paragraph.

Structural Requirements for Reinforced Concrete Walls. The requirements for reinforced concrete bearing walls are included in the ACI *Building Code Requirements for Reinforced Concrete* (13). They include empirical requirements which apply when the dimensions of walls are not determined by structural analysis based on the allowable stresses included in the code. These empirical requirements apply only when the loads are reasonably concentric with the walls. They are as follows.

1. In the case of concentrated loads, the length of the wall to be considered as effective for each shall not exceed the center to center distance between loads, nor shall it exceed the width of the bearing plus four times the wall thickness.
2. Reinforced concrete bearing walls shall have a thickness of at least ¹⁄₂₅ of the unsupported height or width, whichever is the shorter.
3. Reinforced concrete bearing walls of buildings shall be not less than 6 in. thick for the uttermost 15 ft. of their height, and for each successive 25 ft. downward, or fraction thereof, the minimum thickness shall be increased 1 in. Reinforced concrete bearing walls of two-story dwellings may be 6 in. thick throughout their height.

4. The area of horizontal reinforcement of reinforced concrete walls shall not be less than 0.0025 and that of the vertical reinforcement not less than 0.0015 times the area of the reinforced section of the wall if of bars, and not less than three-fourths as much if of welded wire fabric. The wire of the welded fabric shall be not less than No. 10 AS and W gage.

5. Walls more than 10 in. thick, except for basement walls, shall have the reinforcement for each direction placed in two layers parallel with the faces of the wall. One layer consisting of not less than one-half and not more than two-thirds the total required shall be placed not less than 2 in. nor more than one-third of the thickness of the wall from the exterior surface. The other layer, comprising the balance of the reinforcement, shall be placed not less than ¾ in. nor more than one-third the thickness of the wall from the interior surface. Bars if used shall be not less than No. 3 bars nor shall they be spaced more than 18 in. on centers. Welded-wire reinforcement shall be in flat sheet form.

6. In addition to the minimum as prescribed in 4, there shall be not less than two No. 5 bars around all window and door openings. Such bars shall extend at least 24 in. beyond the corners of the openings.

7. Reinforced concrete walls shall be anchored to the floors, or to the columns, pilasters, buttresses, and intersecting walls with reinforcement at least equivalent to No. 3 bars 12 in. on centers for each layer of wall reinforcement.

8. Panel and enclosure walls of reinforced concrete shall have a thickness of not less than 4 in. and not less than 1⁄30 the distance between the supporting or enclosing members.

9. Exterior basement walls, foundation walls, fire walls, and party walls shall be not less than 8 in. thick.

10. Where reinforced concrete bearing walls consist of studs or ribs tied together by reinforced concrete members at each floor level, the studs may be considered as columns but the restrictions as to minimum diameter or thickness of columns shall not apply.

The number and spacing of rods given in Table 29-1 satisfy requirements 4 of this code. They should be placed as specified. For walls thicker than 10 in., see code requirements 4 and 5.

TABLE 29-1

Minimum Wall Reinforcement

Thickness, in.	Spacing of Horizontal Bars	Spacing of Vertical Bars
6	$7\frac{1}{4}$	12
8	$5\frac{1}{2}$	9
10	$4\frac{1}{2}$	$7\frac{1}{4}$

All bars are $\frac{3}{8}$ in. round.

Plain Concrete. For the structural requirements concerning plain concrete walls included in the American Standard Building Code see Art. 30, Sec. D, Pars. 4*g* and 6*e* and Sec. E, Par. 4.

Surface Treatments and Finishes. Various procedures may be followed to produce a suitable finish on exposed surfaces of concrete walls. If a smooth finish with a minimum of form marks is desired, plywood forms or forms lined with plywood are used. The forms may be oiled to protect them for reuse and avoid adherence of mortar, but excess oil will stain the concrete. The forms should be tight, to avoid mortar leakage and the consequent formation of surface defects.

The same brand of cement and the same aggregates and proportions should be used to reduce color variations to a minimum. The consistency of the mix should insure complete filling of the forms including corners and other irregularities. Drier mixtures can be used if the concrete is vibrated.

The concrete should be placed in one continuous operation between predetermined expansion or construction joints or other appropriate locations.

The coarse aggregate should be worked back from the forms with spades or other suitable tools, to permit the mortar to come in contact with the forms and to avoid the formation of voids and aggregate pockets.

The forms must be removed carefully to avoid damaging the surface. They should be removed as soon as feasible to permit any necessary surface repairs to be made promptly. Undesirable projections should be removed and, after wetting the surface, voids should be filled with mortar of the same composition as that in the concrete.

After the defects have been repaired the surface should be saturated, coated with cement grout, immediately scrubbed with a wood or cork float, and finally, after the grout has hardened sufficiently so that it will remain in the small air holes, the excess grout should be removed with a sponge-rubber float.

Various other methods are used for finishing concrete wall surfaces including rubbed finish, formed by rubbing with carborundum stones after the concrete has hardened enough that the aggregate will not be disturbed, with or without the application of mortar while rubbing; tooled finishes, formed on thoroughly hardened surfaces with tools such as those used for finishing cut stone as shown in Fig. 27-2; stucco finish as described in Chapter 12; and painted finish using portland-cement water-base paint or other paints.

White and colored concretes may be used when colored, but not painted, surfaces are desired. White concrete can be made by using white portland cement, preferably with white or light-colored aggregates. Colored concretes are made by using colored aggregates and adding finely ground mineral oxide pigments with the portland cement. The lighter colors may require that some or all of the cement be white. To expose the colored aggregate, the surface may be washed with acid, ground, or tooled as required.

Precast ornamental units may be set in the forms to become parts of a wall, or ornaments may be cast monolithically with a concrete wall by forming the concrete with negative models or molds of the desired form.

Precast and Tilt-Up Construction. Concrete walls and partitions are often made of units which are *precast* and then placed in position, as described in Art. 58, rather than of *cast-in-place* concrete. The simplest precast unit is the concrete block described in Art. 28. Concrete block masonry is not usually called precast concrete. Concrete wall slabs of considerable size are often cast on, or at some distance from, the building site and then placed in the positions they are to occupy. In *tilt-up* construction, they are rotated about their bottom edges from a horizontal position into their final positions, as described in Art. 58.

Flashing. See Art. 25, Flashing and Calking.

Fire Resistance Rating. See Art. 30, Tables 30-3 and 30-4.

30. GENERAL REQUIREMENTS FOR MASONRY WALLS

A. Introduction

This article is primarily devoted to quotations, with minor editorial changes, from the *American Standard Building Code Requirements for Masonry,* prepared under the sponsorship of the National Bureau of Standards, issued by that organization on July 15, 1954, as Miscellaneous Publication 211, and approved by the American Standards Association as American Standard A41. 1-1953. It also includes fire-resistance ratings for masonry walls and partitions from the Uniform Building Code, 1958 Edition, of the International Conference of Building Officials.

This material applies to the common types of masonry walls and partitions as described in Arts. 25 to 29.

Table 30-1

ASTM Requirements for Mortar Compositions

Parts by Volume

Type of Mortar	Portland Cement	Masonry Cement	Hydrated Lime or Lime Putty	Aggregate Measured Damp and Loose
A-1	1	1–Type II		
	1		$\frac{1}{2}$	Not less than $2\frac{1}{4}$ and not
A-2	$\frac{1}{2}$	1–Type II		more than 3 times the sum
	1		More than $\frac{1}{4}$ to $\frac{1}{2}$	of the volumes of the ce-
B		1–Type II		ments and limes used
	1		More than $\frac{1}{2}$ to $1\frac{1}{4}$	
C		1–Type I or II		
	1		More than $1\frac{1}{4}$ to $2\frac{1}{2}$	
D	1		More than $2\frac{1}{2}$ to 4	

B. Materials

1. Masonry Units. Standard specifications for most of the various types of masonry units have been adopted by the American Society for Testing Materials.

2. Mortars. Since the mortars used are mixed on the job, the compositions of mortars for the various types of masonry are given in Table 30-1. The specifications also include minimum requirements for the compressive strengths of small cubes of each kind of mortar. The strongest mortar is listed first, the weakest last. They are not given in the table.

3. Types of Mortar Required. The types of mortar included in the American Standard Building Code Requirements for Masonry for various types of masonry are shown in Table 30-2.

C. Allowable Stresses

1. Compression. The allowable or working stresses for unit masonry depend upon the type and quality of the unit, the type and quality of the mortar, and the quality of the workmanship in laying. The code includes permissible values for compressive stresses under various conditions.

Table 30-2

Types of Mortar Required

Kind of Masonry	Type of Mortar
Foundations	
Footings	A-1 or A-2
Walls of solid units	A-1, A-2, or B
Walls of hollow units	A-1 or A-2
Hollow walls	A-1 or A-2
Masonry other than Foundations	
Piers of solid masonry	A-1, A-2, or B
Piers of hollow units	A-1 or A-2
Walls of solid masonry	A-1, A-2, B, or C
Walls of solid masonry, other than parapet walls or rubble stone walls, not less than 12 in. thick nor more than 35 ft. high, supported laterally at intervals not exceeding 12 times the wall thickness	A-1, A-2, B, C, or D
Walls of hollow units, load-bearing or exterior, and hollow walls 12 in. or more thick	A-1, A-2, or B
Hollow walls less than 12 in. thick where assumed design wind pressure	
(a) exceeds 20 lb. per sq. ft.	A-1 or A-2
(b) does not exceed 20 lb. per sq. ft.	A-1, A-2, or B
Glass block masonry	A-1, A-2, or B
Nonbearing partitions or fireproofing composed of structural clay tile or concrete masonry units	A-1, A-2, B, C, or gypsum
Gypsum partition tile of block	Gypsum

2. Tension. Because of the lack of test information and the many uncertainties involved, the tensile resistance of extreme fibers of non-reinforced unit masonry is neglected in design and not included in the code.

D. Wall and Pier Thickness

The comments in this section are quoted from the *American Standard Building Code Requirements for Masonry.*

1. Lateral Support. The requirements, with minor editorial changes, are as follows.

(a) *Ratio of height or length to thickness.* The ratio of the unsupported height to nominal thickness, or the ratio of unsupported length to nominal thickness (one or the other but not necessarily both), for solid masonry walls or bearing partitions of buildings shall not exceed 20 if of plain concrete or of solid masonry units when laid in Type A-1, A-2, B or C mortar, or 12 when laid in Type D mortar and regardless of type of permitted mortar used, shall not exceed 18 for walls of hollow masonry units or hollow walls. In computing the ratio for cavity walls, the value of the thickness shall be the sum of the nominal thicknesses of the inner and outer wythes. In walls composed of different kinds or classes of units or mortars, the ratio of the height or length to thickness shall not exceed that allowed for the weakest of the combination of units and mortars of which the member is composed. See veneers.

(b) *Method of support.* The lateral support may be obtained by cross walls, piers, or buttresses when the limiting distance is measured horizontally, or by floors or roofs when it is measured vertically. Provision shall be made in the building to transfer the lateral forces to the ground.

(c) *Piers.* The unsupported height of piers shall not exceed ten times their least dimension, provided that when structural clay tile or hollow concrete units are used for isolated piers to support beams or girders, their unsupported height shall not exceed 4 times their least dimension unless the cellular spaces are filled solidly with concrete or Type A-1 or A-2 mortar.

2. General. The thickness of walls shall conform to the requirements of this section, including those for lateral support, and the allowable stresses shall not be exceeded.

3. Change of Thickness. Except for window-paneled backs and permissible chases and recesses, walls shall not vary in thickness between lateral supports. When, because of minimum-thickness requirements, the specified thickness changes between floor levels, the greater thickness shall be carried up to the higher floor level.

When walls of masonry of hollow units or masonry-bonded hollow walls are decreased in thickness, a course or courses of solid masonry shall be interposed between the wall below and the thinner wall above, or special units of construction shall be used that will adequately transmit the loads from the shells above to those below.

4. Thickness of Bearing Walls

(a) *Minimum thickness.* The thickness of masonry bearing walls constructed of solid or hollow units shall not be less than 12 in. for the upper 35 ft. of their height, and shall be increased 4 in. for each successive 35 ft. or fraction thereof measured downward from the top of the wall, except as otherwise permitted by the exceptions that follow.

(b) *Rubble stone walls.* Rough, random, or coursed rubble stone walls, as described in Art. 27, shall be 4 in. thicker than is required in the preceding paragraph, but in no case less than 16 in. thick. The following exceptions do not apply to rubble stone walls.

(c) *Stiffened walls.* Where solid bearing masonry walls are stiffened at distances not greater than 12 ft. apart by cross walls or by reinforced concrete floors, they may be of 12-in. thickness for the upper 70 ft. measured downward from the top of the wall, and shall be increased 4 in. in thickness for each successive 70 ft. or fraction thereof.

(d) *Top-story walls.* The top-story bearing wall of a building not higher than 35 ft. may be 8 in. thick provided it is not over 12 ft. high and the roof construction imparts no lateral thrust to the walls.

(e) *Walls of residence buildings.* In residence buildings not more than three stories high, walls other than coursed, rough, or random rubble stone walls may be 8 in. thick when they are not over 35 ft. high and the roof is designed to impart no horizontal thrust. Such walls in one-story residence buildings, and one-story garages, may be 6 in. thick when not over 9 ft. high, except that the height to the peak of a gable may be 15 ft.

(f) *Penthouses and roof structures.* Masonry walls above roof level, 12 ft. or less in height, enclosing stairways, machinery rooms, shafts, or penthouses, may be 8 in. thick and may be considered to neither increase the height nor require any increase in the thickness of the wall below.

(g) *Walls of plain concrete.* Plain concrete walls may be 2 in. less in thickness than walls constructed of solid or hollow units, but not less than 8 in. thick unless 6-in. walls are permitted.

(h) *Hollow walls.* Cavity or masonry-bonded hollow walls shall not exceed 35 ft. in height, except that 10-in. cavity walls shall not exceed 25 ft. in height above the support of such walls. The facing and backing of cavity walls shall each have a thickness of at least 4 in. and the cavity shall be not less than 2 in. or more than 3 in. wide.

(i) *Faced walls.* Neither the height of faced walls nor the distance between lateral supports shall exceed that prescribed for masonry which forms the facing or the backing.

5. Thickness of Nonbearing Walls and Partitions

(*a*) *Nonbearing walls.* Nonbearing exterior masonry walls may be 4 in. less in thickness than bearing walls must be, but the thickness shall be not less than 8 in. except where 6-in. walls are specifically permitted.

(*b*) *Nonbearing partitions.* The distance between lateral supports of nonbearing partitions of masonry shall not exceed 36 times the actual thickness of partitions, including plaster.

(*c*) *Gypsum tile and block.* Gypsum partition tile or block shall not be used in bearing walls or walls that are subject to continuous dampness. Gypsum partition tile shall not be used for partitions on which portland-cement plaster, ceramic tile, marble, or structural glass wainscots will be used unless self-furring metal lath is placed over the gypsum tile.

6. Foundation Walls

(*a*) *Thickness.* Foundation walls shall be of sufficient strength and thickness to resist lateral pressures from adjacent earth and to support their vertical loads without exceeding allowable stresses. Foundation walls or their footings shall extend below the level of frost action and shall not be thinner than the walls immediately above them, except as noted in paragraphs *b*, *c*, *d*, *e*, and *f*.

(*b*) *Reinforced masonry.* Foundation walls of masonry units supported laterally at vertical intervals not exceeding 12 ft. may be 8 in. thick if reinforced by means of vertical $\frac{5}{8}$-in.-diameter deformed reinforcing bars, or their equivalent, spaced not more than 12 in. apart and not less than $3\frac{1}{2}$ in. from the pressure side of the wall; or $\frac{1}{2}$-in.-diameter deformed reinforcing bars, or their equivalent, spaced not more than 24 in. apart and not less than 5 in. from the pressure side of the wall. Reinforcing bars shall extend from the footing to the top of the foundation wall. Bars should be lapped at least 30 diameters at splices. The space between each bar and the adjacent enclosing masonry surfaces shall be solidly filled with type A-1 grout or mortar.

(*c*) *Allowable depth of 8-inch foundation walls.* Solid foundation walls of solid masonry units, or of coursed stone that do not extend more than 5 ft. below the adjacent finished ground level, may be 8 in. thick; cavity walls and walls of hollow units that do not extend more than 4 ft. below the adjacent finished ground level may be 10 in. and 8 in. thick respectively. Those depths may be increased to a maximum of 7 ft. with the approval of the building official when he is satisfied that soil conditions warrant it. The combined height of an 8-in.

foundation wall and the wall supported shall not exceed the height permitted for 8-in. walls.

(*d*) *Rubble stone.* Foundation walls of rubble stone shall be at least 16 in. thick Rough or random rubble shall not be used as foundations for walls over 35 ft. high.

(*e*) *Plain concrete.* Foundation walls of cast-in-place concrete shall be at least 8 in. thick, provided that when the basement floor does not exceed 4 ft. below average grade level, such walls may be 6 in. thick.

(*f*) *Foundation walls supporting brick veneer or cavity walls.* Foundation walls which are 8 in. thick and conform to the provisions of this section may be used as foundations for dwellings with walls of brick veneer on frame walls or with 10-in. cavity walls, provided that the dwelling is not more than one and a half stories in height and the total height of the wall, including the gable, is not more than 20 ft. Foundation walls 8 in. thick supporting brick veneer or cavity walls shall be corbeled with solid units to provide a bearing the full thickness of the wall above unless adequate bearing is provided by a concrete floor slab. The total projection shall not exceed 2 in., with individual corbels projecting not more than half the depth of the unit. The top corbel course shall not be higher than the bottom of the floor joists, and shall be a full header course of headers at least 6 in. in length.

7. Parapet Walls. Unless reinforced to withstand safely the earthquake and wind loads to which they may be subjected, parapet walls shall be at least 8 in. thick, and their height shall not exceed three times their thickness.

E. Bonding and Anchoring

1. Walls of Solid Masonry Units. Solid masonry bearing and non-bearing walls shall be bonded as required in *a* and *b*.

(*a*) *Bonding with bonders (headers).* The facing and backing shall be bonded so that not less than 4 per cent of the wall surface of each face is composed of bonders, or headers, extending not less than 4 in. into the backing. The distance between adjacent full-length headers shall not exceed 24 in. either vertically or horizontally. In walls in which a single bonder does not extend through the wall, bonders from the opposite sides shall overlap at least 4 in., or bonders from opposite sides shall be covered with another bonder course overlapping the bonder below at least 4 in.

(b) *Bonding with metal ties.* The facing and backing shall be bonded with corrosion-resistant metal ties conforming to the requirements for cavity walls in paragraph 2 of E. There shall be one metal tie for not more than each 4½ sq. ft. of wall area. Ties in alternate courses shall be staggered, the maximum vertical distance between ties shall not exceed 18 in., and the maximum horizontal distance shall not exceed 36 in. Walls so bonded shall conform to the allowable stress, lateral support, thickness (excluding cavity), height, and mortar requirements for cavity walls.

2. Masonry Walls of Hollow Units. Where two or more hollow units are used to make up the thickness of a wall, the stretcher courses shall be bonded at vertical intervals not exceeding 34 in. by lapping at least 4 in. over the unit below, or by lapping at vertical intervals not exceeding 17 in. with units which are at least 50 per cent greater in thickness than the units below; or by bonding with corrosion-resistant metal ties conforming to the requirements of this code. There shall be one metal tie for not more than each 4½ sq. ft. of wall area. Ties in alternate courses shall be staggered, the maximum vertical distance between ties shall not exceed 18 in., and the maximum horizontal distance shall not exceed 36 in. Walls bonded with metal ties shall conform to the requirements for allowable stress, lateral support, thickness (excluding cavity), height, and mortar for cavity walls. Hollow masonry units shall have full mortar coverage of the ends and edges of the face shells in both the horizontal and vertical joints.

3. Stone Walls

(a) *Ashlar masonry.* In ashlar masonry, bondstones uniformly distributed shall be provided to the extent of not less than 10 per cent of the area of exposed faces.

(b) *Rubble stone masonry.* Rubble stone masonry 24 in. or less in thickness shall have bondstones with a maximum spacing of 3 ft. vertically and 3 ft. horizontally, and if the masonry is of greater thickness than 24 in., shall have one bondstone for each 6 sq. ft. of wall surface on both sides.

4. Openings in Walls of Plain Concrete. Reinforcement symmetrically disposed in the thickness of the wall shall be placed not less than 1 in. above and 2 in. below openings and extend not less than 24 in. each side of such openings or be of equivalent developed length with hooks. The minimum reinforcemet both above and below openings shall consist of the equivalent of one ⅝-in. round bar for each 6 in. of wall thickness.

5. Faced Walls. (See definition in Art. 25.)

(a) *Bonding masonry facing.* The actual thickness of materials used for facing shall be not less than 2 in. and never less than one-eighth the height of the unit. Masonry facing shall be bonded to the backing as prescribed in paragraph 1 of E.

(b) *Bonding ashlar facing.* The percentage of bondstones for ashlar masonry shall be computed from the exposed face area of the wall. At least 10 per cent of the face area shall consist of bondstones which extend 4 in. or more into the backing wall and are uniformly distributed. Every bondstone and, except when alternate courses are full bond courses, non-bond stones shall be anchored to backing with $\frac{3}{16}$-in. by 1-in. or larger corrosion-resistant metal anchors. Further details Ref. 1.

6. Cavity and Masonry-Bonded Hollow Walls

(a) *Cavity walls.* The facing and backing of cavity walls shall be bonded with $\frac{3}{16}$-in.-diameter steel rods or metal ties of equivalent stiffness embedded in horizontal joints. There shall be one metal tie for not more than $4\frac{1}{2}$ sq. ft. of wall area. Ties in alternate courses shall be staggered as shown in Fig. 26-5c, and the maximum vertical distance between ties shall not exceed 36 in. rods bent to rectangular shape shall be used with hollow masonry units laid with cells vertical; in other walls the ends of ties shall be bent to 90-degree angles to provide hooks not less than 2 in. long. Additional bonding ties shall be provided at all openings, spaced not more than 3 ft. apart around the perimeter and within 12 in. of the opening. Ties shall be made of corrosion-resistant metal, or shall be coated with corrosion-resistant metal or some other approved protective coating.

(b) *Masonry-bonded hollow walls.* Masonry-bonded hollow walls shall be bonded as required in the paragraph on bonding with bonders.

7. Bonding of Walls to Intersecting Walls, Floors, and Columns

(a) *Where bonded.* Masonry walls shall be securely anchored or bonded at all points where they intersect and where they abut or adjoin the frame of a skeleton frame building.

(b) *Bonding bearing walls.* When two bearing walls meet or intersect and the courses are built up together, the intersections shall be bonded by laying in a true bond at least 50 per cent of· the units at the intersection.

(c) *Walls carried up separately.* When the courses of meeting or intersecting bearing walls are carried up separately, the intersecting walls shall be regularly toothed or blocked with 8-in. maximum offsets and the joints provided with metal anchors having a minimum section of $\frac{1}{4}$ in. by $1\frac{1}{2}$ in. with ends bent up at least 2 in., or with cross pins to form anchors. Such anchors shall be at least 2 ft. long, and the maximum spacing shall be 4 ft.

(d) *Bonding nonbearing walls.* Meeting or intersecting nonbearing walls shall be bonded or anchored to each other in an approved manner.

F. Grouted Masonry

1. Materials. Materials used in grouted masonry shall conform to the specified materials, provided that at the time of laying, masonry units in either the facing or backing, but not necessarily both, shall absorb in 24 hours of cold immersion an amount of water weighing less than 5 per cent of the dry weight of the units.

2. Construction. All masonry units in the outer wythes shall be laid with full head and bed joints of type A-1 or A-2 mortar, and all interior joints shall be filled with grout. Masonry units in the interior wythes shall be placed or floated in grout poured between the two outer wythes. One of the outer wythes may be carried up not more than three courses before grouting, but the other shall be carried up not more than one course above the grout. Each pour of grout shall be stopped at least $1\frac{1}{2}$ in. below the top and properly stirred. The grouted longitudinal vertical joints shall be not less than $\frac{3}{4}$ in. wide. Bonders shall not be used.

G. Veneers

1. Requirements. Installation of veneers shall be in conformance with generally accepted good practice.

2. Load. Veneers shall not be considered as part of the wall in computing the strength of bearing walls, nor shall they be considered a part of the required thickness of walls.

H. Glass Block Masonry

1. Where Permitted. Masonry of glass blocks may be used in non-load-bearing exterior or interior walls and in openings that might otherwise be filled with windows, either isolated or in continuous bands, provided the glass block panels have a thickness of not less than $3\frac{1}{2}$ in. at the mortar joint and the mortared surfaces of the blocks are satisfactorily treated for mortar bonding.

2. Size of Panels. Glass block panels for exterior walls shall not exceed 144 sq. ft. of unsupported wall surface or 25 ft. in length or 20 ft. in height between supports. For interior walls, glass block panels shall not exceed 250 sq. ft. of unsupported area or 25 ft. in one direction between supports.

3. Reinforcement of Exterior Panels

(*a*) *Anchorage.* Exterior glass block panels shall be held in place in the wall opening to resist both external and internal pressures produced by wind. Panels shall be set in recesses at the jambs and, for panels exceeding 10 ft. in horizontal dimension between supports, at the head as well, to provide a bearing surface at least 1 in. wide along the panel edges. When approved by the building official, however, for panels exceeding neither 100 sq. ft. in area nor 10 ft. in either horizontal or vertical dimension, and situated 4 stories or lower and less than 52 ft. above grade level, anchorage may be provided by means of noncorrodible perforated metal strips.

(*b*) *Placing reinforcement.* Glass block panels shall have reinforcement in the horizontal mortar joints, extending from end to end of the mortar joints but not across expansion joints, with any unavoidable joints spliced by lapping the reinforcement not less than 6 in. The reinforcement shall be spaced vertically not more than 2 ft. apart. In addition, reinforcements shall be placed in the joint immediately below and above any openings within a panel. The reinforcement shall consist of two parallel longitudinal galvanized steel wires, No. 9 gage or larger, spaced 2 in. apart, and having welded to them No. 14 or heavier gage cross wires at intervals not exceeding 8 in., or the equivalent approved by the building official.

(*c*) *Mortar.* Glass block shall be laid in type A-1, A-2, or B mortar. Both vertical and horizontal mortar joints shall be at least $\frac{1}{4}$ in. and not more than $\frac{3}{8}$ in. thick, and shall be completely filled.

(*d*) *Expansion joints.* Every exterior glass block panel shall be provided with expansion joints at the sides and top. Expansion joints shall be entirely free of mortar and shall be filled with resilient material.

I. Miscellaneous Masonry Requirements

1. Anchoring of Walls

(*a*) *Meeting or intersecting walls.* Masonry walls that meet or intersect floors or columns shall be securely bonded or anchored if they provide lateral support of the walls.

(b) *Fastening joists or beams.* The ends of floor joists or beams bearing on masonry walls shall be securely fastened to the walls in an approved manner.

(c) *Spacing.* When lateral support for walls is to be provided by anchorage to floor or roof joists that are parallel with the walls, the anchors shall be spaced at intervals not exceeding 6 ft. and shall engage no fewer than three joists; these joists shall be bridged solidly at the anchors.

(d) *Anchoring structural members.* Structural members, including roof members, framing into or supported by walls or piers shall be adequately anchored.

2. Chases and Recesses

(a) *Limitations.* Except as noted in the following paragraph, chases and recesses in masonry walls shall not be deeper than one-third of the wall thickness or longer than 4 ft. horizontally or in horizontal projection, and shall have at least 8 in. of masonry in back of the chases and recesses and between adjacent chases or recesses and the jambs of openings. Chases and recesses shall not be cut in walls of hollow masonry units or in hollow walls, but when permitted they may be built in. There shall be no chases or recesses within the required area of a pier. The aggregate area of recesses and chases in any wall shall not exceed one-quarter of the whole area of the face of the wall in any story.

(b) *Exceptions for 8-inch walls.* In residence buildings not over two stories high, vertical chases not more than 4 in. deep and occupying not more than 4 sq. ft. of wall area may be built into 8-in. walls, except that recesses below windows may extend from floor to sill and be the width of the opening above. Masonry directly above chases or recesses wider than 12 in. shall be supported on lintels.

(c) *Recesses for stairways or elevators.* Recesses for stairways or elevators may be left in walls, but in no case shall the walls at such points be reduced to less than 12 in. unless reinforced by additional piers, or by columns or girders of steel, reinforced masonry, or concrete, securely anchored to the walls on each side of such recesses. Recesses for alcoves and similar purposes shall have not less than 8 in. of material at the back. Such recesses shall be not more than 8 ft. in width and shall be arched or spanned with lintels.

3. Lintels and Arches

(a) *Material.* The masonry above openings shall be supported by arches or lintels of metal or reinforced masonry which shall bear on the wall at each end for not less than 4 in. Stone or other nonreinforced masonry lintels shall not be used unless supplemented on the inside of the wall with iron or steel lintels or with suitable masonry arches or reinforced masonry lintels carrying the masonry backing.

(b) *Stiffness.* Steel or reinforced masonry lintels shall be of sufficient stiffness to carry the superimposed load without deflection of more than $\frac{1}{360}$ of the clear span.

(c) *Design.* Masonry arches shall be designed according to good engineering practice.

4. Beams and Joist Supports

(a) *Beams.* Beams, girders, or other concentrated loads supported by a wall or pier shall have bearing at least 3 in. in actual length upon solid masonry not less than 4 in. in depth or on a metal bearing plate of adequate design and dimensions, or other provision shall be made to distribute the loads on the wall or pier safely.

(b) *Joists.* Joists shall have bearing at least 3 in. in actual length upon solid masonry at least $2\frac{1}{4}$ in. in depth, or other provision shall be made to distribute the loads on the wall or pier safely.

(c) *Support on wood.* Unless specifically approved by the building official, no masonry shall be supported on wood girders or any other form of wood construction.

5. Corbeling

(a) *Maximum projection.* Except for chimneys, the maximum corbeled horizontal projection beyond the face of the wall shall be not more than half the wall thickness, and the maximum projection of one unit shall exceed neither half the depth of the unit nor one-third its width at right angles to the face which is offset.

(b) *Corbeling chimneys.* No chimney shall be corbeled from a wall more than 6 in. nor shall a chimney be corbeled from a wall less than 12 in. thick, unless it projects equally on each side of the wall, provided that in the second story of two-story dwellings, corbeling of chimneys on the exterior of the enclosing walls may equal the wall thickness. In every case the corbeling shall not exceed 1 in. of projection for each course of brick projected.

6. Cornices

The centers of gravity of stone cornices shall be inside of the outer wall face. Terra-cotta cornices and metal cornices shall be structurally supported.

7. Drainage of Hollow Walls

In cavity walls the cavity shall be kept clear of mortar droppings during construction. Approved flashings shall be installed in hollow walls, and adequate drainage provided to keep dampness away from the backing.

J. Precautions during Erection

1. Bracing to Resist Lateral Loads. Masonry walls in locations where they may be exposed to high winds during erection shall not be built higher than ten times their thickness unless adequately braced or until provision is made for prompt installation of permanent bracing at the floor or roof level immediately above the story under construction. Backfill shall not be placed against foundation walls until they are braced to withstand horizontal pressure.

2. Wetting of Brick. Clay or shale brick shall be wetted when laid unless their gain in weight resulting from partial immersion flatwise in ⅛ in. of water for 1 minute is less than ¾ oz. per 30 sq. in. of immersed area.

3. Protection against Freezing. Masonry shall be protected against freezing for at least 48 hours after being laid. Unless adequate precautions against freezing are taken, no masonry shall be built when the temperature is below 32°F. on a rising temperature, or 40°F. on a falling temperature, at the point where the work is in progress.

K. Supplementary Comments

1. Introduction. The comments in this section form a partial abstract, with editorial changes, from the appendix of the *American Standard Building Code*, which consists of explanatory matter referring to various parts of the recommended code requirements. It is not a part of the code but is presented as background material.

2. Nominal and Actual Dimensions. To avoid unnecessary repetition of the adjective "nominal" before each nominal dimension requirement, if the dimension is not nominal the adjective "actual" is used.

3. Vertical Loads on Foundation Walls. Vertical compressive loads on foundation walls resulting from the weight of the building and its contents tend to prevent the development or reduce the magnitude of vertical tensile stresses caused by lateral earth pressures. The resistance to lateral earth pressures of a given foundation wall is therefore increased by an increase in the weight of the superstructure. The use of thinner foundation walls for light structures than for heavy structures, permitted by some codes, is not justified by a consideration of lateral stability (and only in the rare cases where compressive stresses control the design).

4. Parapet Walls. The limits on the ratios of height to thickness specified in this code are believed to be safe for ordinary conditions. In localities subject to high winds or to earthquakes, somewhat more rigid restrictions may be advisable.

Particular attention should be paid to the flashing, dampproofing, and workmanship of parapet walls to prevent disintegration. Through flashing should be provided under the coping, unless the coping is of an impervious material laid with watertight joints, and also at the base of the wall. All joints should be well filled. Coating or sealing the back of the wall with vapor-impermeable materials is not recommended, for this practice prevents rapid drying of the masonry.

L. Fire-Resistance Ratings

The basis for fire-resistance ratings is given in Art. 1. Building codes include fire-resistance ratings for various types and thicknesses of masonry walls and partitions. Comprehensive information on this subject is given in the National Building Code recommended by the National Board of Fire Underwriters. Table 30-3 will serve as an example of such ratings for the more common types of walls and partitions.

Concrete Block. The values in Table 30-4 are estimated ratings by the National Board of Fire Underwriters as given in the 1955 National Code. Thicknesses are minimum *equivalent thicknesses* in inches.

Actual thickness equals equivalent thickness multiplied by ratio of total area to solid area. Values are for conditions where no combustible members are framed into the wall.

Solid Stone Masonry. The rated fire-resistance periods for solid stone masonry walls as given in the 1955 *National Building Code* (16) are as follows: 12 in.—4 hr., 3 hr., and 2 hr.; 8 in.—1hr. No ratings were found for composite masonry walls faced with stone in the references consulted, possibly because of the widely varying fire-resistive properties of the various kinds of stone used in stone masonry for buildings, mentioned in Art. 12.

M. Expansion Joints

To prevent unsightly cracks, expansion joints extending vertically through the entire height of a wall may be required in long walls sub-

Table 30-3

Rated Fire-Resistive Periods for Masonry Walls and Partitions
(Abstracted from *Uniform Building Code*, 1958 edition)

Type of Wall or Partition	4h	3h	2h	1h
	Thickness, in.			
Brick or clay, shale, sand-lime or concrete, and plain concrete				
Solid, unplastered	8			*4*
Plastered	9		*5*	
Hollow clay tile				
End or side construction, one cell thick, plastered				3
Two cells in 8 in. or less thick, unplastered	16	12		8 or 6
Plastered	13	9	7	
Hollow clay load-bearing tile meeting code requirements				
End or side construction, two cells thick, unplastered			6	
Plastered			5	
Combination brick and load-bearing tile				
4-in. brick, 4-in. tile with tile side-plastered	9			
Solid concrete. Not less than 0.2% reinforcement in each direction	6	5	4	2
Hollow gypsum blocks, unplastered	6	*4*	*4*	3
Solid gypsum or portland-cement plaster				
Studless partition with metal lath				*2x*

Thicknesses are minimum allowable including plaster; italics designate nonbearing.

Table 30-4

Fire-Resistance Ratings for Concrete Block Walls

Coarse Aggregate	Min. Equiv. Thickness, in.			
	4h	3h	2h	1h
Expanded slag or pumice	4.7	4.0	3.2	2.1
Expanded clay or shale	5.7	4.8	3.8	2.6
Limestone, cinders, or unexpanded slag	5.9	5.0	4.0	2.7
Calcareous gravel	6.2	5.3	4.2	2.8
Siliceous gravel	6.7	5.7	4.5	3.0

See Concrete Block, p. 294.

Table 30-5

Recommended Maximum Length of Straight Load-Bearing Clay Masonry Walls without Expansion Joints

| Outside Temperature Range from Lowest to Highest Average Temperature | Maximum Wall Length, ft. | | | |
| | Unheated or Insulated | | Heated, Not Insulated | |
	Solid	Openings	Solid	Openings
100°F. and over	200	100	250	125
Less than 100°F.	250	125	300	150

jected to extreme changes in temperature or irregular in plan. The maximum lengths for straight load-bearing clay brick and hollow tile masonry walls shown in Table 30-5 have been recommended by the Structural Clay Products Institute, in *Technical Notes on Brick and Tile Construction,* Vol. 9, No. 3, March, 1958, which includes valuable material on expansion joints.

Walls with less than 20 per cent of the area devoted to openings are considered to be solid.

This publication recommends that "In general, expansion joints should be located at offsets, provided that the wall expanding into the offset is 50 ft. or more in length and at junctions of walls in L-, T-, and U-shaped buildings."

Parapet walls are subjected to extreme conditions of exposure. Cracks tend to develop through such walls and at their junction with the roof. Recommendations for minimizing these defects are included in Vol. 8, No. 9 of the *Technical Notes* previously referred to.

For comments on expansion joints in reinforced concrete construction, see Art. 53.

References

1. *American Standard Building Code Requirements for Masonry,* U. S. Department of Commerce, National Bureau of Standards, Miscellaneous Publication 211, July 15, 1954, American Standards Association Standard, A.41-1953.
2. Cyrus C. Fishburn, *Water Permeability of Walls Built of Masonry Units,* Report BMS 82, National Bureau of Standards, April 15, 1942.
3. Cyrus C. Fishburn and Douglas E. Parsons, *Tests of Cement-Water Paints and Other Waterproofings for Unit Masonry Walls,* Report BMS 95, National Bureau of Standards, March 15, 1943.

4. *Standard Specifications for Building Brick (Solid Masonry Units Made] Clay or Shale)*, ASTM Designation C62-58.

5. *Standard Specifications for Facing Brick (Solid Masonry Units Made from Clay or Shale)*, ASTM Designation C216-57.

6. *Technical Notes on Brick and Tile Construction*, Vol. 5, No. 1, January, 1954, Structural Clay Products Institute.

7. *Technical Notes on Brick and Tile Construction*, Vol. 11, No. 2, February, 1960, Structural Clay Products Institute.

8. Plummer and Blume, *Reinforced Brick Masonry and Lateral Force Design*, Structural Clay Products Institute, 1953.

9. Oliver Bowles, *The Stone Industries*, McGraw-Hill Book Co., 1934.

10. *Technical Notes on Brick and Tile Construction*, Vol. 2, No. 3, March, 1951; No. 6, June, 1951; and No. 11, November, 1951; Structural Clay Products Institute.

11. *Technical Notes on Brick and Tile Construction*, No. 17, November-December, 1962, Part I of IV.

12. *Concrete Masonry Handbook*, Portland Cement Association.

13. *Building Code Requirements for Reinforced Concrete*, American Concrete Institute (ACI 318).

14. *Concrete for Industrial Buildings*, Portland Cement Association.

15. *Design and Control of Concrete Mixtures*, Portland Cement Association.

16. *National Building Code*, National Board of Fire Underwriters, 1955.

17. *Building Code Requirements for Reinforced Masonry*, National Bureau of Standards, American Standard A41.2-1960.

18. *Reinforced Brick Masonry*, Technical Notes on Brick and Tile Construction, Vol. 5, Nos. I to IV, January to April, 1954, Structural Clay Products Institute.

19. *Mortars for Clay Masonry*, Technical Notes on Brick and Tile Construction, No. 8, August, 1961, Structural Clay Products Institute.

20. H. F. Kingsbury, *Glass Block, Windows and Glass in the Exterior of Buildings*, Publication 478, 1957, Building Research Institute, National Research Council.

5 The structural elements

31. INTRODUCTION AND GENERAL DISCUSSION

The structure of all buildings is made up of various combinations and forms of walls, columns, ties, cables, beams, trusses, rigid frames, arches, vaults and domes. Rigid frames are actually forms of arches. The intrados and extrados of solid vaults might be considered to be generated by the horizontal movement of solid arches in the direction normal to the span, and these surfaces of a solid dome, circular in plan, might be considered to be generated by rotating a solid arch about a vertical axis at midspan.

Columns and beams may be constructed of wood, steel, or reinforced concrete. Cast iron was extensively used at one time for columns and for short beams such as lintels, but steel and reinforced concrete have largely taken its place. Wrought iron has been entirely replaced by steel as a structural material.

Trusses are usually constructed of steel, but wood is used extensively and reinforced concrete occasionally. Reinforced concrete is not usually considered an appropriate material for truss construction, although there are many examples of its successful use where local conditions have led to its selection.

Rigid frames are constructed of wood, reinforced concrete, and steel. Arches, vaults, and domes of long span are usually constructed of wood, steel, and reinforced concrete, but aluminum is occasionally used. Arches over openings in masonry walls are usually constructed of brick or stone, as described in Arts. 25, 26, and 27. Steel twisted-wire strand cables are occasionally used to support long-span roofs and cantilever projections of roofs.

The assembling of the various structural elements so that each may perform its function is known as *framing*. One classification of buildings is on the basis of the function of the walls. If the walls carry their share of the dead, live, and other loads, in addition to keeping out the weather, etc., the building is classed as *wall-bearing construction;* but if the loads, including the weight of the walls, are carried by the structural frame consisting of columns, beams, and girders, the building is classed as *skeleton construction.* This term is usually used only for office buildings and similar structures not for industrial buildings.

The classification of buildings according to type of construction, as included in building codes, was given in Art. 1.

Wood frame construction with structural elements consisting of light wood joist and studs is extensively used in dwelling house and small-building construction, but is not used for larger buildings.

Ordinary construction is similar to wood frame construction but has exterior walls of masonry. It is extensively used for dwelling house and small-building construction, but its chief field is for apartment houses, stores, and industrial buildings of various types which require a better class of construction than *wood frame construction,* but which do not need to be especially resistant to fire.

Heavy timber construction consisting of heavy timber beams, girders, columns, floors, and roofs with masonry walls is used for manufacturing plants and industrial buildings requiring a substantial form of construction which will offer considerable resistance to fire.

Steel construction consisting of steel beams, girders, columns, and trusses supporting floors and roofs of light joist construction, of heavy timber construction, or of *fire-resistive construction* is extensively used on all classes of buildings except dwelling houses. The exterior walls may be bearing walls for the lower buildings, but for buildings of more than three or four stories skeleton construction is usually used. In the better class of buildings, *fire-resistive construction* is used throughout. For buildings up to about sixty stories high, steel and reinforced-concrete construction are competitive; but for higher buildings, in this country steel construction is without a rival. Great speed is possible with steel construction. Sometimes the structural frame and floor slabs have been constructed at the rate of a story a day after the foundations are in place. Skyscrapers have been completed in a year.

Reinforced concrete construction may be used for nearly all classes of buildings in which good construction is essential. Dwelling houses are rarely of this type, but apartment houses, hotels, office buildings, school buildings, warehouses, and industrial buildings are often built of reinforced concrete. In buildings with a steel framework, the floors and roofs are usually of reinforced concrete. For tall buildings steel construction has the advantage of smaller columns for the lower floors. The columns of the lower stories may be made of steel, and those above of concrete. For buildings three or four stories high, exterior bearing walls may be used, but above that height skeleton construction is usually adopted. Even for the lower buildings, skeleton construction may be used because of the greater possible speed of construction. When bearing walls are used, each floor must wait until the bearing wall can be built up to carry it, but with skeleton construction the structural frame and floors may be constructed rapidly.

32. COLUMNS AND OTHER COMPRESSION MEMBERS

Forces that tend to shorten or compress a member are called *compressive forces*, and the stresses set up in a member by these forces are called *compressive stresses*. *Bending* or *flexural stresses* are set up in a member when it bends.

The vertical members of a structural frame are called *columns*, and they transfer floor and roof loads to the foundations. Such loads cause stresses in the columns which are chiefly compressive, but because of eccentric loads, rigidity of joints, wind loads and earthquake shocks, columns are also subjected to bending stresses which may be of considerable magnitude.

Classes of Columns. Columns may be divided into three general classes according to the ratio of the longitudinal dimension to the lateral dimension.

If the length of a column is relatively small when compared with its lateral dimension (Fig. 32-1a), the column does not tend to bend to any extent when carrying a load; and, if the load is applied so that its resultant is on the axis of the column, the stresses will be uniformly distributed over each cross section of the column. If the length of a column is great when compared with its lateral dimension, the column

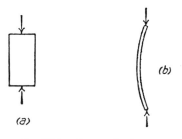

Fig. 32-1. Classes of columns.

will tend to fail by bending or buckling (Fig. 32-1b) when carrying a load, the magnitude of the direct compressive stress being small. A third class includes columns intermediate in ratio of length to lateral dimension to the classes just mentioned; such columns tend to fail by a combination of direct stress and bending or buckling. Reinforced concrete columns are usually of the first class if there are no lateral loads; timber and steel columns may be in either the first or third class. Columns of the second class are not used to any extent.

Other Terms Used. Columns are often called *posts*, especially when made of timber. Truss members carrying compressive stresses are called *struts*, but their action is the same as that of columns. In general, members that carry compressive stresses are called *columns, posts, struts,* or *props.*

The light, closely spaced, vertical, compressive members used in walls and partitions in wood frame construction are called *studs.* Relatively slender blocks or prisms of masonry carrying compressive stresses are called *piers.* Stone or brick columns are sometimes called *pillars,* but this is not a technical term. The term pier has about the same meaning as pillar and is more commonly used. In England, the term *stanchion* is used in place of the term column as used in this country.

Materials. Columns are usually made of timber, steel, or reinforced concrete, but stone columns are frequently used for ornamental purposes.

33. BEAMS AND GIRDERS

A *beam* may be defined as a member supported at one or more points along its length and designed to carry loads acting perpendicular to its length, the reactions at the supports being parallel to the direction of the loads (Fig. 33-1a).

If the line of action of the loads is not perpendicular to the length of the beam, these loads may be resolved into components acting perpendicular to the length of the beam and components acting parallel to the length of the beam (b). In carrying the transverse components, the beam is performing its primary function, and in carrying the components parallel to its length, it is acting as a column.

A beam may be curved or bent (c) if the supports are so arranged that the reactions at the supports will be vertical for vertical loads.

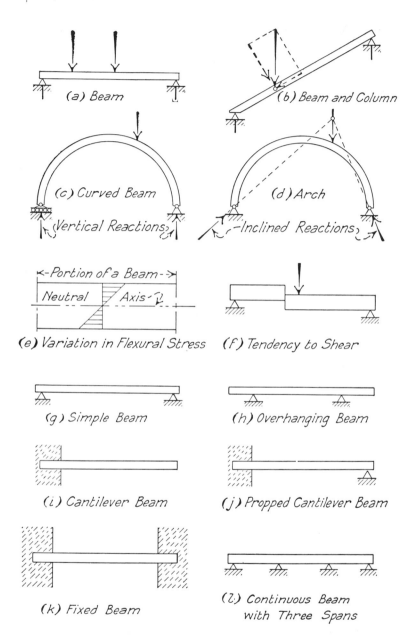

(a) Beam

(b) Beam and Column

(c) Curved Beam
(Vertical Reactions)

(d) Arch
(Inclined Reactions)

(e) Variation in Flexural Stress

(f) Tendency to Shear

(g) Simple Beam

(h) Overhanging Beam

(i) Cantilever Beam

(j) Propped Cantilever Beam

(k) Fixed Beam

(l) Continuous Beam
with Three Spans

Fig. 33-1. Types of beams.

This may be accomplished by placing one end on rollers (*c*) or, to a certain degree, by using plates which permit sliding. If the ends are so arranged that horizontal movement is restricted as the structure deforms, the reaction will no longer be vertical and the structure will be an arch (*d*).

Flexural Stresses. There are two general classes of stresses set up in a beam by the loads, flexural or bending stresses and shearing stresses. The material on the upper side of the beam shown in *a* is compressed or shortened, and that on the lower side is elongated. The stresses causing the shortening are called *compressive stresses*, and those causing the elongation are called *tensile stresses*. Taken together they are called *flexural stresses*. These stresses are greatest at the top and bottom of the beam and are zero at the *neutral axis* near the center of the depth, the exact location of the neutral axis depending upon the shape and composition of the section. For a beam composed of one material, the neutral axis passes through the center of gravity or *centroid* of the transverse section. The variation of stress may be illustrated by the triangles in *e*, the intensity of stress usually varying directly as the distance from the neutral axis, as indicated by the lengths of the horizontal lines in the triangles.

Shearing Stresses. It is evident that the forces acting on a horizontal beam tend to cut it along vertical sections, as shown in *f*. The stresses set up in the beam by this action are called *shearing stresses*.

Classification According to Method of Support. Beams may be divided into the following classes according to method of support.

simple beam. Supported at two points near its ends (Fig. 33-2*g*).

overhanging beam. Supported at two points, but projects beyond or overhangs one or both supports (*h*). It is a special case of the simple beam.

cantilever beam. Supported at one end only but rigidly held in position at that end (*i*).

propped cantilever beam. Supported at two points and rigidly held in position at one of them (*j*).

fixed beam. Supported at two points and rigidly held in position at both points as shown in *k*.

continuous beam. Supported at three or more points as shown in *l*.

Classification According to Use. Beams may be classified according to use as follows.

beam. When any distinction is made between beams and girders, the beam is the smaller member and may be supported by the girder.

girder. See discussion for beam.

lintel. A beam supporting the masonry and other loads over an opening in a wall (Fig. 26-6*i*).

joists. Closely spaced beams supporting a floor or ceiling (Fig. 41-1).

rafters. Closely spaced beams supporting the roof and running parallel to the slope of the roof (Figs. 41-1 and 72-1). The rafters for flat roofs are usually called joists.

purlin. A beam spanning the space principal roof supports, such as roof trusses or arches.

girt. A beam placed horizontally on the sides of a building and fastened to the columns.

header. A beam that carries the ends of beams which are cut off in framing around an opening (Fig. 41-3).

tail beam. A beam which frames into a header instead of spanning the entire distance between supports (Fig. 41-3).

trimmer. A beam at the side of an opening and carrying one end of a header (Fig. 41-3).

collar beam. A horizontal member running between two rafters on opposite sides of a framed roof and usually, but not necessarily, located at some distance above the wall plates. A collar beam does not necessarily act as a beam. It may act as a tie if the rafters are not anchored to prevent the spreading of the lower ends, but if they are securely held at these points the collar beam acts as a strut which reduces the deflection in the rafters.

Materials. Beams may be constructed of wood, steel, or reinforced concrete, as described in the following articles. Stone is occasionally used for lintels but, owing to its low flexural strength, stone lintels are usually supported by steel lintels which do not show on the face of a building.

34. TRUSSES

A *truss* is a framed structure consisting of a group of triangles arranged in a single plane in such a manner that loads applied at the points of intersection of the members will cause only *direct stresses* (tension or compression) in the members. Loads applied between these points cause flexural stresses. The framework shown in Fig. 34-1*a* will illustrate the essential features of a truss, although a truss of this type is of no practical use.

In a truss the ends of a framework must be supported in such a manner that the reactions at the supports are vertical for vertical loads. This result is accomplished by arranging one end so that horizontal

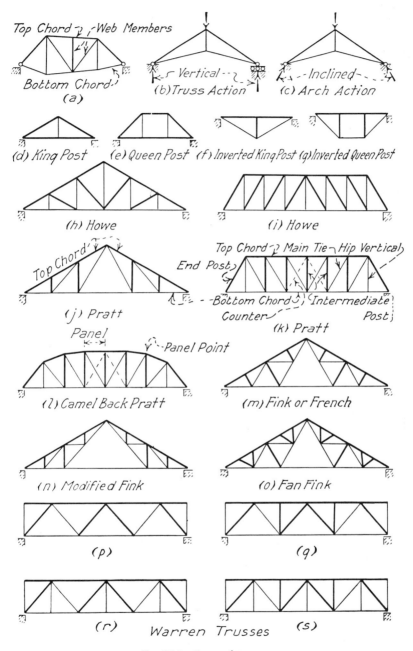

Fig. 34-1. Types of trusses.

movement may take place by sliding or rolling on the bearing plate (*b*) when loads are applied, or when changes of length caused by temperature changes occur.

If the ends are so arranged that horizontal movement is restricted, the reactions will be inclined and the framework will act as an *arch* (*c*). It is not customary to provide sliding or rolling bearings for trusses whose span does not exceed 40 or 50 ft.

Parts of the Truss. The points of intersection of the members of a truss are called *joints,* or sometimes *panel points.* The upper line of members forms the *upper* or *top chord,* and the lower line the *lower* or *bottom chord.* The members connecting the joints on the upper chord to those on the lower chord are the *web members* (*a*). Web members carrying compressive stresses are *struts,* and those carrying tensile stresses are *ties.* The terms *end post, vertical post, hip vertical,* and *panel* apply to special forms of trusses and will be defined later (see *k*). The distance from center to center of the supports is called the *span.*

Materials. Trusses may be built wholly of wood, of wood and steel rods combined, or of rolled-steel sections. Concrete is used to a limited extent but is not usually a suitable material for trusses.

Types of Trusses. Since a truss is composed of a group of triangles, it is possible to arrange innumerable types; but certain types have proved to be more satisfactory than others, and each of these has its special uses. The various types of trusses used in building construction are illustrated by line diagrams in Figs. 34-1 and 34-2. The members indicated by heavy lines normally carry compressive stresses, and those indicated by light lines normally carry tensile stresses, for vertical loads. The types shown with parallel chords may have their top chords made sloping slightly in one or two directions, for roof drainage, without changing the type. The number of subdivisions or panels will depend upon the length of span and the type of construction.

The more common forms of trusses will be discussed in the following paragraphs.

The *king-post truss* (Fig. 34-1*d*), the *queen-post truss* (*e*), and the *inverted king-post* and *queen-post trusses* (*f*) and (*g*) are all used for short spans in wood construction. The members indicated by heavy lines are made of wood, and those by light lines are usually steel rods. The inverted king-post and queen-post trusses are often called *trussed*

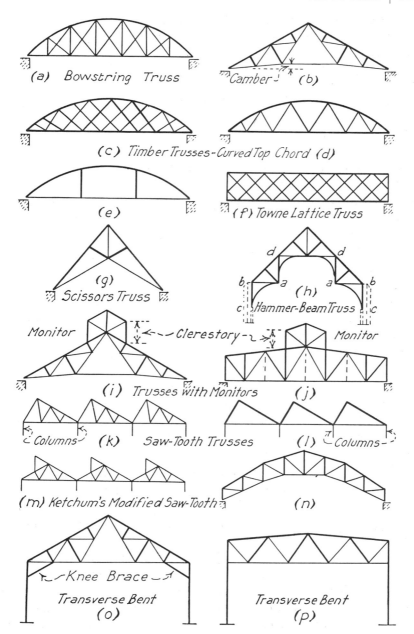

(a) Bowstring Truss

Camber (b)

(c) Timber Trusses-Curved Top Chord (d)

(e)

(f) Towne Lattice Truss

(g) Scissors Truss

(h) Hammer-Beam Truss

Monitor — Clerestory — Monitor

(i) Trusses with Monitors (j)

Columns (k) Saw-Tooth Trusses (l) Columns

(m) Ketchum's Modified Saw-Tooth (n)

Knee Brace

Transverse Bent (o)

Transverse Bent (p)

Fig. 34-2. Types of trusses and transverse bents.

beams and are described in Art. 38. The lower chords of the trusses in *d* and *e* carry tensile stresses but are usually made of wood and therefore are indicated by heavy lines.

The *Howe truss* may be constructed with inclined top chords (*h*) or with parallel chords (*i*). Howe trusses are always constructed with the members indicated by heavy lines made of wood. Those indicated by the light lines may be steel rods. The truss with sloping chords is usually used for pitched roofs, whereas the truss with parallel chords may be used to support flat roofs or floors. Howe trusses may be divided into any number of panels to suit any span or purlin spacing.

The *Pratt truss* may be constructed with inclined top chords (*j*), with parallel chords (*k*), or with broken upper chord (*l*), forming a *camel-back Pratt truss*. Pratt trusses are constructed of wood or steel sections. The truss with sloping chords is used for supporting sloping roofs, and the type with parallel chords may be used for supporting flat roofs or floors. Pratt trusses may be divided into any number of panels to suit any span or purlin spacing.

The *Fink truss* is always constructed with inclined chords (*m*), and all the members are made of steel sections or of wood. Fink trusses are very widely used in supporting sloping roofs. They may be divided into any number of panels to suit any span or purlin spacing. A modified form of Fink truss is shown in *n*, and a *fan Fink* or *fan truss* in *o*.

The *Warren truss* is always constructed with parallel or nearly parallel chords (*f*). Vertical members may be provided to reduce the distance between joints on the upper chord (*q*), on the lower chord (*r*), or on both chords (*s*). The Warren truss is very widely used for supporting floors or flat roofs.

The *bowstring truss* (Fig. 34-2*a*) is usually constructed of wood.

A truss is said to be *cambered* when the bottom chord is raised at the center, as in the cambered Fink truss shown in *b*. Camber improves the appearance of a truss and prevents sagging and the illusion of sagging.

Various special forms of wood roof trusses are shown in *c* to *h*. The trusses shown in *c* and *d* have curved upper chords, the various members being built up of 1- or 2-in. lumber. A curved trussed beam or tied arch is shown in *e*. This beam is built up of light lumber and steel rods. A *scissors truss* is shown in *g*, a *hammer-beam truss* in *h*, and a *Towne lattice truss* in *f*. In the hammer-beam truss shown in *h* the parts of the truss marked *a–b–c* act as brackets to reduce the span to *d–d*. These brackets must be securely fastened to the wall along the vertical member b–c, and the wall must be capable of withstanding the outward thrust produced at the point c. The structural action is complicated.

Other special forms of roof trusses are shown in i to n. *Monitors* are placed on top of roof trusses (i and j) to give better light and ventilation, the vertical face of a monitor, called the *clerestory,* being provided either with glass in sash which will open to provide light and ventilation or with *louvres* for ventilation only.

The *sawtooth trusses* shown in k and l are used to provide light and ventilation, the steeper face of the roof being covered with glass arranged so that a part of the sash will open. This face is usually turned toward the north to secure a uniform light. The type shown in k is constructed of steel, and that in l is constructed of timber and steel rods.

Another form of saw-tooth truss is shown in m. The vertical face is provided with top-hung sash. This type is always constructed of steel sections.

A camel-back Pratt truss with a heavy cambered lower chord is shown in n.

Steel or timber roof trusses may be secured to columns to give lateral rigidity (o and p). Such combinations of trusses and columns are called *transverse bents*. In the transverse bent shown in o, the braces between the truss and columns are called *knee braces*. They are provided to give transverse or lateral rigidity.

A type of truss which is rarely used is the *Vierendeel truss* (Fig. 34-3). It does not satisfy the definition of a truss but is given that designation. Trusses of this type are advantageous where it is necessary to keep unobstructed openings between the vertical posts. They are built of reinforced concrete or steel. Because of the omission of diagonals, all the members are subjected to bending stresses, and the joints must be rigid to make the structure stable.

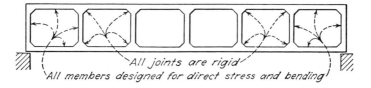

Fig. 34-3. Vierendeel truss or girder.

35. ARCHES, RIGID FRAMES, AND DOMES

Arches. The use of brick and stone arches in building construction has been discussed in Chapter 4. These arches have a structural function but their design is determined largely by appearance.

Arched roofs may have *barrel arches* or *ribbed arches*. A *barrel arch* resembles a segment of a barrel without longitudinal curvature. The vertical cross sections perpendicular to the length of roof are identical. A barrel arch is continuous from one end of a roofed area to the other and forms a *vault*. A *ribbed arch* is one of a series of arches providing structural support for the roof deck which spans the areas between arches and is continuous from one end of the roofed area to the other.

There are two general types of arch ribs (Fig. 35-1). The *solid rib* (*a*) is subjected primarily to compressive stresses but also to flexural and shearing stresses. The *trussed* or *framed* rib (*b*) is made up of members arranged in triangles, as in trusses, each of which is subjected to either tensile or compressive stresses. Arch ribs are also called *arch rings*. Some types of framed arches are not arranged in the form of ribs.

Arched roofs consisting of two or more intersecting arched units are called *groined roofs, vaults,* or *arches*. The lines of intersection of the arched units or the structural members in these locations are called *groins*.

Arched roofs are used chiefly for the long spans required for such structures as armories, exhibition halls, field houses, gymnasiums, and assembly halls. Barrel arches are usually constructed of reinforced concrete, solid arch ribs of reinforced concrete, steel, or wood, and trussed arch ribs of steel or wood.

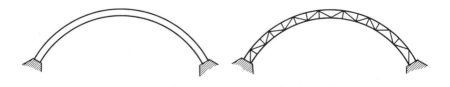

(a) Solid rib arch   (b) Trussed or framed rib arch

Fig. 35-1. Solid and trussed arch ribs.

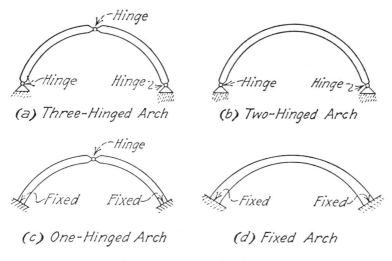

Fig. 35-2. Types of arches.

Arches may be constructed with their ends securely fixed to their foundations or abutments so that no rotation can take place at these points, or hinges which permit rotation may be introduced at these points or at the crown. In the three-hinged arch there is a hinge at each abutment and one at the crown (Figs. 35-2a); in the two-hinged arch there is a hinge at each abutment (b); in the one-hinged arch there is a hinge at the crown but the ends of the arch ring are securely fixed at the abutments (c); and in the no-hinged or fixed arch no hinges are provided and the ends of the arch ring are rigidly anchored to the abutments (d). Steel and wood arches are usually three-hinged or two-hinged. Reinforced-concrete arches may be of the three-hinged, two-hinged, or fixed type. The one-hinged arch is rarely used. Actual hinges may be provided for long-span arches, but often arrangements which offer negligible resistance to rotation are used.

The horizontal component of the thrust at each end of an arch may be transmitted through the foundation to the supporting soil if it has adequate capacity to carry this component as well as the vertical component. Otherwise a steel *tie* may be placed in the soil below the floor level and enclosed in concrete to form a *tie beam* (Fig. 35-3a).

If desired, the enclosed area may be restricted by vertical side walls, shown by dashed lines in the figure, the ends of the arches being left

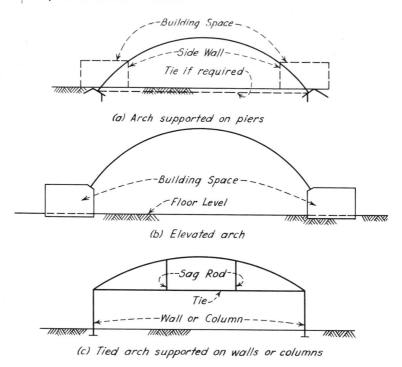

(a) Arch supported on piers

(b) Elevated arch

(c) Tied arch supported on walls or columns

Fig. 35-3. Supports for ends of arches.

exposed, or these ends may be enclosed, increasing the building space. The ends of the arch may be supported on rigid abutments (Fig. 35-3b), these abutments being enclosed in the building space. Such an arch may be provided with a tie, to carry the horizontal components of the end thrusts, and elevated above the floor level by supporting the ends on walls or columns (Fig. 35-3c). *Sag rods* are provided to prevent the tie from sagging.

Rigid Frames. Rigid frames are usually made up of solid members of concrete, steel, or wood corresponding to the solid ribs of arches (Fig. 35-1a), but occasionally their construction is similar to that of the framed arch (b).

The structural action of rigid frames resembles that of arches. However, arches are so proportioned that the stresses in the principal members are primarily compressive, whereas rigid frames are proportioned to provide adequate ceiling height over the entire area even though the structure is supported by foundations located just below the ground surface and not elevated as the arch shown in Fig. 35-3b.

Rigid frames are subjected to large bending and shearing stresses because of their form illustrated by the several types in Fig. 35-4. Rigid frames are often called arches, because their structural action is similar to that of an arch. Several types of single-story rigid frames are illustrated in Fig. 35-4. Multistory rigid frames are also constructed.

The vertical members of rigid frames are called the *legs*. The top members are sometimes called *rafters*. The portion of the frame adjacent to the junction of a rafter and a leg is called a *knee*. If two rafters of adjoining frames meet on a leg, the adjacent portions of these members form a Y. The center of the top member of a symmetrical frame, or a single break in the direction of the top member, is called the *crown*.

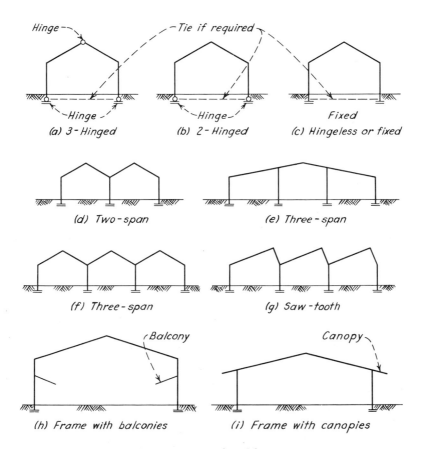

Fig. 35-4. Types of rigid frames.

Three single-span rigid frames are illustrated in *a*, *b*, and *c*, the only differences in them being the types of connections at the bottoms of the legs and at the crown. The frame in *a* is called a *three-hinged frame* because of the hinges at the bottoms of the legs and at the crown; the frame in *b* is called a *two-hinged frame* because there are hinges only at the bottoms of the legs; and the frame in *c* is called a *hingeless, no-hinged,* or *fixed frame* because of the absence of hinges. Actually, no real hinges are provided at any point but, at points where it is assumed in the stress computations that hinges are present, the detail or arrangement provides a negligible resistance to rotation. When it is assumed that bottoms of the legs are fixed, the connection of the leg to the foundation and the foundation itself are so designed that there will be negligible rotation of the legs at these points. The usual assumption is that the connections at these points are hinged.

Steel ties (*a*, *b*, and *c*) may be provided under the floor if necessary to carry the horizontal components of the thrusts of the legs.

Balconies may be cantilevered out from the vertical legs to provide for spectators (*h*), or running tracks may be provided in gymnasiums in this manner. The top members may be cantilevered outward beyond the legs (*i*) to provide *canopies* for protection over loading platforms or other areas.

Rigid frames are used extensively in gymnasiums, field houses, assembly halls, churches, and industrial structures requiring large unobstructed floor areas and ceiling heights.

Domes. Domes (Fig. 35-5) are frequently used as roofs over large circular floor areas for assembly halls, gymnasiums, field houses, and

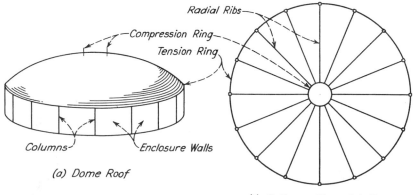

(a) Dome Roof

(b) Pattern with radial ribs

Fig. 35-5. Circular dome roof.

other buildings. They are constructed of self-supporting reinforced concrete shells as described in Art. 55, or the structural members may be various types of wood, steel, and aluminum sections arranged in a great variety of patterns.

A dome exerts outward thrusts continuously around its perimeter. These are resisted by a *tension ring*, as shown in the figure. The dome and tension ring are usually supported on columns spaced around the perimeter and braced to provide lateral stability for the structure. Bearing walls are also used for support. Purlins are commonly provided to span the space between ribs and support the roof deck.

Cables. The roofs of buildings may be supported by steel cables. Each cable consists of a strand of several wires. The wires in a strand are arranged in a helical form. The cables used in supporting roofs are made up of wires produced by cold-drawing steel rods through steel dies. The process of cold drawing produces wires with very high tensile strengths.

6 Wood construction

36. CONNECTING DEVICES

General Discussion. This chapter is concerned with building construction which is primarily of wood. Various terms such as lumber, wood, wooden, frame, and timber are applied to parts of a building constructed of wood. The basic material is always wood, just as steel and concrete are basic materials. According to the definition in the American Lumber Standards, given in Art. 9, *timber* is lumber 5 in. or larger in least dimension, and *lumber* is the product of the saw and planing mill. In general, the term timber is used to designate heavy wood members or construction, and frame is usually applied to light wood construction. There is a tendency to use the term wood in place of the term timber; therefore it is difficult, and probably not worthwhile, to attempt to be entirely consistent in the use of the terms wood and timber.

The rough green size of a piece of lumber is called its *nominal size*. Because of shrinkage and the waste in sawing and dressing, the actual thicknesses and widths of seasoned and dressed lumber are less than the nominal dimensions always used in designating lumber sizes. See the discussion of size standards in Art. 9.

This article will consider various methods used in holding the wood parts of a building together. All the devices considered are not used in framing a structure; many are used on such parts as interior finish. For instance, large nails and spikes are used in framing, but finish nails are not. However, it is convenient to consider finish nails in this article.

Nails. Steel-wire nails are ordinarily used in building construction. The size is designated thus, 8d or 16d, called 8-penny or 16-penny. This method of designation originated in the cost per 100 nails but no longer has this significance.

Wire nails are formed from steel wire of the same diameter as the nails. The common forms of wire nails are shown in Fig. 36-1a to c. Common nails are used where there is no objection to the exposed head and where the wide head is desirable, as in framing, sheathing, sub-floors, etc.

Casing nails are used principally with matched flooring, ceiling, and drop siding. *Finish nails* are used with interior and exterior finish, the heads being sunk below the surface with a *nail set* and the hole thus formed being filled with putty to conceal the nails. Common nails vary in size from 2d, with a length of 1 in., to 60d, with a length of 6 in.; casing nails from 2d, with a length of 1 in., to 40d, with a length of 5 in.; and finish nails from 2d, with a length of 1 in., to 20d, with a length of 4 in. The diameter varies with the length. A *barbed flooring nail* is illustrated in d. *Shingle* and *lath nails* are small nails of the same shape as common nails. *Wire spikes* are the same general shape as common nails, but they may have diamond or chisel points and flat or convex heads. Their size is designated by the length in inches and varies from 6 to 12 in. Wire nails, plain or galvanized, with large heads, are made for use with prepared roofing; galvanized and zinc-coated wire and copper nails are made for tile and slate roofing; and cement-coated nails are made for use where resistance to withdrawal is important. Various other types of wire nails are on the market, and galvanized common nails are available in many sizes.

Cut nails and *spikes* (e) are stamped out of steel plates of the same thickness as the nail. Various sizes and shapes are manufactured to correspond with wire nails and spikes.

The initial holding power of cut nails is greater than that of wire nails, but the holding power when they are partly withdrawn is less. Wire nails are more easily driven than cut nails. Cut nails have a longer life when exposed than wire nails. Wire nails are much more widely used than cut nails.

Boat spikes are made of square bars of steel or wrought iron. They have a wedge-shaped point and a head (f). The size of boat spikes varies from $\frac{1}{4}$ in. sq. by 3 in. long to $\frac{1}{2}$ in. sq. by 12 in. long. Boat spikes are used in heavy timber framing.

The various types of nailed joints used in light wood framing, and the number and size of nails, are shown in Fig. 41-5 and Table 41-2.

Screws. Screws may be divided into two general classes, wood screws and lag or coach screws.

Wood screws may be made of steel, brass, or bronze. Steel wood screws may have the natural steel finish called bright, or they may be

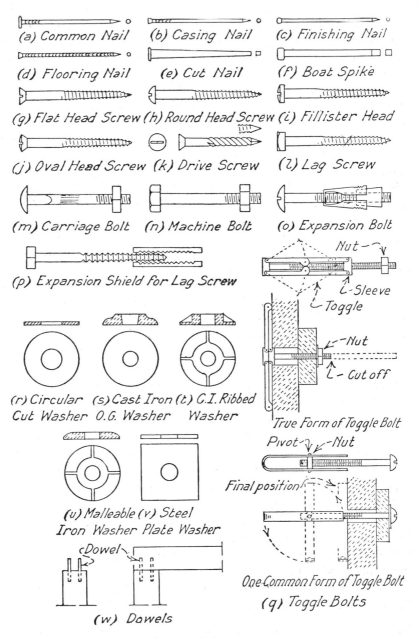

(a) Common Nail   (b) Casing Nail   (c) Finishing Nail

(d) Flooring Nail   (e) Cut Nail   (f) Boat Spike

(g) Flat Head Screw (h) Round Head Screw (i) Fillister Head

(j) Oval Head Screw (k) Drive Screw   (l) Lag Screw

(m) Carriage Bolt   (n) Machine Bolt   (o) Expansion Bolt

(p) Expansion Shield for Lag Screw

Nut —
L-Sleeve
L-Toggle

(r) Circular   (s) Cast Iron (t) C.I. Ribbed
Cut Washer O.G. Washer   Washer

L-Nut
L- Cut off

True Form of Toggle Bolt

Pivot- L-Nut

(u) Malleable (v) Steel
Iron Washer Plate Washer

Final position

Dowel

One Common Form of Toggle Bolt

(q) Toggle Bolts

(w) Dowels

Fig. 36-1.   Nails, screws, bolts, washers, and dowels.

blued, chromium- or nickel-plated, bronzed, lacquered, or galvanized. Various forms of wood screws are shown in *g* to *k*. Except for the *Phillips head screw* (not shown), they all have slotted heads so that they can be driven with a common screwdriver. The Phillips head screw has a cross-shaped depression in a flat head and requires a special screwdriver. With the exception of the *drivescrew* they have gimlet points. Drivescrews have diamond-shaped points and steep-pitched threads so that they may be driven with a hammer. The size of wood screws is designated by the length and gage, several gages being available in each length. Wood screws vary in length from $\frac{1}{4}$ in. to 6 in. They have a great variety of uses in building construction.

Lag screws have a conical point and a square head. *Coach screws* have a gimlet point and a square head, as shown in *l*, but both forms are usually called lag screws. The size of lag and coach screws is designated by the diameter and length of the shank, both being expressed in inches. The lengths vary from $1\frac{1}{4}$ to 12 in., and the diameters from $\frac{1}{4}$ to 1 in. Lag screws are used for heavy timber framing.

A hole should usually be bored to prevent screws from splitting and to make driving easier. This hole should be somewhat smaller than the diameter at the root of the thread.

Bolts. Bolts used in wood construction may be divided into carriage bolts, machine bolts, and drift bolts.

Carriage bolts have a round head shaped as shown in *m* and a square nut. The portion of the shank immediately under the head is square, and the remainder of the shank is round. The square portion of the shank when embedded in a wood prevents the bolt from turning while the nut is being turned. The size is designated by the length of shank and the diameter in inches. Carriage bolts may be obtained in almost any size. They are used in bolting pieces of wood together and are used where the square portion of the shank will be embedded in wood. Cut washers (*r*) are usually placed under the head and nut to give greater bearing area.

Machine bolts may have square or hexagonal heads and nuts (*n*). The entire shank is round. The size is designated by the length of shank and the diameter in inches. Machine bolts are available in almost any size. They are used for bolting steel and cast-iron members to wood and for bolting wood or steel members together during erection or permanently, and for use with timber connectors.

A *drift bolt* is a piece of round or square steel rod, with or without head or point, driven as a spike. Drift bolts are used in heavy framing. Before driving, a hole somewhat smaller than the drift bolt must be bored.

Expansion bolts have many different forms, but in all forms a special nut or shield is used which is so designed that after insertion in a hole the process of turning the bolt will so enlarge or expand the shield that it cannot be withdrawn. One form is illustrated in *o*. Expansion shields shown in *p* are often used with lag screws. Lead expansion shields are available for use with ordinary screws. Expansion bolts are used to fasten wood or iron to masonry which is already in place.

Toggle bolts of various forms are on the market. The head in all bolts is so arranged that, after the bolt has been inserted head first in a hole until the head is free on the other side of the piece, it will rotate or open up in such a manner that it cannot be pulled back through the hole. Two forms of toggle bolt are illustrated in *q*. Toggle bolts are used where bolts cannot be inserted in the usual way because one face is inaccessible.

Washers. Washers are used under the head and under the nut of a bolt in timber construction to provide a larger bearing area and to prevent the crushing of the wood fibers. Washers are of five types, various sizes being available in each type to suit the various sizes of bolts. These types are *circular cut washers* (*r*); *cast-iron O. G. washers* (*s*), the name being derived from the O. G. curve of the sides; *cast-iron ribbed washers* (*t*); *malleable iron washers* (*u*); and *steel-plate washers* (*v*), which are specially made to suit each case.

Dowels. *Dowels* are steel or wooden pins extending into, but usually not through, two members of a structure to connect them (*w*). A *tree-nail* is similar to a wood dowel, but it is used in such a manner that one or both ends are exposed.

Timber Connectors. Various types of metal connectors are designed to connect individual pieces of wood. They are called *timber connectors* and consist of metal rings, plates, and disks embedded in the contact surfaces of two members (Fig. 36-2*a* to *e*). They are embedded to prevent sliding and thereby to make possible the transmission of stress across the surface from member to member. Joints that make use of these connectors are much more effective than the older types. They have greatly extended the possibilities of timber construction for trusses, arches, and other structures.

Many kinds of joints have been devised, but only a few are used to any extent in the United States. The more common types are illustrated in Fig. 36-2. All require bolts passing through the centers of the

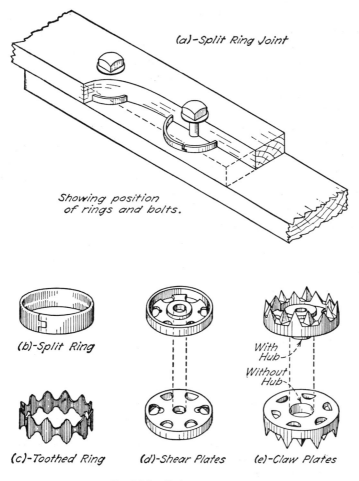

(a)-Split Ring Joint

Showing position
of rings and bolts.

(b)-Split Ring

(c)-Toothed Ring

(d)-Shear Plates

(e)-Claw Plates

With
Hub-

Without
Hub-

Fig. 36-2. Modern connectors.

connectors to hold the timbers in contact and, with some connectors, to force the connectors into the timbers. Special tools are available for preparing the timbers to receive the connectors, when connectors require such preparation, and for pulling the timbers together after the connectors are in position.

The *split ring* in *a* and *b* fits into precut grooves in the timber faces and is used in heavy construction. The *toothed ring* in *c* is placed between the surfaces of two timbers, without previous preparation to receive it, and is forced into the timbers by pressure to produce joints in light construction. The *shear plates* in *d* are used in pairs with each unit let into a prepared depression or *dap* in the timber face until its back is flush with the surface of the timber; or else one unit is inserted into a timber member so that a metal member can be bolted to it (Fig. 36-3). In either case, the stress is transmitted between members by shear in the bolt. The *claw plates* shown in Fig. 36-2e are used in the same manner as shear plates, but the dap is not made deep enough to receive the teeth which are forced into wood below the depth of the dap. These units are made for use singly or in pairs. One has a flush back, whereas the other has a projection which fits into the hole of the other so that stress can be transferred across the joint by the units themselves without producing shear in the bolt. Either unit can be used to connect a metal member to a timber member. If it is desirable to relieve the bolt from the shearing stress, the hole in the metal member is made large enough to receive the projection on the back of the claw.

Each type of connector is available in several sizes and capacities. The number of connectors required in any joint is determined by the stresses in the members and the properties of the wood. When they first came into use many years ago, timber connectors were called *modern connectors* but this designation is rarely used at present.

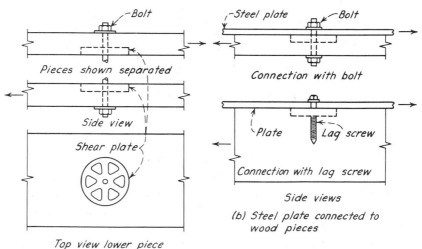

Top view lower piece

(a) Connection between two wood pieces

(b) Steel plate connected to wood pieces

Connectors available with diameters of $2\frac{1}{2}$" and 4"

Fig. 36-3. Use of shear plate connectors.

37. WOOD WALLS AND PARTITIONS

General Comments. Wood is used extensively in the construction of walls and partitions for *wood frame* and *ordinary construction,* defined in Art. 1. The most common use is for the supporting members in wood-stud walls and partitions. These *studs* are vertical members, usually 2-by-4-in. nominal size, but occasionally 2-by-6-in. studs are used. The spacing is normally 16 in., center to center, but may be 12 in. or 24 in. The studs are held in position in various ways, as described in Art. 41.

Methods for providing heat insulation for exterior walls are described in Art. 97. Protective and decorative treatments for exterior and interior wall surfaces are considered in Chapters 10, 11, and 12.

Sheathing. For most forms of outside covering, called *siding,* which are applied to the exterior of wood-stud walls, it is first necessary to cover the studs with *sheathing* to increase the rigidity and heat-insulating properties of the wall and form the base to which siding is attached. This sheathing may be wood boards with a nominal thickness of 1 in., fiberboard $\frac{1}{2}$ and $^{25}\!/_{32}$ in. thick, gypsum board at least $\frac{1}{2}$ in. thick, and plywood $^{5}\!/_{16}$, $\frac{1}{2}$, or $\frac{5}{8}$ in. thick.

Wood sheathing boards may be plain, matched, or shiplapped. They should have a nominal width of at least 6 in. and should be nailed to each stud with not less than two 8d common nails, three nails being desirable in 8-in. boards. They may be placed horizontally or diagonally. Horizontal sheathing is somewhat cheaper than diagonal sheathing but lacks rigidity, and diagonal braces must be provided at the corners of a frame. These are preferably continuous 1-by-4-in. boards let into the studs, but they are sometimes 2-by-4-in. pieces cut in between the studs in a continuous line. Either type of bracing may interfere with the return ducts of forced warm-air heating systems and may be complicated by window openings.

Fiberboard is made of cane fiber, straw, or similar fibrous materials pressed into sheets 2 and 4 ft. wide and usually 8 ft. long, as described in Art. 70. The 4-ft.-wide sheets are placed with the length parallel or perpendicular to the studs and should be nailed with galvanized large-head roofing nails $1\frac{1}{2}$ or 2 in. long, spaced 6 in. apart at intermediate studs and 3 in. apart at the edges. The 2-ft.-wide sheets are edge matched and are placed with the length horizontal. A special board impregnated or coated with bituminous material is available. As explained in Art. 97, it should not be vaporproof.

Gypsum board, as described in Art. 70, is made up of a gypsum core encased in a heavy paper. The width used for sheathing is 2 ft., and the length may be up to 8 ft. The length is placed at right angles to the studs. Sheets are nailed in the manner described for fiberboard.

Plywood is factory-made of three or more layers of wood joined with glue and laid with the grain of adjoining plies at right angles, as described in Art. 70. There are always an odd number of plies. The sheets are 4 ft. wide and up to 8 ft. long. They are nailed to the studs with 6d common nails spaced 6 in. at edge bearings and 12 in. at intermediate bearings.

Tests conducted by the United States Forest Products Laboratory indicated that the relative rigidities of stud walls of various types are about as follows.

1-in. horizontal sheathing without braces	1.0
1-in. horizontal sheathing with cut-in braces	1.6
1-in. horizontal sheathing with let-in braces	4.2
1-in. diagonal sheathing with no braces	4.3
¼-in. plywood sheathing	5.9

Exterior Surfaces. The exterior face of wood-stud walls may be covered with boards of special design called *siding,* placed horizontally and nailed to the studs with or without an intervening layer of sheathing. Noncorrosive nails, such as zinc-coated steel-wire nails or aluminum nails, should be used to avoid rust spots. A heavy specially treated paper such as rosin-sized building paper, or sheathing paper is usually placed under the siding to minimize air infiltration and make the surface more weathertight. As explained in Art. 97, it should not be vaporproof. There are two general types of wood siding: *bevel siding,* which is tapered or beveled so that it is thinner on the upper edge than on the lower edge (Fig. 37-1*a*) and which is lapped in laying; and *drop* or *novelty siding* which has a tongue-and-groove joint or a *rebated* or *shiplap joint* (Fig. 37-1*b* to *h*), some forms of which will give the same effect as bevel siding. Many other designs are manufactured. The common widths are 6 in. and 8 in. (nominal), and the thicknesses ⁹⁄₁₆ in. and ¾ in. (actual); but other widths and thicknesses are available.

Rustic sidings and *colonial sidings* are special forms of drop siding. Bevel siding is sometimes called *weatherboarding.*

Siding is made of Douglas fir, white and yellow pine, spruce, hemlock, redwood, cedar, and cypress.

Clapboards were formerly used as siding. They were sawed from

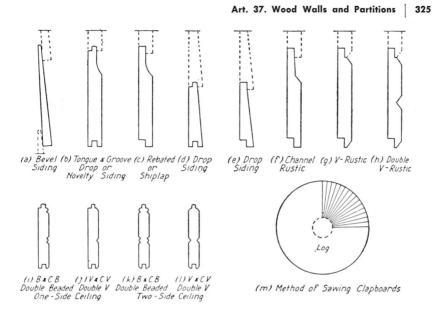

(a) Bevel Siding (b) Tongue & Groove Drop or Novelty Siding (c) Rebated or Shiplap (d) Drop Siding (e) Drop Siding (f) Channel Rustic (g) V-Rustic (h) Double V-Rustic

(i) B & C B Double Beaded One-Side Ceiling (j) V & C V Double V (k) B & C B Double Beaded Two-Side Ceiling (l) V & C V Double V

(m) Method of Sawing Clapboards

Fig. 37-1. Types of wood siding and ceiling.

logs as shown in Fig. 37-1m. The usual width was 6 or 8 in. They were lapped in laying, with 4 or 5 in. exposed or "to the weather." Clapboards are not now a commercial product.

The use of siding without sheathing is illustrated in Fig. 37-2a, that with sheathing in b. The former is an inferior grade of construction.

Wood shingles may be applied to wood-board or plywood sheathing (c). They may be placed with more of the shingle exposed or to the weather than they are when used on roofs. Shingles with a scored face, called *shakes*, are used in the same manner as ordinary shingles, but since their length may be as great as 3 ft. they are laid with a considerable length to the weather. Asbestos-cement or asphalt shingles are also used. For a more detailed discussion of shingles see Art. 73. There are many other types of siding (see Art. 79). Stucco surfaces are sometimes used on the exterior of wood-stud walls. (See Chapter 12.)

In another form of exterior wall construction, using metal lath, the sheathing and waterproof paper are omitted. The scratch coat and brown coat are applied to the exterior, and then a backing coat $\frac{5}{8}$ in. to $\frac{3}{4}$ in. thick is applied from the inside to the interior surface of the exterior lath and bonds to the scratch coat which was placed from the

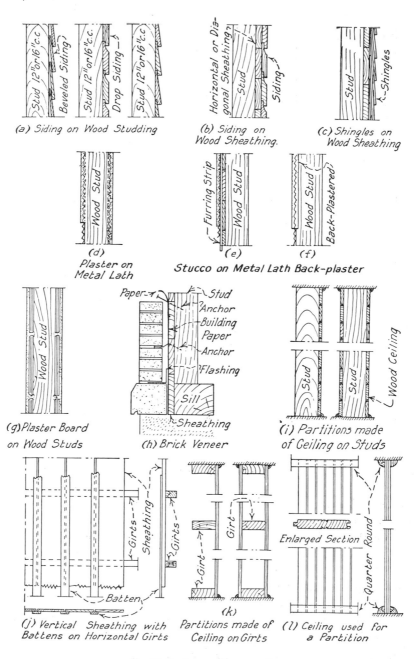

Fig. 37-2. Types of frame walls.

outside. The face of this backing coat should be about ¼ in. back of the face of the studs or, in other words, the studs should be embedded in the plaster about ¼ in. It may be desirable to paint the face of the studs to retard decay. This is known as *back-plastered construction* and is shown in *f*. This type of construction, using metal lath, will be sufficiently rigid if the corners of each wall are braced diagonally by 1-by-4-in. boards let into the studs on the inner side and securely nailed to them.

Square-edged boards placed vertically and attached to horizonal *girts,* with the joints covered with *battens,* may be used for siding (Fig. 37-2*j*). Tongued-and-grooved boards, without battens, may be used in the same manner. In a better type of construction, these types of siding are nailed to 1-in. wood sheathing which is, in turn, nailed to vertical studs. Air infiltration is minimized by placing a layer of sheathing paper between the siding and the sheathing.

Exterior walls with wood studs and some form of sheathing may be veneered with brick (*h*), or with other masonry. The veneer should rest directly on the masonry foundation of the structure and should be tied to the frame structure at intervals not more than 16 in. vertically and horizontally.

The weakest point in this type of construction is the tie between the face brick and the backing. A method which has been used to a considerable extent in the past is shown in *h*. It consists of a nail driven through the sheathing and into a stud. It should be a 40d common galvanized nail which will extend at least 1½ in. into the stud. The usual method of tying is illustrated in Fig. 37-3*a*. The masonry is brought up to the elevation at which the anchor is to be placed, as shown in 1. A corrugated galvanized-steel tie, bent into the form of an L, is placed in the position shown in 2 and attached by a nail driven into a stud. If this method is used, the bend should be sharp, it should be placed at the height of the joint, and the nail should be driven into the bend. This practice is not usually followed, however, and it is possible for the veneer to pull away from the frame. This can be avoided by the procedure illustrated in *b*. The masonry is stopped one course below the elevation of the tie (1); the tie is placed flat along the stud, and the nail is driven into the stud (2); another course of brick is laid (3); and the tie is bent sharply over the head of the nail and into the joint (4). If this procedure is followed the tie cannot yield as it can in *a*. The nail in either method shown in Fig. 37-3 should be not smaller than an 8d common galvanized nail and should always be driven slightly inclined and into a stud.

An air space of about 1 in. should be left between the back of the

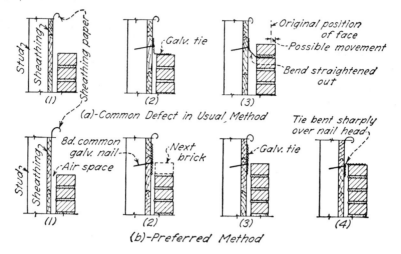

Fig. 37-3. Tying face brick to wood frame.

brick and the sheathing, and a layer of non-vapor-resistant sheathing paper should be placed over the sheathing to increase the tightness of the wall. Openings should be carefully flashed, as shown in Fig. 25-7, to prevent the entrance of moistrue behind the facing. The frame construction should not extend below the first-floor joists. Provision must be made for any shrinkage in the timber frame, or difficulties will be encountered where the window and door frames penetrate the masonry veneer. These are avoided by using the balloon frame described in Art. 41.

Veneered construction resists exposure to exterior fires far better than frame construction. Its resistance to interior fires is about the same as that of frame construction, but if it is not properly firestopped it may be difficult to extinguish fires behind the brick facing.

A plywood ⅜-in. thick, factory-made by hot pressing and by using a waterproof synthetic resin glue, is used for exterior paneling and siding. The edge joints are sealed with a heavy white lead paste and covered with moldings. It is available in several surface finishes.

Interior Surfaces. The interior surfaces of exterior wood-stud walls and both surfaces of wood-stud partitions are usually constructed of a metal-, gypsum-, or fiber-lath base coated with plaster, as shown in Fig. 37-2*d* and *g*. Plaster is applied as described in Chapter 12. Some form of vapor seal, as described in Art. 97, is ordinarily provided on the back of the plastered interior surface of exterior walls.

Dry wall construction as described in the following paragraph is used extensively in residence construction.

Dry wall construction is used instead of lath and plaster to provide for finished interior surfaces on the walls and ceilings of frame construction with wood studs or nailing strips and ceiling joists. The surfaces are provided by gypsum board, fiberboard, plywood or asbestos-cement board as described in Art. 70, wood panels, vertical or horizontal boards with some form of joint treatment, or in some other manner.

Dry wall construction avoids bringing into a building the large amount of water used in the plaster mortar and the tendency of the humid air due to evaporation to cause wood framing members to swell, the necessity for a drying out period before the interior finish can be applied, and the debris which results from plastering operations. Some of the wall boards used result in lower costs than plastered construction and a lower quality of construction. For most types the resistance to sound transmission from room to room is lower than for plastered construction.

38. WOOD COLUMNS, BEAMS, AND GIRDERS

Columns and Studs. Wood columns, as ordinarily used, are square timbers rarely smaller than 4 by 4 in., and usually not larger than 12 by 12 in., although larger timbers can be obtained from some mills. Columns may be built up of small timbers fastened together in various ways to secure unified action of the timbers under load, but, regardless of the means of fastening, except gluing, such columns are not fully effective in supporting loads. One type of built-up compression member is the spaced column (Fig. 38-1*a*), which has a load-carrying capacity much greater than that of the two vertical members not connected by spacer blocks.

Several planks may be spiked together (Fig. 38-1*b*) to form a column, but the arrangement shown in *c* results in a more unified action and is more effective. Columns are sometimes constructed by gluing several pieces or laminations together as described in the paragraph on glued laminated beams, rather than by spiking (Fig. 38-1*b*). Glued laminated columns have the same advantages as beams of this type.

In *wood frame construction,* the vertical closely spaced compression members of walls and partitions, called studs, are usually 2-by-

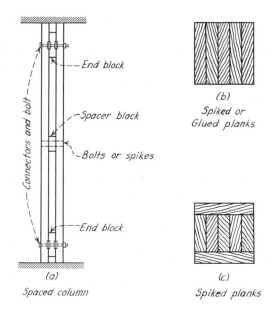

Fig. 38-1. Built-up wood columns.

4-in. lumber placed with the larger dimension perpendicular to the wall surfaces. For dwelling houses and other buildings carrying light floor loads, studs of this size are usually used for bearing and non-bearing walls and partitions of one- and two-story structures. For three-story buildings, 2-by-6-in. studs are ordinarily used for the first story. Occasionally, 2-by-3-in. studs are used for one-story nonbearing partitions.

Studs receive support, in the direction parallel to the length of the wall, from the sheathing of exterior walls and the interior wall surfacing materials attached to them.

In *heavy timber construction,* the minimum dimension permitted for columns is 8 in.

Solid Beams and Girders. Several specific types of flexural members are included under the general designation of beams and girders. Among these are floor and ceiling joists, rafters of sloping roofs, roof purlins, beams, and girders in various locations.

In *wood frame construction,* the closely spaced joists and rafters usually have a thickness of 2 in. and a common depth of from 4 to 8 in. for rafters and 6 to 12 or 14 in. for joists, depending upon the span and loading. Consideration must also be given to the rigidity as determined by the deflection under load. Often rigidity rather than the allowable stress is the factor determining the size. Beams may have a solid section of the required size but, in this type of construction, the required size is often achieved by spiking together 2-in. planks set on edge. Such pieces are readily available and easily assembled, or *fabricated*, on the job.

In *heavy timber construction*, the minimum thickness permitted for joists, beams, girders, and other members of this general type is 6 in., and the minimum depth is 10 in. Much larger timbers are available.

Glued Laminated Beams and Girders. (See reference 1.) If several pieces or laminations of uniform thickness and width are laid flat on each other to form a beam supported at the ends their load-carrying capacity and their vertical rigidity will be relatively low. When a load is applied they deflect downward, slide on each other along the surfaces of contact, and act as individual units. If sliding or relative movement can be prevented, the several pieces will act as a composite or solid unit, and the load-carrying capacity and rigidity will be markedly increased. Various devices have been used more or less satisfactorily, but the most effective procedure consists of gluing the laminations together under pressure applied with clamps, as in *glued laminated beams* (Fig. 38-2a). The usual thickness of laminations is 1⅝ in., or nominal 2 in. Water-resistive glue is used for interior beams and waterproof glue for exterior beams. To secure the desired lengths, laminations are spliced with inclined *scarf joints*, made by pregluing overlapping ends with opposite bevels with slopes of about 1 in 10. After a lamination has been spliced to the desired length, it is surfaced to insure uniform thickness and width throughout its length and is then ready for assembling in the glued beam. Each

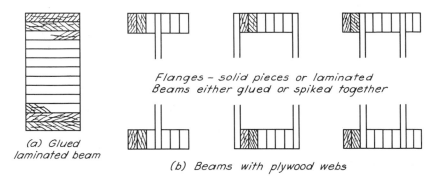

*Flanges – solid pieces or laminated
Beams either glued or spiked together*

*(a) Glued
laminated beam*

(b) Beams with plywood webs

Fig. 38-2. Glued laminated beams and beams with plywood webs.

lamination is usually as wide as the beam, but two laminations may be placed side by side to make up the beam width. The longitudinal vertical joints between adjacent laminations in successive layers are staggered. Full-width top and bottom laminations should be used.

Glued laminated beams and girders are factory-produced. They may have a constant cross section, a tapered top, the maximum cross section at the center or elsewhere, cambering, or other profiles. Girders with spans exceeding 100 ft. have been constructed, and girders with 2-in. laminations have been made as deep as 8½ ft.

Glued laminated construction has advantages compared with solid members because small sizes can be utilized, larger members can be constructed, defects can be eliminated, and there is better opportunity for seasoning. It is sometimes called *gluelam construction*.

Plywood Beams. (See reference 1.) Beams and girders are sometimes constructed with plywood webs and with flanges built up in various ways (Fig. 38-1*b*, *c*, and *d*). The possible depth is limited by the 4 ft. width of the plywood, because horizontal splicing is not feasible. Since their maximum length is 8 ft., vertical web splices are required. The flanges may be made up of vertical laminations or solid sections. If shop-fabricated, the member may be pressure-glued, but if fabricated on the job, the members may be joined by nailing or bolting with or without glue between them. This type of construction is rarely used but is advantageous under some circumstances.

Trussed Beams. Beams, trussed (Fig. 38-3) to increase their load-carrying capacity, are used occasionally.

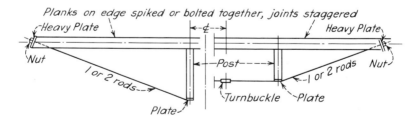

Fig. 38-3. Half-elevations of trussed beams.

39. WOOD TRUSSES

Types of Trusses. The various types of trusses are considered in Art. 34 and illustrated in Figs. 34-1 and 34-2. The most common types used for wood roof trusses for symmetrical sloping roofs are the Howe (Fig. 34-1*h*); the Pratt (*j*); the Fink (*m*); the Belgian, which is similar to the Pratt except that the members which are vertical in the latter are perpendicular to the top chords; and the bowstring (Fig. 34-2*d*).

Flat or gently sloping roofs may be supported by the Howe truss (Fig. 34-1*i*), the Pratt truss (*k*), or the Warren truss (*p* to *s*). These same types may be used to support floors if columns are to be avoided.

Timber Connectors.   Before the development of the timber connectors, described in Art. 36 and illustrated in Figs. 36-2 and 36-3, wood trusses were constructed primarily of rather large timbers with framed joints which were expensive to form, and which reduced the effective sections available for resisting stresses.   Connectors have made it possible to use pieces with small cross sections; these are readily available, require relatively little labor to assemble, and result in only small reductions in the effective cross-sectional areas of the members.   The most common type of connector used for trusses in buildings is the *split ring* (Fig. 36-2*a* and *b*), and the most common sizes have diameters of $2\frac{1}{2}$ and 4 in.   With this type of connector, the only function of the bolts is to hold the surfaces in contact.   One bolt passing through several connectors, with colinear axes, in adjacent pieces at a single joint holds the several adjacent surfaces in contact.

The stress that a single connector will resist depends upon the size of the connector and the properties of the wood in which it is embedded. The number of connectors required between two pieces is determined by the total tendency to slide along the contact surfaces in which the connectors are embedded.

Another commonly used type of connector is the *shear plate* (Figs. 36-2*d* and 36-3) which is used to connect a steel plate to a wood member (Fig. 36-3*a*).   It is also used to make field connections between two wood members, plates being embedded in each member as shown in Fig. 36-3*b*.   In such arrangements the bolts are subjected to the entire shearing stress between the two pieces connected.

If the lumber of which a truss is constructed is not seasoned to a moisture content comparable with what will prevail in service, the bolts should be tightened at intervals until shrinkage has ceased.

General Requirements.   All members, joints, and trusses as a whole should be symmetrical with reference to a vertical plane bisecting the truss longitudinally to avoid any twisting actions that would result from lack of symmetry.   The connectors to which the stress in any piece is transmitted should be located on the center line at the mid-depth of the piece or, if there is more than one row of connectors, they

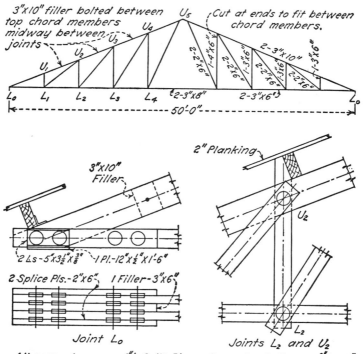

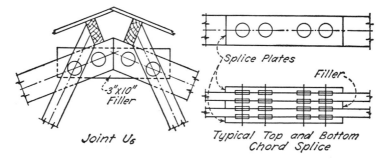

Fig. 39-1. Joint details of wood Pratt truss using connectors.

should be symmetrically arranged with reference to the center line. These requirements are illustrated in the examples referred to in the next paragraph. In addition, the trusses must be suitably anchored to the supports on which they bear, and properly braced to hold them in position to resist the loads to which they are subjected. The roof deck usually provides adequate lateral support for the top chord, but other bracing is usually required.

Examples. A Pratt roof truss with sloping top chords and split ring connectors is illustrated in Fig. 39-1. A Fink roof truss with sloping top chords and split ring connectors is illustrated in Fig. 39-2. It will be noted that the ends of this truss are attached to wood columns, and that knee braces are provided by continuing certain truss members until they can be connected to the columns. This arrangement of truss and columns forms a *transverse bent,* which is capable of resisting lateral or transverse loads on the roof and sidewalls. A Fink truss supported by walls is similar in design to the one shown, but the knee braces are omitted and the stresses in the truss members are changed.

A relatively long-span transverse bent using split ring connectors is shown in Fig. 39-3.

A bowstring roof truss with a two-piece glued laminated top chord, split ring connectors at all joints except the heel joints, and shear plate connectors at the heel joints is shown in Fig. 39-4. An enlarged cross section of the top chord and an enlarged detail of the heel joint are shown. It will be noted that the web members fit in between the divided chords and are fastened to them with split ring connectors. Six pairs of shear plates, illustrated in Fig. 36-2d and Fig. 36-3a, are required at each heel joint.

A typical bowstring roof truss with single-piece glued laminated chords is illustrated in Fig. 39-5. Both chords and all web members have the same width so that the web members can be joined to chords by means of bolted steel-strap end connections. Shear plates are used with the bolts when the stresses require them. Each chord is spliced at midspan by means of steel splice plates attached with bolts and passing through shear plates embedded in the members. A detail of the end connection is shown in the figure. This connection is assembled by welding a heavy inclined thrust plate between two side plates at the required angle to receive the end of the top chord, which is cut normal to the axis of the member. A steel bearing plate is welded to the side plates and projects beyond them far enough on each side to provide for the anchor bolt holes. Trusses of this type are factory-produced with spans up to 150 ft., and trusses with longer spans can be obtained.

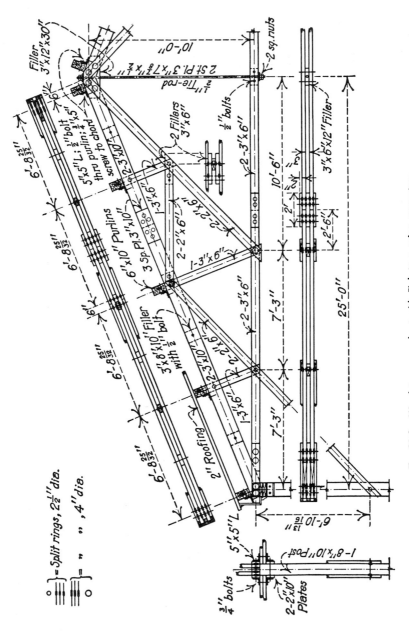

Fig. 39-2. Wood transverse bent with Fink truss using connectors.

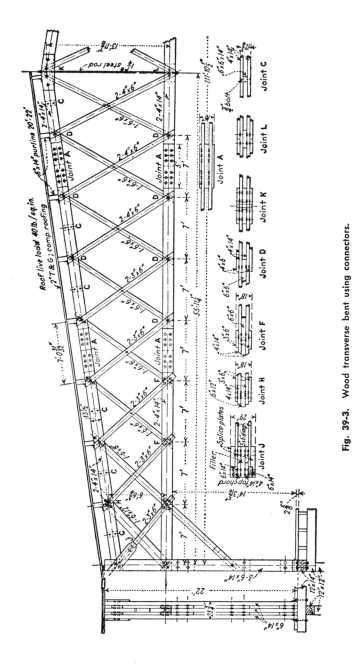

Fig. 39-3. Wood transverse bent using connectors.

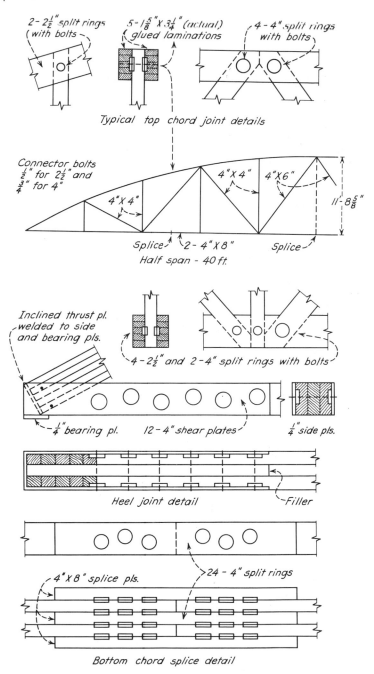

Fig. 39-4. Bowstring truss with two-piece glued laminated top chord. Adapted from Timber Engineering Co. design.

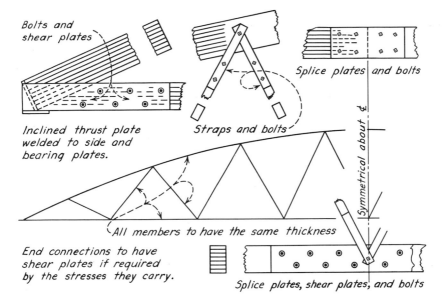

Fig. 39-5. Glued laminated monochord bowstring truss.

Trusses with spans of 250 ft. have been constructed. Because each chord consists of one unit, rather than two units, this type of truss is sometimes called a *monochord* bowstring truss.

40. WOOD RIGID FRAMES, ARCHES, AND DOMES

Introduction. As explained in Art. 35, there is no clear distinction between rigid frames and arches. The distinction made in that article (page 312) will be followed in this discussion, but many authorities would not make such a distinction. The classification based on the number of hinges, as explained in Art. 35, is always followed.

Glued laminated construction, discussed in the paragraph on glued laminated beams in Art. 38, is used extensively in constructing wood rigid frames and arches.

For rigid frames, which include portions with relatively small radii of curvature, it is necessary to use laminations which are thinner than the 1⅝-in. thickness ordinarily used for beams. For example, the minimum permissible radius for 1⅝-in. laminations varies from 30 to 40 ft., and for ¾-in. laminations from 7 to 12 ft., depending upon the species of wood.

The frames are factory-produced and transported to the site. Since it is not feasible to transport completed frames of the usual sizes, they are constructed in sections which are connected by field joints or splices.

Rigid Frames. Typical forms of glued three-hinged laminated rigid frames are illustrated in Fig. 40-1a, for which the slopes of the top members are relatively small, in b, where the slopes are steep, and in c, in which the top member is curved. A more detailed illustration of the frame in a is shown in d. In all of these, outer surfaces of the legs are vertical, but the inner surfaces may be vertical instead. Frames may be curved at the eaves, as shown by the dashed line on the left side of d, rather than angular. Various types of connections are made at the bottom of each leg and at the crown, some of which are shown in Fig. 40-3e to h. Even though the joints at the footings and the crown are considered to be hinged, the usual types of connection develop some resistance to rotation. See paragraph entitled Advantages of Fixing to Foundations in Art. 47.

The two units of the frame are usually raised to position separately, and the leg and crown joints are then secured.

In the crown connections shown in Fig. 40-1f and g, a steel dowel passing through shear plates embedded in adjacent ends of the two

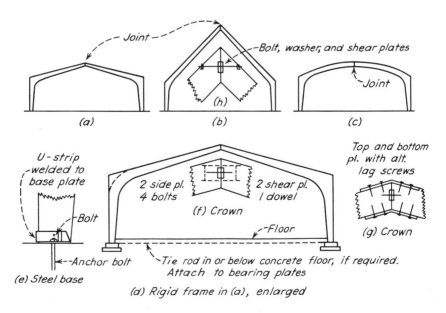

Fig. 40-1. Three-hinged glued laminated rigid frames. Partially from Unit Structures, Inc.

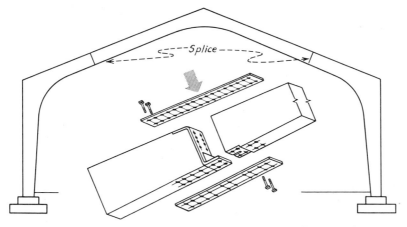

Detail of splice

Fig. 40-2. Detail of splice.

pieces are provided to resist the shear caused by unbalanced loading. To hold the ends together horizontally, splice plates are bolted to the sides of the member and across the joint in *f* and on the top and bottom surfaces in *g*. These plates are not provided to develop resistance to rotation. Shear plates are not required around these bolts. In the crown connection shown in *h*, a bolt with countersunk ends may be used instead of a dowel because of the acuteness of the angle. Therefore splice plates are not required to hold the ends together horizontally.

A simple connection of a leg to a footing is illustrated in Fig. 40-1*e*. If the soil has inadequate resistance to carry the horizontal components of the end thrust of the frames, a steel rod may be provided to tie appropriately designed bases of the two legs together and thus to resist the equal and opposite horizontal components. This tie is placed below the floor level and is embedded in concrete to protect the rod from corrosion. This member is called a *tie beam*.

A two-hinged glued laminated rigid frame is illustrated in Fig. 40-2. It is similar in construction to the three-hinged frame in Fig. 40-1*a* and *d*, but it is constructed in three sections, as shown in the figure. These are spliced together on the job. The splices are located at points where the tendencies to bend, or bending moments, have minimum values. However, since various combinations of dead load, unbalanced snow load, and wind loads from any direction must be provided for, a splice in any location must always be designed to resist bending moments of considerable magnitude.

One effective form of splice is shown in Fig. 40-2. The bent plate is attached to the leg at the factory with nails to hold it in position. Top and bottom splice plates are provided. To receive the leg screws which are to attach these plates, shear plates are embedded in the members and holes are bored to receive the screws. These operations are accomplished at the factory. The shearing resistance of the splice may be increased by means of dowels and shear plates (Fig. 40-1g). The three sections may be assembled flat on the floor, or they may be placed in position separately. If the latter procedure is used, the legs are erected first. After they are in position, the center beam is hoisted and lowered into position on the projecting legs of the bent plates. It is called a *drop-in beam*. It is supported while the lag screws in the splice plates are driven and the splice is made secure.

The roof decks are usually constructed of heavy matched planks spanning the distance between frames or between purlins supported by the frames. The underside of the deck is usually exposed and is appropriately finished.

Glued laminated rigid frames are attractive in appearance. They are used for many kinds of buildings such as gymnasiums, churches, and auditoriums where unobstructed floor areas are required and the clearances provided at the sides by the vertical legs are desired. They are used for spans as short as 30 ft. or less, and have been constructed with spans approaching 150 ft. The type shown in Fig. 40-1b is often used for churches.

Arches. In contrast to rigid frames, arches are so proportioned that the stresses produced by the loads are primarily compressive and the shears and flexural stresses are relatively small. Flexural stresses must be considered, however, in the design of the arch section, splices, and supports. The arch ring commonly has a constant radius and constant cross section, although rings with parabolic profiles and variable cross sections are sometimes used. Glued laminations are usually $1\frac{3}{16}$ or $1\frac{5}{8}$ in., the actual thickness depending upon the species of lumber used and the curvature. The arches may be fixed, two-hinged, or occasionally three-hinged for the longer spans.

A glued laminated arch supported on piers is diagrammed in Fig. 40-3a. Vertical sidewalls may be provided as shown by the inner dashed lines. If such sidewalls are constructed the projecting ends of the arches may be exposed and treated to resist the weather, or they

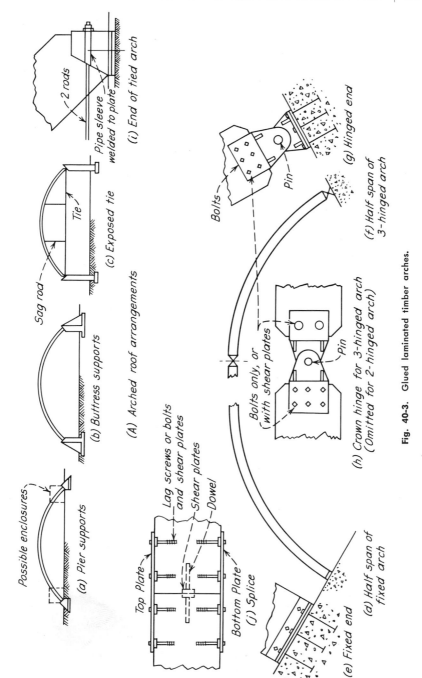

Possible enclosures

(a) Pier supports

(b) Buttress supports

Sag rod

(c) Exposed tie

Tie

2 rods

Pipe sleeve welded to plate

(i) End of tied arch

(A) Arched roof arrangements

Bolts

Pin

(g) Hinged end

(f) Half span of 3-hinged arch

Bolts only, or (with shear plates)

Pin

(h) Crown hinge for 3-hinged arch (Omitted for 2-hinged arch)

Lag screws or bolts and shear plates

Shear plates

Dowel

Top Plate

Bottom Plate

(j) Splice

(e) Fixed end

(a) Half span of fixed arch

Fig. 40-3. Glued laminated timber arches.

may be incorporated in building space. An arch may be elevated (*b*), and supported on rigid reinforced concrete buttresses or on walls or columns with the horizontal thrusts at the ends carried by steel tie rods (*c*). Sagging of the rods is prevented by vertical *sag rods,* or straps. The arches shown in *a* and *b* may have fixed or hinged ends, but the ends of the tied arch in *c* are always considered to be hinged.

An enlarged drawing of half the arch shown in Fig. 40-3*a* or *b,* with fixed end supports, is illustrated in *d,* and a detail of the support is shown in *e.* A hinged end support for these arches is illustrated in the half-arch in *f* and the detail in *g.* They are usually built up of steel plates welded together. If these arches are three-hinged, there is a hinge at the crown as shown in *f* and the detail in *h.* An end support for the tied arch in *c* is illustrated in *i.* This would be attached to a column or bearing wall with appropriate provision made for stability. The horizontal components of the end thrusts are carried by the *tie rods.* To prevent them from sagging under their own weight, *sag rods* may be used as shown in *c.* Tied arches may also be used if the end supports are very near the ground level. Such an arrangement would only be used if the foundation soil were incapable of carrying the horizontal components of the end thrusts.

It may be necessary to fabricate an arch in two or more sections to facilitate transportation or for other reasons. Joints are made normal to the arch axis, and provisions are made at the factory for splicing the adjacent sections together in the field. A type of splice suitable for a heavy long-span arch is illustrated in *j.* The shear plates are embedded in the timbers at the factory, and the necessary holes for bolts or lag screws are bored. For light arches only the top and bottom plates, or only the side plates, held in position by bolts or lag screws, may be adequate. The make-up of the splice appropriate for a given situation is, of course, determined by the designer.

The types of decks used are those described for rigid frames.

Glued laminated arches are used to support the roofs over unobstructed floor areas for many buildings such as auditoriums, churches, recreation buildings, gymnasiums, garages, and warehouses. Spans exceeding 240 ft. have been constructed. They are fabricated at factories.

Light glued laminated arched rafters, spaced as close as 2 ft., are sometimes used for small buildings such as barns. They are covered with 1-in. sheathing.

Lamella Arches. A special form of arched roof known as the *lamella roof* is constructed of short pieces of wood varying in size from 2 by 8 in. to 3 by 16 in., and in length from 8 to 14 ft., as illustrated in Fig. 40-4. The short pieces called *lamellas* are bolted together in diamond-shaped patterns (*a*) to form a complete roof structure, as shown by the roof plan and longitudinal sections of a simple form in *b* and *c*. The diamond-shaped panels are all the same size and shape. The

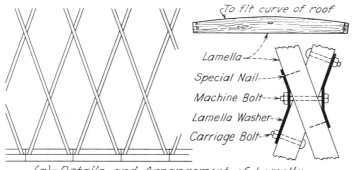

(*a*)—Details and Arrangement of Lamella

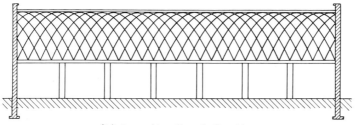

(*b*)—Longitudinal Section

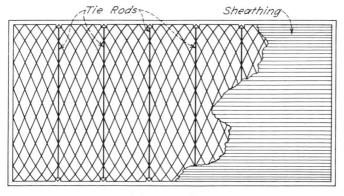

(*c*)—Roof Plan

Fig. 40-4. Wood lamella arch roof.

apparent curvature and distortion of the panels in *c* is caused by the changing slope of the arched roof. The thrust of lamella roofs may be taken by tie rods or by buttressed walls (Fig. 40-3*b* and *c*). Roofs of this type have been used for spans from 25 ft. to 150 ft. on many types of buildings including gymnasiums, dance pavilions, exhibition buildings, auditoriums, churches, garages, warehouses, and sheds.

Domes.   Glued laminated construction is used for the frames of domes covering circular floor areas.   For the building illustrated in Fig. 40-5, the structural supports for the walls and roof consist of sixteen half

Fig. 40-5.   Domed roof with glued laminated rigid frame supports.   Span 96 ft.   Cocoa High School, Cocoa, Florida.   Unit Structures, Inc., Designers and Manufacturers.

Fig. 40-6. 300-ft. diameter dome with 36 glued laminated wood 7 by 16¼-in. ribs. Montana State College Field House. Architects: Wilson and Berg, Jr. Structural Engineer: Ben F. Hurlbutt. Fabricator and Erector: Timber Structures, Inc.

three-hinged, glued laminated timber rigid frames with their legs supported on footings equally spaced around a complete circle, their crowns meeting on a thrust block at the center of the roof. The wedge-shaped roof areas between frames are spanned by equally spaced timber purlins of varying length with their ends supported on the frame by steep strap hangers. These purlins support a timber roof deck.

An outstanding example of another type of heavy timber circular domed roof has arched radial ribs (Fig. 40-6). The dome has a span of 300 ft. and a rise of 51 ft. above the springing line. There are 36 glued laminated ribs with the same radius and cross section. Each rib was factory-fabricated in three equal sections to facilitate transportation and erection, and field-spliced with top and bottom steel plates, shear plates, bolts, and dowels. The outward rib thrusts at the springing line are carried by steel base shoes anchored to the top surfaces of reinforced concrete wall columns, to which the adjacent ends of the 36 straight segments of a built-up steel tension ring are welded. The inward rib thrusts at the crown are carried by a built-up steel compression ring supported radially by 18 steel struts framed together at the center in such a manner that the unit resembles a wheel 18 ft. in diameter. Equally spaced glued laminated straight purlins frame into the sides of the ribs. Light, closely spaced, solid wood subpurlins are attached to the tops of the purlins and are normal to them. These support 3-in. wood-fiber concrete roof deck panels. Each of the 36 sectors between ribs has sets of diagonal steel-strap cross bracing, with one system located immediately above and one immediately below the subpurlins. The ends of the sets of cross bracing in adjacent segments, and in each layer, are welded together to form steel nets enveloping the entire dome. The 36 columns are connected by horizontal reinforced concrete girts, and brick panel walls are constructed between columns to provide lateral support to the columns and the structure as a whole. For a more detailed description, and the erection procedure, see reference 3. This type of construction is suitable for smaller structures.

A dome with wood lamella construction is illustrated in Fig. 40-7. The outside diameter is 142 ft. and the rise 18½ ft. A reinforced concrete tension ring is located around the perimeter of the dome and on top of reinforced columns spaced about 12 ft. apart. Alternate

Fig. 40-7. 140-ft. wood lamella dome roof. Ham, Hanover and Williams, Architects. Roof Structures, Inc., Webster Groves, Missouri, Manufacturers and Erectors.

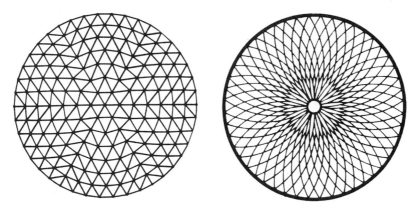

Fig. 40-8. Lamella dome patterns. Lamella Roof Associates.

panels between columns are filled with masonry walls. A crown block is located at the center of the dome to carry the thrusts of the lamella which frame into it. The lamella vary in cross section from 4 by 16 in. for those framing into the tension ring to 2 by 12 in. at the crown. The lamella are connected in the same manner shown for the arch roof in Fig. 40-4. The roof-deck is matched sheathing varying in thickness from 2 in. for the lower portion of the dome to 1 in. for the portion surrounding the crown.

The pattern of the lamella in Fig. 40-7 is shown in Fig. 40-8b. In this pattern the number of lamellas for each concentric passing through the lamella intersections remains constant. The lamellas terminate into collective radial ribs at the crown.

Another pattern is shown in a. For this pattern the 360-degree angle at the crown is divided into from 4 to 12 units, permitting all the lamellas and ring purlins to have the same radius and cross section.

41. WOOD FRAMING

All or a part of the structural elements of many buildings are made of wood. According to the classification based on the types of construction given in Art. 1, there are three classes of buildings which make extensive use of wood structural members. These are *Wood Frame Construction, Ordinary Construction,* and *Heavy Timber Construction.* Consideration will be given to each of these types.

Wood Frame Construction

General. As defined in Art. 1, *Wood Frame Construction* is that type of construction in which the walls, partitions, floors, and roof are wholly or partly of wood or other combustible material.

Wood Frame Construction, commonly called *Frame Construction,* is used extensively for dwellings. Our discussion will be confined to buildings of this type. The height is usually limited to two inhabited stories above the grade line, not including finished habitable attic space, which may be provided under a sloping roof, and a basement. A dwelling with an attic finished with living space is classed as a two-and-a-half-story structure. With minor exceptions, *wood frame construction* is not permitted within fire districts.

The structural frame is constructed of lumber, most of which has a nominal thickness of 2 in. The center-to-center spacing of the various structural members is usually 16 in., but occasionally 12-in. and 24-in. spacings are used. Unless this spacing is made constant throughout, framing difficulties may be encountered. The depths of joists and rafters are determined by the loading conditions, span, allowable stresses, and required rigidity. The studs and plates are usually 2 by 4's. Types of *Wood Frame Construction* are illustrated in Figs. 41-1 and 2.

The exterior wall framing is usually covered with some form of sheathing which is, in turn, covered with finished surfaces consisting of some form of siding or a masonry veneer, as described in Art. 37. The roof framing is covered with a deck consisting of sheathing or other material to receive roofing, as described in Chapter 11. The floor framing is covered with a subfloor on which some type of finished floor, described in Chapter 10, is laid. The wall and roof sheathing are important factors in heat insulation and, together with the subfloors, are essential in providing lateral rigidity.

Before the frame is started, termite shields, described in Art. 9 and illustrated in Fig. 9-1, should be installed on top of all exterior and interior foundation walls constructed of hollow masonry units. Two-inch *sills* or *plates* are then placed on top of the walls and secured by anchor bolts previously installed in the walls. These sills are the first members of the frame to be placed.

If there are unexcavated spaces below the first floor, there should be a clearance of at least 18 in. between the bottoms of the joists and the ground to avoid decay. This is called a *crawl space* because it provides access, by crawling, for inspection and plumbing or other

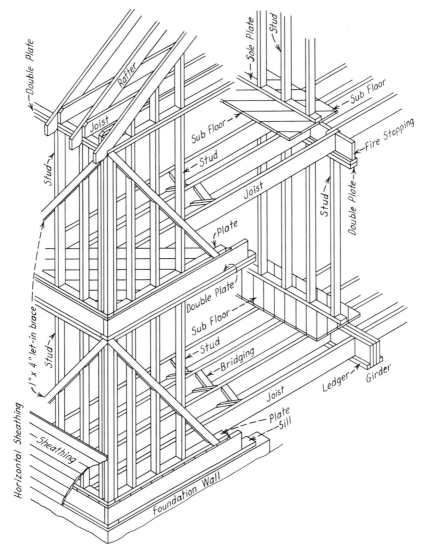

Fig. 41-1. Platform frame. (Adapted from reference 4.)

repairs. Unless adjacent to a basement into which it can be ventilated, a crawl space should be cross-ventilated through adequate screened openings in the foundation walls. If the soil is of a type, such as clay, which conducts moisture upward by capillary action, the surface of the unexcavated soil should be covered with a layer of heavy

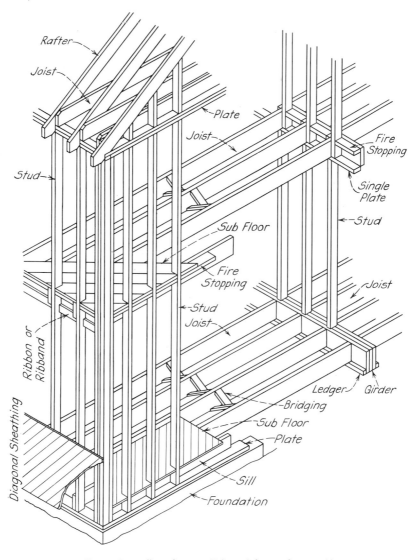

Fig. 41-2. Balloon frame. (Adapted from reference 4.)

polyethylene film to serve as a vapor barrier and assist in humidity control.

There are two types of wood frames commonly used for dwelling houses. These are the *platform frame* (Fig. 41-1) and the *balloon frame* (Fig. 41-2). Each of these can be modified to adapt it to one-story frames, special conditions, or individual preferences. The illustrations are for frames of two-story dwellings. The changes required to adapt them to other types of sloping roofs are obvious. Changes required for one-story frames are considered later.

Platform Frame. This type of frame, for a two-story dwelling, is illustrated in Fig. 41-1. An examination of the drawing will indicate that the framing for the entire first-floor construction, as well as the diagonal *subfloor* which extends to the outer edges of the frame, can be completed to form a platform before work is started on the framing for the first-story exterior walls and the partitions.

Subfloors are laid diagonally to permit a tongued-and-grooved, or matched, wood floor to be laid over them, with the flooring either perpendicular or parallel to the joists. The former is preferred, with the flooring nailed to the joists. In addition, laying the subfloor diagonally adds significantly to the rigidity of the frame.

Cross bridging is provided at the midspan of the *joists*. The function of this bridging is to distribute the effect of concentrated loads over several joists and thereby increase the strength and rigidity of the floor. The same effect is often attained by *solid bridging,* which consists of short pieces, of the same cross section as the joists, which are fitted between the joists at right angles to them and staggered somewhat to permit end nailing.

Framing the first-story walls and partitions is started by nailing the *sole plates* to the subfloor in their proper locations. The first-story *studs* are then erected and capped with doubled *top plates*. The frame is now ready to receive the second-floor joists and sub-floor to complete the second-floor platform.

The framing for the second-story walls and partitions can now be completed, the ceiling joists placed, and the attic subfloor laid if there is to be one.

Double joists are provided under partitions which are parallel with the joists. If these are bearing partitions in either the first or second stories, which are not supported by walls, partitions, or girders, each should be trussed by one or more 1-by-4-in. diagonal braces *let into* notches in the studs and extending the full height of the story and the full length of the partition. Irregular arrangements may be required to avoid door openings.

Finally the roof rafters are erected. They are notched to provide bearing on the top plate on the exterior wall studs. The upper ends of full-length rafters are cut at the proper angle to fit against the vertical sides of the *ridge board* to which they are nailed. Horizontal members, called *collar beams,* are often nailed to every third pair of rafters at approximately their upper third points to strengthen the roof.

The frame is now ready to receive the exterior wall and roof sheathing. For some types of wall sheathing, including horizontal wood sheathing, the frame must be braced laterally by providing *corner bracing* (Fig. 41-1). If such bracing is required, it consists of 1-by-4-in. boards *let into* notches cut in the outer faces of the studs so that the outer faces of the braces are flush with the outer edges of the studs to which they are nailed. See Art. 37.

Often the framing for various portions of the walls and partitions of a story is assembled in a horizontal position on the platform for that story, tilted into the desired vertical positions, and secured ready to receive the framing for the next story or the roof, thus facilitating construction operations.

The frame for a one-story dwelling is identical with the portion of the two-story frame above the tops of the first-story studs. The top plate on these studs becomes the foundation sill. This is the usual type of frame for one-story dwellings that do not have masonry veneers or stucco finishes.

Balloon Frame. This type of frame is illustrated in Fig. 41-2. The basic difference between this type and the platform frame is that the studs for the exterior walls extend from the top of the sill through the two stories and the studs for the interior partitions, which are in the same vertical plane, are interrupted only by a single, or sometimes double, 2-by-4-in. top plate. No header is provided at the exterior ends of the first-floor joists, and the sill on which they rest often consists of two 2-in. pieces rather than one, as in the platform frame.

The two-story exterior wall studs and their double top plates are erected with their lower ends bearing on the sill. The outside ends of the second-floor joists are supported on a 1-by-4-in. *ledger board* let into the inside of the two-story studs by notching them. This board is also called a *ribbon* or *ribband*. The joists are placed in contact with the studs. If there are interior foundation walls under the first-story partitions, the first-story studs are carried down to plates on these walls; otherwise they are supported on girders. The inner ends of the second-story joists are lapped and supported on the single 2-by-4-in. top plates of the first-story bearing partitions. The bottom ends of the second-story joists bear on the top plates of the first-story studs. The relative positions of the first- and second-story bearing partition studs and the second-story joists are shown in the figure.

The lower portion of the frame for a one-story dwelling is the same as the lower portion of the frame for a two-story dwelling. A double wall plate is placed along the tops of the one-story studs to support the ceiling joists and the roof rafters in a manner identical with the upper portion of the second story of a two-story frame.

The comments on the platform frame about bridging, roof framing, double joists, and corner bracing apply also to the balloon frame. Horizontal sheathing requires that the frame be corner braced but diagonal sheathing does not, see Art. 37.

Advantages and Disadvantages of Platform and Balloon Frames. The primary advantage of the platform frame over the balloon frame is its relative ease of construction. The primary advantage of the balloon frame is its relatively smaller vertical shrinkage.

The easier erection of the platform frame results primarily from the use of the platform in each story for assembling the wall and partition framing for that story.

The small vertical shrinkage of the balloon frame results from the continuity of the exterior wall studs through the two stories and the approximate continuity of the bearing partition studs, which take advantage of the negligible longitudinal shrinkage of wood.

The relatively large vertical shrinkage of the platform frame is due to the inclusion of considerable cross-grain wood along the lines of vertical support and the shrinkage of wood in this direction, due to reduction in moisture content, is relatively large.

The major difficulties resulting from vertical shrinkage are produced by unequal vertical movements at different points. These tend to cause plaster to crack, joints to open up, door openings to be out of plumb and distorted, and doors to bind. Such movements can be avoided in both types of frame because the vertical movements which occur in a platform frame can be equalized by equalizing the total vertical thickness of cross-grain wood along all lines of vertical support.

Other difficulties due to vertical shrinkage cannot be avoided by the platform frame if the building is to be faced with a masonry veneer. Such veneers do not shrink with reduction in moisture content, but the frame that supports them shrinks. The relative downward movement of the frame causes defects to develop at the window openings, which are difficult to avoid even if foreseen. They are, of course, more pronounced in two-story than in one-story dwellings. Exterior finishes such as shingles and wood sidings can adjust themselves to vertical shrinkage of the supporting frame, but stucco finishes cannot.

Considering vertical shrinkage, horizontal sheathing is preferable to diagonal sheathing for the platform frame. Diagonal sheathing would restrict the vertical movement due to the vertical shrinkage of the first- and second-floor construction and preclude the equal vertical settlement of all parts of the structure which is an objective of the platform frame.

If the lumber used in constructing a frame were seasoned to the moisture content it would have when the dwelling is in use, there would be no shrinkage problems. This is not feasible for many reasons, including the seasonal variations in indoor temperature and the humidity conditions which result in variations in the moisture content of the framing. The most objectionable shrinkage occurs after the finished wall surfaces have been completed.

Framing around Openings. Typical framings around window and door openings are illustrated in Fig. 41-3a to c. In general, the jambs at these openings are doubled. The heads consist of two pieces on edge, proportioned according to the span and load, supported by the double

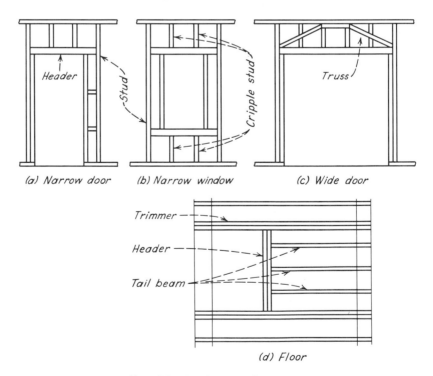

(a) Narrow door   (b) Narrow window   (c) Wide door

(d) Floor

Fig. 41-3. Framing around openings.

jambs as shown in *a*, *b*, and *c*. Short studs above and below openings (*a* and *b*) are called *cripple studs*. A double jamb may be separated (*a*), if blocks are securely nailed between the two studs. Wide door and window openings may be trussed (*c*), or deep headers may be used. The framing must be adequate to resist the loads to which it is subjected without exceeding permissible stresses and deflections. The framing around an opening in a floor is illustrated in *d*, where a *header, trimmers,* and *tail beams* are shown.

Firestopping. Concealed spaces between studs, joists, and rafters, in the clearance space required between masonry chimneys and wood framing, and in other locations which otherwise would permit air currents to pass from one part of a dwelling to another, should be sealed by *firestops* because of the possibility that fire might travel in these spaces.

According to the Code Manual applicable to the New York State Building Construction Code,

Combustible firestopping may be wood blocking of 2-inch nominal thickness or two layers of 1-inch nominal thickness assembled so that there are no through joints.

Noncombustible firestopping may be masonry, concrete, plaster, mortar, wallboard or similar material not less than ¼ inch thick, sheet metal of at least 24 U. S. gage, and slag or rock wool. Metal reinforcement or support such as metal lath should be used when needed to hold firestopping materials in place.

Examples of firestopping given in Fig. 41-4 are (*a*) first-floor platform frame at exterior wall, (*b*) first-floor balloon framing at exterior wall, (*c*) second-floor framing at exterior wall of platform frame, (*d*) second-floor framing at exterior wall of balloon frame, (*e*) second-floor framing over bearing partition of platform frame, (*f*) second-floor framing over bearing partition of balloon frame, (*g*) floor joists resting on girder. Similar to joists supported on steel girders or masonry wall.

Nailed Connections. The most common means for fastening together the 1-in. and 2-in. lumber used in wood frame construction is by nailing. Nails are driven in various ways with reference to the pieces they connect. In the platform and balloon frames the faces of the joist and studs are placed in contact whenever possible (Figs. 41-1 and 2) to permit them to be nailed together.

The types of nailing (Fig. 41-5*A*) are face nailing, end nailing, toe nailing, and blind nailing. In *face nailing* the nails are driven through the face of one piece into the face or edge of another piece (*a*).

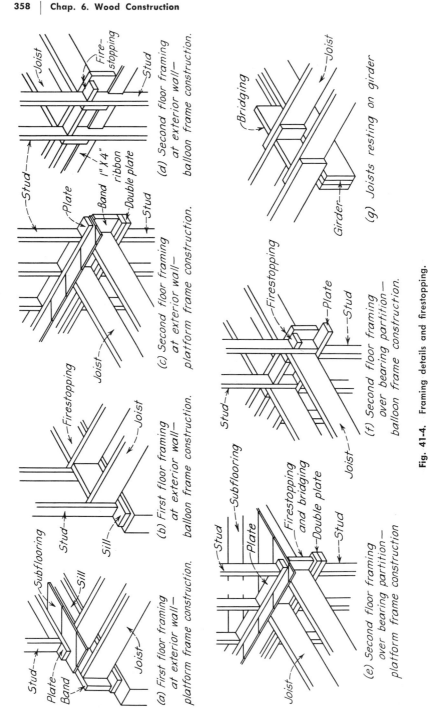

Fig. 41-4. Framing details and firestopping.

(a) First floor framing at exterior wall— platform frame construction.

(b) First floor framing at exterior wall— balloon frame construction.

(c) Second floor framing at exterior wall— platform frame construction.

(d) Second floor framing at exterior wall— balloon frame construction.

(e) Second floor framing over bearing partition— platform frame construction

(f) Second floor framing over bearing partition— balloon frame construction.

(g) Joists resting on girder

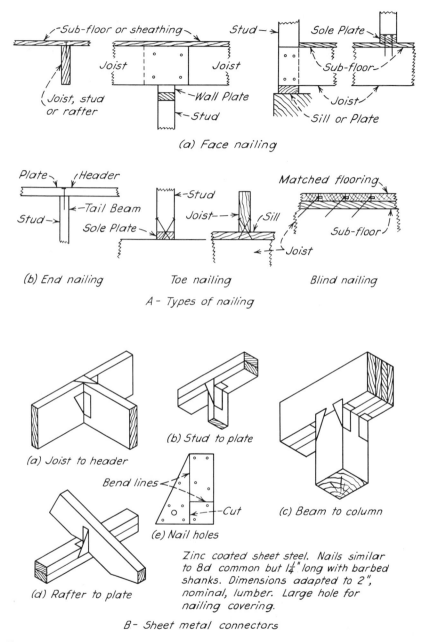

(a) Face nailing

(b) End nailing   Toe nailing   Blind nailing

A - Types of nailing

(a) Joist to header

(b) Stud to plate

Bend lines

Cut

(e) Nail holes

(c) Beam to column

(d) Rafter to plate

Zinc coated sheet steel. Nails similar to 8d common but $1\frac{1}{4}''$ long with barbed shanks. Dimensions adapted to 2'', nominal, lumber. Large hole for nailing covering.

B - Sheet metal connectors

Fig. 41-5(A). Types of nailing. **(B).** Sheet metal connectors. Timber Engineering Company.

In *end nailing,* the nails are driven through the face of one piece into the end of another piece (*b*). In *toe nailing* the nails are driven at an angle of about 30 degrees through the face of one member into the face of another (*c*). Usually toe nails are driven into both faces of the first member, but sometimes, for instance in cross bridging, only one face is accessible. *Blind nailing* is used for nailing matched flooring to the subfloor. The nails are driven at an angle of about 45 degrees, at the top of the tongue, and into the subfloor and joists as shown in *d*. Flooring is not considered a part of the framing. Two-inch matched subflooring is secured by both face and blind nailing to the supporting members.

The type of nailing is determined partially by the accessibility of the nailhead for driving. Nailed joints are strongest when the nails are subjected to shearing stresses. They are weakest when the withdrawing stresses act in the direction parallel with the length of the nail. This is especially true for end nailing, in which the nails are driven parallel to the grain of the wood in the supporting member.

Common wire nails (Fig. 36-1*a*) are used in light wood framing. The lengths of the various sizes of nails are given in Table 41-1. The diameters and head sizes increase with the lengths of the nails.

Box nails are similar to common wire nails but have a more slender shank for a given length or penny size. They are available in sizes up to 16d. They are sometimes called *slim nails.* They cause less splitting than common nails when driven near the end of a piece, but they have less holding power. When splitting cannot be avoided, it is sometimes desirable to predrill holes, somewhat smaller than the nail diameter, with an electric drill.

A nailing schedule giving the types of nailing and the sizes of nails suitable for various connections in light wood framing is given in Table 41-2.

Table 41-1

Lengths of Common Wire Nails

Size	Length	Size	Length	Size	Length	Size	Length	Size	Length
4d	$1\frac{3}{8}$	7d	$2\frac{1}{4}$	10d	3	20d	4	50	$5\frac{1}{2}$
5d	$1\frac{3}{4}$	8d	$2\frac{1}{2}$	12d	$3\frac{1}{4}$	30d	$4\frac{1}{2}$	60	6
6d	2	9d	$2\frac{3}{4}$	16d	$3\frac{1}{2}$	40d	5		

Key: Lengths are in inches.   Odd-numbered sizes are rarely used.

Table 41-2

Nailing Schedule Using Common Nails
Recommended by National Lumber Manufacturers Association (4)

Location	Nailing	Location	Nailing
Joist to sill or girder	T, 3–8d	Continuous header to stud	T, 4–8d
Cross bridging to joist	T, 2–8d	Ceiling joists	
Girder ledger at each joist	F, 3–16d	To plate	T, 3–8d
Subfloor to each joist or girder		Laps over partitions	F, 3–16d
1 by 6 in. or less	F, 2–8d	To parallel rafters	F, 3–16d
Over 1 by 6 in.	F, 3–8d	Rafter to plate	T, 3–8d
2 in.	B and F, 2–16d	1-in. diagonal brace to each	
Sole plate to joist or blocking		stud and plate	F, 2–8d
	F, 16d at 16 in. c.	Sheathing to each bearing	
Top plate to stud	E, 2–16d	1 by 8 in. or less	F, 2–8d
Stud to sole plate	T, 4–8d	Over 1 by 8 in.	F, 3–8d
Double stud	F, 16d at 24 in. c.	Built-up corner studs	F, 16d at 24 in. c.
Double top plates	F, 16d at 18 in. c.	Built-up girders and beams	
Top plates, laps, and intersections		Along each edge	20d at 32 in. c.
	F, 2–16d		
Continuous header, two pieces			
	F, 16d at 16 in. c.		

Key: F, face nail. E, end nail. T, toe nail. B, blind nail. c. denotes center-to-center spacing.

Sheet-Metal Connectors. Zinc-coated sheet-steel connectors of various types are manufactured to replace the usual nailed joints in light wood framing (Fig. 41-5*B*). They are attached to the members with special nails designed for a driving fit in punched holes provided in the connectors.

Plank and Beam Construction (6). A type of framing sometimes used for one- and two-story dwellings makes use of 2-in. planks for subfloors and roof sheathing, supported by beams and rafters spaced from 6 to 8 ft. apart, which are in turn supported at their ends by posts or by trussing the rafters. The planks are laid at right angles to the beams. The wall and partition spaces between the posts are closed by the exterior and interior finished surfaces supported by the required supplementary framing, which is usually nonbearing. The frames resemble platform frames.

The 2-in. plank subfloors and the roof sheathing are usually exposed on their lower sides and should present attractive surfaces when exposed. Because of the wide spacing of the beams, to insure an even surface it is necessary to use tongued-and-grooved planks or planks with grooves on both edges to receive wood strips called *loose tongues* or *splines*. This provision is also necessary to distribute the floor loads laterally. The finished flooring, if of wood, is nailed at right angles to the subfloor planks.

The beams are designed to satisfy structural requirements. They may be solid sections, planks placed on edge and spiked together, or planks separated by blocks. The bottoms of built-up beams should be covered with a single piece because of appearance. Utility lines can be located in separated beams.

The spacings of the columns or posts correspond to the spacings of the beams whose ends they support. These should be large enough to carry their loads and to provide adequate bearing for the ends of the beams. The minimum post size is 4 by 4 in. When the ends of beams abut over a post, its size should be 4 by 6 in. or 4 by 8 in.

Special framing is provided under bearing partitions and heavy concentrated loads. Lateral bracing is required, as it is for the platform frame. Lateral bracing is provided by solid wall panels with diagonal wood or other rigid sheathing, or by diagonal corner bracing. Abutting ends of beams should be tied together with nailed metal straps or in some other manner. The longitudinal joints between the planks of exposed ceilings may be beveled or treated in various other ways to make them attractive.

Limitations in Use. The required fire-resistance ratings and the area and height limitations for *wood frame construction* are illustrated by the values in Tables 1-2 and 1-3.

Ordinary Construction

As defined in Art. 1, *ordinary construction* is that type of construction in which the exterior walls are of masonry or other noncombustible materials having equivalent structural stability under fire conditions and a fire-resistance rating of not less than 2 hours, the interior structural members being wholly or partly of wood of smaller dimensions than those required for *heavy timber construction*.

The various types of masonry walls are described in Chapter 4, and the code requirements for such walls are given in Art. 30. The interior construction is *wood frame construction* as described earlier

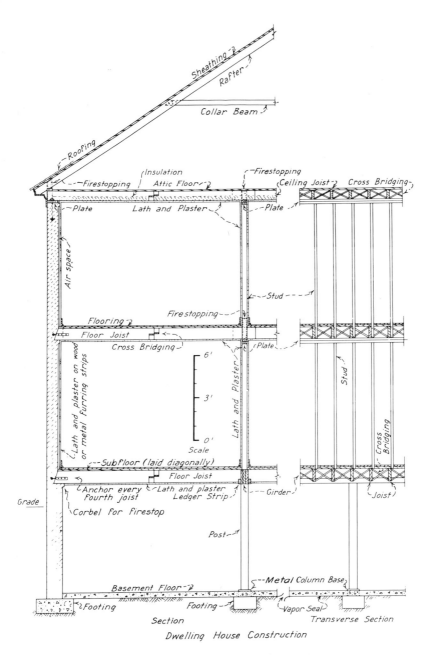

Sheathing

Rafter

Collar Beam

Roofing

Insulation
Attic Floor
Firestopping
Firestopping
Ceiling Joist
Cross Bridging
Firestopping
Plate
Lath and Plaster
Plate

Air space

Stud

Flooring
Firestopping
Floor Joist
Cross Bridging
Plate

6'

3'

Lath and plaster on wood or metal furring strips

Lath and Plaster

Stud

0'
Scale

Subfloor (laid diagonally)
Floor Joist
Cross Bridging
Anchor every Fourth joist
Lath and plaster Ledger Strip
Girder
Joist

Grade

Corbel for firestop

Post

Basement Floor
Metal Column Base
Footing
Footing
Vapor Seal
Section
Transverse Section

Dwelling House Construction

Fig. 41-6. Ordinary construction for dwelling.

in this article, but wood trusses, and steel beams, girders, and trusses, without fireproofing, are often used. This type of construction is used extensively for most types of occupancy when it is not excluded by fire district regulations.

A cross section of a typical two-story dwelling of *ordinary construction* with brick exterior walls is illustrated in Fig. 41-6 and of a typical two-story business building in Fig. 41-7.

Some of the more important features of the buildings follow.

1. The exterior walls of the dwelling are 8 in. thick for both stories, as required by Art. 30, Sec. D, Par. 4*e*, and those of the business building are 12 in. thick, as required by Art. 30, Sec. D, Par. 4*a*.

2. The foundation walls of both buildings are 12 in. thick as required by Art. 30, Sec. D, Par. 6*a*.

3. The story heights for each building are low enough to satisfy the requirements for lateral support in Art. 30, Sec. D, Par. 1*a*.

4. The parapet wall of the business building satisfies the requirement in Art. 30, Sec. D, Par. 7.

5. The exterior walls of both buildings are furred in accordance with Art. 25.

6. The interior brick bearing wall in the basement of the business building is 8 in. thick. This condition is not covered specifically by the requirements in Art. 30, but the 8-in. wall is considered adequate. The girder and post construction shown for the dwelling could be used instead of this wall, and a wall could replace the girder and post in the dwelling. The top of the metal base should be 3 in. above the floor.

7. The outer ends of the first- and second-story joists of both buildings are cut at an angle with the vertical so that their lower edges can bear 4 in. on the masonry and their top edges do not enter the masonry. This arrangement permits the joists to fail, in case of fire, without tending to pull the wall over. Every fourth joist is anchored to the masonry, as required by Art. 30, Sec. I, Par. 1.

8. The outer ends of the ceiling joists of both buildings bear on 2-in. plates which are anchored to the top of the masonry walls.

9. The interior framing of both buildings is *wood frame construction* and corresponds with that of the balloon frame illustrated in Fig. 41-2. This type of construction is superior to the platform frame construction (Fig. 41-1), because it minimizes vertical shrinkage. Minimum shrinkage is important in maintaining level floors, because there is no vertical movement from shrinkage of the exterior walls, as explained under *wood frame construction*. This framing is so similar to the

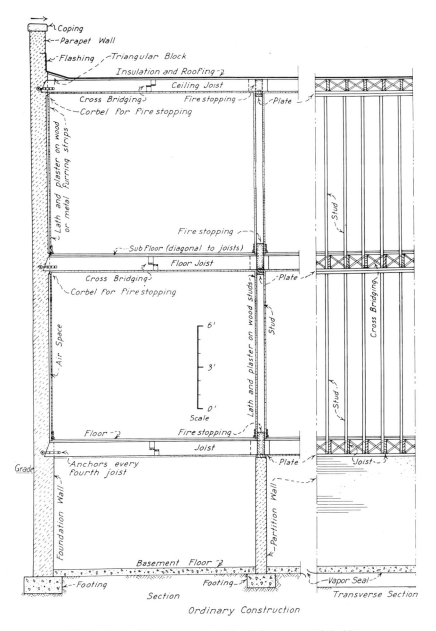

Fig. 41-7. Ordinary construction for light commercial building.

interior framing in the balloon frame, which has been described, that no further description is necessary.

10. The posts in the basement of the dwelling house bear on independent footings and not on the basement floor. They rest on metal bases which prevent the transmission of moisture from the ground through the footing and into the end of the post, thus eliminating the danger of rotting and termites. It is sometimes required that the top of this base be 3 in. above the floor.

11. The air space behind the exterior wall furring of both buildings is firestopped by corbeling the brick masonry. The figures indicate firestopping in other locations by means of brick or other noncombustible materials, but, the methods of firestopping illustrated in Fig. 41-4 are satisfactory and cheaper.

12. Heat insulation, as described in Art. 97, is provided on top of the ceiling surfaces of the second story of each building.

Requirements for *ordinary construction* not illustrated by the figures are as follows.

The wood columns in the several stories of a building should be set directly above one another. The load on a wood column should be transmitted to the column below through connections such as those described under *heavy timber construction*. Columns should not rest directly on floor joists.

Wood joists, beams, and girders supported by masonry walls required to have a fire-resistance rating of 2 hours or more should have not less than 4 in. of masonry between their ends and the outside face of the wall and between the ends of beams that bear on the wall.

If floor or roof joists run parallel to a masonry wall, the wall should be tied to four or more of the joists with metal anchors spaced not over 8 ft. apart for dwellings and 6 ft. for other buildings.

The required fire-resistance ratings and the area and height limitations for this type of construction are illustrated by the values given in Tables 1-2 and 1-3.

Heavy Timber Construction

Definition. As defined in Art. 1, *heavy timber construction* is that type of construction in which the exterior walls are of masonry or other noncombustible materials having an equivalent structural stability under fire conditions and a fire-resistance rating of not less than 2 hours; in which the interior structural members including columns, beams, and girders are heavy timber in heavy solid or laminated masses, but with no sharp corners or projections or concealed or inaccessible spaces; and in which the floors and roofs are heavy plank or laminated wood construction, or any other material providing equivalent fire-resistance and structural properties. Noncombustible structural members may be used in lieu of heavy timber, provided the fire-resistance rating of such members is not less than ¾ hour. This type of construction is sometimes called *slow-burning construction* or *mill construction*.

Laminated masses of heavy timber may be obtained by glued laminated construction described in the paragraph on glued laminated beams in Art. 38. This type of construction is used extensively for heavy timber columns, beams, girders, trusses, rigid frames, arches, and domes. A type of laminated floor and roof deck which is used extensively consists of pieces 2 in. thick and not less than 4 in. deep, nominal dimensions, placed on edge and securely spiked together.

Code Requirements. Building code requirements for *heavy timber construction* may be illustrated by those of the *National Building Code,* recommended by the National Board of Fire Underwriters (8). These requirements are illustrated by the partial vertical cross section and the framing plans of a building with *heavy timber construction* shown in Fig. 41-8.

The foundation walls are poured-concrete walls on spread foundations as described in Chapter 3.

The exterior walls are of masonry, described in Chapter 4, with a fire-resistance rating of at least 2 hours, as required by the code. The specific requirements for these walls are given in Art. 30, Sec. D.

A given building would, of course, make use of only one type of construction and not several types as shown in the figure. The member sizes are not indicated but would be determined by the building dimensions, the structural requirements, and the minimum permissible sizes given by the code. The various framings and other details satisfy the code requirements.

The first-floor framing consists of longitudinal girders (Fig. 41-8). The outer ends of the outer girders project into recesses in the walls and are supported by bearing plates with anchor lugs to tie them to the walls (Fig. 41-9a), leaving adequate ventilation to prevent dry rot. The end of each girder is beveled. If a girder burns in two and falls, the embedded end tilts off of the anchor lug and the girder falls free of the wall, which is not pulled over.

The interior ends of girders are supported by wood columns with chamfered corners, required to increase their fire resistance. The girder ends are supported on the brackets of steel post caps (Fig.

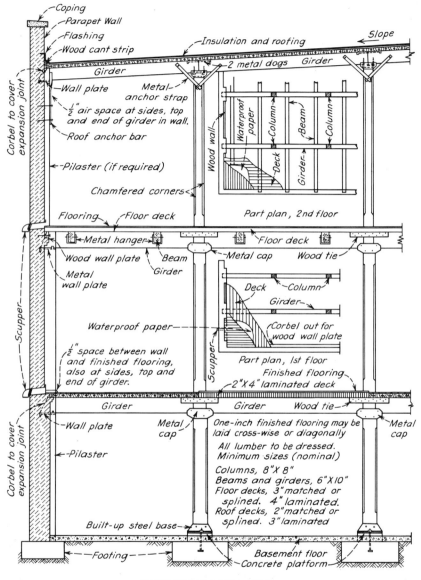

Heavy timber construction

Fig. 41-8. Building with heavy timber construction.

41-8b) to permit the bottom of the second-story column to bear on the post caps as required by the code. The adjacent ends of the two girders which rest on a single post cap are tied together by lateral ties and lag screws through the cap. The bottom of each column bears on a metal base (Fig. 41-9c) which is supported by, and anchored to, a concrete footing.

The outer panels of the first-floor deck are constructed of tongued-and-grooved planks which span the distance between lines of girders. A clearance of ½ in. is left between the edge of the deck and the wall surface to provide for expansion, as required by the code. The top and bottom of this open space are covered by moldings fastened to the wall, or the bottom may be covered by a corbel on the wall.

A laminated deck, consisting of planks 2 in. thick placed on the edge and spiked together, is shown for the interior panels.

The second-floor framing consists of longitudinal girders supported by the wall and the interior columns in the manner described for the first-floor framing. Transverse beams span the distance between lines of girders (Fig. 41-8). These are supported on metal hangers such as those shown in Fig. 41-9d, or they may rest on top of the girders and be tied (Fig. 41-9e). A tongued-and-grooved or a laminated deck may span the space between beams. In the figure, the beams frame into the girders away from the columns, but beams may also frame into the columns. The former arrangement results in simpler column connections, but the latter has some advantages and is usually employed in steel and concrete construction, in which such connections are less complicated than in wood.

The roof framing and the roof deck may be of either of the types described for the floor framing and deck. Types of post caps to support roof girders are illustrated in Fig. 41-9f and g. The latter includes a wood *holster block*. Such blocks are not permitted in floor framing. Requirements for constructing floor and roof decks and finished flooring are included in the code. Waterproof paper is placed between the deck and the finished floor.

Parapet walls may be provided (Fig. 41-8) as required by the code, except under certain conditions. Scuppers are placed in the outside walls at each floor level to discharge water that may have been used to extinguish fires or for other purposes.

Other framing details are used, and many of these are given in reference 7. Heavy timber rigid frames, arches, and domes are described in Art. 40.

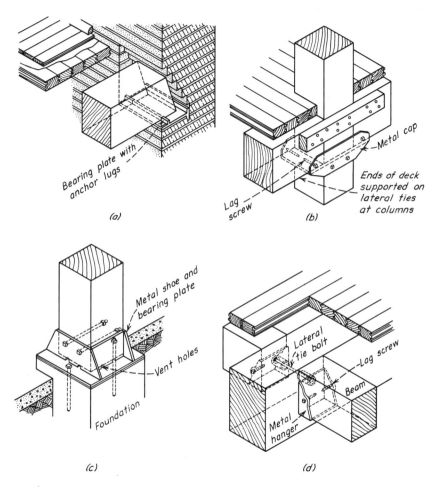

Fig. 41-9. Details for heavy timber construction. (a) Girder bearing on metal wall plate. (b) Metal column cap with two brackets. (c) Built-up steel column base. (d) Metal beam hanger. (e) Beams supported on top of girder. (f) Metal column cap supporting roof girders. (g) Wood bolster block supporting roof girders. (h) Wall beam. National Lumber Manufacturers' Association.

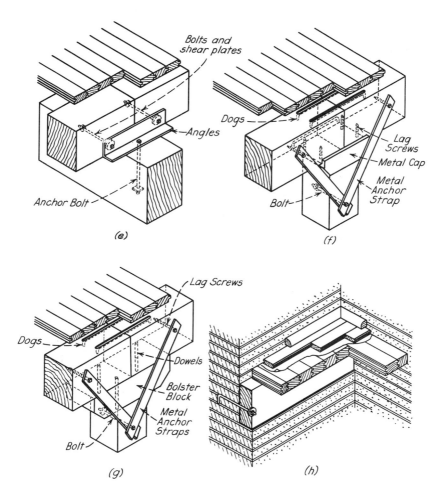

(e)

(f)

(g)

(h)

References

1. *Wood Handbook,* Forest Products Laboratory, U. S. Department of Agriculture, Washington, D. C., 1955.
2. *Typical Designs of Timber Structures,* Timber Engineering Co., Washington, D. C.
3. "Biggest Dome Spans 300 Feet," *Engineering News-Record,* January 10, 1957, p. 32.
4. *Manual for House Framing,* National Lumber Manufacturers Association, Washington 8, D. C.
5. *Plank-and-Beam Framing for Residential Buildings,* National Lumber Manufacturers Association, Washington 8, D. C.
6. *Plank-and-Beam System for Residential Construction,* Construction Aid 4, Housing and Home Finance Agency, Division of Housing Research, Washington, D. C., 1953.
7. *Heavy Timber Construction Details,* National Lumber Manufacturers Association, Washington 8, D. C.
8. *National Building Code,* National Board of Fire Underwriters, 1955.

7 Steel construction

42. ROLLED STEEL SHAPES

Types of Rolled Shapes. The various types of rolled shapes or sections used alone or riveted or welded together to form columns, beams, girders, trusses, and other structural units are shown in Fig. 42-1. The parts of these shapes are designated as *flanges, webs,* and *stems.*

The *wide-flange shapes,* called WF-shapes or sections, vary in depth and weight per foot from a maximum of 36 in. and 300 lb. to a minimum of 4 in. and 7½ lb. Either the inner and outer faces of these shapes are parallel, or the inner face may have a slope of 1 to 20, depending upon the manufacturer. There are two general forms of wide-flange shapes. The shapes which are relatively deep and narrow (*a*) are more suitable for beams and girders, and those which are more nearly square (*b*) are desirable for column sections. The latter are often called H-sections.

The *American standard beams,* called I-beams (*c*), vary in depth and in weight per foot from a maximum of 24 in. and 120 lb. to a minimum of 3 in. and 5.7 lb. The inner face of the flanges of these sections has a slope of 1 in 6.

The *American standard channels,* called channels (*d*), vary in depth and in weight per foot from a maximum of 18 in. and 58 lb. to a minimum of 3 in. and 4.1 lb. The inner face of the flanges of these sections has a slope of 1 in 6.

In addition to the wide-flange and American standard shapes which have been mentioned, *light beams, joists, columns, standard mill beams,* and *junior beams* and *channels* are available.

Angles are divided into those with *equal legs* and those with *unequal legs* (*e*). Equal-leg angles vary in size, thickness, and weight per foot from a maximum of 8 by 8 by 1⅛ in. and 56.9 lb. to 1 by 1

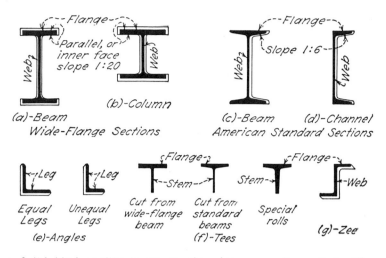

Solid black section represents the minimum section rolled with a given set of rolls. The light area indicates the method of increasing the section by spreading the rolls. Rolls made especially for Tees cannot be spread.

Edges sheared or flame cut in "Sheared Plates", or rolled in "Universal Mill Plates".

(h)-Plates

(i) Square Bars

(j) Round Bars

Wide-Flange Sections	24WF74	Tees	T3X3X6.7
American Standard Beams	15I42.9	Zees	Z6X3½X15.7
American Standard Channels	9⊔13.4	Plates	18X½
Equal Leg Angles	L3X3X¼	Square Bars	1◼
Unequal Leg Angles	L7X4X½	Round Bars	1φ
Structural Tees	ST5WF10.5	Flat Bars	2½X¼

STANDARD DESIGNATIONS FOR USE ON DRAWINGS
American Institute of Steel Construction

Fig. 42-1. Types and designations of rolled-steel sections.

by ⅛ in. and 0.80 lb. Unequal-leg angles vary in size from 8 by 6 by 1 in. and 44.2 lb. to 1¾ by 1¼ by ⅛ in. and 1.23 lb.

Tees (*f*) are commonly made by splitting the webs of wide-flange or American standard beam shapes, and thus are available in sizes which correspond to the sections from which they are cut. These are called *structural tees* and are the ones ordinarily used in structural framing. Other tees are available in depths from 5 in. to 2 in. The latter are classed as *special series* shapes, and the demand for them is small. They are available only by special arrangement and should be used only when the need for a given size is sufficient to justify a special rolling. Shapes which are ordinarily available are called *regular series* shapes.

Square and rectangular tubular shapes are rolled in several sizes and wall thicknesses. Square tubes are available with 1-by-1-in. through 8-by-8-in. outside dimensions. The wall thicknesses vary from about $\frac{1}{10}$ in. for the lightest 1-in. tube to $\frac{1}{2}$ in. for the heaviest 8-in. tube. Rectangular tubes are available with 3-by-2-in. to 6-by-4-in. outside dimensions. The wall thicknesses vary from about $\frac{1}{7}$ in. for the smallest and lightest to $\frac{3}{8}$ in. for the heaviest tube in the largest size. Square tubes as large as 10 in. and rectangular tubes as large as 10 by 6 in. can be rolled but are not now carried in stock. From the structural point of view these shapes have advantages over the wide-flange shapes when used as columns. They have advantages over pipe and wide-flange columns if they are to fit into walls and partitions of masonry and other materials.

Bulb Tees. Tees with the section of the stem enlarged along its edge to form a bulb are used to a limited extent for rafters or sub-purlins to support roof decks consisting of blocks or slabs of various materials. Shapes with heights varying from $1\frac{1}{2}$ in. to $2\frac{5}{8}$ in., widths varying from $1\frac{1}{2}$ in. to $2\frac{1}{4}$ in., and bulb widths from 0.438 in. to 0.938 in. are available.

Zees, as shown in *g,* are rarely used in structural framing. They vary in depth from 6 to 3 in.

Plates, as illustrated in *h,* are one class of flat rolled steel. If the width is 6 in. or less, they are classed as *bars* and if over 6 in. as *plates.* Plates which are over 2 in. thick are called *bearing plates* because they are used to provide bearing areas for the ends of various members. Plates are available in thickness from $\frac{1}{4}$ in. to 2 in., and widths from 6 in. to $15\frac{1}{2}$ ft. Bearing plates are available in sizes up to 56 in., and in thicknesses up to 15 in. For thicknesses up to 2 in. plates are sufficiently smooth and flat to use as bearing plates to receive accurately finished *milled* ends of columns, and plates up to 4 in. can be straightened in presses to the necessary flatness. The top surfaces of plates thicker than 4 in. should be planed over a sufficient area to receive milled-column sections if the plates are grouted on concrete foundations, but both faces should be planed if they rest on steel. Plates on which the edges are rolled when the plates are being rolled are called *universal mill plates*. Plates with sheared edges are called *sheared plates*.

Square and round bars (*i* and *j*) are used for ties, lateral bracing, and hangers in structural-steel framing, and as reinforcing in reinforced concrete structures. Many sizes are available.

The various weights available for the shapes (Fig. 42-1*a* to *g*) are obtained by spreading the rolls that produce the shapes. This process adds to the area of the shapes. The thickness of the flanges, as well as the depth of the wide-flange shapes, increases as the rolls are spread, but all the shapes in a given series are designated by a single *nominal depth* regardless of the *actual depth*. An increase in the flange thickness is desirable because a given amount of material added to the flanges increases the strength and rigidity of a member much more than the same amount of material added to the web. American standard beams and channel sections of a given depth are increased in weight and cross-sectional area by spreading the rolls in such a manner that all the additional material goes into the web, where it is not very effective in increasing the strength and rigidity of the section. The actual depth of all the shapes in a given depth series is the same and is equal to the depth by which the series of sections is designated. Spreading the rolls to increase the thickness of an angle also increases the lengths of the legs, but these increases are not taken into account in designating the size of the angle.

Structural-steel shapes are manufactured at steel mills. The operation of cutting the various shapes to the required size, fastening them together to form columns, girders, trusses, and other structural members, is called *fabrication*. This work is done by fabricating plants. The individual units are shipped to the building site in sizes that can be transported and handled on the job, and are placed in position, or *erected*.

The individual sections are fastened together, in both fabrication and erection, by riveting, welding, or bolting, as described in Art. 43.

Designations of Shapes. The standard designations for structural-steel shapes as adopted by the American Institute of Steel Construction are shown in Fig. 42-1. The meanings of the various terms follow.

wide-flange shapes. The 24 is the *nominal depth* in inches; WF is an abbreviation of wide flange; 76 is the weight per linear foot in pounds. Wide-flange shapes are often designated by giving the nominal depth, the nominal width of flange, and the weight per foot, thus, 24 × 9 WF 76.

American standard beams. The 15 is the *actual depth* in inches; the I signifies I-beam; and 42.9 is the weight per foot in pounds.

American standard channels. The significance of each expression is the same as it is for beams except the I is changed to a channel.

angles. The first symbol designates the type of shape and is followed by the width of each leg and the thickness in inches.

structural tees. ST is an abbreviation of the name of the shape; 5 is the nominal depth of the stem in inches and is equal to one-half the nominal depth of the wide-flange section from which the tee was cut; WF indicates the source of the shape; 10.5 is the weight per linear foot in pounds and is equal to one-half the weight of wide-flange or standard beam shape from which the tee was cut.

ordinary tees. T indicates the type of shape, and the numerals indicate the depth and width of flange, in inches, and the weight per linear foot in pounds.

zees. The designation corresponds to that for tees.

plates. The width and thickness in inches are given.

square bars. The size in inches is followed by the special designation for a square bar, consisting of a square with a vertical or inclined line drawn through it. This line is often omitted.

round bars. The designation corresponds to that of square bars with a different designation for shape, the square being replaced by a circle.

flat bars. The width in inches is followed by the thickness in inches.

The *number of pieces* of a given type, size, and length is always shown by a numeral in front of these designations, and the *length* by a dimension in feet and inches following the designation. For example, 3 − 15I's 42.9 × 12′6″ would indicate three I-beams 15 in. deep, weighing 42.9 lb. per ft. and having a length of 12′6″. The inch and pound symbols are not used in these standard designations except in the length, but they are ordinarily used elsewhere.

Reference. Reference 1 gives complete information on all the significant properties of all structural-steel shapes available and the companies which roll each shape; estimating and detailing; allowable loads on beams, columns, and their connections; standard specifications and codes; and many other pertinent subjects.

43. FABRICATION AND FIELD CONNECTORS

General Comments. The various structural steel shapes and plates of which built-up members are composed are fastened together or *fabricated* in the shop by riveting and welding. The pieces are cut to the required shapes and sizes and fastened together to form a completed member as described later.

The members which are placed in position, or *erected*, in the field to form the structural frame are connected with field rivets, unfinished bolts, or high-strength bolts and by welding, as described in subsequent paragraphs. Field riveting is done with the riveting gun and field welding with manually operated equipment, both of which are described later.

Types of Rivets and Bolts. The various types of fasteners used in shop or field connections are rivets, unfinished bolts, high-strength bolts, and welds. Turned bolts, which were formerly used, have largely been replaced by high-strength bolts.

Drift Pins. Before rivets or bolts are inserted, the holes in a connection are brought into matching positions by means of one or more drift pins. A *drift pin* is a tapered steel rod which is driven into a hole. Specifications do not permit holes that do not match to be enlarged by driving the drift pins. Such holes must be reamed to make them match, but poor connections with poorly matching holes are rejected.

Field Bolts. After the holes of a connection have been matched, an adequate number of temporary unfinished bolts are used to hold the connected parts in position until the final fasteners are installed. The temporary bolts are removed when a sufficient number of the final fasteners are in place.

Rivets. Rivets are made of soft-carbon steel. They are driven in holes $\frac{1}{16}$ in. larger than the shank diameter. They usually consist of a *buttonhead* and a cylindrical *shank* long enough to provide material to form the other head (Fig. 43-1*a*). A rivet with two buttonheads is shown in *b*; with a *flattened head* in *c*; with a *countersunk head* and with a *countersunk* and *chipped head* in *d*.

The buttonhead is the usual type. Countersunk and flattened heads

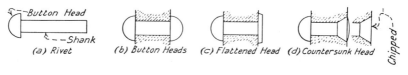

Fig. 43-1. Rivets and rivet heads.

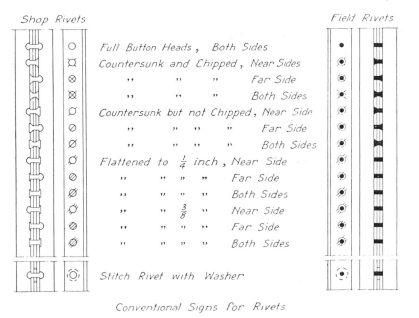

Conventional Signs for Rivets

Fig. 43-2. Conventional signs for rivets.

may be required for clearance, and chipped countersunk heads are required on bearing surfaces.

The methods and equipment used in driving rivets are considered later. Rivets are heated to a cherry red before driving. As they cool, they contract and exert a *clamping force* on the included material. This action results in considerable friction between the surfaces of the material connected, which augments the shearing and bearing resistance of the rivets. This clamping force is not considered in determining the number of rivets required.

The conventions used on structural drawings to represent rivets of the various types are shown in Fig. 43-2. The heads of *shop rivets* are shown in plan by circles the size of the head, but *field rivet* holes are indicated in plan by blackened circles the size of the hole. The longitudinal sections of shop rivets, on the extreme left of Fig. 43-2, are not shown on the drawings, but the blackened sections of field rivet holes, on the extreme right, are shown even though the view of the member is not a section through the rivets.

The line passing through the centers of a row of rivets, in plan view, is called a *gage line*. The center-to-center spacing of rivets is called the *pitch*. The distance from the center of a rivet to the nearest edge is called the *edge distance*. The length of a rivet, determined by the total thickness of the material it penetrates, is called the *grip*.

Unfinished Bolts. Unfinished bolts, or A-307 bolts, are made of low-carbon steel and have rough unfinished shanks and square heads and nuts (Fig. 43-3a). They are used in holes $\frac{1}{16}$ in. larger in diameter than the shank. The permissible carrying capacity is lower than that of rivets of the same diameter. They are relatively inexpensive. They may be tightened with hand wrenches, but when many bolts are used power wrenches may prove more economical and probably give more uniform results.

According to the American Institute of Steel Construction Specifications (2), unfinished bolts may be used in tier building field connections as follows.

1. They may be used for column splices in tier buildings 100 to 200 ft. high if their least horizontal dimension is more than 40 per cent of the height, and in such buildings less than 100 ft. high if their least horizontal dimension is not less than 25 per cent of the height.

2. They may be used for beam and girder connections to columns and any other beams and girder connections in buildings less than 125 ft. high, and for beam and girders on which the bracing of columns is not dependent in buildings over 125 ft. high.

3. They may not be used in roof truss splices and connections of trusses to columns, column splices, column bracing, knee braces, and crane supports in structures carrying cranes of over 5-ton capacity.

4. They are permitted in column splices, with the limitations just given, because the abutting ends of column sections are milled and

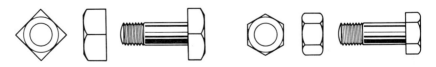

(a) Unfinished bolts   (b) High-strength bolts

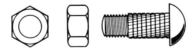

(c) High-strength body bolts

Fig. 43-3. Types of bolts.

the splices so arranged that the compressive stresses are transmitted directly across the splice. Within the specified limits, unfinished bolts are considered satisfactory to resist the flexural stresses in the columns caused by lateral loads. Splice plates are required, regardless of flexural stresses, to hold the column sections in alignment. Unfinished bolts are not permitted for connections of the members of structures that carry large cranes, because the repeated action of the cranes tends to work the joints loose and permit the structure to rock back and forth with the movement of the crane.

A sufficient number of unfinished bolts are used temporarily in erecting members with riveted field connections to hold the members in true position while the field rivets are being driven.

High-Strength Bolts. There are several types of heat-treated bolts made of medium carbon steel, two of which are illustrated in Fig. 43-3b and c. The type shown in b is designated as the *high-strength bolt*, A-325 or A-490, and is inserted in a hole with a diameter $\frac{1}{16}$ in. larger than that of the shank of the bolt. The type shown in c is designated as the *high-strength bearing bolt* or *high-strength interference-body bolt*. It has a raised pattern on the shank, consisting of straight or spiraled ribs or knurls. Since the outside diameter of the shank is greater than the diameter of the hole, the bolt must be driven into the hole with a maul or pulled in with the nut. This process causes the shank to bind in the hole, and the hole is more completely filled than it is when the plain high-strength bolt is used. This is referred to as an interference fit, which gives the bolt one of its names. It also gives better bearing between the bolt and the sides of the hole, which is recognized in the name bearing bolt.

According to the assembly specifications, the type of bolt and the method of tightening, high-strength bolts may or may not require *hardened washers* under either the head or the nut or both. The head is kept from turning initially by gripping with a hand wrench. The high-strength bearing bolt binds in the hole and does not tend to turn when being tightened. The head is button-shaped, as shown in the figure. A hardened washer is generally required under the nut.

The nuts on both types of bolts are tightened with pneumatic impact wrenches. Because of the high strength of the bolts, they are generally tightened so that the clamping forces are sufficient to insure, under most conditions, that the friction between the surfaces of the various parts connected is adequate to prevent any sliding movement due to the applied loads and to make sure that the nuts will not be loosened. In addition, the high tensile strength of the bolts and the initial tension to which they are subjected make them effective in resisting forces that subject them to tension. Under conditions where the tendency to slip is unusually high and where there are abnormal vibrations, bearing bolts are superior to bolts with plain shanks.

The allowable carrying capacities of high-strength bolts are equal to and, under ordinary conditions, greater than those of rivets of the same nominal diameter.

Both types of bolts are used for field connections under the same conditions as rivets. They have the advantage of being cheaper and quieter to install than rivets.

Welding Processes. Many processes are used to weld pieces of metal together. Those used in structural welding are divided into two main groups, *pressure processes*, in which the weld is completed by applying pressure after the pieces to be welded have been placed in contact where the weld is to be formed and have been heated to the required temperature; and the *nonpressure* or *fusion process*, which requires no pressure to complete the weld.

Nonpressure or fusion processes used in structural welding are divided into arc welding and gas welding according to the source of heat.

In *arc welding*, the heat is provided by an electric arc formed between the work to be welded and an electrode held in the operator's hand with a suitable holder or in an automatic machine. The electrode may be a metallic rod, as in *metal-arc welding*, or a carbon rod, as in *carbon-arc welding*.

In *gas welding*, the heat is provided by a gas flame produced by burning a mixture of oxygen and a suitable combustible gas. The flame is formed at the tip of a *blowpipe* or *torch*, which is held in the operator's hand or in an automatic machine. The gas used in structural welding is acetylene, which gives this process the name of the *oxyacetylene process*.

In both the arc and gas processes, the pieces to be welded are placed in contact and the edges are melted so that metal from the two pieces flows together and, when cooled, the pieces are joined by the weld. In order to make a satisfactory joint, additional metal must be supplied.

It is provided by the metallic rod used as the electrode in the metal arc process, but in the carbon-arc and gas processes a metal rod called a *filler* or *welding rod* is used. The end of this rod is melted off into the joint as the joint is being formed.

The only pressure-welding process used in structural work is the *spot-welding process.* In this process, a small area or spot on the surfaces to be joined is heated by placing electrodes against the outer surfaces of the pieces and passing an electric current through the pieces and across the contact surface. The heat required to raise the temperature of the pieces to a welding temperature at the spot where the weld is to be made is generated by the resistance offered by the metal between the electrodes to the flow of electric current. This is, therefore, a *resistance process.* Since the weld is consummated by exerting pressure across the spot, this is a *pressure process.* If spot welds are formed progressively in a continuous overlapping row, the process is known as *seam welding.* Disk electrodes are used to apply the pressure.

Types of Welded Joints. Various types of welded joints used in structural work, with the names applied to the parts of welds, are illustrated in Fig. 43-4. The types of welds illustrated are the *single-* and *double-fillet lap weld* in *a*, the *single-* and *double-vee butt weld* in *b*, the *butt weld* with double-fillet welded backing strip in *c*, the *double-fillet T weld* in *d*, and the *plug* or *rivet weld* in *e*—all of which are fusion welds—and the *spot weld* in *f*, which is a resistance-pressure weld. The electrodes are shown in this figure.

Fabricating Procedures. The following paragraphs on cutting, punching, drilling and reaming, riveting, milling and straightening, bending, and rolling are quoted, with permission, from *Structural Shop Drafting* published by the American Institute of Steel Construction (3).

These procedures apply specifically to riveted members, but the comments on cutting, milling, and straightening, bending, and rolling apply also to welded members.

Cutting. There are several types of cutting operations, each of which is particularly adapted to the class of work involved. Plates are cut in a guillotine type machine, called a *shear.* Angles are cut on a machine with the shear blade shaped and set at an angle to cut both legs with one stroke. Beams, channels, and light columns are usually cut on high-speed saws. There are several types of saws for this purpose, the most common one being the *friction saw,* which cuts through steel as fast as a power crosscut saw passes through timber. Bars are cut by a shear of the guillotine type, the dies and shear blades of which are made in the shape of the material to prevent its distortion. Large bars are cut on a *power hack saw.*

Cutting of material which is over the capacity of the various machines and most cutting of curved and complex forms is done with the acetylene torch and is known as *flame-cutting* or *gas-cutting.* The cutting torch is the most useful and flexible means of cutting steel ever devised. [See *Explanatory Comments.*]

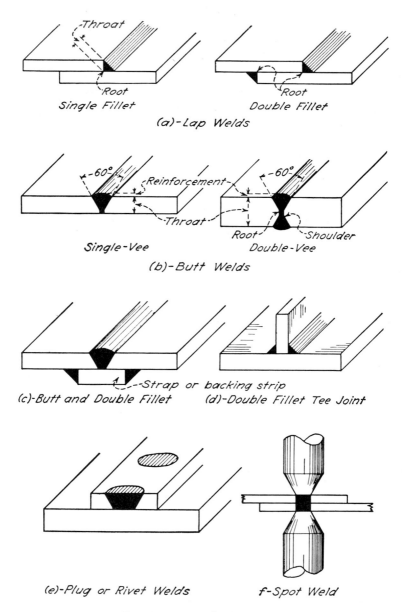

Fig. 43-4. Types of welded joints.

Punching, Drilling and Reaming. Punching is the most economical common method of making rivet and bolt holes in steel. Generally the material is punched rather than drilled, where the size of the hole and the thickness of the metal comes within the range of the machines and when punching is permitted by the specifications. Normally, mild carbon steel up to a thickness one-eighth of an inch greater than the diameter of the rivet can be punched without undue stress on the machine or excessive breakage of the punches.

Except in special cases, all holes are punched with a diameter $\frac{1}{16}$ of an inch larger than that of the rivet or bolt to be used. Some tolerance is required to provide for less than perfect matching of holes in adjacent parts when they are lined up for rivet driving.

Drilling of structural steel is largely confined to making holes in material thicker than the capacity of the punch machines and dies, as in slabs and the heavier wide flange beams and columns, or to meet specification requirements.

Specifications for bridge work and certain other specialized work require all holes to be punched at least one-eighth of an inch smaller than the final size. Then, after the piece has been assembled, it is placed under a battery of reamers operating like jibs or gantries, and the holes are reamed to the desired size. The procedure is usually referred to as *sub-punch and ream.* Reaming produces a clean hole with all burrs and distorted metal removed. Reamed holes are also used for connections which will be field-bolted with close-fitting *turned* or *finished bolts.*

Riveting. Riveting machines of both the pressure and impact type are operated by compressed air at 80 to 100 lb. per sq. in. pressure. The *pressure-type riveter,* frequently known as a *bull riveter,* has a C-shaped frame with a throat depth sufficient to permit a machine to reach halfway across an average girder. Small-size pressure riveters are hung from jib cranes while the larger machines are generally supported from a power-operated gantry or even from an overhead traveling crane. Pressure riveters complete the driving operation with one stroke, the larger machines exerting a pressure of 80 tons.

Impact riveters, generally referred to as *riveting guns,* are portable hand tools which can be connected to the end of a compressed air hose. A rapid succession of blows is delivered to the rivet by means of a plunger moving up and down in the gun barrel much as the piston in a reciprocating steam engine moves back and forth. These tools are also used by the fitter for driving tapered *drift pins* through holes to align the several parts of a member. The gun drives just as satisfactory a rivet as the pressure riveter but, being slower, its shop use is limited to driving rivets inaccessible to the larger machines and scattered rivets where the amount of driving does not warrant taking the work to the machines.

Standard-size rivets used in a structural shop are almost always heated before driving. The heating in most shops is done in either oil or gas-fired furnaces and then raised to a minimum temperature color of light cherry red. In some shops, electric rivet heaters are used. [See *Explanatory Comments.*]

Milling. The ends of columns, struts, and members in compression chords of trusses which are required to bear evenly against another or against supporting base plates are *milled* to a smooth even surface in a *milling machine*. The machine consists of one or more rotating cutting heads fitted with teeth or blades, and a bed on which to securely hold the work in proper alignment during the milling operation.

Column base plates over 4 in. in thickness must be milled over the area in contact with the column shaft. This milling is usually done on a *planing machine*.

Straightening, Bending, and Rolling. All material which is bent or distorted during shipping, handling, or in the punching operation must be straightened before further fabrication is attempted. The machine generally used for straightening beams, channels, angles, and heavy bars is commonly known as a *bulldozer*. This machine has a heavy cast steel frame with a horizontal plunger or ram centered between two lugs about 2 ft. apart set on an anvil or head. With the piece to be straightened placed against the two lugs, pressure is applied by the ram at points along the length of the bent member until it is in alignment once more.

The bulldozer also is used to make long-radius curved beams, channels and angles and to make minor angle bends in heavy pieces and to make other bends within its capacity. Short-radius curves, where material must be heated, are handled by the blacksmith. [See *Explanatory Comments*.]

Long plates which are slightly curved or cambered out of alignment in the direction of their longitudinal center line are usually straightened by cold rolling. By passing these plates between a pair of rolls bearing against their top and bottom faces, with more pressure exerted along the shorter or concave side than along the convex side, the thickness of the plates on the concave side is reduced ever so slightly. The metal thus displaced by the rolls increases the length of this side enough to bring the plate back into true longitudinal alignment.

Explanatory Comments. Certain explanations of the procedures in the foregoing paragraphs seem desirable.

In driving button-headed rivets with the pressure riveter, the heated rivet shown in Fig. 47-1*a* is placed in the hole provided for it. The member is then moved into position between the jaws of the C-frame. A depression is provided to receive the formed head. The end of the plunger is provided, with a depression in which the other button-head (*b*) is formed as the pressure is applied to the projecting end of the rivet. If a rivet is driven with a riveting gun, the formed head is supported in a heavy *dolly*. The other head is formed by several blows from the plunger of the gun, the impact of the plunger being resisted by the dolly, which acts as an anvil. Rivets with one head flattened or countersunk (*c* and *d*) are formed in a similar manner.

Flame cutting or gas cutting is also known as *oxygen cutting*. It includes a group of processes in which the cutting is accomplished by the chemical reaction of oxygen with the base metal at elevated temperatures. These temperatures are attained by means of gas flames resulting from the combustion of oxygen and one of several kinds of gas, the most commonly used gas being acetylene, as in *oxyacetylene cutting*. Steel is also cut by *arc cutting*, a group of processes in which metals are cut by melting them with the heat of an electric arc between an electrode and the base metal (4). Accurate cuts can be made by these procedures regardless of the thickness of the metal.

At least one plant, the Commercial Shearing and Stamping Company, Youngstown, Ohio, is equipped to cold-bend I, H, or wide-flange shapes, with depths as great as 30 in., in the plane of the web. Bends in the plane perpendicular to the plane of web are made more easily. The minimum radius of curvature for bending in the plane of the depth is about fourteen times the depth. A single piece can be bent to various radii along its length. The maximum length of piece which can be handled is 30 ft.

Welding. The following comments on welding procedures are quoted, with permission, from *Structural Shop Drafting*, published by the American Institute of Steel Construction (3):

The process most commonly used in the welding of structural steel is known as *metal-arc welding*. In this process energy is supplied by an electric arc established between the *base* or *parent* metal (the parts being joined) and a metal *electrode*. The instant the arc is formed tremendous heat is concentrated at the point of welding, which is located at the junction formed by the two parts to be welded together. The parent metal melts in a small pool; additional metal supplied by the electrode is transferred through the arc in the form of tiny globules and deposited in the pool. As the electrode (and hence the arc) is moved along the joint, either manually or automatically, the molten metal left behind solidifies as a uniform deposit or *weld*, which joins the parts solidly, thus forming the desired connection.

Electrodes may be either *bare* or *coated*, although most welding is done today with coated electrodes. Bare manually operated electrodes produce welds which are not as reliable as those made with electrodes that are heavily coated. In the case of the coated electrode, the heat from the arc produces from the coating a gaseous and slag flux shield, as shown in Fig. 43-5, which completely envelops the arc and the molten metal, thus preventing contact with the oxygen and nitrogen of the air, contamination from which tends to produce brittle welds. The slag coating which is formed floats on the molten pool thus protecting it from the atmospheric elements. This slag is easily removed after the weld has cooled.

In *manual welding*, the welding operator manipulates the electrode by hand. An insulated gripping device connected by a flexible cable to the source of current is used to hold the electrode. The operator wears proper covering and a helmet which affords protection against *weld spatter* (globules of metal thrown off during welding), heat, the blinding light so characteristic of the process and harmful rays emanating from the arc.

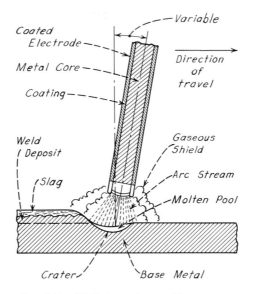

Fig. 43-5. Shielded metal-arc welding process.

Note: Welds in any accessible position can be made by manual welding because the globules of metal from the electrode are forced across the arc almost independently of the action of gravity.

When a weld is terminated abruptly, a *crater* is formed in the base metal by the blast of the arc. It is required that this crater be filled with weld metal so that the finished appearance and the cross section of the weld are uniform.

In *submerged-arc automatic welding,* the electrode is fed by a machine which has a reel for carrying a coiled supply of uncoated wire. With this method, the arc is shielded by a granular flux automatically deposited on the joint ahead of the arc. The welding wire pushes through the flux; the arc is established; part of the flux melts to form a slag flux shield; and the customary slag floats on the molten pool. Unfused flux is recovered for re-use.

44. STEEL COLUMNS

Types of Column Sections. Structural steel columns may consist of a single piece, such as the wide-flange shape (Fig. 44-1a), or they may be built up of various shapes (b to o). The individual shapes are riveted or welded together (p) or welded to form the built-up sections. The small diagonal bars which fasten together the two parts of the sections shown in g are called *lacing bars* or *lacing.* They are indi-

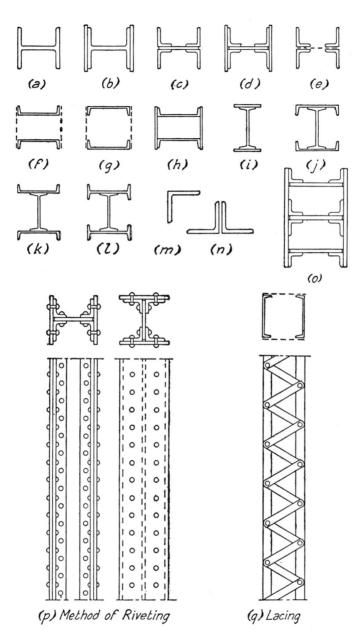

(p) Method of Riveting *(q) Lacing*

Fig. 44-1. Steel columns.

cated on cross sections by dotted lines (*e, f,* and *g*). Lacing bars are rarely used in buildings at the present time.

Wide-Flange Columns. The most commonly used column section is the wide-flange column shown in Fig. 44-1*a*, with nominal depths of 8 to 14 in. Various weights are available for each nominal depth, but it should be noted again that the spreading of the rolls to produce sections with several areas of the same nominal depth increases the actual depths of the sections. For example, the wide-flange shape which has a nominal depth of 14 in. and weighs 87 lb. per ft. has an actual depth of 14 in. and a flange thickness of 0.688 in.; whereas the maximum 14-in. section, which weighs 426 lb. per ft., has an actual depth of 18.69 in. and a flange thickness of 3.033.

Cover-Plated Wide-Flange Columns. Column sections heavier than a maximum wide-flange shape can be obtained by riveting or welding cover or flange plates to such a shape (Fig. 44-1*b*). There is a special 14-in. core shape weighing 320 lb. per ft. to use for this purpose. It has a relatively thick web, as required to adequately support the thick flanges formed by cover plates. Cover plates, each with thicknesses of 1 in. or more, might be riveted or welded to each flange to give a total thickness 3 in. or more for each flange.

Plate and Angle Columns. Columns are built up of four angles and a web plate (*c*) with cover plates also (*d*). Columns of almost any size desired can be built up in this way.

Other Types. The types of sections shown in Fig. 44-1*e* to *l* are not used to any extent. The angle sections (*m* and *n*) may be used in very light corner columns or wherever their form is advantageous. These angle sections are extensively used, however, as members of trusses.

45. STEEL BEAMS AND GIRDERS

The general term *beam* may include various flexural members such as beams, girders, joists, lintels, purlins, and rafters, as explained in Art. 33, which are given specific names because of the manner in which they are used.

Types of Beams. The cross sections of various types of beams are shown in Fig. 45-1. The wide-flange shape shown in *a* and the American standard I-beams shown in *b* are the most commonly used sections.

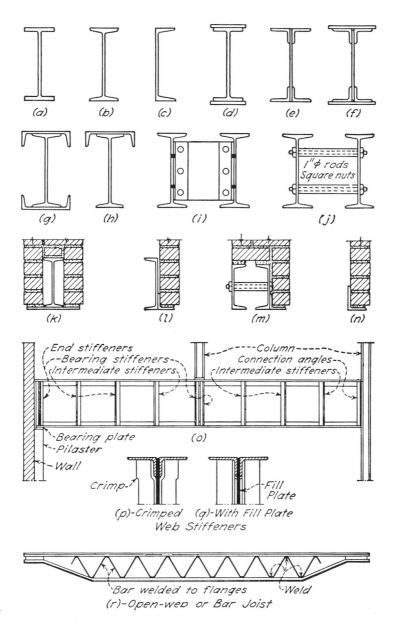

Fig. 45-1. Steel beams.

They are available in a great variety of sizes. The channel shown in c is extensively used for roof purlins. The wide-flange shape or the I-beam may be provied with *cover* or *flange plates* (d). Beams may be built up of plates and angles (e and f) to obtain almost any size desired. The built-up sections shown in g and h are used occasionally.

Separators. In i and j, two beams have been fastened together with *separators* to hold them in position and to make them act more or less as a unit. The *plate-and-angle separator* in i is more effective in this respect than the *pipe separator* in j. If the beams are not too far apart, two overlapping angles, with legs riveted together, can be used as an *angle separator*. Separators spaced 5 or 6 ft. apart are usually required when beams are used in pairs.

Lintels. The sections shown in k to n are lintels arranged to carry brick or stone masonry over openings and can be largely concealed. The single angle shown in n carries the outer layer of masonry, and the remainder of the wall may be carried by a *relieving arch* or another angle may be used.

Plate Girders. A built-up plate girder is illustrated in o. The section consists of four flange angles, a web plate, and cover plates, as shown in f. The web plate is usually made quite thin, a ratio of unsupported depth to thickness of 170 being permitted if *web stiffeners* are provided, to keep the web plate from buckling. Since these stiffeners must project over the flanges, it is necessary to bend or *crimp* them around the vertical legs of the flange angles in order to place them against the web (p); or *fill plates*, equal in thickness to the flange angles, may be placed between the stiffeners and the web plate (q). If the unsupported depth of the web does not exceed 70 times its thickness, *intermediate stiffeners* are not required, but *end stiffeners* are always required. Stiffeners are also required at all points where concentrated loads are supported. The spacing of stiffeners is determined by the shearing stresses. It is often required that the thickness of web plates be at least $\frac{1}{4}$ in.

A girder may be built up of two flange plates and a web plate welded together (Fig. 45-2a), or of a wide-flange section, split along the center of the web and separated to receive a narrow plate which increases the depth (b), the three parts being welded together. Stiffeners are provided by welding plates between the flanges and normal to

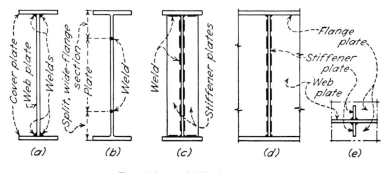

Fig. 45-2. Welded plate girders.

the web (*c* to *e*). Welded girders are lighter than riveted girders with the same carrying capacity.

Joists. When the loads are rather heavy and joists are widely spaced I-beams may prove economical, but special lightweight sections are available for light loads and closely spaced joists. One type of lightweight joists is the *junior beam,* a rolled section of the same form as the standard I-beam, but much lighter because the metal is rolled thinner. The sizes vary from a 6-in. depth weighing 4.4 lb. per ft. to the 12-in. depth weighing 11.8 lb. per ft. The web thickness of the smaller section is less than $\frac{1}{8}$ in., and of the larger section about $\frac{3}{16}$ in. Other sections lighter than the American standard sections are available.

Another form of joist for light loads is the *open-web* or *trussed joist,* one type of which is illustrated diagrammatically in Fig. 45-1*r.* The flanges of joists of this type are made up either of two light angles, two bars, or a tee, with web members consisting of flat bars welded to the flanges, or of a continuous round bar bent back and forth to form the diagonals and welded to the flanges. Some types are called *bar joists,* because they are made up largely of bars.

46. STEEL TRUSSES

Various types of trusses are described in Art. 34 and illustrated in Figs. 34-1 and 34-2. The most common types used for steel trusses for double-pitched roof supports are the Fink and Pratt trusses and, for floor and flat or gently sloping roof supports, the Pratt and Warren trusses. There is no reasonable limit to the span and loads for

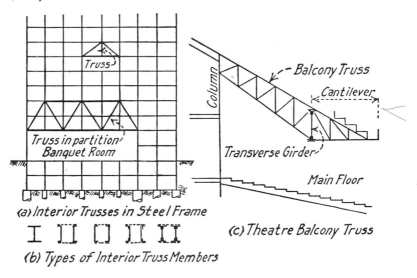

(a) Interior Trusses in Steel Frame

(b) Types of Interior Truss Members

(c) Theatre Balcony Truss

Fig. 46-1. Trusses located in partitions and balcony truss.

which steel trusses can be designed. They are always shop-fabricated and transported to the building site. Spans too long to be transported are made up of two or more sections and are spliced in the field.

Steel trusses are frequently used as a part of the interior framing of tall buildings to span auditoriums, lobbies, banquet halls, dance halls, and other rooms requiring large floor areas free from columns. Such floors are preferably located at the top or near the top of the building for purposes of economy in the structural framing, but other considerations may make it necessary to place these large floor areas in any part of a building. Very often they will be on the first floor with many stories above (Fig. 46-1a). The depth of the truss may occupy one or more stories. It may not be possible to use one of the common types of truss because of doors or hallways, for the floor or floors immediately above may have to pass through the truss and will determine its form. Such trusses have to be of very heavy construction. Some typical cross sections of truss members are given in Fig. 46-1b.

Another common use for steel trusses is the support of the balconies of theaters. Columns are of course objectionable on account of their obstruction of the vision, and they are eliminated whenever possible.

A common form of construction consists of cantilever trusses over-hanging a transverse supporting truss or girder (Fig. 46-1c).

The various members of which a truss is composed are connected at the *joints,* or points where they meet, to form a truss, by riveting or welding, as described in Art. 43.

Riveted Trusses. The members meeting at a *joint* or *panel point* may be connected by attaching them to *connection* or *gusset plates* ¼ in. or more thick and large enough to provide for the number of rivets required by the stresses in the members, and, occasionally, by the stresses in the plates themselves. The rivets may be as small as ⅝ in. in diameter for light trusses but usually are ¾ in. and may be larger for long spans or heavy loads.

For trusses of ordinary spans, there is usually one gusset plate at each joint (Figs. 46-2b and 46-3d). To avoid twisting action, the pieces of each principal member connected to a gusset place should be symmetrically located with reference to the plate. To accomplish this objective the principal members, such as the top and bottom chords, are made up of two units as illustrated by the two angles, placed back to back, of the top chord in Fig. 46-2a and the two channels, placed back to back, for the bottom chord, shown in b and in Fig. 46-3c. These are spaced apart far enough to receive the connection or gusset plate between them (Fig. 46-2b). Members carrying minor stresses may be composed of a single small angle which does not cause significant twisting action because of the low magnitude of the stresses.

If the top chord of a truss is subjected to bending stresses by members such as roof purlins or floor joists not located at the joints, it may be composed of two angles and a plate (Fig. 46-3a), or two channels (c). Similarly, a bottom chord subjected to such stresses may be composed of two angles and a plate (b) or two channels (c). If the member includes a plate, that plate may also serve as a connection plate at the joints.

Truss members consisting of two angles or channels, without a plate, should be provided with *stitch rivets* at intermediate points between the connection plates (Fig. 46-2b). The distance between the backs of the angles or channels is maintained by washers through which the rivets pass. Stitch rivets are provided to make the individual parts act together more nearly as a unit.

Wood or steel purlins may be fastened to the top chords of steel

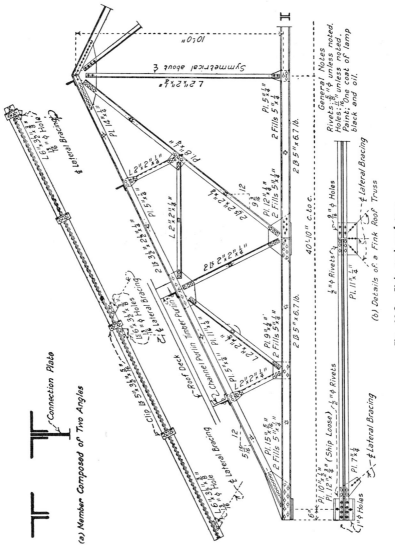

Fig. 46-2. Fink steel roof truss.

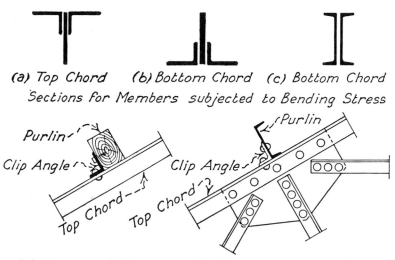

(a) Top Chord   (b) Bottom Chord   (c) Bottom Chord

Sections for Members subjected to Bending Stress

(d) Method of Fastening Purlins to Top Chord

Fig. 46-3. Simple steel roof truss details.

roof trusses by short lengths of steel angles, called *clip angles* (Figs. 46-2*b* and 46-3*d*).

Heavy riveted trusses are made up of large angles and many other types of members such as those shown in Figs. 44-1*a* to *d*.

Welded Trusses. The connection or gusset plates in riveted trusses serve as indirect paths through which stresses are transferred from one member to another member connected to the same plate. A significant advantage of most welded trusses over riveted trusses is the direct transmission of stress from one member to another, which does away with gusset plates. To accomplish this objective, appropriate types of members must be used.

The ends of members to be connected at a joint are so cut and so shaped, by slotting or otherwise, that they will provide suitable opportunities for welding. Most structural welding is done by the electric-arc welding process described in Art. 43. The basic types of welds used are the *butt weld*, by means of which abutting edges or ends of plates and shapes are joined (Fig. 43-4*b*), and the *fillet weld*, formed along the junction of two surfaces which meet at an angle (Fig. 43-4*a* and *d*).

The following comments concerning the structural shapes and arrangements of members at the joints are quoted, with permission and minor changes, from the eleventh edition of the *Procedure Handbook of Arc Welding Design and Practice,* published by the Lincoln Electric Company (4).

Arc-welded trusses may be designed in various ways using T-shapes, H-shapes, or U-shapes for chords. The web members are generally angles or channels. (Various types of arc-welded truss connections are illustrated in Fig. 46-4.)

1. Perhaps the simplest type of truss connection is made of angle sections for web members (Fig. 46-4*a*). This is easy to fabricate and weld because the sections lap each other and fillet welds are used.

2. For a heavier truss, the vertical member can be an I-beam or H-beam. The web of this member is slotted to fit over the stem of the T-section (*b*). The T-section is used for both the top and bottom chord members. The

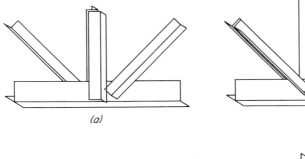

(a)   (b)

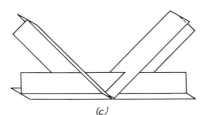   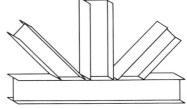

(c)   (d)

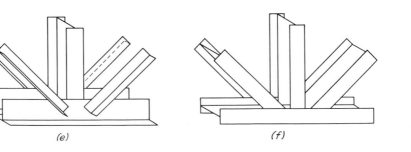

(e)   (f)

Fig. 46-4. Connections for simple welded trusses. Lincoln Electric Company.

diagonal members are made of a double set of angles. (Fillet welds are used.)

3. Some trusses make use of T-sections for their diagonal members (c). The flanges of the diagonal members must be slotted to fit over the stem of the T-section used for the top chords as well as the bottom chords. The stem of the diagonals is also cut back and is butt-welded to the stem of the top and bottom chords. (Fillet welds are used elsewhere.)

4. Quite a few trusses are made completely of H-sections (d). Both top and bottom chords are made of H-sections, as are the web members. This allows loads to be placed anywhere along the top and bottom chords because of the high bending strength of the H-section. With the conventional truss design, loads must be placed only at points where diagonal or vertical members connect to the chord members. Almost all the welds are on flanges of the top and bottom chords and, since they are flat surfaces, there is no unnecessary filling of the members to make these connections. (The welds are all fillet welds.)

5. In the connection shown in e, two T-sections are intermittently welded together at their flanges to form top and bottom chord members. The vertical member is an H-section set in between the stems of the T-sections. Each diagonal member is made of a set of angles. All the welding consists of fillet welds.

6. Sometimes the flanges are made of wide-flange beams and H-sections with the webs of the top and bottom chords placed horizontally (f). The welding of these members consists mainly of butt-welding the flanges together. Under severe loading, gusset plates are added in between the flange connections in order to strengthen the joint and reduce the possibility of concentrated stresses.

The types of connections shown in Fig. 46-4 can be adapted to many forms of truss, including the bowstring roof truss, for which the top chord can be cold-formed with the desired curvature.

The end panels of a heavy riveted Warren roof truss with 12 panels and a span of 150 ft., connected to a column, are illustrated in Fig. 46-5. Because of the large stresses involved, the types of connections in Fig. 46-4 are not suitable and gusset plates are required. The edges of the gusset plates are curved between members, to improve the stress distribution within the welds. This also improves the appearance. They are also made straight, however.

Except at the top of the column the structural section, of which each truss member is composed, ends at a gusset plate. At each end, its web is butt-welded to the gusset plate. The flanges are butt-welded to ends of the stiffener plates, which are welded normal to each side of the gusset plate.

Instead of ending the structural section of the gusset plate, as just described, the web of the section may be cut off at this point and the projecting flanges slotted to form a forked end which fits closely over the gusset plate. The web is butt-welded to the edge of the gusset plate, and the projecting flanges are fillet-welded to the sides of this

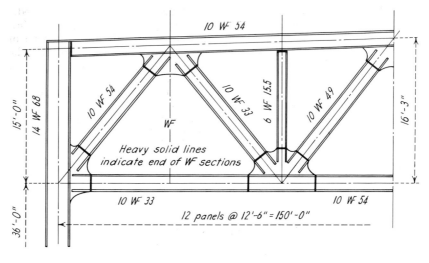

Fig. 46-5. Welded truss with gusset plates. (Lincoln Electric Company.)

plate. No stiffening plates are required. The latter arrangement has the advantage of not breaking the continuity of the flange material, but it requires a longer main section and does not utilize the web material which is cut out in forming the slots.

The end top chord member which connects to the top of the column carries only the relatively small stresses due to lateral loads, such as the wind load. It is butt-welded to the column. The gusset plate at the end of the bottom chord is fillet-welded to the column. A suitable end connection can be devised for a truss, simply supported by a column, ending at the outer end of the lower chord, and the end member of the top chord is omitted. The sizes of the gusset plates are determined by the stresses they must carry and by the lengths of the welds required to transmit the stresses from the members to the plates.

47. STEEL RIGID FRAMES, ARCHES, DOMES, AND CABLE-SUPPORTED ROOFS

Rigid Frames

General Comments. Rigid frames, as defined in Art. 35 and illustrated in Fig. 35-4, constructed of steel are used extensively for auditoriums, gymnasiums, armories, field houses, industrial plants, and buildings with many other classes of occupancy. Steel rigid frames normally are not advantageous for spans of 40 ft. or less. They are widely used for spans up to 100 ft. and have been constructed for spans exceeding 200 ft. For the longer spans, however, steel arches are usually used.

Rigid frames are constructed by connecting structural steel shapes and plates either by riveting or welding them together. Welding is particularly well suited to this type of structure, however, and is usually employed.

The Common Type. The most common type of welded steel rigid frame is illustrated in Fig. 47-1. The vertical legs or columns are provided with flat bases which bear on the tops of the foundations. Actual hinges are never provided at these points, and thus there is always some resistance to rotation. If the column bases are so anchored to the foundation that this resistance is nominal and is not considered in the foundation design, the connections are considered to be hinged in preparing the frame designs. If the bases are securely anchored to the foundations so as to fully resist the moment, and the foundations are designed accordingly, the connections are considered to be fixed. Between these two extremes, the condition of partial fixity is often considered.

Fixing the column bases increases the rigidity of the frame but may increase the cost of the foundations significantly. For that reason, rigid frames are usually designed on the assumption that the joints at these points are hinged. In most, if not all, frames full

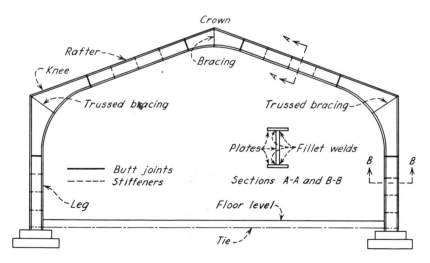

Fig. 47-1. Steel rigid frame.

fixity is provided at the crown. Therefore, the common type of single-span rigid frame is usually considered to be two-hinged for design purposes.

Advantages of Fixing to Foundations. The lateral wind loads on a high, narrow, rigid frame may cause it to deflect laterally enough to damage rigid enclosing walls. In addition, a rigid frame whose columns support a traveling crane may have frequent and excessive lateral deflections caused by the operation of the crane. These might damage rigid enclosing walls and the frame itself and interfere with the operation of the crane. Since fixing the column bases reduces lateral deflections, fixed bases may be essential and fully justify the greater cost of the foundations (4).

Tie between Foundations. The horizontal component of the thrust of each leg at the top of its foundation must be considered in the design of the foundation. The soil may be adequate to resist this component, but if not, the column bases at the two sides may be tied together by steel rods, embedded in concrete to resist corrosion, to form a tie beam located below the floor, as shown in the figure, or the tie rods may be embedded in a concrete floor. Turn buckles

Fig. 47-2. Rigid frame in Field House at University of Colorado.

(Fig. 48-4b) are provided on the tie rods to adjust them accurately to the required length.

Basic Components of a Rigid Frame. The long-span frame (Fig. 47-1) includes two *knees* and a *crown* with I-shaped cross sections, each made up of flange plates fillet-welded to a web plate. The portions of the frame included between the ends of the crown and knees, often called *rafters*, may be wide-flange shapes or, to obtain greater depths, they may be built up of a web plate to which flange plates are fillet-welded, as for the knees and crown. The various sections are butt-welded together, as indicated by the heavy lines in the figure, and the bottom of each leg is fillet-welded to a heavy baseplate with holes to receive bolts to anchor the frame to the foundations.

Stiffeners. Stiffeners consisting of plates fitted between the flanges, normal to the webs, and fillet-welded to the flanges and the web are used in various locations. They must be provided at all points where either of the flanges changes direction, to prevent the flanges and the web from buckling. Such conditions exist at the butt-welded joints between the various sections indicated by the heavy lines on the figure. They also exist at the center of each knee and the crown, as shown by the light solid lines. Stiffeners may be required at intermediate points along the length of each rafter and leg, as shown by the dashed lines. This condition may prevail if the web is relatively thin or if there are heavy roof purlin loads along the rafter.

Lateral Bracing. Effective lateral bracing is required between adjacent frames, at the ridge, and in the diagonal plane through the knee where the stiffeners are located. The latter is called an *eaves strut*. Such bracing often consists of light trussed members.

Each frame and all its parts must be supported laterally, to remain in their true positions. Roof purlins, combined with diagonal cross bracing, consisting of angles in the plane of the top flange and located in alternate panels between frames, usually constitute the principal bracing for this part of the structure. In addition, lateral support must be provided for the legs.

Other Types. Many other types of knees and other parts may be used on rigid frames of the general type illustrated in Fig. 47-1. The top member may be horizontal, steeply pitched, segmental, or curved, as shown in Fig. 35-4.

Two-story buildings have been constructed, with a rigid frame for each story, and multiple-span rigid frames (Fig. 35-4) are rather common. For such frames the knees of the interior columns are re-

Fig. 47-3. Saw-tooth roof with welded steel rigid frames.

placed by Y-shaped units. Rigid frames may be used to support sawtooth roofs (Fig. 35-4*g* and Fig. 47-3).

Rigid frames are often used for craneways by supporting the crane girders on brackets welded to the legs. In addition, balconies for spectators may be cantilevered out from the legs of rigid frames (Fig. 35-4*h*).

Arches

Use. Steel arches are used extensively to support roofs covering large unobstructed floor areas in structures such as hangars, field houses, and exhibition halls with spans that may exceed 300 ft. Often, rigid frames would be preferred for intermediate spans.

Classification according to Hinges. As explained in Art. 35 and illustrated in Fig. 35-2, arches may be three-hinged, two-hinged, one-hinged, and fixed or hingeless. The most common type is three-hinged. Hingeless arches are often used, two-hinged arches are occasionally used, and one-hinged arches are never used.

Comparisons of Classes. The stress computations for three-hinged arches are relatively simple, whereas those for two-hinged and fixed arches are more complex. The stresses in three-hinged arches are not affected significantly by minor movements of the abutments. Horizontal movements of the abutments can be prevented by tying the two abutments together with tie rods (Figs. 47-4 and 5) if the soil supporting the foundations cannot provide adequate lateral support. The stresses in two-hinged arches are unaffected by minor vertical movements of the abutments if the span remains constant. The stresses in fixed arches are affected by vertical or horizontal movements or rotation of the abutments. In general, the three-hinged arch is usually preferred, except when significant savings in material can be achieved by the other types, especially the fixed arch. The latter requires favorable foundation conditions.

Types of Ribs. The arched members are ordinarily called ribs. Arches may be *girder arches,* whose ribs have solid I-shaped cross sections such as those of plate girders or wide-flange shapes, or they may be framed in a manner similar to trusses, in which case they are said to be *trussed arches,* as explained in Art. 35 and illustrated in Fig. 35-1.

Lateral Bracing. Since both chords or flanges of arch ribs are in compression, they must be braced laterally to prevent buckling in that direction. This is usually accomplished by using trussed purlins whose depth commonly is equal to that of the arch rib. If the spacing of the arches is relatively small, rolled sections shallower than the ribs are sometimes used for purlins, in which case the bottom chord or flange may be supported by knee braces located near the ends of the purlins. Other lateral bracing is required to give stability to the structure as a whole. This consists of diagonal bracing between the arches in the curved surface tangent to the top chord and sometimes the bottom chord also, a simple example of which is illustrated in Fig. 48-7b.

Methods of Connecting Parts Together. The various parts of an arch may be either riveted or welded together. The method used for this purpose determines, to a large extent, the structural shapes of which the members are composed.

Girder Arch Ribs. A riveted plate-girder arch rib is built up in a manner similar to a riveted plate girder (Fig. 45-1f) with a web plate and two flanges each consisting of two angles placed back to back and cover plates as required. A welded plate girder arch rib consists of a web plate to which top and bottom flange plates are welded, as for the welded plate girder section shown in Fig. 45-2a.

Riveted or welded plate girder ribs may be made up of straight segments spliced together or they may be fabricated to conform to the curves of the ribs. The flange angles and flange plates for ribs of the latter type are cold-bent to the curve of the arch, and the webs are cut with this curvature. If wide-flange shapes are used for arch ribs, they may be made up of straight or cold-bent segments butt-welded together.

Trussed Arch Ribs. A determining factor in selecting the flange or chord sections of a trussed arch rib is the fact that provisions must be made for connecting the ends of the web members to the chords. In riveted trussed arches, these connections are usually made by gusset plates. Two angles placed back to back with gusset plates between them (Fig. 47-4) is a common form. The cross section of the flange can be varied, without changing the angles, by the use of appropriate cover plates. The web members used with chords of this type are usually composed of two angles placed back to back with the gusset plates between them.

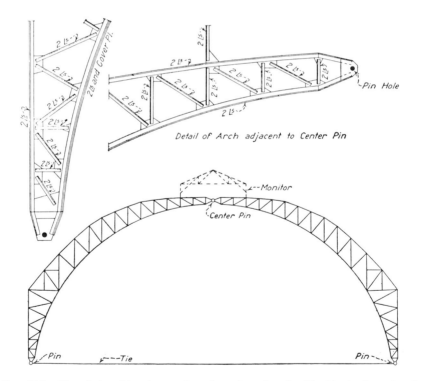

Fig. 47-4. Riveted three-hinged trussed or framed steel arch with 2-L chords and web members.

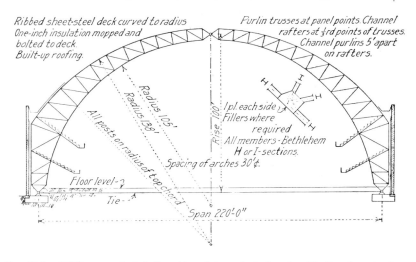

Fig. 47-5. 220-ft. span riveted three-hinged trussed steel arch, with H-section chords and H-section and I-beam web members. University of Minnesota Field House.

Another common arrangement for riveted trussed arches utilizes H-sections for both chord and web members (Fig. 47-5). The webs of all members are placed perpendicular to the plane of the truss. Sections of the same depth, or of such a size that the differences in depth can be compensated for by the use of filler plates, are used. By this arrangement, the members meeting at a joint can be connected by two gusset plates each riveted to a flange of the H-sections, as shown in the figure. The chord members may be straight segments or they may be cold-bent to the required curvature. I-beams are also used.

The ends of members meeting at a joint of a trussed rib may be welded together in the same manner as truss members are welded, described in Art. 46 and illustrated in Fig. 46-4*f*.

Riveted Three-Hinged Constant-Depth Trussed Arch. A long-span riveted, three-hinged trussed arch with a constant depth, except at the hinges, is illustrated in Fig. 47-6. The spacing of the arches is 40 ft. (5). The chords are composed of 14-in. wide-flange shapes with the webs normal to the plane of the arch. They are cold-bent to the desired curvature. The same wide-flange section is used throughout, and the section area is increased, where required, by riveting plates to the webs rather than the flanges, as is the common practice. Each web member consists of two angles, one riveted to the flange on each side

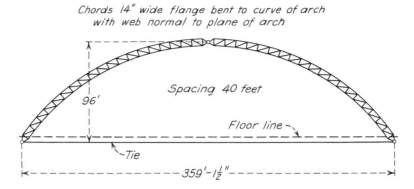

Fig. 47-6. 360-ft. span, riveted constant-depth, three-hinged steel trussed arch with wide-flange chords. Hangar at Edwards Air Force Base. Van Dyke and Barnes, Architects and Engineers.

of the rib. Only a few gusset plates are required. Web members are not provided with lacing or battens except near the center of the arch.

The chords are braced laterally by trussed purlins with depths equal to that of the rib. Other bracing is provided in the surfaces tangent to the chords. The roof deck is composed of the V-beam type of asbestos-protected sheet metal, with glass-fiber insulation applied to the underside of the deck.

Welded Constant-Depth Hingeless Trussed Arch (6). A long-span welded constant-depth trussed arch without hinges is illustrated in Fig. 47-7. The fixed ends are supported by reinforced concrete abut-

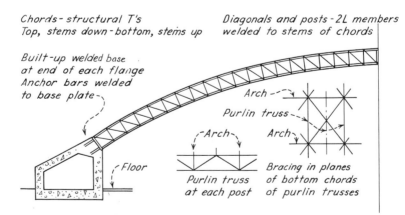

Fig. 47-7. 300-ft. span fixed arch with constant-depth rib welded trussed and structural T chords. U. S. Navy Hangar, Patuxement, Md. Arranged from *Engineering News-Record*.

ments. Each flange consists of a structural T-section, and each web member consists of two angles placed back to back and spaced far enough apart to fit over the stems of the flanges to which their ends are welded. The chord members are made up of segments straight for two panel lengths. The ends of adjacent segments are butt-welded together.

Since both chords are compression members and tend to buckle laterally under stress, they are braced effectively in this direction. The arches are spaced 25 ft. apart. Purlin trusses located between the arches are framed into each radial arch truss member or post to provide lateral support. They are in the same planes as these members, are as deep as the arch ribs, and are welded trusses with T-section chords and angles for web members. Diagonal bracing, consisting of T-sections, is located in surfaces tangent to the top and bottom chords and between the chords of the trussed purlins.

For ease in erection, the chords of each arch are divided into five segments of about equal length and are spliced by field welding. The roof is wood sheathing spanning the distances between the trussed purlins.

Riveted Three-Hinged Girder Arch. A long-span riveted three-hinged girder arch is shown in Fig. 47-8. The ribs have I-shaped cross sec-

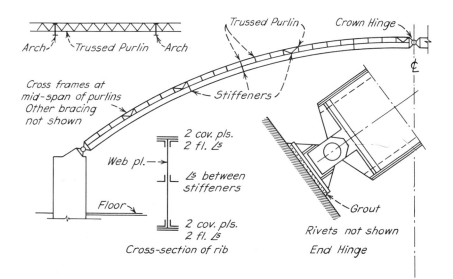

Fig. 47-8. 300-ft. span, three-hinged plate girder rib, riveted arch. Hangar at Idlewild Airport, Port of New York Authority. Arranged from *Engineering News-Record*.

tions built up of four flange angles, a web plate, and cover plates riveted together as shown in the figure. Trussed purlins provide lateral support for the arch ribs as well as for the light-gage-steel roof deck. Other bracing is provided to increase the lateral support of the arch ribs and the structure as a whole. Each arch is erected in four sections, locating the field splices near the quarter points of the arch (7).

Welded Three-Hinged Girder Arch. The framing for the Field House at the University of Vermont, shown in Fig. 47-9, consists of 28 welded three-hinged arches with a span of 153 ft. covering a floor 486 ft. long. The arch ribs consist of 26-by-⅜-in. web plates and 15⅝-by-⅝-in. flange plates shaped to conform to the curvature of the arch and welded together.

The roof deck consists of tongue-and-groove planks 4 in. thick spanning between arches. They are anchored to the arches by 4-by-10-in. wood nailing strips attached to the top flanges of the arches at the fabricating shop. The roof deck is covered with a built-up roofing.

Fig. 47-9. 153-ft. span welded three-hinged girder arch. University of Vermont Field House. Architect, Freeman-French-Freeman. Structural Engineers, Severud, Elstad and Krueger Associates. Steel fabricator and erector, Vermont Structural Steel Corporation. Structural steel furnished by the Bethlehem Steel Corporation.

Each arch was shipped to the site in four sections, assembled on the ground in two halves, and pin-connected to the foundations. The two halves were then raised into position by truck-mounted cranes and pinned at the crown. The two sections of each half arch rib were field-connected with high strength bolts.

Rock Decks. See Art. 72.

Domes

General Comments. Coliseums, field houses, exhibition halls, auditoriums, sports arenas, and other large floor areas are often roofed over with domes that have supporting members of steel. Such domes have been constructed with diameters of nearly 400 ft.

A dome is an integral or self-contained unit. Its perimeter may be supported directly by the foundation, which carries the vertical and horizontal thrusts of the ribs. It is usually provided, however, with a steel tension ring which carries the outward thrusts of the ribs and is supported on steel or reinforced concrete columns located at the bottom ends of the ribs. They may be vertical or their tops may be tilted outward. They are braced together laterally to form a stable structure.

Patterns of Framing. Many arrangements or patterns of steel frames have been used for the support of domes. Most of them provide for a *tension ring* around the perimeter of the dome. Usually there are radial *ribs*, with bottom ends framing into the tension ring and top ends framing into a *compression ring*, with its center at the center of the dome.

Three types of patterns are illustrated in Fig. 47-10. The tension and compression rings and the radial ribs are indicated by heavy lines. The rings are usually made up of straight segments. The number of radial ribs varies from 12 to 48 depending upon the diameter of the dome, the framing patterns, and other factors.

The tension ring is made up of straight segments between ribs. The rim of the compression ring is supported by radial members, shown by the dashed lines, which may be located at every second or third rib, causing the entire assembly to resemble a wheel.

For the pattern shown in the sector *AB* of the figure, the roof deck is supported directly by equally spaced straight purlins spanning from rib to rib. For the pattern in the sector *AC* of the figure, the roof

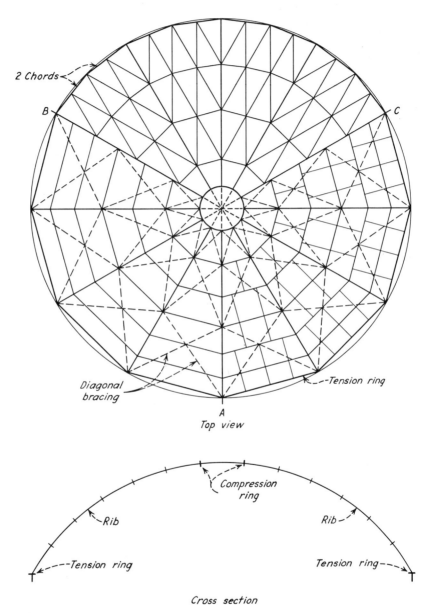

Fig. 47-10. Patterns of dome framing.

deck is supported directly by rafters normal to straight purlins, which are in turn supported by the ribs. An interior view of framing with this pattern would resemble Fig. 47-11. The pattern in the sector BC includes secondary framing members parallel to the main ribs, extending from the tension ring until they meet the ribs to form diamond-shaped patterns as in the *lamella* pattern. The Houston, Texas stadium has a 642-ft. clear-span dome of this pattern with 12 trussed main ribs and secondary ribs dividing the tension ring into 72 segments all supported on 72 steel columns (17).

Types of Ribs.   The ribs may be fabricated by welding or riveting. They may be of the girder or the trussed type, as described under arches. The ends of the ribs may be fixed or hinged at their junctions with the tension and compression rings.

Lateral Bracing.   For all the patterns shown in Fig. 47-10, the ribs receive lateral support from the purlins which frame into them. In the patterns in sectors AB and AC, additional lateral support is provided by diagonal cross bracing, as shown by the dashed lines. The pattern in sector BC is made up of diamond-shaped panels which are subdivided into triangles by the circumferential members or purlins. Since triangles are stable units, each sector is stable against lateral forces.

As has been stated, a dome is usually supported on steel or reinforced concrete columns located at the bottom ends of the ribs. The dome itself, framed as described, is stable against lateral forces, but the lateral forces against the dome are transmitted to the tops of the columns. In addition, provisions must be made to resist the lateral forces on the portion of the structure below the perimeter of the dome. These may consist of rigid framing or of diagonal bracing in the panels between columns.

Dome with Wide-Flange Ribs.   The roof framing for the Field House at Syracuse University (Fig. 47-11) consists of a dome with thirty-six 18-in. wide-flange ribs spanning between a steel tension ring 300 ft. in diameter and a steel compression ring 18 ft. in diameter. It is supported on 36 tapered precast reinforced concrete columns 30 ft. high. The domed roof is surrounded with an overhang which projects 18 ft. beyond the exterior walls of the building.

The ribs consist of segmental sections butt-welded together. There are five intermediate circumferential rings of steel purlins, spanning between the ribs and bulb-tee rafters or subpurlins with a constant spacing of 2-ft.-9-in. spanning between the purlins, as shown in the

Fig. 47-11. Steel framed dome with wide-flange radial ribs. Field House, Syracuse University. Span 300 ft. 36 precast reinforced concrete columns. Seating capacity 2,000. Architects: King and King. Structural Engineers: Eckerlin and Kleeper. General Contractor: R. A. Culotti Construction Co.

figure. These are shimmed to conform to the spherical roof surface. There are three sets of cross-rod bracing in each of the 36 segmental panels of the dome.

Between the tension and compression rings, the roof deck of the dome is made up of 3-in. wood-fiber-cement planks spanning between rafters. These are lightweight and noncombustible and contribute significantly to heat insulation and sound absorption. The planks are covered with a 1-in. rigid insulation, over which is a conventional 5-ply built-up roofing with a marble surface. A 7-in. slab of lightweight concrete 40 ft. in diameter covers the opening within the compression ring and is elevated to provide ventilation. The 18-ft. overhang is constructed of vermiculite concrete on a sheet-metal roof deck with an asbestos-cement board underside. The ventilator slab and the overhang are covered with a conventional 5-ply built-up roofing (15).

Roof Decks. See Art. 72.

Cable-Supported Roofs

General Comments. As stated in Art. 6, cold-drawing of steel bars through dies to form wire markedly increases the strength of the steel. For this reason, cables made up of steel wires are efficient members for carrying loads that subject them to tension. Such action occurs in various forms of roofs which are supported by wire cables and are called *cable-supported* or *cable-suspended roofs*, the former designation being less common but probably preferable because it is more general. Because of the flexibility of cables, special consideration must be given to the effects of unbalanced loads on deflections and the tendency of gusts of wind to cause vibration and flutter which, if excessive, may cause failure.

According to Roebling (16), a group of wires twisted together (Fig. 47-12*a*) is called a *strand* and a group of strands twisted together, as shown in *b*, is called a *wire rope*. Resistance to corrosion is markedly increased by using galvanized wire.

Bridge strand and rope are *prestretched* by the manufacturer to remove constructional looseness which is present when they come from the stranding or closing machines. The process is often called *pre-stressing*, but this term must not be confused with other meanings explained in Art. 57.

Normally, the cables for cable-supported roofs consist of *galvanized*

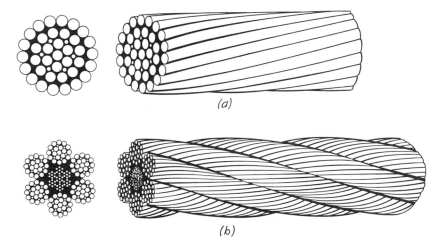

(a)

(b)

Fig. 47-12. Wire strand and rope: (a) Galvanized bridge strand. (b) Galvanized bridge rope. American Steel and Wire Division, U. S. Steel Corp.

bridge strand. It is considered superior to *galvanized bridge rope,* which is also available, because it has higher strength for a given diameter and because it elongates less when subjected to a given unit tensile stress.

Galvanized bridge strand is available, from one manufacturer, in diameters varying from ½ in., made up of 7 or 14 wires, to 3⅝ in., made up of 223 wires. Galvanized bridge rope is available in diameters varying from ⅝ in., with 6 strands and 7 wires per strand, designated as 6 x 7, to 4 in., with 6 strands and 43 wires per strand, designated as 6 x 43. Other manufacturers have corresponding strands and wire ropes differing somewhat in available diameters and numbers of wires. Adjustable connections are available for anchoring the ends of cables.

Single-Layer Cable-Supported Roofs. The single-layer cable-supported roof in Fig. 47-13*a* and *b* shows the basic structural features of a covered stadium, 310 ft. in diameter, with cylindrical exterior walls 85 ft. high, located in Montevideo, Uruguay. The rainfall in this area is very low, there is no snow, and earthquakes do not occur. Such favorable conditions rarely exist. The roof support consists of a reinforced concrete *compression ring* located on top of the 4-in. reinforced concrete wall surrounding the stadium, a steel *tension ring* at the center, and 256 galvanized wire cables radiating between the two rings. The cables are made of strands 0.6 in. in diameter. The roof deck consists of thin reinforced concrete slabs precast to the dimensions of the trapezoidal space each occupies in the completed roof. These slabs are anchored to the cables and to each other by means of projecting ends of the reinforcing rods.

After all the roof slabs were in place, the roof was temporarily loaded with brick to increase the stress in the cables. Loading increased their length and widened the joints between the slabs. The joints were then filled with cement mortar. After the mortar had hardened, the brick were removed and the cables tended to return to their previous length. Their action was resisted by the slabs and joints, which were compressed, and the joints remained tight. This procedure is known as prestressing. The prestressing also increased the stiffness of the roof.

Slabs were not placed in a circular area 65 ft. in diameter at the center of the roof. This was covered with a ventilated skylight (Fig. 47-13*a*). Because of the absence of snowfall, it was not necessary to provide for an unbalanced snow load.

The tops of the slabs were waterproofed. Rainwater that falls on

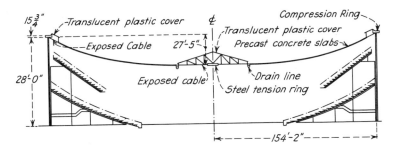

(a) Cross section of one-layer cable-supported roof

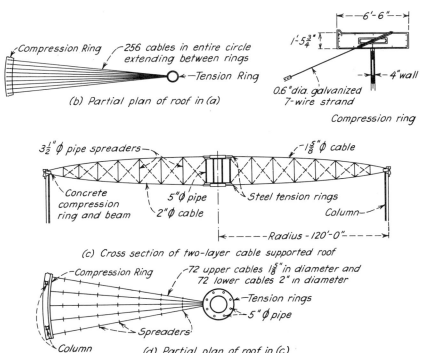

(b) Partial plan of roof in (a)

Compression ring

(c) Cross section of two-layer cable supported roof

(d) Partial plan of roof in (c)

Fig. 47-13. Single-layer and double-layer cable-supported roofs.

the roof is collected in a trough around the central opening and conducted through four pipes, hung from the ceiling, to downspouts on the outside wall and into a storm sewer.

A more detailed description of this project is given in reference 8. The type of roof was conceived by L. A. Mondino, L. I. Viera, and A. S. Miller of Montevideo with the Preload Company, Inc., as special consultant on the design of the roof system.

The single-layer type of cable-supported roof for the Chicago-O'Hare International Airport Restaurant is illustrated in Fig. 47-14. The reinforced concrete compression ring, whose diameter is 190 ft., is supported on 26 reinforced concrete columns 58 ft. above the ground surface with diamond-shaped profiles. The tension ring is a wide-flange shape and has a diameter of 13 ft. The sag of the cables is 10 ft., 6 in. There are 52 lengths of 2-in. prestretched galvanized bridge strand cables with their ends anchored to the compression and tension rings. The roof deck consists of precast reinforced concrete slabs $3\frac{1}{2}$ in. thick which fit between the cables with projecting ends of the reinforcement hooking over the cables. The cables were pre-stressed in the manner described for the Montevideo Stadium, except that pig iron was used for the temporary load instead of brick.

A cable-supported roof similar to that of the Montevideo Stadium was constructed for the Assembly Building at San Antonio, Texas. The span is much smaller, being only 132 ft. There are 200 cables, attached to a welded built-up steel ring. This ring is designed to

Fig. 47-14. Single-layer cable-supported roof. Chicago O'Hare International Airport Restaurant. Architects and Engineers, C. F. Murphy Associates. Roof Contractor, E. H. Marhoefer, Jr. Cables furnished by John A. Roebling's Sons Division, Colorado Fuel and Iron Corp.

carry the compressive and flexural stresses to which it is subjected because it is supported by 20 vertical steel columns spaced about 20 ft. apart around the perimeter. The inner ends of the cables are attached to a welded-steel tension ring 40 ft. in diameter. Steel trusses radiating out from a hub at the center of the roof to the tension ring support the roof over the area surrounded by the tension ring.

The remainder of the roof consists of small trapezoidal shaped precast concrete slabs arranged in concentric rings, supported on the cables, with open joints which were filled with mortar after the cables had been prestressed by loading the roof with brick. All operations follow procedures similar to those used in building the Montevideo Stadium. This comment also applies to the drainage system (13).

Double-Layer Cable-Supported Roof. A roof supported by a double layer of cables is illustrated in Fig. 47-13c and d. This roof covers the Memorial Auditorium at Utica, New York, a circular building 240 ft. in diameter. The supporting system consists of two 72-cable layers. The outer ends of the cables in both layers are anchored to a reinforced concrete compression ring, with a section area of about 20 sq. ft., supported on twenty-four 2-ft.-square reinforced concrete columns equally spaced around the perimeter of the building and supported laterally. The two welded-steel tension rings are 18 ft. apart vertically and are held apart by equally spaced steel pipes 5 in. in diameter. Vertical pipe struts are inserted at intervals of about 14 ft. between each pair of cables, in the same vertical plane and located on concentric circles.

The two tension rings were supported in contact on a temporary scaffold at the center of the building while the cables were being placed and anchored to these rings and to the compression ring. At this stage, the tension rings were at a predetermined elevation. Hydraulic jacks were inserted between the rings and gradually forced them apart. Downward movement of the lower ring was made possible by removing timber blocking which was provided on top of the scaffold. Jacking was continued until the two layers were 18 ft. apart, vertically, at the center. Since the ends of the cables were anchored to the tension and compression rings, the vertical movement produced by the jacks subjected the cables to tension. The operations were so controlled that the stresses in the cables reached predetermined values. The jacks were replaced by permanent pipe separators. The tensions in the cables were then increased to desired values by inserting the vertical struts between the upper and lower cables, as shown in the figure. Diagonal cross bracing, consisting of rods, was placed in each panel between struts. This bracing distributed the effects of concentrated loads due to mechanical equipment and stiffened the roof. Final adjustments were made to insure that the tension in the cables was in close agreement with the desired values.

Inducing tensile stresses in the cables before the loads to be carried are applied is called *pretensioning* or *prestressing*. Pretensioning controls the deflection of the roof and prevents objectionable vibrations which may develop in cable supported structures. Both cables remain in tension under all conditions of loading.

The roof deck is constructed of light-gage steel supported directly on the upper cables except near the perimeter where intermediate channel purlins are required.

A more detailed description of this project is given in reference 9. The structural system was conceived and designed by Lev Zetlin, consulting engineer.

A cable-supported roof, which resembles the roof just described, was provided for the United States Pavillion at the Brussels Worlds Fair. The span is 302 ft. There are two layers of cables, but they are not prestressed (10).

Cable-Supported Cantilever Roofs. Cable-supported cantilevers are used to support the roofs of hangars. They may be of the single- or double-cantilever types. Portions of the structures other than the cables may be constructed of structural steel, reinforced concrete, or various combinations of these materials.

One example of a cable-supported, single-cantilever hangar is illustrated in Fig. 47-15a. The principal roof support consists of a series of heavy wide-flange steel girders, each hinged at one end to a rigid side section of reinforced concrete and supported near the other end by a cable passing over a steel mast erected above the innerside of the side section and anchored to the outer side of that section. The roof deck consists of precast reinforced concrete channel slabs, as described in Art. 58, supported on rolled-steel purlins spanning between the cantilever girders. The relative weights and dimensions of the cantilever and side sections and the anchorage provided must insure stability (11).

A cable-supported, double-cantilever hangar is illustrate in Fig. 47-15b. The steel cantilevers project outward from both sides of a center section. The inner ends of the cantilevers are hinged to the steel frame of the center section. Cables provide support near the outer two-thirds points of the cantilevers and extend inward over steel masts to anchorages on the center section.

Principal structural supports for the roof over the Sports Arena at Squaw Valley, California, is illustrated in Fig. 47-15c. They consist

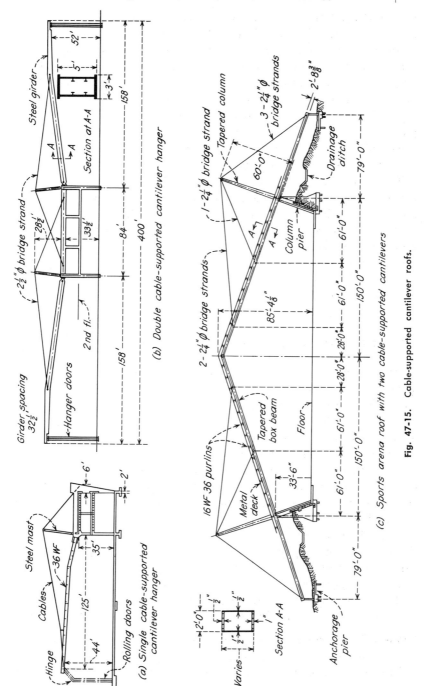

Fig. 47-15. Cable-supported cantilever roofs.

(a) Single cable-supported cantilever hanger

(b) Double cable-supported cantilever hanger

(c) Sports arena roof with two cable-supported cantilevers

of two independent cable-supported cantilevers with free ends meeting at the ridge of the roof. The inclined girders are tapered-steel box sections. The columns or masts are tapered-steel four-flanged cross-shaped sections built up of plates welded together. The cantilever projection of each girder is supported at two points by cables that pass over the top of a column normal to the girder and are anchored to the lower end of the girder. This end is in turn anchored to a pier, the uplift at this point being resisted by the pile foundation. Each column is supported by a column pier. The entire system is arranged as shown in the figure.

The roof deck consists of cellular sheet-steel panels, 4½ in. deep, supported on heavy wide-flange steel purlins spaced about 12 ft. apart and spanning the 32 ft. between the cantilevers, all designed and connected so as to require no further lateral bracing in the plane of the roof. The top surface of the roof panels is arranged to serve as the finished roof surface to receive a plastic coating.

Further information on this project is given in reference 12, on which these comments are based.

48. STEEL FRAMING, CONNECTIONS, AND BRACING

General Comments. The preceding articles in this chapter have been concerned with the structural steel shapes available and their use in constructing the various types of members used in the *frames* or *framing* of buildings. The means employed for fastening pieces together have been considered. Examples of the use of gusset plates in forming the joints of riveted and welded trusses and of welded joints without gusset plates, have been given. This article is concerned primarily with column, beam, and girder splices and connections and with lateral bracing for the frames of tier buildings and mill or industrial buildings.

A tall building with steel frame is often referred to as a *skeleton construction* building because its frame resembles a skeleton; it is called a *tier building* because its stories constitute tiers; and is known as a *skyscraper* because of its height. Buildings of any height which enclose undivided floor areas that can be subdivided to suit the tenants are often called *loft buildings*.

Riveted Construction. Various details used in connections with rivets as fasteners are explained in the following paragraphs.

Lap and butt joints. Joints provided by riveting plates or parts

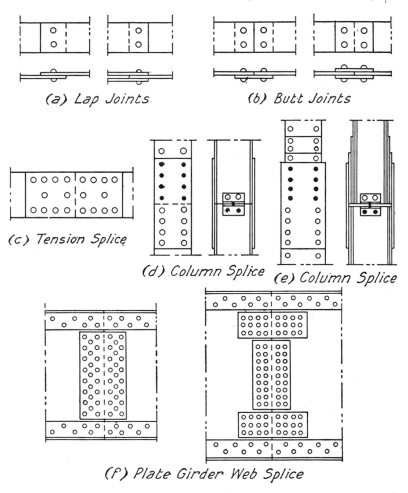

(a) Lap Joints   (b) Butt Joints

(c) Tension Splice

(d) Column Splice   (e) Column Splice

(f) Plate Girder Web Splice

Fig. 48-1. Riveted splices in steel members.

of members which lap over each other (Fig. 48-1a) are called *lap joints*. Those formed by butting the ends of two parts together and fastening them by rivets passing through a splice plate or connection plate (b) are called *butt joints*.

Column splices. Steel column sections are usually made constant for two story heights. Because of the change in the load on a column at each floor, it would be possible to save column material by reducing the column section in each story. This practice would be undesirable because the cost of the splices and the increase in erection costs would probably offset any saving in column section. In order that they will not interfere with the beam and girder connections, the splices are usually made about 2 ft. above the floor line.

The abutting ends of the columns at the splice are accurately *milled* so that the compressive stresses can be transferred directly from the upper column to the lower column by bearing. Splice plates are riveted to the flat sides of the columns and extend a short distance above and below the abutting ends. The functions of these plates are to hold the two sections in line, to resist bending stresses caused by wind and other causes, and to provide lateral rigidity. They are not relied upon to transfer any of the direct load from one section to the other, with the possible exception of columns carrying very light loads.

If the two sections are of the same width, the splice is simple (*d*). If the widths are not the same, the difference in width is taken up by the *fill plates* (*e*). If the difference in width is so great that the flanges of the upper columns do not bear on those of the lower column, a horizontal bearing plate is inserted between the abutting ends as shown in the figure.

Splices in plate-girder webs. The size of plates available for webs of plate girders is limited, and it is often necessary to splice these web plates. Two forms of *web splices* are shown in *f*.

Beam and girder connections. The usual method of connecting beams to girders is with *framed connections*, as illustrated in Fig. 48-2*a*. The size of angles and the number of rivets to be used for each size of beam has been standardized to quite an extent, and such connections are called *standard connections*. One angle is sometimes used instead of two. Very often it is necessary to keep the top flanges of the beam and the girder at the same elevation. The beam flange must then be cut to clear the flange of the girder (*b*), and the beam is said to be *coped*. In many cases the beam may rest on top of the girder and the only connection required is bolts through the flanges (*c*) to hold them together. Channel purlins are usually supported on the sloping top chords of roof trusses by means of the *clip-angle connection* shown in *d*. This connection may be bolted instead of riveted if desired.

Connection of beams and girders to columns. There are two types of connections used between beams or girders and columns, the *framed-connection type* and the *seated type*.

The framed-connection type, illustrated in *e*, consists of two angles riveted to the beam or girder in the shop, the rivets between the angles and the column being driven in the field. A *shelf angle* may

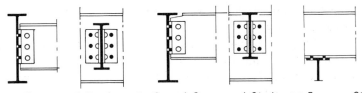

(a) Beam and Girder (b) Coped Beam and Girder (c) Beam on Girder

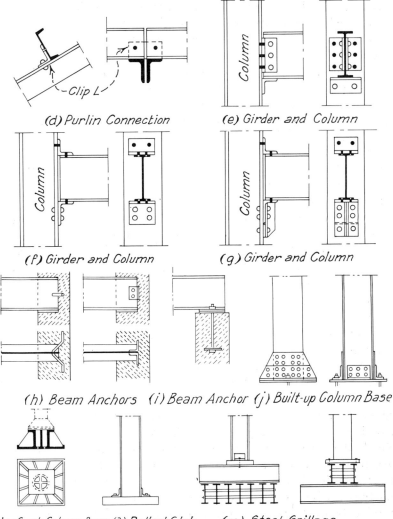

(d) Purlin Connection   (e) Girder and Column

(f) Girder and Column   (g) Girder and Column

(h) Beam Anchors   (i) Beam Anchor (j) Built-up Column Base

(k) Cast Column Base (l) Rolled Slab   (m) Steel Grillage

Fig. 48-2. Riveted beam end connections and column bases.

be provided to support the beam or girder during erection. This is called an *erection seat.*

The seated type of connection shown in *f* consists of an angle at the bottom side of the beam which is shop-riveted to the column and an angle at the top which is field-riveted to the beam and column. For large reactions it is necessary to provide one or two *stiffener angles* to support the outstanding leg of the bottom angle (*g*).

The shop work is simpler on the seated type and fewer field rivets are required, but this type may project through the fireproofing if used in connecting to column flanges, and then the framed connection is used.

Wall supports for beams and girders. Steel beams and girders may be built into masonry walls. *Bearing plates* are provided to distribute the reaction over a larger area, and anchors (*h*) tie the beam and wall together. Where beams and girders are not built into the wall, *anchor bolts* (*i*) are provided.

Column bases. The load at the lower end of a column must be transferred to a concrete footing or pier which in turn transfers the load to the ground. If the end of the steel column were permitted to rest directly on the concrete, the concrete would be crushed where the two came in contact because the working stress in the steel is much greater than the strength of the concrete in bearing. It is therefore necessary to distribute the column load over a large area of the footing. This is done by means of the *column base.* Bases for steel columns may be divided into four classes.

1. Built-up bases made from structural sections (*j*).
2. Cast bases of steel or cast iron (*k*).
3. Rolled-steel slabs (*l*).
4. Steel grillages (*m*).

Built-up bases are suitable for light loads, but where it is necessary to distribute the column load over a considerable area, cast-iron or cast-steel bases may be used, cast steel being much stronger and more reliable than cast iron. These are rarely, if ever, used. Rolled-steel slabs have come into general use. They are more economical and reliable than the cast-iron bases and more economical than the cast-steel bases. The end of the column is milled and bears directly on the steel slab. A simple connection is made between the column end and the slab by means of two angles. Slabs are available up to 12 in. thick, but slabs over 6 in. thick are not usually economical.

Welded Construction. Typical details for welded beam, girder, and column connections are illustrated in Fig. 48-3, together with the pertinent standard welding symbols.

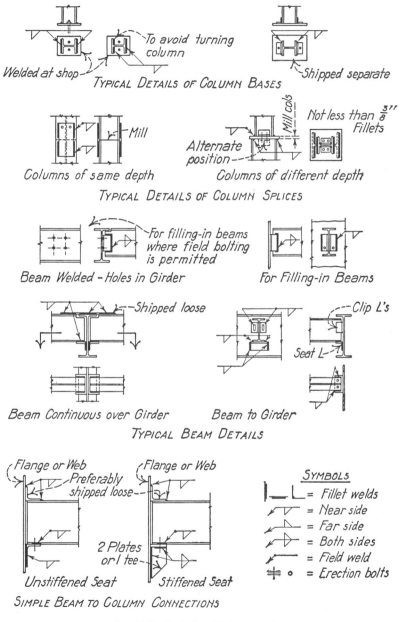

Fig. 48-3. Typical welded connections.

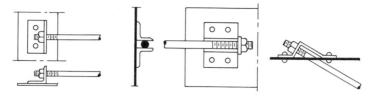

(a) End Connections for Threaded Rods

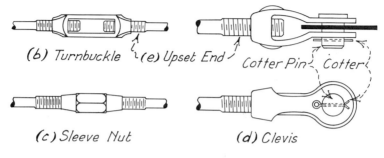

(b) Turnbuckle (e) Upset End Cotter Pin Cotter

(c) Sleeve Nut   (d) Clevis

Fig. 48-4. Connections for rods or bars.

Connections for Rods or Bars. The ends of round or square bars may be threaded to receive nuts to form an end connection. Several connections making use of nuts on *threaded ends* are shown in Fig. 48-4a. When long bars are used, it is usually economical to enlarge the end of the bar so that the area of the section at the root of the threads is somewhat greater than the area in the body of the bar. A smaller bar can then be used, for the threads do not reduce the section area. These enlarged ends are called *upset ends* (b).

The *clevis* shown in *d* is a convenient form of end connection for round and square bars. Upset ends are usually provided. The pin in the clevis may be a *cotter pin,* as shown, or an ordinary bolt and nut. The small split pin inserted in the larger pin is called a *cotter.*

It is often desirable to make tension rods and bars adjustable so that they may be tightened. Two devices are used for this purpose, the *turnbuckle* (b) and the *sleeve nut* (c). In both devices a right-hand thread is used at one end and a left-hand thread at the other so that the abutting ends of the bar may be drawn together or pushed apart by turning the turnbuckle or sleeve nut in the proper direction.

Tier Building Frame. The riveted frame of a tier building formed by assembling the various beams, girders, and columns is illustrated in Fig. 48-5. In this frame no special provision was required for wind bracing. The following points should be noted.

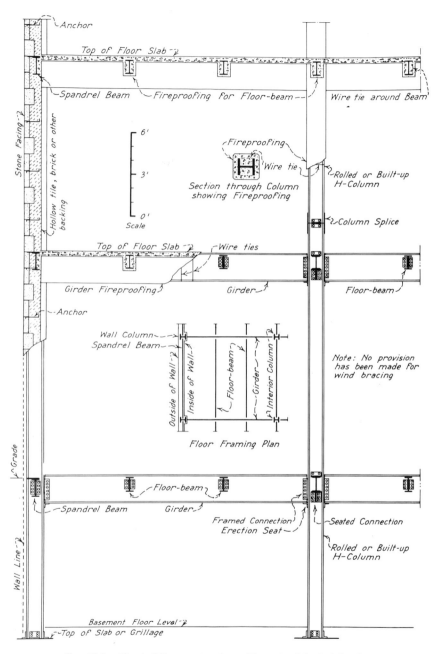

Fig. 48-5. Tier building construction without special wind bracing.

Fig. 48-6. Steel frame for office building, Chase Manhattan Bank Building, New York City. 60 stories and 813 ft. high with 5-story basement. Architects: Skidmore, Owings & Merrill. Structural steel supplied, fabricated and erected by Bethlehem Steel Co. See frontispiece.

1. The outside wall, called a panel or enclosure wall, is supported at each story by the spandrel beams which transmit their load to the outside columns.

2. The panel walls shown are veneered with stone ashlar $3\frac{3}{4}$ in. thick, which is bonded to the backing by a bond course $7\frac{1}{2}$ in. thick

every third course and by anchors at the intermediate joints. The backing may be of brick or of structural clay tile. The anchors are galvanized after bending. One bond course rests on the spandrel beam.

For office buildings and some other occupancies, panel walls with large glass areas, as described in Art. 92, are used extensively. Such walls are usually called *curtain walls* or *window walls*.

3. The floor beams are placed at the third points of the girders where they cause the least moment. They are connected to the girders by framed connections.

4. The floor beams are attached to the columns by seated connections. Framed connections can be used if there is room for them.

5. Framed connections are used between the girders and columns. Seated connections can be used if the stiffener angles can be small enough so that they will not project through the fireproofing.

6. Wide-flange section columns are used. The columns are continuous through two stories, or sometimes continuous for three stories.

7. The column splices are located about 2 ft. above the floor.

8. Reinforced concrete floor slabs supported by steel beams are shown. Many other types of floor, as described in Art. 63, might have been used.

9. The supports for the columns are not shown. The columns would rest on slabs or grillages which would spread the column load over concrete footing or piers.

10. All steel members are fireproofed.

Wind Bracing for Industrial Buildings and Arches. Buildings must be designed to resist the horizontal forces caused by wind as well as the vertical forces from the weight of the buildings and their contents. Provision must also be made for the lateral thrust of cranes and other equipment. Bracing provided to resist all lateral loads is usually called wind bracing.

A simple industrial or steel mill building frame with lateral bracing omitted is shown diagrammatically in Fig. 48-7a. The steel frame for a building with three-hinged arches is shown in *b*. The arches are braced in pairs, as shown by broken lines. Several types of steel industrial building frames are shown in *c*. These are provided with lateral bracing as described in the following paragraphs. Three types of wind bracing are used in steel mill buildings. The simplest type makes use of *knee braces* to brace the columns rigidly to the trusses (Fig. 48-8a), or trusses with considerable depth at the ends are rigidly fastened to the columns (*b*). This type of construction provides bracing to resist wind forces on the sides of the buildings, but wind forces

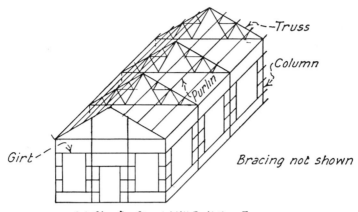

(a) Simple Steel Mill Building Frame

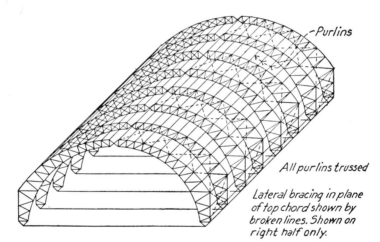

(b) Steel Frame with Three-Hinged Arches

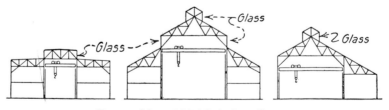

(c) Types of Steel Mill Building Frames

Fig. 48-7. Framing for steel industrial buildings.

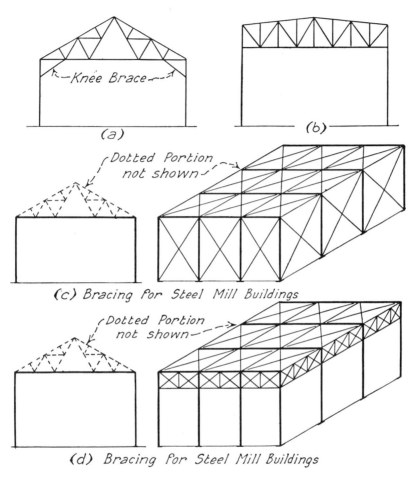

Fig. 48-8. Wind bracing for steel industrial buildings.

against the ends of the buildings are resisted by *cross bracing* in the plane of the sides or by a rigid lattice girder just below the eaves.

Another method of bracing steel industrial buildings to resist wind forces consists of providing cross bracing in the plane of the bottom chord of the truss to make the building rigid from end to end in this plane. In addition to such bracing, the sides and ends are made rigid by *diagonal bracing* so that the whole structure acts like a rigid box (c). It is not necessary to provide diagonal bracing in all the *bays* (spaces between columns) on the sides. Bracing is also provided in the plane of the top chord to hold the tops of the trusses in position, but this bracing is not essential to the wind bracing system and therefore it is not shown in the figure. It is evident that this system might interfere seriously with the windows and doors.

A third system provides lattice girders in the sides and ends to make them rigid. The bracing in the plane of the bottom chord is the same as in the previous method (*d*). Various other arrangements are used.

Wind Bracing for Tier Buildings. In tall buildings of skeleton construction such as office buildings, providing adequate bracing to resist wind is an important feature of the design. If a frame as illustrated in Fig. 48-9*a* is subjected to lateral forces such as wind forces, it would collapse by distorting as in *b*. In low buildings of considerable

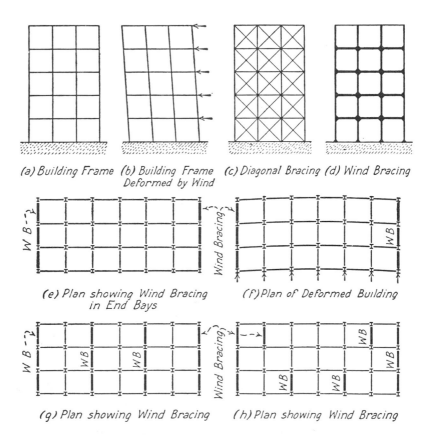

(a) Building Frame (b) Building Frame (c) Diagonal Bracing (d) Wind Bracing
Deformed by Wind

(e) Plan showing Wind Bracing (f) Plan of Deformed Building
in End Bays

(g) Plan showing Wind Bracing (h) Plan showing Wind Bracing

Fig. 48-9. Wind bracing for steel office or tier buildings.

width, the stiffening effect of the panel walls and partitions and the rigidity of the joints between the girders and columns may be sufficient to provide satisfactory resistance to wind forces and earthquake shocks, but this is not true of tall buildings.

Code requirements for wind loads and earthquake shocks are considered in Art. 2. No further mention will be made of bracing to resist earthquake shock except to note that the methods employed are similar but more extensive than those employed for wind bracing.

In designing the wind bracing for a building, the stresses in the structural frame must not exceed allowable values, and the deflections and vibrations of the building must be controlled to prevent discomfort to the occupants and cracking of partitions and other parts of the structure. The maximum permissible lateral deflection at the top of a building is sometimes limited to one-thousandth of the height.

Several types of wind bracings have been devised. The most direct type consists of diagonals crossing the vertical panels between the columns and the floor girders (Fig. 48-8c). It is evident, however, that this method is limited in its application because of its interference with the use of the building and with the locating of windows and doors, even though it is necessary to brace only a relatively small number of panels, as will be explained later.

If sufficiently rigid connections are provided between the girders and columns (d), a skeleton frame will be able to resist the lateral forces. Obviously, there is a tendency to bend the columns and girders when this type of bracing is used, and therefore it is necessary to consider the bending stresses in the design of these members. This type of wind bracing can be arranged to interfere very little with the design and the use of a building.

The group of braced vertical panels in a single vertical plane designed to resist wind stresses is called a *wind bent*. It is not necessary to make all panels of a building rigid, although this may be desirable as it reduces the size of the bracing. Sometimes wind bents can be placed in the outside walls (e). With this arrangement, the floors of a building tend to deform (f) under the action of wind forces. The floors used in modern building construction are usually rigid enough to carry the wind load to the wall bents but, if they are not, special bracing can be provided in the plane of the floors. It may be undesirable or impossible to place all the required wind bracing in the outside bents of a building, and if so some of the interior bents must be utilized. It is desirable but not necessary for these to be continuous across the building (g), but wind bents may be distributed throughout the building (h), each designed to carry its part of the wind load.

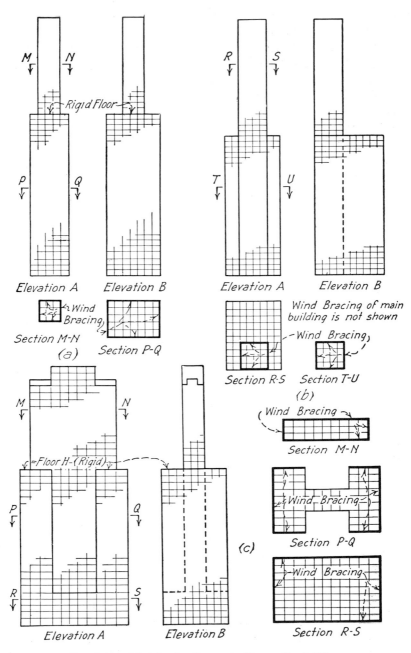

Fig. 48-10. Wind bracing for steel office or tier buildings.

They should be so placed that there is no twisting effect in the frame caused by greater rigidity on one side than on the other, and due consideration must be given to relative lateral deflections.

In buildings that diminish in size in the upper stories, wind bents located in the exterior walls may be continued down through the interior of the lower part of the building, or sometimes it may be desirable to transfer the wind loads to wall bents in the lower stories (Fig. 48-10a). The horizontal effect of the wind on the upper section may be transferred to the wall bents or other bents in the lower stories by means of a heavy concrete floor slab where the building changes section, or by special bracing in the floor. The vertical reactions of the columns of the wind bents are transferred directly down through the corresponding columns in the lower section.

In buildings with towers projecting above a relatively low and broad main building, the towers are usually provided with wind bracing which is independent of the main structural frame (b). The tower bracing may be in the exterior bents only or in the interior bents also.

Buildings of irregular shape and buildings which change in section require special study. The system of bracing shown in c has been used on such buildings. No wind bracing is required for the upper floors. From sections $M-N$, $P-Q$, and $R-S$ it is seen that the wind bracing is placed entirely in the outside walls, but all outside walls do not contain wind bracing. The horizontal thrust on the portion of the building above floor H is transmitted to the wind bents in the outside walls below floor H. In order to transmit this horizontal thrust, floor H must be specially designed. The vertical wind loads in the columns above floor H are transmitted directly down the same columns below floor H.

Walls enclosing elevator shafts and stairways or other walls without openings sometimes can include diagonal wind bracing, and sometimes vertical bents, have been converted into vertical cantilever wind trusses. In addition, instead of using diagonal bracing or vertical trusses, reinforced concrete walls may be installed in such locations. These are called *shear walls*. They are relatively rigid.

For further comments see paragraph entitled lateral bracing in Art. 53.

Wind-Connection Details. Various types of connections between wind girders and columns, using shop rivets and field rivets or high-strength bolts, are illustrated in Fig. 48-11a to f. The *simple connection* in a may be used when the moment is small. It can be used on interior connections as well as on exterior connections, since it does not occupy

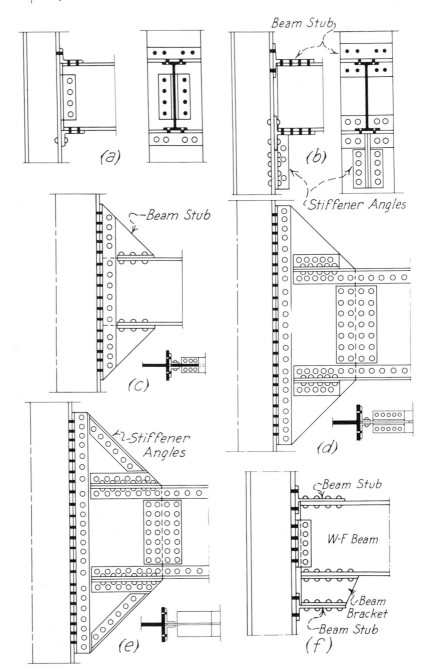

Fig. 48-11. Types of wind connections.

any space. The *knuckle connection* (*b*) will develop considerable resisting moment and occupies very little space. The connecting members are structural tees cut from wide-flanged shapes. A *framed connection* can be used with this detail in place of the *seated connection* shown. The connection shown in *c* is sometimes used. The brackets are wide flange or I-beams which have been cut diagonally. A triangular plate and a pair of angles can be substituted for each wide flange or I-beam bracket, and a plate girder can be substituted for the wide flange or I-beam. The connection shown in *d* can be used to develop large resisting moments. A single plate is used to form both brackets and to replace a part of the web of the girder. This requires the use of splice plates as shown. The connection shown in *e* is similar to that in *d*, except that stiffener angles are provided along the edges of the bracket if necessary to prevent buckling. The connections shown in *d* and *e* can be altered to have only a bottom bracket, and all three types may be changed so as to have top brackets instead of bottom brackets. The connections in *d* and *e* are called gusset-plate connections.

In tall slender buildings the wind moment may place tension in some of the columns. These stresses must be provided for in the design of the column splices, in anchoring the columns to the foundations, and in the design of the foundations.

Many other types of riveted connections have been used, and connections which are suitable for welded construction have been developed.

Before about 1950, all the taller skeleton construction buildings were field-riveted. Since that time, high-strength bolts have come into extensive use to replace rivets with no restriction on the building height. Shop and field welding is also being used for buildings of considerable height and its use will doubtless continue to expand.

Lateral Bracing of Rigid Frames, Arches, and Domes. The lateral bracing for structures of these types is considered in Art. 47.

Fire Protection of Structural Steel. The classification of buildings according to construction is considered in Art. 1. The required fire ratings of the various parts of buildings in each class is given in Table 1-2, these ratings being based upon the behavior of materials in a *standard fire test*, which is explained. The ratings must be sufficient to withstand the hazard involved.

The capacity of structural steel to carry stresses is considerably reduced at the high temperatures that may be expected to prevail during a severe fire. For that reason it is necessary to protect structural

Table 48-1

Thickness of Fire-Resistive Materials

For Protection of Structural-Steel Members for Various Fire Ratings, According to the 1955 Building Code of New York City

Fire-Resistive Materials	Inches Required for Rating			
	4 hr.	3 hr.	2 hr.	1 hr.
Brick, burned clay or shale	$3\frac{3}{4}$	$3\frac{3}{4}$	$2\frac{1}{4}$	$2\frac{1}{4}$
Brick, sand lime	$3\frac{3}{4}$	$3\frac{3}{4}$	$2\frac{1}{4}$	$2\frac{1}{4}$
Concrete brick, block, or tile, except cinder-concrete units	$3\frac{3}{4}$	$3\frac{3}{4}$	$2\frac{1}{4}$	$2\frac{1}{4}$
Hollow or solid cinder-concrete block and tile having a compressive strength of at least 700 lb. per sq. in. of gross area	$2\frac{1}{2}$	2	2	$1\frac{1}{2}$
Solid gypsum block (to obtain 4-hr. rating must be plastered with $\frac{1}{2}$ in. of gypsum plaster)	2	2	$1\frac{1}{2}$	1
Gypsum poured in place and reinforced	2	$1\frac{1}{2}$	$1\frac{1}{2}$	1
Hollow or solid burned clay tile or combinations of tile and concrete	$2\frac{1}{2}$	2	2	$1\frac{1}{2}$
Metal lath and gypsum plaster	$2\frac{1}{2}$	2	$1\frac{1}{2}$	$\frac{7}{8}$
Cement concrete, Grade I *	2	2	$1\frac{1}{2}$	1
Cement concrete, Grade II †	4	3	2	$1\frac{1}{2}$
Cement concrete, Grade II with wire mesh	3	2	2	$1\frac{1}{2}$
Hollow gypsum block (to obtain 4-hr. rating must be plastered with $\frac{1}{2}$ in. of gypsum plaster)	3	3	3	3
Metal lath and vermiculite-gypsum plaster provided that, to obtain a 4-hour rating for columns, a backfill of loose vermiculite shall be employed. For the 3- and 2-hour ratings for floors, the thickness may be $\frac{3}{4}$ in. Thickness shown includes finish coat of plaster.	1	1	$\frac{7}{8}$	$\frac{3}{4}$

* Grade I concrete has aggregate consisting of limestone, traprock, blast-furnace slag, cinders, calcareous gravel.

† Grade II concrete has aggregate consisting of granite or siliceous gravel.

steel members with fire-resistant materials. According to the 1955 Building Code of New York City, the thicknesses of fire-resistive materials, exclusive of air spaces, required to give various fire-resistive ratings are given in Table 48-1.

Methods used in protecting structural steel against the action of fire are shown in Fig. 48-12.

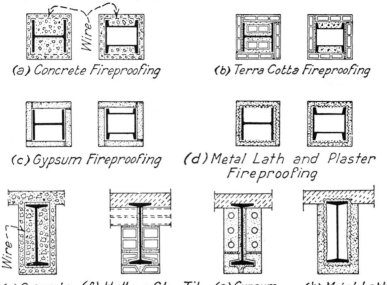

(a) Concrete Fireproofing   (b) Terra Cotta Fireproofing

(c) Gypsum Fireproofing   (d) Metal Lath and Plaster Fireproofing

(e) Concrete   (f) Hollow Clay Tile   (g) Gypsum   (h) Metal Lath and Plaster

Fig. 48-12. Fire protection for steel members.

References

1. *Steel Construction,* American Institute of Steel Construction.
2. *Specifications for the Design, Fabrication and Erection of Structural Steel for Buildings,* American Institute of Steel Construction.
3. *Structural Shop Drafting,* American Institute of Steel Construction, 1950.
4. *Procedure Handbook of Arc Welding Design and Practice,* Lincoln Electric Company, 1957.
5. "Steel Trussed Arches Span 360 ft. in Hangar," *Engineering News-Record,* August 9, 1956, p. 36.
6. Arsham Amirikian, "Navy Builds 300-Ft. Welded Arch Hangar," *Engineering News-Record,* January 26, 1950, p. 24.
7. "Long Steel Arches for Hangars Erected Fast," *Engineering News-Record,* May 25, 1950, p. 40.
8. M. Schupack, "Cable-Supported Roof Cuts Cost," *Civil Engineering,* April, 1958, p. 52.
9. "Prestressing Stabilizes Unusual Cable Roof," *Engineering News-Record,* April 28, 1960, p. 36.
10. "U. S. Pavillion at Brussels Features Cable Supported Roof," *Civil Engineering,* July, 1955, p. 95.

11. Boyd Anderson, "Planning Hangars for Jet Aircraft," *Civil Engineering,* May, 1959, p. 57.
12. "Cable Supported Roof for Olympic Arena," *Civil Engineering,* September, 1959, p. 47.
13. W. E. Simpson, "Cable-Suspended Roof for San Antonio Assembly Building," *Civil Engineering,* November, 1960, p. 63.
14. Howard Seymour, "Suspension Structures," *Architectural Record,* September, 1960.
15. Edward C. Kurt, "Steel Frame Dome Spans Arena," *Engineering News-Record,* May 10, 1962, p. 39.
16. *Suspension Bridge Technological Data,* John A. Roebling's Sons Division, Colorado Fuel and Iron Corp., Trenton, N. J., p. 1.
17. "Record-Span Dome Roofs Air-Conditioned Stadium," *Engineering News-Record,* February 27, 1964.

8 Cast-in-place reinforced concrete construction

49. INTRODUCTION

Classification of Concrete. This chapter is devoted to *cast-in-place* concrete which, as its name implies, is cast in the position it is to occupy permanently, in contrast to *precast concrete*, which is cast in some position other than the one it will finally occupy. *Prestressed concrete* is reinforced concrete in which the reinforcement has been stressed, before the concrete is loaded, to partially counteract the stresses produced by the applied loads. Since most prestressed concrete is precast, precast and prestressed concrete are considered together in Chapter 9.

Concrete without reinforcement, or with only enough reinforcement to provide for shrinkage and temperature changes, is classed as *plain concrete* and included under the general classification of *masonry* as considered in Art. 29. *Reinforced concrete* is concrete into which enough reinforcement is introduced to act effectively with the concrete in resisting forces.

The materials and methods used in making and placing concrete are considered in Art. 11.

Reinforcement. Concrete has a low tensile strength, and therefore is not an effective material for use, without reinforcement, for constructing members subjected to loads that tend to cause them to bend, as will be explained later. In addition, longitudinal rods are provided in columns to reduce the size, or cross-sectional area, required to carry a given load, an area of steel being many times more effective in resisting compressive stresses than the same area of concrete. The usual type of reinforcement is steel rods or bars. Several grades of steel are used for making reinforcing bars, but the most common

Table 49-1

Stock Sizes of Reinforcing Bars
All bars are deformed except No. 2

Bar Number	Nominal Diameter	Bar Number	Nominal Diameter
2	$\frac{1}{2}$ in.	7	$\frac{7}{8}$ in.
3	$\frac{3}{8}$ in.	8	1 in.
4	$\frac{1}{2}$ in.	9	1.128 ($1\frac{1}{8}$) in.
5	$\frac{5}{8}$ in.	10	1.270 ($1\frac{1}{4}$) in.
6	$\frac{3}{4}$ in.	11	1.410 ($1\frac{3}{8}$) in.

Diameters in parentheses are approximate. Bar number equals number of whole one-eighth increments included in its nominal diameter. Larger bars are available on special order.

is an intermediate grade which can be cut and bent easily. To be most effective, the bond between the bars and the concrete must be strong. This objective is accomplished by using, instead of plain bars, round bars whose surface has been deformed in rolling, with the deformations spaced uniformly along the bars, following patterns that tests have shown to be the most effective. The forms of such patterns are controlled by specifications. Most reinforcing bars are of this type, but deformed bars are not available with diameters less than $\frac{3}{8}$ in.

The available sizes of deformed bars have nominal diameters varying by $\frac{1}{8}$-in. increments from $\frac{3}{8}$ in. to about $1\frac{3}{8}$ in. Each diameter of bar is designated by a number, the number being equal to the number of $\frac{1}{8}$-in. increments included in the diameter. For example, a No. 7 bar is $\frac{7}{8}$ in. in diameter.

Reinforcing is also available in the form of welded wire fabric with a rectangular mesh, consisting of cold-drawn longitudinal or carrying wires and usually smaller transverse wires or ties, the two sets of wires being connected at the intersections by welds. The spacing of the longitudinal wires varies from 2 in. to 6 in., and that of the transverse wires from 8 in. to 16 in. Various combinations of wire sizes and spacings are available, as are other less common types.

Concrete. The composition of concrete and its mixing and placing are considered in Art. 11

Code Requirements. The *Building Code Requirements for Reinforced Concrete,* prepared by the American Concrete Institute (1) and adopted by that organization and the American Standards Association, have been included in many building codes and represent the best practice in this country. Specific comments about design, in this chapter, are based chiefly on these requirements.

50. REINFORCED CONCRETE COLUMNS

Types of Columns. Columns constructed of concrete without reinforcing would be unreliable and would be cracked easily by bending stresses caused by differential settlement, temperature changes, unbalanced loads on the surrounding floors, etc. Consequently they are not used except where the least width is large in comparison with the length, when they would be classed as *piers* rather than as columns. Longitudinal bars are placed near the outside surface of concrete columns to provide resistance to bending but, since the principal load on columns causes compressive stresses, the longitudinal bars if used alone would tend to kick out or buckle and spall off the surrounding concrete. To avoid this, circumferential or lateral reinforcement is used in the form of *ties* spaced 8 to 12 in. apart (Fig. 50-1a) or in the form of closely spaced *hoops.*

Because of the difficulty of making individual hoops, a single rod is bent into the form of a helix (b) and acts in the same manner as individual hoops. It is called a *spiral hoop* or simply a *spiral,* although it is really a helix. Columns with ties are called *tied columns,* and those with spiral hoops, although usually called *spirally reinforced columns,* are sometimes referred to as *hooped columns.* The spiral reinforcement serves another purpose. By confining the concrete *core* within the spiral, it prevents sudden and complete collapse of the column and therefore makes it more dependable. Since ties are not as effective as spirals, the allowable load on a tied column is taken as 80 per cent of the allowable load on a spirally reinforced column with the same area and longitudinal reinforcement.

Other types of columns composed largely of concrete are the composite column and the combination column. A *composite column* is one in which a steel or cast-iron structural member is completely encased in concrete containing spiral and longitudinal reinforcement (Fig. 50-1l and m). A *combination column* is one in which a structural steel member, designed to carry the principal part of the load, is wrapped with welded wire mesh and encased in concrete of quality

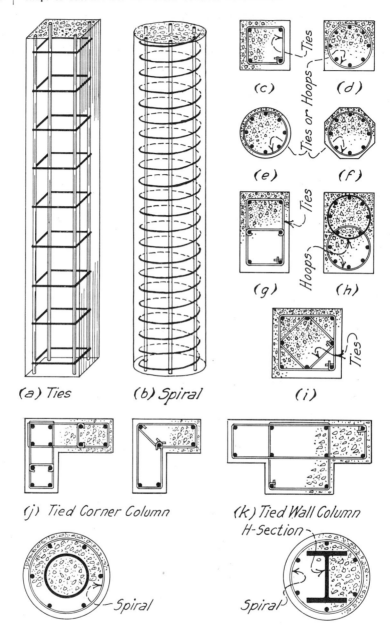

(a) Ties   (b) Spiral   (c)   (d)   (e)   (f)   (g)   Hoops   (h)   Ties   (i)

Ties or Hoops   Ties

(j) Tied Corner Column   (k) Tied Wall Column

(l) Composite Column-Cast-Iron Core   (m) Composite Column-Steel Core

H-Section   Spiral

Spiral

Fig. 50-1. Reinforced concrete columns.

that permits some additional load. This type of column resembles the composite column shown in Fig. 50-1*l*. Another type of combination column is the *pipe column*, which consists of a steel pipe filled with concrete.

The load on a column is considered to be distributed between the concrete and the vertical reinforcement, structural steel, steel pipe, or cast iron included in the column in accordance with specified relationships. Some of the specific requirements for the various types of columns are considered in the following paragraphs.

Spirally Reinforced Columns. This type of column is illustrated in Fig. 50-1*b*, *d*, *e*, and *f*. The cross-sectional area of the vertical reinforcement must not be less than 1 per cent nor more than 8 per cent of the overall or gross cross-sectional area of the column. Reinforcement must consist of at least six No. 5 bars.

The clear spacing between bars must not be less than $1\frac{1}{2}$ in. or $1\frac{1}{2}$ times the maximum size of the coarse aggregate used. The regulations state the minimum permissible amount of spiral reinforcement, and they require the minimum diameter of spiral rods to be $\frac{1}{4}$ in. The maximum permissible center-to-center spacing of spirals is one-sixth of the core diameter, the maximum clear spacing between spirals is 3 in., and the minimum is $1\frac{3}{8}$ in. or $1\frac{1}{2}$ times the maximum size of the coarse aggregate used. The spiral reinforcement must be protected everywhere by a covering of concrete, cast monolithically with the core, whose thickness is not less than $1\frac{1}{2}$ in. nor $1\frac{1}{2}$ times the maximum size of the coarse aggregate nor less than that required by the fire protection and weathering provisions

Tied Columns. This type of column is illustrated in Fig. 50-1*a*, *c*, *d*, *e*, *f*, and *i*. The maximum allowable axial load on columns reinforced with longitudinal bars and separate lateral ties is 80 per cent of such a load on a spirally reinforced column which is identical to it except for the difference in lateral reinforcement. The cross-sectional area of the vertical reinforcement must not be less than 1 per cent nor more than 4 per cent of the overall or gross cross-sectional area of the column. This reinforcement must consist of at least four No. 5 bars. The spacing requirements for vertical reinforcement are the same as for spirally reinforced columns. Lateral ties must be at least $\frac{1}{4}$ in. in diameter and must be spaced apart not more than 16 bar diameters, 48 tie diameters, or the least dimension of the column. When there are more than four vertical bars, additional ties must be provided so that every bar is held firmly to its designated position.

Composite Columns. This type of column is illustrated in Fig. 50-1*l* and *m*. The cross-sectional area of the metal core of a composite column must not exceed 20 per cent of the gross area of the column. If a hollow metal core is used, it should be filled with concrete. The amounts of longitudinal and spiral reinforcement and the requirements for spacing of bars and thickness of protective shell outside the spiral must conform to the limiting values specified for spirally reinforced columns. A clearance of at least 3 in. must be maintained between the spiral and the metal core at all points, except that when a structural steel H-column is used this clearance may be reduced to 2 in.

Metal cores must be accurately milled at splices, and positive provision must be made to maintain alignment. Many requirements are included to insure the unified action of the concrete, the metal core, and the reinforcement included in the column. The metal core must be designed to carry safely any construction or other loads to be placed upon them prior to their encasement in concrete.

Combination Columns. A combination column which includes a structural steel column must provide a concrete encasement at least 2½ in. thick over all metal parts except rivet heads. It must be reinforced by the equivalent of welded wire mesh having wires of No. 10 ASSW gage (diameter 0.135 in.), the wires encircling the column being spaced not more than 4 in. apart and those parallel to the column axis not more than 8 in. apart. The mesh must extend entirely around the column at a distance of one inch inside the outer concrete surface and must be lap-spliced at least 40 wire diameters and wired at the splice. The steel column is designed to carry any construction or other loads to be placed upon it before its encasement in concrete. This type of column has a cross section similar to Fig. 50-1*m* but has different reinforcement. Columns like it are used occasionally in the lower stories of reinforced concrete buildings to reduce the required column size.

The other form of combination column consists of a steel pipe filled with concrete.

Irregular Sections. Column cross sections are usually square, circular, or octagonal. Conditions may make it desirable, however, to use columns with other cross sections, such as the section in Fig. 50-1*h* with interlocking spirals, and the sections in *g*, *j*, and *k* with ties arranged to support the longitudinal rods, following the requirements stated in the paragraph on tied columns. The longitudinal rod in the middle of each side of the square section in *i* is supported in this manner.

Minimum Dimension. Principal columns in buildings must have a diameter of at least 12 in. for circular columns, a thickness of at least 8 in. for rectangular columns, and a gross area of at least 96 sq. in. for any shape of cross section. Auxiliary supports that are not continuous from story to story must have a diameter or thickness of at least 6 in.

51. REINFORCED CONCRETE BEAMS AND GIRDERS

Concrete is strong in compression but weak in tension. If steel rods are placed in the concrete on the tensile side of a beam (Fig. 51-1*a*), they will carry the tensile stresses and a very efficient form of beam will result. A sufficient amount of steel reinforcement is usually used to make the beam as strong in tension as it is in compression.

The simplest form of beam is rectangular in section (*b*), but since the concrete on the tensile side of the beam is not considered to carry any stress, some of this concrete may be left out of wide beams, leaving only enough to carry the steel rods and to provide for the shearing stresses. This forms the T-beam shown in *c*. The outline of the corresponding rectangular beam is shown by the dotted lines. Usually some of the concrete on the compressive side near the neutral axis is also omitted (*d*). By referring to Fig. 33-1*e* (page 302) it may be seen that the stress carried by this material is small so that the strength of the beam is reduced only slightly by its omission.

Sometimes the size of a beam is limited, and it is necessary to design a beam of given strength to fit into a space which is smaller than would be required for an ordinary rectangular or T-beam. The tensile strength may be secured by providing the required amount of tensile reinforcement, but the amount of concrete available for compression is limited by the space to be occupied. The additional compressive strength necessary is secured by placing steel bars on the compression side of the beam, forming a double-reinforced rectangular beam (Fig. 51-1*e*). A given amount of steel is about fifteen times as effective in compression as the same amount of concrete. Because of relative costs, however, it is more economical to use concrete to carry compressive stresses than it is to use steel.

So far only tensile and compressive stresses have been considered, but it is necessary to provide for shearing stresses also. These stresses combined with the tensile stresses cause *diagonal tension stresses,* which tend to cause diagonal cracks near the ends of a beam (*f*). Where these stresses are large, it is necessary to provide reinforcement

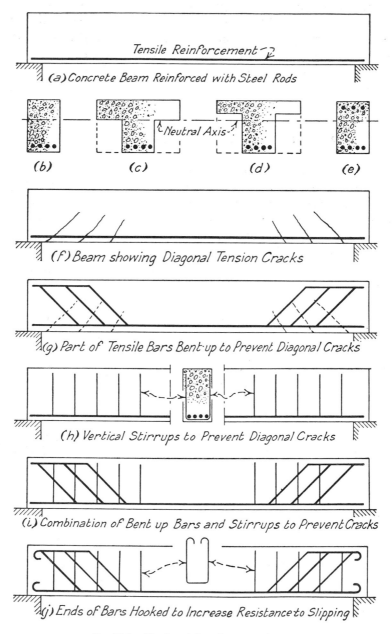

(a) Concrete Beam Reinforced with Steel Rods

(b) (c) (d) (e)

(f) Beam showing Diagonal Tension Cracks

(g) Part of Tensile Bars Bent up to Prevent Diagonal Cracks

(h) Vertical Stirrups to Prevent Diagonal Cracks

(i) Combination of Bent up Bars and Stirrups to Prevent Cracks

(j) Ends of Bars Hooked to Increase Resistance to Slipping

Fig. 51-1. Simple reinforced concrete beams.

to prevent cracks. Reinforcement may be provided by bending up a part of the tensile reinforcement (*g*), or by providing vertical U-shaped members passing around the tensile steel (*h*). These members are called *stirrups* and should not be spaced farther apart than one-half the depth of the beam. Various other forms of stirrups may be used. In rectangular beams reinforced for compression, stirrups have the additional function of holding the compressive steel in position and overcoming the tendency of these bars to kick out. Here the stirrups have an action similar to the ties or hoops in columns. Usually a combination of bent-up bars and stirrups is used (*i*). The ends of stirrups should usually be hooked to increase their resistance to slipping. In beams reinforced for compression, they are bent around the compressive steel. Steel reinforcement does not prevent the formation of cracks on the tensile side of a beam, but if the steel is not overstressed the cracks are very small and are not objectionable.

Still another form of stress which must be provided for is *bond stress*. Bond stresses are caused by the tendency of the steel to slip in the concrete when a beam is loaded. This is frequently a serious matter. To increase the bond strength, deformed bars may be used. They are usually adequate. The resistance to slipping may be increased by *end anchorage* or by hooking the ends of bars (*j*).

The reinforcement in continuous beams must be arranged differently from that in simple beams. If reinforcement were provided at the bottom of the beam only, it is evident that the beam would crack over the intermediate supports (Fig. 51-2*a*), owing to the tensile stresses in the upper part of the beam at those points; and if the ends are continuous over columns, cracks will develop on top, at or near the columns. To prevent these cracks it is necessary to provide steel near the top surface in the parts of the beam near the supports (*b*). Instead of using separate bars at the top, it is more convenient to bend up some of the bars from the bottom where they are no longer needed (*c*). At least one-fourth of the bars in the bottom should be left at the bottom except, in end spans, this proportion should be one-third. Usually the splices in the bars are made over the supports and the bars are arranged as shown in *d*, but not necessarily separated vertically. The ends of plain tensile bars are hooked to increase their resistance to slipping. Hooks are usually not required on deformed bars. The inclined portions of the bent-up bars are effective in resisting diagonal tension stresses and are utilized for that purpose, but it is usually necessary to use stirrups to take care of the parts of the beam where shear reinforcement is necessary which are not provided

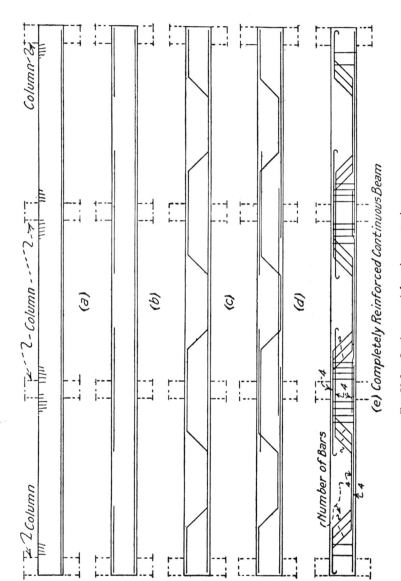

Fig. 51-2. Continuous reinforced concrete beams.

for by bent-up bars. It is desirable to bend up bars at more than one point at each end of each beam as shown in *e*. This figure illustrates a completely reinforced concrete beam built monolithic with the supporting columns. The columns must be reinforced to resist any bending stresses introduced by the beams or from other causes.

In building construction, floor slabs are usually cast monolithic with the beams and girders, as shown in Fig. 52-1*c*. This slab is effective in carrying compressive flexural stresses when such stresses occur in the upper part of the beam, but near the supports the compressive stresses are in the lower part of the beam and the floor slab is not effective in this capacity. At these points the bars which run straight through near the bottom of the beam are utilized to carry a part of the compressive stresses. Continuous beams which are cast monolithic with the floor slabs are therefore T-beams in the central part of the span and double-reinforced rectangular beams over the supports. See Art. 52 for further discussion.

52. REINFORCED CONCRETE SLABS

Ordinary Slabs. Reinforced concrete slabs may be considered wide shallow beams. They are used as floors and roofs of buildings with masonry bearing walls or with reinforced concrete or steel frames. Sometimes, they are supported by timber beams.

The simplest example is that of separate slabs simply supported on steel beams (Fig. 52-1*a*), but this type of construction is not common. Usually the slabs are continuous over the beams (*b*). It is necessary to provide steel near the top of the slabs over the beams, because the tensile stresses are on that side at this point. This may be provided by bending up some of the steel from the bottom of the slab or by short bars over the supports. Although no tensile stresses exist at the bottom of the slab over the supports, it is desirable to run at least one-fourth of the bottom steel straight through. The amount of steel required at the top of the slab over the beams is usually about equal to the amount required at the bottom in the center of the span. In buildings classed as *fire-resistive,* it is necessary to protect the steel beams by surrounding them with concrete (*c*). Effective protection is provided by metal lath and pearlite or vermiculite plaster as shown. See Table 48-1.

Reinforced concrete slabs are commonly constructed monolithic with reinforced concrete beams and girders (*c*). In this case, the slab serves the double function of spanning the space between the beams

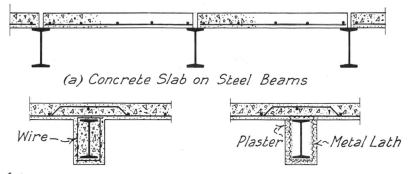

(a) Concrete Slab on Steel Beams

Wire—

Plaster

~Metal Lath

(b) Method for Fireproofing Steel Beams with Concrete

(c) Concrete Slab on Concrete Beams

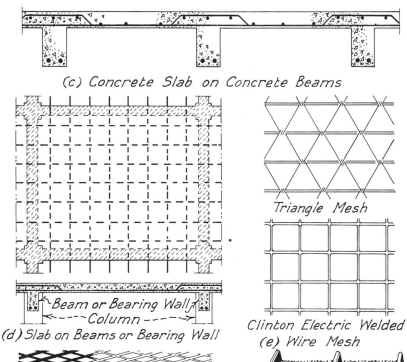

Beam or Bearing Wall

Column

(d) Slab on Beams or Bearing Wall

Triangle Mesh

Clinton Electric Welded
(e) Wire Mesh

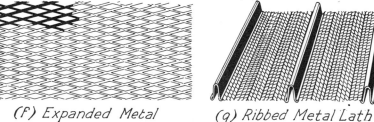

(f) Expanded Metal

(g) Ribbed Metal Lath

Fig. 52-1. Reinforced concrete slabs.

and acting as the flange of the T-beams which support it. The slabs are continuous over the beams and require tensile steel near the top over the beams. Specifications commonly permit the portion of the slab extending eight times its thickness each side of the beam to be considered as the flange of the T-beam. The total width of the slab so considered, however, cannot be greater than the distance center to center of the beams or greater than one-fourth the span of the beams. It is sometimes possible and desirable to support a slab on four sides by means of beams or bearing walls (d).

The principal reinforcement for slabs will, of course, run perpendicular to the supporting members, but it is necessary to provide a small amount of reinforcement parallel to the supports to prevent cracks produced by temperature changes and shrinkage and to assist in the lateral distribution of concentrated loads. The reinforcement usually consists of bars, but light slabs may be reinforced with some form of wire mesh (e), or expanded metal lath (f). The ribbed metal lath shown in g is used on light slabs poured without the usual forms, the ribs being sufficiently rigid to span the distance between supports and the mesh being so fine that the concrete will not run through but can form a substantial grip on the mesh.

Flat-Slab Construction. The ACI regulations define a *flat slab* as a concrete slab reinforced in two or more directions, generally without beams or girders to transfer the loads to the supporting members. The supporting members referred to in this definition are usually columns. To assist in transferring the loads on the flat slabs to the supporting columns, the upper portion of each column may be enlarged to form a *column capital* (Fig. 52-2). To strengthen the portion of the slab immediately surrounding each column or column capital so that it may better resist the stresses which become intensified in this region, the slab may be thickened in this area by adding to its bottom side to form a *drop panel* (Fig. 52-2), which is cast monolithically with the remainder of the slab. Flat-slab construction is suitable for panels which are approximately square. The reinforcement is usually arranged in the two directions parallel to the sides of the panel. Slabs reinforced in this manner are called *two-way flat slabs.*

For purposes of design, a two-way flat slab is considered to consist of strips in each direction as follows.

A *middle strip,* one-half panel in width, symmetrical about the center line of the panel.

A *column strip* consisting of two adjacent quarter panels on either side of the column center line.

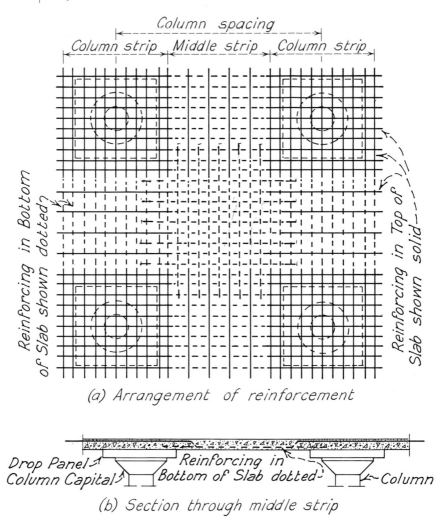

(a) Arrangement of reinforcement

(b) Section through middle strip

Fig. 52-2. Two-way flat-slab construction.

These strips are indicated on Fig. 52-2. The size and spacing of the longitudinal reinforcing bars in each strip are usually made constant. The bars are located near the bottoms or the tops of the strips about as shown in Fig. 52-2 in order to resist the tensile stresses caused by the loads.

The minimum permissible thickness of slabs with drop panels is one-fortieth of the longest span but not less than 4 in. The side of a drop panel must be at least one-third the parallel span. The maximum effective central angle of a column capital is 90 degrees. The minimum permissible column diameter is 10 in. The bottom portion of flat slabs may include recesses or pockets formed by permanent or removable fillers between reinforcing bars, as described later and illustrated in Fig. 52-5*f*. Many other factors are considered in the regulations.

Flat-slab construction such as has been described is used extensively for warehouses and industrial buildings with heavy floor loads. It is not desirable for buildings whose floor areas are to be subdivided by partitions because of the interference of column capitals and drop panels.

Flat-Plate Construction. For lighter floor loads such as those in office buildings, apartment houses, hotels, and dormitories, flat slabs may be designed without column capitals or drop panels (Fig. 52-3*a*). This is called *flat-plate construction* and is used extensively because it gives a flat uninterrupted ceiling, well suited to subdivision. For the

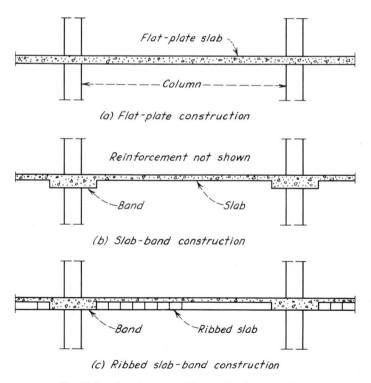

(a) Flat-plate construction

(b) Slab-band construction

(c) Ribbed slab-band construction

Fig. 52-3. Flat-plate and slab-band floor construction.

same clear ceiling height, flat-plate construction results in a lower story height than other forms of floor construction. Such slabs are designed in accordance with flat-slab principles. The shearing stresses in the portions of slabs close to and surrounding the columns limit the loads for which this type of construction is feasible. The slab thickness required depends upon the column spacing, the loading, and the allowable stresses, and varies from about 6 to 10 in.

Slab-Band Construction. *Slab-band construction* consists of wide shallow beams, called *bands,* running continuously along each longitudinal row of columns and supporting one-way slabs spanning the space between bands and cast monolithically with them (Fig. 52-3b). If desired, the space under the bands may be devoted to closets, washrooms, etc., locating the principal rooms under the slabs to achieve flat ceilings. To accomplish this objective, the band is sometimes located off center with the columns. A column may also be set somewhat off center from the other columns in a row. Columns located in partitions may be rectangular in cross section, with a width equal to the width of the band and a thickness sometimes as small as 8 in. The slab thickness depends upon the column spacing, the band width, the loading, and the allowable stresses, and varies from about 5 to 8 in.

A combination of ribbed slabs, described in the following paragraph, and slab-band construction (Fig. 52-3c) may be used to form a flat ceiling. This type of construction is adaptable to longer spans and heavier loads than would be possible with flat-plate construction.

Ribbed Slabs. In reinforced concrete beams and slabs the concrete between the neutral axis and the tension face is not contributing to the flexural strength, but it is effective in resisting a part of the shearing stresses, as explained in Art. 51. The shearing stresses in slabs are usually low, and therefore all this concrete is not necessary. To save concrete and to reduce the weight of the slab, a large part of the concrete on the lower side of the slab is eliminated, leaving only the ribs or joists (Fig. 52-4a), the bottom of the corresponding solid slab being at the bottom of the ribs. These ribs are made wide enough to resist the shearing stresses and to carry the necessary tensile steel, practically the same amount as required for the solid slab except for the saving in steel due to the reduction of the dead load. The remaining flange may extend down to the neutral axis, but usually it does not. This results in a reduction in the compressive resistance, but this is small because the concrete near the neutral axis carries very little stress, as has been explained. The solid slab would be reinforced with relatively small bars closely spaced, but in the ribbed slab two

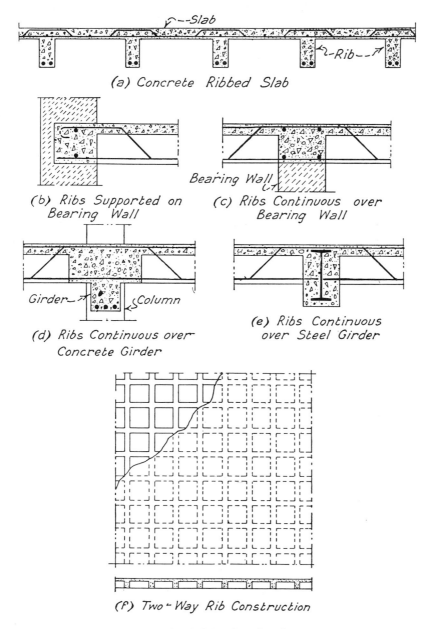

(a) Concrete Ribbed Slab

(b) Ribs Supported on Bearing Wall

(c) Ribs Continuous over Bearing Wall

(d) Ribs Continuous over Concrete Girder

(e) Ribs Continuous over Steel Girder

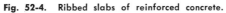

(f) Two-Way Rib Construction

Fig. 52-4. Ribbed slabs of reinforced concrete.

larger bars are ordinarily used in each joist. This results in increased bond stresses, but such stresses are not often a controlling factor. Some conditions require solid bridging between joists, spaced not more than 15 ft. apart, for some types of joist floors. This bridging is commonly 4 in. wide and the full depth of the joists. It is reinforced with one rod near the top and one near the bottom. The function of such bridging is primarily to distribute heavy loads such as those produced by partitions, safes, bookcases, etc., over several joists. The minimum width of joists is 4 in., and the depth below the bottom of the slab is sometimes limited to three times the width. The clear spacing between the joists is limited to 30 in. The thickness of the top slab varies from $1\frac{1}{2}$ to 3 in. depending upon the span and loading.

The detail used where the end of a ribbed slab is supported by a bearing wall is shown in Fig. 52-4b. The details used for slabs continuous over bearing walls, concrete girders, and steel girders are shown in c to e.

Occasionally it may be advantageous to support a slab on four sides and provide ribs in two directions, as shown in f.

Ordinary wood forms would be so expensive for ribbed slabs that their cost would be prohibitive. For this reason, various types of construction have been devised to take the place of such forms. The sides of the joists and the bottom of the slab are formed by structural clay tile, hollow gypsum tile, or sheet-steel cores (Fig. 52-5a to c), or special forms of concrete block. Wood forms are constructed for the bottoms of the joists. These are usually made of 2-in. material and are sufficiently wider than the joists to support the edges of the clay or gypsum tiles or the steel pans. The formwork is therefore very simple.

The clay tile, gypsum tile, and concrete block provide a surface which serves as a plaster base for the ceiling formed by the underside of the slab. Special forms of tile or block cover the bottoms of the joists to provide a uniform plaster base over the whole ceiling. The ends of the end tile may be closed by a thin slab made for that purpose, by using pieces of sheet-metal, wire screen or in some other way.

The sheet-steel cores may be made of heavy material, which will survive being removed after the concrete has set and being used several times. They may also be made of thinner material designed to be left in place. If the removable forms are used, and the ceiling is to be plastered, metal lath is fastened to the underside of the joists to serve as a base for plaster for the ceiling below. Various types of anchors are available for casting in the underside of the joists to receive the metal lath. If the sheet-steel cores are to be left in place, metal lath is laid over the forms before the cores are set. The metal

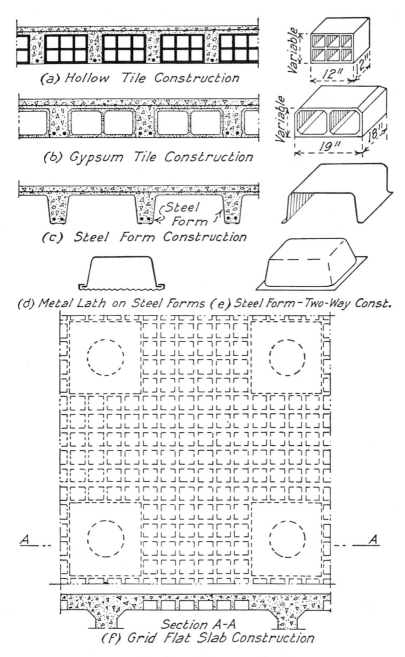

(a) Hollow Tile Construction

(b) Gypsum Tile Construction

(c) Steel Form Construction

(d) Metal Lath on Steel Forms (e) Steel Form – Two-Way Const.

Section A-A
(f) Grid Flat Slab Construction

Fig. 52-5. Cores for ribbed slabs and grid-flat-slab construction.

lath is wired to the reinforcing bars in the joists. In one type of steel core, the lath is fastened to the core as shown in Fig. 52-5d before the core is placed. Sheet-metal closers or end caps are made for the ends of the end cores. It is sometimes necessary to widen the joists at the ends because of excessive shearing stresses. This is accomplished by using tapered cores at the ends of the joists. The most common widths of metal core are 20 and 30 in., used with joist widths of 4, 5, and 6 in. The core depths available vary by 2-in. increments from 6 to 14 in. They are usually corrugated to increase their stiffness and are lapped one or one-half corrugations or more if necessary to provide the exact lengths required. The cores are supported on forms placed under the joists. No forms are necessary between the joists. Removable cores may be used several times. The cost of removing them must be considered, as must the greater cost of placing the lath. The type most suitable for a given case can only be determined by studying all of the factors involved.

For all types of core, the reinforcement in the top slab must be adequate to resist the loads on the slab and to provide for temperature changes and shrinkage of the concrete. It usually consists of $\frac{1}{4}$- or $\frac{3}{8}$-in. rods normal to the joists and spaced from 6 to 12 in., or of wire mesh. No reinforcement is required, however, in the direction parallel with the joists because of the reinforcement in the joists.

Ribbed slabs are suitable for spans varying from 10 to 35 ft. In constructing long-span slabs, consideration should be given to providing camber to offset the deflections caused by elastic deformation and time yield or plastic flow.

Special types of tile and sheet-steel cores are available for two-way construction. A steel core for two-way construction is shown in Fig. 52-5e.

A form of flat-slab construction has been devised to make use of the ribbed slab in place of the flat slab. This is known as the *grid flat slab* and is illustrated in Fig. 52-5f. The reinforcing is not shown in this figure, but would be similar to that used in the two-way system shown in Fig. 52-2 with the rods placed in spaces between the cores.

53. REINFORCED CONCRETE FRAMING

In framing a reinforced concrete building the forms are first constructed, the reinforcing steel is then placed, and finally the concrete is poured, as described in Art. 11. After the concrete has set, the forms are removed. It is obviously impossible to pour an entire building in one operation, and therefore construction joints cannot be avoided. These should be so located and constructed as to impair the strength or appearance of the building as little as possible. The joints in slabs, beams, and girders should be vertical and at the center of the span where the shearing stresses are small. The columns should be poured to the underside of the floor girders for beam and girder construction so that the shrinkage in the concrete of the columns may take place before the floor above is poured.

Forms are usually constructed of wood, but steel forms are quite extensively used, especially for buildings of flat-slab construction. The reinforcing steel is held in position by wiring the bars together at their intersections. The bars for each beam, girder, and column are usually wired together to form a frame which is set in position as a unit. Various devices such as chairs and spacers have been designed to hold reinforcing steel in position.

Reinforced concrete buildings may be of bearing-wall construction or of skeleton construction. The bearing walls may be constructed of brick, stone, structural clay tile, concrete block, plain concrete, or reinforced concrete, described in Chapter 4.

The cross section of a reinforced concrete building with flat-slab construction is shown in Fig. 53-1a and of one with beam and girder construction in b.

Typical details for a building of the beam and girder type are shown in Fig. 53-2. All reinforcing is deformed bars. The features which should be noted in this figure are as follows.

1. The reinforcing in the slab. Reinforcing is provided at the bottom of the slab near the center of the span and at the top where the slab crosses the beams. Some of the bottom steel continues through on the bottom.

2. The reinforcing in the beams is not shown, but it is similar to that in the girders. It consists of horizontal bars in the bottom of the girder and bars bent up from the bottom of the girder at the center to the top in the region near the supporting columns.

3. Shear reinforcing is provided by bent-up bars and vertical stirrups.

4. Spread footings are used. Dowels extend from the footings into the columns. These dowels should be equal in size and in number to the longitudinal bars in the column, since their function is to transfer the stress in the column bars to the footing. They must extend into the column and into the footing a sufficient distance so that their bond stress will not be excessive.

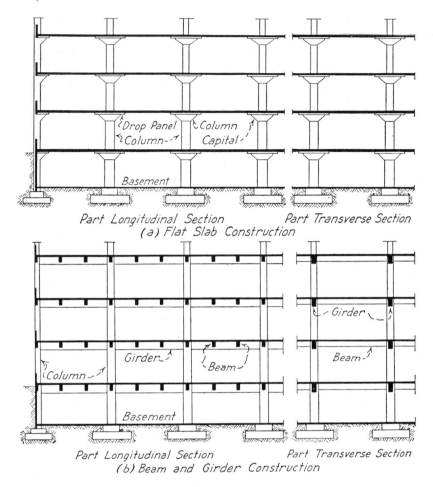

Part Longitudinal Section   Part Transverse Section

(a) Flat Slab Construction

Part Longitudinal Section   Part Transverse Section

(b) Beam and Girder Construction

Fig. 53-1. Types of reinforced concrete framing.

5. The longitudinal bars in the interior columns are arranged around the edge of the columns and are surrounded with closely spaced spiral reinforcing. To avoid confusion all the longitudinal bars are not shown in the elevation, but they are shown in the section.

6. The longitudinal bars of the wall columns are held in position by lateral reinforcement in the form of ties which are not as closely spaced as the spirals of the interior columns. Spirally reinforced columns might have been used.

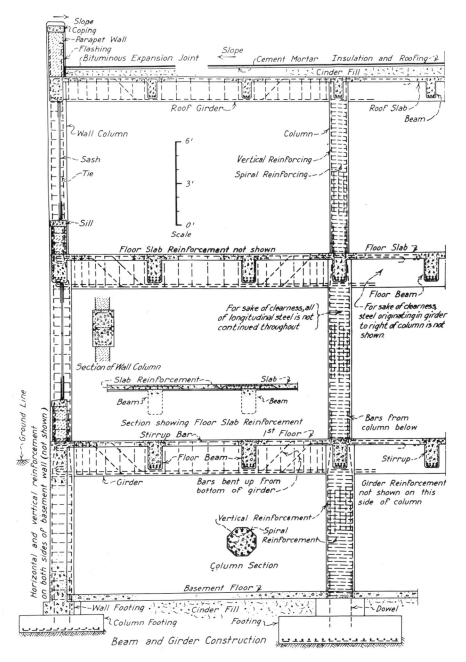

Fig. 53-2. Beam and girder construction.

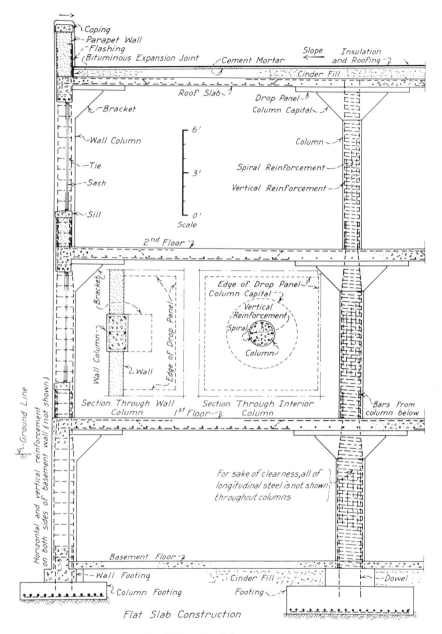

Fig. 53-3. Flat-slab construction.

7. The columns are spliced by running the longitudinal bars from one column upward into the column above. To take care of the smaller size of the upper columns, the bars are bent inward in the part of the column occupied by the floor construction. They are again made vertical after the floor level is passed.

8. The slope of the roof is obtained by a cinder fill with a cement mortar topping to receive the built-up bituminous roofing. The cinder fill also serves as heat insulation. An expansion joint is provided between the filling and the parapet wall so that the topping can expand as it becomes heated. If this provision were not made, the topping would either buckle or push the parapet wall out. Similar expansion joints should be provided at other points in the topping. Some designers object to a cinder fill because, if leaks develop in the roofing, the fill may absorb water and freeze. Under these conditions, the fill may expand and exert a thrust against the parapet walls and cause them to crack. It is usually undesirable to slope the slab for drainage. Good results have been secured with decks which do not slope to drains, because any shallow pools of rainwater which may accumulate do not damage a built-up roof.

9. The panel walls consist of steel sash which occupy the entire width between columns and below which masonry walls are placed.

10. The parapet wall is capped with a coping, the top of which slopes toward the roof so that it will drain toward the roof and not over the face of the building.

Typical details of a building of the flat-slab type are shown in Fig. 53-3. The features which should be noted in this figure are as follows.

1. The substitution of flat-slab construction for the beam and girder construction shown in the previous figure.

2. The drop panels and the column capitals of the interior columns.

3. The brackets and drop panels of the exterior columns.

4. The spiraled interior columns. For the sake of clearness, only a part of the longitudinal bars are shown in the elevation, but they are all shown in the section.

5. The tied wall columns. Since these columns are rectangular, they are provided with intermediate ties. Spirally reinforced columns might have been used.

Other features are the same as the corresponding features of the beam and girder type which have just been explained.

Walls. Reinforced concrete walls are discussed in Art. 29.

Fig. 53-4. Reinforced concrete framed office building. Bank of Georgia Building, Atlanta, Georgia. Tallest reinforced concrete building in the United States with conventional framing. 30 stories and 390 ft. 10 in. high. Architect-Engineer: Wyatt C. Hedrick. General Contractor: Henry C. Beck Co.

Lateral Resistance. The problems involved in designing tall buildings with steel frames to resist the lateral forces caused by wind and earthquake shock were considered in Art. 48. As with steel frame buildings, nonbearing masonry walls and partitions contribute to the lateral rigidity of a reinforced concrete building, but the magnitudes of such contributions are uncertain and they are usually neglected in design. The only resisting elements that are considered are the integral structural parts. Members subject to stresses produced by wind and earthquake forces combined with other loads may be proportioned for unit stresses one-third higher than the allowable stresses for dead and live loads only, but the size of member must not be less than is required for these loads.

The horizontal deflections from lateral loads tend to distort the rectangular partitions constructed between the columns and floor systems and cause them to crack. A similar phenomenon occurs in door and window openings with objectionable results. Therefore, even though a frame may be structurally adequate as far as stresses are concerned, it may not be satisfactory. For that reason, horizontal deflections of a frame as well as stresses must be considered.

A significant factor in determining the special structural requirements for resisting lateral loads of given intensities is the ratio of the height, or the portion of a building above the elevation being considered, to the width, or smallest lateral dimension. Another significant factor is the type of floor construction. Construction with girders framing into the columns and running across the width of a building offer considerable resistance to lateral forces without exceeding allowable stresses in the columns or girders, but construction with flat-plate floors are less effective in this respect.

Usually, tier buildings only a few stories high or the upper few stories of tall buildings do not require special provisions for wind unless they are very narrow in at least one dimension. It will be obvious to experienced designers that under some conditions no special provisions are required, and that under other conditions they are certain to be necessary. Between these two extremes, each case must be given specific consideration.

Tall buildings with long narrow horizontal sections or plans which require special provisions to resist wind loads acting against the broad side of the building do not normally require such provisions to resist the wind load against the narrow side. This condition results from the smaller wind load and the greater lateral strength of the building in the direction parallel to the longer dimension.

When the usual types of construction prove to be inadequate to resist the lateral forces, after the permissible increases have been made in the allowable stresses, a common solution is to include reinforced concrete *shear walls* in some of the vertical bents bounded by continuous columns and the floor systems. These walls are made integral with the structural members by tying them together with reinforcing bars. They are designed to resist the lateral forces on the portions of the building that contribute to the lateral loads they are designed to carry.

A simple arrangement of shear walls to provide transverse rigidity is illustrated in Fig. 53-5a. Pairs of columns in every third row in each story are connected by shear walls to form *wind bents*. To provide for a longitudinal corridor, shear walls are not placed between the two interior columns in each transverse row.

The lateral loads are transmitted horizontally to the wind bents by the floor systems as explained for steel tier buildings in Art. 48. The usual types of reinforced concrete floor systems may prove adequate to transmit these loads, but sometimes special provisions must be made by additional reinforcement or increased sections.

Preferably, shear walls are carried continuously from the foundation to the height above which they are no longer required but, when this is not possible, the lateral loads are transferred horizontally between discontinuous shear walls by the floor systems at the elevations where the discontinuities occur. The vertical loads are transmitted directly downward.

The simple patterns of shear walls illustrated in Fig. 53-5 may be

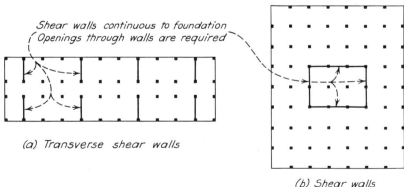

(a) Transverse shear walls

(b) Shear walls around central core

Fig. 53-5. Shear walls.

possible in some buildings but not in others. When it is not possible, shear walls may be located in walls enclosing cores which include elevator shafts and stairwells and in other positions which do not interfere with the desired use of the floor space.

Shear walls vary in thickness from 6 to 12 in. depending upon the prevailing conditions. As has been stated, their function is to resist horizontal shearing forces produced by lateral loads, which in some regions may include earthquake shocks as well as wind. They are not considered to carry any part of the dead and live loads.

Reinforced concrete bearing walls have been used to resist lateral forces in a manner similar to that described for shear walls. Such walls carry the dead and live loads in addition to the lateral loads and, for that reason, must be thicker than shear walls. Under usual conditions, such construction is not economical.

Another means of increasing lateral rigidity and strength is to use rectangular columns with their long dimensions parallel with the short dimension of the plan and with deep floor girders framing into them.

Under any conditions, the provisions to resist lateral forces must be such that the resultant resistance at any elevation is colinear with the resultant lateral force at that elevation. Otherwise, the building tends to twist.

As has been stated, lateral resistance is often provided by a rectangular core bounded by shear walls. In each building of the twin Marina City Towers in Chicago (Figs. 53-6, 53-7, and 53-8), a cylindrical reinforced concrete core is provided to resist lateral forces. Each core is 64 stories and 588 ft. high above the circular reinforced concrete pad or mat on which it bears. The internal diameter of core is 32 ft. for its entire height. The thickness of the core walls varies from 30 in. at the bottom to 15 in. at the top, the changes in thickness taking place in steps.

The diameter of each foundation mat is 58 ft. In the original design the thickness of each mat was 3 ft. but, because of construction difficulties, one mat was made 6 ft. thick. Each mat is supported on two concentric rings of piers extending about 115 ft. through soil and hardpan to rock. The inner ring includes 8 piers located directly beneath the core wall, and the outer ring includes 16 piers, each directly beneath a column located as will be described, and illustrated in Fig. 53-8.

The structure surrounding the core has a height of 60 stories. It is supported primarily on two rings of 16 columns each with their centers located on circles concentric with the core. One ring has a radius of 23 ft. 6 in., and the other of 54 ft. 8 in. The inner ring of columns

Fig. 53-6. Model of Marina Towers in Chicago. Architects and engineers, Bertrand Goldberg and Associates. Consulting Engineers, Severud-Elstad-Krueger Associates. Foundation Consultants, Moran, Mueser and Rutledge and R. B. Peck. Sponsors, Building Service Employees International Union.

Fig. 53-7. Marina Towers in Chicago during construction.

bears on the mat, as has been stated, and each column in the outer ring is supported on a foundation pier extending to rock. Each pier in the outer ring is anchored to the mat by a radial tie beam, and the piers are tied together by circumferential beams.

The upper portion of each pier is reinforced with vertical bars. Some of the piers are reinforced throughout their entire depth. A 6-ft. square steel bearing plate 2 in. thick is placed on top of each pier in

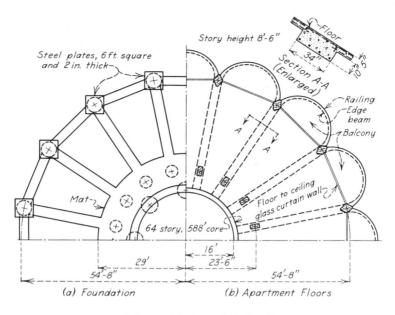

Fig. 53-8. Partial plans of Marina Towers.

the outer ring to facilitate the transfer of the column load to the caisson. The top ends of the reinforcing bars in the pier are welded to the bottom of the plate, and the bottom ends of the reinforcing bars in the column are welded to the top of the plate. Full bearing is assured by placing the concrete in the top of the pier through a hopper extending through a hole in the center of the plate in such a manner as to provide hydrostatic head.

The lower 4 stories of each building are occupied by shops and services, the upper 16 stories by helical ramps providing parking spaces for 448 cars, the next 40 stories by 448 apartments of varying sizes, and the upper 4 of the 64 stories in the core house the elevator machinery, air conditioning equipment, and other mechanical equipment. The elevators, stairways, and various other services are located in the core. At each floor level a corridor surrounds the core.

The core walls, columns, and foundations are of ordinary stone concrete. The ramps and the floors of the apartments are lightweight concrete slabs integral with wide shallow beams radiating outward from the core and over the columns in the two rings (Fig. 55-8). The parking ramps occupy the space between the core and the outer row of columns, and cantilever out 9 ft. 2 in. beyond their centers. On the apartment floors, a semicircular balcony cantilevers out in each bay beyond the columns in the outer row. The apartments are enclosed between exterior columns with floor-to-ceiling glass curtain walls which include sliding glass doors to give access to the balconies. The balconies are open except for railings.

The maximum height of the parapet wall above a street level is 581 ft. In 1963, when these buildings were completed, they were the highest reinforced concrete buildings in the United States. References 10 and 11.

Expansion Joints. The following material on expansion joints is quoted from the Joint Committee Report (6).

a. Expansion joints are expensive and in some cases difficult to maintain. They are, therefore, to be avoided if possible. In relatively short buildings, expansion and contraction can be provided for by additional reinforcement. No arbitrary spacing for joints in long buildings can be generally applicable. In heated buildings joints can be spaced farther apart than in unheated buildings. Also, where the outside walls are of brick or of stone ashlar backed with brick, or where otherwise insulated, the joints can be farther apart than with exterior walls of lower insulating value.

b. In localities with large temperature ranges, the spacing of joints for the most severe conditions of exposure (uninsulated walls and unheated buildings) should not exceed 200 ft. Under favorable conditions buildings 400 to 500 ft. long have been built without joints even in localities with large temperature ranges.

c. In localities with small temperature ranges, the spacing of joints for unheated buildings or with uninsulated walls should not exceed 300 ft. In such localities buildings up to 700 ft. long have been successfully built without joints where other conditions were favorable.

d. In roof construction, provision for expansion is an important factor. The joints in the roof may be required at more frequent intervals than in the other portions of the building because of more severe exposure. In some cases expansion joints spaced 100 ft. apart have been provided in roofs and not in walls or floors.

e. Joints should be located at junctions in L-, T-, or U-shaped buildings and at points where the building is weakened by large openings in the floor construction, such as at light wells, stairs, or elevators. Joints should provide for a complete separation from the top of the footings to the roof, preferably by separate columns and girders.

Maximum Heights. The tallest tier buildings in the world have structural steel frames. The Empire State Building with its height of 85 stories and 1245 ft., excluding the broadcasting tower, has held the record as the tallest building in the world since its completion in 1931.

During the period since World War II, buildings with reinforced-concrete framing have steadily increased in height. The tallest buildings of that type in the United States in 1962 were the twin Marina City apartment buildings in Chicago, with a height of 60 stories and

581 ft. (2). Because of relative cost conditions in some other countries favoring concrete over steel for tall buildings, the tallest concrete buildings are located in other countries. In 1962, the height record was held by a 58-story 614-ft. office and apartment building in Caracus, Venezuela.

54. REINFORCED CONCRETE RIGID FRAMES, ARCHES, AND DOMES

(See also Article 55.)

Rigid Frames. A single-span two-hinged rigid frame is shown in Fig. 54-1. The structure is supported on spread footings with a tie rod under the floor to carry the outward horizontal components of the thrusts on the footings. The roof deck consists of wood plank sheathing supported by reinforced concrete purlins. These are haunched at the ends to improve the lateral support they provide for the frame. The exterior walls are constructed of concrete reinforced for temperature changes and shrinkage and supported by the frame. Concrete slabs might have been used instead of the wood roof sheathing shown in the figure.

Usually, rigid frames can be constructed more economically by precasting rather than casting in place. Rigid frames of that type are considered in Art. 61.

Arches. Long-span reinforced concrete arches have been used extensively to support the roofs of hangars, auditoriums, field houses and other structures requiring unobstructed floor areas.

The cross section of a reinforced concrete thin-shell arched roof with stiffening and carrying ribs supported on cantilever abutments for the War Memorial of Onondaga County in Syracuse, New York, is shown in Fig. 54-2. The span of the arch rib is 160 ft., and the cantilever projection on the abutments is 27 ft. The structure includes twelve identical bays spaced 19½ ft. center to center and arranged in pairs with the dimensions as shown in the figure. Each alternate rib is divided into two half-ribs separated by cane fiber insulation board. This joint provides for expansion and contraction produced by temperature changes and serves as a construction joint which enables two bays to be poured in one operation. Since the arch bays are identical, the same forms were used to cast the six pairs of bays. They were so arranged that they could be moved easily from bay to bay. The cantilever abutments were cast about a month in advance of the arches to enable them to gain sufficient strength to support the arches.

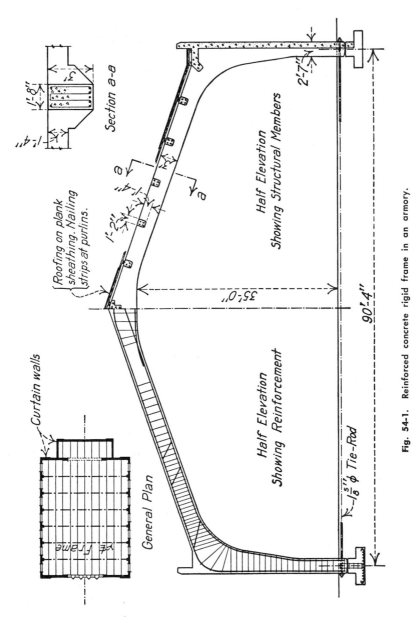

Section a-a

Roofing on plank sheathing. Nailing strips at purlins.

Half Elevation Showing Structural Members

Half Elevation Showing Reinforcement

Curtain walls

General Plan

Fig. 54-1. Reinforced concrete rigid frame in an armory.

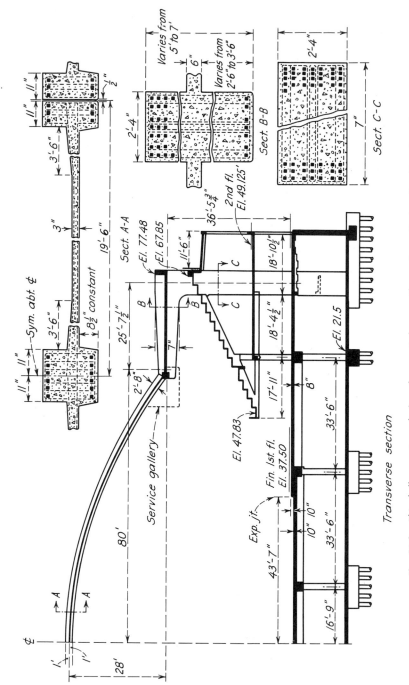

Fig. 54-2. Thin-shell concrete arched roof supported on cantilever piers. *Engineering News-Record.*

The entire roof is covered with wood fiber insulation board 1 in. thick over which a 4-ply asbestos-felt built-up roofing was installed. The ceiling was sprayed with 1 in. of acoustical material.

Edgarton and Edgarton, Architect-Engineer Associates, prepared the design and were responsible for the supervision. Ammann and Whitney were consulting structural engineers. F. S. Merritt, Senior Editor of *Engineering News-Record*, wrote the article on which this description was based and from which the illustration was taken (8).

Various other types of shell arch roofs are considered in Art. 55.

An exterior view of a thin shell arch coliseum is shown in Fig. 54-3.

Domes. Reinforced concrete is used extensively in the construction of roof domes which usually cover circular areas. The simplest form of dome would be generated by revolving a solid arch about a vertical axis through its center. Arches of this type are described in Art. 55 and illustrated diagrammatically in Fig. 55-4. A common form is the ribbed arch illustrated diagrammatically in Fig. 35-1. The spaces between ribs may be spanned by purlins to support the roof deck. A

Fig. 54-3. Thin-shell concrete arch roof of Denver, Colorado, Coliseum. Structural Engineers, Roberts and Schaefer. Courtesy Denver Convention and Tourist Bureau.

simple folded-plate domed roof is illustrated diagrammatically in Fig. 55-7.

A thin-shell dome roof for a theater in San Diego, California, was constructed on a compacted artificial earth mound 36 ft. high with its top surface shaped to serve as the form for the underside of the dome. The dome is a pierced concrete shell 190 ft. in diameter. It is supported around its perimeter by five thrust blocks, and arches between these supports to form openings 9 ft. high. The major portion of the dome is 4 in. thick but the thickness increases to 16 in. at the thrust blocks and the edges between thrust blocks are stiffened with edge beams.

The top of the fill was covered with a skim coat of concrete to form a smooth surface which was oiled to prevent bonding. After placing the reinforcement, the lightweight concrete of the dome was placed pneumatically. Finally, after the concrete had cured, the earth fill and the skim coat of concrete were removed.

Architects were Richard Wheeler and Associates, structural engineers were A. J. Blaylock and Associates, and the contractor was Peter Kiewit Sons.

The domed roof illustrated in Fig. 54-4 consists of 32 arch ribs with the outer end of each supported by an inverted L-shaped pier and its inner end supported by a compression ring into which it frames and

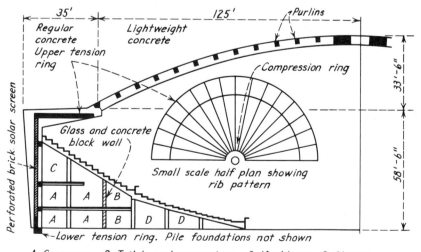

A-Concourse. B-Toilets and concessions. C-Machinery. D-Storage

Fig. 54-4. Concrete ribbed dome, Jacksonville, Florida, Coliseum. Architects, George R. Fisher and A. Eugene Cellar. Structural Engineer, Grumar E. Kraus.

which carries the inward thrusts of the ribs at the crown. The outward thrusts of the lower ends of the ribs which are carried directly by the piers are transferred to an upper tension ring which circles the roof structure between the horizontal portions of the piers. The outward thrusts of the lower ends of the piers are carried by a lower tension ring into which they frame and which is below the ground surface. The spaces between ribs are spanned by purlins spaced about 10 ft. radially. Bulb tees spaced about 33 in. span the space between purlins and support noncombustible compressed fiberboard roofing plank 3 in. thick which, in addition to their structural function, were chosen because of their heat-insulating and acoustical properties.

As shown in the figure, the dome has a span of 250 ft. and the horizontal leg of each pier is 35 ft. long; thus the overall diameter is 320 ft. The ribs and purlins of the dome are constructed of lightweight concrete and the remainder of the structure of regular concrete. The piers and the columns of the seating portion of the structure have pile foundations. The outer wall is a solar screen constructed of perforated brick and the inner walls are constructed of glass and concrete block. The building was constructed to provide for basketball, ice hockey, trade shows, and other events (9).

55. TYPES OF SHELL STRUCTURES

by Milo S. Ketchum, Ketchum and Konkel, Consulting Engineers, Denver, Colorado.

Folded Plates. The folded plate, shown in Fig. 55-1, is the simplest of the shell structures. Its principal advantages are the ease of forming and its simple lines. The structure acts as a concrete slab across the short dimension. At the supports of the plates it is necessary to provide a stiffener to pick up the reactions of the plates and deliver them to the columns. A horizontal tie is also necessary to hold the horizontal forces. At an edge the arrangement of the plates must start with a short plate. A two-element plate with an edge member turned up at an angle is shown in a. A three-element folded plate with a turned-down edge member is shown in b. The advantage of this shape is that the width of individual plates may be less for the same column spacing. A three-element "Z" shell suitable for buildings having clerestory, north-light windows between the edges of adjacent units is shown in c. A five-element folded plate which resembles a barrel shell is shown in d.

The thickness of a folded plate is primarily dependent on the thick-

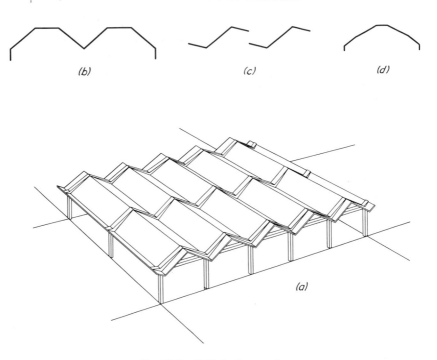

Fig. 55-1. Folded plate roofs.

ness necessary to carry the slab (short) span. This may range from 3 in. for a 5-ft. width to 4½ in. for a 12-ft. width For structures greater than 12 ft. the slab should be haunched. The slope of the plates should not be greater than 45 degrees, and the ratio of depth to span should be about 1 to 12 for simple spans and 1 to 15 for continuous spans.

Barrel Shells. Sketches of long-barrel shells are shown in Fig. 55-2. In this type of cylindrical structure, the approximate ratio of span to width is assumed to be greater than 2 to 1. Short-barrel shells are described in the next paragraph.

The barrel shell acts as a beam in the long direction and as an arch in the short direction. The arch, however, is not supported at its ends, as it is in the usual highway bridge arch, but is supported by the internal shears.

Several cross sections are shown. Figure 55-2a is a circular cylindrical barrel with a turned-up edge. The usual section is a circle, but other shapes are satisfactory. A continuous series of curves as in a corrugated section is shown in b. Discontinuous units suitable for a north-light structure is shown in *c*. Edge members at the junction of each barrel are shown in *d*. The depth of the structure may be increased by this method and longer spans may be used.

The thickness of the barrel is dependent in most cases on the amount of cover over the reinforcing bars and varies from three to four inches. It is customary to thicken the shells slightly at the valley. The ratios of span to depth are about the same as for folded plates. However, the widths may be considerably greater for the same thickness.

Short Shells. The width of a short shell is large in comparison to the span as sketched in Fig. 55-3*a* and *b*. The barrels are picked up by arches or frames which may be either above or below the shell. The arches may have many different forms, two of which are shown in *a* and *b*. The short shell acts as an arch in the upper part of the curve and delivers its thrusts to a beam element at the lower end of the shell. This area must be braced by an upturned or downturned edge member. In *a* the shell is turned down. The thickness of short shells is usually a minimum, about 2.5 to 4 in., except at an edge which is not supported at an edge plate.

Short shells are often used for quite wide openings. A typical width is 250 ft. with the arch elements spaced 25 to 35 ft. The arch is the predominant structural element.

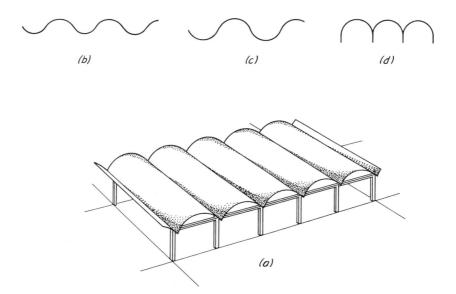

(b)   *(c)*   *(d)*

(a)

Fig. 55-2. Long-barrel shell roof.

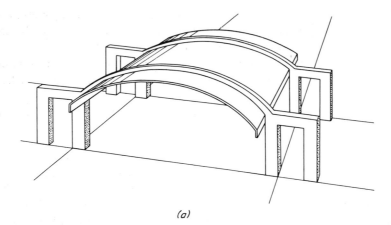

(a)

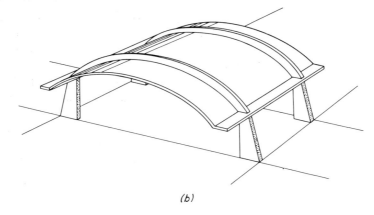

(b)

Fig. 55-3. Short-shell roofs.

Domes of Revolution. A typical dome of revolution is shown in Fig. 55-4a. This is a segment of a sphere. The shell acts as a membrane, and all stresses are direct compression or tension. There is very little bending in the shell except as a secondary stress near the tension ring at the lower edge. The ring holds the shell mainly in compression and may be prestressed by high-strength steel wires wrapped around the ring.

Many cross sections may be used for a dome of revolution, as shown in the figure. In *d*, a central column is used.

The thickness of domes is usually a minimum, and tanks with a diameter of 100 ft. have been built with a roof thickness of 2 in.

The acoustical problems associated with domes may be very difficult.

The Hyperbolic Paraboloid. The hyperbolic paraboloid is the name of a mathematical surface created by twisting a plane surface, and for that reason these structures are often called *twisted surfaces.* The shell has a double curvature, convex in one direction and concave in the other.

If properly arranged, the stresses in a twisted surface are mostly membrane, that is, there is tension in one direction and compression in the other. Ribs are usually necessary at the exterior edges and at the junctions of the surfaces.

Several structures are shown in Fig. 55-5a to c. A series of umbrella shells is shown in a. The support is a column at the center of each square unit. The shell in b is a dome arranged with four square or rectangular surfaces supported by triangular tied arches. A circular dome with the corners clipped off is shown in c. The thrusts from the shell are taken by curved arches. There are an infinite variety of shapes possible using the basic twisted surface.

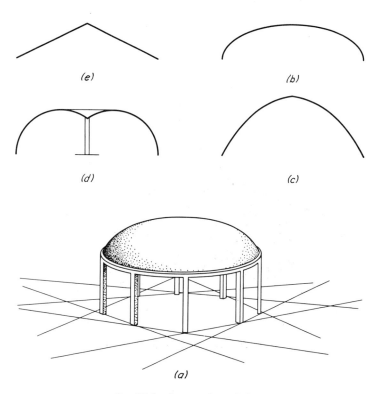

(e)

(b)

(d)

(c)

(a)

Fig. 55-4. Domes of revolution.

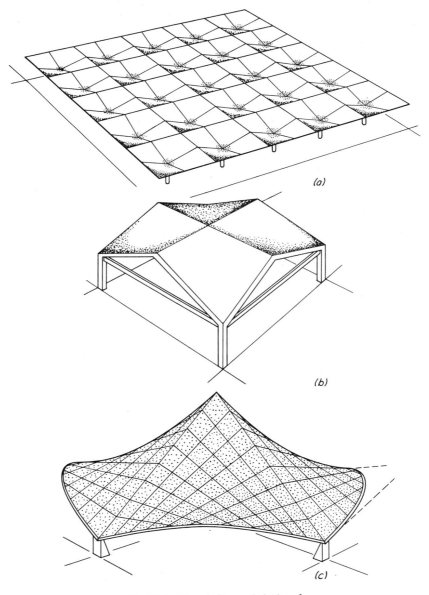

(a)

(b)

(c)

Fig. 55-5. Hyperbolic paraboloid roofs.

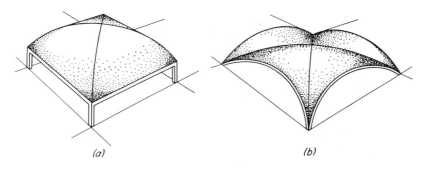

Fig. 55-6. Roofs formed by the intersection of cylindrical units.

The thickness of the shell may be a minimum. If two layers of $\frac{3}{8}$-in. bars are used and $\frac{3}{4}$ in. of cover are required, the thickness should be $2\frac{1}{4}$ in.

Intersection Shell. The dome shown in Fig. 55-6a is made by the intersection of cylindrical units. This structure acts essentially as a short shell, and the intersections form a rib to stiffen the dome. In b the axis of the barrels is reversed, and the shell must be supported by arch ribs at the edges.

Folded-Plate Dome. A dome made with triangular folded plates is shown in Fig. 55-7. The plates exert a thrust in the horizontal ring.

Shell Arch. An arch with the cross section of a folded plate is shown in Fig. 55-8.

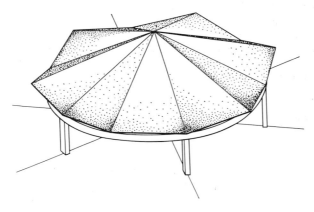

Fig. 55-7. Round folded-plate domed roof.

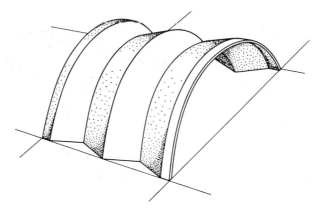

Fig. 55-8. Arch with folded-plate cross section.

Other Types. The structures shown in this article are only a few of the many possible structures available for shell structures, and in this field the creative genius of the architect and the engineer is quite necessary.

References

1. *Building Code Requirements for Reinforced Concrete,* American Concrete Institute.

2. "Tall Concrete Towers for Chicago," *Engineering News-Record,* March 10, 1960.

3. *Reinforced Concrete Floor Systems,* Portland Cement Association, 1956.

4. William Cohen, "How to Stop Partitions from Cracking," *Engineering News-Record,* September 9, 1954, p. 35.

5. J. DiStasio and M. P. Van Buren, and Fred N. Severud, "Flat Plate Floors Designed as Continuous Frames," "Slab Band Floors Are Economical for Apartment Buildings," *Modern Developments in Reinforced Concrete,* No. 20, Portland Cement Association, 1947.

6. *Recommended Practice and Standard Specifications for Concrete and Reinforced Concrete.* Published by American Concrete Institute, 1940, seventh printing, September, 1950.

7. Phil M. Ferguson, *Reinforced Concrete Fundamentals,* John Wiley and Sons, 1958.

8. F. S. Merritt, "War Memorial Serves Many Purposes," *Engineering News-Record,* November 16, 1950, p. 39.

9. Domed Roof for Coliseum," *Engineering News-Record,* December 8, 1960, p. 26.

9 Precast and prestressed concrete construction

56. PRECAST CONCRETE

General Comments. The term *precast concrete* is applied to individual concrete members of various types which are cast in separate forms before they are placed in a structure. In contrast, the term *cast-in-place* or *site-cast* concrete is given to concrete members which are cast or poured in forms in the positions they are to occupy in the finished structure.

Precast members are cast on the building site or at a casting yard located some distance from the structure in which they are to be used, transported by truck or other means of transportation to the site of the structure, and placed in position by cranes or in some other manner. Concrete block, as described in Art. 28, are the simplest form of precast unit although they are not given that designation.

To improve its quality, to permit a low water-cement ratio to be used, and to insure that the forms are completely filled, the concrete is vibrated while being placed, as described in Art. 11. Steam or hot water curing is often used to reduce the setting time. Lightweight concrete, as considered in Art. 11, is often employed. In addition to the advantage of light weight, such concrete has a relatively high heat insulation value.

Types of Members. Nearly every type of concrete member which can be cast in place can be precast, but not always advantageously. Included in these types are floor and roof slabs, wall panels, bearing walls and partitions, joists, beams, girders, columns, rigid frames, arches, domes, and piles. Trusses have been precast, but that form of structural member is not often advantageously constructed of concrete, either precast or cast-in-place. Precast piles are considered in Art. 20.

Building Heights. Except for lift-slab construction, in which the floor and roof slabs are precast as described in Art. 60, most buildings whose main structural members are precast are one-story, but two- and three-story buildings have been constructed. Precast beams, purlins, floor and roof panels, and curtain walls may be used, however, regardless of height.

Prestressing. Precast concrete members may or may not be prestressed, as described in Art. 57. In general, prestressing may be advantageous for members subjected to high flexural stresses such as long-span or heavily loaded slabs, beams, and girders. Examples of various types of precast construction are given in the following articles for illustrative purposes, but this type of construction is advantageous for a great variety of members and structures.

Framing. The structural elements of a building may be assembled in various ways, some of which follow.

1. All the members precast.

2. Precast floor and roof decks supported by cast-in-place concrete or steel girders, columns, or rigid frames.

3. Cast-in-place floor and roof slabs supported directly by precast joists or purlins.

4. Precast wall panels supported by cast-in-place concrete or steel columns or rigid frames.

5. Heavy timber roof sheathing supported directly by precast purlins.

6. Precast arches supporting precast concrete purlins and cast-in-place concrete slabs or heavy timber sheathing.

7. Masonry exterior walls and various types of partitions with precast floor and roof decks.

Connections. The connections between precast members are made in various ways. A common method consists of casting anchored steel plates in the members to be connected, which are so located that they will come in contact when the members are in position (Fig. 56-1*a*). These are called *matching plates*. After the members have been placed in position, the matching plates are welded together to form the connection. Occasionally bolts are used instead of welds and angles are used instead of plates.

Reinforcing bars may be extended beyond the ends of adjacent members so that they overlap (*b*), and they may be joined by weld-

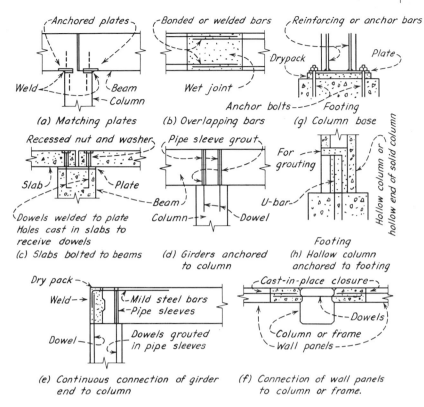

Fig. 56-1. Typical connections for precast members.

ing, the intervening space then being filled with concrete. Instead of welding, the connection may be established by the bond of the over-lapping bars. This is called a *wet joint*.

Pipe sleeves or holes may be cast in members and so located that they will fit over dowels or bolts cast in the supporting members (*c, d,* and *e*). Some form of anchorage is provided on the ends of the dowels which project beyond the end of the sleeve or hole, or the dowels are grouted into the sleeves.

Beams may be connected to the tops of columns in various ways, one of which is shown in *d*. A plate may be welded to the ends of column reinforcing for anchoring a column to its footing (*g*). In *h*, a hollow column is set in position on its footing. A looped bar has been cast in the top of the footing to serve as an anchor. A temporary opening is provided in the side of the column, and the bottom portion of the core is filled with concrete poured through this hole to complete the joint. A hollow end may be cast in a solid column for anchoring in this same manner. Wall panels are connected to columns as shown in *f*.

Numerous other types of joint may be used, some of which are explained in subsequent articles.

Advantages. The use of precast concrete may be advantageous when there are many identical members to be cast, for the same forms can be used many times. In addition to the savings in such form costs, precast concrete has other advantages over cast-in-place concrete. These include the following.

1. Quality of concrete can be controlled more carefully.

2. Smoother exposed surfaces can be achieved, and plastering is not required to produce a finished surface.

3. Less storage space is required at the site.

4. Casting can be carried on under all weather conditions as long as suitable protection is provided.

5. Curing can be done more advantageously.

6. Erection is less restricted by weather conditions.

7. Greater erection speed is possible.

8. Lower cost may be possible under conditions favorable to precasting.

57. PRESTRESSED CONCRETE

General Comments. *Prestressed concrete* is the term applied to concrete members in which the concrete is subjected to compressive stresses, before the external loads are applied, by inducing tensile stresses in the reinforcement to counteract tensile stresses in the concrete caused by external loads. The term *conventional reinforced concrete* applies to members that are not prestressed. To make prestressing advantageous, both the concrete and the reinforcement must have much higher strengths than are required for conventional reinforced concrete members. As will be explained later, the reinforcement consists of high-strength steel wires or cables or high-strength alloy steel bars, all of which are called *tendons*.

The design procedures for prestressed concrete members are the same as those for conventional reinforced concrete members, except that they are extended to provide for the effects of prestressing.

Prestressed concrete is advantageous only under special conditions because of the cost of prestressing. Its use is confined primarily but not exclusively to precast members. Only that use is considered in this chapter.

Basic Principle. To understand the structural action of prestressed concrete members, it is helpful to review this action in homogeneous beams, explained in Art. 33 and illustrated in Fig. 33-1e, and in conventional reinforced concrete beams, considered in Art. 51. As explained in these articles, the lower portion of a horizontal simple beam carrying downward vertical loads is subjected to tensile stresses. Since the tensile strength of concrete is low, a homogeneous concrete beam has very little flexural strength. To offset this deficiency, steel reinforcement is provided near the bottom of simple beams to carry the tensile stresses. The tensile strength of the concrete is neglected in the computations for the flexural strength of conventional reinforced concrete beams.

By subjecting the tensile reinforcement of a beam to tensile stresses before the external loads are applied, by procedures which are described later, compressive stresses are induced in the concrete of the beam. Usually the tensile stresses in the concrete caused by the external load are completely, or almost completely, offset or absorbed by the compressive stresses in the concrete resulting from prestressing the reinforcement which, in turn, prestresses the concrete, as has been explained. The concrete, therefore, is being used effectively in resisting tensile stresses produced by external loads rather than being neglected as it is in conventional design.

Flexural Stresses in Prestressed Concrete. The computed fiber stresses at the section A-A of a homogeneous simple beam with a symmetrical cross section for various designated conditions are shown in Fig. 57-1a to e, and those in a prestressed beam in f.

Before the external forces F are applied, as shown in a, the beam would normally be supported by forms throughout its entire length and there would be no flexural stresses. As soon as the forces F are applied, the beam deflects upward because of the uneven distribution of the compressive fiber stresses in the concrete (a), and it is supported only at the ends (b). In b and the remaining figures the member acts as a simple beam.

It is not feasible to prestress the beam by applying equal and opposite external compressive forces F at the ends. Substantially the same effect is obtained simply by inserting tendons in holes or ducts cast in the concrete (f), prestressing these tendons, and anchoring them at the ends of the beam so that a force F is applied to these ends (a and e).

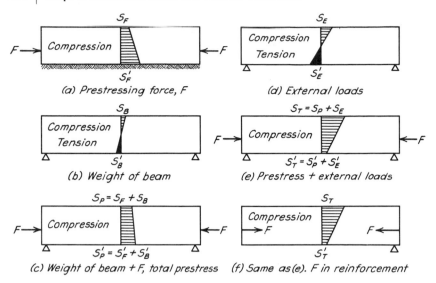

Fig. 57-1. Fibe: stresses caused by various loading conditions.

This procedure is called *posttensioning*, because the prestressing force is applied to the tendons after the concrete has hardened.

A similar objective can be accomplished by prestressing the tendons in the forms before the concrete is poured. After the concrete has set, it becomes bonded to the tendons, which therefore retain most of the prestress after prestressing force ceases to act, and the member is removed from the forms. This procedure is called *pretensioning*.

A significant portion of the initial prestress in the tendons is lost because of various factors which cause the concrete to shorten. Concrete shrinks as it dries out. Concrete also shortens elastically as compressive forces are applied and shortens still further under the action of these forces at a decreasing rate through a long period of time because of a phenomenon called *creep, plastic flow,* or *time yield.* The length of each tendon increases elastically while the prestress is being applied. This does not reduce the prestress. Steel increases gradually in length, or *creeps,* at a decreasing rate, when subjected to a constant unit stress. However, if the length remains constant, as in the tendons of prestressed concrete, the unit stress gradually decreases at a decreasing rate. This is called *relaxation,* and it is the significant factor in prestressed concrete design. Finally, there is a loss of prestress in posttensioning because of the friction between the tendons and the surrounding material. This is especially true if the tendons are curved or *draped,* as explained later. Appropriate allowances are made for these factors which decrease the initial prestress. The value of F in Fig. 57-1f is the final prestress in the tendons.

For a given external vertical load, the stresses in the concrete differ at different sections. The stresses in the tendons remain substantially equal to the final prestress at all sections. It never exceeds the initial prestress. This is also true for different external loads if the stresses do not exceed those caused by working loads.

The discussions in this article refer to the flexural stresses in a prestressed simple beam. Similar procedures apply to prestressed continuous beams, and to columns and piles if they are subjected to loads that would produce important flexural stresses if they were not prestressed.

Types of Tendons. As has been stated, high-strength steel must be used for tensile reinforcement to make prestressing effective. This is true because the loss of prestress from shrinkage, elastic deformation, and creep in the concrete and the relaxation and frictional losses in the steel during prestressing would offset most of the allowable stress in ordinary steel bars, as has been explained.

The individual units, or tendons, which comprise the total tensile reinforcement, corresponding to the bars used in conventional reinforced concrete, usually consist of two or more *parallel wires* about $\frac{1}{4}$ in. in diameter or of *strands* consisting of several of such wires "spiraled" around a straight center wire. Seven-wire strands with diameters of $\frac{1}{4}$ to $\frac{1}{2}$ in. are ordinarily used in pretensioned members. Large-diameter strands with 7, 19, 37, or more wires are used extensively in posttensioned members.

The wires are formed by drawing steel rods, while cold, through dies of smaller diameter than the rods to produce wires of the desired diameter. This process of *cold-drawing* markedly increases the tensile strength of the steel. The wires may be galvanized, after drawing, to resist corrosion.

High-strength alloy steel bars are also used for tendons. Their strength is further increased by heat-treating or cold-stretching. Diameters vary from $\frac{1}{2}$ to $1\frac{1}{8}$ in. They are used principally in posttensioned members. Finally, the tendons are heat-treated to improve their properties.

Casting and Prestressing. Prestressed concrete members are usually precast, as explained earlier in this article. They are divided into two classes, pretensioned or posttensioned, according to the sequence of casting and prestressing.

As has been explained, for *pretensioned* members the tendons are prestressed in place in the forms before the concrete is poured. The *long-line process* is ordinarily used if several members with the same cross section and identical tendons are to be cast. The casting bed on which the forms are placed may be several hundred feet long and arranged as illustrated diagrammatically in Fig. 57-2a.

The bed includes two end abutments. Tendons long enough to provide the tendons for several members to be cast in line are placed on the casting bed. They are anchored to the abutment at one end, and at the other end to hydraulic jacks operating against the other abutment. Various jacking arrangements have been devised. A template through which the tendons pass is provided at each end. Holes in each template are so located as to hold the tendons in the desired positions. Bulkheads are placed in position along the long-line form to subdivide it into forms for several individual members of the desired lengths. These are provided with notches or other devices so that they can straddle the tendons, or the tendons may be threaded through them. The long tendons are prestressed the desired amount by operating the jacks. The ends of the tendons are anchored and the jacks removed.

The concrete is then placed in the forms. After it has gained its initial set, the forms are covered to retain moisture or steam is introduced to hasten setting. When the concrete has hardened sufficiently to carry the prestress, the bulkheads between the ends of the

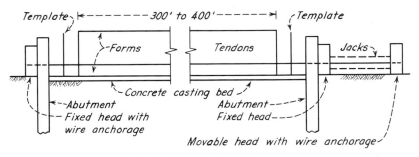

(a) Pretensioning bed for long-line process
Arranged from Portland Cement Ass'n publication

(b) Original position   (c) Draped position

Fig. 57-2. Pretensioning beds and draping of tendons.

members are removed. Usually this process requires about 24 hours. The members are separated by cutting the exposed portions of the tendons with a welding torch or by some other method, removed from the forms by cranes, and stored ready for shipment to the building site.

Stirrups or other steel objects to be cast in the members are, of course, placed in position in the forms before the concrete is poured.

It is often desirable to *drape* some of the tendons of each member so that they will be near the top at the supports and near the bottom in the central portion of a span. The long tendons to be draped are placed near the top of the members and prestressed. They are then pulled downward at the desired points and anchored as shown in Fig. 57-2*b* and *c*. Care must be taken to avoid overstressing the tendons by this operation. Draping improves the distribution of the prestress in the concrete along cross sections near the support, and the inclined portions of the tendons help carry the shearing stresses.

Individual members can be pretensioned without using the long-line process.

For *posttensioned* members, the tendons are inserted in appropriately located holes cast in the concrete or they are placed in position before the concrete is poured. In the former procedure, removable cores are used to form the holes. In the latter, the tendons are surrounded with flexible metal tubes if they are to be bonded as described later. If they are to be unbonded, they are greased to reduce friction during prestressing and to protect against corrosion. They are then wrapped with mortar-tight sheathing such as heavy waterproof paper or plastic films.

The tendons are anchored at one end with various devices. After the concrete has hardened sufficiently and the forms have been removed, the tendons are prestressed by means of hydraulic jacks applied at the free end and anchored to maintain the prestress. The jacks are then removed.

The tendons of posttensioned members may be *bonded* or *unbonded*. If they are bonded, bond is established by forcing cement grout into the annular space surrounding the tendons after prestressing. If they are unbonded, they remain as they were when the prestressing is completed.

Advantages and Disadvantages. As has been stated, most prestressed members are precast, and they have the advantages of this procedure as compared with cast-in-place construction regardless of prestressing. These advantages are explained in Art. 56. In addition, there are advantages to be gained by prestressing when conditions are favorable to its use. Among these are the following.

1. Smaller dimensions of members for the same loading conditions, which may increase clearances or reduce story heights.

2. Smaller deflections.

3. Crack-free members.

4. Smaller loads on supporting members because of the smaller dimensions required.

Among the disadvantages are the following.

1. Higher unit cost of high-strength materials.

2. Cost of prestressing equipment.

3. Labor cost of prestressing.

4. Not advantageous for short spans with low concrete stresses.

58. PRECAST CONCRETE FLOOR AND ROOF SLABS, WALLS, AND PARTITIONS

Floor and Roof Slabs. Precast slabs or panels are used extensively for floor and roof decks. Several types are used. The most common are the channel and double-T in Fig. 58-1.

Channel slabs vary in depth from 9 to 12 in. and in width from 2 to 5 ft. The top slab may be from 1 to 2 in. thick. Spans of 50 ft. or more have been used. The legs of the channels may extend across the ends if desired, and the legs and top slab may be stiffened with occasional cross-ribs. The tensile reinforcement consists of mild steel bars if the channels are not prestressed and of high-strength steel tendons if they are prestressed. The top slab is reinforced with wire mesh. Longitudinal grooves (*a*) are provided along the tops of the legs so that the joints between the slabs can be grouted to form keys between adjacent slabs. The long-line process is ordinarily used.

Double-T's vary in width from 4 to 6 ft. and in depth from 9 to 16 in. Spans as long as 50 ft. have been cast. The top slab varies from $1\frac{1}{2}$ to 2 in. thick and is reinforced with wire mesh. Except for short

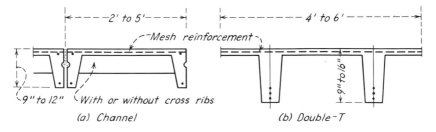

Fig. 58-1. Channel and double-T decks.

spans, the slabs are prestressed, usually by pretensioning using the long-line process. The tendons can be draped as shown in Fig. 57-2*b* and *c*.

Hollow or cored slabs or planks with various dimensions are manufactured and carried in stock. For the longer spans or heavy loads, the bottom reinforcement may be prestressed high-strength tendons, and the top reinforcement may be mild steel bars to withstand prestressing and handling stresses.

Hollow slabs are also manufactured of special forms of concrete block assembled in rows and reinforced with bars grouted in grooves provided in the lower surfaces of the block. The vertical contact surfaces are grouted or ground smooth to obtain good contact.

Solid slabs are sometimes used for roof-decks when the low cost of the forms offsets the saving in material cost that would result from the use of structurally more efficient slabs.

Floor and roof slabs are ordinarily connected to the supporting members by welded matching plates.

Walls and Partitions. Bearing and nonbearing walls and partitions ordinarily consist of panels precast in a horizontal position in a casting yard or on the floor of the building and placed in their vertical positions by cranes or by the tilt-up procedure, described in the next paragraph.

Usually, they are solid reinforced slabs from 5 to 8 in. thick, one or two stories high and with lengths about equal to the clear distances between columns or other supporting members. The actual length depends upon the manner in which the slabs are fastened to the supporting members. The openings required by windows and doors are cast in the slabs. Steel window frames are sometimes cast in exterior wall panels but usually it is preferable to prepare the openings to receive window and door frames. Extra reinforcement should be provided around the openings.

The casting surface usually is a concrete floor slab with a smooth regular surface. Bond between this surface and the wall panels is prevented by covering the casting surface with some form of liquid coating or sheet material, the former being more satisfactory for various reasons. The upper surface of the panel may be finished in several ways such as troweling, floating or brooming.

Precast channel and double-T panels, as described in the preceding paragraph, also may be used for exterior nonbearing walls. The ribs are placed vertically and the designs are adapted to the different loading conditions. Prestressed double-T panels exceeding 60 ft. in height, with one intermediate support, have been used.

Fig. 58-2. Precast Concrete Tilt-Up Construction. Portland Cement Association.

To provide additional heat insulation, *sandwich panels* sometimes are used for exterior walls. They consist of two thin dense reinforced concrete face slabs separated by a core of insulating material such as lightweight concrete, cellular glass, plastic foam, or some other rigid insulating material. The face slabs are tied together with wires, small rods, or in some other manner. The thicknesses vary from 5 to 8 in.

When precast concrete panels, described in Art. 92, are used for curtain walls of multistory buildings, the panels are placed story by story.

Wall panels are often connected to the building frame at their tops and bottoms and to each other by welded or bolted matching plates. Several other types of connections are used (Fig. 56-1*f*).

The joints between wall panels are made watertight by calking on the outside and grouting on the inside.

Tilt-up Construction may be defined as a procedure by which precast wall panels are rotated about their bottom edges to the vertical positions they are to occupy. The panels are designed to resist the lifting stresses. Small panels are sometimes hoisted by hand-operated cranes, but power equipment is usually employed. The simplest means of connecting the hoisting equipment to a panel consists of U-shaped bar loops cast in its top edge, which produce relatively high lifting stresses. A *strongback* made of steel I-beams or channels may be bolted to a panel to reduce the lifting stresses, or a *vacuum pad* may be placed on the panel and held in position by creating a partial vacuum between the panel and the pad. This device is preferred to the strongback because the panel is not disfigured by bolt holes which are cast in the panel for attachment of a strongback. See Fig. 58-2.

Tilt-up construction is also used for placing rigid frames and arches.

59. PRECAST CONCRETE JOISTS, BEAMS, GIRDERS, AND COLUMNS

Joists and Purlins. Small closely spaced beams are usually called joists if used in floor construction and purlins if used in roof construction. They have T- or I-shaped cross sections (Fig. 59-1a and b) and may

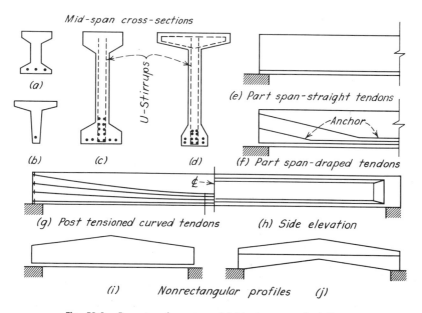

Fig. 59-1. Precast and prestressed joists, beams, and girders.

be prestressed or of conventional design. Several manufacturers carry the common sizes in stock for immediate delivery. Joists with inverted T-sections are available for use in composite construction where they support cast-in-place floor or roof slabs.

Beams and Girders. These terms are often synonymous, but when a distinction is made those with the longer spans are called girders. They may be of conventional precast design or prestressed. The cross sections are usually I-shaped (*c*) except near the ends where they are rectangular. T-shaped cross sections (*d*) are also used. The following discussion refers to prestressed members.

There are structural advantages in curving or inclining some of the tendons upward toward the ends of a girder. In the earlier years of prestressing it was considered necessary that pretensioned tendons be straight, as shown in Fig. 59-1*e*. It has been found, however, that tendons can be *draped* (*f*) by anchoring them at two or more points before or after prestressing, as long as care is used not to overstress the tendons.

In posttensioning girders, the tendons are usually curved (*g*).

The sloping tendons help carry shearing stresses. If additional shearing resistance is required, mild steel stirrups may be used as in the conventional reinforced concrete beams and as shown in *c* and *d*.

Girders may have nonrectangular profiles (*i* and *j*). The profile in *j* raises the center of prestress at the ends, which is advantageous, without curving the tendons as in *g*.

Clear spans exceeding 100 ft. have been constructed.

The girders mentioned are simply supported at the ends. However, they may be continuous with single units or with several units, as shown in Fig. 59-2*a*. Overhanging girders with a *drop-in* beam are illustrated in *b*. The ends of the drop-in beam rest on the ends of the overhangs and are made stable by suitable anchors which do not develop continuity, that is, make them continuous. These types of construction may or may not be prestressed.

The use of a prestressed *cap cable* to develop continuity at a support of adjoining prestressed girders is shown in *c*. After the girders are in position, cables are inserted in ducts which are cast in the concrete, anchored at one end, and prestressed. If the girders are to support a cast-in-place slab, another means of developing continuity is preferable, as explained in the paragraph on composite construction.

Types of connections between girders and columns are illustrated in Fig. 56-1. In the simplest (*a*), matching plates are welded together

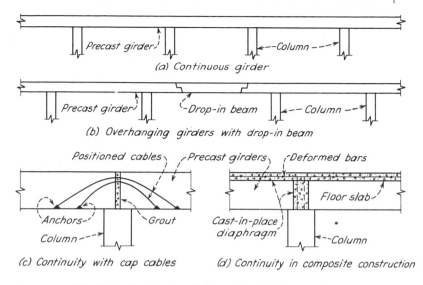

Fig. 59-2. Overhanging girders and continuity connections.

after the members are in position. It develops no continuity. Others which develop partial or full continuity are shown in *d* and *e*. When full continuity is developed, the combination becomes a rigid frame. Such action must be considered in the design of the girders and columns.

Composite Construction. Composite construction consists of precast girders, beams, joists, or purlins on top of which a floor or roof slab is cast in place. The slab and precast units may be considered to act together in resisting the weight of the slab and the applied loads, if provision is made to prevent movement between the slab and the precast units and if the slab is anchored to these units to prevent vertical separation. Horizontal movement of the slab along the beam is prevented by keys consisting of notches, with vertical sides, on the tops of the precast members or by special preparation of the contact surface by sand blasting or other means to insure adequate bond. Vertical separation is prevented by casting vertical steel dowels in the tops of the precast units or by projecting the ends of vertical stirrups in these units.

Beams may be made continuous over supports by including longitudinal reinforcement over the supports in the slab (Fig. 59-2*d*). This procedure is preferable to using cable caps (*c*) if the slab is cast in place.

Columns. Precast concrete columns may be similar to cast-in-place columns as described in Art. 50, or they may be hollow. The hollow column may make use of heavy cardboard tubes to form the core.

Prestressing the longitudinal reinforcement is advantageous only for columns subjected to relatively large flexural stresses. When prestressed, the longitudinal reinforcement consists of high-strength tendons rather than mild steel bars. The tendons may be pretensioned or posttensioned. If they are pretensioned, the long-line process may be used if many identical columns are to be cast. The lateral reinforcement may be small diameter mild steel rods or wires. Columns are cast in a horizontal position and erected by cranes.

A simple type of column base (Fig. 56-1*g*) is suitable for square solid or hollow columns. The type shown in *h* may be used for hollow columns. A looped rod is cast in the column footing and projects upward into the hollow core when the column is set. A temporary opening in the side of the column permits the lower portion of the core to be filled with grout, in which the loop becomes embedded so as to form an effective anchor. The opening is then dry-packed with mortar. Various other types are used.

60. LIFT-SLAB CONSTRUCTION

In lift-slab construction, all the above-ground floor slabs and the roof slab for an entire building are cast in stacks on a previously prepared ground floor. They surround the columns that are to support them. They are lifted into their final positions by simultaneously operating hydraulic jacks mounted temporarily on the tops of the columns, and they are connected, by *lift rods,* to steel *lifting collars* cast in and anchored to the slabs and surrounding the columns.

Because of the tendency of long columns to buckle under load when not supported laterally at intervals, not more than three or four stories are usually constructed in one stage.

Sequence of Lifting Operations. The sequence of operations for a 6-story building, including a basement, which requires two lifting stages is illustrated in Fig. 60-1. It will be noted (*f*) that the columns are extended to their final height at the beginning of the second stage. For taller buildings, more stages are required. These are carried out by extending the two-stage procedure.

Types of Columns. The columns are usually made of steel (Fig. 60-2*a* to *e*), separate units being welded at the corners. They vary in ex-

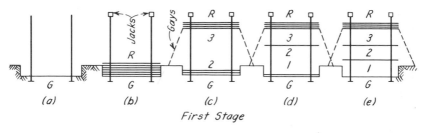

First Stage

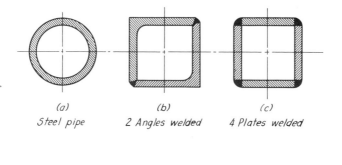

Second Stage

Fig. 60-1. Sequence of lifting operations.

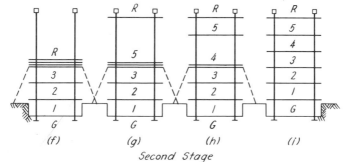

(a)
Steel pipe

(b)
2 Angles welded

(c)
4 Plates welded

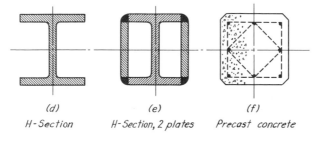

(d)
H-Section

(e)
H-Section, 2 plates

(f)
Precast concrete

Fig. 60-2. Types of columns.

ternal lateral dimension from 8 to 12 in. For a given building this dimension is usually constant. The steel areas are varied by changing the thickness of metal. One dimension is limited by the spacing of the lifting rod attachments on the jacks. Occasionally columns are made of precast reinforced concrete with longitudinal and lateral bar reinforcement (f). Prestressed columns with longitudinal wire tendons and mild steel lateral reinforcement are also used.

The bottoms of the columns are rigidly anchored to their foundations by built-up steel bases to stand vertically. In fire-resistive construction, steel columns are protected by concrete, metal lath and pearlite plaster, or other appropriate noncombustible materials after the slabs are placed. Filling hollow steel columns with concrete improves their fire resistance.

Size of Slab. The jacks that lift a slab must act in unison to avoid local overstressing. All the jacks for one slab are operated from a control console. The usual number of jacks which are operated in this manner is twelve or eighteen, and sometimes equipment has been used which permitted the number of jacks to be increased to 36. For this reason, large floor and roof-decks are usually, but not always, divided into several slabs (Fig. 60-3).

It is desirable, but not always possible, for a slab to cantilever out beyond the exterior rows of columns of a slab, as shown in the figure. The joints between adjacent slabs are located midway between rows of. columns as shown.

Closure Strip. An open space about 3 ft. wide is provided between adjacent slabs. Bars project from the edges of adjacent slabs into this

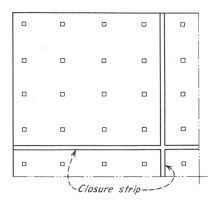

Fig. 60-3. Subdivision of slabs.

Fig. 60-4. Lift-slab buildings. Huron Apartments, Ann Arbor, Michigan. 15 lift slabs, maximum lifting height, 145 ft., 6-ft. cantilevered balconies. Figures illustrates two apartment buildings at different stages of construction. Architects, King and Lewis, Inc. Structural Engineers, R. M. McClurg Associates, Inc. Lift-slab Contractor, Long Construction Co.

space and overlap to permit welding. A *closure* or *pour strip* of cast-in-place concrete fills the space and provides continuity. By providing wider spaces, stairways, elevator shafts, and other vertical shafts can be constructed. In addition, shear walls to provide lateral stability for the building can be built in these spaces as the construction proceeds.

Column Spacing and Slab Thickness and Types. Common column spacings vary from 25 to 30 ft. or more and may differ in the two directions. The slabs are usually solid, and their thicknesses vary from 5 to 10 in. For the longer spans, waffle slabs, similar to the slabs shown in Fig. 52-5, are used frequently, the waffle effect often being obtained by using throw-away cardboard box forms. The areas adjacent to the columns must be solid. The top slabs are reinforced with wire mesh. Waffle slabs must be somewhat thicker than solid slabs under the same conditions.

Prestressing. For the most part, the slabs are prestressed by posttensioning in both directions, as described in Art. 57. Usually the tendons are draped from the lower portion of the slab at the center to the upper portion at the columns and in the cantilevers to resist tensile stresses.

Prestressing causes slabs to deflect upward between columns. This is desirable because such deflections counteract most, if not all, of the deflection due to applied loads. In addition, prestressed slabs are crack-free, a quality which is always desirable and especially to make the roof watertight for roof slabs which do not require that any roofing material be applied.

Lifting Collars. Before each column is erected, the lifting collar required for each slab is placed on the column. A clearance of approximately $\frac{1}{4}$ in. is provided between the collar and the column. Collars are made of cast steel or are built up of steel sections.

Slab Casting. The slabs are cast in contact in the order that they occupy in the building and securely anchored to the lifting collars. These collars increase the resistance of the slabs to shearing stresses near the columns which are caused by the vertical loads. To prevent bonding between slabs during casting, the top of each slab is coated with liquid wax or other liquid preparation or covered with a membrane of film before the next slab is cast.

Connecting Slabs to Columns. After a slab has been lifted to its final position, the lifting collars are welded to steel columns. Provision may be made for temporary support before the final welding takes place. If reinforced concrete columns are used, this connection is made in various ways. If the slabs are to be lifted in two or more stages, it is necessary to park some of the slabs in temporary positions (Fig. 60-1e and f). Several slabs may be lifted simultaneously, the lowest one of which, when fixed in its final position, serves as a temporary support for the slabs above. Slabs may also be parked in any predetermined position by supporting them temporarily on shear pins passing through holes provided in the columns. The rate of lifting varies from 3 to 5 ft. per hour.

Lateral Support. During construction, special lateral support may not be required for low buildings or for the first stage of erection of higher buildings. It may be desirable, however, to provide at least temporary horizontal braces between the tops of the columns and in both directions. A simple method for providing temporary lateral support is by using anchored guy wires (Fig. 60-1). If space is not available for this arrangement, crossed guy wires within the structure in the closure spaces, or around the outside, may be used. Of course, such guy wires can only be placed where slabs are in final position.

Permanent reinforced concrete shear walls may be constructed at stairway or elevator shafts. These may be carried up as the construction proceeds to provide lateral support during construction and for the completed building. Masonry end walls supported laterally at the floor and roof levels may provide permanent lateral support.

The joints between slabs and columns are sometimes designed to resist lateral loads on the building. The provisions for lateral support depend upon the conditions which prevail. Wind loads, and sometimes earthquake shocks, must be considered. One building has been known to withstand earthquake shocks during construction.

Exterior Walls and Partitions. Light exterior enclosure or curtain walls may be located along the outer edges of the cantilever slabs, or these projections may effectively shade exterior walls with south exposure and located along the line of the exterior columns. They are not as effective for shading walls with east or west exposure. Interior partitions are constructed of the same materials as are used in other types of construction.

Advantages and Disadvantages. The primary objectives of lift-slab construction are to reduce form costs to a minimum and to speed up erection. Some of the other advantages follow.

1. Beams are eliminated, as in conventional flat-plate construction, and do not affect partition locations.

2. The lower surface of slabs is as good as a well-trowled floor surface, and does not require plastering to provide a finished surface.

3. Floor construction requires less vertical space than some other types, so that the story height is reduced.

4. If prestressed, deflections are almost eliminated, slabs are crack free, and roof slabs may not require roof covering.

5. Utility lines can be incorporated in slabs from the ground level.

6. Casting of slabs can be carried on in cold weather within a minimum heated enclosure and can be lifted regardless of the weather.

Some of the disadvantages are the following.

1. It is a type of construction with which architects, engineers, and contractors are not generally familiar, and costs may be affected adversely.

2. The column arrangement and other planning features must be favorable.

3. Lifting and prestressing costs are important factors.

The lift-slab method was conceived by Philip N. Youtz and Tom Slick about 1950, and is usually known as the Youtz-Slick Method.

61. PRECAST CONCRETE RIGID FRAMES

General Comments. The general types of rigid frames, regardless of the materials of which they are constructed, are described in Art. 35. Cast-in-place reinforced concrete rigid frames are considered in Art. 54. Similar types can often be precast advantageously.

The joints between girders and columns and the members themselves may be designed to develop full continuity. In such cases the units function as rigid frames but they are not usually so called.

The units included in precast rigid frames are cast in a horizontal position, usually on the finished concrete floor of the building.

Single-span frames may be cast in one piece or in more than one piece to reduce the weight to be hoisted at one time. Multiple-span frames are cast in several appropriate units. They are raised into their vertical positions by cranes and supported temporarily until they receive support from other parts of the building.

The units of the rigid frame are rectangular in cross section, with uniform thicknesses and varying depths. They are usually solid, but occasionally they are made hollow by heavy cardboard tubes cast in the concrete to form cores or in other ways.

The foundations of the outer vertical members, called legs, may be designed to carry the outward horizontal thrusts at the bottoms of each leg, if soil conditions permit. A member consisting of steel bars surrounded with concrete, called a *tie beam*, may also be cast within or under the floor and tie the tops of the foundations together to resist these thrusts. If a building is located in a region subject to earthquake shocks, tie beams may be required.

The hinges in rigid frames may have horizontal pins which offer only frictional resistance to rotation. Instead, they may include bars or dowels which tie the abutting ends of the units together so that the joints offer a negligible resistance to rotation.

Single-span, single-story frame buildings may have adequate longitudinal stability after the members that enclose the building are in place. However, buildings with multiple-span frames usually require precast or cast-in-place horizontal longitudinal struts located between the frames and at the tops of the vertical supporting members of adjacent frames and tied to them. These struts are also called *tie beams*, although they do not function as beams.

A building using precast rigid frames for the main supporting members may be enclosed by precast roof and wall panels, as described in Art. 58, or the exterior walls may be constructed of masonry units, as described in Chapter 4. Precast wall and roof panels are attached to the frames in various ways, as explained in Art. 56. Occasionally the roof construction spanning the distance between widely spaced rigid frames consists of a series of precast folded plates or of thin shell arches as shown in Fig. 62-3.

One of both of the exterior legs of any of the frames considered in this article can be T-shaped in profile to provide cantilevers to support an outside projection of the roof called a *canopy* (Fig. 35-4*i*). These may serve as shelters or to shade the exterior wall from direct sunlight.

Precast frames are sometimes prestressed, but usually they are not. Only frames which are not prestressed are considered in this article. They are designed as conventionally reinforced concrete members.

Single-Span Rigid Frames. Three types of precast single-span rigid frames are illustrated in Fig. 61-1. The two-hinged frame in *a* is cast in two pieces to reduce the weight to be hoisted at one time. A construction joint, called a *wet joint*, is provided in the center of the top member. A detail of this joint is shown. The two-hinged frame in *b* is cast in three pieces by providing two joints in the top member. A precast beam is hoisted in position between the upper ends of the legs. This is called a *drop-in beam*. A detail of the joints at the ends of this beam is shown in the figure. They provide temporary vertical support for the ends of the beam. To establish continuity at each joint, short projecting ends of the reinforcing bars overlap and are welded. The open spaces then are dry-packed with cement mortar.

The three-hinged frame in *c* is cast in two pieces. A detail of the hinge at the crown is shown in the figure. The tie beams shown in these figures are usually not required.

Multiple-Span Rigid Frames. Three types of multiple-span frames are shown in Fig. 61-2. A three-span continuous frame with three drop-in beams and hollow members is illustrated in *a*. The joints at the ends of the drop-in beams are similar to those shown in Fig. 61-1*b*. A longitudinal tie beam is provided between frames at the top of each support. This type of frame can be designed for any number of spans.

A three-span frame consisting of two L-shaped exterior units and two T-shaped interior units is shown in *b*. A joint which functions as a hinge is located at midspan of each top member. The frame functions as a series of three-hinged arches. This type of frame can be designed for any number of spans. Longitudinal tie beams extend between frames as shown.

A three-span frame, cast in two T-shaped pieces which are made

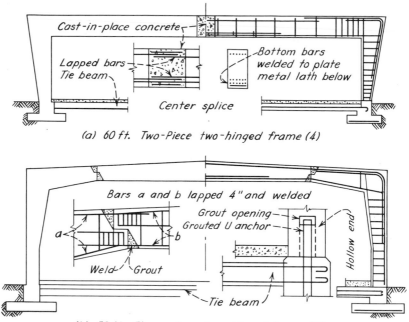

(a) 60 ft. Two-Piece two-hinged frame (4)

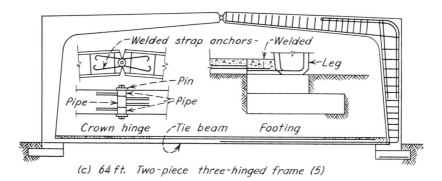

(b) 50 ft. Three-piece two-hinged frame (4)

(c) 64 ft. Two-piece three-hinged frame (5)

Fig. 61-1. Single-span, precast rigid frames. U. S. Navy.

continuous by a wet joint in the center of the top member, is shown in *c*. The outer ends of the frame extend to but are not supported by solid slab tilt-up enclosure walls. Longitudinal tie beams extend between frames as shown.

Multistory Rigid Frames. The two-story two-span frame in Fig. 61-3 is similar to the one-story frames in Fig. 61-1*b* and Fig. 61-2*a*. The

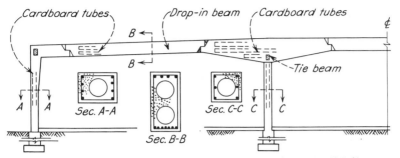

(a) 200 ft. 3-span continuous frame with drop-in beams – U.S. Navy

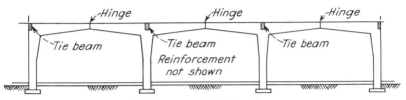

(b) 3-span rigid frame

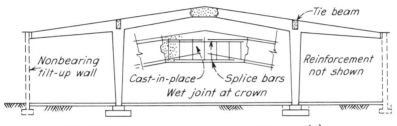

(c) 90 ft. 3-span rigid frame – U.S. Navy (4).

Fig. 61-2. Three-span rigid frames.

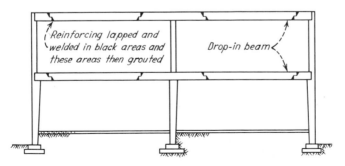

Fig. 61-3. 50-ft. two-span, two-story rigid frame with drop-in beams. Designed by Roberts and Schaefer for U. S. Air Force.

exterior and interior units include cantilever projections to receive the ends of the drop-in beams. Each of these two-story units is erected in one piece. The joints at the ends of the drop-in beams are similar to the type shown in detail in Fig. 61-1b.

Multistory single-span frames are sometimes constructed and erected in one piece.

Reinforcement. As mentioned in Art. 35, the members of rigid frames are subjected to relatively large bending and shearing stresses. As shown in the frames in Fig. 61-1, longitudinal reinforcement is provided near the outer and inner faces of the members. For the sake of clarity, layers of bars are shown to be more widely separated than they actually are. Reinforcement is provided normal to the axes of the members as required. This reinforcement corresponds to the stirrups used in beams. It is looped entirely around the longitudinal reinforcement. In addition to providing for shearing stresses, it holds reinforcement subjected to compressive stresses in position and thereby fulfills one of the functions of spirals and hoops in columns. It is very important in holding both tensile and compressive reinforcement in position in regions where the reinforcement is curved, for example at the knees of the rigid frames in Fig. 54-1, which is a cast-in-place frame but may also be precast.

Lifting Hooks. Appropriately located hooks are cast in the members of frames which are to be lifted, to facilitate erection. The stresses produced in lifting must be provided for in the design of the members of a frame.

Acknowledgments. The various offices of the United States Navy have done much to develop precast construction as described in publications of the Portland Cement Association. The frame illustrated in Fig. 61-3a was patterned after a frame designed for the United States Air Force. It was designed by Roberts and Schaefer Company and described in the April, 1957 issue of *Civil Engineering*. The author wishes to acknowledge the assistance obtained from these sources in preparing this article.

62. PRECAST ARCHES AND PRESTRESSED DOMES

General Comments. The general types of arches, regardless of the materials of which they are constructed, are described in Art. 35. Cast-in-place reinforced concrete arches are considered in Art. 54.

Both rigid frames and arches involve so-called arch action, but they differ in the relative amounts of flexure. Because of the difference in the forms of their profiles, rigid frames are subjected to relatively large flexural stresses, although for arches the stresses are primarily compressive.

The horizontal thrusts on the foundations of both types of structures are comparable, and these thrusts are resisted by the foundations or abutments or by tie beams as described in the preceding article.

Most precast arches are *three-hinged,* but occasionally no hinges are provided and they are called *hingeless* or *fixed arches.* Precast arch ribs are usually solid with rectangular cross sections constant in width and depth. Precast arches may be prestressed, but this practice is not common and is not considered in this article.

The floor area under an arch roof may be limited by sidewalls, as shown in Fig. 35-3a, with the ends of the arches exposed or enclosed within building space constructed along the sides, as shown by the dashed lines. The arches may also be elevated with the side construction designed to carry the arch thrusts as shown in Fig. 35-3b.

Three-Hinged Ribbed Arch. A three-hinged arch precast in two sections included between the hinges, to support the roof of the gymnasium for Citrus Union High School in Azusa, California, is illustrated in Fig. 62-1. Various details are shown on the drawing. Heavy timber purlins and sheathing were used for economy. In doing so, however, fire resistance was decreased.

Other types of deck may be used for precast ribbed arches. Precast concrete purlins with dowel, matching plate or bolted angle end connections to the arches may be used with precast roof panels or a cast-in-place roof slab. The steep roof slopes near the ends of the arches make it difficult to cast the concrete in place. Precast concrete roof panels require secure anchorage to the purlins. These members are designed for the lateral load they carry. Securely anchored precast channel slabs, described in Art. 58, may be used to span the distance between the arches and thereby eliminate the purlins.

Folded Plate Fixed Arch. The arched roof for the Holy Trinity High School Gymnasium at Trinidad, Colorado, shown in Fig. 62-2, is made up of thirteen folded plate arch ribs about 10 ft. wide, as illustrated in the figure. Each rib consists of five identical segments about 31 ft. long.

The segments were supported on falsework during erection. Open spaces were provided between the ends and edges of adjacent seg-

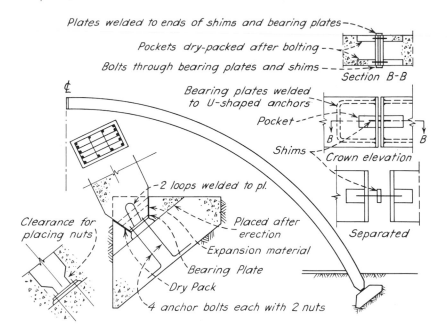

Plates welded to ends of shims and bearing plates--

Pockets dry-packed after bolting --

Bolts through bearing plates and shims --

Section B-B

Bearing plates welded to U-shaped anchors

Pocket--

Shims

Crown elevation

¢

2 loops welded to pl.

Clearance for placing nuts

Placed after erection

Expansion material

Bearing Plate

Dry Pack

4 anchor bolts each with 2 nuts

Separated

Fig. 62-1. 150-ft.-span three-hinged arch. Architects, Austin, Field and Fry. Structural Engineer, Ernest H. Lee.

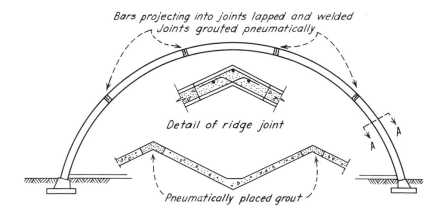

Bars projecting into joints lapped and welded
Joints grouted pneumatically

Detail of ridge joint

Pneumatically placed grout

Section A-A

Welded-wire fabric top and bottom except where grouted joint bars added in ridges and valleys. Lapping bars welded in ridge joint

Fig. 62-2. 115-ft.-span folded plate fixed arch. Architects, Toll and Milan. Consulting Engineer, Henry J. Boland.

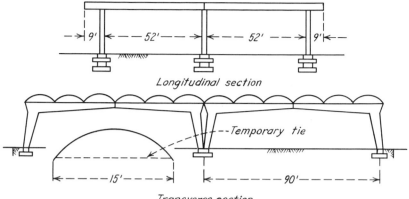

Fig. 62-3. Thin-shell barrel arch roof deck. Architect, Mario Ciampi. Structural Engineer, Isadore Thompson.

ments. Overlapping bars projected from the ends and edges of the segments into the open spaces. These bars were welded and then grouted in pneumatically to establish continuity in both directions. The segments were hoisted by cranes attached to strongbacks bolted to the segments. The roof was waterproofed with a spray-on plastic (10).

Thin-Shell Barrel Arches. A series of precast, thin-shell barrel roof arches supported by precast three-hinged rigid frames are shown in Fig. 62-3.

Each arch unit was constructed of lightly reinforced, lightweight concrete 3½ in. thick, 15 ft. wide, and 61 ft. long, including an exterior cantilever projection of 9 ft. Spreading of the arches during erection was prevented by temporary bar ties located just above the springing lines.

The arches were anchored to the frames. Holes cast in the arches fitted over pipe dowels cast in the supports. After the arches were in position, connections were welded to the tops of the dowels. The tie rods then were cut out. The arches spread slightly to form tight contacts. The edges of adjacent arches were tied together by welding matching plates. Built-up asphalt roofing covers the arches (11).

Prestressed Concrete Domes

Thin-Shell Domes. The common procedure for constructing thin-shell domes is to use conventional types of forms, which require no explanation. This paragraph is devoted to two procedures which make use of compacted earth fills or natural mounds, appropriately shaped, instead of forms. A pierced thin-shell reinforced concrete dome roof, which was constructed in final position by using compacted artificial earth fill as a form, is described in Art. 54. It was not prestressed. Often the tension rings or ring girders of such domes are prestressed by posttensioning as were those described in this paragraph.

A reinforced lightweight concrete thin-shell dome roof, constructed on a compacted earth fill and placed in final position by the lift-slab procedure, is illustrated in Fig. 62-4. It has a diameter of 244 ft., a rise of 43 ft., and a uniform thickness of 4 in. The dome is surrounded with a posttensioned concrete tension ring or ring girder 44 in. wide and 25 in. deep which is, in turn, surrounded with a cantilevered canopy 12 ft. wide.

The ring girder is supported on top of 36 equally spaced steel columns 26 ft. long, founded on spread footings and projecting 16 ft. above the ground surface.

The construction procedure was as follows.

1. Construct the concrete footings and erect the columns.

2. Place steel lifting collars around the columns and in position to become anchored into the ring girder.

3. Form and cast the ring girder or tension ring on the ground.

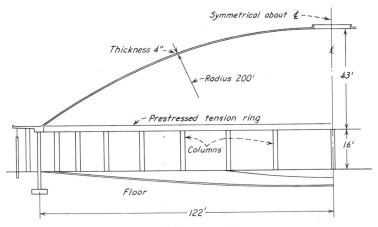

Half cross section

Fig. 62-4. A 244-ft. diameter prestressed concrete dome erected by the lift-slab method. Warner Auditorium, Anderson, Indiana. Architects and Engineers, Johnson, Ritchart and Associates. General Contractor, Lewis Construction Co.

4. Construct an appropriately shaped mound of compacted earth and cover with plastic slabs 1 in. thick to provide the form for the thin shell.

5. Place the reinforcing for the dome on the mound.

6. Pour the concrete dome.

7. Prestress the tension ring, after the concrete in the ring and the dome has set, by wrapping around its outside edge with three rings of ¼-in. steel wire, each ring consisting of 43 wires which are prestressed while being placed.

8. Place a hydraulic lifting jack on top of each column, connect all the jacks to a single console for simultaneous control, and attach the lifting rods to the jacks and lifting collars.

9. Jack the dome into position and secure it by welding the lifting collars to the columns.

10. Construct the canopy.

11. Remove the earth fill and proceed with the completion of the structure. The plastic slabs were left adhering to the underside of the dome to serve as heat insulation.

This structure is the Warner Auditorium constructed in Anderson, Indiana, for the General Ministerial Assembly of the Church of God (16).

A thin-shell dome roof of an auditorium in Albuquerque, New Mexico, was constructed by shaping a natural mound of earth to serve as a form for the underside of the dome. The diameter of the dome is 218 ft.; its rise, 23 ft.; and its thickness 5 in. within a diameter of 160 ft., gradually increasing until the tension ring, or ring girder, is reached. The tension ring is supported by 22 reinforced concrete columns on spread footings.

The steps in the construction procedure were as follows.

1. Excavate for and cast the footings and columns and then backfill.

2. Shape the top of the natural mound to conform with the ceiling of the dome and finish with a layer of fine stone compacted and accurately shaped by rolling. The outer 30 ft., which is exposed, was formed with ¾-in. plywood resting on a rolled surface. Place the forms for the tension ring.

3. Place the radial and circumferential reinforcing for the dome.

4. Place the concrete to form the tension ring and the dome.

5. After the concrete has set sufficiently, prestress the tension ring by winding many turns of highly stressed steel wire around its outer edge and protect with cement grout and concrete.

6. Remove the earth mound and proceed with the completion of the building (17).

Architects; Ferguson, Stephenson and Associates. General Contractors; Lembke, Clough and King.

Circular Folded-Plate Dome Roof. The cross section of a circular arena with a complex folded plate dome roof of lightweight concrete is illustrated in Fig. 62-6. The diameter is 400 ft., and the height from the arena floor to the top of the roof is 128 ft. The arena floor is 24 ft. below the surrounding ground surface.

The roof consists of 24 identical arched folded plate segments, the horizontal thrusts at the lower edges of which are resisted by a post-tensioned tension ring around the perimeter of the roof, and the thrusts at the crown are resisted by a compression ring into which they frame. Catwalks and grid suspended from dome are not shown.

The posttensioning of the tension ring was done before the interior roof supports were removed. It consists of about 600 miles of wire ¼ in. in diameter, which was wrapped progressively while stressed around the outer face of the tension ring to form a band of 44 vertical rows with a total cross-sectional area of 85 sq. in. The voids between the wires were filled with grout, and at the same time a concrete covering, including the gutter, was cast in place around the periphery of the tension ring. After the wire was in place and its protection completed, the interior roof supports were removed. The

Fig. 62-5. Reinforced concrete folded-plate dome roof. Assembly Hall at University of Illinois. Roof dome 400 ft. in diameter with post-tensioned compression ring. Seating capacity: permanent 16,400; temporary 2,000. Architects, Harrison and Abramovitz. Structural Engineers, Ammann and Whitney. General Contractors, Felmley-Dickerson Co.

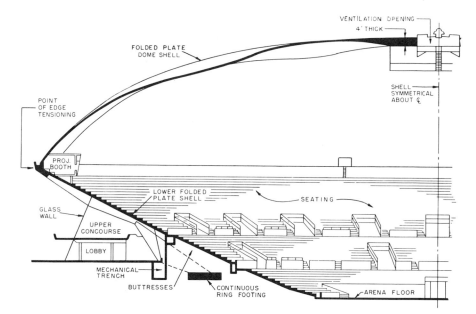

Fig. 62-6. 400-ft. diameter prestressed folded-plate roof dome. University of Illinois Assembly Hall. *Building Construction*, February, 1961.

dome lifted slightly from the forms as the prestressing progressed. The tension ring is supported on 48 equally spaced reinforced concrete buttresses, the bottom ends of which bear on a ring footing with an inner radius of 109 ft. which serves as a compression ring.

The pattern of the roof is illustrated by the 90-degree segment in Fig. 62-7*a* and the 15-degree segment in *b*. A vertical circumferential section at one point is illustrated in *c*. Of course, such sections differ for each radius where they are located.

The maximum depth of the folds is 7½ ft. and the typical depth, about 3½ ft. The radial ribs at the valleys and ridges of the folded plate segments taper from 10½ by 7½ in. to 15½ by 13½ in. in section. The slabs connecting the ridges and valleys are 3½ in. thick and are inclined at an angle of 45 degrees.

Heat insulation and acoustical treatment for the underside of the roof are provided by wood-fiber concrete panels against which the lightweight concrete of the roof structure was poured. The roof is sprayed with three ·coats of waterproofing plastic.

The structure is primarily a basketball and sports arena, but provisions are made to curtain off areas for theatrical and concert events. There are 16,200 permanent and 1800 movable seats (14, 15). At the

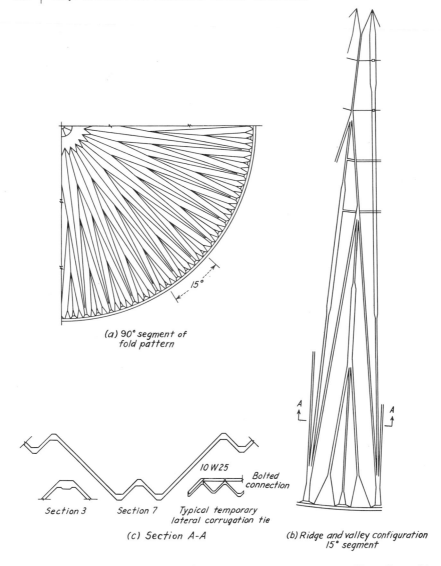

(a) 90° segment of
fold pattern

10 W 25 Bolted
connection

Section 3   Section 7   Typical temporary
lateral corrugation tie

(c) Section A-A

(b) Ridge and valley configuration
15° segment

Fig. 62-7. Pattern of folded-plate roof dome, University of Illinois Assembly Hall. *Building Construction*, February, 1961.

time of its completion in 1963, this was the largest diameter concrete dome roof in the United States.

References

1. *Minimum Standard Requirements for Precast Concrete Floor and Roof Units,* American Concrete Institute Standard ACI 711-58.

2. "Tentative Recommendations for Prestressed Concrete," ACI-ASCE Joint Committee 323, *Journal American Concrete Institute,* 1958, p. 545.

3. Albert C. Smith, "Prestressed Concrete," *Construction Methods,* February, 1957, p. 3.

4. *Modern Developments in Reinforced Concrete,* No. 29, Portland Cement Association, 1953.

5. *Modern Developments in Reinforced Concrete,* Portland Cement Association, 1957.

6. *Navy Builds All Precast Concrete Warehouses,* Portland Cement Association, 1955.

7. *Tilt-Up Construction,* Portland Cement Association, 1952.

8. "Lift Slab Goes Up Six Stories," *Engineering News-Record,* July 3, 1958, p. 37.

9. "Height Record Goes Up Again for Lift Slabs in the U. S.," *Engineering News-Record,* July 3, 1958, p. 37.

10. "Precast Sections Make a Corrugated Roof," *Engineering News-Record,* February 27, 1958, p. 40.

11. "Precast Arches for Gym Roof," *Engineering News-Record,* January 31, 1957.

12. T. Y. Lin, *Design of Prestressed Concrete Structures,* John Wiley and Sons, 1963.

13. Fred E. Koebel and Harvey R. Livesay, Jr., "Precast and Prestressed Concrete," Chapter 13 in *Handbook of Heavy Construction* by Frank W. Stubbs, Jr., editor-in-chief, McGraw-Hill Book Company, 1959.

14. "To Cover This Assembly Bowl: A 400-Ft. Prestressed Saucer," *Engineering News-Record,* June 1, 1961, p. 32.

15. "Designing, Bidding and Building World's Largest Edge-Supported Dome," *Building Construction,* February 1961, p. 28.

16. *Engineering News-Record,* December 14, 1961, p. 38.

17. *Engineering News-Record,* September 27, 1956, p. 36.

10 Floor construction, floor surfaces, and interior wall coverings except plaster

63. TYPES OF FLOOR CONSTRUCTION

Wood Floors on Wood Joists. The most common form of floor construction for *wood frame* and *ordinary construction* buildings consists of wood joists supporting a 1-in. wood subfloor and a matched-wood finished floor as described in Art. 41, preferably with a layer of building paper or other material between the subfloor and the finished floor as shown in Fig. 63-1*a*. Magnesite composition as described in Art. 66 may be used in place of matched flooring, or the construction may be changed to receive tile, terrazzo, or other material.

The joists are usually 2 in. wide and from 6 to 14 in. deep. For heavy loads the joists may be 3 or 4 in. wide. Wider joists are used in *heavy timber construction*, which is considered under another heading. The usual spacings are 12 and 16 in., 24 in. being too great a space for good results with most lath. Light metal lath requires a spacing not greater than 12 in., but greater spacing may be used with heavier lath. In some cases, 1-by-2-in. furring strips, properly spaced for lath and running at right angles to the joists, are nailed to the underside of the joists to receive the lath. Then the spacing of the joists is independent of the lath. This construction enables fire to spread rapidly across the joists and is therefore objectionable. Another objection to the use of wood furring strips, nailed to the underside of wood joists, is the tendency for these strips to become loose and permit the ceiling to fall as the joists dry out and their grip on the nails weakens.

An important function of the subfloor is to provide a floor during the early stages of construction. A subfloor makes the floor more sub-

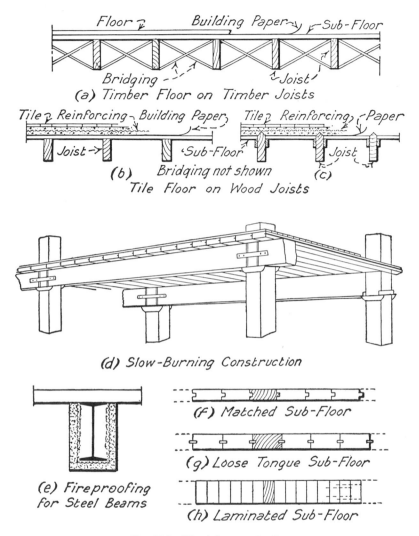

(a) Timber Floor on Timber Joists

(b) Bridging not shown   *(c)*

Tile Floor on Wood Joists

(d) Slow-Burning Construction

(e) Fireproofing for Steel Beams

(f) Matched Sub-Floor

(g) Loose Tongue Sub-Floor

(h) Laminated Sub-Floor

Fig. 63-1. Wood floor construction.

stantial, more fire-resistant, more soundproof, and warmer. When a subfloor is used, there is a tendency to nail the finished floor to the subfloor rather than to the joists. This practice is objectionable because the finished floor does not remain in place as well when nailed to the subfloor and tends to squeak. There is also a tendency to lay the finished floor parallel with the joists, which is objectionable. The subfloor should be laid diagonally, or if strips are placed on the subfloor and over the joists, the finished floor and subfloor may both be laid at right angles to the joists, the strips overcoming the uneven places in the subfloor. The subfloor may be of ordinary sheathing, matched boards, shiplap, or plywood. Sometimes the subfloor is omitted entirely to decrease the cost, and if so the finished floor would probably have to be laid before plastering, during which operation it must be protected from dirt and water. It will absorb moisture given off by the plaster. This will cause swelling, which will be followed by shrinking and the opening of the joints.

The layer between the subfloor and the finished floor may be omitted entirely or may consist of building paper, asphaltic felt, asbestos paper, or gypsum board. Some form of layer should always be used; and, if the cost will permit, the increase in fire-resistance and sound-deadening properties due to a layer of heavy asbestos paper or gypsum board will warrant the additional expenditure.

The joists are held in a vertical position by cross bridging as shown in Fig. 63-1a, one row being used where the span of the joists is over about 8 ft., and two rows where over 16 ft. Cross bridging also serves to distribute concentrated loads over several joists.

If a wood subfloor is laid before rain is excluded from the building, and it usually is, provisions should be made for the swelling of the subfloor or the exterior walls may be cracked and pushed out and other damage may be caused. To prevent this, spaces $\frac{1}{4}$ to $\frac{1}{2}$ in. may be left between the boards, or every tenth or twelfth board may be omitted at first and placed after the building is under cover.

Where a tile floor is to be placed on wood joist construction the floor is usually designed to carry a reinforced-concrete slab (Fig. 63-1b), to act as a base for the tile. The construction shown in c is also used, but is more likely to produce cracks than the construction in b. A thin-setting bed for ceramic floor tile which does not require special construction is described in Art. 67.

This type of floor construction is used in residences and other buildings of *wood frame* and *ordinary construction* and may be used in buildings with steel frames. It is inexpensive, light, and may be made sufficiently strong for heavy loads, but it is very combustible. If protected on the underside by plaster or metal lath its resistance to fire is increased.

Heavy Wood Subfloor on Wood or Steel Beams. Wood subfloors varying in thickness from 3 to 10 in., depending upon the loading and span, may be supported directly by girders running between columns, or by beams which are supported by the girders, as shown in Fig. 41-8 and described in Art. 41. In the first arrangement the lateral spacing of columns commonly is not over 10 or 12 ft. because of the heavy subfloors required for longer spans. .In the second arrangement the beams are spaced 4 ft. or more apart, and the column spacing is not restricted by the strength of the subfloor.

To secure resistance to fire, wood beams and girders are made at least 6 in. wide and 10 in. deep, even though the loads may not require beams of this size. If steel beams are used, they may be protected against fire (Fig. 63-1e), the beam first being covered with metal lath and then plastered.

Heavy wood subfloors may be of three types, matched (Fig. 63-1f), loose-tongue (g), or laminated (h). The matched floor may be used for thicknesses of 3 or 4 in., but for greater thicknesses the waste in matching becomes so large that the hardwood *loose tongue* may be more economical. This loose tongue is also called a *slip tongue* or *spline*.

Floors 4 in. and more in thickness may be constructed by laying 2-in. lumber on edge and securing the adjacent pieces together with spikes spaced about 18 in., 2-by-4's being used for a 4-in. floor, 2-by-6's for a 6-in. floor, and so on. This type of floor is known as a *laminated floor*. A laminated floor is easier to lay than a heavy loose-tongue floor, for the pieces being smaller are more easily handled and drawn into position; however more feet, board measure, are required because 2-in. material is really 1⅝ to 1¾ in. thick. The cost of the loose tongue is saved in the laminated floor.

When the details are properly worked out, this type of construction, using wood in large masses, is called *heavy timber construction*.

Light Steel Joists. Light steel joists are described in Art. 45. Open-web joists (Fig. 45-1r) are spaced 12 to 24 in. apart. They may support a thin concrete or gypsum slab reinforced in both directions with small bars spaced about 12 in. or welded-wire fabric with ribbed expanded metal lath placed over, and fastened to, the tops of the joists (Fig. 63-2a), the metal lath serving as the bottom form for slab. Wood nailing strips running perpendicular to the joists and fastened to the joists (b) may be provided if wood finished flooring is to be used over a thin concrete slab. Instead of providing nailing strips in the concrete slab, nailable concrete, as described in Art. 11, may be used. If wood floors are to be used, nailer joists are available with a wood

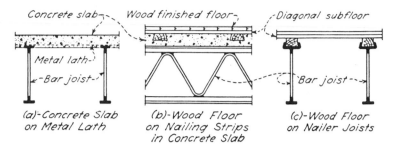

Fig. 63-2. Concrete and wood floors on open-web joists.

nailing strip anchored along the top flange of each joist to permit the nailing of the floor to the joists (*c*). Wood flooring may be fastened directly to the nailing strip shown in *b* and *c* or a wood subfloor may be used. If a subfloor is used, it should be laid diagonally, as has been described.

The light rolled-steel sections manufactured especially for use as floor and roof joists may be used in the same manner as the open-web joists, but nailer joists of this type are not available. The nailing strips are fastened to the joists on the job.

Horizontal or cross bridging is required for open-web joists to correspond to that used with wood joists. This bridging may consist of light steel rods or angles with their ends securely anchored to the flanges of the joists.

Ceilings may be provided on the underside of these types of floor construction by plastering over metal lath, or other plaster base, fastened to the underside of the joists. Such ceilings improve the appearance and are usually required for that purpose as well as to increase the resistance to fire. A 4-hr. rating may be attained by using metal lath and vermiculite gypsum plaster and a noncombustible subfloor.

Reinforced Concrete Floors. Reinforced concrete slabs supported by steel beams are described in Art. 52 and illustrated in Fig. 52-1*a* and *b*. Reinforced concrete slabs supported by reinforced concrete beams are described in Art. 52 and illustrated in *c*. Reinforced concrete flat-slab construction is described in Art. 52 and illustrated in Fig. 52-2.

Reinforced concrete flat-plate and slab-band floors are described in Art. 52 and illustrated in Fig. 52-3. Precast concrete floor decks, which may or may not be prestressed are described in Art. 58 and illustrated in Fig. 58-1. Precast gypsum decks are also used.

Reinforced concrete ribbed slabs supported by steel or reinforced concrete beams are described in Art. 52 and illustrated in Figs. 52-4 and 5.

Cellular Steel and Concrete Decks (1). The floor decks of buildings with structural steel framing are often made of cellular panels consisting of light-gage galvanized or painted sheet steel with cross sections and interlocking edges, such as those illustrated in Fig. 63-3a. These panels span the distance between floor beams which may be 20 ft. or more and are covered with a poured lightweight concrete slab about 2 in. thick. No temporary intermediate supports are required. The panels are attached to the steel beams by welding.

The required fire resistance for the underside is provided by a suspended ceiling of metal lath and plaster. The thickness and composition of this ceiling is determined by the required fire-resistance rating. For example, a ceiling with ⅞ in. of vermiculite plaster on metal lath, suspended to provide at least 2¼ in. of air space between the underside of the panel and the back of the lath, gives the construction a 4-hr. rating. If two coats of sanded gypsum plaster of specified mixes are applied on metal lath to give a total thickness of ¾ in. and no air space is provided, a 1½-hr. rating is given.

This type of deck has light weight, provides a working platform before the concrete slab is placed, and makes possible the placing of present and future wiring in the open cells. It is suitable for use

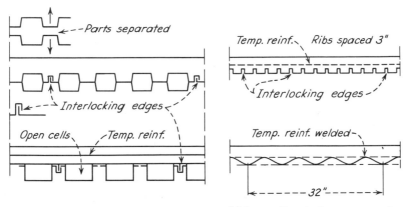

(a) Cellular steel and concrete   (b) Composite steel and concrete
                                           arranged from reference (1)

Fig. 63-3. Types of lightweight steel and concrete decks.

in office buildings, hotels, and apartment buildings because the floors do not carry heavy loads. Its use is permitted, for *fire-resistive* buildings, by many but not all building codes.

Composite Steel and Concrete Decks (1). One type of light-gage, galvanized or painted steel panel which is used in constructing short-span floor decks is illustrated in Fig. 63-3b. It is provided with longitudinal ribs to give rigidity during construction and to provide reinforcement for the concrete floor slab for which it serves as a form. Only the ribs, which are embedded in concrete, are considered effective in providing reinforcement. When necessary, additional reinforcement in the form of bars is included between the ribs as shown. Transverse temperature reinforcement is provided. If the slab is continuous over the supports, reinforcement is placed near the top of the slab in this region, as described elsewhere. The panels are anchored to the steel beams which support them, ordinarily by welding. Temporary supports usually will be necessary between the beams while the lightweight concrete is being placed and hardening.

The light-gage corrugated steel panel (b) is used in a manner similar to the ribbed panel. However, since the temperature reinforcement is welded to the tops of the corrugations, as shown, it anchors or bonds the corrugations to the concrete so effectively that the full cross-sectional area of the corrugated steel is available to resist flexural stresses.

The lower sides of both types of decks are made fire resistant, as required, by providing suspended ceilings constructed of metal lath and plaster of a thickness and composition necessary to provide the specified hourly rating.

Ground Floors. Ground floors are usually constructed of concrete from 4 to 6 in. thick, which is either dampproofed or waterproofed as described in Art. 24. Even after these precautions have been taken, it is quite probable that sufficient moisture will be present to cause some kinds of wearing surface to be short-lived. The various types of wearing surfaces are considered in subsequent articles.

Concrete slabs which serve as the ground floor of basementless houses should be protected against dampness as are other floors in contact with the ground, and in addition, in areas which experience low temperatures, the edges should be insulated with at least 2 in. of rigid waterproof insulation to avoid cold areas and condensation around the outside edges of the floors.

64. SELECTING TYPE OF FLOOR CONSTRUCTION

Factors Involved. Some of the factors involved in selecting the type of floor construction for a building are:

(a) general type of construction used in the building,
(b) plan of the building,
(c) floor loads,
(d) lateral resistance,
(e) floor thickness,
(f) resistance to fire,
(g) sound transmission,

(h) weight,
(i) ceiling, flat or exposed beams,
(j) wearing surface,
(k) position of floor, ground floor or above ground,
(l) installation of utilities,
(m) use of building,
(n) cost.

These factors overlap in many cases, and their relative importance varies with different classes of buildings. Local conditions including prevailing types of construction, availability of labor and materials, weather conditions, time available for construction, and other factors enter into the selection.

Unless precast concrete is specifically mentioned, the comments in this article refer to cast-in-place concrete construction. Special consideration is given to the use of precast concrete construction in Art. 56, to the advantages and disadvantages of precast and prestressed concrete in Art. 57, and to lift-slab construction in Art. 60.

General Type of Construction. The floor system and the structural frame are so interrelated that selections of basic materials and types of construction are made for the building as a whole. For a given building, several alternatives may be investigated, the advantages and disadvantages of each being considered. The local building code requirements must always be satisfied. There are marked differences in the requirements of such codes.

Wood stud walls and partitions would naturally be associated with light wood joist and subfloors. Such floor systems might also be used with wood columns, beams, and girders, or a heavy timber floor system might be used.

If a steel frame is used, the floor system might be one of several types of reinforced concrete plain or ribbed floor systems, except the flat-slab, flat-plate, or slab-band. This type of frame is also suitable for use with thin concrete slabs on light steel or open-web joists or on light-gage steel cellular, ribbed, or corrugated panels. If the framing can be arranged so that there are many identical panels, some form of precast reinforced concrete or gypsum panel may prove advantageous.

If the beams and girders are to be of reinforced concrete, the floor systems will be plain or ribbed reinforced concrete slabs and the columns usually will be reinforced concrete. Such columns will also be used with flat-slab, flat-plate, and slab-band floor systems. Precast concrete or gypsum panels may be advantageous for the same conditions given in the preceding paragraph.

Various types of floor systems can be used with masonry bearing walls, including light wood joist and subfloors; heavy timber floor systems; wood or concrete floors supported on steel I-beams or light steel or open web joists; reinforced concrete beams and slabs; reinforced concrete ribbed slabs; and precast concrete or gypsum slabs supported on steel joists.

Plan of Building. If the floor is divided into panels which are square or very nearly square, reinforced concrete flat-slab or flat-plate construction may be desirable, or the two-way plain or ribbed reinforced concrete slab with beams on the four sides of each panel may be seriously considered. If the spans are short, the plain slab might be used, whereas for long spans the ribbed slabs will be more satisfactory. If the building is to be divided into rooms, flat-plate or slab-band construction may prove desirable, but flat-slab construction is not as satisfactory as it is for undivided areas because of the interference of the column capitals and drop panels with the partitions. Concrete ribbed slabs are particularly suitable for long spans.

The adaptability of a floor system to changes in the locations of partitions to suit changing occupancy is of importance in office and some other types of buildings.

Floor Loads. Reinforced concrete flat-plate floors, light and open-web steel joists, and cellular, ribbed, and corrugated light-gage steel panels all with thin poured concrete slabs are suitable for light and medium floor loads such as those of apartment houses, office buildings, hotels, and schools.

Reinforced concrete slabs supported on reinforced concrete or steel beams, girders, and columns, reinforced concrete flat-slab construction, and heavy timber matched or laminated decks supported on heavy timber or steel beams, girders, and columns are appropriate floor systems for heavy loads.

Even though the distributed floor load may not be heavy, consideration must be given to the possibility that a floor may be subjected to a heavy concentrated load. Such a load may be the determining factor in the thickness of the top slab in ribbed floors or floors with closely spaced joists.

Lateral Resistance. Low tier buildings or even relatively high tier buildings with a low ratio of height to width will usually not require that special provisions be made to resist the lateral forces produced by wind. Girders framing into columns, either steel or concrete, offer the maximum opportunity for providing lateral resistance without the use of shear walls or other special arrangements. Reinforced concrete flat-plate floors and columns are not effective in this respect. Comments might be made on other systems, but these serve as extreme examples. In addition, if shear walls or wind bents are used, the floor systems will be required to transfer the lateral load horizontally to the bents. This factor sometimes requires consideration.

Floor Thickness. The minimum height of building for given number of stories and clear ceiling height is obtained with flat-plate, slab-band, or flat-slab construction.

Thin concrete slabs supported on light-gage cellular steel panels, wood subfloors, or thin concrete slabs supported on open-web steel joists, ribbed concrete slabs, and hollow precast panels form relatively thin floor systems if the girders that support them are located over partitions. Concrete slabs or wood decks supported on beams and girders take up the most room.

Any increase in height means an increase in the cost of walls, columns, elevators, stairways, and many other items, individually small, which may reach a total worth considering. By using thin floor systems, it may also be possible to construct one or more additional stories within a height limitation included in a code.

Resistance to Fire. When a building must be cheaply constructed and resistance to fire is not a decisive factor, ordinary wood joist construction with wood subfloor may be used. These conditions prevail in residence construction more than in any other class of building.

In warehouses and many types of industrial buildings, *heavy timber construction* may offer sufficient resistance to fire and provide a building at a lower cost than that of a more fire-resistive building. This is especially true if automatic sprinkler systems are installed.

In the congested downtown districts of many cities, building ordinances require *fire-resistive construction,* and therefore wood joist construction and *heavy timber construction* cannot be used. Floors constructed of open-web steel joists and concrete slabs protected with suspended ceilings of metal lath and vermiculite or perlite gypsum plaster are approved by some, but not all, cities as *fire-resistive construction.* It is always necessary to consult the local building code to determine the acceptability of the fire resistance of a floor system. The cost of fire insurance is an important factor entering into the choice of floor construction, the rates depending upon the fire resistance of the construction as well as the nature of the contents, the location, and many other factors. The rate is lowered in many classes of buildings by the installation of automatic sprinkler systems which come into action in any part of a building when the temperature in that part is raised by fire.

Sound Transmission. The various types of floor systems differ quite markedly in their effectiveness in resisting the transmission of sound. For some types of occupancy, such as warehouses, this factor is of minor importance, while for other types, such as hotels, schools and apartment houses, it must be given serious consideration. Sound transmission of impact noises is influenced by the type of wearing surface as well as by the floor system. This subject is considered in Art. 98.

Weight. The weight of a floor system to carry a given load is an important factor, because it affects the weight and cost of the supporting members and the foundations. Wood construction is advantageous where its use is permissible. Systems with closely spaced joists which permit the use of thin lightweight slabs are lighter than those which require thicker slabs of reinforced concrete and may satisfy code requirements. Considerable weight reduction can be achieved by using lightweight aggregate in concrete. Various other obvious comparisons might be made, but enough comments have been made for illustrative purposes.

Ceiling. Ordinary wood joist construction, flat-plate construction, slab-band construction, and ribbed concrete slabs provide flat ceilings, but plain concrete slabs supported by beams and girders and some other types of construction require *suspended ceilings* if flat ceilings are desired. Girders running between columns interfere with flat ceilings whenever they are present. In addition to their better appearance, flat ceilings do not interfere with the locations of partitions. Partitions are often located under girders in which case girders are not objectionable.

Plastered ceilings are provided by applying two coats of plaster directly to the underside of ribbed slabs with clay, concrete, or gypsum tile fillers, flat slabs, or plain slabs supported by concrete or fireproofed steel beams. The ribbed slabs and the flat slabs provide a flat ceiling, but the slabs supported by beams necessitate breaks in the ceiling, and the cost of plastering is greater because of the increased area and the additional labor required in finishing around the edges of the beams. Wood joists, heavy timber construction, metal joists, and ribbed slabs with steel forms require lath and preferably three coats of plaster or plasterboard and two coats of plaster on the underside to provide a plastered ceiling. The ceiling supported by wood joists, ribbed slabs with steel forms, and metal joists will be flat, whereas the ceiling supported by heavy timber construction will probably follow around the beams. The cost of the lath and the additional cost of plaster should be considered in selecting the floor construction if plastered ceilings are required. Monolithic concrete ceiling surfaces are often finished by painting directly rather than on plaster.

Wearing Surface. The type of wearing surface, as considered in the following articles, is a factor in selecting the type of floor system, or the reverse may be true.

If wood flooring is to be used for the wearing surface, light wood joist and heavy timber construction have an advantage in cost over other forms of floor construction where nailing strips with concrete fill between have to be provided. The closely spaced light steel joists may be covered with nailable concrete slabs and thereby avoid nailing strips, or nailing strips may be anchored to the tops of the joists with a light concrete slab between nailing strips. Some forms of wood floors may be cemented directly to carefully finished concrete surfaces with bituminous cement.

If the wearing surface is to be linoleum, cork, concrete, composition, asphalt tile, vinyl tile, cork carpet, rubber, ceramic tile, etc., any of the forms of floor construction which provide a concrete top surface are suitable, but the additional cost of providing a finished surface on the concrete must be considered.

With wood joist or heavy timber construction, a concrete surface required as a base for some wearing surfaces would add to the cost. Asphalt tile, vinyl tile, and linoleum, etc., require a matched floor or plywood, but composition can be laid on the wood subfloor.

Ceramic tile, marble, slate, and terrazzo usually require a concrete foundation, and thus the various forms of floor construction which provide a concrete top surface are suitable for the installation of these materials without further expenditure, but wood sub-floors require a

2-in. or 3-in. slab, which increases the cost considerably. The thin-setting bed for ceramic tile described in Art. 67 may, however, be satisfactory.

For many purposes a smooth troweled finish on a concrete slab may be satisfactory. It may be colored or, if subjected only to light traffic, a painted surface may be satisfactory. Such a finish can be provided readily by several floor systems.

Position of Floor. Floors placed on the ground will normally be concrete slabs, and if not subjected to hydrostatic pressure will have light wire mesh or no reinforcing.

Installation of Utilities. The utilities which are installed in a building are not considered in this treatise, but the provisions which often must be made in floor systems to provide for conduits and pipes, wiring, plumbing, and heating, and ducts for ventilating and air conditioning require consideration. Open-web steel joists provide space through which pipes and conduits can be run to any position in a floor and ducts can be placed between joists. Light-gage cellular steel panels afford similar but more restricted opportunities for wiring conduits. The space above suspended ceilings is used extensively for such purposes. Wiring conduits are ordinarily located in concrete floor slabs or in concrete fills placed on top of the structural slabs, but water pipes should not be embedded in this manner because of the cost of repairing leaks. Wood joist floors have the same advantages as open-web steel joists but require that holes be bored for pipes and conduits running perpendicular to the joists.

Use of Building. The use to be made of a building enters into the choice of the type of construction. It is a determining factor in the selection of a particular type of construction only to the extent that it influences the various factors that have been considered.

Cost. Of course, one of the most important factors to be considered in selecting a specific floor system and wearing surface from several which satisfy all of the basic requirements is the cost. The total cost may be divided into the direct cost, the indirect cost, and the continuing annual cost.

The direct cost includes the cost of the floor system, including the wearing surface, the supporting beams, and ceiling surfaces, directly applied or suspended. The indirect costs are the costs of the girders, the columns, and their foundations. The relative effects of floor systems on the total height of a building may also be considered, because differences in cost caused by this factor may be of some significance.

Differences in height are reflected in differences in the costs of exterior walls, columns, elevators, stairways, vertical pipes, conduits, ducts, and other items. The differences continuing annual costs include differences in costs of care and maintenance of the various wearing surfaces.

Finally, the selection of a floor system should take into account the differences in the annual cost of fire insurance. For many classes of occupancy and types of construction, the installation of automatic sprinkler systems may markedly reduce the annual cost or make possible changes in the type of construction which reduce the overall cost.

Because of the many factors involved, including the effects of local customs, and the relative availability and costs of different kinds of labor and materials, no specific comparisons can be made. When cost is an important factor in the selection of the floor system, and it usually is, comparative estimates are made of the costs of the types that warrant consideration after all other factors are considered.

65. WOOD FLOORING

Types. Wood flooring is available in the following forms.

a. Strip flooring, consisting of long narrow pieces or strips with tongued-and-grooved joints along the sides and often along the ends also for hardwoods. Generally called *matched flooring* or simply *flooring.*

b. Plank flooring, consisting of wider boards than strip flooring with tongued-and-grooved joints along the sides and ends.

c. Parquet flooring, consisting of short narrow boards cut to form patterns or mosaics.

d. Industrial wood block flooring, consisting of heavy pieces cut in lengths of from 2 in. to 4 in. forming blocks which are set with the ends of the grain exposed to wear.

e. Fabricated wood block flooring, consisting of small square or rectangular blocks formed by fastening short pieces of strip flooring together, tongued-and-grooved joints being provided on all sides.

Methods of Fastening. Wood flooring may be nailed to wood joists through a wood subfloor. *Nailing strips* are often provided on concrete floor slabs and other types of supporting floors. These strips may be beveled (Fig. 65-1a) and embedded in concrete which holds them in place. Nails may be driven into the sides of the strips to grip the concrete. Expansion bolts or screws may be used as anchors.

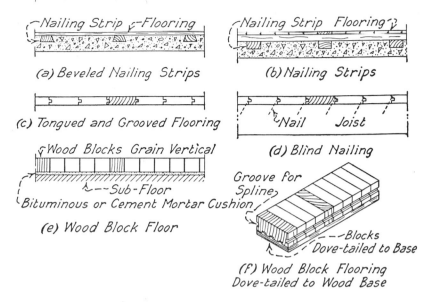

Fig. 65-1. Wood floor surfaces.

Special clips to receive the strips may be embedded in the top of the slab when the slab is poured, or the strips may be nailed to other strips at right angles to them, the whole grid being embedded in concrete (*b*).

Nailable concrete, described in Art. 11, may be used, with more or less satisfactory results, instead of nailing strips. These concretes are of special composition which permits nails to penetrate. They are usually applied in a layer 2 in. thick with the top surface struck very accurately to receive the finished floor.

Industrial and fabricated wood blocks are usually cemented, and parquet, plank, and short pieces of strip flooring are often cemented to concrete floors, or to a concrete fill, with an asphalt mastic. These mastics are of two types, the *hot mastic,* which is made fluid by heating, and the *cold mastic,* which is made fluid by a solvent. The hot mastic is applied to the slab, and the flooring is bedded in it before it cools. The cold mastic gradually solidifies by the evaporation of the solvent after the flooring is placed. The layer of asphalt mastic is called an *underlayment.*

Flooring which is provided with tongue and groove is *blind-nailed* to joists or nailing strips (*d*), so that the nail does not show on the surface. To avoid injuring the floor by the last blow of the hammer which drives the nail home, a square bar, or the square end of a nail set, may be placed in the corner and against the nail head to receive the hammer blow and protect the flooring. Special flooring nails with small heads (Fig. 36-1d) are used in blind nailing. The ends of plank flooring are commonly screwed to the subfloor, the heads of the screws being sunk in holes bored part way in the wood. These holes then are filled with wood plugs which are specially manufactured for that purpose. The plugs are quite visible, but this is the effect desired. To provide for expansion, plank flooring should be laid with temporary metal spacers $\frac{1}{32}$ in. thick placed in the cracks between the planks. Parquet floors are fastened to wood subfloors with brads driven through the face, the brads being set by driving their heads below the surface with a *nail set*. The holes above the heads are filled with putty.

Kinds of Wood. Strip flooring, plank flooring, parquet flooring, and fabricated wood blocks are available in the hardwoods: white and red oak, maple, beech, birch, and walnut. The oaks may be *plain-sawed* or *quarter-sawed*, often called *vertical-grain* or *edge-grain*. Strip flooring is also available in the softwoods: fir, yellow pine, white pine, cypress, and many others, listed in Table 9-1. Only the quarter-sawed or vertical-grain softwoods should be used, except in the cheapest construction or for attics or other floors which are little used. Industrial wood blocks are usually made of yellow pine, oak, gum or Douglas fir.

Size, Grades, etc. *Strip flooring,* which is called flooring or matched flooring, is usually $2\frac{5}{32}$ in. thick. The most common widths of hardwood flooring are $2\frac{1}{4}$, 3, and 4 in. which have exposed faces of $1\frac{1}{2}$, $2\frac{1}{4}$, and $3\frac{1}{4}$ in.; and the common widths of softwood flooring are 3 and 4 in., with exposed faces of $2\frac{3}{8}$ and $3\frac{1}{4}$ in. Oak flooring $\frac{3}{8}$ in. and $\frac{1}{2}$ in. thick and maple flooring $\frac{3}{8}$ in., 1 in., and $1\frac{1}{4}$ in. thick are available. Thicker maple flooring may be obtained on special order. The thinner flooring is for use over old floors and is not usually satisfactory for new buildings because of its tendency to squeak. Thick maple flooring is suitable for severe usage such as in warehouses, factories, and gymnasiums. Heavy trucking may break off the tongues or lower part of the grooves of ordinary strip flooring. Maple, beech, and birch flooring is furnished in three grades depending upon the quality, i.e., first, second, and third. Oak flooring is available in five grades, i.e., clear, sap clear, select, No. 1 common, No. 2 common.

Plank flooring is usually $1\frac{3}{16}$ in. thick and from 3 to 8 in. wide. It is commonly used in random widths and is known as *colonial plank flooring.* The exposed edges may be slightly beveled to form V joints.

Parquet flooring is usually $\frac{5}{16}$ in. thick and 1, $1\frac{1}{2}$, or 2 in. wide with square edges, but $1\frac{3}{16}$-in. flooring, $2\frac{1}{4}$ in. wide, which is side- and end-matched is also available.

Industrial wood blocks vary in thickness from 2 to 4 in., depending upon the severity of the service. The width is from $2\frac{1}{4}$ to 4 in. and the length from 4 to 9 in. The blocks are often provided with wood or metal splines and may be assembled in strips, up to 8 ft. in length, whose width equals the length of a single block, as shown in Fig. 65-1*f*. The joints between the blocks are filled with bituminous filler. Expansion spaces about 1 in. wide should be provided against all walls and around all columns, thresholds, and permanent fixtures.

Fabricated wood blocks are made of flooring usually $1\frac{3}{16}$ in. thick, but $\frac{1}{2}$-in. and 1-in. thick blocks are also available. The squares vary in size from $6\frac{3}{4}$ in. to $11\frac{1}{4}$ in., and the rectangles are about 6 in. by 12 in. The number of strips to a block may be 4, 5, or 6. Expansion spaces should be allowed around all walls, columns, thresholds, and permanent fixtures, the width being about $\frac{1}{16}$ in. for each foot of width or length. These spaces may be partly filled with asphalt mastic, may be completely filled with cork strips, or may contain springs to hold the edge blocks in place. If a room is much longer than it is wide, square blocks should be laid diagonally. The blocks are often sanded, filled, waxed, and polished at the factory.

Uses. Wood floors are warm and elastic and therefore are not tiresome to work on. They are clean and, if proper selection is made and they receive proper care, they are durable. They may be made attractive in appearance and are suitable, from that point of view, for the highest type of use. Wood floors supported by *fire-resistive construction* are used in many buildings classed as fire-resistive, because they burn very slowly in case of fire. However, they are not used in the highest type of fire-resistive buildings. They are one of the most satisfactory floors for residences and are usually the cheapest.

Wood floors should not be placed until after all concrete work and plastering have been completed and the building has had a chance to dry out. The flooring should not be stored in the house during this period. The cracks in wood floors which are permitted to absorb moisture, before they are laid, will open up as the wood dries out. Special care should be used in wood floors laid over concrete to make sure that the concrete has dried out. An asphalt mastic dampproofing layer should preferably be placed over the concrete.

66. CONCRETE, TERRAZZO, AND MAGNESITE COMPOSITION FLOORING

Concrete (2). Concrete wearing surfaces are used very widely where the structural part of the floor is of concrete. The wearing surface may be an integral part of the construction beneath, or it may be added as a separate layer. If the wearing surface is placed before the base has set, a thickness of ¾ in. to 1 in. is satisfactory; but if it is placed after the base has set, the thickness should be 1 in. to 1½ in., and the surface of the base should be roughened, thoroughly cleaned, and coated with cement grout just before the wearing surface is placed. This is done to secure a bond between the wearing surface and the base, but the results are uncertain.

The wearing surface which is an integral part of the floor may be considered as contributing to the strength of the structure; whereas a wearing surface which is added cannot be so considered and its weight increases the dead load that must be carried by all the beams, columns, and foundations. In spite of this disadvantage, a separate wearing surface may be cheaper than the integral wearing surface, for it is placed after the rough work on the building has been completed and does not need to be protected as carefully as the integral surface. The conditions which exist while the structural part of the floor is being placed may be such that the accuracy required of a finished floor is difficult and expensive to secure.

A truer surface can be secured with the separate wearing surface as the deflection due to the weight of the floor and the yielding of the forms has occurred before the surface is placed, and any discrepancies can be taken up in the wearing surface. The separate wearing surface is sometimes made thick enough to permit the placing of electrical conduits on top of the structural slab.

The coarse aggregate is excluded from the wearing surface, and a richer mixture than that used in the structural parts is used. The aggregate grains and not the cement resist the wear, and therefore the grains should have a high resistance to abrasion. Beyond a certain limit, an increase in the amount of cement reduces the wearing qualities of a surface and increases the tendency to crack. Usually the mixture or *topping* for the wearing surface consists of 1 part cement to not less than 2 or more than 3 parts fine aggregate.

For surfaces subjected to severe wear, the mixture should be 1 part cement, not more than 1 part fine aggregate, and not more than 2 parts coarse aggregate with a maximum size of ½ in. Various admixtures, or hardeners, are available for use in the topping to improve its wearing properties.

Concrete wearing surfaces or topping must be carefully laid using a minimum amount of water, troweling as little as possible, and protecting against drying out for at least ten days. Excessive troweling brings excess water and laitance to the surface, causing hair cracks to form and the floor to give off objectionable dust. This process is called *dusting*. Topping applied to a hardened base should be struck off and compacted by rolling or with tampers or vibrators and finished with a steel trowel. The use of dry cement or cement and fine aggregate sprinkled on the surface to stiffen the mix or absorb excess moisture is objectionable because it may cause hair-cracking, scaling, or dusting. Dusting may be prevented or remedied somewhat by the use of *floor hardeners* and other preparations or by painting.

Painted surfaces are satisfactory when the amount of wear is small, but, where subjected to severe use, frequent painting is required. Special paints are manufactured for use on cement floors. A cement-colored paint, of course, shows the wear less than paint of any other color. Paint should not be applied until after the floor has been in place three or four months. Before painting, the surface should be thoroughly scrubbed with a 10 per cent solution of muriatic acid and washed so that the acid is completely removed. The floor should then be allowed to dry before the paint is applied. Paint for the first coat is thinned. Three coats are usually required.

Concrete wearing surfaces are sometimes colored and marked off to imitate tile. Colored concrete floors finished with wax may be attractive in appearance.

If artificial coloring matter is used, only those mineral colors should be employed which will not appreciably impair the strength of the concrete.

Mineral coloring material is preferred to organic coloring material, because the latter fades more than mineral colors and may seriously reduce the strength of concrete. Mineral coloring may reduce the strength of concrete somewhat, but where the quantities used are less than 5 per cent this is not serious. The use of colored aggregates is preferable in obtaining color effects, the surface of the floor being brushed or ground to expose the aggregate.

Concrete floors are inelastic and cold and tiresome to work on, but they are durable if well constructed, are easily cleaned, and are relatively inexpensive. Concrete wearing surfaces should not be used over wood subfloors without taking special precautions to prevent cracking. The construction should be similar to that used for tile floors (Fig. 63-1*b*).

A cement wall base is often used with concrete floors. If a separate wearing surface is used, the wall base may be placed at the same time as the wearing surface with a curving fillet at the junction. This facilitates cleaning. A cement base will not adhere to lime plaster, hard wall plaster, gypsum block, Keene's cement, or plasterboard. The backing should be brick, stone, hollow tile, concrete, or metal lath.

A concrete floor is sometimes called upon to serve the double purpose of a floor and a roof. Under these conditions, a built-up roofing, as described in Art. 77, is placed on the structural slab. A wearing surface, consisting of a concrete slab about 3 in. thick, is placed over this roofing and is divided into sections not over 16 ft. square by expansion joints about ¾ in. wide with a bituminous filler.

Terrazzo (2). Terrazzo wearing surfaces are constructed in a manner similar to concrete wearing surfaces, but a special aggregate of marble chips or other decorative material is always used and this aggregate is exposed by grinding the surface.

The mortar-base course should be at least 1¼ in. thick and should be composed of 1 part portland cement and 4 parts sand with only enough water to produce a mortar of the stiffest consistency that can be struck off accurately with a straightedge.

The *mortar base* can be placed directly on the concrete slab and bonded to it by first cleaning this slab, thoroughly wetting it, and applying a thin coat of neat cement broomed into the surface for a short distance ahead of placing the mortar base; or the surface of the slab can first be covered with a thin smooth layer of fine dry sand about ¼ in. thick, on which is placed a layer of waterproof paper with end and side laps of at least 1 in., on which the mortar base is placed.

The mortar base is struck off at least ¾ in. below the finished floor level. Metal or plastic *dividing strips* are inserted in the mortar base, before it hardens, in positions which will control the cracking and conform to the design or pattern desired. The tops of dividing strips should extend at least 1/32 in. above the finished floor level so that they can be ground down flush with the floor surface when the terrazzo is being ground.

The *terrazzo mixture* should consist of 1 part of gray, white, or colored portland cement, according to the decorative effect desired, to not more than 2 parts by weight of marble chips, other decorative aggregate or abrasive aggregate, or such a mixture of any of these as is desired. The amount of water used should be such as to produce a workable plastic mix. Wet mixtures do not produce good results. Any special coloring agents should be mineral pigments.

After the mortar base has hardened enough to stand rolling, the terrazzo mixture should be placed to the level of the tops of the dividing strips and struck off. It should then be rolled in both directions to secure a thorough compacting. Additional aggregates of the desired color should be spread over the surface during the rolling process until at least 70 per cent of the finished surface is composed of aggregate. As soon as the rolling is completed, the surface should be floated and troweled once without attempting to remove trowel marks. Further troweling is objectionable.

After the terrazzo has hardened sufficiently to hold the aggregate firmly, it should be ground by hand or with a grinding machine, the floor being kept wet during the process. The material ground off should be removed by flushing with water. Any air holes or other defects should be filled with thin cement paste spread over the surface and worked in. After the paste has hardened for at least 72 hours, the floor surface should receive its final grinding. It should be kept continuously wet for at least ten days, scrubbed clean with warm water and soft soap, and mopped dry.

This type of floor is more expensive than concrete and less expensive than tile or marble. It is used for floors of buildings where an attractive and durable floor is desired, but is inelastic and cold. The greatest objection to terrazzo floors is their tendency to crack. Dividing strips greatly reduce this objection.

Terrazzo is not used directly over a wood subfloor. If placed over wooden construction it should have a base similar to that used for tile floors, as shown in Fig. 63-1b.

A terrazzo wall base is commonly used with terrazzo floors. It is usually made in the form of a sanitary cove base, the angle between the floor and the wall having a fillet to facilitate cleaning. A terrazzo base will not adhere to lime plaster, hardwall plaster, gypsum block, or plasterboard. The backing should be brick, stone, concrete, hollow clay, tile, or metal lath.

Magnesite Composition. Several basic types of magnesite composition floors are on the market. In general, magnesite composition floors consist of a dry mixture of magnesium oxide, asbestos or other inert material, fine aggregate such as crushed stone or sand, and a pigment to which liquid magnesium chloride is added on the job to form a plastic material which is troweled to a smooth finish and sets hard in a few hours.

Magnesium oxide is obtained by calcining magnesite, which is magnesium carbonate, the carbon dioxide being driven off in the process. When magnesium chloride is added to magnesium oxide a cementing material, known as magnesium oxychloride, is formed. This is the cementing material in magnesite composition floorings, the asbestos being the inert aggregate. Asbestos is chosen because of its toughness and cushioning effect.

The finished surface is usually $\frac{1}{2}$ or $\frac{5}{8}$ in. thick, but floors as thick as $1\frac{1}{2}$ in. are used. The $1\frac{1}{2}$-in. flooring is usually applied in two layers of about equal thickness. The lower layer is fibrous and serves as a cushion for the upper layer which is harder and forms the wearing surface. Magnesite flooring may be applied to a subfloor of wood, concrete, or steel plates. If the subfloor is wood, a base course or foundation is required in which metal lath or wire mesh is placed to prevent cracking.

A wall base of the same material may be placed at the same time as the floor, and it may be made monolithic with it, with a rounding corner between the two forming a sanitary base which is easily cleaned. This base should not be applied over hardwall plaster, Keene's cement, gypsum blocks, or plasterboard since it will not adhere to these surfaces. It will adhere to hollow clay tile, brick, stone, or concrete masonry and to metal lath. Metal lath should preferably be galvanized.

This type of floor is less attractive and less durable than ceramic tile, terrazzo, and marble, but is more comfortable to work on and less noisy than these floors. It is dustproof, easily cleaned, fire-resistant, and oil and grease resistant.

Magnesite composition, of some type, is appropriately used on the floors of schools, office buildings, industrial buildings, and many other types of buildings.

67. CERAMIC TILE, BRICK, STONE, AND GLASS

General Comments. Hard materials of various kinds, including ceramic tile, brick, stone, and glass, are used in tile or slab form for wall surfaces and, with the exception of glass, for floor surfaces also.

Ceramic tile of various shapes, sizes, thicknesses, colors, and surface finishes are manufactured for use as a surfacing material for interior and exterior floors and walls where a quality surface is desired.

Structural clay facing tile, as described in Art. 28, are manufactured for use as structural units in constructing partitions and interior and exterior wall surfaces. They are manufactured with dull and glazed exposed surfaces to provide a finished wall surface. Extruded wall ashlar, which is similar to structural clay facing tile but is more accurately finished, is available for use as a combined structural and facing wall material and for use as a surfacing material only.

Clay brick, as described in Art. 26, and special paving brick are used for floor surfaces under conditions of heavy wear. Facing brick and brick with glazed and enamel exposed surfaces are used as facing material as well as a structural material for interior and exterior surfaces of brick walls and partitions.

Various forms of natural stone, including marble, travertine, granite, sandstone, limestone, and slate, are used for interior and exterior floor and wall surfaces in the form of tile or large slabs. These materials are discussed in Arts. 12 and 27.

Structural glass is available in the form of tile or slabs in thicknesses from $\frac{1}{4}$ to $1\frac{1}{4}$ in., in various opaque colors, and with polished or honed finish, for use as a finish on exterior and interior wall surfaces. It is known by various trade names such as *Carrara Glass*, *Vitrolite*, and *Opalite*.

These materials may cover the entire wall surface, or they may extend upward only a few feet to form a wainscot and thereby protect the portion of the wall which receives the most severe use. They are all easily cleaned.

All the more important materials, except ceramic tile, are described in other articles and therefore will not be considered further.

Ceramic Tile. Ceramic tile are usually set in portland-cement mortar when used on the interior of buildings. Quarry tile and promenade tile are set in cement mortar over membrane waterproofing on roof gardens or in similar positions where a watertight floor is required. Floor tile are usually set on a concrete slab foundation or base; so wood floors must be specially constructed to receive this base, as described in Art. 63 and illustrated in Fig. 63-1b. Wall tile are set in a bed of portland-cement mortar applied to masonry walls or over portland-cement plaster on metal lath if applied to walls or partitions with wood studs. A thin-setting bed for floor tile has also been developed. It consists of emulsified asphalt and portland cement and is designed for use over wood, steel, and concrete surfaces. Its small thickness of $\frac{1}{16}$ to $\frac{3}{8}$ in. makes possible the use of tile floors in locations which formerly would not have been suitable.

Ceramic tile are divided into many classes depending upon the processes of manufacture, the degrees of vitreousness, and other properties.

These classes are considered more in detail in subsequent paragraphs. The Tile Manufacturers Association divides tile into *exterior* and *interior tile*, according to their exposure, and into *wall* and *floor tile*, according to their position. *Trimmers* are available for angles, corners, recesses, and special uses.

Ceramic tile are made by burning special clays or mixtures of clays which have been pressed into the desired shape. Two processes are used, the plastic process and the dust-pressed process.

In the *plastic process*, the clays are mixed with water and run through pugging machines until a uniform plastic consistency is secured. They are then pressed by hand or machine in dies or molds and, after drying, are burned in kilns. The plastic nature of the materials has a tendency to produce tiles which are slightly irregular in shape.

In the *dust-pressed process* the clays, after being finely ground and mixed with water, are passed into filter presses where the excess water is pressed out. The resulting mass is dried, pulverized, pressed into shape in metal dies, and burned in kilns.

The production of special sizes and shapes in the dust-pressed process involves special dies and handling and is a deviation from the regular routine of manufacture. In the plastic process special sizes and shapes may be produced without distinct departure from the methods of production common to the regular tile.

Ceramic tile may be glazed or unglazed. For use in residences, all types of floor glazes are sufficiently durable for floors, but for public buildings subjected to severe traffic a special high-fire type of glaze is available.

The colors in unglazed tiles are produced either by the selection of clays which will burn to the desired colors or by the addition of certain materials such as the oxides of cobalt and chromium. Some clays and color ingredients can be fired to complete vitrification, producing vitreous tile, while others will not stand this high temperature and produce semi-vitreous tile. A great variety of colors and textures are available.

Unless otherwise noted, the various types of vitreous tile are obtainable in the following colors: white, celadon, silver gray, green, blue-green, light blue, dark blue, pink, cream, and granites of these colors. The semivitreous tiles are available in buff, salmon, light gray, dark gray, red, chocolate, black, and the granites of these colors. The term granite means a mottled color resembling granite.

The most common shapes of tile are square, rectangular, hexagonal, octagonal, triangular, or round; and the sizes vary from ½ in. to 12 in., and the thickness from $\frac{1}{4}$ in. to $1\frac{1}{2}$ in. Trim tile are available for use as wall base or to meet any other decorative or utilitarian demands.

Various names are given to the tiles of different sizes and shapes. The more common types used for floor surfaces are the following. *Ceramic mosaic* include unglazed dust-pressed tile $\frac{1}{4}$ in. thick with an area of less than $2\frac{1}{4}$ sq. in. They are vitreous or semivitreous, depending on the color, and may be square, oblong, hexagonal, or round. These tile usually are mounted with exposed face stuck to paper in sheets about 2 ft. by 1 ft., the paper being removed after the tile are set. If desired the tile can be obtained loose.

Plastic mosaic include the same size and shape tile as ceramic mosaic, mounted or loose, but these tile are made by the plastic process, and the colors are those that result from the firings of natural clays.

Cut mosaic floors are made from unglazed, dust-pressed, vitreous or semivitreous strips, $\frac{1}{4}$ in. thick, and $\frac{1}{2}$ or $\frac{5}{8}$ in. wide, which are cut into the irregular pieces necessary in the production of ungeometric designs and pictorial work. These tile are furnished in loose strips or are assembled in designs mounted with exposed face on paper which is removed after the tile are set.

Vitreous tile and *semivitreous tile* are names applied to unglazed, dust-pressed tile $\frac{1}{2}$ in. thick. These tile are vitreous or semivitreous depending on the color. They are furnished in the same shapes as ceramic mosaic, except round, but are larger, having an area of $2\frac{1}{4}$ sq. in. or greater, the largest vitreous tile being 3 in. square and the largest semivitreous tile, 6 in. square.

Paving tile are unglazed, dust-pressed tile $\frac{3}{4}$ in. thick. Flint tile are vitreous paving tile, and the semivitreous are called *hydraulic tile*. These tile may be square, oblong, hexagonal, or octagonal. With the exception of the oblong tile the smallest size is $4\frac{1}{4}$ in. and the largest 6 in. Oblong tile vary in size from 6 in. by 3 in. to 10 in. by 5 in.

Corrugated paving tile are semivitreous, unglazed, dust-pressed paving tile $1\frac{3}{16}$ in. thick, and 6 in. square with corrugated face.

Rough red paving tile are semivitreous, unglazed, dust-pressed tile, $\frac{1}{2}$ in. or $\frac{5}{8}$ in. thick, depending on the size, and 6 in. or 9 in. square with the corresponding oblong half-tile.

Inlaid or *encaustic tile* are unglazed dust-pressed decorative tile, $\frac{1}{2}$ in. thick, produced by inlaying a figure or ornament of one or more colors into a body of a contrasting or harmonizing color before firing. They are vitreous or semivitreous according to colors.

Quarry tile are machine-made unglazed tile, $3/4$ in. to $1\frac{1}{2}$ in. thick, made from common clays. They are always square, the usual size being 6 in., 9 in., and 12 in. The colors may be various shades, plain red, or the following granites: red, light gray, dark gray, black, chocolate, light brown, dark brown, or green.

Promenade tile are machine-made, unglazed tile 1 in. thick, made from common clays. The size is always 6 in. by 9 in., and the color some shade of red.

Plastic tile are unglazed tile made by the plastic process from natural clays. Any size or shape can be obtained. The thickness is $\frac{1}{2}$ in. or more, depending upon the size.

68. LINOLEUM, CORK, RUBBER, ASPHALT, AND VINYL PLASTIC

General Comments. Elastic or resilient materials of various kinds, including linoleum, cork, rubber, asphalt, and vinyl plastic are used for floor and wall surfaces. These materials are usually cemented to wood, concrete, or plaster surfaces with special cements.

Linoleum. Linoleum is used as a covering for wood and concrete floors. In making linoleum, linseed oil is oxidized by exposure to the air into a tough, rubber-like substance which is mixed with ground cork, wood flour, coloring matter, and other ingredients, and the resultant plastic substance is pressed upon a backing of burlap. It is then passed into drying ovens where it is thoroughly cured and seasoned. There are three common types of linoleum: plain, printed or stamped, and inlaid. Linoleum is furnished in thicknesses varying from $\frac{1}{20}$ in. to $\frac{1}{4}$ in. in rolls usually 2 yd. wide but in some cases 4 yd. wide. It is also available in tile form.

Plain linoleum is a solid color throughout its entire thickness. It is furnished in several thicknesses, varying from $\frac{1}{12}$ in. to $\frac{1}{4}$ in., and in many colors. The thicker grades are known as *battleship linoleum* and are the most satisfactory grades for heavy traffic.

Stamped or *printed linoleum* has a pattern printed on the surface with oil paint. It varies in thickness from $\frac{1}{20}$ to $\frac{1}{12}$ in. and is satisfactory for light service only because the pattern wears off in time. After the pattern shows wear, the linoleum is still serviceable, but is unattractive. Occasional varnishing will preserve the pattern.

Inlaid linoleum consists of small units of linoleum of various colors and shapes arranged in patterns and pressed on a burlap back. The color of each unit is constant throughout the entire thickness; so the pattern remains as long as the linoleum lasts. Inlaid linoleums are furnished in thicknesses varying from $\frac{1}{12}$ in. to $\frac{1}{8}$ in. They are used extensively and will give satisfactory service wherever their use is appropriate.

The best method of laying linoleum on matched wood flooring is to paste a layer of heavy unsaturated felt paper to the wood floor and then to cement the linoleum to the felt. Linoleum is usually cemented directly to smooth concrete, plywood, or hardboard subfloors. Linoleum is sometimes tacked to wood floors, but this method is unsatisfactory.

Linoleum which is cemented directly to a matched wood floor tends to split as the boards shrink. If it is tacked around the edges and not cemented, it buckles because the traffic on linoleum tends to make it spread slightly. Matched floors should be sanded before linoleum is laid. Even if sanded, the outline of matched wood flooring eventually tends to show through linoleum, especially if the boards cup somewhat as they often do. For this reason, $\frac{5}{8}$-in. plywood is an excellent subfloor for linoleum because the joints will be 4 ft. apart and may not show at all if securely nailed. Hardboard $\frac{1}{4}$ in. thick, closely nailed to a wood subfloor, forms a good base for linoleum.

When a suitable linoleum is properly laid it will last for many years. It is sanitary, easily cleaned, resilient, warm, and attractive. Considering the length of life and satisfactory service, it may be classed as an inexpensive floor covering. Linoleum should not be used in basements. A special cove wall base is available for use with linoleum, and special linoleums are available for wall coverings.

Linoleum floors are often used without any surface treatment but if plain and inlaid linoleums are waxed and stamped linoleums are varnished, as often as the use requires, the floors will be more easily cleaned and will last longer.

Linoleum tile are of the same composition as linoleum, and have the same properties and uses, but may be arranged in patterns to form a floor which may be more attractive than linoleum. They are cemented to a wood or concrete floor in the same manner as linoleum.

Cork. Cork flooring is available in two forms, cork carpet and cork tile. Floors of wood or concrete may be covered with *cork carpet,* which is a covering similar to linoleum, and is laid in the same way. It is composed of the same material: oxidized linseed oil, ground cork, and wood flour, pressed to a burlap back, but it is not subjected to as great pressure as linoleum, and so is more resilient and porous and less durable. Cork carpet is ¼ in. thick and is furnished in rolls 2 yd. wide. Many colors are available.

To secure the best service, cork carpet should be laid by first cementing a layer of unsaturated felt to the wood or concrete floor, and then cementing the cork carpet to the felt. Cork carpet is often cemented directly to wood or concrete, and is sometimes tacked to wood floors. The latter method is particularly unsatisfactory.

Cork carpet makes a very quiet floor covering, and is more elastic, more absorbent, and less durable, than linoleum. It is particularly suitable for use in churches, theaters, public libraries, and other places where a noiseless floor covering is essential. Cork carpet should not be used in basements.

Cork tile are made from pure cork shavings compressed in molds to a thickness of ½ in. and baked. They are used over wood or cement floors to which they are cemented. Cork tile are elastic, noiseless, fairly durable, and quite absorbent. They are available in various shades of brown. The rosin in the cork liquefies during the baking process and cements the shavings together when the tile cools. The brown color of cork tile is largely caused by the baking it receives, the darker browns having been baked longer than the lighter browns. Cork tile are used for wall coverings as well as for flooring.

Rubber. Rubber flooring is made of synthetic rubber combined at high temperatures with fillers, such as cotton fiber, various minerals, and with the desired color pigments. It is made in the form of sheet rubber and rubber tile. The thickness varies from ⅛ to ¼ in. Many colors and patterns are available. Rubber flooring is cemented to concrete or wood in the same manner as linoleum. It is attractive in appearance, elastic, noiseless, durable, easily cleaned, but quite expensive. Rubber floors are not resistant to oil, grease, and gasoline and should not be used on floors in contact with the ground. Rubber is used as a wall covering as well as a flooring material.

Asphalt Tile. Asphalt tile are made from asphalt or resinous binders, asbestos fiber, mineral pigments, and inert fillers by amalgamating under heat and pressure. The sheets produced by this process are cut into tile of various sizes usually between 9-in. squares and 18-by-24-in. rectangles, but smaller and larger sizes are available. The thicknesses are ⅛ in., ³⁄₁₆ in., and ¼ in. The thinnest tile are suitable for placing on concrete when the traffic is not heavy. The most commonly used thickness for placing on wood and concrete is ³⁄₁₆ in., and for severe service the ¼-in. thickness is used. Asphalt tile are available in a great variety of colors varying from light to dark. Asphalt tile for industrial use are available in ¼-in., ⅜-in., and ½-in. thicknesses. They are available in various colors. For the lighter colors, the binder is chiefly or entirely resinous.

Asphalt tile floors are cemented to matched wood flooring, plywood, hardboard, or concrete in the same manner as linoleum.

Asphalt tile are resilient, nonabsorbent, reasonably stainproof and acidproof, relatively inexpensive, attractive, and moistureproof so that they can be used on concrete floors below the ground level. They are not resistant to grease and oil, but special "greaseproof" tile are available. Their resistance to indentation is relatively low. They are suitable for use in schools, apartment and office buildings, hospitals, laboratories, residences, and many other kinds of structures. Asphalt tile are used as a wall covering as well as a flooring material.

Vinyl Plastic. Vinyl plastic floor coverings have thermoplastic binders, as described in Art. 8, together with plasticizers and granular mineral fillers and pigments selected and proportioned to give the desired properties and colors. They are manufactured in rolls 6 ft. wide and in tile of many sizes. The thicknesses available are $\frac{5}{64}$, $\frac{3}{32}$, and $\frac{1}{8}$ in. A large assortment of solid colors, as well as marbelized and other patterns, are available. It may be unbacked or backed with various materials.

Vinyl plastics are wear- and indentation-resistant, impervious, resistant to oil and grease, resilient, easily maintained, and attractive.

Vinyl asbestos tile include asbestos fibers in their composition. They are less flexible than the other types, are less resistant to indentation, and are available only in tiles 9 in. square.

Enameled Felt Base. The lowest-cost floor covering consists of an asphalt-saturated felt with a baked enameled design on the top surface and a painted bottom surface. The covering is not usually cemented or fastened in any way to the base, except possibly at door openings, because it is torn easily. Attractive designs are available. It is easily cleaned, but it is not resistant to oil, grease, and alkaline cleaners. It is suitable for use where a low-cost floor covering is desired and it is subjected only to light foot traffic. Widths of 9 ft. are available.

69. SELECTION OF WEARING SURFACES FOR FLOORS

The selection of a proper floor surface is one of the most important and, at the same time, one of the most difficult problems in the construction of a building. The appearance, usefulness, and cost of up-keep of a building are greatly affected by the type of floor installed. Considering the importance of the subject, it is unfortunate that it is not possible to devise a satisfactory basis of selection.

The report of a Committee on Floors of the American Hospital Association has been of considerable value in preparing this article. The definitions of the properties of floor surfaces follow those of the committee quite closely.

The following discussion of the relative merits of the various floor surfaces is prepared, realizing that the value of such discussion is limited because of the great variations in the materials and workmanship, and in the kind of usage and care a floor will receive.

Floors which are manufactured complete and ready for installation, such as tile, linoleum, and rubber, will show less variation in quality than such floors as terrazzo, concrete, and magnesite composition which are manufactured on the job, and are not subject to as rigid control as factory-made products. Natural flooring materials such as marble and slate are also quite variable in quality.

Each property of a wearing surface will be discussed, and an attempt will be made to classify roughly the various materials according to the degree to which they possess that quality.

Appearance. Appearance is the attractiveness of the material, its color range, texture, and its decorative value in an architectural sense.

There are many floor surfaces which are attractive when suitably used, such as hardwood when properly finished, terrazzo, ceramic tile, marble, and, to a somewhat less degree, vinyl plastic, rubber tile, cork tile, linoleum tile, asphalt tile, linoleum, cork carpet, sheet rubber, slate, and magnesite composition. Concrete without special treatment, and industrial wood blocks are not suitable for use where appearance is a factor. Concrete floors may be painted or waxed, and are not unattractive as long as the surface is maintained, but this is difficult to do where the traffic is at all heavy.

Durability. Durability may be defined as the resistance to wear, temperature, humidity changes, decay, and disintegration. The adhesion of a material to its base is also a factor in durability.

The most durable floor surfaces for foot traffic are ceramic tile, terrazzo, slate, and concrete, but terrazzo floors are likely to crack if not divided into blocks by dividing strips or laid in the form of tile. Marble is widely used in floors subject to severe wear, but it does not stand up as well as the materials just mentioned. Some marbles are much more resistant to wear than others. Concrete surfaces to be durable must have durable aggregates.

Hardwood, linoleum, linoleum tile, vinyl plastic, and rubber tile give very satisfactory service, whereas cork carpet, cork tile, asphalt tile, and magnesite composition are fairly satisfactory.

With the exception of concrete, none of the materials mentioned so far is suitable or satisfactory for heavy traffic, such as trucking. Brick and wood block may be used under these conditions. Heavy maple flooring may also be satisfactory.

Comfort. Comfort under foot is determined by the shock-absorbing qualities, sure-footedness, evenness of surface, and conductivity. A floor which is a good heat conductor will always feel cold.

The most comfortable floors to work on are cork tile, cork carpet, and rubber. Wood, linoleum, vinyl plastic, magnesite composition, and asphalt tile, are very satisfactory, but concrete, terrazzo, ceramic tile, marble, slate, and brick are tiresome and cold.

Noiselessness. Cork tile, cork carpet, and rubber are practically noiseless; wood, linoleum, vinyl plastic, magnesite composition, and asphalt tile are slightly less satisfactory but still very good; but concrete, ceramic tile, marble, slate, and brick are the noisiest of flooring materials.

Fire Resistance. Materials may be noncombustible but still suffer severely in case of fire. Concrete, ceramic tile, and brick are probably the most fire-resistant floor surfaces, but terrazzo, marble, and slate are very satisfactory. Magnesite composition, or asphalt tile, will not burn but may suffer seriously in a fire. Linoleum, cork carpet, rubber, vinyl plastic, and wood are combustible, but if laid on a fire-resistant base they are not considered a serious defect in a fire-resistant building.

Sanitation. To be sanitary, a floor surface must be nonabsorbent and easily cleaned. Joints which are not watertight are an unsanitary feature.

The most sanitary floor surfaces are terrazzo, ceramic tile, marble, and slate. Magnesite composition, asphalt tile, rubber, vinyl plastic and linoleum are quite satisfactory. Cork carpet is unsatisfactory because of its porosity, concrete because of the difficulty in cleaning, and wood because of its porosity and the presence of open joints.

Acid and Alkali Resistance. The factors that should be considered under this heading are immunity from damage by occasional spillings of strong acid solutions and resistance to the continuous use of soap, lye, cleaning and scouring compounds, and disinfectants.

Ceramic tile is the most satisfactory floor surface in this respect; asphalt tile and vinyl plastic are quite resistant; rubber, terrazzo, marble, concrete, and magnesite composition are sufficiently resistant for ordinary purposes; but linoleum, cork carpet, and cork tile should not be subjected to the action of acids and alkalies.

Grease and Oil Resistance. Grease and oil are not absorbed by ceramic tile and by vinyl coverings and do not affect these materials. They are absorbed by wood, brick, concrete, terrazzo, linoleum, cork carpet, and cork tile, and therefore detract from their appearance, but they do not seriously affect their durability. Asphalt and rubber floors, except greaseproof asphalt tile, are seriously affected by grease, oil, and gasoline.

Dampness. Ceramic tile, brick, concrete, terrazzo, and asphalt tile are not affected by dampness and are suitable for use on floors located on the ground such as basement floors; but wood, rubber, linoleum, cork carpet, and cork tile are not suitable for use in such locations.

Indentation. The hard flooring materials, such as ceramic tile, concrete, terrazzo, and brick do not suffer indentation from chair legs, heels of shoes, and other objects which rest on them or strike them. Maple and oak flooring yield very little and do not retain imprints. Other materials such as linoleum and rubber yield considerably under such loads but recover quite well when the load is removed. Asphalt and vinyl asbestos tile may become permanently indented.

Trucking. Three factors are pertinent when considering the suitability of a floor for trucking. It must stand the abrasive action of the truck wheels, the tractive effort required to pull the truck must not be excessive, and the flooring must have structural resistance sufficient to carry the load transmitted to it by the truck wheels. Concrete, heavy maple flooring, and industrial wood blocks are satisfactory in all three respects if the materials are of high quality and if the trucking is parallel to the length of the maple flooring rather than crosswise. The maple flooring must be heavy enough so that the weight of the trucks will not break the tongued-and-grooved joint. The aggregate in the concrete may have to be specially selected so as to have a high resistance to abrasion. Rubber-tired wheels are much easier on all types of flooring than wheels which are steel-tired.

Maintenance. This heading includes such items as the ease with which a flooring is cleaned, the necessity for care and surface treatment, such as waxing and painting, the necessity for repairs, and the cost of such operations.

Ceramic tile, marble, terrazzo, slate, vinyl plastic, and rubber tile floors are easily cleaned and require very little care. Linoleum, asphalt tile, and magnesite composition are easily cleaned, but should receive surface treatment occasionally. Cork carpet is not easy to clean, and requires surface treatment. Hardwood floors are fairly easy to clean if in good condition, but require frequent surface treatment. Concrete is not as easy to clean as ceramic tile, linoleum, etc., if it is not painted or waxed. Painting makes cleaning easier but requires frequent renewal.

The monolithic floors such as terrazzo, magnesite composition, and concrete are difficult to repair satisfactorily. Floors composed of separate units of tile, slate, or marble are more easily repaired, but require skilled mechanics. Linoleum, cork tile, and cork carpet may be easily repaired by replacing the damaged parts.

The maintenance costs of wood block, heavy asphalt mastic, brick, and concrete are relatively low except under extremely severe traffic. With the exception of concrete these materials are easily repaired. They receive no surface treatment.

Initial Cost. One of the first factors in selecting a floor surface is the initial cost, but even the most expensive materials do not possess all the desirable features.

Flooring materials may be roughly divided into classes according to their cost in place. In the following list the most expensive materials are given first.

(*a*) Ceramic tile, marble, vinyl tile, and rubber tile.

(*b*) Terrazzo, magnesite composition, cork tile, and hardwood.

(*c*) Cork carpet, linoleum, and asphalt tile.

(*d*) Concrete.

This list assumes that a concrete base is available to receive the wearing surface. Brick and wood block floors are not included in these lists, for they are used for a different class of traffic from that to which the materials included, except concrete, are subjected, and a comparison would be of no value.

Weight. The heavier floor surfaces add indirectly to the cost by requiring stronger floor construction, beams, girders, columns, and foundations. Ceramic tile, marble, and slate are bedded on $\frac{1}{2}$ in. or more of cement mortar which has no structural value; terrazzo requires $1\frac{1}{4}$ in. of material which is simply a dead weight; and hardwood flooring usually requires about 2 in. of filling between the nailing strips if placed over concrete. Rubber tile, magnesite composition, cork tile, cork carpet, linoleum, asphalt tile, and concrete do not require this additional material. This additional weight exists when the structural floor is some form of concrete slab.

70. PLYWOOD, WALL BOARD, AND OTHER BOARDS

Many types of wall boards are available in a great variety of forms to use as finished surfaces for interior walls and ceilings. Some are the cheapest form of finish which can be provided and others compare with ceramic wall tile in cost. They are usually furnished in large sheets 4 ft. wide and up to 12 ft. in length.

Construction which makes use of such boards instead of plastered surfaces is called *drywall construction*, as described in Art. 37. It is used extensively, especially in residences. See Art. 37.

Plywood. Plywood consists of thin layers or *plies* of wood glued and pressed together, with the grain direction of adjacent plies at right angles to each other, to form large rigid panels commonly from $\frac{3}{16}$ in. to $1\frac{3}{16}$ in. thick with widths up to 4 ft. and lengths up to 8 and 10 ft. The number of plies is 3, 5, or 7, the odd number being necessary to avoid warping. The outside plies are called *faces* or *face* and *back*. The intermediate plies with grain parallel to the grain of the faces are called *cores*, and those with grain at right angles to that of the faces are called *crossbands*. The plies are made by softening logs, steaming, and placing them in lathes which are arranged with a cutter to slice off, or *rotary-cut* sheets of veneer in a manner similar to unrolling paper. Douglas fir plywood is available in the *moisture-resistant type*, the *exterior type*, and the *highly moisture-resistant type*, depending upon the moisture resistance of the glue used.

Plywood is made from many different species of wood, the most common being Douglas fir. Plywood is available with faces of Douglas fir, gum, birch, red and white oak, Philippine mahogany, African mahogany, black walnut, and many other woods. See Art. 94.

The faces of plywood may be *good*, which means practically clear, all-heart veneer; the faces may be *sound*, having neatly made patches, sapwood, and stain, but must be smooth and suitable for painting or natural finish; or the faces may be classed as *utility*, and contain knots, splits, pitch pockets, etc., which will not interfere with the use of the panels. A sheet may have two *good* faces, designated G2S; one *good* face and one *sound* face, G1S; or two *sound* faces, S2S.

Moisture-resistant Douglas fir plywood is furnished in *standard panels,* which are used primarily for natural finish and are sanded on both faces; *wallboard,* which is the most widely used plywood product, the principal uses being for facing interior walls and ceilings, and both surfaces being sanded; and *sheathing,* which is an unsanded utility grade for wall and roof sheathing, subflooring, and miscellaneous construction purposes.

Plywood with a highly water-resistant glue is used for concrete forms which can be reused 10 to 15 times.

Exterior plywood is made by the hot-pressed synthetic-resin-bonded process and is intended for permanent exterior use. It is generally considered to have a waterproof, rather than water-resistant, glue bond. It is used for outside paneling and siding of buildings.

Some of the thicker plywoods, with a lumber core rather than the thin plies, are available, for use as cupboard doors, table tops, counter fronts, etc. Either the separate veneers themselves or two-ply panels ⅛ in. thick can be furnished for bending to form curved surfaces.

For decorative effects, the surface of plywood may be finished natural, stained, or painted. Wall paper may be applied to plywood over building felt or muslin.

Various moldings are available for covering the joints of interior plywood, or a V-joint can be made by beveling the edges.

Some of the advantages of plywood are the large sizes available; its freedom from warping, shrinking, or cracking; and the availability of decorative hardwood and plastic face veneers.

Plywood is available with one surface veneered with various species of decorative woods and with a variety of colored plastics.

Fiberboards. Fiberboards are made from masses of cane or wood fibers by pressing them into sheets or boards with thicknesses from ¼ in. to 1 in. or more. The usual widths are 4 ft., and lengths up to 12 ft. are available. The fibers are rather loosely compressed. The surface is usually fibrous, but boards are available veneered with walnut, mahogany, or other woods. Others have an imitation wood finish. Some boards are divided into tile or given other surface design by bevel scoring. Strips called *planks* are made 6 in. to 16 in. wide and up to 12 ft. long. Sheets are cut into individual tile of many sizes, with a varaiety of colors. The large unfinished sheets are sometimes called *building boards.* Fiberboards are used for exposed interior wall and ceiling surfaces, for outside wall sheathing, and for heat insulation and sound absorption. They may be obtained coated with asphalt for protection against moisture when used for sheathing as described in Art. 37. Boards of any thickness are made by cementing thinner boards together with special cement. Some boards have an aluminum-coated back to serve as reflective insulation. See Art. 97.

Gypsum Wallboard. Gypsum wallboard or gypsum board consists of a gypsum core to the surfaces of which are bonded sheets of heavy paper and is intended for use without plaster coatings. The boards are usually 4 ft. wide, 6 to 12 ft. long, and ¼ to ⅝ in. thick. They are fastened to wood studs, furring strips over masonry and ceiling joists with flat head nails which penetrate the supports at least one inch.

Gypsum wallboard is the most widely used interior wall covering used in *drywall construction,* which is often used for residences. The joints may be covered with panel strips battens or beads or they may be concealed. In the latter case, boards with tapered edges are used. The depressions made available in this manner are filled with cement in which a tape is embedded. The surface of the cement covering the joint is made flush with wallboard surfaces. After this cement has set, the joint is finished by sanding. Nail head depressions are filled with cement and sanded.

The exposed surface may be painted or covered with wallpaper, and boards are available with wood-grain patterns and other decorative treatments so that no additional decoration is required.

Boards are available with aluminum foil on one surface to serve as reflective heat insulation, as described in Art. 97, for use on the inside surfaces of outside walls.

Gypsum board is also used for sheathing as described in Art. 37.

Drywall construction is more rapid than lath and plaster construction and avoids the moisture problems which occur when plaster is drying out, but it is less resistant to sound transmission. Some wall boards require no decorative treatment, while others may be painted or covered with wall paper. If fiberboard or gypsum board is used, it is cheaper than lath and plaster construction, but other wall coverings may be more expensive.

Hardboards. *Standard hardboard* is made by subjecting masses of specially treated and separated wood fibers to heat and very high pressure to form a dense, hard, impervious board. Other materials may be added during manufacture to improve certain of its properties. Many species of wood are used, depending on their availability to the manufacturer. *Tempered hardboard* is made from standard hardboard by the addition of certain chemicals and further heat treatment to increase its strength and abrasion resistance and decrease its rate of water absorption.

Hardboard is manufactured with both surfaces smooth or one surface smooth and the other with a screen back, or reverse impression of a screen, on the back. It is also available with special finishes such as striated or rigid, grooved embossed, or marked into tiles, as well as prefinished, prime-coated, and wood-grained patterns. The natural color varies from blond to dark brown depending on the process used.

The width of the sheets or panels is usually 4 ft., although sheets 5 ft. wide are available in some types. The maximum length is 16 ft. The thicknesses vary from $\frac{1}{12}$ to $\frac{3}{4}$ in.

Hardboard is used for interior and exterior wall panels, ceilings, siding, table and counter tops, underlayment for resilient floor coverings, concrete forms, and many other purposes.

Trade names applied to hardboards are: *Masonite, pressed wood,* and *prestwood.*

Asbestos-Cement Board. This type of board is made from asbestos fiber and portland cement molded under pressure to form a dense hardsurfaced sheet usually $\frac{1}{8}$, $\frac{3}{16}$, and $\frac{1}{4}$ in. thick, 4 ft. wide, and up to 8 ft. long. The exposed surface is finished smooth. One type is made in the natural cement color and other decorative colors which extend through the sheet. The sheets may be plain or scored to resemble tile 4 in. square. Other boards are available with various baked-on colored and marbleized surface finishes divided into tile. The tile joints may be cut with a narrow abrasive wheel or be molded. The joints and edges are usually covered with specially designed chromium, aluminum, or stainless-steel moldings. The sheets can be cut with a wood saw, and other operations can be performed with woodworking tools.

Plastic Veneers. Plastics that are impervious, hard, nonbreakable, durable, and attractive are cemented as veneers to plywood, hardboard, and asbestos-cement board to form sheets as large as 4 by 8 ft. The veneer is available separately in sheets $\frac{1}{16}$ and $\frac{5}{32}$ in. thick. A great variety of plain colors and wood and marble imitations are available. The veneer is very resistant to acids, alkalies, and alcohol and can be easily cleaned. Special grades which are cigaret-proof are available. This material is used for wall surfaces, counter tops, table tops, and in many other locations. Various methods of fastening the panels without exposing nail heads have been devised.

High-pressure plastic laminates, as described in Art. 8, cemented to plywood are widely used for table and counter tops subjected to severe usage. The product of one manufacturer is known as *formica*.

References

1. Henry J. Stetina, "Steel Construction," included in *Floors, Ceilings and Service Systems,* Publication 441, Building Research Institute, National Research Council, 1956.
2. *Recommended Practice and Standard Specifications for Concrete and Reinforced Concrete,* report of Joint Committee representing affiliated committees of several societies, 1940. Seventh printing, American Concrete Institute, 1950.
3. Ben John Small, *Flooring Materials.* Circular Series Index F4.6, Small Homes Council, University of Illinois, 1955.
4. *Sweet's Architectural Catalog File,* F. W. Dodge Corporation.

11 Roof decks, roofing and siding

71. TYPES OF ROOFS

Roofs of buildings are divided into various types, depending upon the shape.

Flat roofs (Fig. 71-1a) are extensively used on all kinds of buildings. They are sloped from $\frac{1}{2}$ in. to 2 in. vertical to 12 in. horizontal to insure proper drainage. Some designers make roofs without any slope whatever, since watertight roofs can be secured without any slope to simplify the construction.

Roofs which slope in one direction only (*b*) are called *shed roofs*. This type of roof is used on entire buildings, or in connection with other types shown in *c* to form a *leanto*.

Gable roofs slope in two directions (*d*). This type of roof is widely used, especially on residences. The slope is often as flat as 4 in. vertical to 12 in. horizontal, and occasionally as steep as 20 in. vertical to 12 in. horizontal, but the most common slopes are between 4 in. vertical to 12 in. horizontal, and 12 in. vertical to 12 in. horizontal.

Hip roofs slope in four directions (*e*). This type of roof is widely used. The same slopes are used on hip roofs as on gable roofs.

Gambrel roofs slope in two directions, but there is a break in the slope on each side (*f*). The gambrel roof is used for residences because of the efficient use which can be made of the space under the roof, especially when a long shed dormer (Fig. 71-2a) is used. *Mansard roofs* slope in four directions, but there is a break in each slope (Fig. 71-1g). *Deck roofs* slope in four directions, but have a deck at the top (*h*).

The various types of roof *dormers* are shown in Fig. 71-2a.

The *saw-tooth roofs* shown in Fig. 71-2b and *c* are used quite extensively on industrial buildings because of the opportunities they offer in light and ventilation. The steep face of *b* and the vertical face of *c*

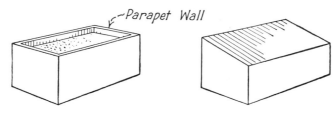
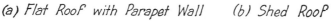

(a) Flat Roof with Parapet Wall　　　(b) Shed Roof

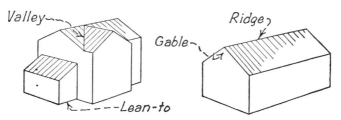
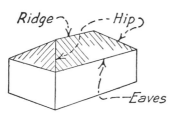
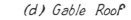

(c) Shed Lean-to　　　(d) Gable Roof

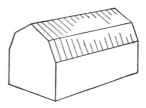
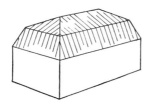

(e) Hip Roof　　　(f) Gambrel Roof

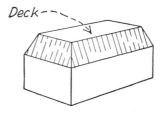

(g) Mansard or Curb Roof　　　(h) Deck Roof

Fig. 71-1. Types of roofs.

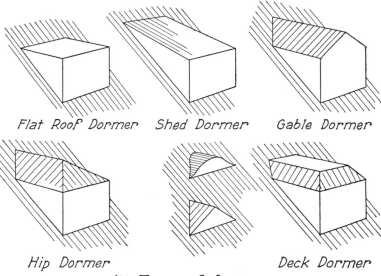

Flat Roof Dormer   Shed Dormer   Gable Dormer

Hip Dormer   Deck Dormer

(a) Types of Dormers

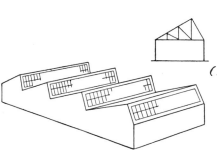

(f) Louvres

(b) Saw-Tooth Roof   (d) Monitor

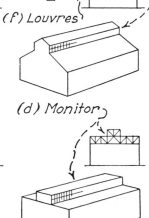

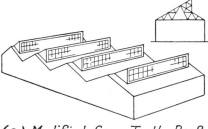

(c) Modified Saw-Tooth Roof   (e) Monitors

Fig. 71-2. Types of dormers and roofs.

are mostly glass and are usually faced towards the north, the light from that direction being more nearly constant throughout the day than light from other directions and the glare and radiant heat of direct sunlight is avoided. The type shown in *c* does not have as large an area of glass as that shown in *b*, but it is more easily made watertight in the valley. At least a part of the windows are arranged to open for ventilation. This is usually the upper half.

The parts of a roof such as *ridge, hip, valley, gable,* and *eaves* are indicated in Fig. 71-1. *Monitors* (Fig. 71-2*d* and *e*) are used extensively to secure better light or ventilation. The vertical face is called the *clerestory*. If only ventilation is desired, *louvres* may be used for ventilation in the clerestory (*f*).

Thin-shell roofs are described and illustrated in Art. 55.

72. ROOF DECKS

General Comments. The roof deck is that portion of the roof construction to which the *roof covering* or *roofing* is applied and through which the loads on the roof are transmitted to the principal supporting members. Roof decks include such parts as sheathing, roof planks or slabs, rafters, purlins, subpurlins, and joists. The principal supporting members include girders, trusses, rigid frames, and the ribs of arches and domes, all of which have been described elsewhere in this book. Sometimes, for example in shell roofs, the decks also serve as principal supporting members. In others, the roof covering and deck are combined in a single unit, for example, the various forms of corrugated roofing which span the distances between purlins.

The deviation of the surface of a roof deck from the horizontal is measured in terms of the ratio of its vertical projection to its horizontal projection and is expressed in inches of vertical projection per foot of horizontal projection. This ratio is called the *slope* or *incline*. It is also called the *pitch*, but the other terms are preferable because the ratio of the *rise*, or center height, to the *span* of a symmetrical roof truss with inclined top chords or a framed roof is also called its pitch. Such a truss with a rise of 10 ft. and span of 40 ft. is said to have a 10/40 or quarter pitch. The roof slope, however, is 10/20 or 6 in. per ft.

The surface area of a roof deck and its covering is expressed in squares, a *square* being 100 sq. ft.

Flat Roof Decks. If the roof of a multistory building is flat, it usually will be constructed according to the same system as that used for the floors. When all of the factors involved are considered, such a procedure is usually cheaper and more satisfactory than any other system of equal quality. Various types of floor construction are considered in Art. 63. Some of such systems will result in level decks. Suitable roof coverings may be applied directly to decks which do not slope to the drains, there being no objection to shallow pools of water remaining in slight depressions of the deck surface until it evaporates. However, slopes of at least $\frac{1}{8}$ in. to the foot often are provided by fills of lean, lightweight concrete placed on top of flat concrete slabs.

For single-story buildings, flat roof systems may be of the same types as some of the floor systems described in Art. 63. Types which are especially suitable for heavy loads, such as the flat-slab, would not be appropriate for such buildings because roof loads are relatively light.

Decks especially designed for roofs include precast gypsum and concrete planks and wood-fiber cement planks in various forms, on steel rafters or purlins. Gypsum is nailable and, by using appropriate aggregates as described in Art. 11, concrete can be made nailable. Cast-in-place or poured gypsum slabs are also used for roof decks but are not extensively used in floor construction. Lightweight, noncombustible, termite-proof planks 2, $2\frac{1}{2}$, and 3 in. thick, made of a compressed chemically treated wood fiber and portland cement are manufactured for use in roof decks. The standard width is 32 in., and lengths up to 9 ft. are available. They are usually supported on bulb-tee subpurlins spaced 2 ft. 9 in. The edges are rabbeted to fit under the bulb projection so as to be anchored when joints are filled with mortar. These planks have good heat-insulation and sound-absorbing properties. They are called *wood-fiber-cement* planks.

Also designed especially for roof decks are lightweight steel-ribbed panels of various types similar to the floor panels illustrated in Fig. 63-3*b*, but with the flat surface on top and without a concrete slab.

The only types of roofing suitable for flat or gently sloping roofs are the built-up roof and the sheet-metal roof with flat soldered seams. The built-up roofs can be used on all types of flat decks, but sheet metal roofing involves nailing and therefore cannot be used directly on nonnailable concrete.

Sloping Roofs. Three arrangements for sloping roof decks and the names of the various parts are shown in Fig. 72-1. The principal supporting members shown in *b* and *c* are trusses, but the same arrangements can be used with other types of such members. A typical arrangement for *wood frame construction* is shown in *a*. Usually, there are no main supports for the rafters between the plate and the

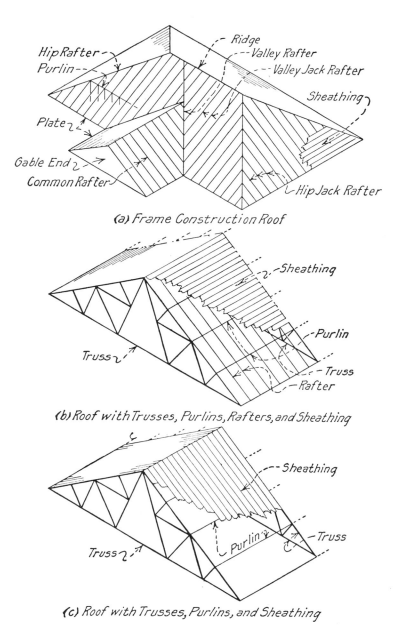

(a) Frame Construction Roof

(b) Roof with Trusses, Purlins, Rafters, and Sheathing

(c) Roof with Trusses, Purlins, and Sheathing

Fig. 72-1. Roof framing.

ridge or hip. The arrangement in *b*, with purlins to support the rafters, is used with 1-in. wood sheathing, light wood rafters, and timber or steel purlins. The arrangement in *c* does not include rafters but the sheathing spans the distance between purlins. The construction might consist of wood sheathing, usually 2 in. thick, and timber or steel purlins; precast gypsum, wood-fiber cement, or nailable concrete planks and steel or precast concrete purlins; or some form of corrugated sheets spanning the distance between timber or steel purlins and serving also as a roof covering.

The arrangements shown in *b* and *c* are suitable for flat roofs, although corrugated sheets would not serve as a roof covering. Horizontal members corresponding to rafters are called joists, the former term being used only for sloping members.

The coverings for sloping roofs must be fastened to the decks with some form of mechanical fasteners, a process which always uses nails if the deck is continuous. For this reason, a type of deck must be selected into which nails can be driven or wood nailing strips can be installed, and in which they will have adequate holding power. Included in such decks are those constructed of wood, gypsum, and nailable concrete. The gypsum and nailable concrete are usually in various forms of precast planks, because this procedure is cheaper and the installation is faster than casting in place.

Cast-in-place decks of ordinary concrete are not nailable, and thus for this form of deck provision must be made for fastening the roofing to the deck. This objective is accomplished by providing wood nailing strips treated with preservatives. For built-up roofs, these strips are placed in the concrete at intervals of 3 ft. running parallel with the slope and with their top surfaces flush with the top surface of the concrete. If rigid insulation with a thickness at least equal to that of 1-in. nominal thickness lumber is used, the nailing strips are placed between the sheets of insulation with their tops flush. The usual method for fastening built-up roofing to poured concrete decks, with slopes of less than 1 in. per foot, is to cement the roofing to the deck with roofing pitch, but this procedure is not suitable for greater slopes because of the tendency of the roofing to creep down the slope.

Heat Insulation. It is desirable to insulate the roof or the ceiling of the top story of many buildings. This reduces the heat losses and the condensation of moisture on the ceilings and reduces summer temperatures. The various materials on the market are described in Art. 97.

Roof Drainage. Roofs may be made flat with no slope whatever; they may be provided with a slight slope as small as $\frac{1}{8}$ in. to the foot;

or they may have considerable slope. Many engineers and architects advocate the absolutely flat or *dead-level roofs* because of the simplicity of construction, maintaining that the water which may stand for short periods on a roof, owing to slight irregularities, does not harm and may actually protect the roof from the effects of the sun. The type of roofing used on dead-level roofs is a built-up roofing consisting of coal-tar pitch and tarred felt with a wearing surface of gravel or slag.

The slopes required for various types of roofing are discussed in Arts. 71 to 78. The rainwater that falls on a roof may be allowed to run off and drip from projecting eaves, but usually it is necessary or desirable to collect the water in *gutters* placed along the eaves of sloping roofs, the water in the gutters being carried off by vertical pipes called *downspouts, conductors,* or *leaders.* Flat roofs or other roofs which do not have projecting eaves are drained by means of downspouts or conductors placed at points where the water is carried by the slight slope provided in the roof. The size of the gutters and conductors is determined by the contributing area and by the intensity of rainfall.

Several types of gutters for sloping roofs are shown in Fig. 72-2. The *hanging gutter* is the simplest form, but is not as attractive as the *crown-mold gutter* or the *wood gutter,* which fit into the design of the cornice. The *standing gutter* is inconspicuous and easily constructed, but the *concealed gutter* is quite expensive. Gutters are sometimes called *eaves troughs.* Cornices which are enclosed so that the rafters do not show are called *box cornices,* and those in which the rafters are exposed are called *open cornices.*

Conductors or downspouts should be provided with strainers at their upper ends (Fig. 72-2), so that leaves, sticks, and other debris cannot clog them. *Conductor* or *leader heads* are used as shown in Fig. 72-2. It is desirable to run conductors down inside of a building rather than to place them on the outside walls, since the heat of the building keeps them from freezing. They may be placed in chases on the inside of outside walls, along columns, or in partitions. If they must be placed on the outside of outside walls, it is desirable to keep them off of north walls if possible. Steam outlets are sometimes provided in exposed conductors so that by discharging steam into them they can be kept from freezing. Cleanouts should be provided so that clogged conductors and the connecting drains can be easily cleaned. Exposed conductors are commonly made of copper and galvanized steel, and copper, cast-iron, and steel pipe are used for concealed conductors or where appearance is not a factor.

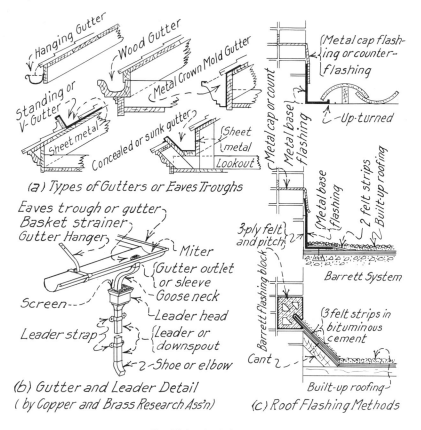

(a) Types of Gutters or Eaves Troughs

(b) Gutter and Leader Detail
(by Copper and Brass Research Ass'n)

(c) Roof Flashing Methods

Fig. 72-2. Roof drainage.

Where a roof surface meets a vertical wall, it is necessary to provide *flashing* to make the joint watertight. Flashing usually consists of strips of some sheet metal such as copper or galvanized iron or steel which is made L-shaped to fit over the joint (Fig. 72-2), one leg of the L running up the wall and the other along the roof. Rainwater which is driven against the vertical face of the wall is kept from running down behind the vertical leg of the flashing by *counterflashing* or *cap flashing*, also made in the form of an L. The L is inverted, the horizontal leg being built or fitted into a mortar joint and the vertical leg fitting over the flashing (Fig. 72-2). Built-up roofing is often flashed, as shown in Fig. 72-2, without the use of sheet metal. To avoid the sharp corner between the wall and the roof, *cant strips* or *boards* or concrete cants are often used. *Flashing blocks*, as shown in the figure, are frequently used. The angle between the back side of a chimney or other projection and a sloping roof is usually protected with a *saddle* or *cricket* which consists of two sloping surfaces meeting in a horizontal ridge perpendicular to the chimney. The valleys on sloping roofs are made watertight by sheet-metal strips, preferably of copper, bent to fit the two intersecting roof surfaces. Roll roofing is often used for valleys on asphalt-shingle roofs, but it is short lived.

73. SHINGLES

Wood Shingles. The best wood shingles are made of cypress, cedar, and redwood, usually by sawing. Standard lengths are 16, 18, and 24 in. Shingles are tapered in thickness, the thickness at the *butt* or thick end being expressed in terms of the number of shingles required to produce a total butt thickness of a designated number of inches. Sixteen-inch shingles are usually 5 butts in 2 in.; 18-in. shingles, 5 butts in 2¼ in.; and 24-in. shingles, 4 butts in 2 in.; called 5/2, 5/2¼, and 4/2, respectively. Regular shingles are variable in width, the maximum width permitted by grading rules being 14 in. and the minimum width 3 in. for 16- and 18-in. shingles, and 4 in. for 24-in. shingles. *Dimension shingles* are cut to specified widths. They are rarely used.

Hand-split shingles are available for use when their rough-textured surface is desired. They are not uniform in thickness, and their minimum thickness is considerably greater than that of sawed shingles. Hand-split *shakes* are similar to the longer hand-split shingles.

Not more than one-third of the length of a shingle should be exposed to the weather on roofs, and not more than one-half on sidewalls. Heartwood is more resistant to decay than sapwood; edge-grain shingles are less likely to warp or cup than flat-grain shingles. Thick shingles warp less than thin shingles, and narrow shingles less than wide shingles. Shingles should be clear, entirely heartwood, and entirely edge grain. It is not economical to use any but the best grade of shingle except for temporary construction.

Shingles should be fastened with steel, hot-dipped, zinc-coated, steel-wire varying in size from 3d to 4d, depending on the thickness of the shingle.

Wood shingles are nailed to wood sheathing or *slats*, each row of shingles being lapped over the row below to give an exposed surface varying from 4 to 7 in., the smaller distance to the weather being used for short shingles on flat slopes and the greater distance for long shingles on steep slopes.

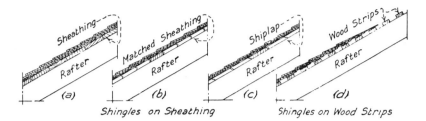

Fig. 73-1. Types of sheathing for wood shingles.

The sheathing may have square edges (Fig. 73-1a); it may be matched (b); or it may be shiplapped (c). The use of wood slats, or *strips,* is illustrated in d.

When the sheathing is without spaces between the boards, or when matched sheathing or shiplap is used, a layer of waterproof paper is sometimes placed between the sheathing and the shingles. This paper makes the roof more air- and watertight, but where there is heavy rainfall it will reduce the life of the shingles by making it impossible for them to dry out from the underside and thus cause cupping or rotting. In general, its use is objectionable.

Shingle roofs with a flatter slope than 4 in. vertical to 12 in. horizontal should not be used but a 6 in. to 12 in. minimum slope is preferred. The chief use of wood shingles is in residence construction. The following discussion of wood-shingle roofs is taken from a report of the Building Code Committee of the Department of Commerce.

Probably no type of roof covering has caused more comment and discussion than the wooden shingle. The great danger of the wooden-shingle roof is from chimney sparks and flying brands from burning buildings or bonfires. The danger from chimney sparks is largely confined to wood or soft coal fires and the sparks resulting from the burning of chimney soot.

The wooden shingle has various well recognized merits. It is light in weight, has excellent insulating value, thus promoting comfort by equalizing temperatures, can be easily applied, furnishes attractive architectural effects, and high grade shingles properly laid produce a roof of excellent durability.

The main objection to the use of wood-shingle roofs is the fire hazard. Sparks or flying embers are more likely to roll or blow off from the smooth surface of a newly shingled roof than from an old roof with weather-worn shingles having curled and broken edges. For this reason any treatment of shingles, such as staining or creosoting, which will tend to maintain a smooth surface incidentally improves their fire resistance. Few if any of the compounds used for treating shingles directly increase their fire resistance.

When wooden shingles are used the very best grades of shingles available should be obtained, as they are more economical to the house owner in the long run than the cheaper grades and prolong the life of a smooth surface roof, thus promoting safety. For best results use edge-grain shingles free from knots and other imperfections and having a thickness at the butt not less than that represented by five shingles in 2 in. (four-tenths inch each). The heads of nails should not be driven into the shingles. Untreated shingles should be thoroughly wet before laying.

Asphalt Shingles. Asphalt shingles are made of heavy felt composed of rag, paper, or wool fiber, saturated and coated with asphalt, with crushed slate or other material embedded in the top surface coating to form a weather-resistant and colored exposed surface. They are made in various sizes, shapes, and colors. A common shape is a strip 12 by 36 in. with the exposed surface cut to resemble three 9-by-12-in. shingles. These are called *strip shingles*. The thickness may be uniform or tapered to give thicker butts. To resist the tendency of winds to raise the exposed butts, some of the types are tapered, as noted above, provided with mechanical fasteners or tabs, made in interlocking shapes, or provided with a band or area of self-sealing adhesive along the underside of the lower edge of the butts.

Asphalt shingles are laid over a layer of roofer's felt and nailed to solid wood sheathing, as described under wood shingles, with hot-dipped, zinc-coated steel nails. The exposure varies with the dimensions of the shingles and will usually give a lap of 2 or 3 in. over the upper end of the second shingle underneath. This is called the *head lap*. The minimum slope that should be used depends upon the characteristics of the shingle. The usual minimum is 4 in. per ft. They are also called *composition shingles*.

Asbestos-Cement Shingles. Asbestos-cement shingles are made of asbestos fiber and portland cement under pressure. They are made in various shapes, sizes, and colors in a thickness of about $5/32$ in. and $1/4$ in. They are laid on a wood deck over a layer of roofer's felt, with a head lap of 2 in., using copper or hot-dipped, zinc-coated steel nails, on a minimum slope of 4 in. per ft.

Asbestos shingles are much stiffer, more fire-resistive, and more durable than asphalt shingles. They are cheaper than clay tile and slate and more expensive than asphalt shingles.

74. CLAY TILE AND SLATE

Clay Tile. Clay tile are made by shaping moist clay in molds and burning. Many different patterns, colors, and textures are available, the most common shapes being French or Ludowici, Spanish, English, and mission or pan tile (Fig. 74-1a to d). Shingle tile are rectangular slabs about ½ in. thick available in various widths up to 9 in. and lengths up to 14 in. Tile of constant width are always used. They are laid in rows to break joints with the length exposed not more than one-half the length of the tile, minus 2 in. The rows may be regular or irregular.

All forms of tile are nailed to wood sheathing. They are laid over a layer of asphalt-saturated rag felt, gypsum, or nailable concrete. The nails should preferably be of copper, but hot-dipped galvanized steel nails are often used. Some forms of tile may be wired to closely spaced steel-angle subpurlins, but this practice is not common.

Special tile are available for the ridges and hips of roofs. The valleys should preferably be made with sheet copper, but in some localities galvanized steel gives satisfactory service. One or two layers of

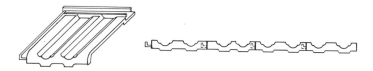

(a) Ludowici Tile

(b) Spanish Tile

(c) English Tile

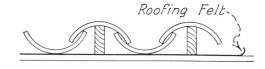

(d) Misson Tile

Fig. 74-1. Clay roofing tile.

roofers' felt should be placed under the tile to serve as a cushion, to keep air currents from lifting the tile from beneath, and to shed water while injuries or defects are being remedied. This is called an *under-layment*.

The usual forms of clay roofing tile should not be used on slopes less than 6 in. vertical to 12 in. horizontal. A special form of tile called promenade tile is placed on a waterproof base to form the floor of roof gardens. They are rectangular and vary in size from 6 to 12 in. with a thickness of 1 in. The waterproof base is constructed in the same manner as a built-up roof, but the surfacing is omitted and the tile are bedded in a 1-in. layer of cement mortar.

Clay tile are fireproof, durable, and attractive, but they are expensive and because of their weight require a strong supporting roof.

Slate. Slate roofing is made from the natural rock by splitting and shaping it into rectangular pieces of the desired dimensions. Slate for roofing should be hard and tough and should have a bright metallic luster when freshly split. It should ring clear when supported horizontally on three fingers and snapped with the thumb of the other hand.

Slate is available in a great variety of colors such as gray, green, dark blue, purple, and red. It is furnished in almost any size from 6 to 14 in. wide, 12 to 24 in. long, and $\frac{1}{8}$ to 2 in. thick, the most common sizes being 12 by 16 in. and 14 by 20 in., $\frac{3}{16}$ and $\frac{1}{4}$ in. thick.

Roofs may be made of pieces of uniform size, thickness, and color, but random sizes, thicknesses, and colors are also used.

Slate may be laid like shingles, each course lapping 3 in. over the second course below or they may be laid at random as long as care is taken to give sufficient lap. They are nailed to matched wood sheathing, nailable concrete or gypsum slabs through holes that are punched in the slate at the factory. A layer *underlay* or *underlay-ment* of asphalt-saturated felt is used between the slate and the deck. The nails should preferably be copper or yellow-metal slater's nails, although redipped galvanized nails and copper-coated nails are often used.

In some regions, slate may be nailed to properly spaced wood strips without an underlay of felt. They are sometimes supported directly on steel subpurlins to which they are wired. Slate roofs should not be used on slopes less than 4 in. vertical to 12 in. horizontal.

Slate flagging may be used on flat roofs for roof gardens by omitting the surfacing on the ordinary built-up roof and by bedding the slate in a 1-in. layer of cement mortar.

Slate roofs are fireproof, durable, and attractive. All the slate used in the United States comes from quarries in Vermont, Pennsylvania, and other Eastern states, and its cost increases in relation to the distance from these sources of supply. Slate roofs may be classed as expensive.

75. SHEET-METAL

Method of Laying. Sheet-metal roofing of galvanized iron or steel, terne plate, copper, zinc, aluminum, or lead is quite widely used. One of the most important factors to consider in the installation of sheet-metal roofs is the large amount of expansion which takes place and which must be provided for to prevent leakage. The expansion of various metals in inches per 10 ft. of length for a temperature rise of 100°F. is as follows. Steel and iron, 0.08; copper, 0.11; aluminum, 0.16; lead, 0.19; and zinc, 0.21. Such expansion is the chief factor controlling the design of the seams and the methods used in fastening the sheet metal to the roof. It may be laid with a *flat seam* (Fig. 75-1a) or with a *standing seam* (b) on steeper slopes and running with the slope of the roof. The seams are clinched tight, the separation shown in the figures being for the sake of clearness. Cross seams are always flat. Flat seams are soldered, but standing seams are not. The sheet

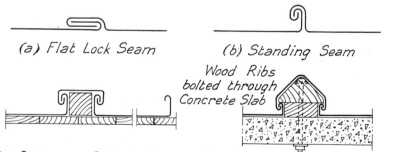

(a) Flat Lock Seam   (b) Standing Seam

(c) Batten or Ribbed Joints on Wood Sheathing and Concrete

(d) V Crimp Roofing

Fig. 75-1. Sheet-metal roofing.

metal is fastened by means of metal cleats 8 to 12 in. apart which are locked into the seams, the cleats being nailed to the deck.

The nails should be of the same material as the roofing when such nails are available in order to avoid galvanic action which may occur between dissimilar metals. Tinned nails should be used with terne plate roofs, copper nails with copper roofs, galvanized nails with galvanized iron or steel and zinc roofs, and aluminum nails with aluminum roofs. Nails should not be driven through the sheets. *Batten* or *ribbed* roofs are formed by using wood battens or ribs running with the pitch of the roof. Special extruded aluminum battens are available for use with aluminum roofs, if desired. Sheet-metal troughs are fitted between these battens and caps are placed over the battens (Fig. 75-1c).

Sheet metal is placed over matched wood sheathing, gypsum, or nailable concrete slabs, a layer of roofing felt being used between the metal and the deck. An important function of this felt is to prevent quick ignition of the wooden decking when the roof is exposed to burning brands or radiated heat. It should be at least $\frac{1}{16}$ in. thick. Tar paper should not be used under tin or terne roofing on account of its possible deleterious effect on the metal, but a rosin-sized paper is satisfactory.

The processes used in manufacturing the various metals used for roofing are described in Arts. 6 and 7.

Galvanic Action. According to a report of the Bureau of Standards (4),

In roofing construction the contact of dissimilar metals is sometimes practically unavoidable, and the question may be raised as to the ultimate effect of such contact upon the general serviceability of the roof.

Galvanic action or *electrolysis* is defined as the deterioration by corrosion of one metal while protecting a dissimilar metal in metallic contact with it. This action will occur only when metals occupying different positions in the electro-potential series (aluminum, zinc, iron and steel, tin, lead, and copper, arranged in order) are in intimate metallic contact in the presence of a suitable electrolyte, such as moisture.

In general, it is believed that galvanic action between the several metals used in roof construction will be negligible, since any accumulation of moisture usually drains off readily and thereby eliminates one of the prime causes of such action. However, adequate precautions should be taken when the conditions previously mentioned occur simultaneously and cannot be avoided.

Longitudinal crimps, shaped like an inverted V, may be formed in sheet-metal roofing (Fig. 75-1d) to increase its stiffness. Such crimps may be only at the edges, but a crimp may also be located in the middle, as shown in the figure. For further stiffness, double crimps are formed along the edges and also in the middle. Triangular wood strips are provided under the outside crimps for nailing. Such roofing is not suitable for flat roofs.

Terne Plate. Tin plates are made by dipping plates of sheet metal or iron in a molten bath of tin to form bright *tin plates* or in a molten bath of tin and lead to form *terne plates*. When taken from the molten bath the plates are usually passed through rolls, the pressure on the rolls determining the thickness of the plate. Bright tin plates are superior to terne plates but are so expensive that terne plates are used for roofing. The common sizes of sheets are 14 by 20 in. and 28 by 20 in. Several sheets may be assembled at the factory by jointing their ends together to form long sheets which are shipped in rolls, but sheets 50 ft. long are also available in seamless rolls.

The sheets are usually painted on both sides at the factory, but if they are not the bottom side must be painted before laying. Terne-plate roofs will last for many years if kept properly painted.

Copper. Sheets of soft copper make an excellent roof covering, which has a high initial cost but is durable and requires no painting. Exposure to the weather causes green copper carbonate to form on the surface. It protects the remainder of the metal and is attractive in appearance. Sheet copper is available in sheets 24, 30, and 36 in. wide and up to 10 ft. long.

Zinc. Zinc sheets may be used to form a durable and satisfactory roof covering. Exposure causes dull gray zinc carbonate to form on the surface, which protects the remainder of the metal. Zinc does not require painting. Zinc is more expensive than terne plate but cheaper than copper. It is rarely used.

Lead. Lead sheets are used for roofing to a limited extent. Lead is particularly suitable for curved or irregular surfaces, for it can be stretched easily and worked to fit such surfaces without cutting. It has a high coefficient of expansion and is difficult to hold in place, particularly on pitched roofs. It has a long life and need not be painted.

A roofing known as *hard lead* is composed chiefly of lead, but antimony is added to increase the elastic limit and decrease the coefficient of expansion. This material has the advantages of ordinary sheet lead without its disadvantages. It may be used on any slope.

Galvanized Iron and Steel. Iron and steel sheets are galvanized by dipping clean sheets in a bath of molten zinc. The zinc protects the sheet from corrosion in proportion to the thickness of the coating. Sheets which are to be sharply bent in forming the joints or for other reasons are given thinner coats to decrease their tendency to flake while being bent. For use in laying galvanized sheet roofing with standing seams, several sheets are assembled at the factory to form continuous sheets, usually 50 ft. long, which can be rolled for shipping. The ends of the sheets are joined by double cross-seam locks. Other forming necessary for the standing seams is done on the job. U-shaped caps are available to place over the standing seam with the sides squeezed together with tongs to form *roll and cap roofing*. *V-crimp roofing* (Fig. 75-1) and sheets with U-shaped edges, which are over-lapped and squeezed to form standing seams, are also available. Galvanized sheet roofing is used extensively, is relatively low in cost, and lasts for many years if kept painted.

Aluminum. Aluminum sheets are available for laying on sloping roofs with standing or batten seams to provide for the relatively high coefficient of expansion. The battens may be of wood or specially designed extruded aluminum. Aluminum is highly resistant to corrosion and has a relatively long life as a roofing material. It does not require painting.

Stainless Steel. Stainless-steel sheets are occasionally used for roofing if the importance of long life, because of inaccessibility or for other reasons, justifies their high cost. They are highly resistant to corrosion and do not require painting.

76. CORRUGATED SHEET ROOFING

Iron and Steel. Corrugated iron and steel are widely used for roofing on industrial buildings. The type ordinarily used has corrugations $2\frac{1}{2}$ in. wide and $\frac{5}{8}$ in. deep (Fig. 76-1a), but other corrugation sizes (shown in the figure) are available. Corrugated sheets are 26 in. wide and may be obtained in lengths up to 10 ft. either painted or galvanized. The thicknesses in common use vary from 24 gage, which is $\frac{1}{40}$ in. thick, to 16 gage, which is $\frac{1}{16}$ in. thick, the gage to be used depending upon the spacing of the supports, the load to be carried, and the quality of the building.

Standing-seam corrugated steel roofing is shown in Fig. 76-1e. This roofing is available in thicknesses from 16 to 28 gage, painted or galvanized. Cleats are used to fasten the sheets to wood or steel purlins. No rivets or nails are used, and the sheets are not punctured in any way in placing. The use of this type of roofing is the same as ordinary corrugated steel.

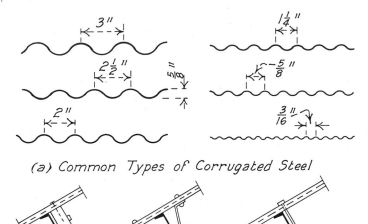

(a) Common Types of Corrugated Steel

(b) Nailing Strip (c) Strap (d) Clinch Nail

Methods of Fastening Corrugated Steel to Purlins

(e) Standing Seam
Corrugated Steel

Fig. 76-1. Corrugated-steel roofing.

Corrugated sheets may be nailed to wood sheathing or may be supported directly by wood or steel purlins spaced 3 to 5 ft., or farther, apart. The sheets are lapped 1½ or 2 corrugations on the sides and 6 or 8 in. on the ends depending on the slope of the roof. On slopes as flat as 2 in. vertical to 12 in. horizontal, standing seams should be used instead of side laps.

Where steel purlins are used they may be provided with nailing strips to which the corrugated steel is fastened (Fig. 76-1b), or the sheets may be held in place by straps passing around the purlins and riveted to the corrugated steel on each side of the purlin (Fig. 76-1c). Long malleable nails called *clinch nails* may be driven through the corrugated steel and clinched around the purlins (Fig. 76-1d). The side laps are held together by galvanized-iron rivets spaced about a foot apart. All rivets and nails should be driven in the tops of the corrugations to prevent leakage. The fasteners should be heavily zinc coated. Lead or plastic washers should be used under the heads of nails not having such provisions on the heads.

When painted sheets which are not galvanized are used, they must be protected against corrosion by frequent painting. Sheets coated with colored plastics are available.

Since galvanized sheets are not subjected to severe bending when forming the corrugations, they may have a heavy coating of zinc. Because of their relatively low cost and fair length of life, they are extensively used on industrial buildings. Their appearance is not suitable for some other classes of buildings.

Aluminum. Corrugated aluminum sheets are illustrated in Fig. 76-2a, and one form of ribbed sheet in b. Sheets 35 and 48 in. wide, 0.024 and 0.032 in. thick, and up to 12 ft. long are available. They are used in a manner similar to corrugated steel, which has been described. Aluminum should not be used in direct contact with steel, however, because of the possibility of galvanic action. For that reason, felt strips should be placed between aluminum sheets, and steel purlins and aluminum fasteners, such as nails, should be used.

Uncoated aluminum sheets are usually employed, but sheets coated with porcelain or baked enamels are available in a great variety of colors. In addition, several colors are obtained by *anodizing* which consists of applying a natural oxide and inorganic dye to the surface by an electrochemical process.

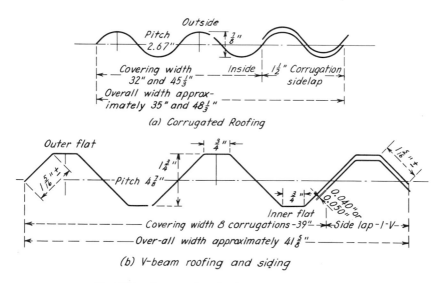

Fig. 76-2. Corrugated and V-beam aluminum roofing.

Stainless Steel. Corrugated stainless-steel sheets are available for use on roofs subjected to the highly corrosive effects of some industrial atmospheres, where their superior resistance to corrosion justifies their higher initial cost.

Asbestos-Protected Metal. Asbestos-protected metal consists of sheet steel covered first with a layer of asphalt, then a layer of asbestos, and finally a heavy waterproof coating. It may be obtained in flat sheets or corrugated sheets of the same size and shape as the plain corrugated sheets just described. The method of application is the same as for plain corrugated steel sheets, but it does not require painting for it is well protected from corrosion. It is a poor conductor of heat and therefore may be used in places where the uncoated sheets are not suitable.

Because of their relatively light weight and fairly good insulating properties, corrugated sheets are extensively used on long-span roofs such as those of hangars and field houses. They are fastened directly to the purlins. The development of plastic coatings has made it possible to obtain sheets of many colors.

Asbestos-Cement Board. Corrugated sheets made of asbestos fiber and portland cement under pressure are used in the same manner as corrugated steel. This material is a good nonconductor of heat, and no trouble is experienced with condensation. It is durable and does not require painting. Sheets are also available with plastic coatings in a great variety of colors.

Wire Glass. Corrugated wire-glass sheets similar in shape to corrugated steel sheets are available for use alone or in connection with corrugated roofing to assist in lighting the interior of buildings. These sheets are $\frac{1}{4}$ in. thick and have wire netting embedded in the glass to strengthen it and to hold it in place when a break occurs. The glass sheets are not laid with side laps, but the joint is covered with metal caps held in place by bolts passing between the sheets. The sheets are held to steel purlins by clips bolted to the metal cap covering the joint between sheets. Strips of asphaltic felt are placed over the purlins to cushion the glass.

77. BUILT-UP AND ROLL ROOFINGS AND PLASTIC COATINGS

Built-Up Roofing. Built-up roofings consist of several overlapping layers of bituminous-saturated roofing felt cemented together with bituminous roofing cement, usually applied so that in no place does felt touch felt. The bituminous material may be tar or asphalt. Tar is a by-product driven off in the process of converting coal to coke and is called *coal tar pitch.* Asphalt is a by-product driven off in the process of refining petroleum. Roofing felt is made from organic or asbestos fibers and is furnished in rolls 3 ft. wide. The organic fibers are primarily graded rags, and for that reason the felts from which they are made are called *rag felts,* but other organic fibrous materials are used along with rag fibers. *Asbestos felt* is composed of at least 85 per cent asbestos fibers, with other materials used to provide desirable properties.

Both asphalt and coal-tar roofing cements are solid at ordinary temperatures. Before applying, they are heated until they become liquid. Tar has a lower melting point than asphalt, a quality which is desirable because it tends to be self-healing if punctured or ruptured but undesirable because tar is less stable on sloping roofs when it is heated by the sun. Tar is also less affected by standing water than asphalts. Asphalt roofing cement is used with asphalt-saturated felts and coal-tar roofing pitch with felts saturated with coal tar. Asphalt is usually preferred for sloping roofs and coal tar for flat or nearly flat roofs.

In addition to the roofing felts and cements, built-up roofs include various surfacing materials, which are embedded in the top layer of roofing cement to protect them from the action of the elements. These are usually fine gravel and crushed slag, but felts with smooth top surfaces designed to be exposed are available. Flat roofs that serve as promenades carrying foot traffic may be covered with built-up roofs surfaced with floor tile or flagstones bedded in a 1-in. layer of portland-cement mortar.

Built-up roofs are adaptable to the various types of *nailable* roof decks, such as those of wood, poured or precast gypsum, precast nailable concrete, and other less common materials, and to those which are *nonnailable,* such as cast-in-place concrete. They are also adaptable to flat and sloping roofs. They can be applied over decks that are not insulated and to decks covered with rigid insulation. A bituminous vapor seal is applied to the deck before the insulation is installed. The seal prevents the accumulation of moisture from the air on the interior of the building in the insulation. The top surface of the insulation is mopped with roofing cement before the first ply of felt is applied. Sheet-steel decks must always be insulated. Wherever insulation is used, it must be adequately secured to the deck.

The simplest form of the best type of built-up roof usually installed is illustrated in Fig. 77-1, in which the roof deck is made of cast-in-place concrete and its slope does not exceed 1 in. per ft. The plies are lapped the distance required to produce a cover whose thickness at every point is equal to the number of plies desired. The roof in the illustration is a 4-ply roof. The plies are laid with their lengths perpendicular to the slope. The laps are made in the direction required to shed water, the direction of flow in the illustration being downward.

The surface of the deck is first covered with a mopping of hot roofing cement, the portion of the surface of each ply which is to be overlapped is similarly covered before placing the next ply, so that in no place does felt touch felt, and finally a uniform coating of hot roofing cement is mopped or poured over the top surface of the top ply, and in this coating clean fine gravel or crushed slag is embedded.

For nonnailable decks with slopes greater than 1 in. to the foot, nailing strips are required, to which each ply can be nailed in a specified manner using tin-plate disks 1 in. in diameter under the nailheads. The nailing strips are made of wood which is creosoted to preserve it. They are usually placed 3 ft. apart, parallel with the slope, with their top surface flush with the surface of the deck and with sides beveled for anchorage or anchored in some other manner.

If a wood or other nailable deck is used, a layer of sheathing paper or unsaturated felt is nailed to the deck. The top surface of this layer

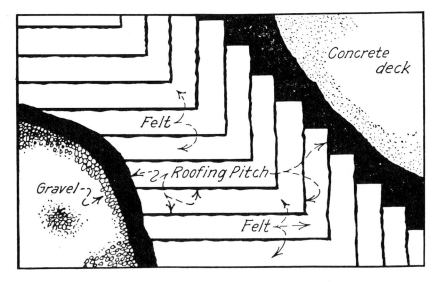

Fig. 77-1. Four-ply built-up roofing on concrete deck.

is mopped with hot roofing cement, and then the desired number of plies of saturated felt are placed and surfaced as for the concrete deck illustrated in Fig. 77-1. A 5-ply roofing on a nailable deck, placed as described, is considered equivalent to a 4-ply roofing on a concrete deck, also placed as described.

Various manufacturers' specifications for laying built-up roofing differ in some respects. They are essentially in accord with the descriptions already given but are more detailed.

Built-up roofs are widely used and durable. Roofs such as those described are guaranteed for twenty years against repair and maintenance expense by the manufacturers if their specifications are followed, but the expected life is much longer. If the number of plies is reduced by one, the guaranty period is reduced five years.

Built-up roofs are sometimes placed by cold processes; in one process the bituminous cementing material is thinned with kerosene to produce what is called a *cutback*. The cementing action occurs as the solvent evaporates. The cold process is used primarily for maintenance rather than new construction.

Brief descriptions of these and other types of built-up roofings are included in Art. 78 under fire exposure.

Roll Roofing. Roofing consisting of sheets composed of a felt base impregnated and coated with asphalt is furnished in rolls and therefore is called *roll roofing*. Because it is prepared ready for application, it is called *prepared* or *ready roofing;* and it is also called *composition roofing*. To prevent sticking when rolled, both surfaces are dusted with mineral matter, such as mica, talc, or fine sand, or the top surface is coated with crushed slate, quartz, burned clay, or other minerals with or without coloring agents embedded in the asphalt coating.

Roofings with smooth surface coatings are lowest in cost, but they are less desirable because coarse mineral surfacing gives considerable protection from the weather and increases the fire resistance. The surfacing also makes possible the manufacture of roofing in a variety of colors.

Roll roofing, available in various weights or thicknesses, is usually furnished in rolls 3 ft. wide and 36 ft. long. It is also furnished in rolled sheets 18 in. wide and 76 ft. long. The most extensive use of roll roofing is over wood decks to which it is nailed with galvanized roofing nails which have large heads. In addition, it is cemented in various ways, using roofing cement which can be applied cold and which hardens as the thinner evaporates.

One type of roof covering composed of roll roofing, when laid on a wood deck, is placed over a layer of lightweight roofing felt laid dry. The roofing is 18 in. wide and is laid with 8 in. exposed, leaving an unexposed *selvage* of 10 in. It is cemented to the ply below over the selvage area. A row of nails is driven along the upper edge of each ply and another above the lower edge of the selvage where it will be covered by the next ply. This arrangement provides 2 plies of protection.

A similar type of construction makes use of roll roofing 36 in. wide, laid with an 11½-in. exposure and a 24½-in. selvage. This arrangement provides 3 plies of protection.

The least expensive and shortest-lived roof covering composed of roll roofing on a wood deck makes use of 36-in. roofing with all its surface except about 2 in. exposed to the weather. This 2-in. edge is side- and end-lapped, cemented, and nailed with the heads of the nails exposed. Because of the distance between rows of nails and its light weight, this type of installation can be blown off by air currents filtering through the deck during windstorms and, being only 1 ply thick, is easily punctured by hail. It is suitable only for temporary structures.

Roll roofings can be used for slopes as flat as 2 in. to the foot.

Plastic Coatings. During recent years several liquid coatings which can be sprayed or rolled on thin-shell concrete roof decks to make them waterproof have been developed. One of them is polyethylene rubber in combination with pigments and fillers. It is resistant to the temperatures to which a roof may be subjected and to atmospheric gases and weathering. The coating forms a membrane which expands and contracts with the base to which it is applied and maintains a continuous covering over hairline cracks which may develop in concrete surfaces. It will not fill visible surface imperfections. The membrane should be reinforced over cracks other than hairline cracks. The coating is available in several colors.

After the surface to be coated has been prepared and cleaned, a prime coat is aplied and permitted to dry for a few hours. A minimum of four topcoats are then applied. The coats may be applied in alternating colors to insure that each coat covers the entire surface. This plastic coating is suitable for application to plywood and metallic surfaces as well as to concrete.

A relatively new product at the time this book is being written, it has been successfully used on many thin-shell roofs, and accelerated weathering tests indicate that it will have a life of at least fifteen or twenty years before requiring renewal.

78. SELECTION OF ROOF COVERINGS

Factors to Be Considered. Many factors enter into the selection of a roofing material for a given building. Some are quite definite, but others vary with local conditions, the class of occupancy, and the preferences of the architect and owner.

The most pertinent factors (not listed in order of their importance) are slope of roof deck, type of roof deck, weight of roofing, climatic conditions, fire exposure, durability, cost, appearance, and maintenance.

Slope of Roof. All forms of shingles, tile, and slate are suitable for use on roofs with a slope of 6 in. or more to the foot and are often used with slopes of 4 in. to the foot. The flatter the slope, the greater the tendency for driving rains to cause leakage. The various kinds of corrugated roofs require a slope of 4 in. to the foot. Special attention should be given to the tightness of the end laps. Sheet-metal roofs can be used on any slope from flat to steep by employing appropriate joints or seams. Built-up roofings can be used on any slope from flat to steep. Roll roofings require a slope of at least 2 in. to the foot.

Type of Roof Deck. All forms of roof covering must be fastened to the decks that support them. The methods of fastening the various types of roof coverings to various types of roof decks have been explained. Because of these relationships, it is seen that the type of roof covering and the type of deck should be selected concurrently.

Weight of Roofing. The weight of the roofing affects the design, weight, and cost of the roof deck and the supporting members. The weight of a given roofing depends upon the specifications being used and range about as shown in Table 78-1.

Climatic Conditions. The durability of roofing materials is affected by the climatic conditions to which they are subjected. *Strong winds* may damage slate, tile, and asbestos-cement shingles, and asphalt shingles and roll roofing are especially vulnerable to their action unless special provisions are made to resist it. *Hail* puncture asphalt shingles and roll roofing and may break tile and slate, the thicker types being less vulnerable than the thinner.

The expansion and contraction of sheet-metal roofs from *extreme temperature changes* may cause the sheets to crack and the joints to

Table 78-1

Weights of Roofing Materials in Place

Material	Weight	Material	Weight
Terne plate	60–75	Built-up roofing	400–675
Copper	80–120	Roll roofing	130–325
Corrugated galvanized steel	120–220	Shingles, wood	200–300
Clay tile	850–1800	Asphalt	130–325
Slate	500–1000	Asbestos-cement	275–600

Values in pounds per square of 100 sq. ft.

leak if adequate provision is not made for this action. Asphalt shingles and roll roofing are also adversely affected by extreme temperatures, especially *high temperatures,* and *sunlight.* Those with mineral surface coatings are more resistant to these actions than smooth surfaces.

Fog, salt air, smoke, and other gases in industrial areas tend to corrode metal roofings. Copper, lead, aluminium, and zinc are highly resistant to *atmospheric corrosion* and do not require protection by painting. Terne plate is resistant to corrosion if protected by painting. Although zinc is resistant to atmospheric corrosion, galvanized steel and iron may corrode because of defects in the zinc coating. Corrugated sheets can be more heavily coated than sheets which are bent sharply to form seams and can be therefore more durable. Galvanized sheet metal should be painted to prolong its life.

Clay tile, slate, asbestos-cement, and built-up roofings are unaffected by the composition of the atmosphere.

Fire Exposure. Building code requirements for roof coverings are based upon their resistance to fire. The classification of roof coverings included in most codes is based on the classifications by the Underwriters Laboratories. These laboratories arrange the coverings into three classes.

Classes A, B, and C include roof coverings which are effective against severe, moderate, and light fire exposures respectively and which are resistant to flying brands. The *National Building Code* of the National Board of Fire Underwriters requires class A or B coverings on all buildings, although class C coverings are accepted on dwellings, buildings of *wood frame construction,* and buildings outside the fire limits which, on the basis of height and area, could be of *wood frame construction.*

The Code Manual of the State Building Construction Code of the State of New York follows the classification of the Underwriters Laboratories but is more complete and includes classes 1, 2, 3, and 4 as specified below. According to that code, "Roof coverings labeled by the Underwriters Laboratories as Class A, B and C, respectively, are acceptable under Code classifications as Class 1, 2 and 3." Some noncombustible roof coverings such as slate, tile, and concrete are not classified by the Underwriters Laboratories. Certain other materials, such as wood shingles and lightweight felt roll roofings, which do not meet the requirements for class 4 roof coverings, are not classified under the Code.

The following classifications are abstracted from the Code Manual, each roof covering to be laid as specified in the manual. All weights are expressed in pounds per 100 sq. ft.

CLASS 1. Clay roof tile with underlay, slate not less than $\frac{3}{16}$ in. thick, asbestos-protected sheet metal.

Asphalt-saturated asbestos felt, smooth-surfaced, 4-ply sheet roofing, laid in a single thickness and with a total weight of not less than 80 lb.

Five layers of 15-lb. asphalt-saturated asbestos felt or equivalent, cemented together with asphalt and surfaced with asphalt paint.

Four layers of 15-lb. asphalt- or tar-saturated asbestos or rag felt or equivalent cemented with asphalt or tar and finished with gravel, stone, or slag in asphalt or tar.

Three layers of 15-lb. asphalt-saturated rag felt or equivalent, cemented with asphalt and finished with asphalt roof tile or $\frac{1}{2}$-in. asphalt-impregnated fibrous board applied with mastic asphalt.

CLASS 2. Asbestos-cement shingles not less than $\frac{3}{16}$ in. thick, laid to provide one or more thickness over underlay.

Asphalt-asbestos felt, smooth-surfaced, 3-ply sheet roofing laid in single thickness and weighing not less than 60 lb.

Asphalt-asbestos felt shingles, surfaced with granular materials laid to have a total weight of not less than 180 lb.

Asphalt mastic shingles surfaced with granular materials.

Sheet roofing of copper, galvanized iron, or tin (terne)-coated iron, with an underlay.

Tile or shingle pattern roofing of copper, galvanized iron, or tin (terne)-coated iron, with an underlay.

Four layers of 15-lb. asphalt- or tar-saturated asbestos or rag felt or the equivalent, cemented with asphalt and finished with asphalt cement.

Three layers of 15-lb. asphalt- or tar-saturated rag felt or the equivalent, cemented with asphalt and finished with gravel, slag, or stone, in asphalt or tar cement.

CLASS 3. Asphalt-asbestos felt, surfaced with sheet or roll roofing, laid in a single thickness with laps, to have a total weight of not less than 48 lb.

Asphalt-saturated asbestos felt, granular-surface sheet or roll roofing laid in a single thickness, to have a total weight of not less than 85 lb.

Asphalt-saturated rag felt, granular-surfaced sheet or roll roofing, laid in a double thickness with laps, to have a total weight of not less than 80 lb.

Asphalt-saturated rag felt individual or strip shingles surfaced with granules, laid with lap, to have a total weight of not less than 80 lb.

Sheet roofing of copper, galvanized iron, or tin (terne)-coated iron, without an underlay or with an underlay of rosin-sized paper.

Tile or shingle pattern roofing of copper, galvanized iron, or tin (terne)-coated iron, without an underlay or with an underlay of rosin-sized paper.

Three layers of 15-lb. asphalt-saturated rag felt or the equivalent, cemented with asphalt and finished with asphalt cement.

CLASS 4. Asphalt-saturated rag felt, smooth-surfaced roll roofing, laid in a single thickness with laps, to have a total weight of not less than 45 lb.

Asphalt-saturated rag felt, granulated-surfaced roofing, laid in single thickness with laps, to have a total weight of not less than 80 lb.

Two layers of 15 lb. asphalt- or tar-saturated rag felt, cemented with asphalt or tar or such other combinations of roofing felt that do not meet the requirements of class 3 built-up roofings.

Wood Shingles. Wood shingles are not classified according to fire exposure. For a discussion of the resistance of wood shingles to fire exposure see Art. 73.

Limitations in Use. The requirements of the *National Building Code* for roof coverings are given earlier in this discussion. According to the New York State Code,

Within the fire limits, roof coverings with or without insulation, shall be Class 1 or 2 except that where the distance separation between buildings is more than 20 ft. and the horizontal projected area of the roof does not exceed 2500 sq. ft., Class 3 roof coverings may be used.

Outside the fire limits, roof coverings, with or without insulation, shall be Class 1, 2 or 3, except that where the distance separation between buildings is more than 20 ft. and the horizontal projected area of the roof does not exceed 2500 sq. ft. and the building does not exceed two stories in height, Class 4 roof coverings or wood shingles may be used.

Specific requirements for the application of roof coverings to satisfy the State Building Construction Code classifications are given in the code manual.

These include requirements concerning lap, sealing for water tightness, nailing shingles or tile, minimum and maximum slopes, and weights of felt and applying built-up roofs. The underlay for tile, shingle or sheet metal roofs, when required, is one or two layers of 15-lb. asphalt-saturated asbestos felt or two layers of 15-lb. asphalt-saturated rag felt. Other building codes include requirements for roof coverings. Those for the New York Code are given as examples.

Durability. The durability of a given roofing material is affected by its quality, its suitability for the purpose used, climatic conditions, quality of workmanship in laying, effectiveness of maintenance, and many other factors. Thus no definite comparisons of different materials may be made.

Considering the best quality of each type, proper installation, and appropriate maintenance, roofing materials may be arranged in groups in decreasing order of length of life somewhat as follows.

1. Sheet copper, lead, stainless steel, aluminum, clay tile, slate, asbestos-protected metal.

2. Terne plate, galvanized iron, asbestos-cement tile, built-up roofing.

3. Wood shingles.

4. Asphalt shingles.

5. Roll roofing.

Cost. The cost of roof coverings in place, exclusive of the cost of the deck, vary with some exceptions in about the same order listed under durability. Special comment should be made about slate because of the transportation costs involved in shipping from the limited sources of supply.

Appearance. Appearance is an important factor in selecting a roof covering for some buildings and is of little consequence in other cases, such as many industrial buildings. Furthermore, some roof coverings are installed on flat or nearly flat roofs where they will usually not be seen. The architectural style of a building and the class of occupancy may be determining factors.

Clay tile, slate, and wood shingles are considered to be attractive roof coverings. Asphalt shingles are surfaced with granular material in a great variety of colors to suit individual preferences. Unless thick butt shingles are used, such coverings have a flat appearance. Copper weathers to a pleasing soft blue-green color. Aluminum weathers to a dull gray color. Terne plate and galvanized sheets are painted to protect them from corrosion, and any color can be applied. Corrugated sheets of various materials are extensively used but are not considered to be attractive unless colored sheets are used.

Maintenance. The initial costs of roof coverings are naturally considered in selecting a roof covering, but the cost of maintenance must also be given consideration.

Copper, aluminum, lead, and stainless-steel roof coverings are non-corrosive and do not require painting. Built-up roofs require very little maintenance. Terne plate and galvanized sheet steel require periodic painting because of the tendency of the base metal to corrode when defects develop in the coatings. Asbestos-protected metal requires little maintenance.

Individual slate, clay tile, and asbestos-cement tile may be broken by large hailstones in some regions or may be broken for other reasons and require replacement; asphalt shingles and roll roofing may be damaged by hail or wind and require repairs.

The life of wood shingles can be prolonged by coating them occasionally with creosote and, less effectively, with shingle stain. Oil paint should not be used because it causes them to warp and curl.

The life of smooth-surfaced asphalt roll roofings can be prolonged by frequent recoating with asphalt roof coatings.

79. SIDING MATERIALS

As explained in Art. 37, siding is a relatively thin covering material which forms the outside surface of many types of exterior walls and is provided to keep out the weather and improve appearance. In many respects siding and roofing materials are similar, and often the same types of materials are used for both purposes. Siding usually serves no structural function.

Some forms of siding, such as wood siding and various types of shingles, are applied over wood sheathing. Other types, such as corrugated or ribbed sheets or panels, do not require sheathing for support but may be used with or without sheathing.

Wood Materials. Siding materials composed of wood include various types of horizontal boards, called siding, and vertical boards with joints covered with battens, as described in Art. 37; plywood with waterproof adhesive, as described in Art. 70; and wood shingles and shakes, as described in Art. 73.

Metal Materials. Corrugated and ribbed aluminum, galvanized iron or steel, stainless steel, and asbestos-protected metal sheets as described in Art. 76 are used for siding on buildings with wood, concrete, or steel frames.

Aluminum and steel corrugated or ribbed sheets with porcelain and baked enamel coatings, galvanized steel sheets with vinyl plastic coatings, and asbestos-protected metal are available in a variety of colors. Various types of sandwich panels with rigid heat insulation included between two metal sheets are available.

Asbestos-Cement Materials. Asbestos-cement shingles and plain or corrugated sheets as described in Arts. 73 and 76 are manufactured in many colors and used for siding materials. Sandwich panels with a core of heat-insulating material and outer surfaces of asbestos-cement boards are manufactured.

Asphalt Materials. Asphalt materials are used for siding in two forms. They may be either in the form of shingles as described in Art. 73 or in rolls as described in Art. 77. Roll sidings are made to resemble brick or stone masonry. They are applied over wood siding.

References

1. *Recommended Minimum Requirements for Small Dwelling Construction,* Building Code Committee, Department of Commerce, 1932.
2. Hubert R. Snoke, *Asphalt-Prepared Roll Roofings and Shingles,* Report BMS 70, National Bureau of Standards, 1941.
3. *Slate Roofs,* National Slate Association, 1953.
4. Leo J. Waldron, *Metallic Roofing for Low-Cost House Construction,* Report BMS 49, National Bureau of Standards, 1940.
5. *Manufacture, Selection, and Application of Asphalt Roofing and Siding Products,* Asphalt Roofing Industry Bureau, 1959.
6. *Test Methods for Fire Resistance of Roof Covering Materials,* UL 790, Underwriters' Laboratories Inc., National Board of Fire Underwriters, 1958.
7. *Code Manual,* generally accepted standards applicable to State Building Construction Code, State of New York, 1959.
8. *Architectural File,* Sweet's Catalog Service.

12 Plaster and stucco

80. GENERAL COMMENTS AND DEFINITIONS

General Comments. The interior wall and ceiling surfaces and the exterior wall surfaces of many types of buildings are usually finished by covering them with two or three coats of a material—consisting of a cementing material, aggregate, and water—which is in the plastic state and is troweled on.

The cementing material for interior surfaces is usually gypsum plaster or hydrated lime, but when such surfaces are to be subjected to extreme moisture conditions or hard usage, portland cement is used. For exterior surfaces mixtures of portland cement and hydrated lime are used.

The aggregate is usually clean well-graded fine sand, but other aggregates may be used for special purposes, as described later. Fiber or hair consisting of manila fiber or goat or cattle hair from $\frac{1}{2}$ to 2 in. long may be added to strengthen or reinforce the mortar during the plastic state and to reduce the amount of dropping while it is being troweled.

Definitions. The following definitions are for the more general terms relating to plaster and stucco.

Plaster. A material in the plastic state which can be troweled to form, when set, a hard covering for interior surfaces, walls, ceilings, etc., in any building or structure (1).

Stucco. A material used in the plastic state, which can be troweled to form; when set, a hard covering for exterior walls or exterior surfaces of any building or structure (1).

Mortar. A material in a plastic state, which can be troweled, and becomes hard in place, to bind units of masonry structures (1).

The terms plaster, stucco, and mortar are used without regard to the composition of the material and are defined only with reference to their use and location (1). The term mortar, however, usually denotes a plastic mixture of a cementing material, fine aggregates, and water regardless of its use.

plaster base. The continuous or discontinuous surface to which plaster or stucco is applied, such as masonry or lath.

lath. A material whose primary function is that of a base or background for the reception of plaster or stucco (1).

cement. A material or mixture of materials, without aggregate, which when in a plastic state possesses adhesive and cohesive properties, and which will harden in place. The word "cement" is used without regard to the composition of the material (1).

neat. This term, when used in connection with cementing materials, refers to the cementing material itself without the addition of aggregates.

Coats. Plaster and stucco are classified, according to the number of coats, into *two-coat work* and *three-coat work.*

The last or final coat is called the *finish coat.* The coat, or combination of coats, applied before the finish coat is called the *base coat.* The coat directly beneath the finish coat is called the *brown coat.* In two-coat work the brown coat is also the base coat and is applied directly to the plaster base. In three-coat work a *scratch coat* is applied to the plaster base before the brown coat is applied. Its outer surface is scratched to improve the bond between the two coats. This operation gives the coat its name. Three-coat work is required over metal lath.

In two-coat work the base coat may consist of a scratch coat, which is not scratched, and a brown coat placed before the scratch coat has set. This is called the *double-up method,* or *double-up work,* and is widely used in applying plaster to unit masonry and gypsum lath. It is also called *laid-off* and *laid-on work.*

Backplastering consists of applying plaster to the inside surface of stucco on metal lath fastened directly to the studs of an exterior wall as described in Art. 37 and shown in Fig. 37-2*f.* The finished interior surface of the wall is applied to the interior surfaces of the studs.

81. CEMENTING MATERIALS, AGGREGATES, AND BASES

Cementing Materials and Aggregates

Gypsum Plasters. The Standards of the American Society for Testing Materials classify the various kinds of gypsum plasters (1) and lime as follows.

Calcined Gypsum. The calcined gypsum shall have a purity of not less than 66.0 per cent by weight of ($CaSO_4 + \frac{1}{2}H_2O$). Commonly known as *Plaster of Paris.*

Gypsum Neat Plaster. Calcined gypsum mixed at the mill with other ingredients to control working quality and setting time. May be fibered or unfibered. Also called *cement plaster* and *hardwall plaster.*

Gypsum Ready-Mixed Plaster. Calcined gypsum plaster mixed at the mill with mineral aggregate and other ingredients to control working quality and setting time. These other ingredients may include fiber.

Gypsum Wood-Fibered Plaster. A gypsum plaster in which shredded, non-staining wood fiber is used as an aggregate.

Gypsum Bond Plaster. Calcined gypsum mixed at the mill with other ingredients to control working quality and setting time and to adapt it for application as a bonding scratch coat over monolithic concrete.

Gypsum Gauging Plaster for Finish Coat. Gypsum plaster prepared for mixing with lime putty for the finish coat. It may contain materials to control setting time and working quality.

Gypsum Molding Plaster. A material consisting essentially of calcined gypsum for use in making interior embellishments and cornices, as gauging plaster, etc.

Keene's Cement. Anhydrous calcined gypsum ($CaSO_4$), the set of which is accelerated by the addition of other materials. It is harder, stronger, and more water resistant than other gypsum plasters and also more expensive.

Lime. The following definitions for quick lime and hydrated lime are included in the Standards of the American Society for Testing Materials.

Quick Lime. A calcined material, the major part of which is calcium oxide in natural association with a lesser amount of magnesium oxide, capable of slacking in water.

Hydrated Lime. A dry powder obtained by treating quicklime with water enough to satisfy its chemical affinity for water under the conditions of its hydration. It consists essentially of calcium hydroxide or a mixture of calcium hydroxide and magnesium oxide and dioxide. It is furnished either unfibered or fibered.

Lime Putty. The product resulting from slacking, soaking and mixing lime and water together.

Portland Cement. Portland cement is the product obtained by finely pulverizing the clinker produced by calcining to incipient fusion an intimate and properly proportioned mixture of argillaceous and calcareous materials with no additions after calcination except water and calcined or uncalcined gypsum. For explanation see Art. 10.

Aggregates. The mineral aggregate used in plaster should be clean and well graded from coarse to fine within specified limits. It is usually sand, but it may be pearlite or vermiculite to improve its fire-resistive and heat-insulating properties. Wood fibers formed by grinding and shredding nonstaining wood may be added at the mill to form gypsum wood-fibered plaster, which is used without other aggregates. Cattle or goat hair, from packing houses, or manila fiber from ½ to 2 in. long may be mixed with gypsum or lime plaster at the mill or on the job. Its function is to keep the keys which bind a plaster base coat to metal lath from breaking off before setting takes place and to reduce the mortar loss caused by dropping.

The mineral aggregate used in stucco is sand.

Water. Water which is suitable for drinking is usually satisfactory. It should not contain mineral or organic substances in amounts sufficient to affect the setting time. Water that has been used to clean equipment should not be used in mixing.

Plaster and Stucco Bases

Classification. Plaster can be applied to properly prepared masonry or lath bases. The masonry bases include brick, stone, hollow clay tile, concrete block, gypsum block, and monolithic concrete. The lath bases include metal lath, gypsum lath, and fiber insulating lath. Gypsum plaster can be applied to any of these bases, but lime or portland-cement plaster should not be applied to gypsum block or lath. Portland-cement plaster should not be applied to fiber insulation lath.

Stucco can be applied to any of these bases except gypsum block, gypsum lath, and fiber insulation lath.

Masonry. A base coat on masonry is held in place by bond. To insure adequate bond, the surface of the masonry must be rough and free from glaze, oil, dirt, or any foreign material that would prevent the development of a strong bond. It may be necessary to roughen monolithic concrete surfaces in some manner. The use of dressed lumber, metal, or plywood forms, the application of oil to the forms, and the vibration of the concrete tend to produce such smooth surfaces that adequate bond is absent.

The first coat of gypsum plaster applied to monolithic concrete should consist of gypsum bond plaster. Lime plaster or stucco should not be applied to monolithic concrete.

Except in arid climates, plaster is not usually applied directly to the interior surfaces of exterior masonry walls, but they are furred for the reasons given in Art. 25, using the methods described in that article and illustrated in Fig. 25-5. In addition, masonry walls which are to be plastered but are not suitable to serve as plaster bases are furred to receive the plaster.

Metal and Wire Lath. Metal lath is lath made of sheet metal, and wire lath is composed of woven or welded wire fabric. Various types of metal lath are manufactured from copper bearing sheet steel and are either coated with a rust-inhibiting paint after fabrication or are made from galvanized sheet steel. The basic types ordinarily used in plastering are *diamond mesh* or *flat expanded metal lath, flat-rib expanded metal lath,* ⅜-*in.-rib expanded metal lath,* and sheet-metal lath, all illustrated in Fig. 81-1. Metal lath are furnished in sheets 18 and 24 in. wide and 8 ft. long. The ribs run in the longitudinal direction.

In manufacturing diamond mesh expanded metal lath, appropriately sized and spaced longitudinal slits are cut into sheets 8 in. wide and expanded laterally, by pulling, to form sheets 24 in. wide. Sheet-metal lath are formed by stamping full-size sheets into the desired pattern of perforations.

Wire lath is made of wire not lighter than about ¹⁄₂₅ in. in diameter arranged with 2½-in. square meshes and a somewhat lighter wire with V-shaped metal *stiffeners* spaced not over 8 in. apart. Both types are galvanized or coated with rust-inhibitive paint. *Paper-backed*

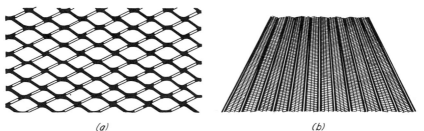

(a)
Diamond mesh

(b)
Flat rib

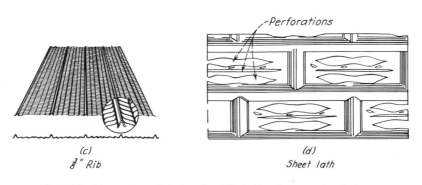

(c)
⅜" Rib

(d)
Sheet lath

Fig. 81-1. Types of metal lath. Metal Lath Manufacturers Association.

wire fabric is made of galvanized wire not lighter than about $\frac{1}{16}$ in. in diameter arranged with 2-in. square meshes, with metal stiffening ribs spaced not over 5 in. apart and a paper backing securely attached with stitch wires to provide adequate embedment of the plaster. Wire lath is 3 ft. wide and is shipped in rolls.

The maximum permissible spacings of vertical and horizontal supports for metal lath and wire lath depend upon the type and weight of the lath and vary from 12 to 24 in. For wire fabric this spacing is always 16 in.

The various types of metal plaster bases are fastened to wood supports with roofing nails, common nails, or staples, the requirements varying with the type and the direction of the supports. They are fastened to concrete ceilings of various types by wires partially embedded in the concrete when it is poured and to open-web steel joists and steel studs by wiring. The attachments should be not more than 6 in. apart. Side laps between supports for metal lath, wire lath, or wire fabric are wired together at intervals of not over 9 in. The long dimension of metal lath sheets is placed normal to the supports, but wire lath and fabric may be placed with the long dimension parallel with the supports.

Metal lath are commonly nailed to both sides of wood studs to form partitions (Fig. 81-2a). Special *prefabricated metal studs* 2 to 6 in. deep are available for use in a similar manner for nonbearing partitions from 4 to $7\frac{1}{2}$ in. thick (Fig. 81-2b). The lath are wired to the studs, which are firmly attached to steel runners anchored to the floor and ceiling or end-anchored in some other manner. The studs are spaced from 16 to 24 in., as determined by the type and weight of the metal lath used. The smallest studs spaced 24 in. are suitable for partitions 9 ft. high, and the largest studs spaced 16 in. can be used for partitions 26 ft. high. Two $\frac{3}{4}$-in. channels braced together may be used instead of a prefabricated stud as shown in Fig. 81-2b.

Solid plaster partitions, which are nonbearing, are constructed by anchoring light hot- or cold-rolled steel studs to the floor and ceiling, wiring metal lath to one side of and normal to the studs, and plastering both sides of the metal lath to completely embed the studs (Fig. 81-2c). The studs vary in depth from $\frac{3}{4}$ to $1\frac{1}{2}$ in., depending upon the partition height, and the stud spacing varies from 12 to 24 in. depending upon the type and weight of lath used. The thicknesses vary from 2 to $3\frac{1}{2}$ in. depending upon the height and the ratio of the height to the unsupported length. For heights over 20 ft. horizontal channel or rod stiffeners, spaced not over 6 ft. vertically, are wired to the channel side of the lath.

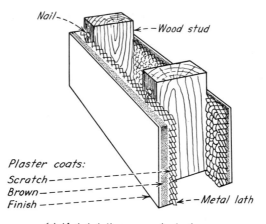

(a) Metal lath on wood studs

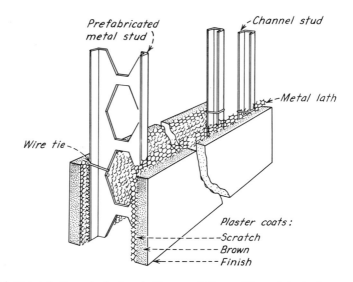

(b) Metal lath and plaster hollow partition with metal studs

Fig. 81-2. Types of metal lath partitions. Metal Lath Manufacturers Association.

Solid studless partitions, which are nonbearing, are constructed by placing sheets of diamond mesh or ⅜-in. rib metal lath with the long dimension vertical and anchoring them at the ends to floor and ceiling runners (Fig. 81-2d). The sheets are edge-lapped and wired together at least every 9 in. of height. Temporary bracing is required until the scratch and brown coats are applied to the unbraced side. The

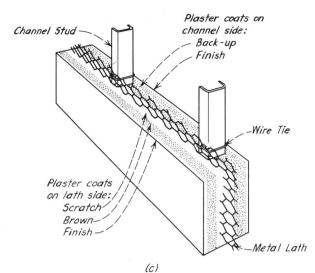

Channel Stud

Plaster coats on
channel side:
— Back-up
— Finish

—Wire Tie

Plaster coats
on lath side:
Scratch
Brown
Finish

—Metal Lath

(c)
Metal lath and plaster solid partition with channel studs

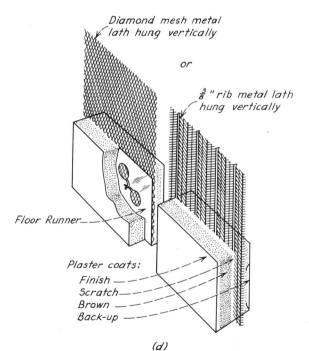

Diamond mesh metal
lath hung vertically

or

$\frac{3}{8}$" rib metal lath
hung vertically

Floor Runner

Plaster coats:
Finish
Scratch
Brown
Back-up

(d)
Studless solid metal lath and plaster partition with diamond mesh or $\frac{3}{8}$" rib lath

Fig. 81-2. (Continued.)

total thickness is usually 2 in., the optimum height $8\frac{1}{2}$ ft. or less, and the maximum permissible height 10 ft.

Wall furring for the inside of exterior masonry walls (Fig. 25-5) is attached to vertical wood strips or light channels anchored to the wall and spaced in accordance with the type and weight of the lath.

Furred and suspended ceilings are constructed with metal lath, supported in such a manner that the permissible spacing of supports for a given type and weight of lath is not exceeded. If structural members are available to support the lath directly, and if their spacing does not exceed the permissible spacing for the lath to be used, no further construction is required.

Sometimes *cross furring* with the appropriate spacing is provided normal to its supports. It consists of $\frac{1}{4}$- or $\frac{3}{8}$-in. rods or $\frac{3}{4}$- or 1-in. channels, the material used depending upon the distance between its supports. When the cross furring is supported directly by attaching to the underside of the structural members, such as joists, the ceiling is called a *furred ceiling*.

When the means of support described are not feasible, when it is desired to provide a flat ceiling surface and this method of support would not provide such a surface, or when there are other reasons, a *suspended ceiling* may be used. For such a ceiling, the cross furring is attached to *main runners* normal to the furring and suspended from the floor system above by heavy galvanized wires, light steel rods, or light strap iron hangers. The main runners are usually $\frac{3}{4}$- or $1\frac{1}{2}$-in. cold-rolled steel channels, the size depending upon the spacing of the hangers. The sizes and spacings of the hangers depend upon the ceiling area each supports. All attachments for metal lath, metal furring, and metal runners are made with annealed galvanized steel wire or special metal clips.

Furred or suspended ceilings may be used to conceal the structural members and provide flat unobstructed ceilings, or they may be used as membranes to increase the fire resistance of floor and ceiling construction. For the latter purpose plaster with vermiculite or pearlite aggregate is more effective than that with sand aggregate.

When stucco cannot be bonded adequately to masonry, when the walls are covered with wood sheathing, or when the structure is of steel frame construction, a stucco surface serves as a thin concrete slab reinforced with expanded or sheet-metal lath or woven or welded wire fabric attached to or applied over waterproof building paper or felt. The paper serves as a backing against which the mortar is forced to provide full embedment of the metal reinforcement in the stucco.

Supports to which the metal reinforcement is attached must not be spaced more than 16 in. The reinforcement should be furred out from the backing at least ¼ in. by some device so that the metal will be completely surrounded with stucco.

Gypsum Lath. Gypsum lath is also called *rock lath* and *plasterboard*. It consists of a gypsum plaster core and surfaces of heavy paper pressed together to form sheets ⅜ and ½ in. thick, 16 and 24 in. wide, and usually 24 in. long, although it may be obtained in longer sheets if desired for special purposes. It may be plain or perforated with holes at least ¾ in. in diameter and spaced 4 in. apart both ways. Plain gypsum lath are available with a sheet of aluminum foil on the back to serve as a vapor barrier and reflective heat insulation as described in Art. 97. The plaster is held to the lath by bond supplemented by keys if perforated lath are used. It is quite fire-resistant.

Gypsum lath are nailed to wood supports spaced not over 16 in. for ⅜-in. lath or more than 24 in. for ½-in. lath. The long dimension is usually placed normal to the supports. Usually the vertical joints are staggered, but they may be continuous if covered with 3-in. strips of metal lath. They are fastened to horizontal or vertical metal supports with special metal clips.

Gypsum lath is used for hollow partitions with metal studs, and for solid partitions with or without metal studs for constructing non-bearing partitions, similar to those constructed with metal lath which have been described. It is also used for furred and suspended ceilings in a manner similar to that described for metal lath.

For solid studless partitions the gypsum lath is ⅜ or ½ in. thick and 16 or 24 in. wide, has a length equal to the ceiling height, and is placed vertically. It is fastened at the top and bottom in a manner similar to that described for the corresponding metal lath partition and braced until the brown coat has been applied to one side. The usual thickness is 2 in.

Fiber Insulation Lath. This type of lath is made of cane fiber or other fibrous materials pressed into sheets ½, ¾, and multiples of half inches thick, made up of a single ply or multiple plies securely joined together to prevent separation. The widths available are 16, 18, and 24 in., and the length 48 in. This type of lath is used because of its good heat insulation property. It may be obtained with a coating of asphalt on the back to provide a vapor barrier as described in Art. 97.

Fiber insulation lath is nailed to wood supports spaced not over

16 in. apart, the size of nail being appropriate for the thickness of the lath. The use of metal clips for attaching to steel supports is not recommended.

82. MIXING AND APPLYING

Proportions. For the base coats of gypsum plaster the proportions of sand, vermiculite, or pearlite to one 100-lb. bag of gypsum neat plaster shall not exceed those given in Table 82-1 (2).

Fibered plaster usually is used for the scratch coat over metal lath. The proportions for lime-cement stucco on metal lath are: *scratch coat*—stiff lime putty 1 part, portland cement 1 part, aggregate 6 parts, all by volume with 6 lb. of hair or fiber per cu. yd.; *brown coat*— stiff lime putty 2 parts, portland cement 1 part, aggregate 9 parts, all by volume with 3 lb. of hair per cu. yd.

The proportions for lime-cement stucco on unit masonry, except gypsum block which do not provide a suitable base for stucco, are: *base coat* of two-coat double-up work—stiff lime putty 2 parts, portland cement 1 part, aggregate 9 parts, all by volume with 6 lb. of hair or fiber per cu. yd.

For portland-cement plaster and stucco, each coat should consist of 1 part of portland cement to not less than 3 or more than 5 parts by volume of damp, loose aggregate.

Materials except cement may be used to increase the workability of portland-cement plaster and stucco. They include lime, finely divided

Table 82-1

Proportions for Plaster

	Sand, lb. Damp, Loose	Vermiculite or Pearlite, cu. ft.
Two-coat work (double-up method)		
Over gypsum lath	150	$2\frac{1}{2}$
Over unit masonry	300	3
Three-coat work		
Scratch coat over lath	200	2
Over masonry	300	3
All brown coats	300	3

clays, and asbestos flour. White portland cement is used in the finish coat for white and the lighter-colored stucco. Colors are obtained by using mineral pigment. Factory-made portland cements are available for use in the finish coat to obtain various colors.

Gypsum ready-mixed plaster is furnished with the sand aggregate added at the mill, and no further additions, except water, are made on the job. *Gypsum bond plaster* is used as the first coat over monolithic concrete surfaces without the addition of aggregate on the job. *Gypsum wood-fibered plaster* is also used in this same manner when applied over all types of lath. When applied to unit masonry, equal parts by weight of damp sand and wood-fibered plaster may be used.

The proportions for lime plaster are as follows.

For the *scratch coat* required only on metal lath—1 cu. ft. lime putty, 2 cu. ft. sand, and 7½ lb. hair or vegetable fiber per cu. yd. of mortar. For all *brown coats*—1 cu. ft. lime putty to 3 cu. ft. sand and 3½ lb. hair or fiber per cu. yd. of mortar.

The *final* or *finish coat* of plaster is extremely important. It must be attractive in appearance with the desired texture, and it must be hard and durable. Many types of finish can be used, the most common being known as the *white-coat finish*. The *sand float* or *sand finish* is also widely used, and the *lime–Keene's* cement finish is used when an especially hard surface is desired. The proportions for these finishes follow.

White-coat finish—1 part of gypsum gauging plaster, which is calcined gypsum, to not more than 3 parts of lime putty by volume. For application over either a gypsum or lime plaster brown coat.

Gypsum–sand float finish—1 part gypsum neat, unfibered plaster to not more than 2 parts of fine sand by weight.

Lime–sand float finish—3 parts lime putty, 3 parts fine sand, and 1 part gauging plaster by weight.

Keene's cement finish—one 100-lb. bag of Keene's cement to 1½ cu. ft. lime putty, for medium hard finish, or ⅝ cu. ft. of lime putty for hard finish.

Lime-cement stucco—The proportions for a smooth trowel finish are stiff putty 5 cu. ft. and portland cement 1 cu. ft.; for sand finish, stiff lime putty 5 cu. ft., portland cement 1 cu. ft., and silica plastering sand or marble dust 500 lb.

Prepared finishes. Several finishes are prepared at the mill and made ready for use on the job by adding water.

Water proportions. Water is added to the specified mixtures in the amounts required to make them workable. If too little water is added, the plaster or stucco will be difficult to spread with the trowel. If too much water is added, the mixture will slide off the trowel or the wall surface. If the mixtures are over-sanded and excess water is added to make them workable, the strength, hardness, and durability are reduced and the service they will render is impaired. Avoiding over-sanding will eliminate the need to add excess water.

Mixing. The ingredients of which the mortar for plaster and stucco is made may be mixed in batches, as required, by means of a mortar mixer.

For lime plasters, hydrated lime, which is a dry powder, is usually used. Water is mixed with the lime on the job to form lime putty. The manufacturers' instructions should be followed in preparing this putty for use. Sometimes it may be used immediately, and sometimes a soaking period of approximately 24 hours is required.

When gypsum is present in the mortar, all tools and equipment should be thoroughly cleaned after the mixing of each batch is completed. Cleaning is important because the presence of partially set gypsum may cause plaster to set too rapidly. Tools should not be washed in water to be used for mixing.

Grounds and Other Guides. The thickness of a plaster coating is of utmost importance to a good job. It is controlled by the use of wood or metal strips, called *grounds,* which are applied around the perimeters of openings (Fig. 82-1*b*) and along the bottoms of walls where wood grounds would be covered with bases or baseboards or where metal grounds would serve as dividers between the plaster and a cement or terrazzo base. Metal *corner beads* (*b*) are applied to projecting corners and around the perimeters of plastered openings to serve as guides and to protect the exposed corners. Wood grounds also serve as bases to which door and window trim or finish is attached. Permanent grounds or corner beads should not be used with stucco.

In locations where guides are necessary and grounds or corner beads cannot be installed, narrow strips of plaster are accurately built up on the first coat with their surfaces flush with the surface to which the brown coat is to be finished. These become incorporated in the brown coat. They are called *plaster screeds.* They are often located horizontally across wall areas and across and around large ceiling areas to assist in forming true surfaces on the brown coat.

Grounds, screeds, and other guides should be set to provide a minimum plaster thickness of $\frac{5}{8}$ in. over metal lath, wire lath, and wire fabric and $\frac{1}{2}$ in. over other types of lath; $\frac{5}{8}$ in. over unit masonry

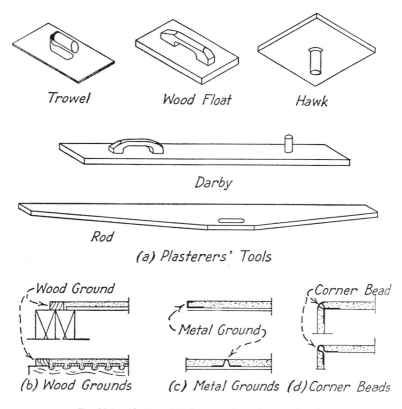

Fig. 82-1. Plasterers' tools, grounds, and corner beads.

and concrete walls; and from ⅛ in. minimum to ⅜ in. maximum over monolithic concrete ceilings. Stucco with metal reinforcement should be at least ⅞ in. thick measured from the face of the reinforcement. Stucco on unit masonry bases should be at least ¾ in. thick.

Application. Plaster is applied by hand or machine methods. If applied by hand, the mortar is dumped on a conveniently located mortar board. The hand tools used by the plasterer are shown in Fig. 82-1a. Mortar is shoved from the board onto the wood or metal *hawk* with a metal *trowel*. It is transferred from the hawk to the wall and spread with the trowel.

In applying the *scratch coat* to metal lath, enough pressure should be exerted to force some of the mortar through the open spaces to form keys which clinch the mortar to the lath. The hair or vegetable fiber included in the scratch coat permits only enough mortar to go through the open spaces in the lathed surface to form good keys. It also adds strength to the key during the early stages of setting. Mortar is thereby held in position and does not drop behind the lath. This coat is about ¼ in. thick and is not accurately finished. Its surface is scratched with appropriate tools while it is still soft, to provide a better bond for the brown coat. Machine application is done by pneumatic plastering machines which blow the plaster into position.

The *brown coat* is applied directly to bases of unit masonry or gypsum lath or to a scratch coat over metal lath after the scratch coat has set firm and hard. It is troweled on and brought to a true surface with a *darby* (Fig. 82-1a), which is given a partial rotary motion, and the *rod* or *straight* edge shown in the figure, the ends of which bear on grounds, screeds, or other guides. Its surface is left rough enough to receive the finish coat.

Gypsum and fiber insulation lath are not wet down. Unit masonry surfaces on which suction must be reduced before applying the brown coat directly to them should be properly wet down. It is often necessary to fill in with mortar irregularities in stone walls before applying the brown coat.

The *finish coat* is applied to a partially dry brown coat or to a thoroughly dry one which has been evenly but not excessively wetted by brushing or spraying.

For a gypsum-lime putty or *white-coat trowel finish* on plaster, the finish mortar is allowed to draw for a few minutes and is then well troweled with water to a smooth finish free from all defects. The *Keene's cement finish* is applied in the same manner. *Sand float finishes* are obtained by applying the mortar with a trowel and finishing by floating with a wood float (Fig. 82-1a), or with such a float with its surface covered by carpet, cork, or other material, forming a plaster surface free from slick spots or other blemishes.

The finish coat of stucco may be given various textures by manipulating trowels and tools of various shapes, using floats with wood, cork, or carpet surfaces, brushing with fiber or wire brushes, dashing small quantities of mortar on the surface and finishing in various ways, or by a great variety of other procedures which may involve many colors.

Ornamental Plastering. Ornamental plastering includes moldings, cornices, panels, decorative ceilings, rosettes, etc., made of plaster or similar material and placed in the interior of buildings.

The base for moldings of small projection is built up solid with the same material as that used for the brown coat. It is built up to approximately the shape of the molding, making sure that there is clearance enough to allow for the finish coat, which is composed of lime putty and gauging plaster. The finish coat is applied to this base and is cut to the desired profile by means of a sheet-metal template operating on guides. The finish coat cannot be cut with sharp outlines in one operation but must be gone over several times, the low places being filled in with mortar each time. For larger moldings the base is built up of metal lath supported on braces.

The moldings and similar ornamental plastering are placed before the finish coat on the remainder of the walls and ceiling because the guides cannot be placed on the finish coat without marring it. Parts of moldings, such as internal and external miters which cannot be run with templates, must be formed by hand, or they may be cast and placed in position before the moldings are run. Parts of moldings such as dentils and brackets may be cast separately and *stuck* in place after moldings are run.

Ornaments that cannot be run are cast in gelatin molds, or they may be purchased from firms that make a specialty of this kind of work.

Acoustical Plaster. Acoustical plasters are special plasters with porous aggregates and are applied with a trowel as a final coat to improve the sound-absorbing properties of walls and ceilings. See Art. 98.

Fireproofing. Fire-resistive plaster applied on metal lath over structural steel members to prolong their resistance to high temperatures is made with pearlite or vermiculite, instead of sand, as the aggregate in gypsum plaster.

References

1. *Standard Definitions of Terms Relating to Gypsum,* ASTM Designation C11-58.
2. *American Standard Specifications for Gypsum Plastering and Interior Lathing and Framing,* American Standards Association, 1955.
3. *Specifications for Lime and Its Uses in Plastering, Stucco, Unit Masonry and Concrete,* National Lime Association, 1945.
4. *Plasterers Manual for Applying Portland Cement, Stucco and Plaster,* Portland Cement Association.
5. *Gypsum Lathing and Plastering,* Gypsum Association.
6. *Metal Lath Technical Bulletins,* Metal Lath Manufacturers Association.
7. *Standard Specifications for Portland Cement Stucco and Portland Cement Plastering,* American Standards Association, 1946.
8. *Standard Specifications for Lime-Cement Stucco,* American Standards Association, 1960.

13 Stairs

83. DEFINITIONS AND GENERAL DISCUSSION

Definitions. A series of steps without an intervening platform, or *landing,* is called a *flight.* A *stair* is a series of steps, or flights of steps connected by landings, for passing from one level to another. The space in a building occupied by the stair is called the *stairwell* or *stairway,* but the latter term is often used in the same sense as stair. A *staircase* includes the entire group of stairs from the bottom floor to the top floor. This term is often used with the same meaning as stair.

The various parts of a stair are shown in Fig. 83-1*a* and *b* and may be defined as follows.

The *tread* is the horizontal top surface of a step or the member forming this surface. The *riser* is the vertical face of a step or the member forming this face. Usually the tread projects a short distance in front of the riser, forming the *nosing.* This makes a stair easier to negotiate.

The *rise* of a step is the vertical distance between treads, and the *run* is the horizontal distance between risers and is equal to the width of tread, not including the nosing. The terms *rise* and *run* are also applied to the corresponding dimensions of a flight of steps. A step whose tread is narrower at one end than the other is called a *winder.* A step with one or both ends rounded in a half or quarter of a circle and ending at the newel or a step with semicircular ends with the newel at the center is called a *bullnose step.* The bottom step is called a *starting step.*

The posts at the top and bottom of a stair which support the *stair-rail, hand-rail,* or *railing* are called *newels* or *newel posts.* The intermediate posts at turns in a stair are also called *newels.* The vertical members running between the ends of the steps and the rails are called *balusters.* A series of balusters and the supporting railing is called a *balustrade.* The parts of a rail located at points where the direc-

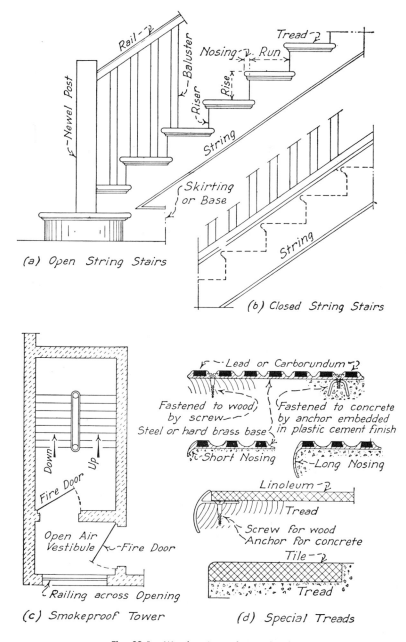

(a) Open String Stairs

(b) Closed String Stairs

(c) Smokeproof Tower

(d) Special Treads

Fig. 83-1. Wood stairs and stair details.

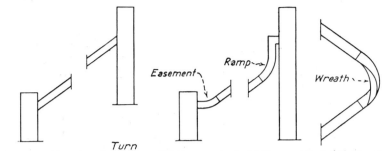

Turn
Starting Newel at Landing (b) Easement at (c) Ramped Rail (d) Wreath
(a) Straight Hand Rail Starting Newel at Turn at Turn

Fig. 83-2. Stair rails, easements, ramps, and wreaths.

tion or slope of the rail changes without running into a newel are called *easements, ramps, easings,* and *goosenecks* or *wreaths,* depending upon their shape (Fig. 83-2).

The inclined member to which the ends of treads and risers are fastened is called the *string.* An *outside string* is one that is not located against a wall. A *wall string* is located against a wall. The upper edge of a *closed* or *curb string* is a continuous line conforming to the slope of the stairs (Fig. 83-1b). If the top edge of a string is notched to follow the treads and risers, it is called an *open string* (Fig. 83-1a).

Inclined surfaces for foot or vehicle traffic are called *ramps.* They are used in preference to stairs where large numbers of people are to be accommodated, as in railway stations, stadiums, etc.; in multistory garages they replace elevators, and their use for many industrial purposes is increasing. The space occupied by ramps is much greater than that required by stairs because of the flat slope necessarily used with ramps. The slope of ramps for foot traffic should not exceed 1 in 8, but a slope not greater than 1 in 10 is preferable. Hand rails should be provided when the slope exceeds 1 in 10. Ramps should be surfaced with some nonslip material.

Proportioning Stairs. The rise and run of a stair are determined by arbitrary rules. For comfort in using a stair, the run must be increased as the rise is decreased. Four of these rules are as follows.

1. The sum of the rise and run should be not less than 17 in. or more than 18 in.

2. Twice the rise plus the run should be not less than 24 in. or more than 25 in.

3. The product of the rise and run should be not less than 70 or more than 75.

4. The product of the rise and the square root of the run should be equal to 23½.

For important stairs a rise of 7 in. and a run of 11 in. will give satisfactory results. In residences a rise of 7 or 7½ in. and a run of 10 in. or even 9½ in. may be used, and unimportant stairs such as those leading to basements are often made with both run and rise equal to 8 in. A rise greater than 8 in. is always objectionable. The nosing may project from ¾ in. to 1½ in.

The pitch or slope of long flights of stairs should be made flatter than would ordinarily be satisfactory, and landings should be introduced to make the stairs less tiresome and less dangerous. The flights between landings should not exceed 12 ft. in height, and the width of the landing should be wider than the tread by an amount equal to the average length of step, or a multiple of this length. The length of step on a landing is less than on the level and may be taken as about 2 ft. The pitch of short flights outdoors should be less than that used inside because of the more rapid pace naturally used outdoors. A 6-in. rise and a 12-in. run are satisfactory.

Building codes include minimum stair requirements for buildings of various types of construction devoted to various uses. For example, the minimum stair width permitted by the National Board of Fire Underwriters is 44 in., except in buildings occupied by no more than 45 persons, where the width may be 36 in. For other buildings the unit of stair width is considered to be 22 in. Stairs with one of such units are not permitted. The number of occupants permitted for a given story per unit of stair width for all stairways serving that story is 60 for assembly, business, educational, industrial, mercantile, and storage and 30 for institutional, residential, and high-hazard. Other codes have corresponding requirements. Requirements for the fire resistance of stairs under various conditions are included in codes.

Smokeproof Towers. Smokeproof towers (Fig. 83-1c) are stairways constructed of incombustible materials enclosed in walls with a fire-resistance rating of from 2 to 4 hours, depending upon the code. Such towers have no openings except the necessary doors and windows. Access to the stairway at each story is by vestibules or outside balconies which have solid floors of incombustible materials and which have exits on a street or a court. The doors are required to be self-closing solid doors of incombustible materials, swinging in the direction of travel from the building. The stairway is separated from the rest of the building by an open-air vestibule so that it cannot become filled with smoke. Codes may require at least one such tower for buildings more than five stories high. Smokeproof towers are sometimes called *fire towers*.

Special Treads. Because of the excessive wear on stair treads and the danger of slipping, special treads of various materials are manufactured for use on stairs. Many types of such treads (Fig. 83-1*d*) are on the market. One consists of an abrasive material embedded in the wearing surface of a cast-iron, bronze, or aluminum tread. In another type the abrasive material is embedded in a clay-tile tread. Strips of lead or lead slugs may be embedded in steel, cast-iron, or brass bases. Rubber, linoleum, and cork treads are used, but they should be protected by a metal nosing, as shown in the figure. They are not especially slip resistant.

Treads and risers for steel and concrete stairs may consist of slabs of bluestone, slate, or marble. Such treads should always be supported throughout their length by steel members or concrete, because if exposed to fire they may become weakened and break when they are most needed. Steel checkered plates and gratings may be used for the treads of steel stairs.

Railings. Stair railings may be of various designs. They may consist of a wood rail and balusters; a wood rail and wrought-iron or steel balusters; ornamental brass, bronze, wrought iron, or steel arranged in various designs; solid plaster with wood or metal rail; pipe rails; solid stone or brick rails; and stone railings with stone balusters. Handrails to be used along a wall are sometimes called *grab rails*. Wide stairs should be provided with center railings.

The type of railing which is appropriate for a given stair will depend to a large extent on the type of construction used for the stair. The various kinds of stairs are described in the articles which follow.

84. WOOD STAIRS

Several methods are used in the construction of wood stairs. One of the most common methods will be described in this article.

Rough Framing. The rough framing required for the support of a wood stair is illustrated in Fig. 84-1*a*. It consists of *carriages* or *horses* accurately cut to receive the treads and risers. A carriage that goes next to a wall should be kept about 3 in. away from the wall so that it

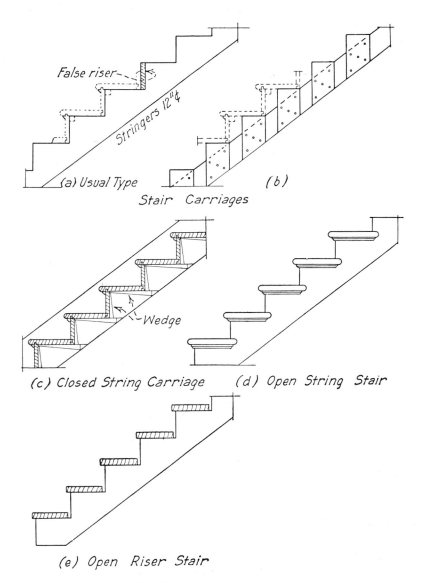

Fig. 84-1. Types of wood stairs.

will not interfere with the wall string to be placed later. Carriages are constructed of 2- or 3-in. material and should be of sufficient strength to carry the load which they are to receive. They are usually spaced 12 in. center to center. On long flights, *false risers* are used on every fifth or sixth step to stiffen the structure. The carriages should be cut so that this riser will clear the finished riser. Rough treads are placed so that the stairs may be used during construction, but these are removed before the finished treads are placed.

Occasionally carriages are constructed as shown in *b*, but this type is undesirable.

Finished Stairs. The finished stairs are prepared at the mill and are placed after the plastering is completed. The ends of the finished treads and risers are housed in a wall string or closed string (Fig. 84-1*c*), provision being made for wedges which are driven up tight and glued to hold the treads and risers firmly in place.

Open-string construction is illustrated in *d*. The string is cut to receive the treads and risers; the nosing is mitered and returned to finish the exposed end of the tread; the riser is mitered with the string; and the lower end of the balusters is dovetailed or doweled to the tread. Tongued-and-grooved joints are usually provided at the junctions of the risers and treads, and blocks may be glued or screwed in the interior angle between the risers and treads.

The treads should usually be $1\frac{1}{8}$ in. thick and the risers $\frac{7}{8}$ in. thick.

Materials. Because of the severe wear to which treads are subjected, they should be made of oak, birch, maple, or yellow pine. Oak and yellow pine should preferably be quarter-sawed. The risers and other parts of the stair may be of softwood if desired.

Plank Stair. A rough stair constructed of planks is illustrated in *e*. It is of open-riser construction with plank treads notched in plank strings.

85. CONCRETE STAIRS

Reinforced concrete stairs are used extensively in fire-resistant buildings. They are usually placed after the structural frame has been completed, and therefore recesses and ties should be provided in the structural frame to receive the stairs.

Structural Details. A simple flight of reinforced concrete is illustrated in Fig. 85-1*a*; a flight ending at a landing in *b*; a flight beginning at a

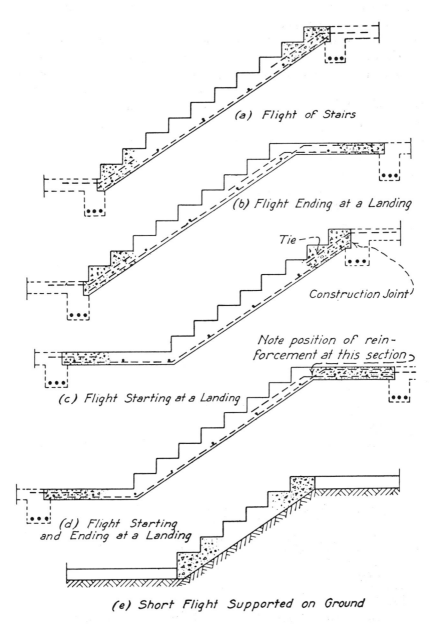

(a) Flight of Stairs

(b) Flight Ending at a Landing

Tie

Construction Joint

Note position of rein-
forcement at this section

(c) Flight Starting at a Landing

(d) Flight Starting
and Ending at a Landing

(e) Short Flight Supported on Ground

Fig. 85-1.   Concrete stairs.

landing in c; and a flight beginning and ending at a landing in d. Particular attention should be paid to the position of reinforcement at an interior angle on the tension side. If the reinforcement follows around the tension side of the stair slab at the angle, it will tend to straighten out and separate from the slab. The drawings show how this can be prevented. In b to d, the stair and the landing act together as a bent slab supported at each end. Instead of being designed as an integral part of the stair, the landing may be supported by beams running between walls enclosing the stairs, by beams suspended from the structural frame of the floor above, or by beams supported by props resting on the structural frame of the floor below. Short flights are frequently supported on the ground.

Concrete is probably the most suitable material for stairs of complicated design, such as winding stairs.

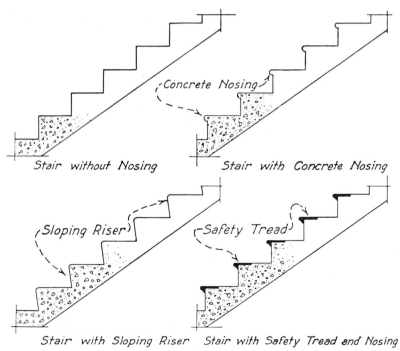

Stair without Nosing   *Stair with Concrete Nosing*

Stair with Sloping Riser   Stair with Safety Tread and Nosing

Details of Steps

Fig. 85-2. Types of concrete stairs.

Details of Steps. Various details of steps are illustrated in Fig. 85-2. The simplest type of step has a vertical riser and the tread is without a nosing, but this detail should not be used on important stairs. Unless proper precautions are taken, the form boards for the risers in stairs with concrete nosings may swell and crack off the nosings. To prevent this, the tops of the boards should be beveled and the boards should be removed as soon as possible. Oiling the boards also helps. The effect of a nosing can be secured at little expense by sloping the riser outward at the top. One form of cast-iron tread provides the nosing and thus simplifies the formwork. The nosing can be formed of concrete and can be used with or without a special tread. Other types of treads, as described in Art. 83, can be used with concrete stairs. A terrazzo finish is frequently used on concrete stairs where appearance is an important factor. Parts of concrete and terrazzo nosings are frequently broken off when moving furniture and are difficult to repair.

86. STEEL AND CAST-IRON STAIRS

Steel stairs are of three general types. The simplest consists of strings of steel channels and treads of steel checkered plate, concrete supported on steel angles or channels, or steel grating (Fig. 86-1a). The risers are usually open, and the treads are fastened to the strings by light shelf angles. The railings and posts may be of angle irons, or a pipe rail may be used. Stairs of this kind are suitable for industrial buildings.

Another type of steel stair consists of strings of steel channels or plates, and risers and structural treads formed of steel plates, all finished to be suitable for high-quality buildings. Typical details of this type of stair are shown in *b*, but a large number of designs are on the market. Stairs of this type are supplied by manufacturers who make stair building a specialty. The illustration shows treads of various materials supported by the subtread which consists of a steel plate. The railings are made attractive in design to suit the rest of the stair.

The third type consists of steel strings and precast reinforced concrete combination tread and riser as shown in *c*. Spiral stairs (Fig. 86-2) are suitable only where they will receive very little traffic and where the space available is small. They are usually made of cast-iron winders arranged around a pipe newel.

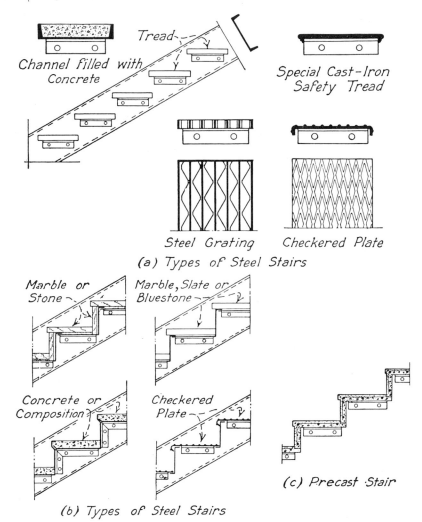

Tread

Channel filled with Concrete

Special Cast-Iron Safety Tread

Steel Grating

Checkered Plate

(a) Types of Steel Stairs

Marble or Stone

Marble, Slate or Bluestone

Concrete or Composition

Checkered Plate

(c) Precast Stair

(b) Types of Steel Stairs

Fig. 86-1. Types of steel stairs.

87. STONE AND BRICK STAIRS

Stone steps and stairs are used extensively in the approaches and entrances to buildings and occasionally in the entrance halls, foyers, or lobbies of public and monumental buildings.

The stone used must have superior wearing properties to withstand

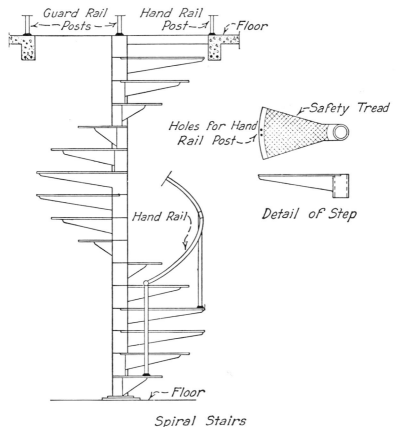

Spiral Stairs

Fig. 86-2. Cast-iron spiral stairs.

foot traffic, and if used on the exterior it must be resistant to weathering action. Granite has these qualities to a high degree, and some sandstones, limestones, and marbles may be used with good results. The steps are supported at their ends and at intermediate points where necessary by masonry or in some other manner. The *hanging stairway* is a special form of construction which is rarely, if ever, used in modern buildings. In this construction one end of each step is solidly built into a masonry wall, and the steps are so shaped at their areas of contact that each step receives vertical and horizontal support from the steps below and horizontal support from the step above.

Short outdoor flights of brick steps supported on concrete masonry are often used in residential construction. Only hard, durable brick bedded in cement mortar with rich cement concave mortar joints compacted and struck with a jointing tool should be used. The forward brick in the treads should be headers, preferably laid on edge.

The treads of all outdoor steps of stone, brick, or concrete should slope forward about ¼ in. to the foot to provide for drainage.

14 Windows and curtain walls

88. DEFINITIONS AND GENERAL DISCUSSION

In general, a *window* is an opening in a wall of a building to provide any or all of the following: natural light, natural ventilation, and vision. The term also refers to the construction installed in the opening to provide protection against entry and the weather. To be satisfactory, windows must be durable, weathertight, reasonable in cost, readily installed, and, for many uses, attractive in appearance. Windows are also used to a limited extent in partitions for vision from room to room, for *borrowed* light, or for other reasons.

Only exterior windows are considered in this chapter. In addition to the glass, they are made of wood, steel, aluminum, stainless steel, and bronze. They are available in a great variety of types to suit many requirements and individual preferences.

Much has been done by the associations representing the manufacturers of windows of each material to standardize the types, sizes, and construction details of their windows. Lower costs and prompter deliveries are possible if *stock*, rather than *custom-made*, windows can be used.

Parts of a Window. A window frame includes the members which form the perimeter of a window; it is fixed to the surrounding wall or to other supports. The horizontal top member of a frame is the *head;* the vertical side members, the *jambs;* and the horizontal bottom member, the *sill.* A vertical member that subdivides a frame or a vertical member placed between and attached to adjacent frames is called a *mullion.* Similar horizontal members are also called mullions.

A *sash* is a framed unit which may be included within a window frame and may be fixed in position or arranged to open for natural ventilation or cleaning. The top member of a sash is the *top rail;* the bottom member, the *bottom rail;* and the side members, the *stiles.*

If one sash is placed above another, the adjacent rails are called *meeting* or *check rails*. If one sash is placed beside another, the adjacent stiles are called *meeting stiles*. If a separate member is placed between adjacent sash, as described, it is called a meeting rail or meeting stile.

The units of glass included within a window frame or sash area are called *panes* or *lights*. If more than one light is included in this area, the vertical and horizontal members between panes, and those that directly support them, are called *muntins*. The panes of glass are held in position by putty, glazing compounds, metal clips, wood or metal moldings, or beads. The last one mentioned is called a *glass bead* or *stop*. Placing the glass in position is called *glazing*. Windows may be designed for glazing from the outside or the inside.

Narrow strips of sheet material in various forms made of metal, felt, rubber, or plastic, called *weatherstrips* or *weatherstripping,* may be placed around the edges of operating sash to exclude moisture and air infiltration.

A *screen* consists of wire mesh surrounded with a rigid frame which is placed in a window or sash opening to exclude insects. A *storm window* or sash is an additional glazed unit placed in a window opening to reduce the heat loss during winter. It is usually placed on the outside of the sash but may be inside. It is often interchangeable with a screen. A *shutter* is a panel provided to cover a window to exclude light, obscure vision, or to provide protection or decoration. Usually one edge is hinged to a jamb and shutters are usually provided in pairs. They are rarely used, and then only for decorative purposes, on residences, in which case they are often fixed in the open position. They are also called *blinds*. A *fire shutter,* also called a *fire window,* is fire-resistant and provides protection against outside exposure fires. It usually operates automatically.

Window Types. The usual types of windows, regardless of the materials of which they are constructed, are shown diagrammatically in Fig. 88-1. The glass areas in these examples are subdivided in various ways which may have no significance to the type of window illustrated. Some windows may include only a single pane of glass. Subdivisions may be made to permit the inclusion of ventilating units, for convenience in cleaning, to limit glass size for safety, for architectural effect or for other reasons. Various types of windows or sash are often combined in a single window opening.

A *fixed window* is illustrated in *a*. It makes no provision for natural ventilation.

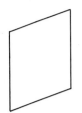
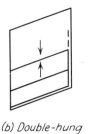

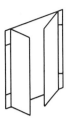

(a) Fixed   (b) Double-hung   (c) Horizontal Siding   (d) Outswinging Casement

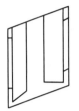
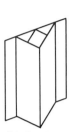

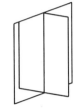

(e) Inswinging Casement   (f) Folding   (g) Horizontal Pivoted   (h) Vertical Pivoted

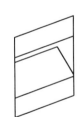
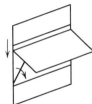

(i) Top-hinged Outswinging   (j) Top-hinged Inswinging   (k) Bottom-hinged Inswinging   (l) Outward Projecting

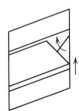

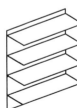
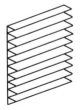

(m) Inward Projecting   (n) Hopper   (o) Awning   (p) Jalouise

Fig. 88-1. Window types—outside views for open positions.

A *double-hung window* is shown in *b*. Both sash slide vertically, with the weight of each counterbalanced by sash weights, spiral spring balances, or tape spring balances similar to clock springs; the sash is easily operated and edge friction will hold it in any set position. For a *single-hung window*, only the lower sash operates. Some types are arranged so that the sash can be removed from the inside.

A *horizontal sliding window* is shown in *c*. One or both sash may be arranged to slide. Some types are arranged so that the sash may be removed from the inside. Heavy sash are often provided with nylon rollers for ease in operation. Sash are sometimes suspended from rollers operating on overhead tracks.

In general, any hinged window is a *casement window*. It may swing out or in and may be hinged at either side, the top, or the bottom, but the term is usually applied only to side-hinged windows. An *outswinging casement window* with two sash is shown in *d*. Each sash swings on extension hinges attached to the hanging stile of the sash and the jamb of the frame. The extension provides an open space between the hanging stile and the jamb to facilitate cleaning the outside. An *inswinging casement window* is shown in *e*. Extension hinges are used to make the sash swing clear of the inside surface of the wall. One or more casement of either type may be included in a single opening. For example, three sash could be included by providing a mullion between a single sash and a pair of sash. Outswinging casements are much more widely used than inswinging. The *folding window* is illustrated in *f*. It is a form of outswinging casement window with the two sash hinged together on their meeting stiles rather than each to its outside stile. Projection arms, which are shown in the figure, are so arranged that the sash operate symmetrically.

A *horizontal pivoted sash*, pivoted at the center, is shown in *g*. Such sash are often arranged in a row to form a continuous or *ribbon window* located in a sawtooth roof or monitor and are operated in unison from the floor by a mechanical operator.

A *vertical pivoted sash* is shown in *h*. Such sash are often arranged to swing in a full circle.

Sash may be *top-hinged* and swing out (*i*) or top-hinged and swing in (*j*). They may also be *bottom-hinged* and swing in (*k*).

Windows with ventilator sash which operate like those in *l* are called *projected windows*. The ends of the arms are pivoted to the stile of the sash and to the frame. Shoes are attached to the top rail of the sash and move vertically along the stiles. They are guided by tracks attached to the vertical members at the sides of the opening.

The window shown in *l* is an *outward-projecting window,* and that shown in *m* is an *inward-projecting window.* If the latter is located at or near the bottom of a window (*n*), it is called a *hopper ventilator.* If several outward-projecting ventilators are located vertically adjacent to each other (*o*) and are arranged to be operated simultaneously by a single operator, the window is called an *awning window.* Fixed meeting rails sometimes are provided between adjacent sash. The downward movement of the top rail of projected sash provides an opening through which the outside of outward-projecting sash can be cleaned.

A *jalousie window* is shown in *p.* It is similar to an awning window except the ventilating units are heavy glass slats from 3 to 8 in. wide with metal end supports to which the operator is attached. Adjacent edges of the slats overlap ½ in. or more to exclude rain and reduce air infiltration. There is considerable air leakage when closed, and they are usually used only for enclosed porches or where air leakage is not objectionable.

A *wicket panel* is a small sliding or hinged panel in an inside screen provided so the operating mechanism of an outswing sash can be reached from inside.

Designations. A procedure for indicating the type of rotating operating units included in a window is illustrated in Fig. 88-2*a.* The meeting point or intersection of the two diagonal lines on a ventilator is located on the axis about which the ventilator rotates. The procedure does not indicate whether the movement is outward or inward. There is no distinction between ventilators rotating about horizontal or vertical axes through their centers, but the axis is usually horizontal.

A system has been devised for designating windows according to the arrangement of lights and ventilators. This designation consists of digits arranged in the following order: Lights wide; lights high; number of ventilators; lights in lower, or only, ventilator; lights in upper ventilator, if any; lights between lower or only ventilator and bottom; lights between upper ventilator, if any, and bottom. Items not present are omitted in designation. The use of this legend is illustrated in Fig. 88-2*b.* The legend was devised for steel windows and is used occasionally for aluminum windows.

Factors in Selection of Type. Several of the factors considered in the selection of the type of window for a specific use are given in the following paragraphs.

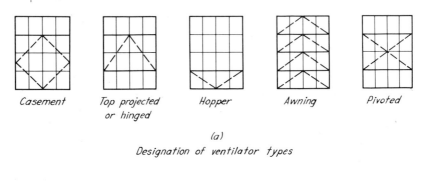

Casement   Top projected or hinged   Hopper   Awning   Pivoted

(a)

Designation of ventilator types

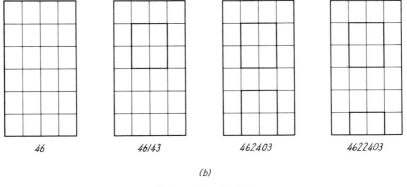

46   46/43   462403   4622403

(b)

Designation of windows

Fig. 88-2. Designations of ventilators and windows.

Ventilation. The following comments refer primarily to buildings that are not air-conditioned but depend on natural ventilation. A vertical or horizontal sliding sash has little effect on the direction of flow of outside air into a room. A rotating ventilator tends to guide the flow in the direction at which the sash is set. For this reason projected hopper, awning, jalousie, and horizontal pivoted sash, as usually arranged, direct the inflowing air upward toward the ceiling, an effect which is usually, but not always, desirable. Similar but horizontal effects result from the directions at which casement and vertical pivoted sash are set. Outswinging casements can be set to direct air currents flowing parallel to the wall surface into a room. Outward projecting sash, awning windows, or jalousie windows serve as canopies in deflecting rain while the sash are open for ventilation. Folding windows are said to have a chimney effect which tends to draw air out of a room. Ribbon or continuous horizontal pivoted or projected ventilators operated mechanically in groups and located high up on the walls of industrial buildings or in roof monitors or sawteeth are especially effective in ventilating industrial buildings.

Screening. Any operating unit can be screened, but sometimes screening is difficult. The screen wire mesh is installed in frames and is renewable. The wire mesh may be painted or galvanized steel, plastic-coated glass fiber, aluminum, or bronze, the last two being the most durable. Screens are arranged to be installed from the inside.

Double-hung, single-hung, horizontal sliding, inswinging casements, and ventilators which open inward (Fig. 88-1) may be provided with outside screens. Ventilators which open out, also shown in this figure, may be provided with inside screens. The inside screens for outswinging casement, awning, and jalousie windows do not interfere with the operators, but special provision must be made for operating outward-projecting ventilators. Horizontal and vertical centrally pivoted ventilators are difficult to screen.

A special type of screen is available which keeps all or a part of the direct sunlight from entering a window, depending upon the exposure. Instead of horizontal wires, the screen has flat miniature metal slats corresponding to the slats of a venetian blind. The slats are set at the angle for greatest effectiveness. The vertical wires are more widely spaced than the usual screen wires. This type of screen, if placed outside, is quite effective in reducing temperatures during the summer, especially for rooms with south exposure.

Cleaning and Repairing. The possibilities for cleaning, replacing broken lights, or eliminating water leakage are important factors to consider in selecting the type of window. Double-hung, single-hung, and horizontal sliding sash are often removable for cleaning or repair from the inside. Outswinging casements are fitted with extension hinges which provide an open arm space between the hanging stile and the jamb. Sometimes the entire outside surface of a window can be reached from the inside for cleaning by adjusting the position of the ventilator. In others the ventilator or movable sash provides for access to the outside for the window cleaner. Except for windows close to the ground or an adjacent roof surface, anchors for the safety belts of window cleaners are often attached to the jambs of windows. Various types of installations have been devised to provide for window washing to be done entirely from the outside even if all the windows are fixed.

Vertical pivoted sash which can rotate through a full circle and top-hinged inswinging sash are designed especially for use in air-conditioned buildings where the sash are only opened while their outsides are being cleaned. Off-season and emergency ventilation may be provided by including a hopper ventilator in the window with one of the types of sash mentioned.

The suitability of the various types of windows for cleaning can be judged by examining Fig. 88-1. If the windows are screened, it will be necessary to remove the screens on some types.

Other Factors. Many other factors must be considered in selecting the type of window, regardless of the material of which it is constructed. A ventilator which projects inward may interfere with the use of space adjacent to a window and with the operation of shading equipment such as window shades and venetian blinds; vertical and especially horizontal members in a window may interfere with desired vision through a window; large glass areas may result in personal injury from glass breakage when someone falls against a window; need for access to the controls of operating units may restrict the placing of furniture or equipment against walls; and the type of occupancy and the appearance may have a significant effect on the selection. Such factors as durability and cost are more closely related to the designs and the materials used in construction than to the type of window.

Minimum Area. According to the code of the National Board of Fire Underwriters every habitable room, that is, every room arranged for living, eating, or sleeping purposes, must be provided with natural light and ventilation by one or more windows opening on a street, alley, or court. The total glass area in the windows must be not less than $\frac{1}{10}$ of the floor area, with a minimum total glass area of 10 sq. ft. except in bathrooms where it is 3 sq. ft.

Window or other openings required for ventilation must have a total openable area of at least 50 per cent of the glazed area required for lighting.

This requirement does not apply to rooms provided with artificial ventilation or air conditioning. Windowless rooms are common, and even windowless buildings are frequently constructed because of the better control they afford for illumination, ventilation, temperature, and humidity than is possible with windows.

Special requirements are included which apply to other types of occupancy and to artificial lighting and ventilation.

Solar Heat Through Windows. See Art. 97.

89. WOOD WINDOWS

General Comments. Wood windows are used extensively in many types of buildings when not excluded by the fire-resistive requirements of building codes.

Wood windows have been used for many centuries. The large-scale production of such windows by machines in factories started in this country about 1840 (1). They are now used more than windows of any other material for residences. The most widely used type is the double-hung window, as illustrated in Fig. 88-1*b*, although outswinging casement in *d* is quite common, and horizontal sliding in *c*, the outward projecting in *l*, the hopper in *n*, the awning in *o*, and the jalousie in *p* are also used.

Double-Hung Window. A detailed drawing illustrating the various parts of a wood double-hung counterweighted window for placing in a masonry wall is given in Fig. 89-1. It consists of three principal parts: the frame, the sash, and the interior trim. The principal parts of the frame, including the head, jambs, and sill and those of a sash, including the top rail, bottom rail, and stiles, are defined in Art. 88. These and the other parts of a double-hung window are shown in Fig. 86-1, and the other parts may be defined as follows.

sash weights. Metal weights to counterbalance the weight of a sash and facilitate its operation and to hold it in a set position when raised.

weight box. The box in which the weights operate.

sash cord or chain. Cord or chain which connects a sash to the weight.

sash pulley. A metal unit consisting of a box containing a sheave or special type of wheel over which the sash cord extends between the sash and a sash weight. Also called a *frame pulley.*

pulley stile. The part of a weight box adjacent to the sash and along which sash slides.

back lining. The part of a weight box next to the masonry.

box casing. The side of a weight box.

pocket. The removable section of a pulley stile which gives access to the interior of the weight box.

pendulum. A thin partition of wood or sheet metal in the weight box to keep the weights from interfering with each other. It is fastened at the top only, so that it can be pushed aside to reach both sides of the weight box through the pocket for repairs.

parting strip. The guide between the two sash.

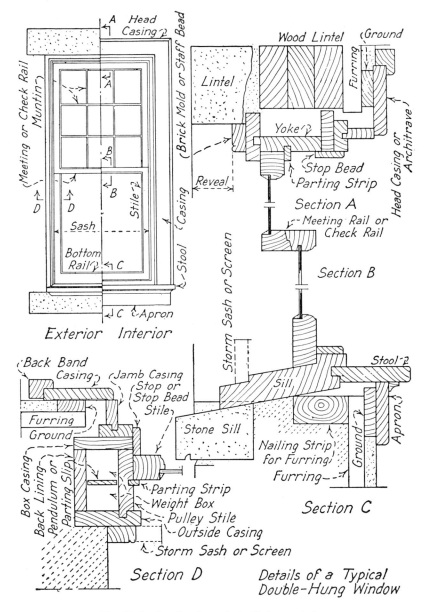

Fig. 89-1. Details of wood double-hung window.

stop or stop bead. The outer and inner guides for sash.

yoke. The top member of the frame, also called the head.

sill. The bottom member of the frame.

stool. The sill of the interior finish.

apron. The part of the finish below the stool.

casing. The interior trim at the sides of the opening.

head casing. The interior trim at the top of the opening.

grounds. The strips under the interior trim arranged to serve as guides to fix the thickness of plaster and as nailing strips for the interior finish.

brick mold. The mold in the outside corner between frame and brickwork.

staff bead. The general term for brick mold to apply to other materials.

reveal. The exposed masonry on the jamb between the frame and the outside face of the wall. Also, the corresponding surface on the inside.

jamb casing. The interior trim on jambs of the opening where the frame is set to give a reveal on the inside of the opening.

To permit the use of narrower interior trim on window openings, narrow rectangular sash weights may be used instead of the common cylindrical sash weights. The same result is accomplished by spiral-coiled springs instead of sash weights. These are placed in recesses in the exposed faces of the frame stiles and the sliding edges of the sash stiles. Sash balances consisting of flat coiled-steel springs, like clock springs, with metal housings are mounted at the tops of the frame stiles with their ends attached to the edges of the sash stiles. They balance the weights of the sash by coiling and uncoiling as the sash are operated.

The sash of all types of counterbalanced double-hung windows are held in set positions by friction between the stiles of the frame and the sash.

Casement Windows. An outswinging casement window with two sash for a masonry wall is illustrated in Fig. 89-2a and an inswinging casement window in *b*. The principal parts of each window are the frame, the sash, and the trim. Many of the parts of these windows have corresponding parts in the double-hung window, which were defined. They are illustrated in the figures. A part peculiar to this type of window is the *astragal* which may be provided to cover the joint between meeting stiles and make it more weathertight.

Casement windows may include one or more sash, the two-sash casement being the most common. All types can be controlled by operators located on the inside.

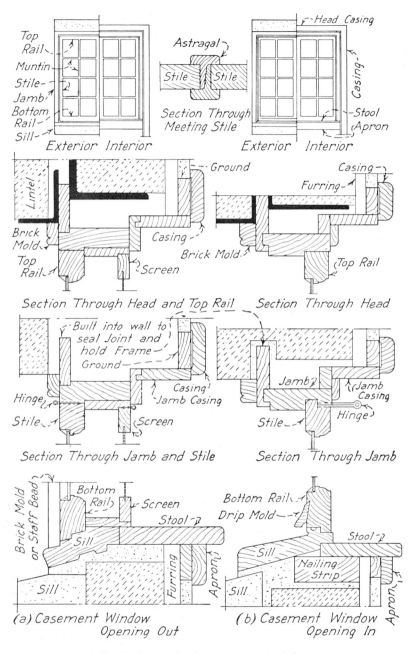

Fig. 89-2. Details of wood casement windows.

Species of Wood. The wood used for the exposed parts of wood windows should be highly weather-resistant and should not warp or shrink. The most commonly used wood is ponderosa pine, but white pine, sugar pine, fir, redwood, cypress, and cedar are also used extensively, the selection being governed largely by relative availability at a given location. The jambs of double-hung windows are subjected to considerable wear, and therefore they should be made of some relatively hard wood such as yellow pine. They are sometimes protected with aluminum. The parts which are exposed only on the inside are made of the same wood as the interior trim.

Frames and sash should be treated with water-repellent wood preservative. All exposed exterior surfaces of wood windows should be protected by periodic painting and interior surfaces by appropriate finishes, except the contact surfaces of double-hung and sliding windows which should be protected by oiling.

Thickness of Sash. The actual thickness of sash most often used is $1\frac{3}{8}$ in., but $1\frac{3}{4}$-in. material is used for the better class of construction and $2\frac{1}{4}$-in. for the best large windows. Small basement sash may be $1\frac{1}{8}$ in. thick. Screens are normally $\frac{3}{4}$ or $1\frac{1}{8}$ in. thick and storm sash $1\frac{1}{8}$ in. thick.

90. METAL WINDOWS

Metals used for window construction are aluminum, steel, bronze, and stainless steel arranged in order of the quantity used. Steel windows were introduced in the United States early in the twentieth century. The use of aluminum windows on a commercial scale started about 1930.

Steel Windows. Steel windows are constructed of hot-rolled solid sections and of cold-roll-formed strip steel. The solid sections are used for nearly all industrial types of window and for the casement and projected types for nonindustrial buildings. Cold-formed strip steel is used principally for double-hung windows in nonindustrial buildings. It has not proved to be economically feasible to shape steel for window construction by extrusion through dies. Almost any form, type, or size of steel window can be manufactured if the cost can be disregarded. Because of the high cost of the equipment used for forming solid sections or cold-formed sections and for assembling the shapes into windows, the shapes of sections and types and sizes of windows have been standardized to a considerable extent,

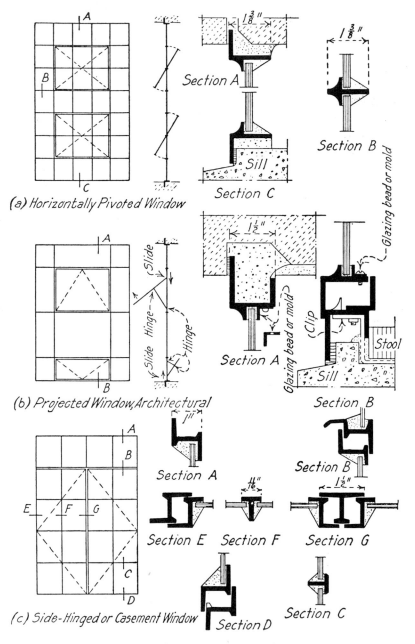

(a) Horizontally Pivoted Window

Section A

Section B

Section C

Sill

$1\frac{3}{8}$"

Glazing bead or mold

(b) Projected Window, Architectural

Slide

Slide Hinge

Hinge

Hinge

Section A

Section B

Glazing bead or mold

Glazing bead or mold

Clip

Stool

Sill

$1\frac{1}{2}$"

(c) Side-Hinged or Casement Window

Section A

Section B

Section E

Section F

Section G

Section C

Section D

1"

$\frac{4}{16}$"

$1\frac{1}{2}$"

Fig. 90-1. Solid-section steel windows.

but substantial savings could be made by further standardization (1). All the types of window illustrated in Fig. 88-1 are available.

Solid hot-rolled section steel windows are classified according to the kinds of building for which they are best suited: *Architectural* for buildings in which appearance and quality are of major importance, such as residences, apartments, hotels, office buildings, school buildings, and hospitals; and *commercial* and *industrial* for which a plain substantial design is suitable, such as stores, factories, warehouses, storage buildings, and power houses.

Cross sections of some of the members of three types of steel windows are shown in Fig. 90-1. All the members of these windows are made of hot-rolled sections.

Windows made of hot-rolled sections are usually protected against corrosion by a special factory treatment of the surface, called *bonderizing,* to improve the adhesion of paint, and then by painting periodically as required. Windows made of hot-rolled steel sections are sometimes galvanized by hot-dipping the completed window, but this practice is not common.

Aluminum Windows. All types of aluminum windows are made from sections or shapes made by extruding an aluminum alloy through dies which produce cross sections of the desired size and shape. The thickness of the metal used for windows in residences and low-cost housing projects varies from about $\frac{1}{16}$ to $\frac{1}{8}$ in., and for those in industrial, commercial, and monumental buildings such as stores, factories, schools, and office buildings the thickness varies from about $\frac{1}{16}$ to $\frac{3}{16}$ in. All the window types illustrated in Fig. 88-1 are available. The most widely used type is probably the projected window.

The cross sections of the members of aluminum windows are similar to those of corresponding solid-section steel windows shown in Fig. 90-1.

Aluminum windows will not corrode, except under extreme conditions, and thus do not require painting. The usual types of finish are the mill or natural finish; the satin finish produced by etching, belt polishing, or rubbing with abrasives; the bright finish produced by buffing; and the anodized finish, which is an electrolytic finish that provides a much thicker and more protective oxide coating than the one that forms naturally. The anodized finish or coating can be given any one of the three finishes first mentioned. Aluminum windows should always be coated with a special temporary clear lacquer applied by the manufacturer to protect against the action of mortar and plaster during construction (1).

Any possible galvanic action between aluminum and other metals, as explained in Art. 75, should be avoided. This possibility should be considered in the selection of hardware and weatherstripping. The preferable nonaluminum metals for use with aluminum are nonmagnetic stainless steel, heavily galvanized steel, and zinc. Copper and nickel alloys should be avoided. Since moisture must be present for galvanic action to occur, watertightness and drainage are important precautions against galvanic action, as are protective coatings, suitable gaskets, and seam compounds. The drainage of salts from non-aluminum metals over aluminum windows should also be avoided. Window details which require one aluminum surface to slide over another such surface should not be used because of the excessive wear which may occur (1).

Bronze and Stainless Steel. Bronze and stainless steel are attractive materials which do not corrode and are highly weather-resistant. The shapes used in constructing bronze windows are extruded in the same manner as those for aluminum windows. For this reason any of the window types available in aluminum can also be constructed of bronze.

Stainless-steel windows are made from cold-roll-formed strip metal following details similar to those used for double-hung steel windows. The vertical pivoted type is also manufactured using similar details.

Windows constructed of these materials are expensive and therefore are used only on the highest type of buildings. Because of the small demand they are custom-made.

91. GLASS AND GLAZING

Composition of Glass. Glass is composed of about six parts white sand, one part lime, and one part soda, with small amounts of alumina and other materials.

Classification. Glass for glazing purposes is classified as follows by Specification 123 of the Federal Specification Board.

Polished plate glass..... $\begin{cases} \text{Second silvering quality} \\ \text{Glazing quality} \end{cases}$

Clear window glass...... $\begin{cases} \text{Single-strength.........} \begin{cases} \text{A quality} \\ \text{B quality} \end{cases} \\ \text{Double-strength........} \begin{cases} \text{A quality} \\ \text{B quality} \end{cases} \\ \text{Heavy sheet...........} \begin{cases} \text{Glazing quality} \\ \text{Factory-run quality} \end{cases} \end{cases}$

Processed glass.........
- Chipped..............
  - No. 1 processed
  - No. 2 processed
- Ground..............
  - Acid-ground
  - Sand-blasted

Rolled figured sheet.....
- Figured sheet.......... Large variety of patterns
- Colored figured sheet

Wire glass ....
- Polished wire
- Polished (one side)
- Figured
- Corrugated
- Colored

Ornamental........... Figured plate (polished one side)

Prism glass...........
- Pressed tile
- Rolled sheet
- Rolled and pressed sheet

Definitions and Manufacture. The definitions and brief statements of the methods of manufacture of the various kinds of glass, as given by Specification 123 of the Federal Specification Board, are as follows.

Plate glass. Transparent, flat, relatively thin glass having plane polished surfaces and showing no distortion of vision when viewing objects through it at any angle. Plate glass is made at present by casting and rolling large sheets periodically or by rolling a continuous sheet. The sheets are then ground and polished.

Clear window glass. Transparent, relatively thin, flat glass having glossy, fire finished, apparently plane and smooth surfaces, but having a characteristic waviness of surface which is visible when viewed at an acute angle or in reflected light. Clear window glass is made at present by hand blowing or by machine blowing and drawing into cylinders and flattening, or by drawing directly into a sheet, the surface finish being that obtained during the drawing process.

Processed glass. There are three kinds of processed glass either in plate or window glass, viz., ground glass, chipped one process, and chipped two processes. The ground glass is made by either sandblasting or acid etching one surface. The chipped glass is made by applying either one or two coatings of glue to the ground surface. The glue is applied hot and in cooling and drying shrinks and pulls small chips off of the surface of the glass.

Rolled figured glass. A flat glass in which the vision is more or less obscured either by the roughened surface produced in rolling or by the impression of a large variety of decorative designs in one surface of the sheet.

Wire glass. Rolled flat glass having a layer of meshed wire incorporated approximately in the center of the sheet. This glass is produced with polished or figured surfaces.

Ornamental plate. A figured plate glass made by rolling or rolling and pressing and having the plane surface ground and polished.

Prism glass. A flat glass having prism-shaped parallel ribs designed for deflecting light. This is made as a rolled plate or as a pressed plate, of which one side may be ground and polished, or as a pressed tile.

Thicknesses and Grades. The most common thickness of polished plate glass is $\frac{1}{4}$ to $\frac{5}{16}$ in., but $\frac{1}{8}$-in. and $\frac{3}{16}$-in. glass is fairly common. Other thicknesses up to $1\frac{1}{4}$ in. are obtainable by special order. *Second silvering quality* is used where the highest quality is desired, but most of the glass used is known as *glazing quality*.

The most common thicknesses of clear window glass are *single strength*, varying in thickness from $\frac{1}{12}$ to $\frac{1}{10}$ in., and *double strength*, varying in thickness from $\frac{1}{9}$ to $\frac{1}{8}$ in. Other thicknesses up to $\frac{1}{5}$ in. are obtainable. All clear window glass should be relatively flat, but a slight regular curvature is not objectionable if it does not exceed 0.5 per cent of the length of the sheet. Glass with a reverse curve or which is crooked should be rejected. A small amount of AA quality window glass is sometimes selected for special purposes and may be obtained at a high price. The grade most often used in windows where appearance is an important factor is A quality, but B quality is used quite extensively. Two grades inferior to B quality are on the market. They are Fourth quality and C quality. Fourth-quality glass contains many defects and distorts the objects viewed through it. It should never be used where vision is important. C quality is too poor for use in buildings.

Rolled figured sheet glass is made in thicknesses from $\frac{1}{8}$ to $\frac{3}{8}$ in. It is made in a great variety of surface finishes which obscure the vision, diffuse the light, and give decorative effects.

Wire glass is made in thicknesses from $\frac{1}{8}$ to $\frac{3}{4}$ in., the standard thickness being $\frac{1}{4}$ in. Only one quality is manufactured for glazing purposes. It is made with polished surfaces and with a great variety of surface finishes which obscure the vision, diffuse the light, and give decorative effects. The wire is in the form of a wire mesh, the standard size of mesh being $1\frac{1}{4}$ by $\frac{7}{8}$ in. and the weight of wire No. 24 B & S gauge.

The wire is placed in the glass by any of three methods: (1) by rolling a sheet of glass, placing the mesh on it while the glass is still plastic, pressing the mesh into the glass, and finishing the surface; (2) by rolling a thin sheet of glass, placing the mesh, and rolling another sheet of glass on the first sheet; (3) by placing the wire on the casting table and holding it in position while the glass is poured around it. Polished wire glass is not of the same quality as polished plate glass.

Safety and Bulletproof Glass. Laminated glass, built up of layers of glass between which are cemented layers of a colorless transparent plastic resembling celluloid, is called *shatterproof* or *safety glass*. The chief use of glass of this type is in automobiles, but it is also used for skylights and in the windows of asylums. *Bulletproof glass* or *bullet-resisting glass* is a thick safety glass used in banks. Ordinary safety glass is ⅛ to ¼ in. thick, but bulletproof glass has several laminations built up to thicknesses of ½ to 2 in. The thickness most commonly used is 1⅛ in. This glass will not be penetrated by bullets from most firearms, although 2-in. glass is recommended to resist shots from a 30-30 rifle. These types of glass will crack under impact, but the plastic layers hold the various pieces of glass together so that it does not shatter.

Tempered Plate Glass produced as described in Art. 96 for glass doors is also used for windows. It is available in thicknesses from ¼ to 1¼ in.

Glass with Special Composition. *Heat absorbing* or *actinic glass* is a kind of glass which, because of its special composition, excludes a high percentage of the ultraviolet rays to which it is exposed, transmits less solar heat into a building than other kinds of glass, and has less bleaching effect on colored fabrics.

Quartz glass transmits a larger percentage of ultraviolet rays than ordinary window glass. Since these rays are beneficial to the health, this kind of glass may be used where this quality is desired.

Double-Glazing. Windows are often glazed with factory-produced panes consisting of two parallel sheets of glass separated by a thin dehydrated air space maintained by a tight seal between the sheets and located around their edges. Because of the seal and the dehydrated air, there is no condensation or accumulation of dirt within the air space. The heat loss through the window is substantially reduced during the winter, and the heat gain during the summer is correspondingly reduced, especially if the outer sheet is heat-absorbing glass. Various other combinations, which may include tempered plate, are used. Double glazing also reduces sound transmission. This type of installation is called *insulating glass* and is also known by the trade name of *thermopane*.

Selection of Glass. Polished plate glass is used for exposed windows in the better grades of buildings. It is much superior to window glass in appearance and in the clearness of vision through it, but is much more expensive. Large windows such as show windows are always made of polished plate glass.

Clear window glass is extensively used in all classes of buildings.

Chipped and ground glass are used to a limited extent where light is to be admitted but vision is to be obscured. Chipped glass is more attractive than ground glass and is used in interior partitions. Rolled figured glass serves the same purposes as chipped and ground glass, is usually cheaper, and is available in more attractive designs.

Rolled figured glass is extensively used on the exterior and interior of buildings to obscure the vision or diffuse the light. Many attractive designs are available, and the cost is less than that for clear window glass.

Wire glass may be used in outside windows because of its resistance to fire. When heated and drenched with water it will crack but, owing to the action of the wire mesh, it will remain in position and protect the interior of a building from fires originating outside except when exposed to extremely high temperatures. Wire glass is also used in doors and in other positions where breakage is likely to occur. It will continue to give service even though badly fractured.

Prism glass is used to light areas remote from a window. Light striking the glass is deflected so that it is effective for a considerable distance away from the glass. A common use for prism glass is in the upper part of store windows where the stores are deep and windows are in the front only.

It is desirable to use some type of figured glass in basement windows below grade because such windows cannot be kept clean and dirt is conspicuous on clear glass. The diffusing effect of figured glass is also usually desirable.

The selection of glass and the shading of windows to reduce the heat transfer through them are considered in Arts. 92 and 97.

Glazing. The process of placing glass in windows is called *glazing*. Rebates or rabbets are provided in the edges of the members that support the panes of glass. They must be deep enough to receive the glass and provide the space required by the medium which holds the glass in place. This medium may be putty, glazing compounds, and wood or metal moldings called *glass beads* or *stops*. Before putty is placed, the panes of glass in wood sash are held in place by small triangular or diamond-shaped pieces of zinc called *glazier's points*, driven into the rabbet. For metal windows, glass is held in a similar manner, before the glazing compound is placed, by spring wire *glazing clips* or other devices.

Wood windows are usually glazed from the outside. Some types of

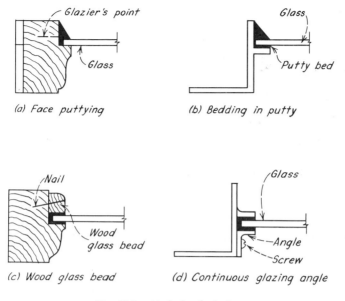

Fig. 91-1. Methods of glazing.

metal windows are glazed on the outside and others on the inside. If a pane of glass is set in position and the putty applied with a putty knife or by other means as shown in Fig. 91-1a, the operation is called *face puttying*. *Back puttying* consists of forcing putty into any spaces that may be left between the edges of the sash and the back of the glass. Before the glass is placed in position, a layer of putty may be spread on the surfaces of the sash to receive the glass, which is then placed. This operation, called *bedding* the glass in putty, is illustrated in *b*, where the final step consists of face puttying. In *c*, a pane which is bedded in putty in a wood frame is held in position by a wood *glass bead*. In *d*, a similar pane in a steel frame is held in position by a steel *glazing angle*. Such continuous metal moldings are required on industrial windows by the National Board of Fire Underwriters. The objectives of bedding are to provide a cushion for uniform support of the glass in order to avoid cracking and to make a water- and airtight seal. Other means are used for holding panes of glass in position.

The selection of glass and the shading of windows to reduce the solar heat transmitted through windows are considered in Arts. 92 and 97.

92. CURTAIN WALLS

A. Metal Curtain Walls

by W. S. Kinne, Jr., Director, University Facilities Research Center, Madison, Wisconsin

A metal curtain wall is an exterior building wall which carries no roof or floor loads; it is fastened to the structural frame and acts solely as an enclosing envelope. It usually consists of metals in combination with glass, plastics, and other surfacing materials, supported on metal unit frameworks. There are three basic types of curtain walls now in general use. *Custom* walls are designed specifically for one major project, using parts and details made specially for this purpose. *Commercial* walls are made up principally of parts, components, and details standardized by a manufacturer and assembled either in the fabricator's stock patterns or in accord with the architect's general design. *Industrial* walls are those in which ribbed, fluted, or otherwise preformed metal sheets in stock sizes are used for major surface coverage, along with standard metal windows, as the principal elements. The commercial and industrial types are sometimes referred to as *window walls.*

Custom curtain walls are most often used for high-rise buildings or multibuilding complexes—office buildings; large-scale housing and apartment developments; corporate building programs; large municipal service expansions such as airport terminals; and major new campus expansions of high school, junior college, college, and university organizations. Commercial curtain walls have had their most frequent use for local educational buildings at the primary, elementary, and secondary school levels, for commercial and industrial office accommodations, and for semispeculative buildings built primarily for rentals to others than the original owners. Industrial curtain walls have been used for large-scale, essentially low-cost wall enclosures for factory and loft types of occupancies, as well as for low-budget applications sometimes considered to be adequately serviced by the commercial curtain wall types.

In metal curtain walls, major emphasis is placed on repetitive factory parts production and prefabricated assembly of reasonably thin, large-area wall surface units, with the objective of keeping assembly and erection labor on the building site at a minimum.

The chief functions of a metal curtain wall are to *withstand* the actions of the natural environment—wind, rain, snow, hail, sleet, and sunlight; to *prevent* access by intruders, the absorption or retention of water vapor, and damage by fire; and to *control* the flow of heat and the passage of air, light, and sound. It must be aesthetically appropriate and have permanence consistent with the design life expectancy of the building enclosed by the wall. The possibility of curtain wall replacement, or substitution, within the useful life of the basic structural frame, is always present.

. The principal elements of a metal curtain wall are the supporting curtain wall frameworks, usually vertical but sometimes horizontal *mullions;* the *glazing units,* operating windows (see Art. 88) or fixed glass panels; the opaque enclosing *panels;* the *anchors* for the attachment of the curtain wall system units to the structural frame of the building; and the *joints* and *sealants* at the junctions between wall units, which compensate for movements within the curtain wall caused by external forces of nature, by movements of the building frame, and by thermal changes. *Solar screens* are often made an integral part of the curtain wall to be a means of controlling the thermal effect of sunlight both on the wall itself and on the internal building spaces enclosed by the wall.

The *mullions* are usually manufactured to a structurally stable profile made from extruded aluminum or aluminum sheet and soil stock, often protected with electrochemical anodic coatings, or they are made of rolled stainless or carbon steel or extruded bronze. Color can be applied to the mullions as part of the basic manufacturing process by the use of coatings of porcelain, baked enamel, vinyl, and other plastics or specialized anodic treatments. Vertical mullions usually extend through one or two stories of the building's height, with slip joints to provide watertight junctions while allowing linear expansion movement.

Sash frames for *glazing units* are usually attached to, or are an integral part of, the mullion system. Operating window sash are often chosen primarily for the ease of washing glass surfaces, since many buildings of the kind that use metal curtain wall have year-round air conditioning, and window ventilation is not an important factor except in between the seasons. Where fixed glass is used, exterior glass washing is often accomplished by power-driven vertical stagings suspended from the roof and restrained from side sway by movable attachments to the mullion system portions of the curtain wall.

Panels are usually composite fabrications of two or more materials into a single assembly. Two principal types are produced, classified by the method of assembly. *Mechanical panels* are held together by screws, rivets, or other mechanical fasteners, and *laminated panels* are held together with adhesives. Panels are designed to provide adequate strength, dimensional stability, thermal insulation, resistance to weather and corrosion, control of condensation, sufficient sound isolation, the necessary degrees of fire resistance, and desired appearance. Structural glass is sometimes used as a panel, backed up with an air space and a secondary panel to provide the desired physical qualities. Composite panels are covered with a wide variety of exterior facings in a wide variety of color and texture ranges. Porcelain on steel sheet or aluminum sheet, thin-set ceramic tile, thin precast concrete or terrazzo, preformed chemically treated metal sheet, and plastic-coated inorganic sheets are frequently employed. Among the more common core materials for laminated panels are treated paper expanded honeycomb, foamed closed-cell insulation units, and compressed glass fiber insulation boards. Vapor barriers on the warm side of the assembly are advisable for all conditions needing condensation control.

Several notable custom curtain wall systems have been designed with the idea of having a preformed metal panel of large size become the entire curtain wall unit assembly. Here the large single-sheet metal units have the structural capability of acting as substructural mullions, present an arrangement possible for the introduction of glazing elements within their unit area, and make possible logical jointing and sealing junctures with adjacent similar units. These units can be laminated to, or backed up with, other materials to make overall physical performance acceptable.

Anchors which provide for the support of curtain wall units at the points of contact with the building frame are usually factory-fabricated from structural steel shapes which are protectively coated by being galvanized or bonderized for corrosion resistance; these frequently employ stainless steel bolts and point-of-contact fasteners. Anchor assemblies must be designed to allow rather sizable dimensional tolerances, in the range of $\frac{1}{2}$ in. to $\frac{3}{4}$ in. plus or minus, adjustable during the field erection process in three directions: *vertical; horizontal, parallel* to the curtain wall surface; and *horizontal, perpendicular* to the wall.

Curtain wall units and assemblies are manufactured and fabricated to closely predictable sizes, but the basic building structural elements to which the wall will be attached are much less precisely dimensioned at the erection site. Thus flexibility of anchorages is very important in assuring a logical and sure junction of wall and structure.

Joints and *sealants* for metal curtain walls are perhaps more critical to the satisfactory performance of the wall than they have been to conventional stone and brick masonry exterior walls. For the metal curtain wall, materials are essentially nonabsorbing. Infiltrated water or internal condensation in an essentially metal assembly will normally collect in substantial quantities. Then it may be forced through the wall as a leak or remain entrapped, causing most undesirable effects on insulation materials and metal fittings subject to corrosion. In contrast, moisture in more absorbent masonry and its joints can be evicted by flashings and removed by slow evaporation without serious local effects.

Metal curtain walls are essentially *multimaterial* assemblies. The variety of materials used have varying coefficients of thermal expansion, as shown in Table 92-1.

Thus it may be seen that large metal curtain wall units or their components will grow and shrink in different magnitudes within ranges of temperature encountered on the exterior of a building. The *joints* between the units, and within them, are designed to provide for these movements mechanically. Then they are sealed to control air and water migrations within the wall, with the idea of repelling and expelling water to the outside while preventing inward or outward air movements which might be disturbing to control of interior air conditioning and ventilation. The *sealants* or gaskets must have qualities of long life, adequate elongation without failure, and good adhesion. They may be considered to be of two types, *liquid sealants* and *preformed gaskets,* both manufactured as synthetic plastics. The usual sealants are polysulfide polymers, known as Thiokol (a trade name). These are applied in liquid form, but at room temperature they convert to flexible synthetic rubber. The preformed gaskets are factory-made as extrusions in profiles appropriate for their use. They are most often polyvinyl chloride plastics or synthetic neoprene rubbers, chemically designed to provide desirable properties of hardness, durability, elongation, and adhesion.

Table 92-1

Dimensional Change, in Inches, Caused by 100°F. Temperature Difference for 10 Lineal Feet of Material

Aluminum	0.156	Glass	0.060
Stainless steel	0.115	Concrete	0.096
Porcelain on steel	0.084	Stone	0.048
Bronze	0.113	Reinforced plastic	0.194
Carbon steel	0.084		

Solar screens, discussed in Art. 97, should be considered an integral part of metal curtain walls or as a potential adjunct. The idea of controlling the effect of solar energy on the interior of a building has long been understood; but the metal curtain wall assembly, using materials with relatively high coefficients of heat transmission and relatively large glass areas, emphasizes the desirability of diverting or reflecting solar heat before it touches the wall surface. This solar energy can then be dissipated in the atmosphere before it enters the interior of the building envelope.

Glass normally covers a rather substantial surface area of metal curtain walls, ranging from less than 20 per cent to about 80 per cent of the total exposed surface of the wall. The general subject of glass is covered in Art. 91. It might be well to describe here the variations of heat transmission expected from the kinds of glass that are usually employed in metal curtain wall assemblies.

Heat transmission, sunlight through glass

$\frac{1}{4}$-in. plate glass—88% heat transmitted through.

$\frac{1}{4}$-in. heat-absorbing glass—66% heat transmitted through.

$\frac{1}{4}$-in. heat-absorbing glass, air space, $\frac{1}{4}$-in. plate glass—50% heat transmitted through.

These data represent the sum of reradiation and transmission. For further information see Art. 97.

There are three types of exterior solar controls now in general use: *horizontal overhangs,* canopies, or eyebrows. These may be solid or louvered and are usually fixed but sometimes movable. They are most effective for southern exposures in the Northern Hemisphere but can be quite effective on northern exposures in the tropics. Perforated *vertical screens,* or preassembled grid systems placed parallel to the wall and window system, can be effective for all orientations. They are usually fixed installations and often become a rather dominant aesthetic factor, for they are literally a screen wall outside of the curtain wall. Outside *vertical fins* or *louvers* are most effective for eastern and western exposures in the middle and high latitudes of the Northern Hemisphere, especially when the fins are movable to compensate for varying early-morning and late-afternoon sun angles through the year.

Interior solar screens, although somewhat less effective than the exterior type because the diverted solar energy is trapped within the building, are still important components of metal curtain walls with large glass areas. With their use, trapped heat can be isolated on the inside of glazed areas and diverted by air-conditioning installations designed for the purpose. Horizontal or vertical retractable venetian blinds placed in pockets or tracks built into the curtain wall system, often in conjunction with heating or cooling elements of mechanical systems, are common. One prime advantage of the interior solar screen idea is that it allows greater flexibility of use under the direct control of the individual building occupant—dictated by considerations of sun position, cloud cover, and glare implications.

B. Concrete Curtain Walls

Precast concrete curtain walls are considered in Art. 58. They are appropriate for use when windows occupy a relatively small portion of the wall area. The following discussion is concerned with such walls when appearance is an important factor. It is based on a bulletin entitled *Concrete Curtain Walls* published by the Portland Cement Association (8).

Concrete curtain walls are made up of precast reinforced concrete slabs whose size and shape can be selected to meet specific requirements. A common size of slab is 8 by 14 ft. The thicknesses range from 4 to 6 in., depending upon code requirements and upon the degree of fire-resistance and heat insulation required.

Composition. The slabs are constructed of lightweight concrete not only to reduce their weight but also to improve their heat insulation properties. They may be of the same composition throughout, or a layer about 1 in. thick, adjacent to the exposed face, may have a special composition for decorative effect.

Color. Various colors are provided for the facing layer by selecting appropriate aggregates or mixtures of aggregates and mortars. Some of the aggregates used are quartz, marble, granite, gravel, tile and ceramic, and other vitreous materials. Each of these is available in a wide range of colors. The ceramic and vitreous materials are manufactured and thus can be produced to match samples submitted by the architect. Ceramic facing tile are available in a great variety of colors and patterns. The tile are laid in cement mortar applied to the face of the concrete slab and are usually laid in regular rows which occupy up to 90 per cent of the exposed surface. They are often 1-in. square or 1-by-1½-in. rectangular tile.

The mortar or matrix in which the aggregate is embedded has a marked effect on the color. Curtain walls whose color depends primarily on the color of the matrix can be made. White portland cement is usually employed in the facing mix to insure purity of color even for the darker shades. The matrix is colored by using mineral oxide pigments. Practically all colors can be obtained in this manner.

Texture. The textures of the exposed surfaces of curtain walls are important factors in their appearance. They vary from glossy to rough or rugged textures, depending upon the kind of surfaces against which they are cast, upon the treatment the surfaces receive after removal from the forms, and upon the size and shape of the aggregates. An exposed aggregate finish is often used. It is produced by using various techniques in casting and finally brushing the surface to expose the aggregate. Exposed aggregate facings may be ground smooth to resemble terrazzo. Desired effects are sometimes secured by mechanical means such as bush-hammering, tooling, and sandblasting. Finally, the characteristics of the surface against which the facing is cast largely determines its texture unless the surface is treated after removal from forms.

Patterns. Patterns of various designs are created on the exposed faces of panels by high and low relief in adjacent areas, by differences in the aggregate colors, and by contrasting textures. In addition, any desired form can be produced on the exposed face by casting against an appropriate mold.

Panel Shapes. Panels of almost any desired shape can be manufactured. The most common shapes are rectangular and square, but diamond-shaped panels have been used.

Panels are cast with open grillwork over a part or all of their surface to serve as a solar screen on the outside of glazed areas. The same effect is achieved by building a wall of small perforated units and located just outside the wall in which the windows are located.

Erection. The procedures followed in placing panels in position and anchoring them in place correspond to those described in Art. 58.

Heat Insulation. The effectiveness of lightweight concrete aggregate curtain walls can be increased by plastering the inside surfaces with pearlite or vermiculite plaster. Sandwich panels, described in Art. 58, are also used to achieve a high degree of insulation.

Fire Resistance. Concrete curtain walls can be constructed with the thickness and quality of concrete necessary to conform to any building code requirements.

C. Other Materials

Curtain walls are also constructed of brick masonry as described in Art. 26, stone masonry as described in Art. 27, and structural clay tile, concrete block, and glass block as described in Art. 28.

D. Fire-Resistance Requirements

Curtain walls as an important feature in the architectural treatment of buildings have developed markedly in recent years. Few building codes have been modernized to recognize this development adequately. There are also major differences in those that have been modernized. As one example, the requirements of the National Building Code of the National Board of Fire Underwriters for the highest-quality *fire-resistive building* are quoted in part. The requirements for lower types of buildings are less severe. According to this code, with minor editorial changes,

Horizontal separation means a permanent open space between the building wall under consideration and the nearest line to which a building is or may be legally built. One-half of the street width shall be used in determining the distance of horizontal separation for walls facing on a street and one-half of the narrowest space between two buildings on the same lot shall be used in determining the distance of horizontal separation between walls of buildings on the same lot.

Bearing portions of exterior and interior walls shall have a fire-resistance rating of not less than 4 hours.

Nonbearing portions of exterior and interior walls shall be of approved noncombustible material.

(1) Where a horizontal separation of 3 ft. or less is provided, nonbearing portions of exterior walls shall have a fire-resistance rating of not less than 3 hours and the total area of windows in such portions of an exterior wall shall not exceed 40 per cent of the total wall area.

(2) Where a horizontal separation of more than 3 ft. but less than 20 ft. is provided, nonbearing portions of exterior walls shall have a fire-resistance rating of not less than 2 hours and the total area of windows in such portions of an exterior wall shall not exceed 40 per cent of the total wall area.

(3) Where a horizontal separation of 20 ft. to 30 ft. is provided, nonbearing portions of exterior walls shall have a fire-resistance rating of not less than one hour and the total area of windows in such portions of an exterior wall shall not exceed 60 per cent of the total wall area.

(4) Where a horizontal separation of 30 ft. or more is provided, no fire-resistance rating is required for the nonbearing portions of exterior walls.

(5) Where there are two or more buildings on the same lot and the total area of the buildings does not exceed one-and-a-half times the allowable area of any one of the buildings, no fire-resistance rating is required for the nonbearing portions of exterior walls of buildings that face each other.

(6) Openings in exterior walls shall be protected, and vertical separation between openings in exterior walls shall be provided in accordance with the requirements given below.

Except as listed below every opening in an exterior wall of a building shall be protected by an approved fire window, fire door or other approved protective when such opening: Faces on a street and is less than 30 ft. from the opposite building line; less than 30 ft. distant in a direct unobstructed line from an opening in another building or from a wood frame building; is above and less than 30 ft. from any part of a neighboring roof of combustible materials or any roof having openings within this distance; faces on and is located less than 15 ft. from an adjacent lot line.

Except as listed below the exterior openings located vertically above one another shall have not less than 3 ft. vertical separation provided by an assembly of noncombustible material having a fire-resistance rating of not less than 2 hours between the top of one opening and the bottom of the one next above, or the exterior openings shall be separated by such an assembly extending outwardly from the building wall a horizontal distance of not less than 3 ft. No vertical separation is required between exterior openings under certain specified conditions.

References

1. James Arkin, "Wood Windows," William Guillett, "Steel Windows," and John P. Jansson, "Aluminum Windows," *Windows and Glass in the Exterior of Buildings,* Publication 478, Building Research Institute, National Research Council, 1957.
2. *Selecting Windows,* Circular Series Index Number F11.1, Small Homes Council, University of Illinois.
3. *Sweet's Catalog Architectural File,* F. W. Dodge Corporation, issued annually.
4. *Curtain Walls of Stainless Steel,* 1955, *Data on Stainless Steel Curtain Walls,* 1957, *Joints in Metal Curtain Walls,* 1957, *Thermal Behavior of Curtain Walls,* 1957, American Iron and Steel Institute, Princeton University School of Architecture (pamphlets).
5. *Metal Curtain Walls,* Publication 378, 1955, *Sealants for Curtain Walls,* Publication 715, 1959, Building Research Institute, National Research Council (pamphlets).
6. William Dudley Hunt, Sr., *The Contemporary Curtain Wall,* F. W. Dodge Corporation, 1958.
7. *Metal Curtain Wall Manual,* National Association of Architectural Metal Manufacturers, 1960 (looseleaf binder).
8. *Concrete Curtain Walls,* Portland Cement Association.
9. Peter P. F. Dejongh, "The New Look in Buildings," *Civil Engineering,* August, 1958, p. 52.
10. Marianne Stern, "What You Should Know About Thin-Wall Buildings," *Engineering News-Record,* April 14, 1958, p. 38.
(See also references 8 and 9 of Chapter 15, page 676.)

15 Doors

93. DEFINITIONS AND GENERAL DISCUSSION

General Comments. A *doorway* is an opening through a building wall
or partition, provided for the passage of persons, vehicles, etc.; the
opening may be closed by a movable barrier called a *door*. A door
is held in position by a door frame, the members of which are located
at the sides and top of the opening. A doorway is often considered
to be the clear opening within the frame. Sills are provided at the
bottom of exterior doorways.

Classes of Doors. Ordinary doors, whose primary function is to permit the passage of persons, are classed as *exterior* and *interior doors.*
Doors at the principal entrances are commonly called *entrance doors.*
Light doors mounted on the outside of the frames of exterior doors,
much of whose area is covered with insect screen, are called *screen
doors.* During the winter months screen doors are often replaced with
storm doors with glass panels. Doors with interchangeable screened
and glazed panels which can serve both as screen doors and storm
doors are called *combination doors.* Doors designed to resist the
passage of fire are called *fire doors.* A *wicket door* is a small door
within a large door, provided to permit passage without opening the
large door.

In addition to the classes of doors mentioned in the preceding paragraph, there are many others, such as elevator doors, garage doors,
hangar doors, and industrial doors of various kinds, which are given
little if any consideration in this treatise. See reference 1.

Operation of Doors. Doors usually open by swinging about a vertical
axis or by sliding horizontally, but sometimes they may swing about
a horizontal axis or slide vertically. These axes are provided by means
of *hinges* or *pivots* fastened to the door and the door frame. Horizontal sliding doors are suspended from *hangers* containing wheels

which operate on tracks placed at the top of the door openings. Vertical sliding doors move between guides provided at the sides and are operated by cables or chains passing over pulleys in much the same way that double-hung windows are operated. They may be either counterweighted or counterbalanced, as will be explained later.

The most common type of door is the swinging door shown in Fig. 93-1a. When ordering hardware for doors it is necessary to specify the *hand* and *bevel* of the doors. The hand of a door is determined by the side on which it is hinged. A door is *beveled* when the outer edge of the lock stile is not at right angles to the face of the door. Doors are beveled to keep them from binding when opening and shutting. It is evident that the direction of the bevel is determined by the direction in which the door swings when opened. If a person is standing on the outside of a door and the hinges are at his left, the door is a *left-hand door*, but if they are at his right it is a *right-hand door*. If the opening door swings away from him, it requires what is called a *regular bevel*, but if it swings towards him, it requires a *reverse bevel*. In Fig. 93-1a, if the outside of the door is the side toward the lower edge of the page, the door would be designated as left-hand, reverse bevel. The corridor side of interior doors is taken as the outside, as is the room side of closet doors.

Two doors hinged at opposite sides of an opening (*b*) are referred to as *double doors*. Such doors are extensively used at the entrances of buildings and of large rooms and even in the small rooms of residences to give a more spacious effect than would be secured with single doors.

The *double-acting door* (*c*) is provided with special hinges which keep the door closed when it is not held open. The door can easily be pushed open in either direction.

The *folding* or *accordion doors* shown in Fig. 93-1d and *e* are used singly or as folding partitions so that two rooms may be used together as a single room or separately. They may be made for very wide openings. Doors are also hinged together (*e*).

The sliding doors shown in *f* and *g* were once used extensively in residences. Swinging doors or *cased openings* without doors have largely taken their place. They slide into pockets provided in the partitions and are out of sight when not in use. Sliding doors are used in many other locations.

Doors sliding on one side of a wall or partition (*h* and *i*) are extensively used for fire doors which nominally stand open but which are released by a *fusible link* in case of fire. They may be made self-

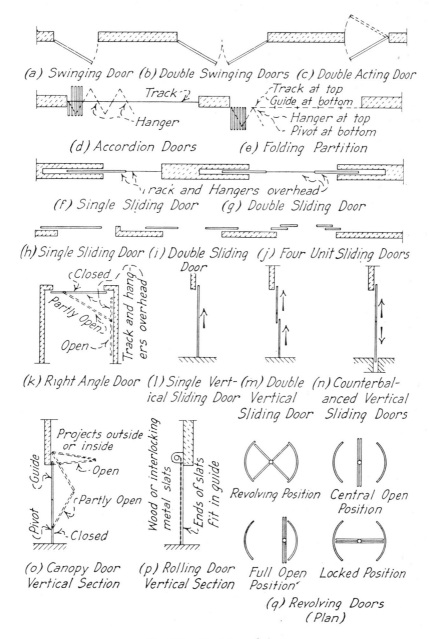

(a) Swinging Door (b) Double Swinging Doors (c) Double Acting Door

(d) Accordion Doors (e) Folding Partition

Track at top
Guide at bottom
Hanger
Hanger at top
Pivot at bottom

(f) Single Sliding Door (g) Double Sliding Door

Track and Hangers overhead

(h) Single Sliding Door (i) Double Sliding (j) Four Unit Sliding Doors
Door

(Closed
Partly Open
Open
Track and hangers overhead

(k) Right Angle Door (l) Single Vert- (m) Double (n) Counterbal-
ical Sliding Door Vertical anced Vertical
Sliding Door Sliding Doors

Projects outside
or inside
Guide
Open
Pivot
Partly Open
Closed

Wood or interlocking
metal slats
Ends of slats
fit in guide

Revolving Position Central Open
Position

Full Open Locked Position
Position

(o) Canopy Door (p) Rolling Door
Vertical Section Vertical Section

(q) Revolving Doors
(Plan)

Fig. 93-1. Operation of doors.

closing by sloping the tracks from which they are suspended or by properly arranging weights and pulleys.

Sliding doors (i and j) are often used for elevator doors. They are so arranged that they will all open when one is pulled back. The inner doors in j are arranged to move faster than the other two so that they will all be completely open at the same time. Two doors opening to the same side are more extensively used than the four-door unit shown.

The right-angle door (k) is used to a limited extent on garages. The doors are suspended from an overhead track.

The vertical sliding doors in l and m are counterweighted and may be operated electrically. They are pulled up by cables or chains which are placed at each side of the opening and which operate over pulleys in the same manner as for double-hung window sash. Such doors are used for large openings in industrial buildings, particularly for freight elevator doors.

Where conditions permit their use, the counterbalanced vertical sliding doors shown in n are convenient. They are used for freight elevator doors and can be easily operated by hand. When one moves up, the other moves down an equal distance.

The canopy door shown in o is used for large openings in industrial buildings. The door is counterweighted and may be electrically operated. If desired, it may open outward to form a canopy over the opening.

The rolling door shown in p operates in the same manner as a window shade. The roller on which the door rolls is operated by hand or electrically or by a spring which counterbalances the weight of the door. The door is made flexible by using wood slats or interlocking slats of sheet metal. The ends of the slats are held behind guides at the sides of the doors. Wood rolling doors are used to form movable partitions in the same manner as accordion doors and folding partitions shown in d and e. Steel rolling doors are used extensively for large exterior doors of industrial buildings and for fire shutters which will close automatically in case of fire.

The revolving door shown in q is used extensively at the entrances of public buildings, banks, stores, etc. It does not permit much cold air to come in from outside when it is in use. During mild or warm weather when it is not in use the revolving part may be moved out of the way as shown. The door may be locked when desired.

Two forms of garage doors which move vertically to open are illustrated in Fig. 93-2. The door in a consists of four leaves which are

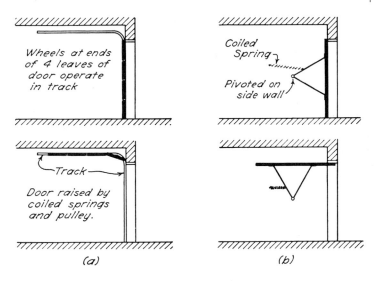

Fig. 93-2. Vertical-opening garage doors.

hinged together as shown. Wheels in the sides of the doors move in guides so that the door takes the position shown in the figure when it is open. A coiled spring balances the weight of the door so that it is easily operated. It may be operated electrically and is often called an *overhead door*. The door shown in *b* consists of a single leaf, which is pivoted on each side as shown. It is opened by lifting vertically and rotating around the pivots. A spring is arranged to assist in opening the door and to hold the door open. This door requires a wall or other support close to each side of the opening to which the pivots can be attached.

Door Materials. Wood, aluminum, carbon steel, and glass are the materials most extensively used in the manufacture of doors, but stainless steel, bronze, and copper are also used, as are auxiliary materials such as hardboard, fiberboard, asbestos, and plastics.

Door Sizes. The sizes of ordinary stock doors whose primary function is to permit the passage of persons vary with the types and the materials used in their construction.

The common widths of single wood doors are 2 ft. 6 in., 2 ft. 8 in., and 3 ft. for interior doors, and 2 ft. 8 in., 3 ft., and 3 ft. 4 in. for exterior doors. Heights are 6 ft. 6 in., 6 ft. 8 in., and 7 ft. for interior doors and 6 ft. 8 in. and **7** ft. for exterior doors. Thicknesses $1\frac{3}{8}$ in. and $1\frac{3}{4}$ in. for interior and exterior doors, but doors 3 ft. 4 in. wide are available only with a minimum thickness of $1\frac{3}{4}$ in. Exterior doors with a thickness of $2\frac{1}{4}$ in. are not unusual, and such doors with heights of 7 ft. 6 in. and 8 ft. are sometimes used.

When double doors are used (Fig. 93-1b), each door may be somewhat narrower than a single door. Storm doors, screen doors, and combination doors are usually $1\frac{1}{8}$ in. thick. For complete information on stock sizes of ponderosa pine doors see reference 2, and for hardwood veneered doors see reference 3.

The stock sizes of metal doors are more limited than those for wood doors but correspond quite closely with the sizes mentioned. For complete information on the sizes of such doors see reference 1.

Panel and Flush Doors. The most common type of door is the *panel* or *framed door*, usually consisting of vertical and horizontal members which frame rectangular areas in which opaque panels or panes of glass or louvers are located. Such doors with glass panels are called *sash doors*.

Another common type of door is the flush door, which usually consists of flat, relatively thin, face panels the full height and width of the door; the door is rigidly bonded or otherwise attached to a solid or hollow core with finished edges. Openings may be provided in flush doors for the insertion of glass for vision or light or of louvers for ventilation. Doors with panels that are of approximately the same thickness as the stiles and rails are called *flush panel doors*.

Panel and flush doors of various materials correspond in appearance with the wood doors illustrated in Fig. 94-1. A great variety of other types with standard sizes are manufactured and carried in stock as *stock doors*. Other sizes and types are manufactured on order, following special designs prepared by the architect.

For complete information on the various types of stock wood doors see references 1, 2, and 3, and for metal doors see reference 1.

Parts of Panel Doors. The parts of panel doors, regardless of the material of which they are constructed, have the same designations as those of wood doors illustrated in Fig. 94-1. These parts may be defined as follows.

stiles. Vertical members at each side of the door which extend its full height. For doors swinging about a vertical axis located on one edge, the stile to which the hinges or pivots are attached is called the *hinge* or *hanging stile*. The stile to which the lock, latch, push, or pull is attached is called the *closing* or *lock stile*.

rails. Horizontal members extending the full width between stiles and framing into them. The rails at the top and bottom of the door are called the *top rail* and the *bottom rail.* Rails located between these two rails are called *intermediate* or *crossrails.* The crossrail at lock height is called the *lock rail.*

mullions. Relatively heavy vertical members which subdivide the areas between stiles and rails. *Muntins* are light vertical or horizontal members corresponding in position to mullions and crossrails.

panels. Members which fill the areas between, and which are surrounded by, the stiles, rails, mullions, and muntins. Wood panels may be *flat panels* of plywood or *raised panels* with a border thinner than the remainder of the panel. One or more panels of a door may be replaced by glass to form a *sash door* for vision, light, or achitectural effect or by louvers for ventilation.

Parts of Flush Doors. Flush doors vary widely in their construction, but all types include *face panels* which form the faces; a *core* which is the construction between the face panels to which they are attached, which gives them support, and which may be solid or hollow; and *edge strips* which surround the rim of the core to provide finished edges to match the material in the face panels. Hollow cores may include vertical or horizontal *ribs*, rectangular *grids*, or small *cells.* Some cores include *stiles* and *rails.* Cores may include special provisions for attachment of locks and other hardware. Openings may be provided through flush doors for the insertion of panes of glass for light or vision or of louvers for ventilation.

Parts of Door Frames. The sides and top of a doorway are provided with a *door frame* which holds the door in position. Door frames may be set in masonry walls at the time the walls are constructed, and if so they are anchored to the walls by metal anchors fastened to the frames and built into the walls. Wood blocks may be built into masonry walls to form an anchorage for frames which are set after the walls are built. Openings to receive door frames are provided in walls and partitions with wood studs by doubling the members forming the jambs and the head. Masonry partitions are provided with *door bucks,* which are rough frames (Fig. 94-2) set at the time the partitions are built and anchored to the masonry by metal anchors. These bucks are constructed of wood for wood frames and doors and of steel channels or pressed steel for hollow metal doors. The openings provided are larger than the outside dimension of the frames to permit the frames to be plumbed.

An exterior doorway may also be provided with a *sill* located across the bottom of the opening. A *threshold* is a relatively thin member with beveled top edges located below the bottom of an exterior door and on top of the sill. It raises the bottom of a swinging door to provide clearance so that it will swing free above the floor or floor covering but will be reasonably weathertight when closed. Hardwood thresholds (Fig. 90-2) are used with wood doors and metal thresholds with wood and metal doors. They may be used with all types of exterior doors. Thresholds are sometimes used with interior doors, especially when the flooring materials on the two sides of a door are different.

The side members of a door frame are called the *jambs,* and the top member the *head. Door stops* are projections or strips on the faces of the jambs and head against which one-way swinging doors close (Fig. 94-2). The term is also applied to projections or strips between which doors slide and to others in similar locations.

The term *frame* is also applied to the portion of a door consisting of stiles and rails framed together.

An *astragal* is a member which may be attached to the closing stile of one of a pair of swinging doors and against which the closing stile of the other door closes. Its function is to cover the crack between the doors (Fig. 94-2). An astragal may also be used to close the crack between a pair of sliding doors.

A small sash, called a *transom,* which may be fixed or operated for ventilation, may be located above a door and included in the same frame. A horizontal bar, called a *transom bar,* is used to separate the door and the transom. Formerly transoms were very common, but now they are rarely used. A *vision panel* is a small glazed panel at eye level to enable a person approaching a door to see a person approaching the door from the opposite side or for other reasons.

The members ordinarily used to provide a finish around door openings are called the *trim.* Trim consists primarily of vertical side members called *casings* and a horizontal top member called a *head casing* which, as used for a wood door in a wood stud partition, are illustrated in Fig. 94-2. Metal frames and casings are often included in a single unit (Fig. 95-1c). A metal covered frame is illustrated in Fig. 95-1e.

Door Hardware. Detailed discussions of building hardware are not included in this book. It seems desirable, however, to mention some of the various items of hardware required for the operation of swinging doors. Swinging is provided for by two or three hinges or pivots mounted on the hanging stile. Door hinges attached to the door edges are commonly called *butt hinges* or *butts,* because the edges of doors are sometimes called *butts.* Butt hinges are usually listed in pairs, three butts being listed as $1\frac{1}{2}$ pair.

Push plates or *door pulls* are provided on the closing stile as required. *Push bars* extending across the entire width of the door are provided on doors with large glass panels to protect the panels from breakage. Metal *kick plates* are sometimes provided on the bottom rail to prevent scuffing when the door is pushed open or shut with the foot.

Door closers, which close a door automatically after it has been opened, are mounted near the top of a door and frame and on the hinge side or are recessed in the floor or head and attached to the door. They also check doors against slamming and thus are often called *door checks.* They may be arranged to hold doors in an open position when desired, serving as *door holders,* although separate devices called door holders are available for this purpose.

Fastening Devices. Various types of devices are attached to the lock stile of doors to fasten them in the closed position when the devices are activated. Several arrangements are made for operating these devices. If they automatically fasten the door when it moves into the closed position, they are called *latches.* Various mechanisms, such as *knobs, levers, thumb turns,* and *thumb presses,* are provided to release latches so that the door can be opened. A *bolt* is a sliding bar which functions in a manner similar to a latch but does not fasten the door automatically when it is closed. A *lock* is a latch which can be set, when desired, to require a key to open from the outside; or a *bolt,* operated by a key, which is often called a *dead lock.* A separate latch and dead lock are often included in a single unit, called a lock. Bolts are usually placed at approximately lock height, but they may be placed to operate vertically at the top or bottom of the door and are then called *top* or *bottom bolts.* A *panic bolt* is a latch and cross bar mounted at lock height on the inside of an outswinging door so that the door can be opened by pressure on the bar.

The distinctions in this paragraph between a *latch,* which fastens the door shut automatically; a *bolt,* which must be thrown to fasten or unfasten the door; and a *lock,* which requires that a key be used in at least one phase of its operation, are not always made.

Preparation to receive hardware is usually done on the job for wood and at the factory for metal and metal-covered doors, glass doors and their frames.

Code Requirements. Building codes include requirements that doors must provide for the safety of the occupants and restrict the spread of fires. Among these are included requirements relating to the type, number, width, location, direction of swing, and fastening of exit doors, and to the fire-resistance ratings and operation of fire doors.

The following extracts from two codes are included for illustrative purposes, but many other factors are considered in codes. When considering a specific project, the governing code should be consulted. Buildings to which these extracts apply are those constructed primarily for human occupancy.

The total width of exit doorways or openings shall not be less than required to provide for the total number of persons served by such exit doorways or openings in accordance with code requirements. (4)

The minimum clear width of a door opening serving a required exit way or leading to a required exit way shall not be less than 28 in. (5)

No single swing door in a doorway of an exit way shall be more than 44 in. or less than 28 in. in width except that each leaf of a pair of doors shall not be less than 24 in. in width and doors in supplementary exits from assembly space shall not be more than 60 in. in width. (4)

No doorway shall be less than 6 ft. 8 in. in height. (4)

Vertical sliding doors and rolling shutters shall not be used in a required exit doorway or doorway leading to a required exit way. (5)

Revolving doors shall not be used in *required* exit ways from portions of buildings used as places of assembly or for educational or institutional occupancy. (5)

Doors in required exits shall swing outward in the direction of exit travel, except that doors from individual rooms may swing inward provided that such rooms are not occupied by more than 50 persons, do not contain high hazard occupancy, are not more than 1000 sq. ft. in area, and wherein the distance to a door does not exceed 50 ft. (4) [This requirement does not apply to space which is under constant supervision, such as that in educational buildings, where doors may swing inward except in assembly space for more than 99 persons.]

All doors in a required exit way or leading to a required exit way from rooms occupied by 45 or more persons and all doors in a required exit way from places of assembly shall be hung to swing open in the direction of exit travel. (5)

Exit doors shall be readily openable from any floor area or occupied space, shall be arranged so that they cannot be locked against exit from such area or space. . . . (4)

Exit doorways opening directly to the exterior from places of assembly with a capacity of 500 occupants and exterior exit doorways of school buildings housing in excess of 100 students, shall be equipped with approved panic release devices. Such devices shall operate when pressure of not more than 15 pounds is applied to the releasing device in the direction of exit travel. (5)

Codes include provisions for the degree of fire resistance required for doors in fire walls, stair towers, corridors, and exterior doors. Fire doors are designed for the protection of openings in walls and partitions against fire when they are installed as required. The rating of 3, $1\frac{1}{2}$, 1, or $\frac{3}{4}$ hours indicates the duration of exposure to fire. The letters A, B, C, D, and E following the hourly rating designate the location for which the door is designed. Fire doors produced under the factory inspection and label service program of the Underwriters Laboratories are identified by labels which give the hourly rating, location, and the testing temperatures for which the doors are designed. Doors labeled in this manner are called *labeled doors* (8, 9).

94. WOOD DOORS

Material. The most common wood used for door construction is ponderosa pine, a species of yellow pine. A considerable portion of the wood resembles white pine in appearance and texture (6) and is usually accepted when specifications call for white pine unless true white pine is specifically called for. It is used for constructing panel doors, as the base to which veneers are applied, and sometimes for the construction of cores for flush doors. Among the other woods used for constructing panel doors are Douglas fir, western red cedar, and sitka spruce.

Veneers of various decorative woods are used for facing panel and flush doors. These include ponderosa and white pine, red and white oak, walnut, hard maple, gum, red and white birch, and African and Philippine mahogany. These face veneers are bonded directly to the solid cores of the stiles and rails of panel doors. They are also used for exposed outer plies called *face veneers,* for plywood used for the panels of panel doors, and for the face panels of flush doors. For a description of plywood see Art. 70. The required width of face veneers is obtained by assembling separate strips matched for grain and color. The selection of the species of wood for face veneers is based on the appearance and suitability to receive the surface coating to be applied. The cross bands of plywood used for face panels of flush doors are usually hardwood.

The face veneers of flush doors are often made of thermosetting laminated plastics. Such veneers are available in a great variety of colors, are not painted or surface treated in any way, and are durable and easily cleaned. Patterns can be obtained if desired. The veneer thickness is usually $\frac{1}{16}$ in. Edge strips which match the face veneer are used.

Manufacture of Veneer. Veneers are thin sheets of wood. They are made by three processes: the sawing process, the slicing process, and the rotary-cut process. In the *sawing process* the thin sheets of wood are cut from large blocks of wood by a circular saw. This process is wasteful because of the wood consumed in the saw-kerf, but it produces the best grade of veneer because it injures the wood less than the other processes. In the *slicing process* the thin sheets are sliced off of the large blocks with a cutting knife. The wood is softened by steaming to make cutting without splitting possible. In the *rotary-cut process* a log which has been softened by steaming or boiling is placed in a lathe and revolved against a wide stationary blade which gradually moves toward the center of the log and cuts off a continuous slice. The entire log cannot be cut up in this manner; a core which must be discarded, as far as this use is concerned, remains.

Before the exposed surface is finished by sanding, sawed veneers are from $\frac{1}{8}$ to $\frac{1}{4}$ in. thick. They are more natural in appearance and more durable than the veneers produced by the slicing and rotary-cut processes. Rotary-cut veneers are from $\frac{1}{28}$ to $\frac{1}{16}$ in. thick and sliced veneer $\frac{1}{20}$ in. and less thick. See Art. 70.

Panel Doors. Many designs and layouts are used for wood panel doors, some of which are illustrated in Fig. 94-1. The *French door* shown in this figure is also called a *casement door*. The various parts of a panel door are defined in Art. 90 and illustrated in Fig. 94-2. The ends of the rails are usually fastened to the edges of the stiles, against which they abut by wood dowels held in position by water-resistant glue and assembled under pressure, but glued blind mortise and tenon joints, which do not show at the exposed edges, may be used. Panels are fastened to the stiles and rails in grooves provided in these members (Fig. 94-1), or a separate continuous mold, called *sticking,* may be used which is usually on one side only.

The panels of doors with solid stiles and rails may be solid raised panels not less than $\frac{7}{16}$ in. thick or flat plywood with a minimum thickness of $\frac{1}{4}$ in. The panels of veneered doors are usually flat plywood at least $\frac{1}{4}$ in. thick, but they may be raised.

The stiles and rails of veneered doors have cores built up of low-density wood blocks not more than $2\frac{1}{2}$ in. wide (Fig. 94-1b) and of varying lengths with end joints in adjacent rows staggered. These core blocks are bonded with water-resistant adhesive. Side edge strips of the same species of wood as the veneer are provided. Top and bottom edge strips may be of any suitable species of wood. The face veneers of stiles and rails should be not less than $\frac{1}{8}$ in. thick before sanding.

The panes of glass in sash doors are held in position by *glass beads* of the same species of wood as a solid door or as the veneer of a veneered door. The panes of outside doors are bedded in putty for watertightness.

Ledged and Braced   Flush   One Panel   Two Panels   Four Panels

Five Panels   Six Panels   Louvered   French   Dutch

(a) Types of Doors

Solid Door with Raised Panels   Solid Door with Raised Panels, Flush Molding   French Door Glass set with Stops

Glass Bead

Raised Panel   Flat Panel

Veneered Doors

(b) Types of Door Construction

Fig. 94-1. Types and construction of wood doors.

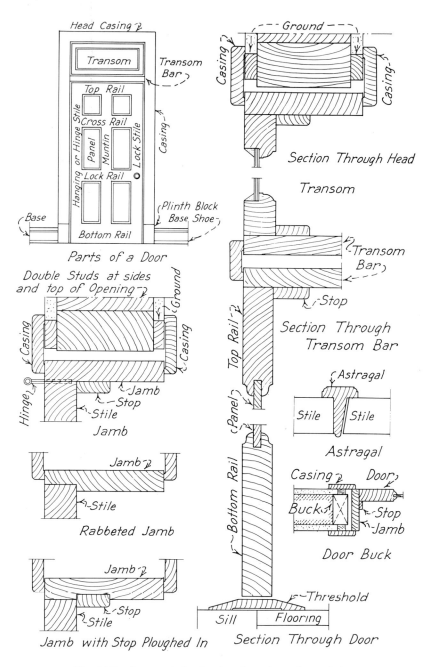

Fig. 94-2. Parts and details of a framed wood panel door.

Flush Doors. Various types of flush doors are illustrated in Fig. 94-3. Any of these may have openings to provide for panes of glass or louvers. The parts of flush doors are defined in Art. 93. Stile and rail frames with or without intermediate rails are used for many kinds. The rails are connected to the stiles by glued dowels.

There are two general types of flush doors, the solid-core door and the hollow-core door (Fig. 94-3). The cores of both types are usually made entirely of ponderosa pine or other low-density kiln-dried wood, but other materials are used especially in special-purpose doors.

The face panels are usually constructed of plywood, and each may have 1, 2, or 3 plies. The face panels should include at least 1 ply

(a) 5-ply
Glued-up Core

(b) 3-ply
Glued-up Core

(c) 5-ply
Floating Core

(d) 5-ply
Mineral Core

Wood solid core flush doors

(e) 7-ply
Horizontal and vertical ladder cores

(f) 5-ply

(g) 7-ply
Grid Core

(h) 7-ply
Ring Core

Wood hollow core flush doors

Fig. 94-3. Wood flush doors.

whose grain runs in the direction normal to the predominant direction of the grain of the units that make up the core. The face panels are bonded to the core under pressure with water-resistant adhesives and surfaced by machine sanding. The exposed edges of the core are covered with matching edge strips about ¾ in. thick, of the same species of wood as the face veneer. The face veneer is always placed with the grain of the wood vertical.

The core of the most common type of *solid-core door* is built up of vertical strips made of wood blocks about 2 in. wide and several inches long, with the ends of blocks in adjacent strips staggered (Fig. 94-3a). The strips are glued together to form a solid panel. No frame is required, but matching edge strips are provided. Each face panel is plywood with 2 plies for a 5-ply door and 3 plies for a 7-ply door, the core being counted as 1 ply.

The *solid-core door* shown in b consists of a doweled stile and rail frame with one or more intermediate rails and horizontal blocks glued together and assembled in the frame. Each face panel usually consists of 1 ply of sawed veneer ¼ in. thick for doors 1¾ in. thick and 1 ply ⅛ in. thick for 1⅜-in. doors. Matching edge strips are provided.

The *solid-core door* shown in c is made up of a doweled stile and rail frame with one or more intermediate rails and horizontal blocks or strips interspaced between the rails. Since these blocks are not glued together, the core is called a *floating core*. The entire core is bonded to the face panels, however. Matching edge strips are provided. The doors may be 5-ply or 7-ply.

Fire-resistive solid-core doors of the type shown in d are constructed with incombustible mineral or asbestos-type cores or impregnated wood chip cores, plywood face panels, each with 2 or 3 plies, and impregnated matching edge strips.

A solid-core door similar in construction to the door in a has the core, cross bands, and edge strips chemically impregnated to improve its fire resistance.

Several general types of *hollow cores* are used in the construction of flush doors. Various kinds of spacers are located between the face panels, to which they are glued, and assembled within stile and rail frames with matching edge strips. The bond to the face panels holds the spacers in position, and the spacers provide lateral support for the panels. A door with a core which includes closely spaced horizontal fiberboard strips is shown in Fig. 94-3e. This is called a *ladder core*. One with wood or fiberboard strips placed vertically is shown in f.

Another type (g) includes thin vertical and horizontal wood strips located and interlocked to form a *mesh, lattice,* or *grid,* with cells or spaces between the strips. A core that includes closely spaced fiber rings is shown in *h.*

To provide for the face attachment or mortising of locks and other hardware to hollow-core doors, *lock blocks* are provided on each stile, as shown in the figures, so that the door can be hung at either edge.

Solid-core doors are heavier, more fire-resistant, and better insulated against the transmission of heat and sound than wood panel and wood hollow-core doors. They are more suitable for curved heads than either of these types and can be more easily adapted to receive glassed and louvered openings than hollow-core doors.

Door Frames. The parts of door frames are defined in Art. 93. The parts of wood door frames for wood swinging doors and the trim for a doorway located in a wood stud partition are illustrated in Fig. 94-2. Metal frames and trim (Fig. 95-1) for hollow metal doors are also used with wood doors.

As shown in Fig. 94-2, the stops on wood frames may be applied to the faces of the jambs and head. These members may also be *rabbeted* or *rebated* to provide the stops, or the stops may be *ploughed* or *plowed* in.

95. METAL AND METAL-COVERED DOORS

General Discussion. The metals most commonly used in the manufacture of doors are aluminum and carbon steel, but bronze, stainless steel, and copper are also used.

The metal members for door construction are usually hollow, with or without some form of nonmetallic filling, and therefore such doors might be classed as hollow metal doors. The usual practice, however, is to class aluminum and bronze doors separately and restrict the use of the term *hollow metal doors* to doors constructed of hollow members of steel with fillings or core materials other than wood, except plywood cores in the panels. Aluminum and bronze doors have hollow metal members, but they are usually classed separately. In addition, doors with metal facings fitting tightly over wood cores are called *metal-covered doors.* Finally, crudely formed solid-wood fire doors covered with terne plate, although covered with metal, are called *tinclad doors.* There are many other special types.

Aluminum Doors. Both panel and flush doors are constructed of aluminum. The most common type is the panel door with tubular ex-

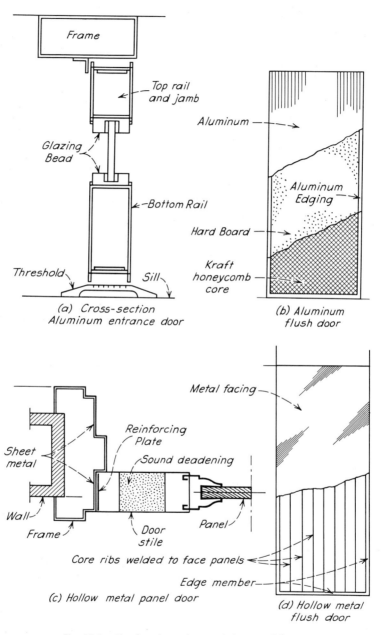

Frame

Top rail
and jamb

Glazing
Bead

Bottom Rail

Threshold

Sill

(a) Cross-section
Aluminum entrance door

Aluminum

Aluminum
Edging

Hard Board

Kraft
honeycomb
core

(b) Aluminum
flush door

Metal facing

Reinforcing
Plate

Sound deadening

Sheet
metal

Wall

Frame

Door
stile

Panel

Core ribs welded to face panels

Edge member

(c) Hollow metal panel door

(d) Hollow metal
flush door

Fig. 95-1. Metal and metal-covered doors and frames.

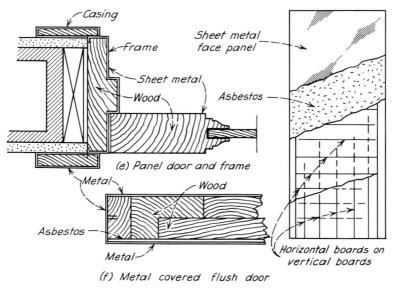

Fig. 95-1. (Continued.)

truded aluminum stiles and rails approximately rectangular in cross section (Fig. 95-1a), with a minimum thickness of $\frac{1}{8}$ in. The members are joined by electric-arc welding with the joints located and finished to be invisible. The frames are constructed of the same material and are also tubular and rectangular in cross section. The doors are usually $1\frac{3}{4}$ in. thick, with stiles and top rails varying in width from $2\frac{1}{8}$ to 5 in. and bottom rails from 4 to 10 in. wide. The frames vary in cross section upward from a minimum width of $1\frac{3}{4}$ in. and a depth of 4 in. The finish of the doors and frames is usually a special polished or satin finish but may be of various architectural colors.

For entrance doors the space between the stiles and rails is usually occupied by a plate-glass panel but may be divided by a narrow aluminum center cross panel. The glass is held in position by continuous aluminum glass stops with vinyl glazing beads, or in other ways, to make putty unnecessary.

Instead of using two glass panels, the lower panel is often faced with aluminum sheets. It is of sandwich construction with a core $\frac{3}{4}$ in. thick of resin-impregnated honeycomb, with $\frac{3}{4}$-in. hexagonal cells, on each face of which is bonded a hardboard layer $\frac{1}{8}$ in. thick, to each of which is bonded an outer layer of sheet aluminum about $\frac{1}{32}$ in. thick. The bonds are formed under heat and pressure.

Aluminum *flush doors* have face panels of fine vertical ribbed or fluted aluminum sheets. For one type of door (Fig. 95-1b) these sheets are about $\frac{1}{32}$ in. thick and are bonded to $\frac{1}{8}$-in. hardboard which are in turn bonded to a resin-impregnated honeycomb core, with $\frac{3}{4}$-in. hexagonal cells, under heat and pressure. The edges of the door may be extruded aluminum sections to which the surface sheets are securely attached. Various types of flush doors are available. They may be pierced for one or more lights of glass or for louvers.

Another form of flush door consists of a framework with extruded aluminum stiles, a top and a bottom rail, and intermediate rails, with the space between rails filled with a solid fibrous core and faced with aluminum sheets.

The *flush panel door* has a stile and rail frame with panels of about the same thickness as that of the stiles and rails.

Hollow Metal Doors. Hollow metal doors are either the panel or flush types. They are usually $1\frac{3}{4}$ in. thick. They are constructed primarily of cold-rolled sheet steel especially processed to give smooth flat surfaces. They ordinarily have a factory finish consisting of one or more coats of baked enamel.

The *panel doors* resemble in appearance the wood panel doors of various designs (Fig. 94-1). The stiles and rails are made of sheets about $\frac{1}{20}$ in. thick and are accurately formed as shown in Fig. 95-1c, with the joints welded and ground smooth. The edges of the doors are usually reinforced internally with channels welded in position. Reinforcement is provided where hardware is to be attached. The stiles and rails are filled with mineral wool, asbestos, or other material for sound deadening so that the doors will not have a metallic sound when closing.

The panels are of sandwich construction with sheet-metal faces about $\frac{1}{20}$ in. thick and cores of asbestos, composition board, sheetrock, hardboard, or other material.

Flush doors (Fig. 95-1d) consist of sheet-metal face panels about $\frac{1}{20}$ in. thick and the full size of the door. They are separated by vertical sheet-metal ribs of various forms, spaced 6 or 8 in., to which they are spot-welded at frequent intervals.

The rim of the door is closed and strengthened by channels or in some other manner, and the face panels are firmly secured to the rim. Sound-deadening material may be bonded between the stiffening ribs on the inside of the face panels or the entire space between ribs may be filled with asbestos or mineral wool insulation or other sound-deadening material. Provisions are made for the attachment of hardware. Other types are available.

The frames for hollow metal doors are made with various profiles which are break-pressed from steel sheets welded and ground smooth at the corners (Fig. 95-1c).

Metal-Covered Doors. Doors of this general type, which are commonly called *kalamein doors*, consist of sheet-metal facings securely bonded or attached to nonresinous kiln-dried wood interior construction (Fig. 95-1e). All joints in the metal covering are recessed locked joints finished with solder and ground smooth. The metal is usually galvanized steel or furniture steel, which is a sheet steel specially processed to give a smooth flat surface. Copper, bronze, aluminum, and stainless steel are also used. The usual thickness is $1\frac{3}{4}$ in.

Panel doors are constructed of doweled or mortised and tenoned stile and rail frames with wood cores and sheet-metal coverings tightly filled by drawing through dies. The panels consist of cores of asbestos board, for the maximum fire resistance, or of composition, plywood, or other board to which metal facings are glued under heat and pressure. The types of panel doors available are similar to those for wood panel doors, some of which are shown in Fig. 94-1.

A common type of *flush door* (Fig. 95-1f) consists of a wood core with a horizontal and a vertical ply, which may·have a thin covering of sheet asbestos glued to one or both sides, both sides covered with sheet metal without seams pressure-glued to the core. The edges are reinforced with wood strips covered with sheet metal. The frames and trim may be sheet metal break-pressed to the desired profile, or wood with metal-covered exposed surfaces.

Tin-Clad Doors. Tin-clad doors consist of a wood core covered with terne plate. The cores are made of either two or three layers of 1-in. boards, preferably tongued-and-grooved, and not more than 8 in. wide. If two layers are used, one is vertical and the other horizontal. If three layers are used, the outer layers are vertical and the inner layer horizontal. The layers are securely fastened together by clinched nails or in some other manner to give smooth surfaces. The covering of terne plate is made up of 14-by-20-in. sheets, preferably with double-lock joints. Solder, if used, must serve only to improve the appearance. The terne plate is held flat against the core by nails.

The 3-ply doors are required where the most effective resistance is desired, and the 2-ply where only a moderate degree of protection is necessary.

Steel-Plate Doors. Steel-plate doors consist of steel plates fastened to one side of an angle-iron frame or both sides of a channel frame, the frames being braced by intermediate members.

Corrugated-Steel Doors. This type of door is constructed of heavy corrugated-steel sheets supported by a structural steel frame. The better doors consist of two thicknesses of corrugated sheets, one with corrugations vertical and the other with corrugations horizontal, with an asbestos lining between the sheets. This lining is from $\frac{1}{8}$ in. to 1 in. thick. Sometimes the structural steel frame is covered with a $\frac{1}{8}$-in. layer of asbestos. A cheaper and less fire-resistant door is made of one thickness of corrugated steel with corrugations vertical, riveted to an angle-iron frame, intermediate braces being provided where necessary.

Steel Rolling Doors. This type of door consists of a curtain of interlocking corrugated steel slats which rolls up on a roller or drum in much the same way as a window shade (Fig. 93-1p). The edges of the curtain operate in vertical guides, and the roller is housed in a steel hood. The curtain may be counterbalanced by springs so that it can be easily raised or lowered by hand; it may be operated by an endless chain with sprocket and gear, by a crank, or by electric motor. Devices for closing the door automatically in case of fire are available.

96. GLASS DOORS

This article is concerned with the common type of *tempered-plate-glass* single- or double-acting swinging door.

In the tempering process plate glass is heated to a high temperature and then cooled suddenly. The sudden cooling has an immediate effect close to the surfaces only. As the interior of the glass slowly cools to a normal temperature, it contracts. This action causes compressive stresses to develop near the surface and balancing tensile stresses to develop in the interior, an equilibrium which remains permanently.

Tempered plate glass is much more resistant to pressure and impact than normal plate glass and is more flexible. It cannot be cut, drilled, or altered in any way after tempering. The glass thicknesses used are $\frac{1}{2}$ and $\frac{3}{4}$ in. The surfaces of the glass are usually smooth and polished, but rough-textured glass is available when it is desired to obscure vision. The edges of the glass are finished smooth.

All fittings to receive hardware to be attached to the door are cemented in position to the glass at the factory.

Aluminum, bronze, or stainless steel hardware is used. Top and bottom pivots are used rather than hinges to provide for the swing of the doors. Pivot door checks or closers are recessed in the floor. Push bars and plates, door pulls, and other hardware required are adapted when necessary for use on this type of door, with appropriate connections to the door.

Cross sections of one type of glass door, with its frame and metal fittings designed to receive the glass and to provide for hardware connections at the top and bottom of a door are illustrated in Fig. 96-1a and b. They may extend entirely across a door, or may be located in any of the positions near the edges shown in c, or in others as required. Holes to receive bolts for attaching certain hardware may be drilled in the glass before tempering but not after.

The frames for glass doors are tubular metal approximately rectangular in cross section, reinforced with steel channels, with the rods located inside the members (Fig. 96-1a and b). The metals used in

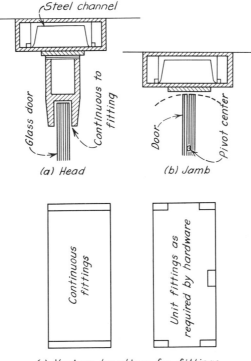

(a) Head   (b) Jamb

(c) Various locations for fittings

Fig. 96-1. Tempered plate-glass doors and their frames.

their construction are extruded aluminum or bronze, or stainless-steel sheets pressed into shapes similar to the extruded shapes.

Sliding doors are also available.

References

1. *Sweet's Architectural Catalog File,* F. W. Dodge Corporation.
2. *Ponderosa Pine Doors,* Commercial Standard CS120-58, U. S. Dept. of Commerce.
3. *Hardwood Veneered Doors,* Commercial Standard CS171-58, U. S. Dept. of Commerce.
4. *State Building Construction Code,* State of New York.
5. *National Building Code,* National Board of Fire Underwriters.
6. *Wood Hand Book,* U. S. Department of Agriculture.
7. *Exterior and Interior Solid Core Flush Doors,* Architectural Woodwork No. 5, Architectural Woodwork Institute.
8. *Standard of National Board of Fire Underwriters for the Installation of Fire Doors and Windows,* No. 80, 1961.
9. *Building Materials List,* Underwriters Laboratories, Inc., January, 1961, p. 137.

16 Heat insulation and acoustics

97. HEAT INSULATION

General Discussion. There has been an increasing interest in making the air in occupied buildings more comfortable and healthful and in conditioning the air in manufacturing buildings to suit the manufacturing processes. There has also been interest in reducing the operating costs involved in such improvements. Two important factors in bringing about these conditions are the temperature and the humidity of the air in the buildings. Both factors are closely associated with the construction of the building. In winter the problem is largely one of providing additional heat and additional humidity, whereas in summer these may be present in excessive amounts. There is a considerable operating cost involved in increasing or decreasing the temperature of the inside air. Usually the savings in this cost which can be brought about by proper design and construction, including insulation, will much more than justify the additional expenditure involved. The direct cost of increasing humidity is not large, but humidities of 35 to 40 per cent and more, which are often maintained, may cause condensation in the outside walls and the roof or ceiling of the top story, which can only be avoided by appropriate types of construction. Decreasing the humidity, as may be desirable in many parts of the country during the summer, is not as easily and cheaply accomplished as increasing the humidity, but this does not require any special consideration as far as the construction of buildings is concerned, except where unusually low humidities or temperatures are employed.

Heat Transmission. Heat is transmitted from one side of the walls and roof of a building to the other in the following ways.

1. By *air infiltration,* or leakage through cracks and other open spaces. The volume of air entering a building is offset by an equal

volume leaving the building. Since the temperature of the two volumes would normally be different, there is a transfer of heat with the air change.

2. By *transmission* through the walls, windows, doors, and roofs.

Air infiltration is minimized by good construction, which reduces or eliminates cracks and other openings through the walls, around cornices, along the sills on foundation walls, and through the roof construction; by the proper design, construction, and installation of doors and window sash and their frames; by calking between frames and surrounding masonry; by covering the sheathing of frame walls with a good quality of building paper with tight joints; and by plaster surfaces on masonry walls. Air infiltration through an unplastered brick wall is many times as great as through the same wall after plastering. The effectiveness of storm sash depends upon how tightly they fit and is relatively high on windows that are not weatherstripped.

Because of the "chimney effect" in tall buildings, the tendency for air infiltration at the lower stories, and for a corresponding outward movement in the upper stories, is large enough to require special provisions to be made to reduce this effect. These provisions consist of closing, with doors or by other means, all openings from floor to floor such as stairways and elevator shafts. This is also a necessary fire-protection measure. Heat losses by air infiltration increase rapidly as the wind velocity increases and may exceed the losses due to the difference in temperatures inside and outside a building.

Heat is transmitted through walls and roofs in three ways.

1. By *conduction* from molecule to molecule of the wall material and, to a certain extent, from molecule to molecule of the air in open spaces in the wall.

2. By *convection* by air currents, which circulate in open spaces within the wall or roof construction and which absorb heat as they pass upward over a warm boundary surface of the air space and release heat as they pass downward over a cold boundary surface of that space. The circulation is produced by the decrease in density of air, which accompanies increase in temperature.

3. By *radiation*, the process by which energy, called *radiant energy*, is transmitted from one body or surface to another body or surface by electromagnetic waves.

Heat passes through a solid wall entirely by conduction, but if there is an air space inside the wall it will cross this space by radiation, convection, and conduction. The resistance which a given homogeneous material offers to the passage of heat varies directly with its thickness and inversely with its density, and decreases with increases in the moisture content of the material. The resistance of an air space, such as a stud space in a frame wall or a cell space in a hollow tile wall, to the passage of heat by radiation is independent of the width of the space but is greatly affected by the nature of the boundary surfaces, being low for the surfaces of ordinary building materials but very high for bright metallic surfaces. The resistance by an air space to the passage of heat by convection is practically independent of the width of this space if it exceeds ¾ in., but it decreases very rapidly as the width decreases below ¾ in. More than half of the heat transmitted through an air space over ¾ in. wide bounded by ordinary materials is radiant heat.

Solar Heat. Solar heat, or radiant heat from the sun's rays, which is transmitted through windows, is an important factor in heating the air in a building. During the winter months this effect is usually desirable, but in many parts of the country it increases the inside temperatures above the comfort range unless excess heat is removed by air conditioning, which significantly increases the initial and operating costs of a building.

As outlined in Section A of Art. 92, there are several ways for reducing the solar heat gain through windows. These include shading windows from the sun's rays, double glazing, and the use of heat-absorbing glass as described in Art. 91.

Canvas awnings, which were extensively used in the past, and the more modern types made of aluminum or plastics are very effective especially if they are so designed as to permit the heated air beneath them to escape.

A detailed discussion of window shading is included in reference 11, which has been helpful in preparing these comments and Table 97-1. The table gives the relative values of solar heat transfer for various fenestrations under the conditions stipulated in the table.

The relative values in Table 97-2 will be of interest in comparing results achieved by several methods for reducing heat gain from all sources, including solar heat, through various types of glazing with the heat gain through ordinary glass which is considered 100 for comparative purposes. Values for sunlit surfaces, with and without sunscreens, are given in the first column, and those for surfaces which are not sunlit are given in the second column. It will be noted that the values for sunlit areas with sunscreens are approximately the same as those for corresponding areas which are not sunlit. Some of the areas listed as sunlit would be sunlit if sunscreens were not provided.

Table 97-1

Relative Values of Solar Heat Transfer for Various Fenestrations

Type of Fenestration	Relative Value
Regular window glass	100 *
Heat-absorbing glass	69
Double glass—heat-absorbing glass outside, regular plate inside	52
Regular window glass, inside venetian blinds	58
Glass block panel	50

* 100 equals heat transfer of 183 Btu per sq. ft. per hour.
Regular window glass considered as 100.
Conditions: typical clear afternoon in midsummer at 40° North latitude with fenestration facing southwest.
Arranged from paper by Donald J. Vild in reference 11.

Heat loss by residential buildings during the winter months is often reduced by replacing window screens with storm sash. Heat gain by such buildings during the summer is sometimes reduced by attic fans which ventilate the attic and replace air heated by solar heat transmitted through the roof with cooler outdoor air. Hot attic air, of course, transmits heat to the rooms beneath. An insect screen is

Table 97-2

Relative Merits of Heat Gain Reducing Methods through Glass

Type of Area	Sunlit	Not Sunlit
Single glass	100	33
Double glazing	73	22
Heat-absorbing glass	68	24
Double-glazed heat-absorbing glass	51	17
Sunscreen on single glass	35	17
Sunscreen on double glazing	26	12
Sunscreen on heat-absorbing glass	24	12
Sunscreen on double-glazed heat-absorbing glass	18	9

As given by G. R. Munger in reference 12.

available with the horizontal wires replaced by thin flat metal strips and vertical wires about ½ in. apart to form venetian blinds with miniature slats. Because they are located outside, they act as sunscreens and are quite effective for windows with south exposure but less effective for those with east or west exposure.

Radiant Heat and Comfort. The effect of the temperature of the surrounding air on the comfort of a person is well known. Air temperatures which are considered desirable for comfort depend upon various factors, but normally they are within the range of 70 to 75°F. The effects of the temperatures of the surfaces of the walls, ceilings, and floors which surround a person are not, however, always understood. If any such surfaces are cooler than the desired air temperatures, a person will feel too cool even though the temperature of the intervening air is within the desirable range. Conversely, if any of the surrounding surfaces are warmer than the desirable range in air temperature, he will feel uncomfortably warm. These conditions are due to the loss or gain of heat by the body caused by the radiation of heat between the body and the surrounding surfaces. Therefore it is important that the temperatures of these surfaces be maintained to a reasonable extent within the comfort range. This factor is significant in selecting insulation.

Condensation. The amount of water vapor that air can contain increases with the temperature of the air. The ratio of the amount actually present to the maximum amount that can be present at that temperature is called the *relative humidity* or simply the *humidity*. It is expressed in percentage. As the temperature of air containing a given amount of water vapor falls, the relative humidity rises until the saturation or *dew-point temperature* is reached and some of the vapor is condensed. This condensation may occur on cold interior wall surfaces and be apparent; but the water vapor tends to pass through the walls and, since the interior of a wall becomes progressively colder toward the outside, a temperature may be reached at which the vapor will condense within the wall. The conditions favorable for this action are an inside humidity of 35 or 40 per cent and higher and a long-continued cold outside temperature. The amount of water that condenses gradually increases and, if the temperature where the water collects is below freezing, ice will form. If porous insulation is present, it will accumulate water as ice and largely lose its effectiveness. The ice will melt when the outside temperature rises sufficiently. Condensation may also occur in insulation over the ceiling of the top story or on the underside of the roof sheathing, particularly around the points of protruding roofing nails. The condensation that forms in the walls, ceiling, or roof construction may come through the finished wall and ceiling surfaces and spoil the decorations, disintegrate the plaster, cause any wood present to swell with resultant cracking, cause paint on exterior wood surfaces to peel off, and damage a building in other ways. These effects are sometimes wrongly attributed to leaking walls and roofs. In wood construction, the wall may be so tightly sealed with sheathing paper that evaporation occurs very slowly, causing the studs and sheathing to decay. Insulation may make conditions worse by causing the outer portions of a wall to be colder, and porous insulation accumulates the water. Some of the higher grades of sheathing paper used on stud walls retard or prevent the escape of water vapor from the walls and increase the condensation effect.

To prevent condensation of this type, avoid high humidities during long periods of low temperatures; place a *vapor barrier* or *seal* under the lath in stud walls and on the bottoms of ceiling joists of the top story and use a sheathing paper which is sufficiently airtight but not an effective vapor barrier; place a vapor seal under the lath on furred masonry walls; place a vapor seal under the insulation on wood or concrete roof-decks, if insulation is used; and ventilate attic spaces. A glossy-surfaced tar paper or a polyethylene film are good vapor seals for use under lath. They must be lapped and tightly fastened at all joints. The longitudinal joints should be over the studs or joists, and the paper should extend from the floor to the ceiling without end joints in the paper. Slaters' felt is considered a satisfactory sheathing paper. On roof decks, a 2-ply seal should be made of saturated felt applied by mopping with hot asphalt or roofing pitch. The vapor seal should always be on the inside.

Some of the rigid insulating materials are coated with bituminous material or encased in bituminous paper to exclude water vapor; many insulating quilts have so-called vaporproof paper coverings; and mineral wool batts are available with vaporproof backs which are placed next to the lath in wood stud walls. These are not regarded as high types of vapor barriers.

Types of Insulating Materials. Insulating materials may be divided into two general classes according to the way they function. In the first group may be included all the low-density, porous, or fibrous materials with low conductivity or high resistance to the passage of heat, whose effectiveness is due to the minute air spaces of which they are largely composed. This group includes three general types of insulating materials as follows: *rigid* or board and slab insulation, *flexible* or quilt, blanket, and batt insulation, and *fill* insulation. As stated in reference 7, "Still air is the best heat insulator we know. But air is seldom still. The slightest change in temperature will make air expand or contract; the warmer air becomes lighter and floats above the cooler, heavier air. So the job is to keep still air still."

Without going into detail, it may be said that insulating materials confine the air which they contain, and upon which their effectiveness depends, in cells, voids, or other spaces, some or all of whose dimensions are so small that there can be little if any movement of the air within their boundaries.

The second group of insulation materials includes those of the *reflective* type which is used to form boundaries of air spaces and whose insulating value lies in its effectiveness in reflecting radiant energy.

The rigid, flexible, and fill insulators consist of wood, cane, and other vegetable fibers, mineral wool, cork, hair felt, expanded mica, foamed glass or plastics, or light granular materials. They owe their insulating properties to the minute air spaces they contain. The insulating value per inch of thickness is about the same for all these materials. It is approximately equal to the insulating value of 3 in. of wood, 17 in. of glass, 31 in. of brickwork, and 40 in. of concrete.

Reflective insulation consists of some form of sheet metal, metal foil, or a metallic coating which is made very thin because its effectiveness is practically independent of the thickness. The most effective insulation of this type will reflect about 95 per cent of the radiant energy that strikes its surface. Since a large proportion of the heat which passes through an insulated wall is produced by radiant energy, reflective insulation can be very effective.

Rigid Insulation. Fiberboards, described in Art. 70, are used for insulating purposes. To be effective, the fibers are not highly compressed as in the hardboards. Moisture and water vapor are partially excluded from some of the fiberboards if the boards are coated with asphalt or encased in a bituminous waterproof paper. For increased insulating value, fiberboards and gypsum boards are available with aluminum foil coating on one surface to serve as reflective insulation. Another form of rigid insulation is corkboard made of pressed cork. It is available in thicknesses up to 6 in. Some forms of rigid insulation serve the dual purposes of insulation and sheathing or insulation and lath. The common thickness for sheathing is 1 in., but any desired thickness may be obtained.

Flexible Insulation. This type of insulation may be in the form of *quilts* or *blankets* and *batts*, often spelled *bats*. The quilts and blankets consist of a fibrous material such as treated wood fiber, hair felt, flax fiber, eel grass, or shredded paper stitched between sheets of waterproof paper to form a flexible material available in various thicknesses up to 1 in.

Another form of flexible insulation is made from *mineral* or *rock wool,* formed by blowing molten rock into fibrous form by steam under pressure. This produces a fluffy, noncombustible product weighing about 6 lb. per cu. ft. It is usually furnished in batts 15 by 24 or 48 in., to fit between studs and ceiling joists spaced 16 in. center to center. The thickness is ordinarily about 4 in. to fill the space completely between 2-by-4-in. studs, but batts 2 in. thick are available. Batts are furnished plain or with a waterproof paper cemented to the back and projecting about 2 in. on each side to provide *nailing flanges,* which lap over the studs or joists to which they are nailed and form a seal. This paper is supposed to serve as a vapor barrier or seal, but if it is to be effective the end joints must be tight. It is better practice to provide an additional vapor barrier, as previously described, over the batt insulation after it is in place, and under the lath. Mineral-wool insulation is also furnished in roll form and as fill insulation, as described in the next paragraph. *Glass wool* is a fibrous glass insulating material similar to mineral wool. It is available in batt, blanket, and fill form.

Fill Insulation. This material consists of granulated rock wool in the form of nodules or pellets, granulated cork, expanded mica, and other material which is blown through large tubes or dumped into open spaces in the walls and ceilings of buildings, such as the stud space in frame walls and the ceiling joist space. Fibrous mineral wool and glass wool are also furnished in loose form for packing by hand into open spaces.

Reflective Insulation. Reflective insulation is placed in air spaces and functions by reflecting a large percentage of the radiant energy which strikes it. The materials used for reflective insulation are very thin tin plate, copper or aluminum sheets, or aluminum foil on the surface of rigid fiberboards or gypsum boards. A common form of reflective insulation is aluminum foil mounted on asphalt-impregnated kraft paper, the strength of which may be increased by the use of jute netting. This material is used for lining air spaces or for curtains to increase the number of air spaces in a given overall space. To be effective, the edges of such curtains must be tightly sealed.

Methods of Installation. *Rigid insulation* can be used as sheathing on the outside of wood studs (Fig. 97-1a); as building board without

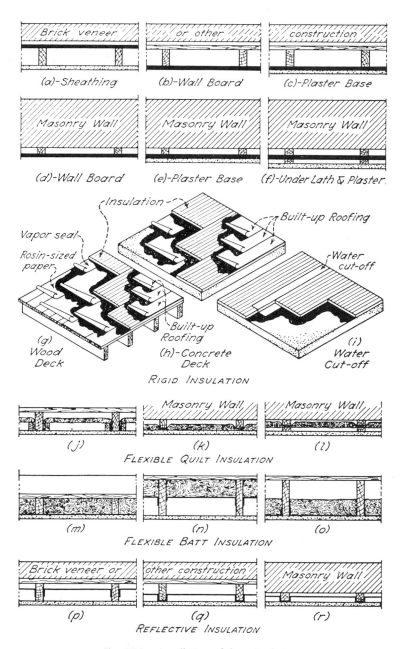

Fig. 97-1. Installation of heat insulation.

plaster on the inside of wood studs (b); and on the lower side of ceiling joists or rafters. It may also be used as lath to receive plaster on the inside of wood studs (c), and on the lower side of ceiling joists. When used with masonry walls, it is nailed to furring strips (d). It may be exposed; it may serve as a plaster base (e); or it may be covered with lath and plaster, with furring strips between the insulation and the lath and on top of the other furring strips or at right angles to them (f).

Rigid insulation may be used on wood and concrete roof decks under built-up roofing (g and h). Wood decks are first covered with one or two layers of rosin-sized building paper, lapped at the joints and securely tacked down. This paper keeps asphalt from running through the cracks between the roofing boards. Over this paper or directly on concrete roofs a layer of asphalt-saturated felt is mopped with hot asphalt or roofing pitch. This layer serves as a temporary roofing. If there is to be considerable vapor in the room below, another layer of asphalt-saturated felt is applied by mopping with hot asphalt or roofing pitch to improve the vapor seal. The insulation is applied by coating the surface of the felt with hot asphalt or roofing pitch just before placing the insulation. Each board is bedded in the hot asphalt or roofing pitch. As many layers of insulation as desired are placed in this way. Finally, with staggered joints, a built-up roofing is applied by mopping the first ply to the top of the top layer of insulation. Slate and tile wearing surfaces can be placed on top of the built-up roofing if desired.

In placing the insulation, precautions must be taken to protect the insulation from rain or other moisture by placing, at one time, only such an area as can be covered in a short period and never leaving the insulation unprotected over night. It is also good practice to localize the effect of any leakage that may occur and to provide a place where work can be stopped, by dividing the roof into about 30-ft. squares with *water cutoffs*. These are made by inserting a 16-in. strip of asphalt-saturated felt at joints (Fig. 97-1i), the strip being tightly cemented to the surface below the insulation and to the insulation itself. Other cutoffs should be located parallel to the parapet walls and about 2 ft. from them. All interruptions in work should occur at waterstops, and the insulation that has been placed should be protected temporarily with at least one ply of the built-up roofing extending to waterstops on all sides. Insulation laid on wood decks sloping more than 3 in. to the foot should be nailed to the deck. Insulation applied in this manner should not be used on concrete decks with such slopes.

Flexible insulation is installed in open spaces in the wall, ceiling, or roof construction where it will not be subjected to loads, for it is easily compressible. Quilts or blankets are installed between the studs and ceiling joists in frame construction or between furring strips on masonry walls (*j*, *k*, and *l*). More than one layer of quilt, together or separated, can be used if desired. Quilt insulation divides the space it occupies into two or more air spaces. To be efficient, the insulation should be so fastened at the sides and ends that there will be no air leakage between spaces. Batts are inserted between studs (*o*). If they are provided with vaporproof back and with nailing flanges, they are lapped over the studs, as shown. If the studs, joists, or rafters are deeper than the thickness of the batts, the nailing flanges are nailed to the sides of these members (*n*). Ceilings are insulated (*o*), or the batts may be inserted from below (*n*), before the lath are placed.

Fill insulation is installed by pouring the loose granulated or nodulated form into open spaces between the studs of stud walls and between ceiling joists, or it is installed by blowing this material into place through large flexible tubes using low air pressure. Fibrous mineral wool and glass wool are available in bulk form. They are packed by hand into the space between studs and joists. Great care is necessary to insure the complete filling of stud spaces.

Reflective insulation is applied between studs, joists, or rafters (Fig. 97-1*p*). Nailing strips may be used to hold it more tightly. Some forms may be installed by lapping over the studs (*q*), or by inserting between furring strips on masonry walls (*r*). This insulation divides the space into two or more air spaces. For the most effective results the insulation must be fastened at the sides, top, and bottom, and at all laps, so that there will be no circulation of air between the two spaces.

98. ACOUSTICS

Definitions. *Acoustics* may be defined as the science of sound. *Sound* may be defined as the sensation of hearing caused by stimulation of the auditory nerves, usually by vibrations transmitted in air affecting the ear. It may also be defined as the vibrational energy which is the physical cause of that stimulation.

General Comments. Improvements in construction during recent years have often resulted in buildings with poorer acoustical properties owing to the more rigid materials and construction used. On the other hand, radios, television, motion pictures, the increased use of mechanical office equipment, the increase in street noise from the automobile, and many other factors have emphasized the importance of improvement in acoustical conditions.

Largely because of its increasing importance, knowledge in the field of architectural acoustics has been developed so that the necessary acoustical features can be determined when the plans and specifications of a building are being prepared. By this procedure the construction of buildings with good acoustics can be assured, and the embarrassment and inconvenience of remedying defective acoustical conditions while a building is in use, usually at much greater cost, can be avoided.

The various acoustical considerations which enter into the design of buildings are considered briefly in this article so that the problems involved will be appreciated, but no effort is made to present material which can be used in the solution of specific problems. To secure good results, specialized advice is usually required.

Good acoustics of building space contribute to the comfort of its occupants, the efficiency of office and factory workers and their supervisors, the effectiveness of classroom instructors, and understanding and appreciation by the audiences in assembly and concert halls.

Nature of Sound. As stated by Paul E. Sabine (1),

A vibrating body will impart a portion of its energy to the air surrounding it, i.e. it will generate sound waves. The *frequency of vibration*—the number of complete round trip excursions per second—is expressed as so many cycles per second or, more brefly, *cycles*. Consider one to and fro movement of the surface of a vibrating body. Its forward movement compresses the layer of air adjacent to it, causing an increase in pressure above the normal atmospheric pressure. The returning movement will cause a decrease in pressure below the normal. This fluctuation of the air pressure above and below the normal will be transmitted with a definite velocity in successive layers. The transfer of energy through the air by successive pressure variations in it is called a *sound wave*. Experiment shows that the velocity of sound of all frequencies is approximately 1120 feet per second. . . . It varies slightly with temperature. . . . The *pitch* of a sound is determined by its frequency.

The *intensity* of sound at a given point is the amount of energy transmitted by the fluctuations in air pressure at that point per unit of area perpendicular to the direction of travel.

Measurement of Sound Intensity. In dealing with acoustical problems, it is necessary to make use of a unit of measure for the intensity of a sound. The range of intensities in the sounds of every day experience is very great. In terms of watts, the unit commonly used for measuring energy,

The intensity of the faintest sound which a normally acute ear can hear is slightly more than 1. The intensity of the sound of the voice speaking in a confidential tone is of the order of 10,000, ordinary conversation is 100,000 to 1,000,000, street noise 10,000,000 to 1,000,000,000, and a painfully loud sound is from one trillion to ten trillion of these units. As an acoustical device, the ear is unsurpassed in the vast range of intensities to which it will respond without being damaged. Because of the awkwardness of handling numbers of such magnitudes and because of the roughly logarithmic response of the ear, the practice has been adopted of expressing sound intensities on a logarithmic scale. (1)

On this basis, intensities, or amounts of energy, proportional to 10, 100 and 1000 produce sensations in the ear proportional to 1, 2 and 3 respectively. A slight modification of this logarithmic scale has come into general use to measure sound energy and the amount of noise reduction. It is called the *decibel scale*. The scale merely multiplies the numbers of the logarithmic scale by 10. The unit of the scale, the *decibel,* is a convenient unit, since it is approximately the smallest change in energy that the average ear can detect. For this reason, the unit has frequently been called a *sensation unit.* The decibel scale is suitable for measuring ratios of sound intensity. To measure absolute noise levels the zero value is assigned to a definite level, that is, a level of 20 decibels corresponds to an energy 100 times that corresponding to the zero value. (3)

Loudness. The relation between loudness and intensity is explained as follows.

The loudness of sound (sensation) depends upon the intensity, but it also depends upon the frequency of the sound and the characteristics of the human ear. The intensity of sound is a purely physical quantity, whereas, the loudness depends upon the characteristics of the ear. . . .

The relationship between frequency, intensity and loudness is quite involved. We do have, however, a sense of relative loudness in that there is a fair measure of agreement among trained observers in their judgments as to when one sound is one-half, one-third and so on as loud as another. . . . Speaking generally one may say that the quantitative evaluation of the magnitude of sensations is a psychological rather than a physical problem so that the acoustical engineer prefers to deal with those aspects of sound that are subject to physical measurement. (1)

The significance of the decibel scale is illustrated by the comparisons in Table 98-1. By consulting this table it is seen that, according to the decibel scale, the difference in loudness between a very faint sound and one that is deafening is about 120 decibels.

Classification of Sounds. Sounds are usually classified into three types, noise, music, and speech, but this classification is not always clear-cut. In general, *noise* is unwanted sound (4). If one is listening to music,

Table 98-1

Noise Levels in Decibels

Db.	Condition	Noise	Db.	Condition	Noise
120		Threshold of feeling	60		
	Thunder of artillery			Noisy home	
	Nearby riveter			Average office	
110		Deafening	50		Moderate
	Elevated train			Average conversation	
	Boiler factory			Quiet radio	
100			40		
	Loud street noise			Quiet home	
	Noisy factory			Private office	
90		Very loud	30		Faint
	Unmuffled truck			Average auditorium	
	Police whistle			Quiet conversation	
80			20		
	Noisy office			Rustle of leaves	
	Average street noise			Whisper	
70		Loud	10		Very faint
	Average radio			Soundproof room	
	Average factory				
			0		Threshold of audibility

Arranged from reference 1

sounds produced by a person speaking nearby are considered as noise; if one is speaking to this person, the music is considered noise.

Since the physical properties of speech differ considerably from those of music, the acoustical properties of speech rooms should differ appreciably from those of music rooms (4).

Requirements of Good Acoustics. "In the design of rooms intended for speaking purposes the prime objective is intelligibility of speech. In the design of music rooms the prime objective is the most favorable enrichment of tonal quality and total blending of the sounds." (4)

Basic Factors in Acoustical Design. Some of the more important factors which must be considered in the planning of buildings to obtain satisfactory acoustical conditions are as follows.

1. Selection of the building site.

2. Arrangement, dimensions, and shapes of rooms and other planning features.

3. Insulation and control of sound transmission within the building.

4. Installation of absorptive materials within the building.

Each of these factors will be discussed briefly in the following paragraphs. For a more comprehensive and descriptive list see reference 4.

Site Selection. In selecting the site for a building for which acoustical considerations are important, attention should be paid to any effects which present or foreseeable prevailing noises in that area may have on the acoustical conditions in the building. Some of the important sources of objectionable noises are automobile traffic on busy streets, traffic arteries, and highways; railroads; airfields; and industrial establishments.

In considering future developments that may be objectionable, the zoning ordinances and any long-range plans prepared for the city should be consulted. Often the site for a building has already been selected, but even then the factors mentioned are important because they affect the acoustical design of the building.

Building Plans. After the site has been selected and when the plans are being prepared, much can be done to promote good acoustical conditions, often at little or no increase in cost or interference with the efficient functioning of a building. Involved in this phase of the planning are certain factors which affect the acoustics in the various rooms in the building and do not include special acoustical treatment. Some of the desirable planning provisions follow.

1. Locate rooms that require a quiet environment where they will have the minimum exposures to objectionable outside noises.

2. Provide horizontal and vertical separation of rooms that require a quiet environment from those that are inherently noisy.

3. Stagger the doorways on the two sides of a hall or corridor.

4. Provide doors at the entrances to long corridors, stairways, and elevator foyers.

5. Provide appropriate shapes for auditoriums, recital halls, music studios, and practice rooms.

6. Provide appropriate shapes for wall and ceiling surfaces of auditoriums.

7. Provide room sizes acoustically compatible with their proposed uses.

Sound Transmission, Insulation, and Absorption. When a sound originating in a room under consideration strikes the surface of the wall, floor, ceiling, or other barrier, a part of it is *reflected* from the surface, a part is *transmitted* through the barriers, and a part is *absorbed* by the barriers and its energy dissipated in the form of heat. The reflected part of the sound remains in the room and is represented by the *reflection coefficient*. The part absorbed by the barrier and the part transmitted through it are considered together as being absorbed and are represented by the *absorption coefficient*. When the part of the sound transmitted through a barrier is considered separately, the reduction in sound energy in passing through a barrier is called the *transmission loss*. It is expressed in decibels and is a measure of the effectiveness of a barrier in *insulating* against the transmission of outside sound into a room.

Obviously, a barrier with a low transmission loss is effective in reducing the sound level in a room caused by inside sounds but is ineffective in insulating the room against outside sounds. For example, fiberboard or porous concrete block partitions whose surfaces are not painted or plastered have low transmission losses and are effective in reducing the sound level in a room caused by inside noises but are ineffective in insulating a room against sounds originating in adjoining rooms or from other outside sources. This difference is not always appreciated.

Transmission Loss and Insulation. The following comments are based largely on the National Bureau of Standards Report BMS 17 by W. L. Chrisler entitled *Sound Insulation of Wall and Floor Constructions* (2), on BMS Report 144 with the same title (3), and on two supplements to these reports.

Sounds may enter a building or room in the following ways.

1. By transmission of *airborne sounds* through openings, such as windows or doors, cracks around doors, windows, water pipes, conduits, ducts of ventilating systems, and in other ways.

2. By transmission of structural vibrations or *structure-borne sounds* from one part of a building to another. Such sounds, with rare exceptions, finally reach the ear through the air.

3. By direct transmission through various portions of the structure itself which act as diaphragms and are set in motion by the sound waves striking them.

Transmission loss is determined by measuring, under specified conditions, the difference between the intensity of sound in decibels in the room where the sound originates and the intensity of the sound in a room separated from the first by the wall, ceiling, or floor being tested.

For a given barrier the transmission loss varies with the frequency or pitch of the sound being lower for low pitched sounds than for those with high pitch. Studies have demonstrated that a frequency of 512 cps is the most satisfactory frequency to use for acoustical design under ordinary conditions.

Airborne sounds are lowered by reducing the openings to a minimum and even eliminating windows entirely. The amount of sound admitted through a closed window of a room may be many times that admitted through the walls, ceiling, and doors, and that admitted by a closed door may be as much as is admitted by the remainder of the enclosing structure of a room except the window. The amount of sound admitted through a window or door only partly opened is many times that admitted by a closed window. These qualitative relationships emphasize the importance of windows in noise control. Most of the noise from ventilating ducts can be eliminated by inserting acoustic filters.

Sounds transmitted by structural vibrations may be reduced by giving special consideration to them when designing the building and by selecting materials which do not transmit vibrations readily.

The weight of a homogeneous wall per unit of area is the most important factor in determining its sound-insulation efficiency. The kind of material and the way it is held in position are of secondary importance. Because of its lightness, fiberboard is not an effective sound insulator. The sound-insulating value of a given material does not increase directly with the thickness or weight per unit of area, but as the logarithm of this weight; therefore a high degree of sound insulation cannot be secured with a homogeneous wall unless it is excessively thick. This relationship is illustrated in Table 98-2.

Table 98-2

Relation of Transmission Loss to Weight (13)

Wt.	Loss	Wt.	Loss	Wt.	Loss	Wt.	Loss
1	22.7	10	37	40	45	100	51.3
5	32	20	41	60	48	400	60

Key: Weight in lb. per sq. ft. Transmission loss in decibels. For frequency of 512 cps.

The insulating value of a wall of a given weight can be increased considerably by dividing the wall into two or more layers. In an ordinary lath and plaster partition, with wood studs to which the lath are fastened, most of the sound is transmitted directly through the studs and only a small portion indirectly from one layer of lath and plaster across the air space to the other layer. Stiff studs transmit less sound than flexible studs, but hard strong plaster is a poorer insulator than soft weak plaster, which unfortunately is not sufficiently durable for use. A partition constructed of gypsum lath fastened to the studs with resilient metal clips is a more effective insulator than one in which the lath are nailed directly to the studs.

Staggered studs may be used, with each plaster layer fastened to a different set of alternate studs. This prevents the transmission of sound directly through the studs, but a considerable amount of sound is transmitted indirectly by the studs through the top and bottom plates to which they are attached. The sound-insulating value of a stud partition may be decreased, rather than increased, by using a filling material between the studs. If the filling material is elastic and exerts pressure against the layers of lath and plaster, it may improve the sound-insulating properties of the partition.

A double or cavity masonry wall is more effective in sound insulation than a single wall of the same weight, but fillers placed in the intervening space seem to have little value. Partitions constructed of 3- or 4-in. hollow tile with plaster applied directly to the tile may be too light to give satisfactory sound insulation. If furring strips are fastened to the tile, a waterproof paper is placed over the furring strips to cut off any possible contact of the plaster with the tile, and lath and plaster are then applied to the furring strips, the insulating properties of the partition are increased considerably. Experiments indicate that the method used in fastening the furring strips to the tile is of little importance.

The sound insulaion of a concrete floor can be improved by using a *floating floor* of wood and a suspended ceiling. The method of attaching the nailing strips seems to be of little importance, but rigid hangers should not be used for the suspended ceiling. Flexible supports such as springs or wires are satisfactory.

Impact noises caused by walking or moving furniture or by a direct transfer of vibration from machines and musical instruments, such as pianos and radios, form another class of noise which is more difficult to insulate than airborne noise. A machine often sounds as noisy in the room below as in the room where it is located. A so-called floating floor is sometimes built by laying a rough subfloor on wood joists and over this placing a layer of fiberboard which supports a finished wood floor nailed through the fiberboard to the rough floor. Experiments show that the fiberboard, laid in this manner, has no sound-insulating effect. A floor constructed in a similar manner to that just described, but with nailing strips above the fiberboard to receive the full length of the nails holding the finished flooring, is much more effective. The method of fastening the nailing strips is not very important. They can be nailed every 3 or 4 ft. or can be held in position by straps, springs, or small metal chains containing felt. Conversation is not audible through such a floor, but it is not effective in reducing impact noises such as those caused by footsteps.

Floors constructed with separate wood joists for the floor and ceiling below do not give experimental results quite as good as the floating floor. A floating floor added to this construction is very satisfactory as far as airborne noises are concerned, but not as satisfactory in reducing impact noises.

Impacts applied directly to a masonry floor are almost as audible in the room below as in the room where they are applied. A floating floor results in decided improvement, and a suspended ceiling gives still further improvement. The reduction in airborne noise is better than that for impact noise, but the latter noise is much less than that for a concrete slab alone. Concrete construction with a floating floor and a suspended ceiling gives better results than a wood floating floor with floor and ceiling joists separated as described.

Soft and yielding floor coverings act as cushions in reducing the transmission of impact noises produced by walking on the floor or from other causes. Heavy carpet on a pad is very effective and rubber or cork tile are beneficial but to a much lesser degree.

The noise level in a room caused by outside noises can be reduced by increasing the total absorption units in the room, but this reduction is not large. A much greater reduction can usually be obtained at less cost by increasing the sound insulation of the walls, ceiling, and floors of the room. Absorbent materials are necessary to keep down the noise level resulting from noises originating in the room. Absorbent materials in corridors prevent them from acting as speaking tubes transmitting sound from one room to another when the doors are open.

The *masking effect* due to other noises is important. If a room is located in a quiet area, it may be possible to hear sounds clearly from an adjoining room, but if the room is located where the sound level is high, very little may be heard.

Airborne machinery noises are usually much smaller than those caused by the vibration of the foundation or other support for the machinery. The noise caused by the vibration of the support can be reduced by placing machines on layers of cork, asbestos, rubber, or felt, and sometimes by mounting them on springs.

Values for the transmission losses in decibels through many types of partition, floor, and ceiling construction are given in references 2, 3, and 4. The losses through various common types of construction are given in Table 98-3 for illustrative purposes (3). Larger losses can be achieved by special types of construction as have been described and more fully considered in reference 3. The addition of acoustical materials has little effect on transmission losses because of the light weight of these materials.

Sound Absorbent Materials. As stated by Paul E. Sabine (1):

Absorption of sound involves the dissipation in the form of heat of the vibrational energy of sound waves. Speaking generally, materials that are absorbent in any considerable degree are either *porous,* inelastically *flexible* or inelastically *compressible,* or they may possess two or more of these properties in varying degrees. In porous absorbent materials, the pores are intercommunicating and penetrate the surface. The alternating pressure in the sound wave forces the air particles into the narrow channels of the pore structure where their vibrational energy is dissipated by the viscosity of the air and the friction against the walls of the channels. Sealing the surface of such a material may decrease in considerable degree the sound absorbing efficiency. Felts, fabrics and fibrous materials of vegetable and mineral fiber absorb sound largely by virtue of their porosity and to a certain extent because of their inelastic flexibility and compressibility. Hard nonyielding absorbents owe their absorbent properties entirely to their porosity. Fibrous wallboards with an impervious surface and plywood owe what absorbent properties they have to their forced, inelastic flexural vibration under the alternating pressure of the sound waves at their surface.

Various means have been found of increasing the absorbent coefficients of commercial absorbents as by slotting, perforating, fissuring or otherwise providing small apertures into the body of the materials. The mechanics of this effect is not completely understood. Depth, diameter and distribution of the holes over the surface of the material have been found to have an important effect on the sound absorbing efficiency. An important property of absorbents of this type is that painting does not, to any measurable degree, decrease the absorbing efficiency so long as the paint does not clog the holes.

It has also been found that covering the surface of a porous material with a thin perforated screen of metal or other hard material produces a negligible effect on its sound absorbing efficiency. The explanation lies in the fact that a thin membrane of this type in which the perforated area may be as small as 10 per cent of the total area transmits practically 100 per cent of the sound energy to the absorbent back of it. At high frequencies, say 2000 cps, the effect of the perforated screen is measurable.

Table 98-3

Transmission Losses in Decibels for Various Constructions (2) (3).

Construction	Weight	Loss
Partitions		
Load-bearing structural clay tile $\frac{5}{8}$-in. sanded gypsum plaster both sides		
1. 8-by-12 by 12-in. 6 cell	48.0	44
2. 6-by-12 by 12-in. 6 cell	39.0	42
3. 4-by-12 by 12-in. 3 cell	29.0	40
4. 3-by-12 by 12-in. 3 cell	28.0	36
Hollow cinder block, $\frac{5}{8}$-in. gypsum plaster both sides		
5. 4-by-8 by 16-in.	35.8	44
6. 3-by-8 by 8-in.	32.2	42
7. 2-by-4-in. wood studs 12-in. c. metal lath, $\frac{7}{8}$-in. gypsum plaster both sides	20.0	38
8. Same except lime plaster	19.8	44
9. 2-by-4-in. wood studs 16-in. c., $\frac{3}{8}$-in. gypsum lath $\frac{1}{2}$-in. gypsum plaster both sides	14.2	42
10. 2 by 4-in. wood studs 16-in. c., $\frac{5}{8}$-in. tapered edge gypsum wall board. Joints taped	7.2	37
11. 2-by-4-in. wood studs 16-in. c., $\frac{1}{2}$-in. wood fiberboard both sides, joints filled	5.1	24
12. Same with $\frac{1}{2}$-in. gypsum plaster both sides	13.3	47
13. $\frac{3}{4}$-in. steel channels 12-in. c. metal lath one side, gypsum plaster both sides, solid 2 in. thick	16.4	34
14. $\frac{3}{4}$-in. steel channels 16-in. c. perforated gypsum lath one side, gypsum plaster both sides, solid 2 in. thick, $\frac{3}{4}$-in. channels	19.4	31
15. 12-in. brick, not plastered	121.0	53
16. 8-in. brick, $\frac{5}{8}$-in. gypsum plaster both sides	97.0	49
Floors		
1. 2-by-8-in. wood joists 16-in. c. Ceiling-metal lath $\frac{7}{8}$-in. plaster Subfloor-$\frac{13}{16}$-in., finish floor $\frac{13}{16}$-in. oak	17.1	34
2. 4-in. reinforced concrete slab	53.4	45
3. 6-by-12 by 12-in., 3-cell hollow tile 18-in. c., 6-in. concrete joists between tile, 2-in. slab	83.0	47
4. Same as 3 except 2-in. cinder concrete and 1-in. topping on floor side	109.0	48
Single Sheets		
1. $\frac{1}{4}$-in. 3 ply plywood	0.78	20
2. $\frac{1}{2}$-in. wood fiberboard	0.75	20
3. $\frac{1}{8}$-in. double-strength glass	1.60	27
4. $\frac{1}{4}$-in. plate glass	3.50	31

Key: Values in decibels for frequency of 512 cps. Weights in lb./sq. ft. Expanded metal lath. Sanded plaster.

c. = center-to-center.

The *absorption coefficient* of a material is equal to the proportion of the sound energy in absorbs of that which strikes it. The absorption coefficient of an open window is 1.00.

Absorption coefficients for various common materials are given in Table 98-4 for illustrative purposes.

Many kinds of special acoustical materials are available with absorption coefficients varying from 0.45 to 0.99 (6). They include tile made up of various materials such as felted or perforated wood or mineral fiber, thin perforated metal or asbestos-cement board facing

Table 98-4

Absorbent Coefficients for Various Common Materials (6)

Item	Coefficient
Open window	1.00
Brick wall, painted	.017
unpainted	.03
Plaster, gypsum, or lime, smooth finish on tile or brick masonry	.025
Same as above on lath	.03
Plaster, gypsum, or lime, rough finish on lath	.06
Wood panelling	.06
Glass	.027
Marble or glazed tile	.01
Concrete and terrazzo floors	.015
Wood floors	.03
Linoleum, asphalt, rubber, or cork tile on concrete	0.3–0.8
Carpet, unlined	0.20
Carpet, felt-lined	0.37
Fabric curtains	
Light, 10 oz. per sq. yd., hung straight	0.11
Medium, 14 oz. per sq. yd., hung straight	0.13
Heavy, 18 oz. per sq. yd., draped	0.50
Audience seated, units per person depending on character of seats, etc.	3.0–4.3
Chairs, metal or wood, each	.17
Theater and auditorium chairs, each	
Wood veneer seat and back	.25
Upholstered in leatherette	1.6
Heavy upholstered in plush or mohair	2.6–3.0

Values for 512 cps.

backed with a mineral wool sound absorbing pad, and mineral wool with fissured surface. Surface coatings, consisting of mineral fibers with a binder, which can be sprayed on and granular aggregates with portland cement, lime, or gypsum binders which can be troweled on, are available.

The thicknesses of most types of tile vary from $\frac{1}{2}$ in. to 1 in., not including an air space and furring if these are provided. Some tile are as thick as 2 or 3 in. without air space or furring. Tile may be square or rectangular. A common size of square tile is 12 by 12 in. and of rectangular tile 12 by 24 in., but larger sizes are also available. Perforated tile have holes from $\frac{1}{8}$ in. to $\frac{3}{16}$ in. in diameter, usually spaced about $\frac{1}{2}$ in. each way, although some have a random spacing.

Tile may be attached in various ways to the surface over which they are applied including cementing, nailing to wood furring strips spaced in accordance with the tile sizes and with or without mineral wood between the strips, or mounting on special metal supports with or without furring strips.

Detailed information about these materials are given in reference 6, and illustrations and brief descriptions in references 13 and 14.

Ordinarily the ceilings of rooms are the most feasible locations for the installation of acoustical materials. If rooms are wide and have low ceilings, side-wall installation locations may be preferable to ceiling locations.

Echoes. When the reflection of a sound is heard as a distinct repetition of the original sound, the reflection is called an *echo*. For an echo to be formed, the time difference between the two sounds must be at least $\frac{1}{20}$ of a second. If the difference is smaller than this the reflected sound merely reinforces the original sound. Echoes do not occur in small rooms. Successive repetitions of the same sound by reflections from several surfaces are called *multiple echoes*.

Build-Up and Decay of Sound. When a constant source of sound is introduced into a room, each successive wave it produces spreads in all directions. As it strikes the various surfaces in the room, it is partially absorbed and partially reflected from the several surfaces it strikes. The average intensity of the sound builds up to a maximum at which it continues because the rate of introduction of sound energy equals the rate of absorption by the enclosing surfaces and the contents of the room. If the sound source is cut off, the sound in the room does not cease immediately but gradually decays because of absorption. This phenomenon is illustrated in Fig. 98-1.

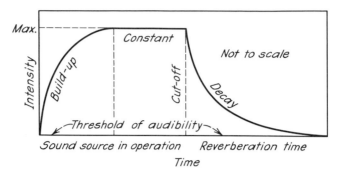

Fig. 98-1. Build-up, continuation, and decay of sound.

Reverberation. Sound which continues in a room after its source has been cut off is called *reverberation*. It may be considered as a series of multiple echoes of decreasing intensity which are so closely spaced that they produce a continuous sound. Reverberation tends to cause spoken syllables to overlap and become indistinct and individual musical notes to be prolonged. The *reverberation time* is the period included between the cut-off time and the time when the sound becomes inaudible. A quantitative definition for reverberation time and specific procedures for its measurement are used in acoustical studies. Reverberation time is illustrated in Fig. 98-1.

The reverberation time for existing rooms can be established by experiment under standardized conditions. W. C. Sabine developed the following formula, based on theoretical studies and many experiments.

$$T = 0.5 \frac{V}{A} \quad \text{or} \quad A = 0.5 \frac{V}{T}$$

T is the reverberation time in seconds for 512-cycle sounds, V is the volume of the room in cubic feet, and A is the total of the absorption units in the room and is equal to the sum of the products of each absorbing area in the room and its absorption coefficient. Appropriate allowances are made for occupants and for seats and other furnishings including carpets, window draperies, etc., such as those included in Table 98-4.

This formula is extensively used in acoustical design but has limitations. Other more precise but more complex procedures are also used. From this formula, the value of A which must be achieved by installing special sound absorbing materials to yield the desired reverberation time can be computed for a given value of V.

Auditoriums. The reverberation time of a large room such as an auditorium, assembly hall, concert hall or theater is of paramount importance. The most desirable or *optimum reverberation time* for a room depends upon the purposes for which it is to be used. It is longer for music than for speech. It also depends upon the volume of the room, which increases with the size of the room.

The acoustical properties of rooms used for speech may be impaired by long reverberation times, but such rooms with very short reverberation times seem dead and unnatural because the ear is accustomed to some reverberation. The acoustical properties of a room used for music may be impaired by reverberation times which are too short or too long. Optimum reverberation times for various conditions have been established by measuring the reverberation times of rooms of various sizes used for various purposes and which are considered by trained observers to have good acoustical properties. One factor which must not be overlooked is the size of the audience for which the time is to be selected because audiences account for much of the sound absorbed.

Reverberation times recommended by the Acoustical Materials Association may be obtained from Fig. 98-2 (1). In this figure, the vol-

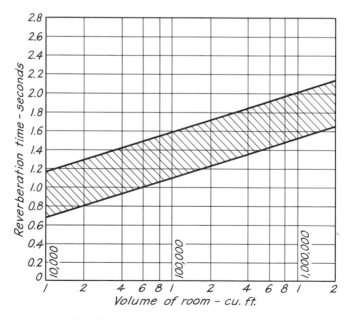

Fig. 98-2. Optimum reverberation times (1).

umes are plotted on a logarithmic scale and the reverberation times on a linear scale. The shaded area represents acceptable reverberation times for various room sizes and a frequency of 512 cycles per second. For moving picture theaters or auditoriums which have public address systems, the reverberation times should fall near the lower limit of the shaded area and for churches and concert halls, they should fall near the upper limit. It will be noted that for a room with a volume of 10,000 cu. ft., the optimum reverberation times vary from 0.88 to 1.16 seconds and for a room with a volume of one million cubic feet the variation is from 1.5 to 2.0 sec. The seating capacities for rooms with these volumes depend upon their ceiling heights, whether or not there are balconies in the larger rooms, and other factors, but they are of the order of magnitude of 80 to 100 and 3000 to 4000 respectively.

Another factor is the shape of the enclosing surfaces. Concave surfaces such as curved rear walls and domed ceilings tend to focus reflected sound waves to produce concentrations of sound in certain areas which result in annoying echoes and loss of intelligibility of speech. Since convex surfaces reduce the intensity of reflected sound and do not cause echoes, they are not objectionable and may be desirable.

Consideration should be given to reducing the sounds transmitted into the auditorium from outside sources. The size and proportions of a room are important. It has been recommended that the volume of a room in cubic feet should not be greater than two hundred times the number of seats (1). The presence of a stage or balcony requires special consideration.

Many other factors are involved. The problems are very complex and require the services of an expert.

Work Rooms. The significance of good acoustics to the occupants of building space has been mentioned previously. The multiple reflections of sound from the enclosing surfaces build up the sound level in a room far above what it would be without such reflections. Increasing the total absorption units in a room results in a proportionate reduction in the contributions to the noise level by reflections.

Except in small rooms, reverberation in untreated rooms may interfere with the intelligibility of speech, including telephone conversations. When the occupants raise their voices to overcome this effect they increase the general noise level.

Reductions in noise level are accomplished by means of acoustical materials with high absorption coefficients. Usually these need be applied only to the ceilings, but they may also be applied to the walls of small rooms with low ceilings. It is not possible to compute the amount of acoustical material which must be applied to accomplish a desired result. In general, the use of absorbent materials for office quieting is not likely to be overdone (1). Sound absorption treatment is usually required in nearly all parts of school buildings and restaurants and in library reading rooms and in rooms used for many other purposes. Corridors often require special consideration, even though other parts of a building may not require treatment.

"Acoustical treatment of offices, banks, schools, etc. often reduces the noise level 6-db. compared with that before treatment. A 6-db. reduction is equivalent to 30 to 50% noise reduction judged by the human ear." (14)

Acknowledgments. This article is based largely on the reports by V. L. Chrisler prepared for the National Bureau of Standards, references 2 and 3, and a bulletin prepared by Paul E. Sabine for the Acoustical Materials Association (1).

References

1. Paul E. Sabine, *Theory and Use of Architectural Acoustical Materials,* Second Edition, Acoustical Materials Association.
2. V. L. Chrisler, *Sound Insulation of Wall and Floor Constructions,* National Bureau of Standards Report BMS 17, 1939, Supplement 1940.
3. *Sound Insulation of Wall and Floor Constructions,* National Bureau of Standards Report 144, 1955.
4. Vern O. Knudsen and Cyril M. Harris, *Acoustical Designing in Architecture,* John Wiley and Sons, 1950.
5. Richard H. Holt and Robert B. Newman, "Architectural Acoustics" included in *Architectural Engineering,* F. W. Dodge Corporation, 1955.
6. *Sound Absorption Coefficients of Architectural Acoustical Materials,* Bulletin XII, Acoustical Materials Association, 1950.
7. *Fundamentals of Building Insulation,* Insulation Board Institute, 1950.
8. Tyler Stewart Rogers, *Design of Insulated Buildings for Various Climates,* F. W. Dodge Corporation, 1951.
9. *Heating, Ventilating and Air-Conditioning Guide,* American Society of Heating and Ventilating Engineers, published annually.
10. *Sweet's Architectural Catalog File,* F. W. Dodge Corporation, published annually.
11. Donald J. Vild, *Principles of Heat Transfer Through Glass Fenestrations;* Alfred L. Jaros, Jr., *Design for Solar Heat Gain and Loss; Windows and Glass in the Exterior of Buildings,* Publication 478, Building Research Institute, National Research Council, 1957.
12. G. R. Munger, "There Are Six Ways to Bring Down the Cost of Air Conditioning," *Refrigerating Engineering and Air Conditioning,* October, 1957, p. 46.
13. C. W. Glover, *Practical Acoustics for the Constructor,* Chapman and Hall Ltd., 1933.
14. G. W. Handy, Section 17, Acoustics, Building Construction Handbook by Frederick S. Merritt, Editor, McGraw-Hill Co., 1958.

Index